Gaining and Sustaining Competitive Advantage

Jay B. Barney

The Ohio State University

Addison-Wesley Publishing Company

Reading, Massachusetts   Menlo Park, California
New York   Don Mills, Ontario   Harlow, United Kingdom
Amsterdam   Bonn   Sydney   Singapore
Tokyo   Madrid   San Juan   Milan   Paris

Executive Editor: Michael Payne
Senior Acquisitions Editor: Beth Toland
Senior Project Manager: Mary Clare McEwing
Marketing Manager: Mark Thomas Childs
Production Supervisor: Patsy DuMoulin
Prepress Services Buyer: Caroline Fell
Manufacturing Supervisor: Hugh J. Crawford
Production Services: Beth Stephens
Compositor: Publishers' Design and Production Services
Illustrator: Publishers' Design and Production Services
Cover Designer: Diana Coe
Cover Photographs: Tony Stone Images

Library of Congress Cataloging-in-Publication Data

Barney, Jay B.
    Gaining and sustaining competitive advantage / Jay B. Barney.
      p.   cm.
    Includes bibliographical references and index.
    ISBN 0-201-51285-8
    1. Industrial management.   2. Strategic planning.   3. Competition.
    I. Title.
    HD31.B36838   1996
    658.4--dc20   96-7024
                                                        CIP
Reprinted with corrections October, 1996.

ISBN 0–201–51285–8

4 5 6 7 8 9 10 — MA—009998

About the Author

Jay Barney is Professor of Management and holder of the Bank One Chair for Excellence in Corporate Strategy at the Max M. Fisher College of Business at the Ohio State University. He received his undergraduate degree from Brigham Young University and his master's and doctorate degrees from Yale University. After completing his formal education, Professor Barney joined the faculty of the Anderson Graduate School of Management at UCLA. He moved to Texas A&M University in 1986 and joined the faculty of Ohio State in 1994.

Professor Barney teaches organizational strategy and policy to M.B.A. and Ph.D. students at Ohio State. He also has taught in executive training programs at Ohio State, Texas A&M, UCLA, Southern Methodist University, the University of Michigan, and Bocconi University (in Milan, Italy). Professor Barney received the George Robbins Teaching Award at UCLA in 1983 and the Association of Former Students' Distinguished Teaching Award at Texas A&M in 1992.

Professor Barney's research focuses on the relationship between idiosyncratic firm skills and capabilities and sustained competitive advantage. He has published over thirty articles in journals such as the *Academy of Management Review, Strategic Management Journal, Management Science*, and the *Journal of Management*. He has been on the editorial board of the *Academy of Management Review* and the *Strategic Management Journal*, has been Associate Editor of the *Journal of Management*, and is currently senior editor of *Organization Science*. Professor Barney has delivered scholarly papers at the Harvard Business School, the Wharton School of Business, the University of Michigan, the University of Illinois, Northwestern University, the University of Minnesota, and over twenty other universities throughout the world. He has published two books: *Organizational Economics* (with William G. Ouchi) and *Managing Organizations: Strategy, Structure, and Behavior* (with Ricky Griffin). He won the College of Business Distinguished Research

Award at Texas A&M in 1992, and he presented the Holger Crafoord Memorial Lecture at the University of Lund, in Lund, Sweden, in 1993.

Professor Barney has consulted with a wide variety of public and private organizations, including Westinghouse Electric, the Masonite Corporation, McDonnell-Douglas, Wells Fargo Bank, Honeywell Information Systems, Mead, Hewlett-Packard, Texas Instruments, Tenneco, Arco, and Koch Industries Inc. His consulting focuses on implementing large-scale organizational change and strategic analysis.

Preface

So—why do we need another book on business policy and strategic management? What does this book bring to its readers that other books don't? To answer these questions, it is important to understand (1) how business education has evolved in business schools and (2) strategic management's disciplinary status in colleges of business.

RESEARCH AND TEACHING IN BUSINESS SCHOOLS

In 1959, two evaluations of the status of undergraduate and graduate business education were published. The first, sponsored by the Carnegie Foundation, concluded that "the central problem facing this branch of higher education is that academic standards need to be materially increased" (Pierson, 1959:ix). The second, funded by the Ford Foundation, described in more detail what these academic standards should be by arguing that "business educators in increasing numbers are recognizing that it is insufficient to transmit and apply present knowledge. It is the function of higher education to advance the state of knowledge as well. A professional school of business that aspires to full academic status must meet this test" (Gordon and Howell, 1959:v).

These evaluations of business education in the 1950s have had a profound impact on the structure and function of business schools. Before the Carnegie and Ford studies, business school professors were often retired managers, and business school classes consisted primarily of discussions about and applications of various informal rules of thumb for managing different business functions. Today, most business school professors have Ph.D.s in either a business discipline or a related nonbusiness discipline, and business school classes focus on discussions about and applications of various models, concepts, and theories that have been developed by academic research. Where previously the discussion of business practices was not well connected to any base academic disciplines, now teaching and research in business draw directly from, and often contribute to, these base disciplines—including economics, psychology, sociology, and mathematics.

Of all the functional areas in the business school, none began making the transition to a theory-grounded, research-based discipline earlier than organizational behavior and finance. As early as the 1930s, organizational behavior researchers were attempting to apply rigorous research methodologies to study the behavior of individuals and groups in organizations. The now-famous studies of the Western Electric plant in Hawthorne, New Jersey, demonstrated not only that social science research methods, originally developed by social psychologists, could be applied in an organizational context, but that they could be used to describe complex social phenomena inside firms (Roethlisberger and Dickson, 1939). In finance, Modigliani and Miller's (1958; 1963) work on capital structure and the cost of capital, and Markowitz's (1959) and Tobin's (1958) work on portfolio selection, led the way in the application of economic theory to financial decision making in firms. Since this early work, finance has become, in a real sense, a subfield of microeconomics. Moreover, theoretical and empirical work in finance has had a significant impact on the field of microeconomics more generally.

Many of the other disciplines in business schools have gone through similar evolutions. Where marketing used to be taught by retired marketing executives, and marketing classes focused on the experiences of these managers, now marketing classes are typically taught by faculty with Ph.D.s in marketing or related disciplines, and marketing classes focus on understanding and applying models and concepts derived from economics, psychology, and statistics. Where operations management used to have an uncertain discipline grounding, it now has become an arena where psychological, sociological, mathematical, and statistical models are applied in managing quality, plant location, logistics, and other critical operational activities in firms. Finally, where accounting used to focus solely on generally accepted accounting rules, accounting research now draws more broadly on economics, psychology, and computer science to develop those accounting rules and to anticipate their implications for firms.

Some have been concerned that this increased emphasis on rigorous business research has reduced the quality of a business education (Hayes and Abernathy, 1980). These observers have argued that although we now have much more rigorous methods for analyzing a firm's business situation, we have lost the human touch that is required to manage real firms—a human touch that used to be communicated to students by retired executives in the classroom. Of course, there is a great deal of truth in this criticism. It is certainly the case that if all a manager did was to apply research-derived models in a firm, the firm would probably not perform very well. The management of a real organization is not something that can easily be reduced to a computer algorithm. Discipline-based faculty must strive to expose students to this human touch. This is one reason for the continued popularity of case-based teaching in business schools. Not only do cases provide students opportunities to apply the theoretical models they are learning, they also simulate the socially complex context within which the application of these models must actually occur.

It is also the case that much of this rigorous business research is irrelevant to real business managers. In any given issue of a research journal, maybe only one or two articles actually have the potential to be applied in real organizations. The rest of this work is basic research. It is designed to address theoretical problems, problems that often have limited application potential. However, this basic research is often necessary before the applied work can be done. Moreover, when rigorous business research can be applied in real firms, its implications can be staggering. For example, there is little doubt that the way firms are managed today is fundamentally different from how they were managed thirty years ago and that much of this change is traceable to work done in organizational behavior and related business disciplines (for example, Ouchi, 1981; Peters and Waterman, 1982). There is also little doubt that theoretical advances in finance have had an enormous impact on the structure and function of the modern economy. Leveraged buyouts, futures markets, derivatives, and capital budgeting are all examples of economic phenomena that have been fundamentally altered by work in financial economics. Also, there is little doubt that the quality movement that swept the world through the 1980s and early 1990s found its intellectual roots, and many of its management tools, in the work done by operations management researchers. Indeed, there really isn't anything quite as practical as a good theory.

THE ACADEMIC STATUS OF STRATEGIC MANAGEMENT

Where does the discipline of strategic management stand in this evolutionary process? It is probably safe to say that strategic management is the least developed and the least mature of all the disciplines in the business school. Finance and organizational behavior were well on their way to becoming rigorous, discipline-based fields by the 1950s, and marketing, accounting, and operations were well on their way to this same status by the 1960s. But it was not until the late 1970s and early 1980s that work on a theoretically rigorous underpinning for the field of strategic management was begun. Before this time period, strategic management was often taught by retired managers, and course content focused primarily on describing the activities and decisions of general managers in organizations.

In many ways, the delayed maturity of the field of strategic management is quite understandable. Strategic management is an inherently integrative activity in a firm—forcing managers to bring the skills and expertise of different business functions together to conceive of and implement a strategy. Thus research on strategic management is an inherently multidisciplinary task. To fully mature as an academic discipline, each of the specialties on which strategic management scholars rely must also mature. Thus it is not surprising that the evolution of the field of strategic management was delayed until other business functions had matured from their pre-academic state to become more discipline-based, research-oriented specialties. However, although the maturing of strategic management has been delayed, it is certainly occurring.

Two events signaled the beginning of the evolution of the field of strategic management from its pre-academic stage to a modern, discipline-based research field: the publication (in 1980) of Michael Porter's book *Competitive Strategy* and the publication (in 1974) of Richard Rumelt's book *Strategy, Structure, and Economic Performance*. As I indicate in Chapter 3, Porter adapted concepts from industrial organization economics to the analysis of threats and opportunities in a firm's competitive environment. Before Porter, the analysis of a firm's competitive environment was not well structured and involved generating long, idiosyncratic lists of threats and opportunities facing a firm. After Porter, the critical threats in a firm's environment, as derived from IO economics, could be described and opportunities facing a firm could be deduced from the structure of a firm's industry. Porter had begun to provide a theoretical structure for analyzing one critical component of the business-level strategy formulation problem.

As I indicate in Chapter 11, Rumelt took ideas that had been explored by business historians (for example, Chandler, 1962) and business scholars (for example, Wrigley, 1970) to develop a theory explaining the conditions under which corporate diversification strategies could add economic value to a firm, as well as a model describing the organizational structure firms would need to realize the potential value of a diversification effort. Before Rumelt, discussions of corporate strategy were mired in not very rigorous discussions of synergy and the appropriate level of centralization and decentralization. After Rumelt, the kind of product relatedness needed to achieve synergy was described, and the specific organizational structure needed to realize these synergies was detailed. Rumelt had begun to provide a theoretical structure for analyzing some critical components of the corporate-level strategy formulation and implementation problem.

Just as Porter and Rumelt were completing their work, research in other disciplines began to be published that was destined to have a significant impact on the evolution of the field of strategic management. In organizational behavior, Ouchi's (1981) work on Japanese management systems significantly opened up the strategic implementation problem. In economics, transactions-cost economics (Williamson, 1975) and the evolutionary theory of the firm (Nelson and Winter, 1982) provided some powerful tools for analyzing a firm's competitive position. In organization theory, population ecology theory was beginning to provide insights to the competitive process facing firms (Hannan and Freeman, 1977). In finance and accounting, agency theory (Jensen and Meckling, 1976) and positive accounting (Watts and Zimmerman, 1978) were providing insights into the economics of organizational structure and organizational processes. Many of these theoretical developments were described in a book I published with Bill Ouchi in 1986 titled *Organizational Economics*.

The result of these theoretical breakthroughs in the field of strategic management and related disciplines has been a rapid growth in the intellectual maturity of strategic management. The number of people studying strategic phenomena in organizations has increased dramatically over the last several years. Currently, the Business Policy and Strategy Division of the Academy of Management is one of the largest of all Academy divisions. Scholars with a wide variety of disciplinary backgrounds, from finance to organizational behavior, are publishing in the strategic management literature. New ideas are constantly being developed and tested.

Moreover, this growth in interest in strategic management phenomena has not been limited to just business school academics. Much of the best of this work has had important implications for how real firms are managed. Porter's books, including *Competitive Strategy* (1980) and *Competitive Advantage* (1985), have been read and applied by many practicing managers. C. K. Prahalad and Gary Hammel's *Harvard Business Review* article (1990) on core competencies—an article solidly grounded in strategic management academic research (for example, Prahalad and Bettis, 1986; Wernerfelt, 1984)—is the all-time best selling reprint at *HBR*. Like earlier work in finance, OB, and operations, research in strategic management has had, and continues to have, a profound impact on management practice.

THE PURPOSE OF THIS BOOK

Unfortunately, many students of strategic management—whether they are full-time students, part-time students, or practicing managers—have found it difficult to get their minds around this rapidly evolving field. Individual articles or books generally push only a single point of view and do not provide the overall integrative framework necessary to apply strategic management concepts in real organizations. With a couple of exceptions, most textbooks do not include information on the most up-to-date research in strategic management, nor do they provide guidance to students or practitioners about how this research might be applied. *The purpose of this book is to summarize and integrate the latest research in strategic management and related disciplines in a way that is accessible to students and practitioners and in a way that facilitates its application.*

UNIQUE ATTRIBUTES OF THE BOOK

I have taken several actions to ensure the realization of this purpose.

INTEGRATING STRATEGIC MANAGEMENT RESEARCH

One of my purposes is to present an integrated view of the field of strategic management. To facilitate this integration, the first five chapters develop a framework (summarized in Chapter 5) that is then used as an organizing framework for the rest of the chapters. Moreover, this framework recognizes that understanding threats and opportunities in a firm's competitive environment and understanding the competitive implications of a firm's organizational strengths and weaknesses are both important in strategy formulation and implementation.

Thus, unlike Porter (1980) and others, this book is not organized around different types of competitive environments that firms might face. Such a structure unduly emphasizes environmental determinants of firm performance over organizational determinants of performance. Instead, after the organizing framework is developed, chapters focus on specific strategic options that firms may choose to gain competitive advantages. At the business level, these options include cost leadership (Chapter 6), product differentiation (Chapter 7), tacit collusion (Chapter 8), and strategic alliances (Chapter 9). At the corporate level, these options include vertical integration (Chapter 10), diversification (Chapters 11 and 12), mergers and acquisitions (Chapter 13), and global strategies (Chapter 14). How these strategic options help neutralize environmental threats and exploit environmental opportunities is discussed in each of these chapters, in connection with a discussion of how organizational strengths and weaknesses affect the ability of firms pursuing these strategies to gain sustained competitive advantages.

Another way in which the integration of the field of strategic management is facilitated is that strategy formulation and strategy implementation are not discussed in separate parts of the book. Many books and articles seem to adopt the fiction that it is possible to study strategy formulation and strategy implementation independently. This is obviously incorrect. It would clearly be a mistake for firms to formulate their strategies without considering how they were going to implement those strategies. Moreover, it is not possible to evaluate the quality of a firm's strategy implementation efforts independent of the strategy that the firm is trying to implement. Yet many strategy scholars focus either on strategy formulation or on strategy implementation, and many strategy texts address these topics separately, in different parts of the book.

In this book, strategy formulation and strategy implementation are discussed together for each of the strategic options facing firms. Thus, beginning with Chapter 6, the conditions under which pursuing a strategy will be economically valuable, along with the conditions under which pursuing a strategy will be a source of sustained competitive advantage, are discussed. Following this strategy formulation discussion, the actions that a firm must pursue to implement this strategy are also discussed. For all but one of the strategic options facing firms (diversification), the strategy formulation and implementation discussions occur in the same chapter. For diversification strategies, the formulation discussion is in one chapter (Chapter 11), and the implementation discussion is in the subsequent chapter (Chapter 12), because the diversification implementation literature is so large.

INCLUDING THE LATEST RESEARCH

Another of my purposes is to summarize the latest research findings in strategic management and related disciplines. Several things have been done to accomplish this purpose. For example, within each chapter, current thinking and research—some of it not yet published—is incorporated in the discussion. In Chapter 2's discussion of firm performance, a variety of measures of firm performance that have only recently begun to appear in the strategy literature are discussed, including the Treynor index, Sharpe's measure, Jensen's alpha, and Tobin's q. Other popular measures of performance that have not been widely discussed in other strategy books are also introduced, including event study methodologies for analyzing firm performance. Also, Chapter 5's discussion of organizational strengths and weaknesses is a state-of-the-art summary of what has come to be known as the resource-based view of the firm (Wernerfelt, 1984; Barney, 1986a; 1991). Chapter 8's discussion of tacit collusion draws on recent developments in game theory, and Chapter 9's discussion of trust in strategic alliances draws on some very recently published work. Chapter 11's discussion of diversification strategies is well grounded in current work in strategic management and finance. Chapter 14's analysis of global strategies draws on some of the most recent developments in this rapidly growing literature.

Each chapter reflects the latest developments in strategic management research, and my choice of which strategies to focus on in Part 2 (business-level strategies) and Part 3 (corporate-level strategies) reflects currently important topics in the field. Many books limit their discussion of business-level strategies to competitive strategies (including cost leadership and product differentiation), but this book includes discussions of cooperative business-level strategies as well. Moreover, two classes of these cooperative strategies are discussed— tacit collusion and strategic alliances. Collusion strategies have been much in the business news lately and are important phenomena about which students and practitioners need to be aware. Strategic alliance strategies—including nonequity alliances, equity alliances, and joint ventures—are becoming increasingly important for firms and especially for firms looking to expand their business opportunities in non-domestic markets.

At the corporate level, this book includes a chapter on vertical integration strategies (Chapter 10). In an era of downsizing and out-sourcing, decisions about what business functions to keep within the boundaries of a firm are extremely important. Chapter 10 presents the latest thinking about these issues. Moreover, although most strategy books have chapters on diversification and global strategies, fewer have discussions on merger and acquisitions strategies—even though mergers and acquisitions are often popular means of implementing diversification and global strategies. Chapter 13 presents the latest research on merger and acquisition strategies.

To ensure that my text includes the full range of the most recent work in strategic management and related disciplines, each article in each issue of the *Strategic Management Journal*, the *Academy of Management Review*, the *Academy of Management Journal*, the *Academy of Management Executive*, and the *Rand Journal of Economics* for the last ten years was read and summarized. Then, if it was determined that an article had a strategic focus, the article was classified as being germane to one or more of the chapters of this book. Not all of these articles are cited in the text, but I am quite confident that any current major research stream published in these journals is reflected in the content of the book. For example, I was able to relate every article published in *SMJ* to one of the chapters of this book with the exception of a few articles on strategic management in small firms and a few articles on the process of managing innovation in firms.

ENSURING ACCESSIBILITY AND APPLICATION

If students and practitioners cannot read, understand, and apply all this research, it will be of limited value to them. Thus it was not enough to include all the major research streams in strategic management and related disciplines; it was also important to make this work accessible and applicable. I have done several things to accomplish this. First, the book is full of examples. Most of them come from *Fortune* or the *Wall Street Journal*. Indeed, each issue of *Fortune* for the last eight years, and most editions of the *Wall Street Journal* over this same time period, have been read in search of examples of the phenomena discussed in this book. If no examples of a particular strategic phenomenon discussed in the research literature could be found, a discussion of this strategic phenomenon was usually omitted from the book. The logic here is straightforward: If we can't find examples of a phenomenon in the popular business literature, then the phenomenon, though perhaps theoretically interesting, is probably not practically important and thus can be omitted without loss.

In addition, each chapter ends with a chapter summary and review questions. The summary highlights the key issues discussed in the chapter, and the review questions force readers to go beyond what is written in a chapter, to try to understand its implications for managing real firms.

One characteristic that enhances the accessibility and applicability of many strategic management texts is missing in this book—cases. The lack of cases does not mean that cases are irrelevant in the teaching of strategic management. Indeed, I think that case teaching is a very important component of any strategic management class. However, to be most useful, cases should provide students and managers an opportunity to see how a set of ideas, a model, or a technique can actually be used to engage in a strategic analysis and make a strategic decision. In this book I focus on these ideas, models, and techniques, and I assume that teachers will choose their own cases in which these tools can be applied.

There are numerous sources for case material that can be used in conjunction with this book. Moreover, the structure of my text makes choosing cases relatively easy. Since much of the text is organized around specific strategic options facing firms, cases that focus on firms trying to decide whether to pursue a particular strategic option help demonstrate how the ideas and models in a chapter can be applied in a realistic setting. Thus, for example, to help the discussion of cost-leadership competitive business strategies to come alive, cases on Nucor Steel and Wal-Mart are good options, for these firms tend to focus on cost leadership. To help the discussion of strategic alliances to come alive, cases on General Motors, AT&T, and Corning are good options, for these firms have all been pursuing alliance strategies, albeit in very different ways and for very different reasons. The discussion of vertical integration can be greatly enhanced by cases that focus on firms going through outsourcing decisions and by cases that focus on firms that exist because of outsourcing (such as EDS).

ACKNOWLEDGMENTS

I began writing this book in 1984, while I was an assistant professor at UCLA. Over the years, I have continued to work on and refine the text, first as a faculty member at Texas A&M University and most recently as the Bank One Chair for Excellence in Corporate Strategy at the Fisher College of Business at Ohio State University. Colleagues, students, and friends at all these institutions have had a profound impact on my ability to finish this book—a book that, for a long time, I called the "alleged book." At UCLA, Bill Ouchi, Dick Rumelt, and Bill McKelvey helped form my approach to academic life and research. Early work with Bill Ouchi and Dick Rumelt had a significant impact on my development as an economically oriented strategy scholar. At UCLA, I was also lucky to have some unusually talented Ph.D. students who influenced me. These students included Jim Robins, Bill Hesterly, Todd Zenger, Julia Liebeskind, and, most important, Kathleen Conner.

When I arrived at Texas A&M, I found a thriving strategy group. My colleagues there also had a significant impact on my work. These people included Mike Hitt, Bob Hoskisson, Bert Cannella, Barry Baysinger, Tom Turk, "Aggie" Abby McWilliams, and Javier Gimeno. My work was also influenced by some talented Ph.D. students at A&M, including Beverly Tyler, Lowell Busenitz, Jim Fiet, Doug Moesel, and, most recently, Mark Hansen. Much of the hard work of developing the organizing framework and applying it to the analysis of several strategic options occurred while I was at Texas A&M. I am grateful to Mike Hitt and Don Hellriegel, my department heads at A&M, for helping to create a setting within which this kind of work was possible.

Since my arrival at the Fisher College at Ohio State, I have found the support and friendship of my department head, Steve Mangum, to be very important. However, in truth, this book would have remained the "alleged book" without the help of two people: Kathy Hutton, my very talented and dedicated secretary, and Woong-he Lee, a Ph.D. student at Ohio State who has helped with the numerous references in the text.

I am also grateful to the following reviewers for their valuable comments on the manuscript: Kimberly Boal, Texas Tech University; Kathleen Conner, University of Michigan; Patrick DeGraba, Cornell University; Derrick Dsouza, University of North Texas; Ari Ginsberg, New York University; Constance Helfat, The Wharton School; R. Duane Ireland, Baylor University; Danny Kinker, Washburn University; Marvin Lieberman, UCLA; John Pearce, George Mason University; Julia Porter Liebeskind, University of Southern California; Mark Shanley, Northwestern University; Stephen Tallman, University of Utah; Natalie Taylor, Babson University; Thomas Turk, Chapman University; Keith Weigelt, The Wharton School; and Todd Zenger, Washington University.

Throughout this time period, there has been only one constant in my life—my family. Without them, none of this would have been possible or worthwhile. Thus it is to my family—my wife, Kim, and my three children, Lindsay, Kristian, and Erin—that I dedicate this book.

J.B.

Contents

PART I

THE LOGIC OF STRATEGIC ANALYSIS

CHAPTER

1

What Is Strategy?

In 1969, two students at the Lakeside School in Seattle, Washington, began learning about computers. By using an ASR-33 Teletype terminal, these students were able to gain access to a General Electric Mark II "time sharing" computer located in the eastern part of the United States. They spent this precious computing time devising programs to solve difficult mathematical problems, as well as designing some simple computer games, including ticktacktoe. Later that year, they formed their first company, Traf-O-Data, a company that used a rudimentary computer to automatically count the number of cars that passed through busy intersections (Schlender, 1995).

Six years later, in 1975, one of these students was a dissatisfied sophomore at Harvard University; the other was unemployed. The unemployed student, Paul Allen, spotted an article on the MITS Altair 8800 in the January 1975 issue of *Popular Electronics* and called his old friend, Bill Gates. The Altair 8800 was one of the first commercially available personal computers, and Allen and Gates decided to create another new company to try to exploit the opportunities promised by this new technology. This new company was called Microsoft.

Microsoft's first major products were programming languages for the Apple II and other early personal computers. However, in 1980, Microsoft became IBM's supplier of an operating system for the forthcoming IBM personal computer. This operating system was known as MS-DOS, for Microsoft Disc Operating System. In August 1981, IBM introduced its first line of personal computers, with MS-DOS as the operating system. IBM PCs soon gained over 75 percent of the personal computer market, although competitors quickly developed numerous lower-priced IBM clones. MS-DOS was the operating system both for IBM PCs and for IBM clones.

MS-DOS was an unwieldy, difficult-to-use operating system. Beginning in the early 1980s, Microsoft began a joint development project with IBM to build the next generation of operating system. This new system was to be called OS/2. However, in 1990, Microsoft introduced its own next-generation operating system—Windows 3.0. Windows emulated the user-friendliness of Apple's Macintosh computer and trumped IBM's effort to build strength in the PC operating systems market. Windows also created problems for many applications software firms—firms that had invested heavily in software that could run with the OS/2 operating system. These firms, including WordPerfect and Lotus, began scrambling to make their application software compatible with Microsoft's Windows.

Of course, Microsoft did not leave this opportunity unexploited. While other applications firms scrambled to modify and improve their software, Microsoft began introducing its own applications software. Beginning in 1991, Microsoft went from having essentially no market share in personal computer applications software to having the largest market share in many of these applications. In addition to enjoying 82 percent of the market share in personal computer operating systems in 1995, Microsoft also controlled 64 percent of the Windows word-processing software market, 61 percent of the market for Windows spreadsheet software, 60 percent of the market for Macintosh word-processing software, and 89 percent of the market for Macintosh spreadsheet software (Schlender and Kirkpatrick, 1995). In 1994, nearly two-thirds of Microsoft's revenues came from applications software. From 1990 through 1994, Microsoft's profits, revenues, and stock price all quadrupled. Sales in 1994 were $4.9 billion, up 25.4 percent from 1993, and net profits were $1.2 billion, up 24.4 percent from 1993. The average annual return to Microsoft investors from 1989 through 1994 was 45.4 percent.

The evolution of Microsoft from a limited operating systems company (with MS-DOS), to a more sophisticated operating systems company (with Windows), to an operating systems and applications company (with Windows and Microsoft applications) has generated enormous wealth, but Microsoft has faced serious challenges and difficulties. For example, Microsoft's rapid growth in the early 1990s was fueled by the continuing demand for personal computers—personal computers that needed operating and applications software. However, as this market approached saturation, the ability of Microsoft to continue selling software to new customers diminished. More users began to require only less-profitable software upgrades. This upgrade plateau is one explanation of why Microsoft's sales growth slipped from 56 percent in 1990 to 24 percent in 1994.

Also, Microsoft's domination of the operating systems and applications software businesses has led many to accuse the firm of monopolistic practices. Both the U.S. Federal Trade Commission and the Department of Justice have investigated Microsoft, seeking evidence of anticompetitive behavior. Antitrust litigation is still pending against Microsoft, although the company denies any wrongdoing (Schlender and Kirkpatrick, 1995). This cloud of antitrust litigation has slowed Microsoft's effort to expand its base of applications software. For example, Microsoft's 1994 effort to purchase Intuit—maker of Quicken, the most popular line of personal finance software—received unusually high levels of regulatory scrutiny.

Despite these challenges and difficulties, it is nevertheless the case that Bill Gates, building on Microsoft's original success in the operating systems business, has built a powerful and very successful personal computer software company.

■   ■   ■

In 1984, the Walt Disney Company earned profits of $242 million. Most of its profit (77 percent) in 1984 came from its theme park operations—in California, Florida, and Japan. Consumer products that exploited Mickey Mouse and other famous Disney characters generated 22 percent of these profits; filmed entertainment generated only 1 percent. Then Disney hired Michael Eisner from Paramount Studios to be president of the Walt Disney Company (Huey, 1995).

Eisner made three decisions that fundamentally altered the way the Disney organization did business. First, Eisner increased admission prices for Disney's theme parks (Huey, 1995). Reasoning that the price of admission was actually a small percentage of the total cost of attending one of these "destination resorts," Eisner concluded that it would be possible to raise ticket prices without adversely affecting attendance. Moreover, since the Disney theme parks exploited so many assets unique to the Disney Company, customers were unlikely to begin attending different theme parks in response to this price increase. In addition to raising prices, Eisner also expanded and upgraded the Disney resorts. The results were spectacular. In 1984, Disney's theme parks generated only $186 million in profits; by 1989, these same parks generated $787 million in profits.

Second, Eisner reasoned that the ability to charge premium prices for Disney products and services depended critically on the stable of characters that Disney had been able to develop through its movies and television programs. But many of these characters were beginning to age. Moreover, it was not clear that the characters that had appealed to children in the 1950s and 1960s would still be appealing to children in the 1980s and 1990s. None of this would have been a problem if Disney had been able to constantly develop new characters through its studio operations. However, by 1984, these production operations were moribund. It had been so long since a Disney movie had created marketable characters that it was not clear that the studio still could do so. Eisner emphasized film production and invested in a series of highly successful animated and live-action movies. This effort culminated in 1994 with an animated feature—*The Lion King*. *The Lion King* was the second-highest-grossing movie of all time, with a worldwide box office take of $740 million. An additional $1 billion in revenues came from sales of retail merchandise associated with *The Lion King*. And this revenue does not yet count the millions (billions?) of dollars *The Lion King* is expected to generate through home video sales. In 1984, film production generated only $2.42 million in profits for Disney; by 1994, it generated $845 million in profits.

Third, Eisner reasoned that the numerous unique resources possessed by Disney were not fully leveraged through the film and theme park operations. In an effort to exploit these capabilities, Eisner broadly diversified Disney's operations. In 1984, the Disney Company was essentially a theme park operator; by 1995, Disney operated in a complex set of businesses, including movie studios, the Disney Channel, broadcast television (through their acquisition of Capital Cities/ABC), a television production company, theme parks in the United States, Europe, and Japan (including real estate, construction, hotel, and restaurant operations associated with these theme parks), consumer products, retail stores, mail order operations, a publishing company, a record company, live theater operations, a National Hockey League franchise (the Mighty Ducks), and a cruise line. All these businesses complement each other and build on many of the traditional strengths at Disney.

Eisner's actions have had a profound effect on the Disney Company. In 1994, Disney had over 65,000 employees. Over 23 percent of Disney's 1994 revenues came from overseas, and Disney has consistently reported annual increases in profits and return on equity of more than 20 percent. In 1984, the market value of the Disney Company was only $2 billion. By 1994, its market value was $28 billion—bigger than, for example, the Ford Motor Company (Huey, 1995).

Of course, Disney has faced some challenges under Eisner. For example, EuroDisney has yet to be profitable. By 1994, EuroDisney had cost the Disney Company over $500 million in write-offs. A recent restructuring of EuroDisney financing has still not made it profitable. Also, during 1994, many of the senior managers who had helped make Disney what it has become resigned to pursue other opportunities.

Among those who left were Jeffrey Katzenberg (former head of Disney's film and television production units) and Richard Frank (former head of Disney's television production unit). Finally, in this same year, Disney—in the face of public pressure—had to abandon plans for a new theme park (called America) to be built in Virginia.

Despite these setbacks and challenges, Michael Eisner has clearly implemented a series of decisions, the results of which have substantially enhanced the performance of the Walt Disney Company.

■   ■   ■

By 1962, Sam Walton and his brother, Bud, owned and operated sixteen Ben Franklin five-and-dime stores in rural Arkansas. Early on, Sam Walton recognized the economic potential of locating discount retail outlets in relatively rural cities but was unable to convince the owners of the Ben Franklin chain to pursue this opportunity. In response, he created his own company and called it Wal-Mart Stores.

Wal-Mart began operations in the fiercely competitive discount retail business. Through the late 1960s, several discount retailers—including King's, Korvette's, Two Guys, and Woolco—were forced out of business. Profit margins in the surviving stores were paper thin—often averaging only 2 or 3 percent of sales. Despite this challenging industry, Wal-Mart began to prosper and grow. By the mid-1980s, while more established retailers, including Kmart and Zayre's, had a return on equity averaging about 14 percent, Wal-Mart's return on equity averaged about 33 percent. Despite the fact that Wal-Mart was only one-third of Kmart's size, Wal-Mart's market value was more than two times Kmart's market value (Ghemawat, 1986).

Walton attributed the success of his firm to a combination of three factors. First, by locating many of its stores in relatively rural cities, Wal-Mart was providing a much-needed service to customers who lived in or near these cities. Moreover, these cities were only large enough to support one large discount retail operation. Thus the Wal-Marts that operated in these rural locations were able to charge prices that were as much as 6 percent higher than the prices at Wal-Marts that were operated in more urban areas—all without attracting additional retail companies into these markets (Ghemawat, 1986).

Second, Wal-Mart was able to develop one of the most effective and cost-efficient distribution networks in the retail industry. Built around several large warehouse facilities, Wal-Mart's distribution system began with detailed inventory information gathered at each store. This information was used to order just enough product to ensure that inventory would be on hand, but not so much that large amounts of inventory would have to be warehoused. By operating its own fleet of trucks, and by cooperating with its suppliers, Wal-Mart was able to obtain a 6 or 7 percent cost advantage over its competition, including the much larger Kmart (Ghemawat, 1986).

Third, Sam Walton himself helped create an organizational culture and way of doing business that motivated and inspired his employees. To emphasize the importance of low costs, he built a headquarters building that looked a great deal like a warehouse. Sam rode around in a beat-up old truck—even though at the time of his death he was the richest person in the United States. Employees responded to Sam's way of doing business and generated higher-than-industry-average levels of productivity and lower-than-industry-average levels of shrinkage.

Of course, Wal-Mart faced its own challenges as well. First, by the early 1990s, most of the rural markets that had allowed Wal-Mart to charge relatively higher prices were already exploited. To continue its growth, Wal-Mart had to begin to expand its operations in much more competitive urban settings. Second, in response to developments in the warehouse segment of the retail industry, Wal-Mart introduced Sam's Discount Warehouses. Although discount warehouses have several attractive features, they work on even narrower margins than discount retail stores do. Finally, Wal-Mart began to experience resistance to its growth efforts. Local merchants and community leaders in several New England states, for example, worked together to keep Wal-Mart from destroying the existing retail distribution network—and the lifestyles associated with it (Ortega, 1995).

Despite these difficulties and challenges, Wal-Mart continues to be a growing and successful company. At the time of Sam Walton's death, in 1992, he was widely hailed as one of the most influential and successful entrepreneurs in the retail industry (Ortega, 1995).

Most observers would agree that Microsoft, Disney, and Wal-Mart have at least one thing in common: They have been uncommonly successful. They have all generated enormous wealth for their stockholders and at least some of their employees. They have all had a profound impact on how business in their industry is conducted. And they have all had an important effect on consumers throughout the world.

Most observers would also agree that these three firms have pursued strategies that were carefully chosen and brilliantly executed. Microsoft's strategy was to leverage its foothold in the PC software industry, through the MS-DOS operating system, to become a *software* powerhouse. Disney's strategy was to build, nurture, and exploit its characters and brand names in the development of an *entertainment* powerhouse. Wal-Mart's strategy was to exploit its rural locations and cost advantages to build a *retailing* powerhouse.

1.1   DEFINITIONS OF STRATEGY

Most would agree that much of the success of those firms can be attributed to their strategies, but there is much less agreement about what actually constitutes a firm's strategy. Indeed, there are almost as many different definitions of strategy as there are books written about strategy. Some of the most important definitions of *strategy* and of *strategic management* are listed in Table 1.1. Some are long and complex—for example, Quinn (1980) and Schendel and Hatten (1972). Others are deceptively simple—for example, Hatten and Hatten (1988:1). Some stress the relationship between strategy and a firm's objectives; some focus on matching environmental opportunities with corporate strengths; and some emphasize the subjective and psychological character of strategies.

Some of the variety in the definitions of strategy and strategic management presented in Table 1.1 reflects the relative youth of teaching and research on these organizational phenomena. Although the intellectual roots of strategy teaching and research can be traced back to economists like Marshall (1891), Chamberlin (1933), and Schumpeter (1934), and to research on the role of the general manager in organizations conducted at the Harvard Business School over the last several decades (Learned, Christensen, Andrews, and Guth, 1969), strategy only emerged as an independent area of teaching and research well into the 1960s (Ansoff, 1965). As a result, many of the definitional debates that were resolved long ago in more mature disciplines, like finance and organizational behavior, continue to linger only partially resolved in the field of strategy.

However, this definitional variety is not just the result of the relative youth of research on strategy. It reflects the complexity and multifaceted nature of strategic phenomena in organizations. The study of strategy and strategic management is the study of the integration of numerous business functions in a firm (Steiner and Miner, 1977). It unfolds at several distinct levels of analysis—from corporate headquarters to single businesses—and even extends to the analysis of specific functions within a single business (Thompson and Strickland, 1987) and specific business actions within those functions. It involves the collection and analysis of data about general competitive conditions; the strengths, weaknesses, and likely actions of current competitors, potential competitors, suppliers, customers, and so forth (Porter, 1980); and a firm's own internal strengths and weaknesses (Learned et al., 1969; Porter, 1980:xiii–xx).

Phenomena as complex and multifaceted as strategy and strategic management are not easily described in crisp 25-words-or-less definitions. Most efforts at creating these kinds of definitions inevitably stress

**TABLE 1.1
Alternative
Definitions of
Strategy and
Strategic
Management**

Strategic management: "The process of determining and [maintaining] the relationship of the organization to its environment expressed through the use of selected objectives, and of attempting to achieve the desired states of relationship through resource allocations which allow efficient and effective action programs by the organization and its subparts" (Schendel and Hatten, 1972:5).

Strategy: "The formulation of basic organizational missions, purposes, and objectives; polices and program strategies to achieve them; and the methods needed to assure that strategies are implemented to achieve organizational ends" (Steiner and Miner, 1977:7).

Strategic management: "The process whereby managers establish an organization's long term direction, set specific performance objectives, develop strategies to achieve these objectives in light of all the relevant internal and external circumstances, and undertake to execute the chosen action plans" (Thompson and Strickland, 1987:4).

Strategy: "Concerned with drafting the plan of war and shaping the individual campaigns, and within these, deciding on the individual engagements" (Von Clausewitz, 1976:177).

Strategy: "A pattern in a stream of actions or decisions" (Mintzberg and McHugh, 1985:161).

Strategy: "A complete plan: a plan which specifies which choices [the player] will make in every possible situation" (Von Neumann and Morgenstern, 1944:79).

Strategic management: "The process of managing the pursuit of organizational missions while managing the relationship of the organization to its environment" (Higgins, 1983:3).

Strategic management: "The process of examining both present and future environments, formulating the organizational objectives, and making, implementing, and controlling decisions focused on achieving these objectives in the present and future environments" (Smith, Arnold, and Bizzell, 1988:5).

Strategy: "A unified, comprehensive, and integrated plan designed to ensure that the basic objectives of the enterprise are achieved" (Glueck, 1980:9).

Strategy: "The pattern or plan that integrates an organization's major goals, policies, and action sequences into a cohesive whole. A well formulated strategy helps to marshal and allocate an organization's resources into a unique and viable posture based on its relative internal competencies and shortcomings, anticipated changes in the environment, and contingent moves by intelligent opponents" (Quinn, 1980).

Strategic management: "The process by which an organization formulates objectives and is managed to achieve them" (Hatten and Hatten, 1988:1).

Strategy: "The way to achieve organizational objectives" (Hatten and Hatten, 1988:1).

some facets of these phenomena over others (Mintzberg, 1988). Once one set of definitions has been proposed that emphasizes one aspect of strategy, another set is proposed that emphasizes a different aspect. This leads others to propose still another set of definitions, and so on. In the end, there is little agreement about definitions of strategy and strategic management.

However, although there may not be much general agreement about the definitions of these two concepts, it does not necessarily follow that competing definitions are contradictory. Indeed, if each definition emphasizes a different facet of strategy as it exists in organizations, then these different definitions are more likely to be complementary than contradictory. In this chapter we investigate the relationship between different definitions of strategy by reviewing, evaluating, and comparing the most important of these definitions currently in the literature. By examining how different definitions complement one another, we can obtain a more complete picture of what strategy is in real organizations.

1.2   HIERARCHICAL DEFINITIONS OF STRATEGY AND STRATEGIC MANAGEMENT

The oldest definition of strategy relates this concept to a firm's mission, objectives, and tactics (Steiner and Miner, 1977; Andrews, 1971; Quinn, 1980). This definitional approach imagines the hierarchy presented in Fig. 1.1. Here, strategy is defined as the way that a firm attains its objectives or fulfills its mission, and strategic management is the process by which a firm's mission and objectives are decided, how its specific strategies are chosen, and how those strategies are implemented through specific policies or tactics.

COMPONENTS OF HIERARCHICAL DEFINITIONS

The terms *mission, objectives, tactics,* and *policies* all have specific meanings in this hierarchical definition of *strategy* and *strategic management.* As suggested in Fig. 1.1, a firm's *mission* is top management's view of what the organization seeks to do and become over the long term (Thompson and Strickland, 1987:5). Often, this view of the future is expressed in the form of a mission statement: a publicly available summary of the long-term goals of a firm's top managers. Two examples of mission statements are presented in Table 1.2. Hershey Foods sees its mission as "to become a major diversified food company." MCI sees its

**FIGURE 1.1
Hierarchical
Definitions of
Strategy and
Strategic
Management**

Mission: Top management's view of
what the organization seeks to do and
become over the long term

Objectives: Specific performance
targets in each of the areas covered
by a firm's mission

Strategies: Means through which
firms accomplish mission and objectives

Tactics/Policies: Actions that firms
undertake to implement their strategies

mission as "leadership in the global telecommunications services industry" and "profitable growth" (Thompson and Strickland, 1987:6–7).

Objectives in the hierarchical definition of strategy are the specific
performance targets that firms aspire to in each of the areas included in
a firm's mission statement. It is usually not enough for a firm just to
assert that it wants to be a "leader" in its industry or that it wants to
become a "major diversified company." In addition, a firm needs to
specify what it means to be a leader in its industry, what being a
"major" diversified company means. Often, objectives are stated in
financial or economic terms. Thus for one firm being a "leader" in an
industry may mean having the largest market share, but for other firms
leadership might mean being the most profitable firm in the industry,
having the highest-quality products, or being the most innovative. In
the same way, being a "major diversified company" may mean unrelated diversification across a wide variety of industries for one firm,
and it may mean a relatively narrow product and industry focus for
another. In this hierarchical definition of strategy, comparing actual
behavior with objectives is the way that managers can know whether
they have fulfilled a firm's mission.

Neither Hershey nor MCI includes specific objectives in its mission
statement (see Table 1.2). It is not difficult, however, to imagine what
these firms' objectives might be. For Hershey, becoming a "diversified
food company" may mean having a specific percentage of its sales and
revenue come from noncandy food businesses, and becoming a "major"
company may mean obtaining a certain level of sales or profits. For MCI,

TABLE 1.2
Examples of
Corporate Mission
Statements

Hershey Foods Corporation Mission Statement

Hershey Foods Corporation's basic business mission is to become a major, diversified food company. The company uses four approaches in pursuit of its mission: (1) to capitalize on the considerable growth potential of the company's existing brands and products in current markets, (2) to introduce new products, (3) to expand the distribution of Hershey's long-established, well-known brands and new products into new markets—domestic and foreign, and (4) to make acquisitions and other types of alliances. These approaches are pursued within the context of maintaining the financial strength of the company.

A basic principle which Hershey will continue to embrace is to attract and hold consumers with products and services of consistently superior quality and value.

MCI Communications, Inc., Mission Statement

MCI's mission is leadership in the global telecommunications services industry. Profitable growth is fundamental to that mission, so that we may serve the interests of our stockholders and our customers.

To maintain profitable growth, MCI will: provide a full range of high-value services for customers who must communicate or move information electronically throughout the United States and the world; manage our business so as to be the low-cost provider of services; make quality synonymous with MCI to our growing customer base; set the pace in identifying and implementing cost-effective technologies and services as we expand our state-of-the-art communications network; continue to be an entrepreneurial company, built of people who can make things happen in a competitive marketplace.

the fundamental mission of "profitable growth" may have been translated into specific sales growth and profitability targets.

With a mission and objectives in place, a firm, according to the hierarchical definition of strategy, can then turn its attention to strategies. Strategies thus become the means through which firms accomplish their objectives and mission (Thompson and Strickland, 1987:13; Hatten and Hatten, 1988:1). Strategies are so important that they are sometimes included as part of a firm's mission statement. Thus Hershey Foods not only states its mission ("to become a major diversified food company") but also specifies how it will accomplish this mission (by expanding current products in current markets, introducing new products, expanding distribution of current products into new markets, and acquisitions). In the same way, MCI states that, to become a leader in the international telecommunications services industry, it will provide a full range of services, be a low-cost provider, emphasize quality, continue technological innovation, and retain a spirit of entrepreneurship. These specific actions that MCI will take to reach its objectives and fulfill its mission thus constitute, at least according to this definition, its strategy.

The final level of analysis in the hierarchical definition of strategy presented in Fig. 1.1 is the policy or tactic level. In this definition, *policies* or *tactics* (the words are almost synonymous) are the specific actions that firms undertake to implement their strategies (Steiner and Miner, 1977:22–23). That Hershey may engage in acquisitions to reach its mission of becoming a "major diversified food company" suggests one of the strategies it might use. Which particular firms Hershey will acquire, how much the company will pay for them, and how it will integrate an acquisition into Hershey's ongoing operations would be its tactics. MCI states that one of its strategies is to remain a technological leader. Spending money on research and development and purchasing technological advances developed by others might be its tactics.

STRENGTHS OF HIERARCHICAL DEFINITIONS

The hierarchical definition of strategy presented in Fig. 1.1 has three important strengths. First, it emphasizes the link between strategy and performance. Virtually all strategic management researchers, and most practicing managers, are interested in the relationship between the actions taken by a firm and a firm's performance (Rumelt, Schendel, and Teece, 1991). The hierarchical definition provides explicit criteria for judging the performance quality of a firm's strategies—"good" strategies enable an organization to reach its objectives and fulfill its mission; "bad" strategies make it more difficult for a firm to reach its objectives and fulfill its mission.

Second, this hierarchical definition focuses on the multiple levels of analysis that are important in formulating and implementing strategies (Thompson and Strickland, 1987). These levels of analysis vary in their degree of abstraction. Company missions are very abstract concepts. They specify what a firm wants to become but say little about how a firm will get to where it wants to go. Objectives translate missions into specific goals and targets and thus are less abstract. Strategies specify which actions firms will take to meet their objectives. Tactics, the least abstract concept, focus on specific actions that need to be taken to implement strategies.

These levels of strategic analysis roughly correspond to different levels of authority in the formal hierarchy of large diversified firms. These formal hierarchical levels are discussed in more detail in Chapter 12. However, for purposes of this discussion, the three levels of hierarchy presented in Fig. 1.2 will suffice (Williamson, 1975). At the corporate level in firms, strategic efforts focus on defining and refining a firm's mission and objectives. The results of these efforts have been called "grand strategy" by some authors (Hitt, Ireland, and Palia, 1982). Within separate business divisions, strategic management efforts focus on specific strategies that might be used to reach a firm's objectives and missions (Thompson and Strickland, 1987). Finally, within functional specialties inside different business divisions, specific tactics that might be used to implement strategies are formulated.

By emphasizing the multiple levels of analysis in the strategic management process, hierarchical definitions appropriately emphasize the need in organizations to gather information, ideas, and suggestions from all parts of the firm in order to formulate effective strategies. In this conception of strategy, each part of a firm plays an important role. Senior corporate managers specialize in establishing missions and objectives, division general managers specialize in strategy formulation, and functional managers focus their efforts on tactics. No one of these tasks is more important than any other. Missions and objectives without strategies and tactics will never be reached. Strategies without missions and objectives will be unfocused. Strategies without tactics are usually not implemented. And tactics without strategies or missions are not likely to improve a firm's performance. The hierarchical definition presented in Fig. 1.1 helps communicate that strategy and strategic management are companywide issues, not issues that are held in reserve for top managers.

A third strength of the hierarchical definition is that it emphasizes that strategy, in order to have an impact on performance, cannot remain simply an idea in an organization. Rather, it must be translated, through resource allocation, into action. An organization's mission is often a statement of an idea, or a manifestation of the values, of top

FIGURE 1.2
Levels of Analysis in the Hierarchical Definition of Strategy Compared to Levels in a Firm's Formal Hierarchy

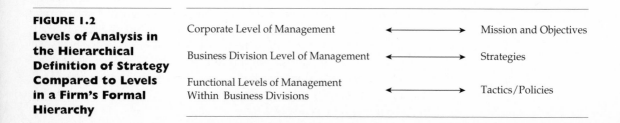

Corporate Level of Management	⟷	Mission and Objectives
Business Division Level of Management	⟷	Strategies
Functional Levels of Management Within Business Divisions	⟷	Tactics/Policies

management. However, by itself, a mission statement is likely to have little impact on firm performance. Rather, this mission statement must be linked with objectives, strategies, and tactics. In choosing objectives, strategies, and tactics, managers must make tough decisions, set priorities, and allocate resources.

Firms that translate their mission into actions increase the probability that they will improve their performance. For example, General Electric (GE) has recently gone to great lengths to make its mission of becoming a flexible, innovative company a reality. Led by Jack Welch, president and CEO, GE has moved well beyond just stating that it wants to become flexible and innovative. Top management has made difficult strategic and operational decisions (such as selling GE's consumer electronics business to concentrate on medical imaging) that help make this mission a reality. Early reports suggest that GE has been quite successful in its efforts (Stewart, 1991; Huey, 1991).

Sony also invests heavily in its effort to fulfill its mission of remaining one of the most innovative firms in the world (Schlender, 1992). Sony's 9,000 engineers and scientists, working 10- and 12-hour days, spend approximately $1.5 billion a year on developing new products—6 percent of Sony's revenues! To facilitate innovation, Sony encourages its engineers to seek out interesting projects, no matter where they are in the firm. Creative engineers rapidly rise to key technical positions in Sony. This investment, of time, money, and other organizational resources has enabled Sony to introduce a blizzard of products in the 1990s, including the PalmTop personal computer (a powerful personal computer that weighs less than a pound), the Discman (a portable CD player), the Data Discman (a portable CD ROM data storage device), and the Mini Disc (a digital recording and playback system) (Schlender, 1992).

WEAKNESSES OF HIERARCHICAL DEFINITIONS

The hierarchical definition of strategy has weaknesses as well as strengths. First, it has a very underdeveloped notion of the competitive environment's impact on strategy formulation and implementation. Mission statements summarize where top management wants an organization to be in the long run, but the development of these statements tends to be too inwardly focused. In choosing a mission, top managers are encouraged to look inward, evaluating their own personal priorities and values. Certainly, this kind of internal analysis is an important step in developing a firm's mission. Indeed, in Chapter 5 we suggest that these kinds of internal analyses are essential for firms seeking sustained competitive advantages. Such internal analyses, however, must be linked with an analysis of the competitive environment in order for firms to choose missions (and thus objectives, strategies, and tactics) that will add value to a firm.

There are numerous examples of firms that have failed to link internal and external analyses when choosing missions, objectives, strategies, and tactics. Polaroid's effort to create a "perfect" instant photography camera—the SX-70 camera—led to a camera that was too expensive for its market niche (Porter and Fuller, 1978). Coca-Cola's decision to protect its market share from Pepsi by abandoning its traditional flavor in favor of the sweeter New Coke failed to anticipate the almost fanatical commitment of loyal Coke drinkers (Hartley, 1991). Yugo's strategy to exploit unmet demand for inexpensive cars failed to recognize the need for quality, reliability, and safety in this market niche (Hartley, 1991).

A second weakness of the hierarchical definition is that it tends to focus, almost exclusively, on formal, routinized, bureaucratic strategy-making processes. In this definition, strategic choices are made through systematic study and analysis. These analyses result in a coherent, self-reinforcing sets of strategies that, taken together, lead a firm to reach its objectives and mission. There is little doubt that many organizations choose at least some of their strategies in this logical and systematic way. An enormous amount of research on formal strategic planning suggests that more and more firms are adopting explicit and formal planning systems to choose their strategies (Armstrong, 1982; Pearce, Freeman, and Robinson, 1987; Steiner, 1983). The hierarchical definitions presented in Fig. 1.1 tend to emphasize this formal, systematic aspect of choosing and implementing strategies.

Yet not all strategies are chosen in this way. Firms choose strategies by discovering an unanticipated opportunity and exploiting that opportunity to improve performance (Barney, 1986a). Firms also choose strategies "retroactively"—that is, they engage in certain kinds of behavior over time, and then, only after that pattern of behavior has existed, senior managers label these actions as a coherent or consistent strategy (Mintzberg, 1978; Mintzberg and McHugh, 1985). Some firms "stumble into" their strategies by chance (Barney, 1986a). All these are ways that firms can "choose" strategies, yet none of them is consistent with the formal, systematic strategic management process presented in Fig. 1.1.

Honda's initial entry into the U.S. motorcycle market is a good example of a firm that did not choose its strategy in a formal, hierarchical manner. When Honda executives first arrived in the United States in 1959, they anticipated selling large motorcycles to confirmed motorcycle riders. They did not want to market the small, 50cc Honda Cubs that were popular in Japan. Unfortunately, Honda's large motorcycles were plagued by mechanical failure and were not well received in the United States. At the same time, however, Honda executives were riding their Cubs throughout Los Angeles, running business errands. These small motorbikes received a great deal of attention from Honda's distributors, but Honda preferred to focus on its larger bikes. Then, in desperation, Honda started selling its small motorbikes. Exploiting this opportunity—although it was not part of Honda's mission, objectives, strategies, or tactics as the company entered the U.S. market—proved to be the key that opened the door through which Honda was able to establish a presence in this market. Honda's subsequent success in medium and large motorcycles was an outcome of its willingness to exploit this unforeseen opportunity (Pascale, 1984).

A final limitation of hierarchical approaches to defining strategy and strategic management is that, despite their apparent rigor and clarity, they often fail to give significant guidance to managers when they are applied in real organizations. There are literally thousands of objectives that an organization could choose to support any given mission statement. Which of these objectives a firm should choose, which should be given priority, and which should be ignored are questions that must be answered with logic and ideas that are not provided within the hierarchical definition. Moreover, there may be thousands of different strategies that firms could choose to support any given set of objectives. Which particular strategies a firm should choose goes beyond the hierarchical model. The same is true for the thousands of tactics that may or may not support a firm's strategies.

In the end, while the hierarchical definition points to some of the critical dimensions of strategy, it fails to provide sufficient guidance to firms seeking to choose and implement strategies.

1.3   ECLECTIC DEFINITIONS OF STRATEGY AND STRATEGIC MANAGEMENT

Several authors have responded to the formal, bureaucratic emphasis of the hierarchical definition by suggesting that more flexible, inclusive definitions of strategy are more appropriate. A leader in this eclectic approach to defining strategy is Henry Mintzberg. In a series of articles and books, Mintzberg has developed a perspective on strategy and strategic management that includes a much wider range of organizational phenomena than would be included in the hierarchical definition.

COMPONENTS OF ECLECTIC DEFINITIONS

Although Mintzberg has adopted a single definition of strategy in some of his work—for example, "strategy is a pattern in a stream of decisions or actions" (Mintzberg, 1975, 1985)—his preference is apparently to adopt multiple definitions or characterizations of strategy, to obtain the multiple insights that each of these different definitions provides. These multiple characterizations (all beginning with the letter p) are presented in Table 1.3. (After all, marketing has its four p's, so why shouldn't strategy have its five p's?)

For Mintzberg (1988:14), strategy is a *plan*, "a consciously intended course of action, a guideline (or set of them) to deal with a situation." This notion of strategy is closely related to the hierarchical definition discussed earlier, for strategies (according to this definition) are presumed to be developed before they are needed, and they are developed consciously and purposefully. In Mintzberg's (1973) language, these are intended strategies.

Strategy is also a *ploy*, a maneuver to outwit an opponent. An example cited by Mintzberg (1988:14) is a firm that threatens to expand plant capacity to stop a competitor from building a new plant. This firm does not actually want to expand capacity; its intention is to prevent its competitor from building a new plant. Thus its strategy to threaten to expand capacity is a ploy. A growing literature on these kinds of ploys is discussed in Chapter 3 in the analysis of contrived deterrence strategies as a barrier to entry into an industry.

For Mintzberg (1988), strategy is also a *pattern*. As suggested above, many of the strategies that firms end up pursuing may have been strategies they intended to pursue. Others, however, may be actions and decisions that they did not, ahead of time, intend to pursue but strategies that nevertheless emerged. These emergent actions are strategies if they form consistent patterns over time, whether or not they were intended.

TABLE 1.3 **Mintzberg's Eclectic Approach to Defining Strategy**	**Strategy as . . .**	
	Plan:	a consciously intended course of action to deal with a situation
	Ploy:	a maneuver to outwit an opponent
	Pattern:	a pattern of actions that emerge, unintendedly, over time
	Position:	the way a firm relates to its competitive environment
	Perspective:	the way that managers in a firm see themselves and the world around them

Honda's entry into the U.S. motorcycle market is a good example of an emergent "strategy as a pattern." So was McDonnell-Douglas's entry into the software and computer services industry. McDonnell-Douglas did not "plan" on becoming a major actor in the data-processing industry. However, as it developed data-processing skills to support its core business of manufacturing commercial and military aircraft, it discovered it had built an expertise in data processing (*Business Week,* 1983). After some time, it began to market those skills—that is, to implement a "data-processing strategy." Yet the ability to implement that strategy had been neither conceived of ahead of time nor intentionally developed. It was purely a byproduct of other efforts at McDonnell-Douglas. Later, once this strategy became clear and articulated, efforts were made to further improve McDonnell-Douglas's skills in this area. These efforts included the acquisition of TymShare, Inc. At this point, the exploitation of McDonnell-Douglas's data-processing skills had become an intentional strategy. But it began simply as an emergent pattern of actions, an unforeseen byproduct of other efforts.

Some firms do almost nothing to choose a particular strategy, but one emerges anyway. PEZ Candy Inc. manufactures and sells small plastic candy dispensers with cartoon and movie character heads, along with candy refills. This privately held firm has made few efforts to speed its growth, yet demand for current and older PEZ products continues to grow. In 1991, PEZ had to double the size of its manufacturing operation to keep up with demand. Old PEZ dispensers have become something of a collector's item. In 1993 alone, two national conferences on PEZ collecting were held, and some particularly rare PEZ dispensers were auctioned at Christie's. This demand has forced PEZ to raise the price of its dispensers to $1.29 and the price of its candy refills to $1.39, all without increases in advertising, sales personnel, and movie tie-ins so typical in the candy industry (McCarthy, 1993).

Strategy is also *position* (Mintzberg, 1988:15)—that is, the way that a firm relates with its competitive environment. This concept is very closely linked to the matching definition of *strategy* discussed in Section 1.4. A firm's position (its competitive niche, its product market domain, and so on) can be arrived at either by plan or by pattern. But no matter how a firm gets to the position it is in, this position comes to define its strategy.

Finally, strategy is also *perspective.* By perspective, Mintzberg means the way that managers in a firm perceive themselves and the world around them. This perspective is sometimes very deeply ingrained into the character of a firm (Selznick, 1957). IBM sees itself as a "marketing firm"; Hewlett-Packard and Westinghouse see themselves as "engineering firms." These self-conceptions profoundly influence how these firms organize themselves, who is promoted, the kinds of actions that are taken, the kinds of decisions that are made, and so forth. Although it may not be the case that a firm deliberately chooses to see itself as an engineering or a marketing firm, once this culture and world-view exists, it has an important impact on the subsequent actions and decisions of firms.

STRENGTHS OF ECLECTIC DEFINITIONS

Mintzberg's approach to defining strategy and strategic management has numerous strengths. Primary among them is that it points to a wide range of phenomena that can affect a firm's performance, besides its formal, hierarchically chosen strategy. By pointing out these effects, the eclectic approach can help managers become aware of opportunities that a rigid commitment to hierarchically derived strategies would ignore. Honda would have had a much more difficult time becoming established in the U.S. motorcycle market, and McDonnell-Douglas a more difficult time becoming established in the data-processing market, if managers in these two firms had remained rigidly committed to their organizations' narrowly defined missions, strategies, and tactics.

The eclectic approach also helps emphasize the subjective and qualitative nature of strategy formulation and implementation. Earlier, we suggested that strategy cannot *just* be an idea, or a concept. Rather, to have an impact on firm performance, ideas must be translated into resource allocation decisions, priorities, and programs. However, although this translation into policies and practices is important, it is also important to remember that strategies are also ideas—ideas that can motivate, even inspire, managers and organizations. Assumptions about what an organization is, and what it can become, are at the core of strategy formulation and implementation efforts. Firms that can exploit these core assumptions when they add value to a firm can expect to gain competitive advantages (Barney, 1991). Firms that are able to change these core assumptions when their competitive environments change can also gain these advantages (Huey, 1991). The eclectic approach to defining strategy and strategic management helps remind managers that strategy is both an idea and the policies and procedures that operationalize that idea.

An example of a firm that has exploited strategy as a motivating tool is the Scandinavian airline SAS. The president and CEO of SAS, Jan Carlzon, believes it is possible to develop customer loyalty in the airline business if an airline responds quickly and efficiently to customer needs. In hundreds of meetings with employees at all levels in SAS, Carlzon constantly emphasizes the twin messages of service and quality. Employees have heard the message, and SAS is now widely cited as one of the highest-service-quality airlines flying. This vision of a high-quality, high-service airline has also translated into high performance. In years when other international airlines, including TWA, Pan Am, and Alitalia, lost money, SAS was able to retain its profitability (Labich, 1991).

WEAKNESSES OF ECLECTIC DEFINITIONS

The weaknesses of eclectic definitions of strategy parallel the strengths of these definitions. First, although the eclectic approach includes a wide range of phenomena in the study of strategic management, it may, in the end, not exclude any phenomena. Since *any* idea or action that might exist in a firm can be thought of as a strategy (according to one or another of the approaches in the eclectic definition), the study of strategy is not limited to any specific phenomena. Second, some of the attributes of the hierarchical definition that are very appealing—including the emphasis on the relationship between strategy and firm performance, and the emphasis on resource allocation—are blurred or lost altogether in some of the approaches included in the eclectic definition. Some of these approaches, while provocative, fail to provide the kind of managerial guidance that is a core objective of much strategic management teaching and research.

Even Mintzberg (1990) recognizes some of the limitations of various parts of the eclectic approach, suggesting that different approaches to defining strategy will be more or less effective depending on the competitive contexts in which a firm finds itself.

1.4   MATCHING DEFINITIONS OF STRATEGY AND STRATEGIC MANAGEMENT

A final approach to defining strategy focuses on the matching process depicted in Fig. 1.3. Here, a firm's strategy is defined as actions that the firm takes to respond to threats and opportunities in its environment while exploiting its strengths and avoiding or fixing its weaknesses (Learned et al., 1969; Quinn, 1980). Strategic management is defined as the process through which firms analyze their competitive environments to discover their threats and opportunities, the process through which they analyze their own resources and capabilities to discover their competitive strengths and weaknesses, and the process of matching these two analyses to choose strategies. Strategic management also includes organizing to implement the strategies chosen in this manner.

The matching approach depicted in Fig. 1.3 is perhaps the dominant approach currently. Virtually every strategy textbook written over

FIGURE I.3
A Matching Definition of Strategy and Strategic Management

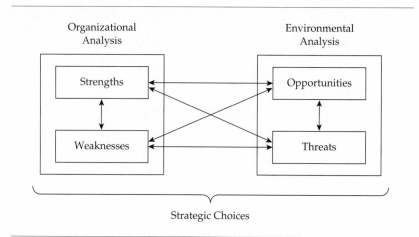

the last ten years begins with one form or another of this definition. Even authors who seem to prefer the more traditional hierarchical approach to defining strategy move quickly to focus attention on this matching process in choosing strategies (for example, Thompson and Strickland, 1987:4–16, 44–54; Steiner and Miner, 1977:17–22, 41–54). Porter (1981a) suggests that this matching approach to defining strategy underlies virtually all teaching and research in the field.

For reasons that are not altogether clear (but may have something to do with product differentiation in the marketplace of ideas—see Chapter 7 for further discussion), matching definitions of strategy have given rise to a whole range of catchy acronyms to describe the process of choosing strategies. These include WOTS-UP analysis (weakness, opportunities, threats, and strengths underlying planning), SWOT analysis (strengths, weakness, opportunities, and threats), and TWOS analysis (threats, weaknesses, opportunities, and strengths), to name just a few (Thompson and Strickland, 1987; Rowe, Mason, and Dickel, 1982). Whatever the acronym, the underlying characterizations of strategy and strategic management are the same.

STRENGTHS OF MATCHING DEFINITIONS

Matching definitions of strategy have several strengths. Some of them overlap the strengths of the hierarchical and eclectic definitions; others are unique to the matching approach.

First, matching definitions recognize the important impact of a firm's environment on strategic choices. This emphasis on the environment is considerably greater than is the case in the hierarchical approach. Application of the matching approach necessarily involves analyzing threats and opportunities in a firm's environment and analyzing how a firm can neutralize threats and exploit opportunities. A firm implementing this approach is less likely to choose strategies with limited market potential than a firm implementing the hierarchical approach. If Polaroid had analyzed its competitive environment more closely, it probably would not have invested as much money as it did in the SX-70 camera. If Coca-Cola had understood the loyalty of its traditional customers better, it probably would not have introduced New Coke. And if Yugo had understood the importance of safety, reliability, and quality—along with price—it may have been more successful in the U.S. automobile market.

Second, matching definitions recognize the important impact of a firm's internal strengths and weaknesses on strategic choices. In this model, strategic choices cannot depend solely on environmental threats and opportunities. In addition, a firm's unique resources and capabilities—its strengths and weaknesses—and how these can be applied in neutralizing threats and exploiting opportunities are important considerations. This internal focus suggests that there may be some environmental threats and opportunities that certain firms—firms without the required strengths—cannot neutralize or exploit.

This internal aspect of the matching model excludes the neutralization of some threats and the exploitation of some opportunities as options for some firms, and it may point to important sources of competitive advantage for others. If several competing firms are pursuing the same strategies, using the same underlying resources and capabilities, then none of them can be expected to gain a competitive advantage. But if a firm with unusual strategic strengths can pursue a strategy more efficiently than its competitors, then this efficient firm can gain a competitive advantage (Rumelt, Schendel, and Teece, 1991). Such unusual resources and capabilities are called distinctive competencies. A firm's distinctive competencies cannot be isolated by using a model of strategic choice that focuses only on a firm's competitive environment (Barney, 1991).

Consider, for example, a set of highly skilled manufacturing firms (such as Japanese automobile companies) competing with one another. Each of these firms may have developed to a high level its resources and capabilities in manufacturing. Each may have done this by investing in sophisticated equipment, focusing on quality, and so forth (Hayes and Wheelwright, 1979). However, if all of these firms are *equally* skilled, then these manufacturing resources and capabilities cannot give any one of them a competitive advantage. But if one of these firms, in addition to high-quality manufacturing, has also developed a *better* design process, or a *larger* distribution network, or *better* relations with suppliers, these internal resources and capabilities may be sources of competitive advantage. These issues are discussed in more detail in Chapter 5.

Third, like the hierarchical definition, the matching definition of strategy emphasizes the allocation of resources to implement strategies—while not denying the importance of a firm having a clear vision of its strategic goals and objectives. Mintzberg (1988) and others appropriately remind us that ideas underlie strategic management. Several authors have pointed to the importance of senior management's vision of the future of an organization as a determinant of a firm's performance (Tichy and Devanna, 1986). Having a clear vision that can be shared with members of an organization can help motivate change and improvement.

However, to have an effect on firm performance, vision must be translated into reality. In the hierarchical approach, this translation occurs through strategies, policies, and tactics that support a mission statement. In the matching approach, the translation of vision into policies and procedures occurs when organizations implement specific strategies that neutralize threats and exploit opportunities while taking advantage of strengths and avoiding or fixing weaknesses.

Finally, like the hierarchical definition, the matching definition of strategy emphasizes firm performance and provides explicit criteria for judging the quality of a firm's strategies. In the hierarchical approach, "good strategies" support a firm's objectives and mission. In the matching approach, a "good" strategy is one that (1) neutralizes threats while (2) exploiting environmental opportunities and (3) capitalizing on internal strengths and (4) fixing or avoiding internal weaknesses.

WEAKNESSES OF MATCHING DEFINITIONS

There are two major weaknesses of the matching definitions of strategy. First, this approach (just like the hierarchical definition) tends to emphasize formal, intended strategies. Although it is possible to use the matching approach to evaluate why a firm's emergent strategies improved a firm's performance *after* those strategies have emerged, this definition tends to focus more managerial attention on anticipating environmental opportunities and threats, and proactively exploiting strengths and avoiding or fixing weaknesses. This kind of emphasis focuses on intended rather than emergent strategies.

A second weakness of the matching definition is that although this approach is very helpful in describing the *kinds* of questions that managers should ask to choose and implement strategies (for example, what are a firm's environmental threats and opportunities, what are its internal strengths and weaknesses), it provides little guidance in how to answer these questions. All these definitions suggest is that managers should somehow "match" an organization's strengths and weaknesses with its threats and opportunities. What an organization's strengths and weaknesses might be, what its specific threats and opportunities are, what a match between these sets of variables means for strategic choice, and how firms should go about determining whether a match exists (Schoonhoven, 1981; Van de Ven and Drazin, 1985) are questions without answers in the matching definition of strategy. In short, this approach defines the process by which strategic choices should be made; it does not describe the content of those choices.

Some authors have argued that attempts to move beyond helping managers ask the right kinds of questions in choosing strategies are misguided (Churchman, 1971; Cosier, 1978, 1981). Mason and Mitroff (1981), for example, argue that strategic choices made by firms are ill structured in the sense that the formulation of the decision problem is itself a key issue. These authors see "solving" a strategic management problem by choosing a particular strategy as much less problematic than choosing the correct formulation of the problem in the first place. Implementing the right strategic "solution" to the wrong question is seen as more likely to get a firm into financial and other difficulties than is implementing an imperfect strategic solution to the right question. Helping managers to learn to ask the right questions when choosing their strategies is thus a very important objective.

There certainly may be circumstances where all that can be done is to help managers ask the right questions when choosing strategies to implement. In these settings, the definitions presented in Fig. 1.3 are very helpful in specifying the kinds of questions firms should ask. However, it may be possible to move beyond simply specifying the questions that should be asked, to begin to specify how those questions can be answered. The purpose of this book is to begin to answer the questions posed by the matching definition of strategy.

As suggested in Table 1.4, this book uses the matching definition of strategy as a primary organizing framework. The rest of Part 1 focuses on defining the concept of firm performance (Chapter 2) and developing models for analyzing a firm's environmental threats (Chapter 3), opportunities (Chapter 4), and organizational strengths and weaknesses (Chapter 5). Part 2 focuses on strategies that firms can choose to exploit their opportunities and strengths while neutralizing threats and avoiding or fixing weaknesses in a single business. These business-level strategies include competitive strategies—including cost leadership (Chapter 6) and product differentiation (Chapter 7)—and cooperative strategies—including tacit collusion (Chapter 8) and strategic alliances (Chapter 9). Part 3 examines strategies that firms can choose to exploit their opportunities and strengths while neutralizing threats and avoiding or fixing weaknesses across several businesses simultaneously.

TABLE 1.4
The Structure of This Book and Matching Definition of Strategy

Part 1:	The Logic of Strategic Analysis	
Chapter 1:	What Is Strategy?	Introduction
Chapter 2:	What Is Performance?	
Chapter 3:	Evaluating Environmental Threats	Environmental Analysis
Chapter 4:	Evaluating Environmental Opportunities	
Chapter 5:	Evaluating Firm Strengths and Weaknesses: Resources and Capabilities	Organizational Analysis
Part 2:	Business Strategies	
Chapter 6:	Competitive Strategies: Cost Leadership	Gaining Competitive Advantage in a Single Business
Chapter 7:	Competitive Strategies: Product Differentiation	
Chapter 8:	Cooperative Strategies: Tacit Collusion	
Chapter 9:	Cooperative Strategies: Strategic Alliances	
Part 3:	Corporate Strategies	
Chapter 10:	Vertical Integration Strategies	Leveraging Resources to Gain Competitive Advantage in Multiple Businesses
Chapter 11:	Diversification Strategies	
Chapter 12:	Organizing to Implement Diversification Strategies	
Chapter 13:	Merger and Acquisition Strategies	
Chapter 14:	Global Strategies	

These corporate-level strategies include vertical integration strategies (Chapter 10), diversification strategies (Chapters 11 and 12), merger and acquisition strategies (Chapter 13), and global strategies (Chapter 14). Much of the content of the book can be understood as an attempt to provide models, ideas, and theories that help managers answer the questions posed by the matching definition of strategy. Thus this book assumes that it is possible to move beyond process in strategy and strategic management, to begin to specify the strategies that firms seeking to enhance their performance should implement.

1.5 WORKING DEFINITIONS OF STRATEGY AND STRATEGIC MANAGEMENT

What then are strategy and strategic management? Based on the definitions of strategy reviewed above, the following definitions will be used throughout this book. Strategy is *a pattern of resource allocation that enables firms to maintain or improve their performance.* A "good" strategy is *a strategy that neutralizes threats and exploits opportunities while capitalizing on strengths and avoiding or fixing weaknesses.* Strategic management is *the process through which strategies are chosen and implemented.*

These definitions build on many of the strengths of the other definitions discussed earlier. They emphasize resource allocation and performance. They acknowledge the existence of both emergent and intended strategies. And they provide explicit criteria for judging the quality of a strategy. However, until models are developed for analyzing a firm's environmental threats and opportunities and organizational strengths and weaknesses, and for linking these to strategic choices facing firms, these definitions remain nothing more than a description of important strategic questions that should be asked. It is to the task of developing models to answer these questions that we now turn.

Based on these definitions of strategy and strategic management, it is now possible to describe the strategies of Microsoft, Disney, and Wal-Mart. Microsoft's strategy has been to exploit its strengths in operating systems by developing new operating systems and application software to address numerous opportunities in the personal computer software industry. In so doing, Microsoft has been able to neutralize threats from other software firms as well as from hardware companies.

Disney's strategy has been to exploit its strengths in theme park operations and brand name characters by exploiting a wide range of opportunities in the entertainment industry. Concerned that some of its core brand names may have been aging, Disney has moved to avoid this weakness by investing in new characters. These new characters have reduced the threat of competitive entry into Disney's core entertainment business.

Wal-Mart's strategy has been to exploit its strengths in small southern towns, its distribution network, and its organizational culture to take advantage of retail opportunities throughout North America. Wal-Mart is now looking at ways to neutralize some potential threats due to the relative maturity of the discount retail industry, resistance to Wal-Mart's expansion, and Sam Walton's death.

1.6   SUMMARY

Defining the concept of strategy is not easy. Teaching and research in this area are relatively new, and thus little agreement exists about definitions. Moreover, this phenomenon is complex and multifaceted, and such phenomena are always difficult to describe and define.

One of the most common definitions of strategy emphasizes the relationship between a firm's mission, objectives, strategies, and tactics or policies. Some of the strengths of this hierarchical approach include (1) an emphasis on the linkage between strategy and performance, (2) a recognition of multiple levels of analysis in strategic choices, and (3) the focus on the importance of translating ideas into resource allocation decisions. Some of the weaknesses of this hierarchical approach are (1) an underdeveloped sense of the impact of the competitive environment on firm performance, (2) the emphasis on formal, routinized strategy-making processes in organizations, and (3) a lack of practical guidance when firms seek to choose among numerous strategic and tactical alternatives.

Mintzberg has rejected any single definition of strategy in favor of an eclectic set of definitions. For Mintzberg, strategy can be a plan, a ploy, a pattern, a position, or a perspective. Strengths of the eclectic approach are that it (1) incorporates a broad range of phenomena that may have an impact on firm performance and (2) recognizes the subjective and qualitative aspects of strategy—that strategy can be a motivating idea or vision in a firm. Weaknesses of the eclectic approach are (1) its inclusiveness, which prevents it from defining any uniquely strategic phenomena, and (2) the lack of emphasis on performance and on resource allocation issues in at least some of the eclectic definitions.

A third approach to defining strategy focuses on matching a firm's internal strengths and weaknesses with its competitive threats and opportunities. The strengths of this matching approach include (1) a recognition of the importance of a firm's competitive environment as a determinant of its performance, (2) a recognition of internal strengths and weaknesses as important components of the strategic choice process, (3) a focus on translating ideas and visions into concrete resource allocation decisions, and (4) an emphasis on strategy and performance, together with explicit criteria for evaluating the quality of a firm's strategy. Weaknesses of the matching approach include (1) a tendency to emphasize intended strategy over emergent strategy and

(2) an emphasis on specifying the questions to ask in making strategic choices but a failure to suggest how those questions should be answered.

The definitions of strategy and strategic management used throughout this book draw on all previous definitions. Strategy is defined as patterns of resource allocation that enable a firm to improve or maintain its performance, and strategic management is the process through which firms choose and implement their strategies. Drawing most closely from the matching definition, a "good" strategy is defined as one that neutralizes threats, exploits opportunities, takes advantage of strengths, and avoids or fixes weaknesses. Much of the rest of the book develops rigorous models for choosing "good" strategies.

REVIEW QUESTIONS

1. Some firms widely publicize their corporate mission statements by including them in annual reports, on company letterheads, and in corporate advertising. What, if anything, does this practice say about the ability of these mission statements to be sources of sustained competitive advantage for a firm? Why?

2. There is little empirical evidence that having a formal, written mission statement improves a firm's performance. Yet many firms spend a great deal of time and money developing mission statements. Why?

3. Is it possible to distinguish between an emergent strategy and an ad hoc rationalization of a firm's past decisions? Can the concept of an emergent strategy be prescriptive? Why or why not?

4. SWOT analysis is a very general organizing framework. Can it be applied in analyzing a person's career strategies? If no, why not? If yes, apply it to the analysis of your career.

5. Both organizational and environmental analyses are important in the SWOT framework. Is the order in which these analyses are done important? If yes, which should come first—environmental analysis or organizational analysis? If the order is not important, why not?

CHAPTER 2

What Is Performance?

2.1 PERFORMANCE IN THE DEFINITION OF STRATEGY

In Chapter 1, we reviewed and compared definitions of strategy ranging from the complex to the simple, from the straightforward to the subtle. There is significant variety in those definitions, but most have at least one attribute in common: They focus on the impact of a firm's strategies on its performance. This emphasis on performance was made explicit in the working definition of strategy proposed in Section 1.5: a pattern of resource allocation that enables firms to *maintain or improve their performance* (emphasis added).

As applied to organizations, what is performance? The notion of performance in some settings seems to be clear enough. In athletics, the fastest runner, the highest jumper, the person who throws the discus farthest—all these people outperform their competition. But in organizations, performance is a somewhat more complicated concept. There are numerous definitions of *organizational performance* but relatively little agreement about which definitions are "best," let alone agreement about the criteria against which definitions should be judged (Cameron, 1981, 1986, Hannan and Freeman, 1977; McKelvey, 1982; Scherer, 1980; Fisher and McGowan, 1983).

In this chapter we discuss one reasonable approach to defining *performance* and then evaluate a broad range of measures of this approach. In the end, we suggest that no single measure of performance is without flaws and that multiple approaches can be useful in actual strategic analyses.

2.2   A CONCEPTUAL APPROACH TO DEFINING PERFORMANCE

The definition of organizational performance explored here is based on a conception of organizations developed by Simon (1976), Jensen and Meckling (1976), Coase (1937), and Alchian and Demsetz (1972). These authors all suggest that an organization is an association of productive assets (including individuals) who voluntarily come together to obtain economic advantages. Simon (1976), in his analysis of this "coming together," talks about an equilibrium between "inducements" and "contributions" that must exist in order for individuals and other productive assets to be willing to remain associated with an organization. Jensen and Meckling (1976) and Coase (1937) define an organization as "a nexus of contracts" among owners of capital, labor, managers, and other productive assets. These contracts can be formal and written down, or they can be informal and implicit. No matter the formality of these contracts, these authors again emphasize the importance of owners of productive assets being satisfied with the use of those assets in an organization for an organization to continue to exist. Alchian and Demsetz (1972) also emphasize this important voluntary character of organizations: Owners of productive assets will make those assets available to an organization only if they are satisfied with the income they are receiving—and in particular, if the total income they are receiving (adjusted for risk) is at least as large as the income they could expect from any reasonable alternatives.

Building on these insights, it is possible to develop a conceptual definition of organizational performance that compares the value that an organization creates using its productive assets with the value that owners of these assets expect to obtain. If the value that is created is at least as large as the value expected, then it is likely that owners of productive assets will continue to make those assets available to be used by a particular organization. When value created is less than what is expected, owners of assets are likely to be dissatisfied and look for alternatives where the use of their asset can obtain its full expected value (Tirole, 1988).

Consider, for example, the performance of the three hypothetical electronics firms in Table 2.1 (Zenger, 1989). Assume (for convenience) that the only productive asset used by these three firms is their engineers. Firm A hires the best engineers ("A"-level engineers) and pays them a wage commensurate with high expectations about their value to the firm (an "A" level of compensation). However, if this organization is poorly managed or unlucky or has a bad strategy, it will get only a "B" level of performance out of these "A"-level engineers. In that case, in the long run Firm A will not be able to generate sufficient

TABLE 2.1	**Firm A**	**Firm B**	**Firm C**
The Performance of Three Hypothetical Electronics Firms	Hires "A"-level engineers, pays them "A" wages, generates "B" performance	Hires "A"-level engineers, pays them "A" wages, generates "A" performance	Hires "B"-level engineers, pays them "B" wages, generates "A" performance

revenue to pay its "A"-level engineers their "A" wage, and these engineers will have to look elsewhere for employment.

Firm B hires "A"-level engineers, pays them an "A"-level wage, and is able to get "A" levels of performance out of these engineers. Engineers in this setting are likely to remain satisfied, and the firm will generate just enough revenue with these engineers to be able to pay them their market wage.

Firm C is in yet another situation. For some reason, Firm C is either unable or unwilling to hire the best-trained "A"-level engineers. Instead, it hires competent but not superstar "B"-level engineers and pays a corresponding "B"-level wage. However, if Firm C is particularly well managed, if it has an innovative strategy, or if it is lucky, it may be able to get "A" levels of performance out of its "B"-quality managers. In this context, Firm C is generating greater-than-expected value with its engineering assets and will have more than enough revenue to fully compensate its engineers.

This same kind of analysis can be done for each of the productive resources attracted to and used by a firm, including labor, management, entrepreneurial skill, physical capital, and financial capital. Each of these resources can be used by firms to create value, and each has an expected value associated with it. Whether a firm is able to generate the expected value determines the firm's level of performance.

The relationships between expected value and actual value suggest the three-way classification of performance presented in Table 2.2. First, a firm obtains *normal performance* when the value it generates with the resources it employs exactly equals what the owners of those resources expected. They thought their resources were worth $10, and the firm creates $10 in value using them. A firm obtains *below-normal performance* when it generates less than the expected value of a resource. The owners of resources thought their resources were worth $10, and the firm creates $8 in value using them. Finally, a firm obtains *above-normal performance* when it generates greater-than-expected value from the resources it employs. In this final case, the owners think their resources are worth $10, and the firm creates $12 in value using them.

TABLE 2.2 The Relationship Between the Expected Value of a Firm's Resources, Their Actual Value, and Firm Performance		
Normal economic performance	A firm generates with its resources economic value *equal to* what owners of those resources expect
Below-normal economic performance	A firm generates with its resources economic value *less than* what owners of those resources expect
Above-normal economic performance	A firm generates with its resources economic value *greater than* what owners of those resources expect

This positive difference between expected value and actual value is known as an economic profit or an economic rent.

"Normal," "below-normal," and "above-normal" performance are terms derived from traditional theory in microeconomics and refer to the level of firm performance under conditions of perfect competition. Under perfect competition, the value created by a firm with its resources is just large enough for the firm to fully compensate the owners of all those resources, including a risk-adjusted rate of return for suppliers of capital (Porter, 1980). These firms are surviving. When firms generate below-normal value, owners of assets take those productive resources away from a firm and move them to a context where they can obtain their full expected value. When all of a firm's assets migrate, economically (though perhaps not legally) a firm no longer exists. Finally, a firm generating above-normal value will be able to retain its productive assets and will be able to attract even more. This kind of firm is prospering.

In general, firms that are earning above-normal economic profits enjoy some sort of competitive advantage in their market or industry. A firm has a competitive advantage when it is implementing a value-creating strategy not being implemented by numerous other firms in that market or industry. Firms that are earning normal economic profits are usually in a state of competitive parity, and firms earning below-normal performance face a competitive disadvantage.

This approach to defining performance has many advantages. It is consistent with the received view from microeconomics, it is consistent with most definitions of performance developed in organization theory and organizational behavior, and it is helpful in analyzing the impact on performance of a firm's environment and its internal strengths and weaknesses. Unfortunately, this definition of performance is difficult to measure.

2.3   MEASURING FIRM PERFORMANCE

There are a wide variety of techniques for measuring firm performance as defined in Table 2.2. None of these approaches is without limitations, and it is usually advisable to apply multiple measures of performance when conducting the strategic analysis of a firm. Four major approaches to measuring performance are reviewed here: (1) survival as a measure of performance, (2) accounting measures of performance, (3) stakeholder approaches to performance measurement, and (4) present-value approaches. Some additional measurement techniques are also discussed.

FIRM SURVIVAL AS A MEASURE OF PERFORMANCE

From the distinctions listed in Table 2.2, it is possible to conclude that a firm that survives over a relatively extended period of time must be generating *at least* normal economic value. Firms generating less than this level of value will not survive over the long run unless they receive some government or private subsidy (Demsetz, 1973). Thus the very survival of a firm is at least one measure of performance (Hannan and Freeman, 1977; McKelvey, 1982, Alchian, 1950).

Strengths of Survival Measures

The primary strength of survival as a measure of firm performance is that it is apparently easy to use. Application of this measure does not require detailed information about a firm's economic condition. The only information that is required concerns whether a firm's operations are continuing. If a firm's operations are ongoing, the firm is surviving and thus generating at least normal economic value.

Weaknesses of Survival Measures

Using firm survival as a measure of firm performance has some important limitations. For example, it is often difficult to decide when, exactly, a firm no longer exists. The decision is relatively easy for some very small firms—such as restaurants, gas stations, and small newspapers. Indeed, most researchers who have studied the determinants of firm survival have chosen to focus on these kinds of smaller firms, whose "death" is easy to determine (Freeman, Carroll, and Hannan, 1983; Carroll and Delacroix, 1982). However, determining when a firm no longer exists is not so easy for medium-size and larger firms. For example, does a firm cease to exist after it is taken over by another firm? Legally, it no longer exists as an independent entity, but most of its productive assets may remain intact, and it may make the same products, service the same customers, and compete in the same markets. In what sense has this firm ceased to exist?

Also, when a firm declares bankruptcy, does it cease to exist? Again, many of its productive assets continue to be used, it still has customers, and it still has competitors. Recently, the development of so-called strategic bankruptcies suggests at least the possibility that firms can maintain or perhaps even *improve* their performance by declaring bankruptcy. Texaco's bankruptcy, Manville's bankruptcy, and Continental's two bankruptcies over the last several years all appeared to have had some strategic, performance-enhancing attributes (Engel, 1984; Thompson, Tell, Vogel, Davis, Norman, and Mason, 1987).

A second limitation of using survival as a measure of firm performance is that sometimes the "death" of a firm (however defined) can occur over a protracted period of time. This is particularly the case for firms that at some point in their history generated above-normal value and thereby acquired numerous valuable assets whose liquidation can prolong survival. During this time, it is often not clear whether a firm is actually in the process of going out of business or simply facing temporary setbacks. Using "firm survival" as the only definition of performance in this context can lead to ambiguous results.

One example of a firm whose survival was probably *not* a good measure of its actual performance was Pan Am. One of the first truly international airlines, Pan Am probably earned substantial levels of above-normal performance for several years in the 1930s. The Second World War also helped Pan Am's performance (Pulley, 1991). However, beginning in the late 1950s, Pan Am began to face severe financial pressures. In the 1980s, Pan Am began selling off assets to survive. These assets included most of its air routes to Europe and Asia, as well as its domestic network (Pulley, 1991). During this entire time, Pan Am survived but probably did not earn even normal levels of performance. In 1991, Pan Am finally declared bankruptcy, and the final liquidation of its assets was concluded.

Even firms that do survive for long periods of time may transform themselves so completely that analyzing them as a single firm may be misleading. For example, the Hudson Bay Company has survived as a legal entity for almost two centuries. However, the business activities of the Hudson Bay Company in the 1700s (building and maintaining trading posts to facilitate the fur trade) are very different from the business activities of the Hudson Bay Company in the 1990s (owning and operating large department stores). In an important sense, the old Hudson Bay Company has been replaced by the new Hudson Bay Company, although focusing solely on firm survival as a measure of performance would miss this transition.

A final limitation of using firm survival as a measure of performance is that this approach provides no insights concerning above-normal performance. Firm survival can only distinguish between firms generating below-normal levels of value and at least normal levels of value. However, among those firms generating at least normal economic value, some may be obtaining just normal performance, others slightly above-normal performance, and still others very high levels of above-normal performance. Strategists may be interested in understanding the conditions that enable their firms to generate above-normal performance. A sole focus on survival makes it impossible to gain these kinds of insights (Rumelt, Schendel, Teece, 1991; Porter, 1980).

Thus although survival is an important issue in evaluating the performance of firms, it is usually not the only issue. Kanter and Brinkerhoff (1981:335) suggest that survival, as a measure of firm performance, is limited because (1) it is not applicable to new organizations (Freeman, Carroll, and Hannan, 1983), (2) it provides no guidance to short-term decision making, (3) it may be "artificial" (that is, organizations may survive because of another's willingness to continue support), and (4) firms that focus exclusively on their survival may lose track of other important objectives and purposes.

ACCOUNTING MEASURES OF PERFORMANCE

By far the most popular way of measuring a firm's performance is through the use of accounting measures (Scherer, 1980; Fisher and McGowan, 1983). Accounting measures of performance are publicly available for many firms. They communicate a great deal of information about a firm's operations. For these reasons, most early teaching and research in strategy and strategic management focused on the impact of strategy on a firm's accounting performance (Hofer and Schendel, 1978).

Accounting approaches to characterizing a firm's performance often rely on ratio analysis (Aragon, 1982; Smith, Arnold, and Bizzell, 1988:248–257). Accounting ratios come in various shapes and sizes. Some of the most important accounting ratios, and what they suggest for a firm's performance, are listed in Table 2.3. The major categories of accounting ratios are (1) profitability ratios (ratios with some measure of profit in the numerator and some measure of firm size or assets in the denominator), (2) liquidity ratios (ratios that focus on the ability of a firm to meet its short-term financial obligations), (3) leverage ratios (ratios that focus on the level of a firm's indebtedness), and (4) activity ratios (ratios that focus on the level of activity in a firm's business).

It is also possible to integrate a firm's financial ratios to obtain a more complete picture of a firm's economic performance. Altman (1968) has applied multivariate discriminant analysis to estimate the impact

TABLE 2.3
Ratio Analysis Using Accounting Measures of Firm Performance

Ratio	Calculation	Interpretation
Profitability Ratios		
1. Return on total assets (ROA)	$\dfrac{\text{profits after taxes}}{\text{total assets}}$	Measure of return on total investment in a firm
2. Return on equity (ROE)	$\dfrac{\text{profits after taxes}}{\text{total stockholders' equity}}$	Measure of return on total equity investment in a firm
3. Gross profit margin	$\dfrac{\text{sales} - \text{cost of goods sold}}{\text{sales}}$	Measure of sales available to cover operating expenses and still generate a profit
4. Earnings per share (EPS)	$\dfrac{(\text{profits after taxes}) - (\text{preferred stock dividends})}{\text{number of shares of common stock outstanding}}$	Measure of profit available to owners of common stock
5. Price-earnings ratio	$\dfrac{\text{current market price per share}}{\text{after-tax earnings per share}}$	Measure of anticipated firm performance—high p/e ratio tends to indicate that the stock market anticipates strong future performance
6. Cash flow per share	$\dfrac{\text{after-tax profits} + \text{depreciation}}{\text{number of common shares outstanding}}$	Measure of funds available to fund activities above current level of costs
Liquidity Ratios		
1. Current ratio	$\dfrac{\text{current assets}}{\text{current liabilities}}$	A measure of the ability of a firm to cover its current liabilities with assets that can be converted into cash in the short term
2. Quick ratio	$\dfrac{\text{current assets} + \text{inventory}}{\text{current liabilities}}$	A measure of the ability of a firm to meet its short-term obligations without selling off its current inventory
Leverage Ratios		
1. Debt to assets	$\dfrac{\text{total debt}}{\text{total assets}}$	Measure of the extent to which debt has been used to finance a firm's business activities

(continues)

TABLE 2.3
Ratio Analysis Using Accounting Measures of Firm Performance (continued)

Ratio	Calculation	Interpretation
2. Debt to equity	$\dfrac{\text{total debt}}{\text{total equity}}$	Measure of the use of debt versus equity to finance a firm's business activities
3. Times interest earned	$\dfrac{\text{profits before interest and taxes}}{\text{total interest charges}}$	Measure of how much a firm's profits can decline and still meet its interest obligations
Activity Ratios		
1. Inventory turnover	$\dfrac{\text{sales}}{\text{inventory}}$	A measure of the speed with which a firm's inventory is turning over
2. Accounts receivable turnover	$\dfrac{\text{annual credit sales}}{\text{accounts receivable}}$	Measure of the average time it takes a firm to collect on credit sales
3. Average collection period	$\dfrac{\text{accounts receivable}}{\text{average daily sales}}$	Measure of the time it takes a firm to receive payment after sale has been made

of different financial ratios on the probability that a firm will declare bankruptcy. Altman's (1968) estimated equation was

$$Z = .012 \text{ (working capital/total assets)} + \qquad Eq.\ 2.1$$
$$.014 \text{ (retained earnings/total assets)} +$$
$$.033 \text{ (earnings before interest and taxes/total assets)} +$$
$$.0006 \text{ (market value of equity/book value of total debt)} +$$
$$.999 \text{ (sales/total assets)}$$

Altman concluded that if a firm's "Z score" is less than 1.8, the firm will fail; if it is between 1.8 and 3.0, the firm will probably not fail; and if it is greater than 3.0, the firm will not fail. This model successfully predicted corporate failures five years prior to their occurrence 69.8 percent of the time. Dambolena and Khoury (1980) improved on Altman's

(1968) prediction rate, from 69.8 to 78 percent, by including the standard deviation of some financial ratios in their discriminant function (Altman, Haldeman, and Narayanan, 1977).

Limitations of Accounting Measures

The accounting measures of performance summarized in Table 2.3 are powerful tools for understanding a firm's performance, but they are not without limitations. Three particularly important limitations of accounting measures of performance are discussed below.

Managerial Discretion.   Managers often have some discretion in choosing accounting methods, including methods of counting revenues, valuing inventory (for example, LIFO versus FIFO), rates of depreciation (straight-line versus accelerated), depletion, amortization, and so forth (Watts and Zimmerman, 1978, 1990). Thus to some degree at least, measures of accounting performance reflect managerial interests and preferences. The relationship between a variety of different managerial interests and accounting methods has been examined in the accounting literature.

When the value of a manager's bonus depends on the firm's accounting performance, managers have a strong incentive to adopt accounting practices that increase the level of reported current-period performance. Empirical work suggests that, under these conditions, managers often do adopt such accounting practices (Watts and Zimmerman, 1986; Healy, 1985). For example, when Archie McCardell was president of International Harvester (IH), he had a management bonus contract that substantially increased his income if certain of IH's accounting performance ratios equaled the industry average. Apparently, McCardell adopted some accounting method changes (such as changing depreciation rules and changing inventory-valuing methods) that drove up IH's reported accounting performance above industry averages. In the end, McCardell received his bonus, although IH was bankrupt within two years (Hamermesh and Christensen, 1981).

Also, when a firm's performance violates the expectations of capital markets, managers have an incentive to adopt accounting practices that increase the level of reported current-period profit. In so doing, they may avoid potential employment instability that might be associated with very low stock prices leading to unfriendly takeovers or to the violation of debt contract covenants leading to bankruptcy (Kalay, 1982). Managers apparently reason that adopting these accounting methods may give them time to get their organization's performance in order. Again, empirical work is generally consistent with this expectation (Press and Weintrop, 1990; Duke and Hunt, 1990; Bowen, Noreen, and Lacey, 1981).

For example, in the late 1980s, IBM was able to downplay some of its impending economic problems through such accounting method changes, including booking shipped goods as revenue even though they might be returned by customers, booking the lifetime revenue of long-term computer leases at the time they were signed, and adopting accounting methods that pushed the cost of equipment and retirement into the future (Miller and Berton, 1993). None of these actions were illegal or inconsistent with generally accepted accounting principles. However, they all had the effect of increasing IBM's current-period reported profits. Given IBM's history of very conservative accounting practices, some have suggested that these changes were misleading (Miller and Berton, 1993).

On the other hand, managers have an incentive to report lower current-period profits when high current-period profits might create potential antitrust liability for themselves and their firm. In this context, high accounting profits could be interpreted as a signal of anti-competitive monopolistic behavior. By adopting accounting methods that reduce the level of reported current profits, managers can avoid this antitrust liability (Watts and Zimmerman, 1990). Empirical results generally support this relationship between the threat of antitrust activity and the adoption of profit-reducing accounting methods (Zmijewski and Hagerman, 1981; Zimmerman, 1983).

Finally, managers have an interest in reducing the level of current profitability when doing so gives them power in negotiations with external stakeholders. For example, owners of major-league baseball teams have at least three reasons for understating the profitability of their teams: (1) to obtain tax write-offs to offset the profits of other businesses they own, (2) to present a bleak picture in labor negotiations with players, and (3) to scare cities into subsidizing the construction of additional baseball infrastructure, including new roads, parking lots, and even stadiums (Smith and Norton, 1993). In 1984, baseball owners reported a collective accounting loss of almost $42 million, although representatives of the players' union concluded, using the same data, that the teams that year collectively had a $9 million accounting profit (Smith and Norton, 1993). Despite these accounting problems, the market value of baseball franchises has doubled every nine years, for the last ninety years. The Baltimore Orioles, for example, were purchased for $70 million in 1989. Their potential sale price in 1993 was $145 million. In this industry, it may well be the case that reported accounting performance is not a particularly accurate measure of economic performance.

What this research on managerial interests and accounting methods suggests is that accounting measures of performance cannot be understood independent of the interests and preferences of managers (Watts and Zimmerman, 1990). Thus if two firms have exactly the same underlying "true" performance, but one firm has large management bonus plans tied to accounting numbers or is not meeting capital market expectations about accounting performance, while the second is under threat of government antitrust action or in the midst of labor negotiations, management choices about accounting methods can lead these firms to have very different "reported" accounting performance.

Short-Term Bias.   Second, most accounting approaches to measuring performance have a built-in short-term bias, because longer-term, multiple-year investments in a firm are usually treated, for accounting purposes, simply as costs in those years where they do not generate revenues that exceed cost. Consider, for example, a firm that has a research and development budget of $50,000 per year. For convenience, assume that this firm knows, with absolute certainty, that five years of investing in R&D at this level will create a product that will generate $3,000,000 in revenue in the sixth year. If this firm calculates its return on investment (ROI) in each of the first five years of R&D, the ROI for each of those years looks very bad ($0/$50,000 = 0% ROI). However, if this firm calculates the ROI for the entire six-year period ($3,000,000/$250,000 = 1200% ROI), the return is very good. Unfortunately, since most accounting measures of performance are calculated on an annual basis, the longer-term positive impact of R&D for this firm could easily be understated.

Some authors have suggested that an overreliance on short-term accounting measures of performance by managers in U.S. firms has led many of these firms to take an overly short-term perspective and fail to invest in their long-term success (Hayes and Abernathy, 1980). One reason often cited for the emergence of many Japanese firms in world markets over the last twenty years is that Japanese managers are reported to be less reliant on short-term accounting numbers as a measure of their firms' performance (Ouchi, 1980). There now seems to be a growing understanding of the dangers of an overreliance on short-term accounting numbers to measure performance, and more firms are adopting additional measures, and modifying their accounting practices, to accommodate longer-term investments in the firm (Hayes and Abernathy, 1980).

Valuing Intangible Resources and Capabilities.   A third limitation of accounting measures of firm performance is that they generally undervalue a firm's intangible resources and capabilities. A firm's intangible resources and capabilities are productive assets that are difficult to observe, describe, and value but that nevertheless can have a significant impact on a firm's performance (Itami, 1987). Intangible resources and capabilities such as "close relationships with customers," "close cooperation among managers," "a sense of loyalty to the firm," and "brand awareness" are fuzzy and difficult to describe yet are often important determinants of a firm's success (Dierickx and Cool, 1989; Barney, 1991).

The challenge facing accounting measures of performance is that intangible resources and capabilities, just like their more tangible counterparts, are the result of investments made by firms over long periods of time (Dierickx and Cool, 1989). However, instead of investing in such physical assets as plant and equipment, firms invest in nonphysical assets such as teamwork, reputations, loyalty, and relationships. If these investments in intangible resources and capabilities are not included in a measure of firm performance, computed accounting rates of return can substantially overstate a firm's actual performance.

Of course, accountants have understood this problem for some time and have developed the accounting category of "goodwill" to include these kinds of investments (Spiller and Gosman, 1984). However, more often than not, "goodwill" is simply a residual accounting category. For example, when one firm buys another and pays a price in excess of that target firm's book value, the difference between the acquisition price and the book value is called "goodwill." Thus instead of being estimated directly, "goodwill" is defined as what is left over, after the book value of the acquired firm has been accounted for. Few techniques exist for valuing "goodwill" directly—despite the fact that the intangible assets that often constitute "goodwill" can be, strategically, very important.

Impact of Accounting Limitations

Accounting measures of performance are limited. But if these limitations are very small in size, accounting numbers might still be an extremely accurate—and convenient—measure of firm performance. Unfortunately, a great deal of research suggests that these measurement problems can, in fact, be very large. The magnitude of these measurement problems has been examined in detail by Fisher and McGowan (1983) and their colleagues (Fisher, 1979; Livingstone and Solomon, 1971; Solomon, 1970; Stauffer, 1971). In a series of simulation studies, Fisher and McGowan (1983) show very significant effects of differences in accounting practices on accounting measures of performance. Indeed, Fisher and McGowan (1983:83) conclude: "the[se] effects can be large enough to account for the entire inter-firm variation in the accounting rates of return among the largest firms in the United States. A ranking of firms by accounting rates of return can easily [be] invert[ed]."

This assertion has created quite a stir among those interested in understanding the determinants of a firm's performance. Recall that most of the early teaching and research that has focused on the link between a firm's strategies and its performance has adopted accounting measures of performance. Among others, Long and Ravenscraft (1984) criticized Fisher and McGowan's (1983) use of simulations.

However, empirical work by Ijiri (1980) and Solomon (1985) is consistent with the simulation studies of Fisher and McGowan (1983).

Recent attempts to develop activity-based accounting methods recognize important limitations of traditional accounting methods as a measure of economic performance (Pare, 1993). In activity-based accounting, instead of being assigned to broad standard categories, costs and revenues are assigned to the specific activities required to design, manufacture, and sell a product. This form of accounting avoids some of the short-term biases that are inherent in more traditional forms of accounting (Spiller and Gosman, 1984).

All this does not suggest that traditional accounting measures of performance are, somehow, bad. Nor does it suggest that accounting numbers should be ignored. It does suggest, however, that care and judgment must be used when applying accounting measures of firm performance.

THE MULTIPLE STAKEHOLDERS VIEW OF PERFORMANCE

Another popular way to measure performance is called the multiple stakeholders approach (Kanter and Brinkerhoff, 1981; Connolly, Conlon, and Deutsch, 1980). In many ways, this approach to measuring performance is closest to the conceptual definition of performance presented in Section 2.2. In this view, an organization's performance should be evaluated relative to the preferences and desires of stakeholders that provide resources to a firm (Cameron, 1986).

Several authors have developed lists of the different stakeholders for firms (Mason and Mitroff, 1981). A typical list of an organization's stakeholders includes customers, labor, management, top executives, suppliers, partners, equity holders, debt holders, and society at large. To be a stakeholder, a party must make important resources (such as labor, money, and loyalty) available to a firm. Because stakeholders provide resources, they have an interest in how those resources are used and applied. Moreover, since each stakeholder provides different resources to a firm, each stakeholder can have a different interest in how it would like to see the firm managed. In this multiple stakeholders approach, one set of stakeholders may believe that a firm is a very high performer, another set may conclude that a firm is only a mediocre performer, and still another might conclude that a firm is performing poorly.

Applying the Stakeholder Approach

Because different firm stakeholders use different criteria to judge the performance of a firm, rarely will it be possible for an organization to implement strategies that completely satisfy all of its stakeholders. A firm that, for example, fully satisfies its employees and managers by providing expensive non-business-related perquisites (such as chauffeur-driven limousines, numerous corporate jets, extra-thick carpeting in offices) may be reducing the economic wealth of its stockholders (Jensen and Meckling, 1976; Barney and Ouchi, 1986). Both of these stakeholding groups will not simultaneously be fully satisfied. A firm that fully satisfies its customers by selling high-quality products at very low prices may be reducing its profits, an action that reduces the potential gain of stockholders (Titman, 1984). Also, a firm that fully meets the needs of its stockholders, by borrowing money for low-risk projects but investing in high-risk projects, can end up increasing the risks borne by its debt holders (Copeland and Weston, 1983).

Because firms can rarely implement strategies that fully satisfy all of their stakeholders, the interests of certain stakeholders are usually emphasized over the interests of other stakeholders. This was demonstrated empirically in Cameron's (1978) research on the performance of institutions of higher education. Beginning with a list of 57 indicators of the performance of colleges and universities, Cameron developed a set of 9 dimensions along which these organizations' performance can be judged. These dimensions represent different stakeholders for colleges and universities, and they range from student education satisfaction to faculty and administrator employment satisfaction to organizational health. These 9 dimensions, and how 6 kinds of institutions of higher learning rate along these dimensions, are presented in Fig. 2.1.

One of Cameron's strongest findings is that no single type of college or university is a high performer along all nine dimensions. These organizations apparently choose from among all their stakeholders those they will focus on, and they either just satisfy or ignore the rest. Thus, for example, major research institutions (Institution 5 in Fig. 2.1) tend to do well along the dimensions of student educational satisfaction, the ability to acquire resources, and organizational health, and they do poorly along the student career development and system openness and community interaction dimensions. Junior colleges (Institution 4 in Fig. 2.1), on the other hand, fare well along the student career development and system openness dimensions but do rather poorly along student educational satisfaction, student academic development, and related dimensions.

The multiple stakeholders approach to measuring performance suggests not only that different types of firms choose different criteria for evaluating their performance but also that different individuals within a single firm choose different criteria to judge a firm's performance (W. R. Scott, 1977; Kanter and Brinkerhoff, 1981). Scott, Flood, Ewy, and Forrest (1978), for example, suggest that an organization's

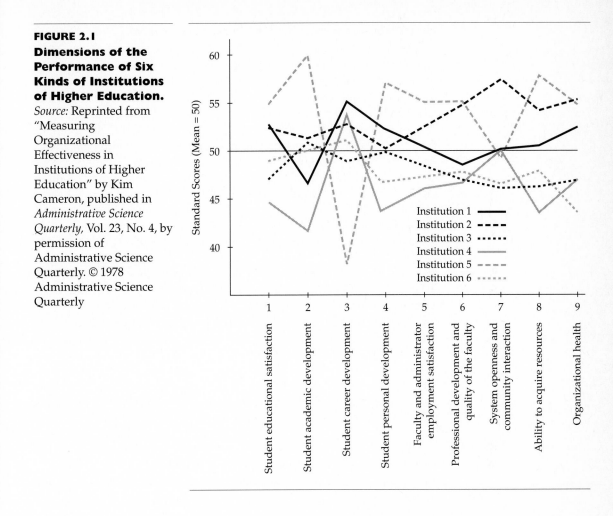

FIGURE 2.1
Dimensions of the
Performance of Six
Kinds of Institutions
of Higher Education.
Source: Reprinted from
"Measuring
Organizational
Effectiveness in
Institutions of Higher
Education" by Kim
Cameron, published in
*Administrative Science
Quarterly,* Vol. 23, No. 4, by
permission of
Administrative Science
Quarterly. © 1978
Administrative Science
Quarterly

managers will typically prefer to describe performance with reference to structural measures of organizational characteristics (such as number of employees and overhead costs) because they have control over these factors. But these authors argue, employees may prefer measures of performance that emphasize their level of personal involvement and satisfaction on the job and that customer groups will typically prefer measures of performance that focus on organizational outcomes like the quality of goods produced and the prices charged (Quinn, 1978). Consistent with these findings, Mahoney and Weitzel (1969) have shown that managers in research and development units of companies evaluate the performance of their firms in ways very different from the ways used by managers of less specialized business units.

Limitations of the Multiple Stakeholders Approach

In many ways, the multiple stakeholders approach to measuring performance is the most intuitively appealing of all the measures examined in this chapter. It certainly is very close to the conceptual definition of performance provided in Section 2.2 by examining the value created by each of a firm's critical resources (Weick and Daft, 1982; Venkatraman and Ramanujam, 1987). But, unfortunately, it is often very difficult to apply multiple stakeholders measures of performance in real strategic analyses. If the multiple stakeholders point of view is taken to its logical conclusion, there is no such thing as "organizational performance." Rather, there are numerous "organizational performances" associated with each firm (W. R. Scott, 1977; Scott et al., 1978; Cummings, 1978; Kanter and Brinkerhoff, 1981). Each stakeholding group, and perhaps each individual stakeholder, may define performance in an idiosyncratic way.

Understanding the performance implications of strategies becomes extremely complex in this situation (Goodman, Atkin, and Schoorman, 1983). The implications of a particular strategy for each of a firm's numerous stakeholders would need to be isolated. As long as there is the possibility of significant variance in these stakeholders' interests, this task is almost overwhelming, for strategy analysts and managers alike. The answer to the question "Will this strategy improve this firm's performance?" will always be "Yes and no, depending on whom you talk to." In this context, it is necessary for managers and analysts alike to adopt simplified measures of performance, measures that emphasize a few dimensions of performance over others.

PRESENT-VALUE MEASURES OF PERFORMANCE

Another popular way of measuring firm performance focuses on the present value of the cash flows generated by a firm. Rooted in the theory of finance (Copeland and Weston, 1983), the present-value approach addresses several of the limitations of other measures of performance. For example, by examining cash flows over time, it avoids the short-term bias of accounting measures of performance. Also, the value of resources made available to a firm is included in present-value measures through the concept of the discount rate.

Calculating a Firm's Present Value

Calculating a firm's present value requires two important numbers: a firm's net cash flow and the discount rate applied to that net cash flow. Calculation of these numbers is discussed below.

Net Cash Flows.   Firms have a pattern of cash flow over time. Often, as a firm begins operations or implements new strategies, this cash flow is negative (that is, revenues are less than investment costs). Hopefully, over time, a firm's cash flow becomes positive (revenues are greater than investment costs).

The relative size of a firm's revenues and costs can be conveniently measured for any time period by the amount of cash, net new investment, generated by a firm in a given time period. This amount of cash is a firm's *net cash flow (NCF)*. Copeland and Weston (1983:40) define NCF as

$$NCF_{j,t} = (Rev_{j,t} - C_{j,t}) - \tau_j(Rev_{j,t} - C_{j,t} - dep_{j,t}) - I_{j,t} \qquad Eq.\ 2.2$$

where,

$NCF_{j,t}$ = Firm j's net cash flow at time t

$Rev_{j,t}$ = Firm j's operating revenues at time t

$C_{j,t}$ = Firm j's operating costs at time t (this includes variable costs and fixed cash costs such as property taxes and corporate overhead)

τ_j = Firm j's marginal corporate tax rate

$dep_{j,t}$ = Firm j's depreciation (and other noncash charges) during time t

$I_{j,t}$ = Firm j's new investment during time t

The first term in Eq. (2.2) is simply the difference between operating income ($Rev_{j,t}$) and operating costs ($C_{j,t}$, fixed and variable) in time t. This defines the "base" amount of cash generated by a firm during time t. Of course, the net amount of cash generated depends on the taxes paid by the firm on this base amount. Thus the second term in Eq. (2.2) multiplies this base level of cash times a firm's marginal tax rate and subtracts this tax payment from the base cash generated by a firm.

This second term in Eq. (2.2) also includes depreciation and other noncash charges ($dep_{j,t}$). The role of $dep_{j,t}$ can be seen more clearly by rearranging the terms in Eq. (2.2). This is done in Eq. (2.3):

$$NCF_{j,t} = (1 - \tau_j)(Rev_{j,t} - C_{j,t}) + \tau_j(dep_{j,t}) - I_{j,t} \qquad Eq.\ 2.3$$

In Eq. (2.3), $[(1 - \tau_j)(Rev_{j,t} - C_{j,t})]$ is simply after-tax cash. Now, however, it becomes clear that the tax benefits of a firm's depreciation and other noncash charges should be treated as cash inflows in computing $NCF_{j,t}$. The term $\tau_j(dep_{j,t})$ is the amount of money saved by a firm on taxes through depreciation.

After calculating the base level of cash, subtracting taxes paid on that cash, and adding back tax savings from depreciation, the only task left in calculating $NCF_{j,t}$ is to subtract any new investment ($I_{j,t}$) made by a firm. Notice that this new investment is over and above the operating costs associated with maintaining a firm's current operations. It might be the case, for example, that a firm may decide that to enhance its value, it needs to spend on a strategic investment more money than just standard operating expenses. This additional investment reduces the net cash flow and thus needs to be subtracted to calculate NCF.

Discounting.   The net cash flow for each period t of a firm's operations is a reasonable measure of performance, closely related to return of investment (ROI). But examining only one period of NCF can create the short-term biases associated with traditional accounting measures of performance. What is important is not *just* the performance of a firm in any one period but its performance across all periods. The simplest way to capture this entire pattern of cash flows is to sum them for the time a firm is operating—that is,

$$\sum_{t=0}^{N} NCF_{j,t} \qquad\qquad Eq.\ 2.4$$

where N is the number of time periods

This simple solution, however, fails to take into consideration the time value of money (Copeland and Weston, 1983). Because money has a time value associated with it, a dollar earned today is more valuable than a dollar earned twenty years from now. After all, the dollar earned today can be invested in other strategic activities, put in the bank, or consumed in other ways, but the dollar earned twenty years from now has little value until that future date. Operationally, the time value of money suggests that a firm's net cash flows many years into the future need to be discounted, for they are less valuable than net cash flows in the current period or in the near future, which consequently need not be discounted as much. Thus an appropriate measure of firm performance is

$$NPV_j = \sum_{t=0}^{N} \frac{NCF_{j,t}}{(1+k)^t} \qquad\qquad Eq.\ 2.5$$

where,

NPV_j = net present value of Firm j's cash flow

$NCF_{j,t}$ = net cash flow of Firm j at time t

N = economic life of investment i

k = the discount rate

Conceptually, what this discount rate, k, should be is clear. Earlier, we suggested that the performance of a firm needs to judged relative to the expectations of owners of resources that are made available to a firm. Thus, k, the discount rate, should equal the expected value of the assets employed by a firm.

As a measure of performance, Eq. (2.5) has several attractive properties. If the discount rate k actually equals the expected value of a firm's assets at each point in time, t, then a firm with a positive present value ($NPV_j > 0$) is generating above-normal value (that is, value greater than expected), a firm with a zero present value ($NPV_j = 0$) is generating normal value, and a firm with a negative present value ($NPV_j < 0$) is generating below-normal value. The relationship between present-value measures of performance and the conceptual definition of performance provided in Section 2.2 is summarized in Table 2.4.

Several approaches for calculating the discount rate, k, exist. Most of them depend on the assumption that, in efficient capital markets, the expected value of a firm will be reflected in a firm's cost of capital (Copeland and Weston, 1983). With this assumption, it is possible to apply the capital asset pricing model to estimate k. The capital asset pricing model can be written as

$$E(R_{j,t}) = RFR_t + \beta_j[E(R_{m,t}) - RFR_t] \qquad Eq.\ 2.6$$

where,

$E(R_{j,t})$ = the expected rate of return of Firm j's securities at time t

RFR_t = the risk-free rate of return in time t

β_j = Firm j's systematic risk

$E(R_{m,t})$ = the expected rate of return on a fully diversified portfolio of securities at time t

and where, theoretically,

$$\beta_j = \frac{COV(R_j, R_m)}{VAR(R_m)} \qquad Eq.\ 2.7$$

where,

$COV(R_j, R_m)$ = the covariance between returns from Firm j's securities and the overall securities market

$VAR(R_m)$ = the variance of overall security market returns

Under the assumption that capital markets are efficient, the discount rate, k, is conceptually equivalent to the expected return on a firm's securities, $E(R_{j,t})$—that is, $k = E(R_{j,t})$.

TABLE 2.4
The Relationship Between a Firm's Net Present Value and Economic Performance

$NPV = 0 \rightarrow$ normal economic performance

$NPV < 0 \rightarrow$ below-normal economic performance

$NPV > 0 \rightarrow$ above-normal economic performance

Empirically, each of the variables in the capital asset pricing model, except one, can be directly measured. For example, a reasonable measure of the risk-free rate of return in a time period (RFR_t) is the interest rate on government securities during that time period. A reasonable measure of the expected market rate of return during a time period [$E(R_{m,t})$] is the actual rate of return of various stock market indices, including the New York Stock Exchange index of common stock or the Standard and Poor's composite index. The remaining variable in Eq. (2.6), β_j, can be estimated by rewriting Eq. (2.6) in the form of a statistical multiple regression equation as,

$$R_{j,t} = a_j + b_j R_{m,t} + e_{j,t} \qquad\qquad Eq.\ 2.8$$

where,

$R_{j,t}$ = the return of Firm j's securities at time t

a_j = a constant equal to $(1 - b_j)RFR_t$

b_j = an estimate of β_j

$R_{m,t}$ = the rate of return on a fully diversified portfolio of securities at time t

$e_{j,t}$ = the error in estimating $R_{j,t}$

The value of b_j in Eq. (2.8) can be estimated through regression analysis and is an empirical estimate of β_j.

Application.   These analytical tools can be applied to calculate net-present-value measures of firm performance. Suppose that a firm has a cash flow pattern as presented in Table 2.5. Also, suppose that an empirical estimate of β_j for this firm, using the regression in Eq. (2.8), is $b_j = 1.3$. With this pattern of cash flow and estimate of β_j, it is possible to calculate the net present value of this firm. This present value, calculated in Table 2.5, is –334.82. Assuming this firm's capital market is reasonably efficient, a net present value of –334.82 implies that this firm is generating below-normal economic value.

TABLE 2.5

Calculating the Net Present Value of a Firm

The regression estimate of β_j for this firm is $b_j = 1.3$. All other parameters vary over time for this firm.

Period	NCF_t	RFR_t	$E(R_{m,t})$	$E(R_t)$	PV_t
0	−400	.04	.12	$.04 + 1.3(.12 − .04) = .144$	$\dfrac{−400}{[1 + .144]^0} = −400$
1	−300	.03	.10	$.03 + 1.3(.10 − .03) = .121$	$\dfrac{−300}{[1 + .121]^1} = −267.62$
2	+100	.02	.09	$.02 + 1.3(.09 − .03) = .098$	$\dfrac{+100}{[1 + .098]^2} = +82.99$
3	+150	.02	.09	$.02 + 1.3(.09 − .03) = .098$	$\dfrac{+150}{[1 + .098]^3} = +103.23$
4	+300	.05	.12	$.05 + 1.3(.12 − .05) = .115$	$\dfrac{+300}{[1 + .115]^4} = +125.58$
5	+600	.03	.10	$.03 + 1.3(.10 − .03) = .121$	$\dfrac{+600}{[1 + .121]^5} = +96.48$
6	+900	.04	.11	$.04 + 1.3(.11 − .04) = .131$	$\dfrac{+900}{[1 + .131]^6} = +17.52$

$$NPV = −334.82 \text{ (below-normal economic profits)}$$

Strengths of Present-Value Measures

The present-value measure of performance has several strengths. First, it has been shown in finance that firms that apply NPV performance measures and invest in positive NPV strategies maximize the wealth of their stockholders (Copeland and Weston, 1983). While only one stakeholder in the multiple stakeholders approach to measuring performance, stockholders are, nevertheless, consistently cited as one of the most important stakeholders in a firm (Mason and Mitroff, 1981).

A second strength of present-value measures is the close link between this measure and the conceptual definition of firm *performance* presented in Section 2.2. That definition depended critically on comparing a firm's actual performance to what was expected. The present-value measure provides a rigorous definition of a firm's actual performance (*NCF*) and of its expected performance (*k*). If both these parameters are estimated correctly, then this present-value measure is a very accurate measure of firm performance.

Limitations of Present-Value Measures

Although, in principle, present-value measures of performance have much to recommend them, important measurement and conceptual problems limit the usefulness of this approach.

Measurement Problems: NCF.   Ex post, it is usually not difficult to estimate the past pattern of net cash flow (NCF) generated by a firm. This is largely an accounting problem. Also, ex ante, there may be some firms that have relatively easy-to-predict patterns of future cash flow. However, for many firms, accurately *anticipating* future cash flow patterns can be very difficult. This is especially the case for firms with long anticipated product life cycles that are pursuing highly innovative strategies in uncertain environments. One might be able to accurately predict net cash flow in the first year or two, but anticipating net cash flow in year 15 or 20 is very difficult, if not impossible. Though highly discounted, these far-in-the-future cash flows can still have a significant impact on a firm's present value. The inability to accurately anticipate future cash flows has an important impact on the accuracy of present-value measures of performance.

Measurement Problems: β_j.   Not only can net cash flows be difficult to anticipate, but the discount rate, k, applied to those cash flows can be difficult to measure as well. This difficulty reflects problems in estimating β_j with b_j.

The traditional approach for estimating β_j described previously seems straightforward enough—that is, simply estimate the statistical regression in Eq. (2.8). However, slight modifications in how the variables in Eq. (2.8) are measured can lead to different beta estimates. For example, Merrill Lynch's approach to estimating b_j is based on monthly capital gains for an individual security ($R_{j,t}$) and for the market as a whole ($R_{m,t}$), where market returns are estimated using the Standard and Poor's 500 Index. The resulting regression equation is then adjusted according to the criteria developed in Blume (1975). Value Line, on the other hand, estimates b_j using weekly capital gains return data and uses the New York Stock Exchange Composite Index as a measure of market returns. The resulting regression equation is again adjusted according to Blume (1975). Unfortunately, the betas calculated in these different ways can be different. Indeed, Statman (1981) has shown that these two estimates of beta are statistically different from one another even though they use the same empirical equation—Eq. (2.8)—and only slightly different measures of variables.

Moreover, the estimate of β_j typically requires a relatively long data series, both for the returns of an individual firm's securities and for expected market rates of returns. This requirement is not a problem for firms that have existed for long periods of time or for calculating expected market rates of return. However, if a firm has a relatively brief history, it may be statistically impossible to estimate its β_j.

Theoretical Mis-specification of the CAPM. A final limitation of present-value measures of performance concerns the theoretical validity of the capital asset pricing model (CAPM). As suggested above, the capital asset pricing model is essential to the calculation of the discount rate, k. The discount rate, in turn, has an enormous impact on the calculation of a firm's present value. Unfortunately, there is a growing consensus that the capital asset pricing model is an incomplete explanation of how returns on a firm's securities are generated (Copeland and Weston, 1983:207).

If the CAPM is complete, and if capital markets are efficient, then empirical estimations of Eq. (2.8) should reveal (1) that a_j is not significantly different from zero and (2) that b_j should be the only statistically significant factor to explain a firm's security performance. Unfortunately, empirical research is simply not consistent with these expectations: (1) a_j is often significantly different from zero, and (2) other factors, besides b_j, have a significant impact in explaining a firm's security returns, even when controlling for b_j (Copeland and Weston, 1983; Basu, 1977; Banz, 1981; Reinganum, 1981). These results suggest that the CAPM is an incomplete model, that capital markets are not efficient, or both. Roll (1977) has concluded that it is logically *impossible* to conduct separate tests of the completeness of the CAPM and capital market efficiency, and thus not possible to fully evaluate the completeness of the CAPM. Ross's (1976) development of arbitrage pricing theory is an effort to overcome the limitations of the CAPM.

However, as was the case with the firm survival, accounting, and multiple stakeholders approaches to measuring performance, simply because this present-value approach has limitations does not mean it is not useful. Calculating a firm's present value can be very important in understanding its economic performance, despite problems in measuring future net cash flow, in estimating β_j, and theoretical limitations of CAPM.

OTHER MEASURES OF FIRM PERFORMANCE

Although the firm survival, accounting, multiple stakeholders, and present-value approaches to measuring firm performance have received a great deal of attention in the literature, there are a variety of other useful techniques as well. Some of the most important of these are discussed in this section.

TABLE 2.6
Tobin's *q* for a sample of firms *(continued)*

Company	1960–1977 Average *q* Ratio	Company	1960–1977 Average *q* Ratio
Congoleum Corp.	1.17	Federal-Mogul Corp.	1.35
Continental Group	1.15	Federal Paper Board Co.	.52
Continental Oil Co.	1.69	Federated Department Stores Inc.	2.06
Cooper Industries, Inc.	1.24	Ferro Corp.	.97
Copperweld Corp.	.69	Flintkote Co.	.86
Corning Glass Works	3.75	Foote Mineral Co.	1.07
Crane Co.	.72	Foster Wheeler Corp.	.86
Crown Cork & Seal Co., Inc.	1.41	GAF Corp.	1.27
Crown Zellerbach	1.08	GATX Corp.	1.10
Culbro Corp.	1.07	Gamble-Skogmo	.97
Cummins Engine	1.35	Gardner-Denver Co.	1.57
Curtiss-Wright Corp.	.95	General Gable Corp.	1.64
Cutler-Hammer, Inc.	1.35	General Electric Co.	2.07
Dan River, Inc.	.67	General Foods Corp.	2.10
Dart Industries	1.41	General Motors Corp.	1.59
Diamond International Corp.	1.50	General Portland, Inc.	1.09
Diamond Shamrock Corp.	1.55	General Refractories Co.	.70
Dome Petroleum, Ltd.	2.94	General Telephone & Electronics	1.32
Dow Chemical	1.62	Georgia-Pacific Corp.	1.63
Du Pont (E.I.) De Nemours	2.47	Gillette Co.	3.92
Duquesne Light Co.	.90	Goodrich (B.F.) Co.	.89
Eastern Gas & Fuel Assoc.	1.11	Goodyear Tire & Rubber Co.	1.05
Eaton Corp.	1.17	Grace (W.R.) & Co.	1.16
Ethyl Corp.	1.48	Graniteville Co.	.55
Exxon Corp.	1.05	Great Northern Nekoosa Corp.	.79
FMC Corp.	1.57	Grumman Corp.	1.06
Fairchild Camera & Instrument	2.12	Gulf Oil Corp.	1.25

TABLE 2.6
Tobin's *q* for a sample of firms (*continued*)

Company	1960–1977 Average *q* Ratio	Company	1960–1977 Average *q* Ratio
Halliburton	1.86	Libbey-Owens-Ford Co.	1.47
Hammermill Paper Co.	.68	Liggett Groups	1.02
Hercules, Inc.	1.86	Lilly (Eli) & Co.	4.02
Hershey Foods Corp.	1.83	Lone Star Industries	.89
Holly Sugar Corp.	.50	Long Island Lighting	1.28
Honeywell, Inc.	2.28	Lowenstein (M.) & Sons, Inc.	.61
Ideal Basic Industries, Inc.	1.08	Lucky Stores, Inc.	1.58
Imperial Oil, Lts.-CL A	1.67	Lukens Steel Co.	.74
Ingersoll-Rand Co.	1.76	Mallory (P.R.) & Co.	1.22
Inland Steel Co.	.95	Marathon Oil Co.	1.81
Insilco Corp.	1.39	Maremont Corp.	1.24
Interco, Inc.	.98	Marshall Field & Co.	1.14
Interlake, Inc.	.75	Maytag Co.	2.71
International Business Machines Corp.	4.21	McGraw-Edison Co.	1.28
International Paper Co.	1.17	McLouth Steel Corp.	.74
Iowa-Illinois Gas & Electric	.85	Mead Corp.	.97
Iowa Power & Light	.73	Medusa Corp.	.60
Johns-Manville Corp.	1.24	Melville Corp.	2.21
Johnson & Johnson	3.64	Midland-Ross Corp.	1.02
Kmart Corp.	1.99	Minnesota Mining & Manufacturing Co.	4.87
Kaiser Aluminum & Chemical Corp.	.80	Mobil Corp.	1.20
Kaiser Cement & Gypsum Corp.	.96	Monsanto Co.	1.38
Kaiser Steel Corp.	.78	Motorola, Inc.	1.97
Kellogg Co.	3.20	NCR Corp.	1.74
Kimberly-Clark Corp.	1.51	NI Industries	1.56
Koppers Co.	.88	Naico Chemical Co.	3.69
Kraft, Inc.	1.35	National Distillers & Chemicals	.94

(*continues*)

TABLE 2.6
Tobin's _q_ for a sample of firms *(continued)*

Company	1960–1977 Average _q_ Ratio	Company	1960–1977 Average _q_ Ratio
National Gypsum Co.	3.69	Pullman, Inc.	.91
National Steel Corp.	.53	Quaker State Oil Refining	1.92
National Tea Co.	.97	RCA Corp.	1.67
Owens-Corning Fiberglass Corp.	1.71	Revere Copper & Brass, Inc.	1.17
Owens-Illinois, Inc.	1.30	Reynolds (R.J.) Industries	1.90
PPG Industries, Inc.	1.05	Reynolds Metals Co.	.81
Pabst Brewing Co.	1.31	Robertshaw Controls	1.11
Pennwalt Corp.	1.36	Robertson (H.H.) Co.	.89
Pepsico, Inc.	2.31	Rohm & Haas Co.	2.09
Pfizer, Inc.	2.49	Rubbermaid, Inc.	2.03
Phelps Dodge Corp.	1.71	SPS Technologies, Inc.	.80
Philip Morris, Inc.	1.45	Safeway Stores, Inc.	1.14
Phillips Petroleum Co.	1.74	St. Joe Minerals Corp.	1.91
Pitney-Bowes, Inc.	1.92	Schering-Plough	4.30
Polaroid Corp.	6.42	Scott Paper Co.	1.46
Potlatch Corp.	.82	Scovill Manufacturing Co.	1.05
Public Service Electric & Gas	1.12	Searle (G.D.) & Co.	5.27
Publicker Industries, Inc.	.59		

1981:16–17). Nevertheless, because _q_ combines accounting information with market information in characterizing a firm's performance, it is often a superior measure of performance compared to simple accounting ratios of the sort listed in Table 2.3.

Stock Market Measures: Event Studies

Market measures of performance, which figure so prominently in the calculation of Tobin's _q_, can be used to develop another measure of a firm's performance. This measure of performance is rooted firmly in the theory of finance and assumes that capital markets are efficient in the semistrong form—that is, that the price of a firm's debt and equity fully reflects all publicly available information about the economic value of a firm (Fama, 1970). This approach has been come to be known as the *event study method* (Fama, Fisher, Jensen, and Roll, 1969; Ball and Brown, 1968; Brown and Warner, 1980, 1985).

The logic behind these event studies is quite simple. Imagine that a firm chooses and implements a valuable new strategy. A valuable new strategy will generate higher levels of economic performance for a firm after it is implemented, compared to the economic performance of that firm before the strategy is implemented. This greater economic performance, in efficient capital markets, will be reflected in higher stock market performance for this firm, compared with its stock market performance before the strategy was implemented. In this approach to measurement, the implementation of a new strategy marks the beginning of an event. An event ends when the capital markets fully adjust to the additional value created by a firm's new strategy. The period of time between the beginning of an event and the end of an event is called an *event window.*

A measure of the total value created by a strategic event is that event's cumulative abnormal return, or CAR. An event's CAR is computed in several stages. First, an individual firm's capital asset pricing model parameters (a_j and b_j) are estimated. This is done by regressing the stock market rate of return in time t ($R_{m,t}$) on a firm's actual rate of return in the stock market in time t ($R_{j,t}$), as in Eq. (2.10).

$$R_{j,t} = a_j + b_j R_{m,t} + e_{j,t} \qquad \text{Eq. 2.10}$$

All these variables are defined as in Eq. (2.8).

It is important that these parameters be estimated using a firm's market return data *outside* the event window of interest. Thus if a firm implements a new strategy in January 1997, the estimates of a_j and b_j for that firm should be based on its returns before January 1997. These parameter estimates can then be used to calculate excess returns for that firm ($XR_{j,t}$) in the event window, as in Eq. (2.11).

$$XR_{j,t} = R_{j,t} - (a_j + b_j R_{m,t}) \qquad \text{Eq. 2.11}$$

In this equation, $R_{j,t}$ is the actual stock market return that a firm experiences in the event window—that is, after the firm has implemented its new strategy—and ($a_j + b_j R_{m,t}$) is the return this firm would have obtained if its historical performance had continued. If $XR_{j,t}$ is greater than zero for each time period, t, then the firm earned a greater than historically expected return in that period. $XR_{j,t}$ thus becomes a measure of above-normal performance. Of course, if $XR_{j,t}$ is less than zero, then a firm will have earned less than its historically expected return (that is, a below-normal return) on its new strategy in each time period, t. If $XR_{j,t}$ is equal to zero, the firm would have earned just its historically expected return (a normal return) in each time period.

The cumulative effect of a new strategy on a firm's stock market performance is then measured by its cumulative abnormal return (CAR),

$$CAR_j = \sum_{t=T_1}^{T_2} XR_{j,t} \qquad\qquad Eq.\ 2.12$$

where T_1 is the beginning of the strategic event and T_2 is the end of the strategic event. Whether or not a firm's cumulative abnormal return is large enough to conclude that it did not occur by chance (that is, large enough to be statistically significant) can be calculated by dividing a firm's CAR by the standard deviation of excess returns during the event window, as in,

$$t_j = CAR_j/s_j \qquad\qquad Eq.\ 2.13$$

where s_j is the standard deviation of $XR_{j,t}$ from time T_1 to time T_2. This statistic is normally distributed when the number of time periods in an event window is large. A t_j greater than 2.0 means that the probability that a firm's CAR was generated by chance is less than .05.

Event studies are powerful measures of a firm's performance, but they too have limitations. First, it is sometimes difficult to specify a strategic event's beginning date. As is described in Chapter 5, firms sometimes have a strong incentive to keep the implementation of new and valuable strategies proprietary (Barney, 1991; Bettis, 1983). Thus specifying with any precision when a strategy is implemented can be difficult. Moreover, emergent strategies, in an important sense, have no starting date (Bromiley, Govekar, and Marcus, 1988). They are described as strategies only after they have been implemented.

Second, even when a strategic event does have an explicit beginning date, information about a pending strategy may leak out to the capital markets before the strategy is officially implemented. As this information becomes public, it will be reflected in a firm's stock prices. Thus by the time of the official announcement, much of the rise in the price of a firm's stock will already have occurred because investors will have anticipated the valuable strategy that was announced. In this situation, a firm's CAR in the event window may not be statistically significant even though the strategy itself added significant value to the firm (Bromiley, Goveker, and Marcus, 1988).

Given these limitations, event study measures of economic performance are most applicable for analyzing the performance implications of intended and discrete strategies (Lubatkin and Shrieves, 1986), such as mergers and acquisitions, organizational restructurings, and changes in management compensation.

Finally, these event study methods depend on the capital asset pricing model. Measurement problems associated with the CAPM, along with possible theoretical mis-specification, continue to be limitations for event study measures of firm performance.

Alternative Market Measures

Three additional market-based measures of performance have been proposed in the literature: Sharpe's measure, the Treynor index, and Jensen's alpha.

Sharpe's Measure.   In the Sharpe (1966) measure, a firm's stock market performance is compared to a firm's total risk. Stock market performance is computed by taking the difference between a firm's stock market performance in some time interval ($R_{j,t}$) and the average risk-free rate of return during that same interval (RFR_t). A firm's total risk is measured as the standard deviation of its stock market returns in the time interval (sd_t). Thus, S_j is computed as

$$S_j = \frac{R_{j,t} - RFR_t}{sd_t} \qquad\qquad Eq.\ 2.14$$

The numerator in Eq. (2.14) can be thought of as a measure of the risk premium earned by a firm, and the denominator is a firm's total risk. Thus, S_j is a measure of a firm's return dollars per unit of risk. The higher the value of S_j, the greater is the dollar return per unit of risk, and the greater is the economic performance of a firm.

The Treynor Index.   Treynor's (1965) index is similar to the Sharpe measure. However, where Sharpe's measure compares a firm's returns to total risk, the Treynor index compares returns to a firm's systematic risk, measured by β_j:

$$T_j = \frac{R_{j,t} - RFR_t}{\beta_j} \qquad\qquad Eq.\ 2.15$$

Jensen's Alpha.   A final alternative market-based measure of performance was proposed by Jensen (1968). This measure is computed by comparing a firm's stock market performance to its risk-adjusted expected performance, as in

$$R_{j,t} - RFR_t = a_j + b_j(R_{m,t} - RFR_t) + e_j \qquad\qquad Eq.\ 2.16$$

where,

$R_{j,t}$ = Firm j's stock market returns at time t

RFR_t = the risk-free rate of return at time t

a_j = an empirically determined CAPM parameter

b_j = an estimate of Firm j's systematic risk, β_j

$R_{m,t}$ = the stock market return for a fully diversified portfolio of stocks at time t

e_j = error

Notice that, in Eq. (2.16), a_j is the only difference between the risk premium actually earned by Firm j $(R_{j,t} - RFR_t)$ and that firm's expected market performance, given its economic history $[b_j(R_{m,t} - RFR_t) + e_j]$. A Jensen's alpha greater than zero suggests that a firm is outperforming the market (above-normal returns); an alpha less than zero suggests that a firm is underperforming the market (below-normal returns); and an alpha equal to zero suggests that a firm is performing at market levels (normal returns).

Limitations of Alternative Market Measures. Each of these alternative performance measures was originally designed to evaluate the performance of an investment portfolio. Only recently have they begun to be applied to measuring firm performance (Hoskisson, Hitt, Johnson, and Moesel, 1993). However, they continue to rely on assumptions that are usually more appropriate for valuing investment portfolios than for valuing firms. For example, both the Sharpe and the Treynor measures implicitly assume that the cost of capital for firms is equal to the risk-free interest rate (Khoury, 1983). This is why both of these measures, in the numerator, calculate the difference between a firm's actual returns $(R_{j,t})$ with the risk-free return (RFR_t). Fully diversified investment portfolios are more likely to be able to obtain capital at this low risk-free rate. However, a firm's cost of capital is usually higher than this risk free rate. Also, the Treynor index only compares a firm's actual returns to systematic risk (β_j), implicitly assuming that the firm has fully diversified away any unsystematic risk. Again, although this may be a reasonable assumption for investment portfolios, relatively few firms diversify away all unsystematic risk. Indeed, in Chapter 11, we argue that such diversification often reduces the wealth of a firm's shareholders. Finally, both the Treynor index and Jensen's alpha depend on the capital asset pricing model to compute a firm's systematic risk. All the limitations of this model, discussed earlier, also apply to these measures.

Despite these limitations, these three alternative market measures, in combination with other measures of firm performance, can provide insight to a firm's economic position. Empirically, Sharpe's measure, the Treynor index, and Jensen's alpha are highly correlated. In a study of 160 diversified and nondiversified firms, Hoskisson and his colleagues (1993) found that the correlations among these performance measures ranged from .84 to .90 and were all statistically significant. However, the correlation between these three measures and two accounting measures of performance (firm ROA and ROE minus industry average ROA and ROE) while consistent, were much lower, ranging from .15 to .30. These correlations were still statistically significant. These results suggest that these alternative market measures of firm performance provide information about performance over and above accounting measures of performance.

2.4   SUMMARY

This chapter has examined the role of performance in strategic management. Conceptually, *firm performance* was defined by comparing the actual value created by a firm with its expected value. Firms that earn just what they are expected to earn are generating a normal level of performance, firms that earn less than they are expected to earn generate a below-normal level of performance, and firms that earn more than they are expected to earn generate an above-normal level of performance.

Several measures of this conceptualization of performance were discussed and evaluated. These include firm survival, accounting measures, the multiple stakeholders approach, present-value measures, and other measures of performance (including Tobin's q, event studies, Sharpe's measure, the Treynor index, and Jensen's alpha). All of these measures have both strengths and weaknesses, and thus multiple measures of performance should often be used in strategic analyses.

REVIEW QUESTIONS

1. A firm is currently earning an economic profit (realized value is greater than expected value). What impact will this current performance have on the expected value of the firm in the future? What

implications, if any, does your answer have for the strategizing efforts of managers?

2. Should a firm's managers attempt to gain normal or above-normal profits from their strategizing efforts? Justify your answer from the point of view of stockholders, employees, customers, and society at large.

3. Economic definitions of *firm performance* have been criticized for focusing on only one of a firm's stakeholders—stockholders. Do you agree with this criticism? Why or why not?

4. Accounting measures of firm performance are an imperfect indicator of a firm's economic performance. This condition is problematic only if economic performance is somehow a "better" way than accounting performance to think about firm performance. Is economic performance a "better" way to think about firm performance? Why or why not?

5. You are on an airplane, sitting next to the president of a company, and she begins boasting about her firm's high ROA. What questions should you ask her to fully evaluate the performance of her firm? Suppose she boasts about her firm's high earnings per share (EPS). What questions should you ask to fully evaluate her firm's performance? Suppose she boasts about her firm's ability to attract managerial and professional talent. What questions should you ask to fully evaluate her firm's performance?

CHAPTER
3

Evaluating Environmental Threats

Chapter 1 suggested that firms that wish to maintain or improve their performance need to choose strategies that exploit opportunities and strengths while neutralizing threats and avoiding or fixing weaknesses. With Chapter 2's discussion of performance in place, it is now possible to use SWOT analysis to explore how a firm's strategic choices affect its performance. This chapter describes models for evaluating a firm's environmental threats. Chapter 4 describes models for evaluating its environmental opportunities, and Chapter 5 describes models for evaluating its organizational strengths and weaknesses.

The fundamental objective in analyzing the threats and opportunities in a firm's environment is to evaluate the overall economic attractiveness of an industry. The average performance of firms in economically very attractive industries (industries with low levels of threat and high levels of opportunity) will be greater than the average performance of firms in economically unattractive industries (industries with high levels of threat and low levels of opportunity). Thus, firms in the pharmaceutical industry, an industry most observers agree is economically very attractive, typically outperform firms in the U.S. airline industry, an industry that most agree is not economically attractive. Of course, industry analysis must go beyond an arbitrary listing of threats and opportunities in an industry. This listing approach to industry analysis is not only arbitrary, it may be incomplete. Rather, what is required is an approach to analyzing industry attractiveness that is grounded in a theory of competition in an industry.

This chapter discusses a general theoretical framework that can be used to inform the analysis of environmental threats and opportunities: the structure-conduct-performance (S-C-P) model in industrial organization economics. The chapter examines how the S-C-P model has been used to develop a framework for analyzing environmental threats (Porter, 1980) and applies this framework to the analysis of threats in the pharmaceutical and textile industries.

3.1   THE STRUCTURE-CONDUCT-PERFORMANCE MODEL

In the 1930s, a group of economists began developing an approach for understanding the relationship between a firm's environment, its behavior, and performance (Mason, 1939; Bain, 1968). The original objective of this work was to describe conditions under which perfect competition dynamics in an industry would not unfold (Mason, 1939) in order to assist government regulators in isolating those industries within which competition-enhancing regulations should be implemented (Porter, 1981a; Barney, 1986c).

The theoretical framework that developed out of this effort became known as the structure-conduct-performance model (Scherer, 1980). The term *structure* in this model refers to industry structure, measured by factors such as the number of buyers and sellers in an industry, the level of product differentiation, barriers to entry, cost structure, and vertical integration. *Conduct* refers to specific firm actions in an industry, including pricing behavior, product strategy, advertising, research and development, and investment in plant and equipment. *Performance* in the S-C-P model has two meanings: the performance of individual firms and the performance of the economy as a whole. The structure-conduct-performance model is summarized in Fig. 3.1.

The logic that links industry structure to conduct and performance is well known. Attributes of the industry structure within which a firm operates define the range of options and constraints facing a firm. In some industries—those approaching the perfectly competitive ideal of neoclassical microeconomics (Conner, 1991; Tirole, 1988)—firms have very few options and face many constraints. In these competitive industries, most firms are simple price takers and respond to changes in supply and demand, rather than attempting to influence the level of supply or demand (Hirshleifer, 1980). Firms in these industries generate, at best, normal economic value in the long run, and social welfare (as traditionally defined in economics) is maximized. Thus if an industry's structure is perfectly competitive, firm conduct is completely determined (firms are price takers), as is long-run firm performance (normal).

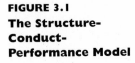

FIGURE 3.1
The Structure-
Conduct-
Performance Model

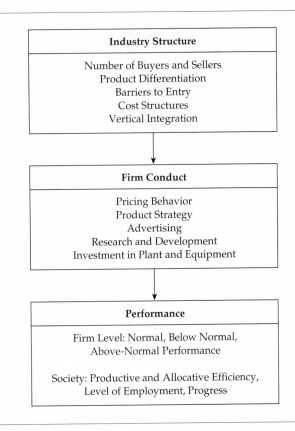

However, in other industries—less competitive industries—firms face fewer constraints and a greater range of options. Some of these options may enable firms to obtain competitive advantages and above-normal economic performance. However, even when firms have more conduct options, industry structure still constrains the range of those options. More importantly, other attributes of industry structure—including barriers to entry—determine how long firms in an industry will be able to earn above-normal performance (Bain, 1968). Without barriers to entry, any above-normal performance by firms in an industry will be quickly competed away by new entrants (Porter, 1980). Thus even in this case, industry structure (both the range of options open to firms and the existence of barriers to entry) determines firm conduct (product differentiation, oligopolistic cooperation, and so forth) and firm performance (temporary or sustained competitive advantages).

The regulatory implications of the S-C-P framework fall out of this emphasis on barriers to entry preventing an increase in competition in an industry (Porter, 1981a). When barriers to entry into an industry exist, natural competitive forces will not generate the social welfare benefits of perfect competition. In such settings, the government must intervene with antitrust lawsuits, forced divestitures, or other competition-enhancing activities (Demsetz, 1973).

Strategy researchers have turned the traditional objectives of the S-C-P model upside-down. Instead of seeking ways to increase the competitiveness of industries, strategy researchers have used the S-C-P model as a way to describe the attributes of an industry that make it *less* than perfectly competitive, and thus to help firms find ways to obtain above-normal economic performance (Porter, 1980).

3.2   THE FIVE FORCES MODEL OF ENVIRONMENTAL THREATS

To a strategy researcher and manager, an environmental threat is any individual, group, or organization outside a firm that seeks to reduce the level of that firm's performance (Christensen, Andrews, Bower, Hamermesh, and Porter, 1980). Threats increase a firm's costs, decrease a firm's revenues, or in other ways reduce a firm's performance. In S-C-P terms, *threats* are forces that tend to increase the competitiveness of an industry and force firm performance to a normal level (Porter, 1980).

The objective of developing a model of environmental threats is to assist managers in analyzing these threats so that they can be more effective in developing strategies to neutralize them. The model of environmental threats Porter developed—the five forces framework—is presented in Fig. 3.2. The five attributes of industry structure that, according to Porter (1979, 1980) can threaten the ability of a firm to either maintain or create above-normal returns are (1) the threat of entry, (2) the threat of rivalry, (3) the threat of substitutes, (4) the threat of suppliers, and (5) the threat of buyers.

THE THREAT OF ENTRY

New entrants are firms that have recently begun operations in an industry or that threaten to begin operations in an industry soon. For General Motors' automobile operations, new entrants have included, over the years, Toyota, Nissan, and more recently the Hyundai Motor Corporation. For IBM in its multiple computer businesses, relatively new entrants have at various points included Amdahl Computers, Hewlett-Packard, and Digital Equipment Corporation. Recently, IBM

FIGURE 3.2
The Five Forces Model of Environmental Threats. *Source:* Porter (1980).

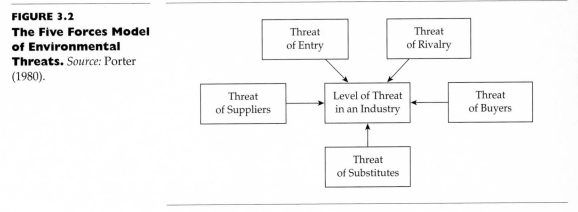

has faced additional significant new entry from numerous personal computer firms.

According to the S-C-P model, new entrants are motivated to enter into an industry by the above-normal economic profits that some incumbent firms in that industry may be earning (Baumol, Panzar, and Willig, 1982). Firms seeking a piece of that above-normal pie enter the industry, thereby increasing the level of industry competition and reducing the performance of incumbent firms. Absent any barriers, entry will continue as long as any firms in the industry are earning above-normal performance, and entry will cease when all incumbent firms are earning normal returns (Hirschleifer, 1980).

The extent to which new entry acts as a threat to an incumbent firm's performance depends on the cost of entry. If the cost of entry into an industry is greater than the potential profits a new entrant could obtain by entering, then entry will not be forthcoming, and new entrants are not a threat to incumbent firms. But if the cost of entry is lower than the return from entry, entry will occur until the profits derived from entry are less than the costs of entry.

The threat of entry depends on the cost of entry, and the cost of entry, in turn, depends on the existence and "height" of barriers to entry (Bain, 1968). Barriers to entry are attributes of an industry's structure that increase the cost of entry. The greater the cost of entry, the greater is the "height" of these barriers. With significant barriers to entry in place, potential entrants will not enter into an industry even though incumbent firms are earning above-normal economic performance. Five barriers to entry are broadly cited in the S-C-P and strategy literatures (Bain, 1968; Porter, 1980). These five barriers, listed in Table 3.1, are (1) economies of scale, (2) product differentiation, (3) cost

TABLE 3.1
Barriers to Entry into an Industry

1. Economies of scale
2. Product differentiation
3. Cost advantages independent of scale
4. Contrived deterrence
5. Government regulation of entry

advantages independent of scale, (4) contrived deterrence, and (5) government regulation of entry. Three other barriers to entry often cited in the literature are actually special cases of these basic five.

Economies of Scale as a Barrier to Entry

For economies of scale to act as a barrier to entry, the relationship between the volume of production in a firm and firm costs must have the shape of line A in Fig. 3.3. This curve suggests that any deviation, positive or negative, from an optimal level of production (point X in Fig. 3.3) will lead a firm to experience much higher costs of production. Empirical research seems to suggest that the economies-of-scale curves in many industries are not as steeply sloped as line A in Fig. 3.3 (Scherer, 1980). Rather, in many industries there is a broad range of volume of production that can lead to low costs of production, as depicted by line

FIGURE 3.3
Economies of Scale and the Cost of Production.
The figure shows two economies of scale: steeply curved (line A) and not steeply curved (line B).

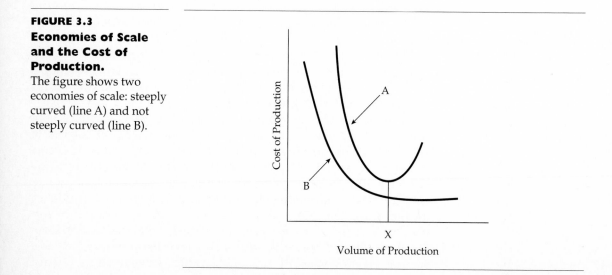

B in Fig. 3.3. Nevertheless, some industries seem to have very narrow ranges of optimal sizes of production, including, perhaps, metal-can manufacturing, steel manufacturing, and aluminum smelting.

To see how economies of scale can act as a barrier to entry, consider this example. Imagine the following: There are five incumbent firms in an industry (each firm has only one plant), the optimal level of production is 4,000 units ($X = 4,000$ units); total demand for the output of this industry is fixed at 22,000 units; the economies-of-scale curve is as depicted by line A in Fig. 3.3; and there are few, if any, opportunities to differentiate products in this industry. Total demand in this industry (22,000 units) is greater than total supply ($5 \times 4,000$ units $= 20,000$). From traditional price theory, it follows that the five incumbent firms in this industry will be earning above-normal economic profits. The S-C-P model suggests that, absent barriers, these above-normal economic profits should motivate entry.

However, look at the entry decision from the point of view of potential entrants. Certainly, incumbent firms are earning above-normal economic profits, but potential entrants face an unsavory choice. On the one hand, new entrants could enter the industry with an optimally efficient plant and produce 4,000 units. However, this form of entry will lead industry supply to rise to 24,000 units (20,000 + 4,000). Suddenly, supply will be greater than demand (24,000 > 22,000), and all the firms in the industry, including the new entrant, will earn below-normal performance. On the other hand, the new entrant might enter the industry with a plant of smaller-than-optimal size (say 1,000 units). This kind of entry leaves total industry demand larger than industry supply (22,000 > 21,000). However, the new entrant faces a serious cost disadvantage in this case, because it does not produce at the low-cost position on the economies-of-scale curve. Faced with these bleak alternatives, the potential entrant does not enter, even though incumbent firms are earning above-normal economic profits (Bain, 1956).

Of course, there are other options for potential entrants besides entering at the efficient scale and losing money or entering at an inefficient scale and losing money. First, potential entrants can attempt to expand primary demand (that is, increase total demand from 22,000 to 24,000 units or more) and enter at the optimal size. This alternative relaxes the assumption that industry demand is fixed. Second, potential entrants can attempt to develop new production technology, shift the economies-of-scale curve to the left (thereby reducing the optimal plant size), and enter. Such new technology makes production in this industry less "lumpy" and may enable firms to enter and earn normal or even above-normal returns. Finally, potential entrants may try to differentiate their products, thereby charging higher prices to offset higher production costs associated with a smaller-than-optimal plant (Bain, 1956).

Any of these actions, or combinations of them, may enable entry into an industry. However, these actions are costly. If the cost of engaging in these barrier-busting activities is greater than the return from entry, entry will not occur, even if incumbent firms are earning above-normal economic performance. Moreover, not only can potential entrants engage in these activities, but so can incumbent firms. If incumbent firms act to increase primary demand, introduce new production technology, or differentiate their product, these incumbent firms may be able to obtain any above-normal returns that could have been appropriated by new entrants, and new entry will not occur. As we discuss in Chapter 5, which firms act to appropriate these above-normal returns depends on firms' unique resources and capabilities.

Historically, economies of scale acting as a barrier to entry discouraged entry into the worldwide steel market. To fully exploit economies of scale, traditional steel plants had to be very large. If new entrants into the steel market had built these efficient and large steel manufacturing plants, they would have had the effect of increasing the steel supply over the demand for steel, and the outcome would have been reduced margins for established and incumbent firms. The likelihood of this outcome tended to discourage new entry. However, in the 1970s, the development of alternative mini-mill technology shifted the economies-of-scale curve in the steel industry to the left by making smaller plants very efficient in addressing some segments of the steel market. This shift had the effect of decreasing barriers to entry into the steel industry. Recent entrants, including, for example, Nucor Steel, have significant cost advantages over firms still using outdated, less efficient production technology (Ghemawat and Stander, 1992).

Product Differentiation as a Barrier to Entry

Product differentiation means that incumbent firms possess brand identification and customer loyalty that potential entrants do not possess. (Porter, 1980). Brand identification and customer loyalty serve as entry barriers because new entrants not only have to absorb the standard costs associated with starting production in a new industry but also have to absorb the costs associated with overcoming incumbent firms' differentiation advantages. If the cost of overcoming these advantages is greater than the potential return from entering an industry, entry will not occur, even if incumbent firms are earning above-normal performance (Bain, 1956).

Care must be taken when comparing the costs that incumbent firms face in creating product differentiation barriers to entry and the costs that potential entrants face in overcoming those barriers. In general, if the cost of entry deterrence borne by incumbent firms is equal to the value of entry deterrence in deterring entry, then incumbent firms will earn only normal economic performance, even though they have successfully deterred entry (Barney, 1986a). For example, suppose a firm could earn $1,000 of above-normal economic profits if there was no entry into its industry. However, because there are potential entrants, this firm may feel compelled to invest in product differentiation (through advertising, customer service, and so forth) to deter entry. These activities are costly. If the total cost of the product differentiation needed to deter new entry is $1,000, then this incumbent firm would earn only normal economic profit ($1,000 in potential economic profit – $1,000 in costs for deterring entry = $0 economic profit), even if it successfully deterred entry. Only if the cost of entry deterrence is less than the value of deterred entry can incumbent firms obtain above-normal economic performance.

There are numerous examples of industries within which product differentiation tends to act as a barrier to entry. In the brewing industry, for example, substantial investments by Budweiser, Miller, and Coors (among other incumbent firms) in advertising (will we ever forget the Bud Bowl?) and brand recognition have made large-scale entry into the U.S. brewing industry very costly. Whether these efforts to forestall entry have reduced the returns to these incumbent firms to normal is a difficult question, although some recent research seems to suggest that this may have occurred for the largest firms in U.S. brewing (Montgomery and Wernerfelt, 1991).

Cost Advantages Independent of Scale as Barriers to Entry

In addition to the barriers previously cited, incumbent firms may have a whole range of cost advantages, independent of economies of scale, not available to new entrants. These cost advantages can act to deter entry, since new entrants will find themselves at a cost disadvantage vis-à-vis incumbent firms with these cost advantages. New entrants can engage in activities to overcome the cost advantages of incumbent firms, but as the cost of overcoming them increases, the economic profit potential from entry is reduced. In some settings, incumbent firms enjoying cost advantages, independent of scale, can earn above-normal profits and still not be threatened by new entry—since the cost of overcoming those advantages can be prohibitive. Five examples of these cost advantages, independent of scale, have been discussed in the literature: (1) proprietary technology, (2) know-how, (3) favorable access to raw materials, (4) favorable geographic locations, and (5) learning-curve cost advantages.

Proprietary Technology.   In some industries, proprietary (secret or patented) technology gives incumbent firms important cost advantages over potential entrants. To enter these industries, potential entrants must develop their own substitute technologies or copy the proprietary technologies. Both of these activities can be costly. Developing substitute technology can involve expensive and risky research and development efforts. Copying proprietary technology can be costly in terms of potential lawsuits for patent violations (Barney, 1991). If the cost to new entrants of duplicating incumbent firms' cost positions is greater than the economic potential from entering an industry, new entry will not be forthcoming even though incumbent firms may be earning above-normal economic profits. Notice that this proprietary technology need not be linked with economies of scale to act as a barrier to entry.

Know-how.   Even more important than technology per se as a barrier to entry is the know-how built up by incumbent firms over their history (Kogut and Zander, 1992; Conner, 1991). Know-how is the often-taken-for-granted knowledge and information that is needed to compete in an industry on a day-to-day basis (Polanyi, 1962; Itami, 1987). Know-how includes information about countless details that has taken years, sometimes decades, to accumulate in a firm, that enables a firm to interact with customers and suppliers, to be innovative and creative, to manufacture quality products, and so forth. New entrants, typically, will not have access to this know-how and thus may find themselves at a cost disadvantage compared to incumbents. Moreover, it may be difficult (costly) for new entrants to build this know-how in relatively short periods of time. Together, these attributes of know-how can discourage new entry.

One industry where this kind of know-how is very important is the pharmaceutical industry. Success in this industry depends critically on having high-quality research and development skills. The development of world-class research and development skills takes decades, as firms accumulate the knowledge, abilities, ideas—the know-how—needed to succeed. New entrants face enormous cost disadvantages for decades as they attempt to develop these abilities, and thus entry into the pharmaceutical industry has been quite limited (see Section 3.3).

Favorable Access to Raw Materials.   Incumbent firms may also have cost advantages, compared to new entrants, based on favorable access to raw materials (Scherer, 1980). If, for example, there are only a few sources of high-quality iron ore in a specific geographic region, steel firms that have access to these sources may have a cost advantage over steel firms that must ship their ore in from distant sources.

Of course, in order for favorable access to raw materials to be a source of cost advantage for incumbent firms, firms with this access must not have paid its full value when they acquired it. If a firm is able to save a million dollars a year because it does not have to ship its raw materials long distances, but it has to pay an extra million dollars a year for access to its raw materials, this firm obviously does not earn above-normal economic profits. However, if a million-dollar savings was obtained for a $25,000 investment, then this firm has a cost advantage over potential entrants and can be expected to earn above-normal profits that will not motivate entry.

There are a variety of reasons why an incumbent firm may pay less for access to raw materials than what that access is really worth (Barney, 1991). First, at the time access to raw materials is obtained, the full value of this access may not be known. Thus, for example, a farmer may purchase land to grow cotton, only to discover that the land rests on a very valuable reservoir of oil. Second, changes in technology or demand may increase the value of a source of raw materials in ways that were not anticipated when the source was acquired. Porter (1980) cites certain deposits of sulfur that were thought to have relatively little value when they were sold by some oil companies to several sulfur-mining companies. However, changes in sulfur-mining technology made these sources of raw materials much more valuable than had been anticipated.

In general, new entrants are less likely to be able to acquire favorable access to raw materials for a price less than the full value of that access, compared to incumbent firms. When incumbent firms earn economic profits on their favorable access to raw materials, these economic profits reveal the full value of that access. In the future, firms that attempt to duplicate that access will have to pay its full economic value. Thus the above-normal profits earned by incumbent firms that motivate new entry ensure that new entrants will not be able to earn economic profits from acquiring special access to raw materials.

Favorable Geographic Locations.   Incumbent firms may have all the favorable locations locked up, thereby gaining a cost advantage compared to potential entrants. Like favorable access to raw materials, favorable locations are only a source of cost advantage if incumbent firms acquire these locations at a price that is less than their true value (Ricardo, 1817).

One firm that has built its success at least partly on the early acquisition of favorable geographic locations is Wal-Mart. By moving early to put its large retail outlets in small and medium-size markets, Wal-Mart was able to acquire many retail locations before the full value of these locations was apparent. New entrants into these markets would have to compete not only with Wal-Mart's impressive economies of scale but also with Wal-Mart's cost advantage stemming from the timing of the acquisition of its locations. Given these two factors, it is not surprising that few other retail firms have moved into these same small and medium markets (Ghemawat, 1986).

Learning-Curve Cost Advantages.   It has been shown that in certain industries (such as airplane manufacturing) the cost of production falls with the cumulative volume of production (Scherer, 1980). Over time, as incumbent firms gain experience in manufacturing, their costs fall below those of potential entrants. Potential entrants, in this context, must endure substantially higher costs while they gain experience, and thus they may not enter, despite possible above-normal returns being earned by incumbent firms. These learning-curve economies are discussed in more detail in Chapter 6.

Contrived Deterrence as a Barrier to Entry

Economies of scale, product differentiation, and cost advantages independent of scale can all be thought of as "natural" barriers to entry. In each case, incumbent firms are engaging in activities designed to improve their efficiency (economies of scale and cost advantages independent of scale) or give themselves an advantage over current competition (product differentiation). A secondary consequence of these activities is that they also deter entry. However, firms would engage in these activities even if they did not deter entry, because they improve a firm's efficiency and enhance its competitive position in an industry.

An alternative approach to studying entry focuses on "contrived deterrence" (Tirole, 1988). Here, incumbent firms engage in activities whose sole objective is to deter new entry even if these activities may *reduce* the efficiency of incumbent firms.

Most of the barriers previously cited could be used in contrived deterrence ways. For example, to prevent possible entry, a firm might invest in more product differentiation than current competition requires. Also, to deter entry, a firm might invest in more than economy-of-scale maximizing levels of manufacturing capacity. In all cases, the objective of this additional investment is to send a signal to potential entrants that if they enter they are likely to face intense competitive pressures from incumbent firms.

Of course, these contrived deterrence investments are costly and can actually reduce the efficiency of incumbent firms. As with all strategic decisions, the benefits of these investments (in the form of deterred entry) must be weighed against the costs (reduced efficiency).

Consider, for example, the situation analyzed by Dixit (1982) and presented in Fig. 3.4. Here, there is one incumbent firm and one potential entrant. In panel A, the incumbent firm has made no contrived deterrence investments. The first decision made in the game depicted in panel A is made by the potential entrant. If this firm decides not to

FIGURE 3.4
Contrived Deterrence Strategies.

P_m = monopolist profits; P_d = duopolist profit; P_w = "warring" duopolist profit; C = costs. Profit results assume that $C < P_d$. The incumbent's profit is listed first in each ordered pair. *Source:* A. K. Dixit, "Recent developments in oligopoly theory," *Papers and Proceedings of the American Economic Association (94th Annual Meeting),* 1982, 72(2), pp. 12–17. Reprinted with permission.

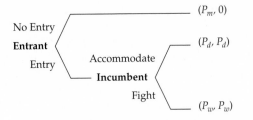

A. There is one incumbent and one new entrant, and the incumbent makes no contrived deterrence investments.

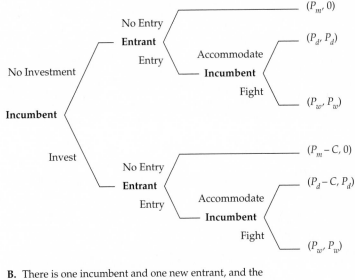

B. There is one incumbent and one new entrant, and the incumbent makes a contrived deterrence investment that costs C.

Profit implications: $P_m > (P_m - C) > P_d > (P_d - C) > P_w > 0$

enter this industry (perhaps because of substantial "natural" barriers to entry), the incumbent firm will earn a monopolist profit (P_m) and the new entrant will earn (at least in this industry) zero profits (0).

If, on the other hand, the potential entrant decides to enter, the incumbent firm has to decide whether to accommodate new entry (by, for example, reducing its level of output) or fight new entry (by, for example, maintaining or even increasing its output in order to drive the new entrant out of business). If the incumbent firm decides to accommodate the new entrant, then both the new firm and the incumbent earn profits equal to P_d (the duopolist profit). If the incumbent firm decides not to accommodate, both incumbent and new entrant earn profits equal to P_w (the "warring" profit). It is not difficult to see that $P_m > P_d > P_w > 0$. Accommodating new entrants is discussed in more detail in Chapter 8.

These profitability results present a dilemma for the incumbent firm. Clearly, the incumbent firm is much better off if the potential entrant decides not to enter. In this case, incumbent firms earn profits equal to P_m. To help ensure this level of profitability, the incumbent is likely to "threaten" the potential entrant with dire consequences if it actually enters—especially if there are no "natural" barriers to entry protecting the incumbent firm. However, these threats, in general, are not credible. Once entry actually occurs, the incumbent firm has a strong incentive to accommodate the new entrant, since P_d is greater than P_w. Of course, accommodating a new entrant sends to other potential entrants the signal that the original incumbent firm will accommodate, which increases the probability of subsequent entry.

An incumbent firm can partially resolve its dilemma by engaging in a contrived deterrence strategy. This is shown in panel B of Fig. 3.4. In panel B, the incumbent makes the first decision whether to invest in contrived deterrence. If the incumbent does not invest in contrived deterrence, then the outcomes are as shown in panel A. But if the incumbent decides to invest in contrived deterrence, the potential entrant must then decide whether to enter, and the incumbent must then decide whether to accommodate or fight if new entry is forthcoming. If the investment is made and no new entry is forthcoming, the incumbent firm earns $P_m - C$ (where C is the cost of the entry-deterring investment), and the potential entrant earns zero. If the investment is made, new entry occurs, and the incumbent accommodates, then the incumbent earns $P_d - C$, and the new entrant earns P_d. If the investment is made, entry occurs, and the incumbent fights, then both the incumbent and the new entrant earn P_w. The cost of deterring entry is not counted against the incumbent firm in this case because it is being used in a productive activity.

If the cost of deterring entry (C) is less than the profits of a duopolist (P_d), then the following relationships hold in panel B of Fig. 3.4: $P_m > (P_m - C) > P_d > (P_d - C) > P_w > 0$. The implications of these inequalities for an incumbent are clear. The best situation to be in is to be a monopolist not threatened by entry (or a monopolist protected by "natural" barriers to entry) and to earn the highest level of performance (P_m). Thus incumbent firms should invest in contrived deterrence only if they are not protected from entry by "natural" barriers—economies of scale, product differentiation, or cost advantages independent of scale. If this is not the case, the next best situation is to *effectively* deter entry (since $P_m - C > P_d$). Indeed, there may be significant leeway in making these entry-deterring investments. As long as the cost of deterrence (C) does not reduce an incumbent firm's performance to the level of a duopolist profit (P_d), this investment should be made. Also, this analysis suggests that if an investment to deter entry is going to be made, it should not fail, for ($P_d - C$) is less than P_d.

Researchers have suggested that contrived deterrence investments are most likely to succeed if they have three attributes (Tirole, 1988). First, an incumbent firm should invest in ways that, to the extent possible, forces it to fight if entry occurs. The object of these investments should be to reduce managerial discretion to accommodate to zero. It is, perhaps, ironic, but firms in this contrived deterrence world gain advantage by limiting their strategic options (Schelling, 1960).

Second, contrived deterrence investments must be highly specific. Specific investments have value in a limited range of economic activities. Nonspecific investments can be used to engage in a wide range of activities, including those that could accommodate new entrants. Specific investments may not be useful in accommodating new entrants. Indeed, their only use may be to fight new entrants. Thus an investment in excess general-purpose manufacturing space or in general-purpose warehouse space does not pose a credible threat to a potential entrant, but an investment in highly specialized excess manufacturing capacity or in highly specialized warehouse space does. Also, the costs of transforming these specialized investments into alternative uses must be high, so that they remain specific (Schelling, 1960; Tirole, 1988).

Finally, contrived deterrence investments must be made in a very public setting. If an incumbent firm makes these investments but fails to inform a potential entrant, their deterrence impact is limited. It is much more effective for an incumbent to publicly announce its deterring investment as widely as possible.

The model developed by Dixit (1982) applies to a monopolist attempting to deter entry into its industry. It can easily be generalized to industries with closely cooperating oligopolists (Tirole, 1988). Indeed, as we describe in detail in Chapter 8, virtually all contrived deterrence research focuses either on monopolists or on closely cooperating oligopolists. When numerous firms of equal size are competing in an industry, no one firm is likely to be able to create a sufficiently credible threat to be able to deter entry (Tirole, 1988).

One industry where this kind of contrived deterrence seems to have been operating was the U.S. electric turbine industry in the early-to-mid 1960s. All indications were that this industry was significantly case, cash flow projections associated with entry may not be affected, but the discount rate associated with this investment may be very high. If returns to entry cannot be expected for some time, and if the costs of entry are substantial, applying large discount rates may very well make entry a negative present-value investment. In this case, even if firms wanted to enter, they would not be able to obtain the capital to do so. However, entry is deterred not by the sheer size of capital required but by the advantages incumbent firms possess that raise the discount rates of potential entrants. Thus if capital is a barrier to entry, it is a barrier because one (or several) "natural" barriers are in place.

One important managerial implication of this discussion of capital barriers to entry is that firms that are unable to raise the capital they need to implement their entry strategies, on average, should spend less time worrying about capital markets and more time developing the resources and capabilities they will need to compete with incumbent firms. Once they develop the resources and capabilities they need to compete, capital will be forthcoming—assuming, of course, that capital markets are reasonably efficient.

Customer-switching costs have also been cited as a possible barrier to entry (Porter, 1980). Customer-switching costs are one-time costs borne by customers when they switch from one firm's products to another's. For certain products and services, customers must make substantial investments to learn how to use the product, to support it, and to fully exploit it. For example, when a company purchases a mainframe computer system from IBM, it makes substantial investments in buildings and rooms that are specifically designed for these computers, for hardware peripherals (including printers, disk drives, and terminals) that support their operations, and for software and trained computer operators to make the system work. The value of these investments can easily be larger than the cost of the mainframe computer itself.

When customers have made such investments to use incumbent firms' products, new entrants must convince these customers not only that their products are somehow preferable to the incumbent firms' but also that their products or services will add value over and above the switching costs that customers will have to bear to purchase a new entrant's products or services. If switching costs are substantial, potential entrants may not be able to begin operations even though incumbent firms are earning an above-normal return (Klein, Crawford, and Alchian, 1978).

However, upon reflection, it becomes clear that customer-switching costs are a special case of "natural" cost or product differentiation barriers to entry in an industry. Absent monopoly, customers in an industry will be willing to accept high switching costs as a condition to using a firm's products if they perceive the value of that firm's products to be much greater than the value of alternatives. Higher perceived value, in turn, is a function of the level of product differentiation or lower costs of incumbent firms in an industry. Thus customer-switching costs operate as a barrier only under conditions of product differentiation or cost advantage.

Finally, access to distribution channels has also been cited as a barrier to entry (Porter, 1980). If incumbent firms have all the logical distribution channels in an industry already locked up, then new entrants will have to absorb substantial costs to create new distribution channels to compete. However, if it is recognized that prior access to distribution channels is logically equivalent to having special access to some important raw material, geographic location, or know-how, then distribution channels become a special case of cost advantages independent of scale acting as a barrier to entry. Because of this, all the conditions that must hold for these cost advantages to generate entry deterrence must also hold for access to distribution channels. Most notably, the full value of access to distribution channels cannot have been reflected in the cost to incumbent firms when that access was originally obtained.

Even when incumbent firms have prior access to distribution channels, new entrants may still be able to create new channels. This has occurred in the U.S. television broadcasting industry with the entry of several new television networks, including the Fox and Warner Brothers networks (Jensen and Robichaux, 1993). In the end, if the profit potential of new entry is greater than the cost of new entry, entry is likely to occur even if the cost of creating new distribution networks is significant.

THE THREAT OF RIVALRY

New entrants are an important threat to the ability of firms to maintain or improve their level of performance, but they are not the only threat cited by Porter (1980). A second environmental threat isolated by Porter is the level of rivalry in an industry—the intensity of competition among a firm's direct competitors. GM's rivals in the automobile business have historically included Ford and Chrysler. More recently Toyota and Nissan have emerged from the status of new entrants to become rivals. IBM's rivals in mainframe computers include Unisys and Honeywell-Bull, and in other competing products include Compaq, Hewlett Packard, Gateway 2000, and Apple.

Rivalry threatens firms by reducing their economic profits. High levels of rivalry are indicated by such actions as frequent price cutting by firms in an industry (for example, price discounts in the airline industry), frequent introduction of new products by firms in an industry (continuous product introductions in consumer electronics), intense advertising campaigns (the "Pepsi Challenge" and Coke's "It's the Real Thing" advertising campaigns), and rapid competitive actions and reactions in an industry (competing airlines quickly matching the discounts of other airlines).

Some of the attributes of an industry that are likely to generate high levels of rivalry cited by Porter (1980) are listed in Table 3.2. First, rivalry tends to be high when there are numerous firms in an industry and these firms tend to be roughly the same size and have the same influence on total industry supply. Such is the case in the lap-top personal computer industry. Over 120 firms, worldwide, have entered the laptop computer market (Saporito, 1992). Historically, prices in this industry have fallen from 15 to 20 percent a year, mostly because of improved technology and manufacturing. However, since the early 1990s, prices have been declining from 25 to 30 percent a year. Profit margins for lap-top personal computer firms that used to be in the 10-to-13 percent range have rapidly fallen to 3 and 4 percent (Allen and Siconolfi, 1993).

Large numbers of suppliers and retailers in the consumer electronics industry have also led to intense rivalry. For example, the average wholesale price of televisions in the United States has fallen 37 percent, in real dollars, since 1977 (Saporito, 1992). Sony experienced an operating loss in its consumer electronics business in 1993; Toshiba's earnings in this industry fell 67 percent in 1992. While all this is going on, more than fifteen thousand bankrupt consumer electronics retail companies continue selling products in the U.S. market.

Second, rivalry tends to be high when industry growth is slow. When industry growth is slow, firms seeking to increase their sales must acquire market share from established competitors. This tends to increase rivalry. It is interesting to note that the "cola wars" between Pepsi and Coke began in earnest in the mid-1970s, when a combination of increased sugar costs and increased interest in consumer health led

---

**TABLE 3.2
Attributes of an
Industry That
Increase the Threat
of Rivalry**

1. Large number of competing firms

2. Competing firms that are the same size and have the same influence

3. Slow industry growth

4. Lack of product differentiation

5. Productive capacity added in large increments

to a flattening in demand growth in soft drinks (Christensen et al., 1980). In order to continue to grow, Coke and Pepsi had to begin to acquire market share from each other, thereby increasing the rivalry between two already highly competitive firms.

Slow growth has been a factor igniting rivalry in other industries as well. In the office furniture business, sales are expected to decline by about 5 percent each year over the next several years. This negative growth has prompted firms in this industry to slash their prices 60 percent and more (Mitchell, 1991). Slow growth in the luxury segment of the automobile industry has intensified rivalry among established firms (including Mercedes and BMW) and between established firms and new entrants (Toyota and Nissan) (Taylor, 1991). Rivalry in this market has focused primarily on introducing new technologies and improving performance and reliability. However, price reductions recently have become more common in this luxury segment.

Third, rivalry tends to be high when firms are unable to differentiate their products in an industry. When product differentiation is not a viable strategic option, firms are often forced to compete only on the basis of price. Intense price competition is typical of high-rivalry industries. In the airline industry, for example, intense competition on longer routes—such as between Los Angeles and New York and between Los Angeles and Chicago—has kept prices on these routes down. There are relatively few product differentiation options on these routes. However, by creating hub-and-spoke systems, certain airlines (American, United, Delta) have been able to develop regions of the United States where they are the dominant carrier. Hub-and-spoke systems enable airlines to partially differentiate their products geographically and thus reduce the level of rivalry in segments of this industry. There may also be substantial economies of scale associated with hub-and-spoke systems.

In some industries, previously "unassailable" product differentiation advantages have eroded, to be replaced by intense rivalry. In the U.S. cigarette market, for example, discount brands have been capturing an increased share of sales, rising from less than 5 percent in 1981 to 30 percent in 1992. In response to this trend, Philip Morris recently began discounting the price of its brand leader, Marlboro. Philip Morris concluded that such discounts were necessary to maintain Marlboro's market share, although they resulted in a 40 percent reduction in pretax profits from Philip Morris's U.S. tobacco operations (Shapiro, 1993).

On the other hand, some brand names continue to protect firms from intense rivalry. Despite the cola wars of the 1970s and 1980s, Coca-Cola remains among the world's best-known brands. By carefully exploiting that product differentiation advantage, especially overseas (thereby avoiding direct confrontations with PepsiCo), Coca-Cola was able to obtain 1992 sales of $13.5 billion, with a net profit of $1.7 billion and return on equity of 42.5 percent. Not surprisingly, Coca-Cola's market value rose from $4 billion in 1980 to over $51 billion in 1993 (Huey, 1993).

Finally, rivalry tends to be high when production capacity is added in large increments. If, in order to obtain economies of scale, production capacity must be added in large increments, an industry is likely to experience periods of oversupply after new capacity comes on line. This overcapacity often leads to price cutting (Tirole, 1988). Much of the growing rivalry in the commercial jet industry among Boeing, McDonnell-Douglas, and AirBus can be traced to the large manufacturing capacity additions made by AirBus when entering this industry (Labich, 1992).

A particularly pernicious form of rivalry exists when capacity can be added only in large increments, when there are large sunk costs, and when demand is uncertain. Telser (1978) calls industries with these attributes "empty core markets." In empty core markets, there is no stable competitive equilibrium, and firms often engage in cutthroat competition by charging prices that generate revenues less than costs.

There is now a growing consensus that the airline industry has many of the attributes of an empty core market, not the least of which is severe price cutting. Cutthroat competition in this industry has generated operating losses of over $10 billion in the 1990s alone. To see how empty core markets can create cutthroat competition, consider several airlines competing for a single route. If demand on this route were completely predictable, aircraft manufacturers could build optimally sized planes. However, route demand is generally not so predictable, and jet aircraft come in only a few (fixed) capacities. Suppose that, for some period of time, demand on this route is greater than supply. With demand greater than supply, firms already flying this route will be able to earn an above-normal return. Of course, these above-normal profits will motivate entry, either by an airline already flying the route adding capacity, or a new airline entering into a route. However, since capacity can be added only in large increments (a plane at a time), these actions will often lead to oversupply. Price reductions (to fill planes) will ensue, leading to below-normal returns—until one or more carriers reduce their service. Thus this route is chronically either oversupplied or undersupplied.

Of course, one might ask, If a carrier knows that expanding service or entering into a route will lead to oversupply and below-normal returns, why would the carrier do it? The answer depends on these firms' sunk costs. If the only productive assets a firm owns are airplanes, and if a firm wants to remain in the airline business, then this is the game that must be played (McWilliams and Barney, 1995).

McWilliams and Barney (1995) have shown that traditional competitive strategies cannot generate normal returns in this setting. Rather, what is required is firms cooperating in allocating airplanes to routes. This cooperation can be voluntary (see Chapter 8's discussion of tacit collusion), or it can be imposed by government regulations (Telser, 1978).

THE THREAT OF SUBSTITUTES

A third environmental threat discussed by Porter (1980) is substitutes. The products or services provided by a firm's rivals meet approximately the same customer needs in the same ways as the products or services provided by the firm itself. *Substitute* products or services meet approximately the same customer needs but do so in different ways. Substitutes for GM's automobile products include bicycles, buses, trains, and airplanes. There are relatively few obvious substitutes for IBM's computer products.

Substitutes place a ceiling on the prices firms in an industry can charge and on the profits firms in an industry can earn. For example, during the oil price shocks of the 1970s and 1980s, members of OPEC were able to collude, reduce output, and drive the price of crude oil to over $40 per barrel. At this price, a broad range of substitutes that had previously not been economically viable suddenly became more attractive. Substitutes included oil shale, oil sands, solar energy, and even conservation. If the price of oil had remained at (inflation adjusted) over $40 per barrel, several of these substitutes might have reached a critical mass and become long-term viable alternatives to crude oil, and they could have acted as constraints on the profits of oil companies and oil-producing countries. The collapse of crude oil prices in the 1980s made these substitute products less attractive, but at the cost of reducing the profits of oil-producing countries.

In the extreme, substitutes can ultimately replace an industry's products and services. This happens when a substitute is clearly superior to previous products. Examples include electronic calculators as substitutes for slide rules and mechanical calculators, electronic watch movements as substitutes for pin-lever mechanical watch movements, and compact discs as substitutes for long-playing records (although some audiophiles continue to argue for the sonic attributes of LPs).

Substitutes are playing an increasingly important role in reducing the profit potential in a wide variety of industries. For example, in the legal profession, private mediation and arbitration services are becoming viable substitutes for lawyers (Pollock, 1993). Computerized texts are becoming viable substitutes for printed books in the publishing industry (Cox, 1993). Television news, especially services like CNN, are very threatening substitutes for weekly news magazines, including *Time* and *Newsweek* (Reilly, 1993). In Europe, so-called superstores are threatening smaller food shops (Rohwedder, 1993). In Britain, the number of large superstore outlets increased by 41 percent from 1992 to 1993, while the total number of food stores decreased by 20.6 percent. In Austria, the number of large stores increased by 50.2 percent during the same period, while the total number of food stores fell by 12 percent. In the United States, riverboat gambling, an emerging industry in many states, has begun to threaten the traditional dominance of gambling at horse race tracks (Helyar, 1991).

THE THREAT OF SUPPLIERS

Porter's (1980) fourth environmental threat is suppliers. Suppliers can threaten the performance of firms in an industry by increasing the price of their supplies or by reducing the quality of those supplies. Any above-normal profits that were being earned in an industry can be transferred to suppliers in this way. In the automobile industry, for example, there is substantial evidence that the above-normal performance of General Motors in the 1950s and 1960s was captured by labor unions, as suppliers of labor, in the form of high hourly wages (Scherer, 1980). Recent conflicts between Microsoft and IBM, together with the joint venture between IBM, Apple, and Motorola, can all be understood as an effort by IBM to reduce the power of Microsoft as a software supplier in the personal computer industry (Zachary, 1991).

Some supplier attributes that can lead to high levels of threat are listed in Table 3.3. First, a firm's suppliers are a greater threat if the *suppliers'* industry is dominated by a small number of firms (Porter, 1980). In this setting, a firm has few options but to purchase supplies from these firms. These few firms thus have enormous flexibility to charge high prices, to reduce quality, or in other ways to squeeze the profits of the firms they sell to. Much of Microsoft's power in the software industry reflects its dominance in the operating systems market, where MSDOS and Windows remain the de facto standard for most personal computers. For now, at least, if a company wants to sell personal computers, it is going to need to interact with Microsoft.

Conversely, when a firm has the option of purchasing from a large number of suppliers, suppliers have less power to threaten a firm's profits. For example, as the number of lawyers in the United States has increased over the years (up 40 percent since 1981, currently 770,000), lawyers and law firms have been forced to begin competing for work (Tully, 1992a). Some corporate clients have forced law firms to reduce their hourly fees and to handle repetitive simple legal tasks for low flat fees (Tully, 1992a). Also, as the percentage of a firm's workers in a labor union shrinks, the ability of that union to threaten the firm falls (Nulty, 1993).

TABLE 3.3
Indicators of the
Threat of Suppliers in
an Industry

1. Suppliers' industry is dominated by a small number of firms.
2. Suppliers sell unique or highly differentiated products.
3. Suppliers are *not* threatened by substitutes.
4. Suppliers threaten forward vertical integration.
5. Firms are *not* important customers for suppliers.

Second, suppliers are a greater threat when what they supply is unique or highly differentiated. There is only one Michael Jordan, as a basketball player, as a spokesperson, and as a celebrity (but *not* as a baseball player!). Jordan's unique status gives him enormous bargaining power as a supplier. Much of the economic profit that is earned by the Chicago Bulls is extracted by Michael Jordan and other Chicago basketball players in the form of salary and bonuses. In the same way, Intel's unique ability to develop, manufacture, and sell microprocessors gives it significant bargaining power as a supplier in the personal computer industry.

The uniqueness of suppliers can operate in almost any industry. For example, in the highly competitive world of television talk shows, some guests, as suppliers, can gain surprising fame for their unique characteristics. For example, Sherrol Miller has been a guest on three episodes of *Donahue*, two episodes of *Sally Jessy Raphael*, one episode of *Geraldo*, one episode of *Joan Rivers*, and one episode of *Attitudes*. Ms. Miller's claim to fame: She was the tenth wife of a gay, con-man bigamist (Jensen, 1993b).

Third, suppliers are a greater threat to firms in an industry when suppliers are *not* threatened by substitutes. When there are no effective substitutes, suppliers can take advantage of their position to extract economic profits from firms they supply to. When there are substitutes for supplies, supplier power is checked. In the metal can industry, for example, steel cans are threatened by aluminum cans as a substitute. In order to continue to sell to can manufacturers, steel companies have had to keep their prices below the price of aluminum. In this way, the potential power of the steel companies is checked by the existence of a substitute product, aluminum (Christensen et al., 1980).

Fourth, suppliers are a greater threat to firms when they can credibly threaten to vertically integrate forward into an industry. In this case, suppliers cease to be suppliers alone but become suppliers *and* rivals. The threat of forward vertical integration is partially a function of barriers to entry into an industry. When an industry has high barriers to entry, suppliers face significant costs of forward vertical integration, and thus forward integration is not as serious a threat to the profits of incumbent firms (vertical integration is discussed in detail in Chapter 10).

Finally, suppliers are a threat to firms when firms are *not* an important part of suppliers' business (Porter, 1980). Steel companies, for example, are not too concerned with losing the business of an artist or of a small construction company. But they are very concerned about losing the business of the major can manufacturers, major white-goods manufacturers (that is, manufacturers of refrigerators, washing machines, dryers, and so forth), and automobile companies. Steel companies, as suppliers, are likely to be very accommodating and willing to reduce prices and increase quality for can manufacturers, white-goods manufacturers, and auto companies. Smaller, "less important" customers, however, are likely to be subject to greater price increases, lower-quality service, and lower-quality products.

THE THREAT OF BUYERS

Porter's final environmental threat is buyers. Where sellers act to increase a firm's costs, buyers act to decrease a firm's revenues. The greater the power of buyers, the more that the profitability of firms in an industry can be threatened. Except for large customers, including the federal government and auto rental companies, GM's buyers do not individually represent a significant threat to GM's automotive profitability. The same can be said of individual IBM customers. Some of the important indicators of the extent to which buyers are a threat are listed in Table 3.4.

First, if a firm has only one buyer, or a small number of buyers, these buyers can be very threatening (Porter, 1980). Firms like McDonnell-Douglas and Westinghouse that sell a significant amount of their output to the Department of Defense recognize the influence of this buyer on their operations. Recent reductions in defense spending have forced defense companies to try even harder to reduce costs and increase quality to satisfy government demands. All these actions reduce the economic profits of these defense-oriented companies (Perry, 1993).

Travel agencies buy travel services from the major airlines. As the number of travel agencies has grown, agencies have become progressively more important customers. In the last several years, airlines have had to increase agency commissions to ensure that agencies will continue purchasing tickets on their airlines. These increased commissions reflect the increasingly powerful role of travel agents in the travel industry. Recent efforts by airlines to lower travel agency fees have met with mixed success—and charges of unfair collusion leveled at airlines by travel agencies (Dahl, 1993).

TABLE 3.4
Indicators of the
Threat of Buyers in
an Industry

1. Number of buyers is small.

2. Products sold to buyers are undifferentiated and standard.

3. Products sold to buyers are a significant percentage of a buyer's final costs.

4. Buyers are *not* earning significant economic profits.

5. Buyers threaten backward vertical integration.

Second, if the products or services that are being sold to buyers are standard and not differentiated, then the threat of buyers can be greater (Porter, 1980). For example, farmers sell a very standard product. It is difficult to differentiate products like wheat, corn, or tomatoes (although this can be done to some extent through the development of new strains of crops, the timing of harvests, the use of no pesticides, and so forth). In general, wholesale grocers and food brokers can always find alternative suppliers of basic food products. These numerous alternative suppliers increase the threat of buyers and force farmers to keep their prices and profits low. If any one farmer attempts to raise prices, wholesale grocers and food brokers simply purchase their supplies from some other farmer.

Third, buyers are likely to be more of a threat when the supplies they purchase are a significant portion of the costs of their final products (Porter, 1980). In this context, buyers are likely to be very concerned about the costs of their supplies and constantly on the lookout for cheaper alternatives, including the possibility of backward vertical integration. For example, the metal can is approximately 40 percent of the final cost of a can of Campbell's soup (Christensen et al., 1980). To reduce this cost and gain control over a significant portion of its total costs, Campbells Soup Company has vertically integrated backward and has become one of the largest can-manufacturing companies in the world. The U.S. Postal Service, as a buyer of air transportation services, has considered building its own fleet of jets to operate its overnight mail delivery service (McGinley and Karr, 1991). Such a move would be a threat to the airlines that have traditionally sold these services to the post office.

Fourth, buyers are likely to be more of a threat when they are *not* earning significant economic profits. In these circumstances, buyers are likely to be very sensitive to costs and insist on the lowest possible cost and the highest possible quality from suppliers. This effect can be exacerbated when the profits earned by suppliers are greater than the profits earned by buyers. In this setting, buyers have a strong incentive to vertically integrate backward to capture some of the economic profits being earned by suppliers.

Finally, buyers are more of a threat to firms in an industry when buyers have the ability to vertically integrate backward. In this case, buyers become both buyers and rivals and lock in a certain percentage of an industry's sales. The extent to which buyers represent a threat to vertically integrate, in turn, depends on the barriers to entry that are in place in an industry. If there are significant barriers to entry, buyers may not be able to engage in backward vertical integration, and their threat to firms is reduced.

It is interesting to note, for example, that Home Box Office, Inc., began producing its own movies (that is, it vertically integrated backward) when the level of competition in cable services increased. One explanation of this move is that Home Box Office could no longer gain high levels of performance in the cable business, so instead began operations in a higher-profit supply industry, the film production industry (*Wall Street Journal*, 1992).

THE FIVE FORCES AND AVERAGE INDUSTRY PERFORMANCE

Porter's (1980) five forces model has three important implications for managers seeking to choose and implement strategies. First, this model describes the most common sources of threat in industries. Second, it can be used to characterize the overall threat in industries. Finally, it can be used to anticipate the average level of performance in an industry.

In an important sense, the five forces model describes processes that tend to move an industry toward the economic condition of perfect competition. Although there are numerous definitions of *perfect competition* in the literature, most of them are consistent with an industry characterized by high levels of threat from new entry, rivalry, substitutes, suppliers, and buyers (Scherer, 1980). Firms in this kind of industry earn at most normal economic profits, or a level of performance just large enough to enable a firm to survive. Any above-normal profits that might exist in this type of industry are quickly competed away by potential entrants entering, rivals reducing their prices, substitutes becoming more attractive, suppliers raising their prices or lowering their quality, and buyers demanding lower prices or higher quality.

When a firm operates in an industry that is not perfectly competitive, it may be possible to earn above-normal economic profits. Industries where the threat of new entrants, rivals, substitutes, suppliers, and buyers is less pronounced will, on average, have higher levels of performance.

3.3 APPLICATIONS

To see how the five forces model can be used to analyze the threats in an industry, consider the performance potential of the two industries described in Table 3.5, the pharmaceutical industry and the textile industry.

**TABLE 3.5
Application of Five Forces Model to Analysis of Threats in the U.S. Pharmaceutical Industry and the U.S. Textile Industry**

Pharmaceutical Industry

The pharmaceutical industry consists of firms that develop, patent, and distribute drugs. There are not significant production economies in this industry, but there are important economies in research and development. Product differentiation exists as well, as firms often sell branded products. Firms compete in research and development. However, once a product is developed and patented, competition is significantly reduced. Recently, the increased availability of generic, nonbranded, drugs has threatened the profitability of some drug lines. Once an effective drug is developed, there are usually few, if any, alternatives to that drug. Drugs are manufactured from commodity chemicals usually available from numerous suppliers. Major customers include doctors and patients. Recently, increased costs have led the federal government and insurance companies to pressure drug companies to reduce their prices.

Textile Industry

The textile industry consists of firms that manufacture and distribute fabrics for use in clothing, furniture, carpeting, and so forth. Several firms have invested heavily in sophisticated manufacturing technology, and many lower-cost firms located in Asia have begun fabric production. Textiles are not branded products. Recently, tariffs on some imported textiles have been implemented. There are numerous firms in this industry; the largest have less than 10 percent market share. Traditional fabric materials (such as cotton and wool) have recently been threatened by the development of alternative chemical-based materials (such as nylon and rayon), although many textile companies have begun manufacturing with these new materials as well. Most raw materials are widely available, although some synthetic products may be periodically in short supply. There are numerous textile customers, but textile costs are usually a large percentage of the final product's total costs. Many users shop around the world for low prices on textiles.

ANALYZING THE PHARMACEUTICAL INDUSTRY

The pharmaceutical industry consists of organizations that develop, patent, and distribute drugs. Some of the major players in this industry include Johnson & Johnson (1994 sales of $15.7 billion), Bristol-Myers Squibb (1994 sales of $11.9 billion), and Merck (1994 sales of $14.9 billion).

Threat of Entry

The threat of new entry into the pharmaceutical industry is quite low. Although there are not significant production economies of scale in this industry, there are very important economies in the research and development process. Firms with large research and development labs are able to engage in basic research that can simultaneously benefit several lines of inquiry. For example, basic research on retroviruses in the 1970s enabled Burroughs Wellcome to develop AZT, an AIDS-fighting drug, in the 1980s (HIV, which causes AIDS, is a type of retrovirus) (O'Reilly, 1990).

There are important product differentiation advantages for incumbent firms in the pharmaceutical industry. Brand names such as Tylenol, Bayer, and Sudafed help differentiate what would otherwise be commodity products (Deveny, 1992). Incumbent firms also enjoy cost advantages over potential entrants. These cost advantages reflect the proprietary technology and research and development know-how that has developed in pharmaceutical firms over decades. Government policy also plays a role in deterring entry, since the approval of new drugs for sale in the United States can take up to twelve years. As suggested earlier, new entrants not only face the challenge of developing the R&D skills to compete in this industry, but also must wait several years before selling their products.

Threat of Rivalry

The threat of rivalry in this industry is low. Firms compete in research and development, and the first firm to develop a particular class of drugs gains important advantages. However, once this R&D competition is resolved, there are few other indicators of high rivalry. For example, there were only thirteen pharmaceutical firms in the 1994 Fortune 500 ("The Fortune 500," May 5, 1995). The median growth in sales of these firms from 1993 to 1994 was 9 percent; some firms (Ivax) grew as fast as 76 percent. All this suggests that the pharmaceutical industry is not a slow-growth industry.

Product differentiation in this industry is very significant, as different firms carve out different product niches based on their individual R&D skills. Also, new capacity is not added in large increments.

Indeed, because of government regulations that encourage the development and sale of so-called orphan drugs—drugs that cure rare diseases and thus have relatively small demand—new drugs can be introduced in the market with very low volumes of production (Starr, 1993).

Threat of Substitutes

The threat of substitutes in the pharmaceutical industry is moderate to low. Substitutes do exist for some key products. Acetaminophen (the key ingredient in Tylenol), for example, is a substitute for aspirin (the key ingredient in Bayer aspirin). However, in prescription drugs, fewer substitutes exist, especially during the time when a firm holds a patent on a drug. After the patent expires, so-called generic drugs may be substitutes for brand-name drugs.

Threat of Suppliers

The threat of suppliers in the pharmaceutical industry is low. There are large numbers of suppliers for the basic raw materials. These supplies, more often then not, are commodity chemicals. Because of the barriers to entry cited above, the threat of forward vertical integration by suppliers into this industry is small.

Threat of Buyers

Historically, the threat of buyers in the pharmaceutical industry has been very small. Recently, however, pressures by insurance companies, health maintenance organizations, and the federal government to reduce the price of drugs have become more intense (Tanouye, 1993; Birnbaum and Waldholz, 1993). Legislation that limits the time that pharmaceutical companies can retain patents on drugs has been introduced. Also, many states have passed legislation that requires pharmacists to offer consumers nonbranded generics in place of branded drugs. However, much of this threat has been reduced by the strong product differentiation that exists in the pharmaceutical industry. Thus, overall, the threat of buyers is moderate.

Performance

Given this five forces analysis of the pharmaceutical industry, it is not surprising that the level of threat in this industry, overall, is quite low and that the level of performance is quite high. In 1994, the thirteen largest firms in this industry had a median profit as a percentage of revenue of 16 percent, a median ROA of 13 percent, and a median ROE of 28 percent ("The Fortune 500," 1995). These results rank the pharmaceutical industry among the top performing industries in the United States ("The Fortune 500," 1995).

ANALYZING THE TEXTILE INDUSTRY

The textile industry consists of firms that manufacture and distribute fabrics for use in clothing, furniture, carpeting, and so forth. Major players in this industry include Shaw Industries (1994 sales of $2.7 billion), Burlington Industries (1994 sales of $2.1 billion), and Springs Industries (1994 sales of $2.0 billion).

Threat of Entry

Threat of entry into the textile industry is very high. While firms like Burlington and Springs have invested heavily in technology to try to increase economies of scale and gain cost advantages over new firms, entry by low-cost firms in Asia has continued (*Economist*, 1993). Although textiles come in innumerable colors, patterns, and textures, only a few possess any brand-name recognition, and thus little or no product differentiation exists in the industry. There are few, if any, cost advantages independent of scale, although a few firms have developed some expertise in sophisticated weaving machines. In fact, entry by foreign competitors has been so common in the textile industry that the industry has sought protection from foreign competition (Bowers, 1993). Tariff and trade policy are among the only effective barriers to entry currently operating in this industry.

Threat of Rivalry

The level of rivalry in the textile business is very high. There are numerous firms in this industry. Each of the largest has less than 10 percent of the market. Growth in industry sales has also been slow; the median sales growth in the largest eleven textile firms was equal to 5 percent from 1993 to 1994 ("The Fortune 500," 1995). As suggested earlier, relatively little product differentiation exists among different textiles.

Threat of Substitutes

Several chemical companies have developed substitutes for traditional textiles. These chemical substitutes include rayon, nylon, and spandex. However, over the years, several traditional textile companies have developed the skills needed to make these new textiles as well as more traditional textiles. Thus, overall, the threat of substitutes has been lessened, and it is now moderate to low.

Threat of Suppliers

Suppliers to traditional textile materials (such as cotton and wool) are numerous and do not pose a significant threat. However, suppliers of synthetic fabrics (such as Du Pont) can have a significant impact on the profitability of textile firms if these supplier firms have patent protections on the fabrics they make. For example, recent demand for Du Pont's spandex has been so great that Du Pont has had to allocate supplies to key customers (Roman, 1990). Overall, the power of suppliers in the textile industry is moderate to low.

Threat of Buyers

There are numerous buyers of textiles. However, most of these firms are relatively small, and the cost of textiles represents a large percentage of the costs of their final products (that is, clothing). Because of this, these small firms are very interested in reducing their textile costs as much as possible. Moreover, because textiles are not well differentiated, buyers of textiles can shop the entire worldwide market for the cheapest prices. Overall, the threat of buyers is moderate.

Performance

It might appear that the level of threat in the textile industry is mixed: The threat of entry and rivalry are very high, but the threat of suppliers, buyers, and substitutes is moderate to low. However, the level of new entry and rivalry are so high that they effectively outweigh the moderating influence of the threat of suppliers, buyers, and substitutes. Overall, the level of threat in this industry is quite high, and the expected level of performance is very low (and certainly lower than the level of performance of the pharmaceutical industry). In fact, textiles is one of the lowest-performing industries listed in the Fortune 500. The top eleven firms in this industry in 1994 had a median profits as a percent of revenues of 3 percent, a median ROA of 5 percent, and a median ROE of 13 percent.

3.4 SUMMARY

The structure-conduct-performance framework was originally designed to evaluate the competitiveness of industries to assist government regulators. This framework suggests that a firm's conduct and performance are largely determined by industry structure. Thus sources of above-normal economic performance must be sought in the structural characteristics of industries.

Strategy scholars have turned the original objectives of the S-C-P framework upside-down by attempting to describe industry conditions under which firms may be able to obtain competitive advantages and above-normal economic returns. In doing so, strategy scholars have developed powerful models of environmental threats and opportunities, two key components of SWOT analysis.

The most influential model of environmental threats has been developed by Michael Porter (1980). His five forces (threats) in an industry are (1) threat of entry, (2) threat of rivals, (3) threat of substitutes, (4) threat of suppliers, and (5) threat of buyers. The level of threat of new entrants is a function of barriers to entry, including (1) economies of scale, (2) product differentiation, (3) cost advantages independent of scale, (4) contrived deterrence, and (5) government regulation of entry. There are also numerous indicators of the other threats in an industry.

Although S-C-P-based models of environmental threat are important tools in strategic analyses, they must be linked with models of environmental opportunities and models of organizational strengths and weaknesses to choose strategies that maximize the performance of firms. These models are examined in the next two chapters.

REVIEW QUESTIONS

1. Your former college roommate calls you and asks to borrow $10,000 so that he can open a pizza restaurant in his hometown. In justifying this request, he argues that there must be significant demand for pizza and other fast food in his hometown because there are lots of such restaurants already there and three or four new ones are opening each month. He also argues that demand for convenience food will continue to increase, and he points to the large number of firms that now sell frozen dinners in grocery stores. Will you lend him the money? Why or why not?

2. According to the five forces model, one potential threat in an industry is buyers. Yet unless buyers are satisfied, they are likely to look for satisfaction elsewhere. Can the fact that buyers can be threats be reconciled with the need to satisfy buyers?

3. If several competing firms are aware of the five forces model of environmental threats and make their strategic choices solely on the basis of this model, what is the expected level of performance for these firms? Why?

4. Government policies can have a significant impact on the average profitability of firms in an industry. Government, however, is not included as a potential threat in the five forces model. Should the model be expanded to include government (to make a "six forces" model)? If yes, why? If no, why not?

5. Strategic management scholars turned the original social welfare-maximizing objectives of the S-C-P framework upside-down. What, if any, are the social welfare implications of this approach, and should managers be concerned about these implications (if they exist)?

CHAPTER 4

Evaluating Environmental Opportunities

In Chapter 3 the structure-conduct-performance model is used to describe a framework for analyzing a firm's environmental threats. Chapter 4 also applies the structure-conduct-performance model. However, instead of focusing on environmental threats, this chapter describes frameworks for analyzing environmental opportunities. When joined together, the analyses of threats and opportunities complete the environmental aspects of SWOT analysis. The internal components of SWOT analysis (analyzing organizational strengths and weaknesses) are discussed in Chapter 5.

Chapter 4 examines opportunities associated with each of the threats listed in Porter's (1980) five forces model, and then describes a set of generic industry structures developed by Porter (1980), along with the kinds of opportunities that are likely to exist in each. The chapter ends with a discussion of some of the limitations of the S-C-P framework as it is applied to the study of environmental threats and opportunities. An appendix to Chapter 4 describes an additional environmental analysis tool: strategic groups analysis.

4.1 ENVIRONMENTAL THREATS AS OPPORTUNITIES

Although Porter's (1980) five forces model certainly describes some important threats facing firms, it also describes some possible opportunities. In an important sense, each threat is also an opportunity—the opportunity to choose strategies that neutralize threats. Strategies can be chosen that may be able to neutralize each of the five forces, although firms may also face important constraints as they attempt to implement these strategies. Important threat-neutralizing opportunities associated with each of the five forces are listed in Table 4.1.

NEUTRALIZING THE THREAT OF ENTRY

The primary opportunity associated with the threat of entry is the erection of barriers to entry. Firms may erect any of the barriers to entry discussed in Chapter 3—economies of scale, product differentiation, cost advantages independent of scale, contrived deterrence, and government policy. The success of these barriers depends on substantially increasing the cost of entry of firms into an industry but doing it in such a way that the cost of erecting these barriers is less than the profits protected by deterring entry (Barney, 1986a).

Two outcomes of erecting barriers to deter entry are likely to make it difficult for firms to retain above-normal economic profits if they take advantage of this opportunity. First, the absolute cost of erecting barriers may be very high. For example, a firm that invests in new

---

**TABLE 4.1
Threats as
Opportunities**

Threats	Opportunities to Neutralize Threats
Entry	*Erect barriers to entry:* create and exploit economies of scale, differentiate products, reduce costs independent of scale, implement contrived deterrence, use government policy to deter entry
Rivalry	*Compete on dimensions besides price:* cost leadership, product differentiation, cooperation, diversification
Substitutes	*Improve product attractiveness compared to substitute:* cost leadership, product differentiation, cooperation, diversification
Suppliers	*Reduce supplier uniqueness:* backward vertical integration, development of second sources
Buyers	*Reduce buyer uniqueness:* forward vertical integration, product differentiation, seeking additional customers

technology to reduce its costs and deter entry has to absorb the large development costs associated with that new technology. Moreover, this firm has to absorb the substantial risk that the new technology will not perform adequately, despite the expense. A firm that increases its advertising to differentiate its product and deter entry absorbs substantial direct costs from this activity. Even a firm that lobbies for government protection from entry will often have to give up a great deal to obtain that protection. For example, many utility companies (until recently) were protected from new entry by government regulation. However, the cost of obtaining this barrier was government-imposed limits on profitability (Maremont, 1994). When the cost of erecting an entry barrier is greater than the profits protected by that barrier, exploiting this opportunity will not be a source of above-normal performance for a firm.

Second, erecting barriers to entry is likely to create free-rider problems. A barrier to entry deters entry into an *industry*. Thus a barrier implemented by any one firm has the effect of deterring entry for all incumbent firms. Indeed, an entry barrier can be thought of as a collective good for firms in an industry (Olson, 1965). A collective good exists when the benefits of an investment cannot be limited to just those firms who make an investment. The firms that invest to create barriers to entry will gain whatever advantages are associated with those barriers, and they will also have to absorb the cost of erecting them. The firms that do not invest in erecting the barriers will gain all the benefits resulting from barriers but will not have to absorb the cost of erecting them. Thus a firm that does not invest to erect a barrier is actually better off than a firm that does invest, assuming, of course, that at least one firm invests and that the investment actually deters entry. The likelihood of free riding implies that firms have a strong incentive to wait until one of their number invests to create a barrier. Of course, if all firms in an industry wait for another to invest in creating an entry barrier, that entry barrier will never be created.

The obvious solution to this free-rider problem is for a firm to invest in barriers that uniquely benefit it. Such investments, however, are no longer industry-level barriers to entry but rather are firm-level "barriers to imitation" (Rumelt, 1984). These firm-level phenomena are quite common and reflect the valuable, rare, and costly-to-imitate resources and capabilities controlled by a firm. These kinds of resources and capabilities are discussed in detail in Chapter 5.

Although numerous challenges are associated with erecting barriers to entry, there are nevertheless examples of industries where such barriers have been created. In breakfast cereals, for example, product differentiation—in the special form of brand proliferation—has continued for many decades. It is now the case that virtually every combination of grain, sugar, and artificial colors that could be invented has already been invented. Moreover, breakfast cereals take up a large percentage of the available shelf space in most grocery stores. Entry into this market is very difficult, because incumbent firms have already filled just about all possible entry points (Schenk, 1987). It appears that the soft-drink industry, with the introduction of caffeine-free colas, sugar-free colas, fruit-based soft drinks, and clear colas, is moving in a similar direction, making entry into this market very difficult.

NEUTRALIZING THE THREAT OF RIVALS

A second important threat to firm profitability is rivalry. As suggested in Chapter 3, rivalry is most intense when firms compete solely on the basis of price. This implies that the most important opportunity associated with reducing the threat of rivalry is shifting the basis of competition away from price and toward other dimensions.

There are, of course, numerous bases of competition besides price. A firm may compete on the basis of its lower costs (cost leadership) or on the basis of special features of its products (product differentiation). Also, firms may choose to cooperate with competing firms (tacit collusion or strategic alliances). Finally, firms can compete on the basis of the mix of businesses within which they operate (diversification). These rivalry-reducing opportunities are discussed in detail in Parts 2 and 3. It is sufficient to note here that each of these strategies represents an effort by firms to turn away from competition based primarily on price and to compete on other dimensions.

The fast-food business is an example of an industry that for years was able to avoid high rivalry and price competition through the implementation of product differentiation strategies. Different fast-food firms focused their marketing efforts on different segments of the fast-food industry—for example, McDonald's for children, Jack in the Box for adults, Taco Bell for Mexican food, Kentucky Fried Chicken for chicken. However, the use of product differentiation as a rivalry-reducing strategy has broken down in the fast-food industry and has been replaced by fierce price competition. Value meals, free soft-drink refills, sale items, and lower everyday food prices are all indicators of the higher level of rivalry in this industry (DeGeorge, 1994).

On the other hand, relationships between U.S. and Japanese automobile companies are now characterized by less rivalry than they were a few years ago. Through much of the 1980s, U.S. and Japanese automobile firms competed head-to-head on price, performance, quality, and service. However, since the mid-1980s, these former direct competitors have learned to cooperate with each other—through joint ventures and strategic alliances—in ways that have reduced rivalry and increased profits. Now, whenever Mazda sells a car in the U.S. market, Ford benefits; whenever Mitsubishi sells a car in the United States, Chrysler benefits; and so forth. Indeed, a recent effort to establish import quotas reducing the number of Japanese cars that could be imported into the United States did not receive required political support from *U.S.* automobile companies (Ingrassia and Nomani, 1993). The use of cooperative strategies has enabled U.S. automobile companies to reduce the threat of rivalry.

NEUTRALIZING THE THREAT OF SUBSTITUTES

The same strategies that can reduce the threat of rivalry can also be used to reduce the threat of substitutes. A firm threatened by substitutes can reduce the cost of its products (cost leadership), can improve the quality or performance of its products (product differentiation), can cooperate with substitute manufacturers in joint ventures and strategic alliances, or can diversify its operations and begin producing substitute products. This diversification opportunity is often a particularly attractive one, especially when the substitute poses a substantial threat.

As suggested in Chapter 3, the rising price of crude oil in the 1970s and 1980s made several energy substitutes—oil shale, tar sands, wind energy, solar energy—look economically attractive. Rather than simply focusing on crude oil, most international oil companies began diversifying their operations to include one or more of these substitute energy sources. As long as the price of crude oil was high, these energy substitutes were important components of the business of these firms. However, the oil bust of the 1980s prompted most of these firms to divest these diversified operations. Such divestitures were consistent with the observation that these activities were no longer close substitutes for crude oil (Hamilton, 1983).

NEUTRALIZING THE THREAT OF SUPPLIERS

Suppliers are a threat to firms in an industry when there are not many of them. The primary opportunity associated with neutralizing this threat is to reduce the uniqueness of suppliers. There are several ways to do so. The threat of suppliers can be reduced if a firm vertically integrates backward and becomes its own supplier (Porter, 1980). Backward vertical integration not only directly reduces the threat of suppliers but also increases the number of suppliers in an industry. The conditions under which backward vertical integration is a viable strategic option are discussed in detail in Chapter 10.

Another action that can reduce the power of suppliers is for a firm to license second sources for key supplies. Such second sources are particularly common in the electronics industry, where a potential supplier will develop a unique technology and a firm wishing to use the technology will need to redesign its entire product to do so. Before redesigning its product, a firm will often require the original supplier to license several other firms that can also be its suppliers. With these multiple, less threatening suppliers in place, a firm is more willing to redesign its product to take advantage of the new technology (Klein, Crawford, and Alchian, 1978).

Many Japanese firms have taken an alternative approach to managing the threat of suppliers. Suppliers can be a threat when a buying firm depends on a supplying firm more than the supplying firm depends on the buying firm. A way to create a balance in this dependence is for a supplier to purchase a substantial equity position in its critical customer and for a customer to purchase a substantial equity position in its critical supplier. This cross-equity holding gives both parties incentives to cooperate. Indeed, this ownership structure can be thought of as a form of strategic alliance (see Chapter 9). Such cross-equity ownership is very common in Japan. Indeed, it is not unusual for four or five of the largest equity holders in a Japanese firm to be major suppliers to that firm. These large equity holders will include not only suppliers of raw materials and parts but also suppliers of capital (that is, banks) and suppliers of labor (company labor unions). These cross-equity relations tend to be very stable and form the basis of very cooperative relations among Japanese firms and their suppliers. Recently, several U.S. firms have begun to implement similar cooperative approaches to managing supplier relations (Ouchi, 1984).

NEUTRALIZING THE THREAT OF BUYERS

Like suppliers, buyers become a threat in an industry to the extent that there are relatively few of them. As with suppliers, the major opportunity in reducing the threat of buyers is to make buyers less unique. Specific ways to realize this opportunity include forward vertical integration (to become one's own buyer), product differentiation (to make one's product unique), and seeking additional customers (to reduce dependence on a small set of buyers).

An example of forward vertical integration to neutralize the power of buyers can be found in the metal container industry. In this industry, traditional steel can manufacturers refused to invest in technologies for manufacturing aluminum cans. Without this technology in place, aluminum firms such as Alcoa would not have been able to exploit a significant market opportunity they believed existed for aluminum cans. In response to the unwillingness of metal can manufacturers to invest in aluminum can manufacturing technology, Alcoa began manufacturing its own aluminum cans. This forward vertical integration move neutralized the potential threat of Alcoa's customers and led Alcoa to become a major player in the worldwide metal container industry (Hamermesh and Rosenbloom, 1989).

4.2 OPPORTUNITIES IN INDUSTRY ENVIRONMENTS

Although neutralizing threats is important for firms seeking to maintain and protect their above-normal performance, the options are limited. In particular, this type of opportunity analysis focuses more on how firms can protect their profits and less on how firms can create above-normal economic profits in the first place.

In light of S-C-P logic, it seems reasonable to look at the structural characteristics of industries for environmental opportunities to create above-normal economic returns (Bain, 1956). Porter (1980) does this when he suggests that the kinds of opportunities firms can exploit vary, depending on the kinds of industries in which they are operating. Porter and others have examined opportunities for creating superior performance in five generic industries: (1) fragmented industries, (2) emerging industries, (3) mature industries, (4) declining industries, and (5) international industries. The kinds of opportunities associated with each type of industry are summarized in Table 4.2.

OPPORTUNITIES IN FRAGMENTED INDUSTRIES: CONSOLIDATION

Fragmented industries are industries in which a large number of small or medium-size firms operate and no small set of firms has dominant market share or creates dominant technologies. Most service industries, retailing, fabrics, and commercial printing—to name just a few—are fragmented industries.

Industries can be fragmented for a wide variety of reasons. For example, there may be few barriers to entry into a fragmented industry, thereby encouraging numerous small firms to enter. There may be few, if any, economies of scale, and even some important diseconomies of scale, thus encouraging firms to remain small. Also, there may be a need for close local control over enterprises in an industry—for example, local movie houses and local restaurants—to ensure quality and to minimize losses from theft (Scherer, 1980).

The major opportunity facing firms in fragmented industries is the implementation of strategies that begin to consolidate the industry into a smaller set of firms. Firms that are successful in this consolidation

TABLE 4.2
Industry Structure and Environmental Opportunities

Industry Structure	Opportunities
Fragmented industry	Consolidation
	■ Discovery of new economies of scale
	■ Altering ownership structure
Emerging industry	First-mover advantages
	■ Technological leadership
	■ Preemption of strategically valuable assets
	■ Creation of customer-switching costs
Mature industry	Product refinement
	Investment in service quality
	Process innovation
Declining industry	Leadership strategy
	Niche strategy
	Harvest strategy
	Divestment strategy
International industry	Multinational organization
	Global organization

effort can become industry leaders and obtain benefits from this kind of effort, if they exist (Scherer, 1980).

Consolidation can occur in several ways. For example, an incumbent firm may discover new economies of scale in an industry. In the highly fragmented funeral home industry, Service Corporation International (SCI) found that the development of a chain of funeral homes gave it advantages in acquiring key supplies (coffins) and in allocating scarce resources (morticians and hearses) (Jacob, 1992c). By acquiring numerous previously independent funeral homes, SCI was able to reduce its costs substantially and gain higher levels of economic performance.

In the highly fragmented paper and office supplies industry, Century Paper found that owning several geographically contiguous supply outlets enabled the organization to reduce warehousing costs, reduce corporate overhead, and apply professional management techniques to otherwise inefficiently managed operations. By building on its base in Houston, Texas, Century Paper was able to acquire supply operations in San Antonio, Dallas, New Orleans, and other locations in a way that helped make the company one of the largest suppliers in the United States (personal communication).

Incumbent firms may also adopt different ownership structures to help consolidate an industry (Porter, 1980). KOA uses franchise agreements with local operators to provide camping facilities to travelers. KOA provides these operators with professional training, technical skills, and access to brand name reputation. Local operators, in return, provide KOA with local managers who are intensely interested in the financial and operational success of their campgrounds. Similar franchise agreements have been instrumental in the consolidation of other fragmented industries, including fast foods (McDonald's), muffler repair (Midas), and motels (La Quinta, Holiday Inn, Howard Johnson's) (Porter, 1980).

The benefits of implementing a consolidation strategy in a fragmented industry turn on the advantages larger firms in such industries gain from their larger market share. As we will discuss in Chapter 6, firms with large market share can have important cost advantages over firms in the same industry with small market share. However, as is the case with all opportunities facing a firm, the benefits of exploiting this opportunity must be weighed against the cost of exploiting this opportunity. If the value of becoming an industry leader (by implementing consolidation) is less than the cost of becoming an industry leader, then exploiting this opportunity will lead to below-normal economic performance. However, as we will discuss in the case of mergers and acquisitions (Chapter 13), there is reason to believe that consolidation strategies in fragmented industries will sometimes (but not always) enable firms to earn above-normal economic profits.

OPPORTUNITIES IN EMERGING INDUSTRIES: FIRST-MOVER ADVANTAGES

Emerging industries are newly created, or newly re-created industries formed by technological innovations, changes in demand, the emergence of new customer needs, and so forth (Porter, 1980:215). Over the last thirty years, the world economy has been flooded by emerging industries, including the microprocessor industry, the personal computer industry, and the medical imaging industry, to name a few. Firms in emerging industries face a unique set of opportunities, the exploitation of which can be a source of superior performance for some time for some firms.

The opportunities that face firms in emerging industries fall into the general category of first-mover advantages. First-mover advantages are advantages that come to firms that make important strategic and technological decisions early in the development of an industry (Lieberman and Montgomery, 1988). In emerging industries, many of the rules of the game and standard operating procedures for competing and succeeding have yet to be established. First-moving firms can sometimes help establish the rules of the game and create an industry's structure in ways that are uniquely beneficial to them. According to Lieberman and Montgomery (1988), first-mover advantages may arise from three primary sources: (1) technological leadership, (2) preemption of strategically valuable assets, and (3) the creation of customer-switching costs.

Technological Leadership

Firms that make early investments in particular technologies in an industry may be able to obtain two advantages. First, these firms may obtain a low-cost position based on their greater cumulative volume of production with a particular technology. These cost advantages have had important competitive implications in such diverse industries as the manufacture of titanium dioxide by Du Pont (Ghemawat, 1984) and Procter & Gamble's competitive advantage in disposable diapers (Porter, 1981b). However, recent work suggests that learning-based cost advantages can give a firm a sustained advantage only when learning is proprietary (Spence, 1981) and that, in most industries, learning is rapidly diffused through competing firms (Mansfield, 1985; Lieberman, 1982, 1987). Thus although early investment in a technology may give a firm a head start, maintaining that head start is usually difficult. The relationship between a firm's cumulative volume of production and its costs is discussed in detail in Chapter 6.

Second, firms that make early investments in a technology may obtain patent protections that enhance their performance (Gilbert and Newbery, 1982). Xerox's patents on the xerography process (Bresnahan, 1985) and General Electric's patent on Thomas Edison's original light bulb design (Bright, 1949) were important for these firms' success when these two industries were emerging. However, although there are some exceptions (for example, the pharmaceutical industry and specialty chemicals), patents per se seem to provide relatively small profit opportunities for first-moving firms in most emerging industries. Mansfield, Schwartz, and Wagner (1981) found that imitators can duplicate first movers' patent-based advantages for about 65 percent of the first mover's costs. Thus there may be cost advantages in being an efficient "second mover," especially in industries where returns to investing early are very uncertain. Mansfield and his colleagues (1981) also found that 60 percent of all patents are imitated within four years of being granted—without legally violating patent rights obtained by first movers. As we will discuss in detail in Chapter 5, patents are rarely a source of sustained competitive advantage for firms, even in emerging industries.

Preemption of Strategically Valuable Assets

First movers that invest only in technology usually do not obtain sustained competitive advantages. However, first movers that move to tie up strategically valuable resources in an industry *before their full value is widely understood* can gain sustained competitive advantages. Firms that are able to acquire these resources have, in effect, erected formidable barriers to imitation in an industry (Rumelt, 1984; Barney, 1986a). Some strategically valuable assets that can be acquired in this way include (1) access to raw materials, (2) particularly favorable geographic locations, and (3) particularly valuable product market positions.

When an oil company like Royal Dutch Shell (because of its superior exploration skills) acquires leases with greater development potential than was expected by its competition, the company is gaining access to raw materials in a way that is likely to generate sustained competitive advantages (Main, 1955). When Wal-Mart opens stores in medium-size cities before the arrival of its competition, Wal-Mart is making it difficult for the competition to enter into this market (Ghemawat, 1986). And when breakfast cereal companies expand their product lines to include all possible combinations of wheat, oats, bran, corn, and sugar, they are using a first-mover advantage to deter entry (Schmalensee, 1978; Robinson and Fornell, 1985).

Of course, such first-moving actions must take place before their full value is known. If the full value of these resources is known before their acquisition, in general, their price will rise to equal their value in generating first-mover advantages (Barney, 1986a). If the cost of acquiring these resources exactly equals their value for a firm, then the firm will earn only normal economic profits.

Creating Customer-Switching Costs

Early decisions by firms in an emerging industry can also have the effect of increasing customer-switching costs. This is what occurs when a firm in an emerging industry sets a standard in technology, service, or production and customers accept this standard and adjust their policies and procedures accordingly (Klemperer, 1986; Wernerfelt, 1986, 1988). These adjustments tie customers to a particular firm and make it more difficult for them to begin purchasing from different firms.

As suggested in Chapter 7, switching costs can be thought of as a form of product differentiation. The ability to set the standard differentiates an early mover's product from other firms' products. Such switching costs are important factors in industries as diverse as operating systems for personal computers (Gross, 1995), prescription pharmaceuticals (Bond and Lean, 1977; Montgomery, 1975), and groceries (Ries and Trout, 1986; Davidson, 1976).

The Sony Corporation is an example of a firm that has attempted over the years to move early, set standards, and create switching costs (Schlender, 1992). Sometimes, these efforts have been successful (for example, the 8mm video format). At other times, Sony has moved early and attempted to set a standard but failed to make that standard available for other manufacturers. In the competition between Sony's Beta video format (the first mover) and Matsushita's VHS format (a relative latecomer in the video industry), VHS has become dominant.

Creating customer-switching costs can be so important that in some industries firms actually have an incentive to almost give their products away early in the industry's development, so that customers will commit to a particular technology and it will become the de facto standard. For example, Conner and Rumelt (1991) have shown that in some circumstances it is in the interest of software companies for customers to make and use unlicensed copies of their software. Conner and Rumelt argue that (1) these customers are unlikely to buy the software in question anyway, (2) customers who are likely to buy the software are concerned about the number of people who are using a particular software, and (3) so-called pirated software increases the number of people using a particular software, thereby increasing the chance that buying customers will choose to purchase the often-pirated software.

First-Mover Disadvantages

Of course, the opportunities for investing in new technologies, acquiring strategically valuable resources, and creating buyer switching costs must be balanced against the risks associated with first moving in emerging industries. These kinds of industries are characterized by a great deal of uncertainty. When first-moving firms are making critical strategic decisions, it may not be at all clear what the right decisions are (Wernerfelt and Karnani, 1987). In general, first moving is desirable when first movers can influence the way that uncertainty in an industry is resolved. However, when the evolution of technology, consumer demand, and production technology cannot be influenced by first-moving firms, whether or not first-moving efforts will be successful is indeterminate (Wernerfelt and Karnani, 1987).

There are numerous cases in which first movers did not gain significant advantages in their industry. Sony's experience with the Beta video format has already been described. Also, Microsoft's MS-DOS operating system was not a true first mover but came after the short-lived CPM system was developed and marketed.

Indeed, there are organizations that specialize in being second movers. In computer technology, IBM has usually been described as a second mover, waiting for other firms to develop new technology and then quickly moving to duplicate that technology (Carroll, 1993). Crown Cork & Seal has adopted an explicit second-mover strategy in food container research and development (Hamermesh and Rosenbloom, 1989). And Procter & Gamble has generally been seen as a very effective second mover in its industry (Porter, 1981b). Given that a second mover's product development costs can be just 65 percent of a first mover's product development costs, the advantages that accrue to a first mover must be very substantial to justify first moving as a strategy.

OPPORTUNITIES IN MATURE INDUSTRIES: PRODUCT REFINEMENT, SERVICE, AND PROCESS INNOVATION

Emerging industries are often formed by the creation of new products or technologies that radically alter the rules of the game in an industry (Schumpeter, 1934). However, over time, as these new ways of doing business become widely understood, as technologies diffuse through competitors, and as the rate of innovation in new products and technologies drops, an industry begins to enter the mature phase of its development. Common characteristics of mature industries include (1) slowing growth in total industry demand, (2) the development of experienced repeat customers, (3) a slowdown in increases in production capacity, (4) a slowdown in the introduction of new products or services, (5) an increase in the amount of international competition, and (6) an overall reduction in the profitability of firms in the industry (Porter, 1980:238–240).

One industry that may be mature is the fast-food business. Indeed, McDonald's is beginning to have difficulties finding locations for new restaurants that do not impinge on the sales of existing outlets. In the early 1990s, McDonald's first began to see declines in its operating profit, a possible indication that the rapid growth that characterized the fast-food industry since the early 1960s may have slowed (Gibson, 1991), to be replaced by higher levels of interfirm rivalry.

Opportunities for firms in mature industries typically shift from the development of new technologies and products in an emerging industry to a greater emphasis on refining a firm's current products, an emphasis on increasing the quality of service, and a focus on reducing manufacturing costs and increasing quality through process innovations.

Refining Current Products

In mature industries such as home detergents, motor oil, and refrigerators, there are likely to be few, if any, major technological breakthroughs. However, this does not mean that there is not innovation in these industries. Innovation in these industries focuses on extending and improving current products and technologies. In home detergents, innovation recently has focused on changes in packaging and on selling more highly concentrated detergents (Demetrakakes, 1994). In motor oil, recent packaging changes (from fiber foil cans to plastic containers) and new additives that keep oil cleaner longer are recent examples of this kind of innovation (Reda, 1995). And in refrigerators, the availability of crushed ice and water through the door and units that can be installed flush with kitchen cabinets are recent improvements (Quinn, 1995).

Emphasis on Service

When firms in an industry have only limited ability to invest in radical new technologies and products, efforts to differentiate products often turn toward the quality of customer service (Porter, 1980). A firm that is able to develop a reputation for high-quality customer service may be able to obtain superior performance even though the products it sells are not highly differentiated.

This emphasis on service has become very important in a wide variety of industries. For example, in the financial planning and insurance industries, Aetna is reemphasizing customer service. In one case, an elderly couple that had been burglarized was visited by the Aetna claims adjuster within one hour of the police, simply to reassure these customers that Aetna was aware of their needs (Jacob, 1992b). Bell Atlantic cut in half the time it needed to hook its customers up to AT&T, MCI, or Sprint by taking a process that had involved twenty-eight handoffs between functions and restructuring it so that it could be accomplished by a single team. Alcoa has reduced the time it takes to fill orders for aluminum sheets by 60 percent through its increased emphasis on service (Jacob, 1992b).

Process Innovation

Hayes and Wheelwright (1979) have studied the relationship between process innovation, product innovation, and the maturity of an industry. This work, summarized in Fig. 4.1, suggests that in the early stages of industry development, product innovation is very important, as firms struggle to create technological advantages, preempt valuable strategic resources, and create buyer-switching costs. However, over time, product innovation becomes less important, and process innovations designed to reduce manufacturing costs, increase product quality, and streamline management become more important. In mature industries, firms can often gain an advantage by manufacturing the same product as competitors, but at a lower cost. Alternatively, firms can

FIGURE 4.1
Process and Product Innovation and Industry Structure.
Source: Hayes and Wheelwright (1979).

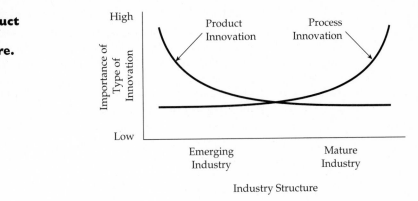

manufacture a product that is perceived to be of higher quality, and do so at a competitive cost. Process innovations facilitate both the reduction of costs and the increase in quality.

Some recent research on manufacturing in the automobile industry points to the importance of process innovations. In a study of over seventy auto assembly plants, Krafcik and MacDuffie (1989) measured both the quality of the assembled cars and the cost of these cars. The cars assembled in these plants were midsize family sedans—a relatively mature segment of a relatively mature industry, the automobile business. These researchers found six plants in their sample that simultaneously had very high quality and very low costs. These six plants were designated "world-class manufacturers." The management of these plants had several things in common; among them was a constant, unending focus on improving the manufacturing process as well as the process for managing the entire plant. This emphasis on process innovation enabled these plants to gain competitive advantages in an otherwise very mature segment of the industry.

One firm that has been successful in creating profits through its emphasis on process innovation is Johnson Controls' automobile battery division. The price of automobile batteries has not increased in over ten years. Indeed, sales of Johnson's batteries through Sears and Wal-Mart dropped significantly in the early 1990s. Yet during this same time, profits from the battery division increased by 12 percent (Tetzeli, 1993). Johnson's CEO at the time, Jim Keyes, attributed this continued profitability to a 40 percent reduction in the time required to transform raw materials into automobile batteries. Such cycle-time reductions are characteristic of intense process innovation (Hayes and Wheelwright, 1979).

OPPORTUNITIES IN DECLINING INDUSTRIES: LEADERSHIP, NICHE, HARVEST, AND DIVESTMENT STRATEGIES

A declining industry is an industry that has experienced an absolute decline in unit sales over a sustained period of time (Porter, 1980:254; Harrigan, 1980). One of the most obvious examples of a declining industry is the U.S. defense business. Since the end of the cold war, defense spending has dropped rapidly, from a high of $127 billion in 1985 to a low of $54 billion in 1993 (all in constant 1993 dollars) (Perry, 1993). The total number of civilians employed in the defense industry is expected to drop by over 800,000 through the mid-1990s (Smith, 1993). In addition, U.S. military forces are expected to drop by an additional 400,000 individuals during this time period. At the beginning of the 1990s, these changes represented significant threats to some historically successful firms in the defense industry, including McDonnell-Douglas (45 percent of 1991 sales in defense contracts), General Dynamics (85 percent of 1991 sales in defense contracts), Raytheon (43 percent of 1991 sales in defense contracts), and Northrop (54 percent of 1991 sales in defense contracts) (Smith, 1993).

Obviously, firms in a declining industry face more threats than opportunities. Rivalry in a declining industry is likely to be very high, as is the threat of buyers, suppliers, and substitutes. However, even though threats are significant, there are opportunities that firms must recognize and, where appropriate, exploit. The major strategic options that firms in this kind of industry face are (1) leadership, (2) niche, (3) harvest, and (4) divestment (Porter, 1980:267; Harrigan, 1980).

Leadership Strategy

An industry in decline is often characterized by overcapacity in manufacturing, distribution, and so forth. Reduced demand often means that firms in this kind of industry will have to endure a significant shakeout period as this overcapacity is brought off-line and capacity is brought more into line with demand. But after this shakeout has occurred, it may be the case that a smaller number of lean and focused firms may enjoy a relatively benign environment with few threats and several opportunities. If the industry structure that is likely to exist after a shakeout is quite attractive, firms in an industry before the shakeout may have an incentive to weather the storm of decline, to survive until the situation improves to the point that they can begin to earn higher profits.

If a firm has decided to weather the storm of decline in hopes of better environmental conditions in the future, it should consider various steps to increase its chances of survival. Most important of these is that a firm must establish itself as a leader in the pre-shakeout industry, most typically by becoming the share leader in that industry (Porter,

1980). The purpose of becoming a leader is *not* to facilitate tacit collusion (see Chapter 8) or to, necessarily, obtain lower costs from economies of scale (see Chapter 6). Rather, in a declining industry, the leader's objective should be to try to facilitate the exit of firms that are not likely to survive a shakeout, thereby obtaining a more favorable competitive environment as quickly as possible.

Leaders in declining industries can facilitate exit in a variety of ways, including (1) purchasing and then deemphasizing competitors' product lines, (2) purchasing and retiring competitors' manufacturing capacity, (3) manufacturing spare parts for competitors' product lines, and (4) sending unambiguous signals of their intention to stay in an industry and remain a dominant firm (Porter, 1980). For example, overcapacity problems in the European petrochemical industry were partially resolved when ICI traded its polyethylene plants to British Petroleum for BP's polyvinylchloride (PVC) plants (Aguilar, Bower, and Gomes-Casseres, 1985). In this case, both firms were able to take some excess capacity in specific markets (polyethylene and PVC) off-line while sending clear signals of their intention to remain in these markets.

In the defense industry, two firms seem to exemplify this leadership strategy: Loral and Martin Marietta. Since 1987, Loral has spent over \$1.8 billion buying several high-technology military electronics businesses, including Ford Aerospace and LTV's missile division. Clearly, management at Loral is committed to the defense industry. In the early 1990s, Martin Marietta acquired General Electric's aerospace businesses for \$1 billion in preferred stock (Perry, 1993). In 1994, Martin Marietta consolidated its position even more substantially with its \$10 billion merger with Lockheed to form Lockheed Marietta (Pare, 1994). As is the case at Loral, top management at Lockheed Marietta seems to be convinced that the defense business will remain a viable one—after an industry shakeout—and wants to be well positioned to exploit any possible opportunities there.

Niche Strategy

A firm in a declining industry following a leadership strategy attempts to facilitate exit by other firms, but a firm following a niche strategy in a declining industry reduces its scope of operations and focuses on narrow segments of the declining industry. If only a few firms choose this niche, then these firms may have a favorable competitive setting even though the industry as a whole is facing shrinking demand.

Two firms that have used this niche approach in a declining market are GTE Sylvania and General Electric in the vacuum tube industry (Harrigan, 1980). The invention of the transistor and then of the semiconductor just about destroyed demand for vacuum tubes in new products. GTE Sylvania and General Electric rapidly recognized that new-product sales in vacuum tubes were drying up. In response, these firms began specializing in supplying *replacement* vacuum tubes to the consumer and military markets. To earn high profits, these firms had to refocus their sales efforts and scale down their sales and manufacturing staffs. Over time, as fewer and fewer firms manufactured vacuum tubes, GTE Sylvania and General Electric were able to charge very high prices for their replacement parts.

In the defense industry, several small firms seem to be implementing niche strategies. Signal Technology, a supplier of microwave and radio frequency components to Raytheon, Loral, and Hughes, grew from $40 million in sales in 1990 to $90 million in 1993 by acquiring unwanted businesses and divisions from other businesses. However, in most of these acquisitions, Signal Technology remained focused on its relatively narrow market segment—microwave and radio frequency components (Perry, 1993). In the future, it seems likely that Signal Technology will be a major player in this narrow segment of the defense industry.

Harvest Strategy

Leadership and niche strategies, though differing along several dimensions, have one attribute in common: Firms that implement these strategies intend to remain in the industry despite its decline. Firms pursuing a harvest strategy in a declining industry do not expect to remain in the industry over the long term. Instead, they engage in a long, systematic, phased withdrawal, extracting as much value as possible during the withdrawal period (Porter, 1980).

The extraction of value during the implementation of a harvest strategy presumes that there is some value to harvest. Thus firms that implement this strategy must normally have enjoyed at least normal economic profits at some time in their history, before the industry began declining. Firms can implement a harvest strategy by reducing the range of products they sell, reducing their distribution network, eliminating less profitable customers, reducing product quality, reducing service quality, deferring maintenance and equipment repair, and so forth. In the end, after a period of harvesting in a declining industry, firms can either sell their operations in an industry (to an industry leader) or simply cease operations.

In principle the harvest opportunity sounds simple enough, but in practice it presents some significant management challenges. The movement toward a harvest strategy often means that some of the characteristics of a business that have long been a source of pride to managers may have to be abandoned. Thus where prior to harvest a firm may have specialized in high-quality service, quality products, and excellent customer value, during harvest the quality of service may fall, product quality may deteriorate, and prices may rise. These changes may be difficult for managers to accept, and high turnover in a harvesting firm may be the result. It is also difficult to hire first-rate managers into a harvesting business, for such individuals are likely to seek greater opportunities elsewhere (Harrigan, 1980).

For these reasons, few firms explicitly announce a harvest strategy. However, examples can be found. General Electric and Westinghouse both seem to be following a harvest strategy in the declining electric turbine business (Klebnikov, 1991). Also, USX and Bethlehem Steel seem to be following this strategy in certain segments of the steel market (Rosenbloom and Christensen, 1990). In the declining defense industry, GM's Hughes Electronics may be engaging in a harvest strategy. Hughes recently consolidated its four separate missile plants into a single facility. This consolidation enabled Hughes to reduce its R&D expenditures and manufacturing costs, although it also limited the range of missile products the company was manufacturing (Perry, 1993).

Divestment Strategy

The final opportunity facing firms in a declining industry is divestment. Like a harvest strategy, the objective of a divestment strategy is to extract a firm from a declining industry. However, unlike harvest, divestment occurs quickly, often soon after a pattern of decline is established. Firms without established competitive advantages may find divestment a superior option to harvest, since they have few competitive advantages they can exploit through harvesting (Porter, 1980).

In the 1980s, General Electric used this rapid divestment approach to virtually abandon the consumer electronics business. Total demand in this business was more or less stable during the 1980s, but competition (mainly from Asian manufacturers) increased substantially. Rather than remain in this business, GE sold most of its consumer electronics operations and used the capital to enter into the medical imaging industry, where the organization has found an environment more conducive to superior performance (Finn, 1987).

In the defense business, divestment is the stated strategy of General Dynamics, at least in some of its business segments. General Dynamics managers recognized early that the shrinking defense industry could not support all the incumbent firms. When General Dynamics concluded that it could not remain a leader in some of its businesses, it decided to divest those, to concentrate on a few remaining businesses (Perry, 1993). Since 1991, General Dynamics has sold businesses worth over $2.83 billion, including its missile systems business, its Cessna aircraft division, and its tactical aircraft division (maker of the very successful F-16 aircraft and partner in the development of the next generation of fighter aircraft, the F-22). These divestitures have left

General Dynamics in just three businesses: armored tanks, nuclear submarines, and space launch vehicles (Smith, 1993; Perry, 1993). During
this time, the market price of General Dynamics stock has gone from
$25 per share to $110 per share.

Of course, not all divestments are caused by industry decline.
Sometimes firms divest certain operations to focus their efforts on
remaining operations, sometimes they divest to raise capital, and
sometimes they divest to simplify operations. These types of divestment reflect a firm's diversification strategy and are explored in detail
in Chapter 11.

OPPORTUNITIES IN INTERNATIONAL INDUSTRIES: MULTINATIONAL AND GLOBAL STRATEGIES

It is an assumption of business in the late twentieth century that competition is becoming more international in scope. Even industries that
appear likely to be national or regional in focus (Broadway plays, for
example, are by definition produced only in New York City) have, over
the last several years, become more international in character (many
Broadway hits are transfers from the West End in London, and regional
traveling companies exhibit these plays throughout the world).
International competition has some very obvious effects on the level
and kinds of threats in an industry. International competition tends to
increase rivalry, the threat of new entry, and the threat of substitutes
(Porter, 1980). However, the internationalization of a business also creates opportunities for firms. The key decision that firms in international businesses must make is whether to compete with a multinational strategy or with a global strategy. The elements that combine to
determine this choice are described in detail in Chapter 14. Some of the
basic opportunities associated with these options are discussed here.

Multinational Strategies

Firms pursuing a multinational strategy simultaneously compete in
numerous national or regional markets. However, these national or
regional operations are independent of each other and free to choose
their own strategies in response to national or regional competitive
pressures (Bartlett and Ghoshal, 1989). In Chapter 14, two types of
multinational strategies are described: a decentralized federation strategy and a coordinated federation strategy (Bartlett and Ghoshal, 1993).
Some well-known multinational firms are Nestlé, CIBA-Geigy, and
General Motors. Each of these companies operates in several countries,
but divisions in those countries are highly autonomous.

Pursuing a multinational strategy has at least two advantages.
First, decentralization enables firms to respond rapidly to changing

conditions in a country or region. If threats or opportunities appear in one part of the world but not in others, a multinational firm can quickly move to neutralize threats or exploit opportunities in those geographic regions where action is needed (Bartlett and Ghoshal, 1989). For example, by following a multinational strategy, McDonald's enables many of its European franchises to sell beer and wine alongside Big Macs and fries (Gatling, 1993).

Second, although there are relatively few operational interactions between divisions and headquarters in a multinational company, impressive organizational resources can be quickly marshaled should they be required to exploit an opportunity or neutralize a threat in a particular country or region. McDonald's, for example, has been able to use all of its technological and management skills to open franchises in Moscow and other eastern European cities (Blackman, 1990).

Global Strategies

Whereas firms pursuing a multinational strategy operate in countries or regions in an independent manner, those pursuing global strategies seek to optimize production, distribution, and other business functions throughout the world in addressing all the markets in which they operate (Bartlett and Ghoshal, 1989). If manufacturing costs are very low and quality is very high in plants located in Singapore, global organizations will locate manufacturing facilities there. If particular research and development skills and technology are widely available in Great Britain, global organizations will locate research and development operations there. If capital is less costly in New York, global organizations will locate financial functions there. In this manner, the cost and quality of each organizational function can be optimized. Two types of global strategies are also described in Chapter 14: centralized hub strategies and transnational strategies (Bartlett and Ghoshal, 1989, 1993). Examples of global organizations include IBM, Texas Instruments, General Electric, and Westinghouse. Global strategies have the obvious advantage of locating operations in geographic positions that reduce costs and maximize quality in all business functions. A firm like the Danish company that manufactures and sells the Lego brand of children's toys can use its global approach to manufacture its toys at the lowest possible cost (Kestin, 1986).

However, global strategies also have some costs and risks associated with them. First, since the delivery of products or services in a global organization requires inputs from numerous operations all over the world, a global strategy puts a great deal of emphasis on coordination (Porter, 1986). Coordination can be difficult across divisions within a single country; it can be even more difficult across divisions in different countries or regions. Differences in language, culture, legal systems, and traditional business practices may complicate coordination efforts (Bartlett and Ghoshal, 1989). To help control this problem, Lego does not allow any of its national subsidiaries to develop or market their own products, thus making sales, inventory, and accounting practices across the subsidiaries very similar to one another.

Second, locating interdependent units in geographically disparate areas can create significant transportation costs (Bartlett and Ghoshal, 1989). The very low cost of manufacturing transmissions in Mexico may be effectively increased by the need to transport those transmissions to Japan to be installed in automobiles. This is less of a problem for a firm like Lego, since the products it ships (small plastic toys) are relatively light and have very high margins (Kestin, 1986).

Finally, global strategies may limit a firm's ability to respond to local needs, opportunities, and threats. Firms pursuing global strategies are well designed to respond to global markets and less well designed to respond to a series of local markets. If the structure of the markets in which a firm operates does not significantly vary by country or region, a global strategy may be a particularly attractive opportunity (Porter, 1986). Again, this approach fits Lego's needs, since stacking plastic blocks seems to be a universal form of play. Moreover, rather than modifying products to meet local needs (by, for example, painting Asian features on figurines sold in Asia), Lego has chosen a more generic product (all figurines, sold anywhere in the world, have the same yellow undifferentiated smiling face) (Kestin, 1986).

4.3   LIMITATIONS OF S-C-P-BASED MODELS OF ENVIRONMENTAL THREATS AND OPPORTUNITIES

There is little doubt that S-C-P models of environmental threats and opportunities are important strategic tools and vital for firms looking to choose strategies (Porter, 1981a). However, like all models, they have some important limitations, and managers and scholars alike must be aware of these limitations as they attempt to apply S-C-P models. Three particularly important limitations are (1) assumptions about firm profits and entry, (2) the role of inefficient firm strategies, and (3) the limited concept of firm heterogeneity.

ASSUMPTIONS ABOUT FIRM PROFITS AND ENTRY

Traditional S-C-P logic suggests that entry into an industry is motivated by incumbent firms earning above-normal economic profits— that above-normal profits are a signal to potential entrants that opportunities in an industry exist. Empirically, S-C-P logic suggests that the rate of entry into an industry will be positively correlated with the level of firm performance in that industry.

There is, however, an alternative point of view. According to this point of view, a high level of performance by incumbent firms sends exactly the opposite signal to potential entrants: Instead of encouraging entry, high performance by incumbents discourages entry because it suggests that incumbent firms are very effective and efficient (Demsetz, 1973). Incumbent firms with important competitive advantages are able to meet customer needs very effectively and at very low cost and thus generate above-normal performance. Potential entrants decide against entering because of the likelihood that they will not be able to duplicate the effectiveness and efficiency of incumbent firms. Empirically, this alternative view suggests that the rate of entry into an industry will be negatively correlated with the level of firm performance in that industry.

Not surprisingly, there is mixed empirical evidence concerning these alternative views of profits and entry. It seems that when incumbent firms earn above-normal profits based on monopolistic/oligopolistic price and output strategies (see Chapter 8), high levels of performance in an industry generally encourage entry. The reason for this outcome is that incumbent firms in this context are usually not very efficient or effective in meeting customer needs (Scherer, 1980) and are easy prey for efficient and effective new entrants. But if incumbent firms are earning above-normal performance because of their exceptional ability to meet customer needs in a low-cost and efficient manner, high levels of firm performance in an industry actually discourage entry (Demsetz, 1973).

These conflicting points of view concerning profits and entry have a wide variety of implications. At a societal level, antitrust regulation has traditionally been based on the S-C-P assumption that high levels of firm performance in an industry are evidence of collusion, contrived deterrence, monopoly, or other anticompetitive actions (Porter, 1981a). The alternative view of profits and entry is only now beginning to have an influence on government policy. In fact, sometimes it is difficult to tell whether high profits encourage or deter entry. IBM, for example, enjoyed very large market share and very high profits in the mainframe computer industry for at least thirty years. Did IBM's dominant position in this industry reflect monopolistic, anticompetitive behavior, or did it reflect IBM's unusual skills and abilities in designing, selling, and servicing mainframe computers?

At the firm level, assumptions about whether high incumbent profits encourage or deter entry go a long way in determining whether a firm should choose to enter an industry. If incumbent firms are earning high profits because of their oligopoly/monopoly actions, then entry may be an attractive alternative. But if the profits of incumbent firms are high because of competitive advantages that those firms possess, entry is likely to be more costly and thus a less desirable option.

THE ROLE OF INEFFICIENT FIRM STRATEGIES

Most of the strategic options that emerge from an S-C-P analysis of environmental threats and opportunities have the effect of improving a firm's ability to meet customer needs or reduce a firm's costs. These strategies focus on improving a firm's efficiency and effectiveness in order to gain competitive advantages and above-normal economic profits. These strategies suggest that the best way to gain and maintain advantages is to be more effective and efficient than current or potential competitors.

However, certain S-C-P strategies (such as contrived deterrence strategies) seem to suggest that firm performance can be maximized by *decreasing* a firm's efficiency and effectiveness (Tirole, 1988). This occurs when an S-C-P model suggests that a firm invest in more productive capacity than is required for current and anticipated operations, invest in more product differentiation than is required to meet customer needs, or gain access to more low-cost factors of production than are required for efficient operations.

In general, implementing strategies that *decrease* firm efficiency in order to improve a firm's performance seems likely to be very risky and applicable only in very unusual circumstances. For example, in Dixit's (1982) model, presented in Chapter 3, there was only one incumbent firm and one potential entrant. More typically, firms that reduce their efficiency encourage new entry, rather than discourage it. As suggested earlier, inefficient and ineffective incumbent firms are easy prey for efficient and effective rivals and new entrants. In general, the most reasonable strategic advice must be for incumbent firms to learn how to meet customer needs more efficiently and effectively. This choice not only will give firms the opportunity for competitive advantages within an industry but will usually have the effect of deterring new entry as well (Williamson, 1991).

THE LIMITED CONCEPT OF FIRM HETEROGENEITY

S-C-P models of environmental threats and opportunities have only a weakly developed sense of the heterogeneity of firms in an industry. Firms in an industry can differ in an S-C-P framework, but differences are restricted to variance in the threats and opportunities a firm faces.

This variance, in turn, reflects differences in economies of scale, in product differentiation, in production costs, and so forth. This level of firm heterogeneity in the S-C-P approach is significantly less than the level of firm heterogeneity assumed to exist in traditional approaches to strategic management (Barney, 1991; Conner, 1991).

This lack of firm heterogeneity in S-C-P models of environmental threats and opportunities is not surprising and stems directly from the unit of analysis in these models: the industry. The S-C-P framework is designed to study industry structure and leads to a powerful model of environmental threats and opportunities. It was never intended to be a general model of strategic choice (Porter, 1981a). A general model of strategic choice must include both environmental analyses (of threats and opportunities) and organizational analyses (of strengths and weaknesses) (Barney, 1991). Alternative theoretical frameworks that focus on unique firm characteristics must be used to complete the internal analyses required by SWOT. These frameworks are described in the next chapter.

4.4   SUMMARY

Two ways of thinking about environmental opportunities exist. First, opportunities associated with neutralizing the five threats to firm performance discussed in Chapter 3 are outlined. Though important for firms protecting normal or above-normal performance, these opportunities focus more on protecting profits than on creating profits. A second approach to the study of environmental opportunities is based on the analysis of five generic industries described by Porter and others: (1) fragmented industries, (2) emerging industries, (3) mature industries, (4) declining industries, and (5) international industries. The most common types of opportunity in each of these industries have been identified.

Although S-C-P-based models of environmental threats and opportunities are very powerful, they are subject to some limitations. Some of the most important of these are (1) the impact of incumbent firms' profits on entry by new firms, (2) the impact of strategies that reduce incumbent firms' efficiency and effectiveness on new entry, and (3) an underdeveloped sense of firm heterogeneity. These limitations suggest that the S-C-P framework is not a general model of strategy formulation but must be coupled with additional theoretical frameworks that enable scholars and managers to analyze the strengths and weaknesses of individual firms.

REVIEW QUESTIONS

1. Under what conditions, if any, can a firm earn above-normal profits from erecting industry barriers to entry? Explain your answer.

2. Can neutralizing some environmental threats increase other environmental threats? For example, can neutralizing the threat of substitutes (through product differentiation) increase the power of suppliers? Explain your answer.

3. How should firms choose from among the four opportunities they face in declining industries?

4. Given the ideas developed in Chapter 4, is it appropriate to say that there are really no unattractive industries? If yes, what implications does this statement have for the ideas presented in Chapter 3? If no, describe an industry that has no opportunities.

5. Is the evolution of industry structure from an emerging industry to a mature industry to a declining industry inevitable? Why or why not?

6. Under what conditions, if any, would it make sense for firms to implement strategies that reduce their competitive efficiency?

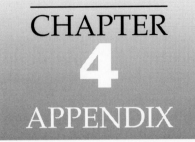

CHAPTER
4
APPENDIX

Strategic Groups Analysis of Environmental Threats and Opportunities

The analysis of environmental threats and opportunities outlined in Chapters 3 and 4 assumes that the appropriate unit of analysis for this type of strategic work is the industry. On the threat side, entry into an industry, rivalry among firms within an industry, substitutes for products in an industry, the power of suppliers to firms in an industry, and the power of an industry's buyers are the most relevant points of analysis. On the opportunity side, different opportunities are assumed to depend on the structure of the industry within which a firm operates. This industry focus is not too surprising, since the theoretical underpinnings of the models presented in these two chapters—the structure-conduct-performance paradigm—also takes the industry as its unit of analysis.

Unfortunately, adopting the industry as the unit of analysis in evaluating a firm's threats and opportunities is not without limitations. First, the definition of what constitutes an industry is often ambiguous. The traditional definition of an industry focuses on cross elasticities of demand among a set of firms. When increases in the price of one firm's products or services lead to an increase in demand for another firm's products or services, then these two firms have a high cross elasticity of demand and can be thought of as being in the same industry.

However, in practice, studies of such cross elasticities of demand between firms are rarely done. And even when they are done, how high cross elasticities need to be to constitute an industry is somewhat of a judgment call. More often than not, firms are classified into the same industry when they seem, to some outside observers, to produce similar goods or services. Rigorous definitions of how similar products or services need to be, the dimensions along which products or services are similar, and other important issues are rarely examined. Indeed, most decisions about what industry a firm is in depend more on a firm's standard industrial classification (SIC) code and less on the economic situation facing the firm.

Second, the adoption of the industry as the unit of analysis implicitly assumes that firms within an industry are essentially identical in terms of the threats and opportunities they face (Porter, 1981a). But even when there is high cross elasticity in demand between firms, it does not follow that different firms, or different groups of firms, will face exactly the same threats and opportunities. For example, there is probably high cross elasticity of demand between Mercedes and Lexus. Both are in the luxury end of the automobile market, and changes in the price of one of these types of cars are likely to affect demand for the other. Yet the threats these two firms face are different. For example, Lexus, a division of Toyota Motor Corporation, needs to deal with the threat of import quotas being applied to Japanese automobile firms—a threat that has yet to emerge for Mercedes and other German automotive companies.

Given these limitations of using the industry as a unit of analysis, several scholars have suggested that a level of analysis between the individual firm and the industry would be appropriate. This level of analysis is the strategic group.

THE CONCEPT OF STRATEGIC GROUPS

The first authors to propose this new level of analysis in the evaluation of a firm's threats and opportunities were Hunt (1972) and Caves and Porter (1977). These authors defined a *strategic group* as a set of firms that face similar threats and opportunities that are different from the threats and opportunities facing other firms in an industry (see McGee and Thomas, 1986; Barney and Hoskisson, 1990). Notice that this definition requires that a set of firms face threats and opportunities that are similar to each other yet simultaneously different from the threats and opportunities faced by other firms in an industry. If only the first criteria holds (similar threats and opportunities) without the second, the strategic group is logically equivalent to an industry, and traditional

S-C-P based analyses of threats and opportunities are appropriate (McGee & Thomas, 1986).

This concept of strategic groups allows both for ambiguity about the boundaries of an industry and for variance in the structure of threats and opportunities that face firms in an industry. Boundary ambiguity is made less relevant by focusing on the set of firms that face very similar threats and opportunities relative to a particular firm. Defining industry boundaries becomes less important, in this context, than defining group boundaries. If more than one group exists in an industry, then variance in the structure of threats and opportunities can be included in an industry analysis.

Many of the concepts that are applicable in the analysis of industry structure have analogies in the analysis of strategic groups. Most important of these is *mobility barriers,* a concept that is directly analogous to entry barriers at the industry level. Whereas entry barriers restrict entry into an industry, mobility barriers restrict movement of firms between strategic groups in an industry. Industry characteristics that limit entry into an industry can also limit mobility between strategic groups. Thus, for example, economies of scale, product differentiation, cost advantages independent of scale, government policy, and even contrived deterrence can all be mobility barriers in an industry. Firms seeking to reduce mobility by erecting mobility barriers face the same cost/benefit kinds of constraints (including the free-rider problems discussed in Section 4.1) as firms seeking to erect barriers to entry (Caves and Porter, 1977).

APPLYING THE CONCEPT

The concept of strategic groups has been applied in order to understand the structure of threat and opportunity in a wide variety of industries. One recent application by Cool and Dierickx (1993) focused on the evolution of competition within and between strategic groups in the pharmaceutical industry. The first task in this type of analysis is to isolate several key mobility barriers that might be operating in an industry. Recall that these mobility barriers are intra-industry versions of any of the barriers to entry cited earlier. Cool and Dierickx (1993), building on the work of Cool and Schendel (1987), described three major mobility barriers operating in the pharmaceutical industry: research and development skills, marketing skills, and product-positioning skills (that is, differentiated versus generic drugs). These mobility barriers are all examples of combinations of economies of scale, product differentiation, and cost advantages independent of scale barriers to entry operating within the pharmaceutical industry.

With these mobility barriers isolated, it is possible to measure the conduct of firms in an industry with respect to these mobility barriers. Some firms emphasize their own research and development skills; others rely on the research and development skills of other firms by licensing products that these other firms develop. Some firms have invested in huge marketing forces to sell their drugs; others have invested in less elaborate marketing organizations.

With the conduct of each firm measured relative to the mobility barriers in an industry, a similarity matrix can be formed. Different measures of similarity can be used, but most researchers apply simple correlational analysis to form an ($n \times n$) correlation matrix (where n is the number of firms in an industry). Each element of this correlation matrix (i,j) is the correlation between the vector of measures of conduct for firm i with the vector of measures of conduct for firm j.

To actually form groups of firms that face similar threats and opportunities but that are also different from the threats and opportunities facing other firms in an industry, this similarity matrix can be subjected to cluster analysis. The resulting clusters are strategic groups—that is, sets of firms that are pursuing similar sets of strategies and actions and thus are likely to face similar sets of threats and opportunities. Cool and Dierickx (1993) conducted this type of analysis on firms in the pharmaceutical industry, using data on firm conduct from 1963 to 1969. They then repeated this analysis of firms in the pharmaceutical industry from 1980 to 1982. The results of these analyses are presented in Fig. 4A.1.

Cool and Dierickx (1993) are able to describe in some detail the evolution of competition within and between strategic groups in the pharmaceutical industry. They observe, for example, that the strategic group that they label "ethical houses" lost some of its members over time, as three firms (Abbott, Lederle, and Squibb) were unable to keep pace with the innovative output of research and development leaders in the industry (Lilly, Merck, and Upjohn). Second, as revealed in the dimensional analysis in Fig. 4A.1, the "ethical houses" in the 1980–1982 period had some difficulty remaining distinct from the "commercial houses" during this same period (this is indicated by the closeness of the "commercial houses" to the "ethical houses" in the dimensional diagram in the figure). Also, Lederle, a member of the "ethical houses" group in the 1963–1969 period, left this group in the later period and seemed to follow a unique strategy. In the 1980–1982 period, Lederle used its relatively large marketing group to push commodity generic drugs, a strategy not pursued by any firm in the earlier period.

FIGURE 4A.1

Strategic Groups in the U.S. Pharmaceutical Industry, 1963–1969 and 1980–1982.
Groups are represented in three dimensions. Each axis represents a critical attribute or firm conduct in this industry: research and development skills, marketing skills, and product-positioning skills. The size of the spheres reflects the total sales of the firms in each strategic group. *Source:* K. O. Cool and D. Schendel, "Strategic Group Formation and Performance: The Case of the U.S. Pharmaceutical Industry, 1963–1982, *Management Science,* 33, 1987, pp. 1102–1124. © 1987 The Institute of Management Sciences (currently INFORMS), 290 Westminster Street, Providence, RI 02901.

Strategic groups during 1963–69

Strategic groups during 1980–82

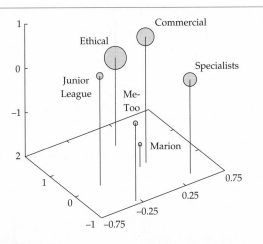
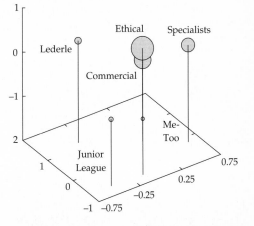

Ethical houses
Abbott
Lederle
Eli Lilly
Merck
Squibb
Upjohn

Commercial houses
American Home Products
Bristol-Myers
SmithKline
Sterling Drug

Junior league
Johnson & Johnson
Morton Norwich
Pfizer
Merrell-National
Schering-Plough
Syntex

Specialists
G.D. Searle
Warner-Lambert

Me-too
Carter Wallace
A.H. Robins
Rorer

Marion Labs

Ethical houses
Eli Lilly
Merck
Upjohn

Commercial houses
Abbott
American Home Products
Bristol-Myers
Pfizer
SmithKline
Warner-Lambert

Junior league
Johnson & Johnson
Schering-Plough
Squibb
Sterling Drug

Specialists
G.D. Searle
Syntex

Me-too
Carter Wallace
Marion Labs
Merrell National
Morton Norwich
A.H. Robins
Rorer

Lederle

LIMITATIONS OF STRATEGIC GROUPS ANALYSIS

If carefully applied, strategic groups analysis can be an important supplemental tool for analyzing environmental threats and opportunities in an industry. In particular, it can be used to study the evolution of competition between sets of firms in an industry over time. Unfortunately, the use of this concept can also be misleading.

WEAKNESSES OF CLUSTERING AND RELATED TECHNIQUES

At first, cluster analysis seems ideally suited for the isolation of strategic groups in an industry. These algorithms are designed to discover groups of individual firms that are similar to one another but different from other groups (Hartigan, 1975). If the strategies that firms pursue in an industry are used as the basis of these cluster analyses, the resulting clusters seem likely to qualify as strategic groups. This logic underlies the empirical work of Hatten (1974), Hatten, Schendel, and Cooper (1978), Harrigan (1985), Hergert (1983), and many others (see McGee and Thomas, 1986).

Although this logic seems enticing, it has significant limitations. As Hatten and Schendel (1977) acknowledge, the application of clustering algorithms and related techniques to discover strategic groups in an industry rests on the "untested assertion" that these groups actually exist. Assuredly, any clustering algorithm, when applied to the analysis of any data set, will generate clusters. Thus the development of clusters cannot be used to demonstrate the existence of strategic groups. In this analytic approach, one is left in the uncomfortable position of assuming that strategic groups exist, applying algorithms that are guaranteed to generate clusters, and then concluding that the obtained clusters demonstrate that strategic groups exist in an industry.

This issue is particularly problematic for practicing strategic managers. Such managers may make strategic decisions based on the strategic group structure that is "discovered" in an industry through a cluster analysis—even though that group structure may be simply an artifact of cluster analysis. For example, the fact that Lederle emerged as a one-firm group in the 1980–1982 analysis of the pharmaceutical industry (Cool and Dierickx, 1993) might lead some pharmaceutical firm to begin to explore Lederle's strategy as a viable opportunity in that industry. Also, the fact that three firms dropped out of Cool and Dierickx's (1993) ethical group between 1963–1969 and 1980–1982, together with the observation that the "ethical houses" and the "commercial houses" are almost indistinguishable in the second time period, might be interpreted as suggesting that the strategies pursued by firms in the ethical group are not likely to be viable over the long run. Unfortunately, all these competitive implications are drawn from an analysis that *assumed* that groups in this industry actually exist, and from a data aggregation approach that created those groups, whether or not they actually existed. Put differently, managers cannot tell whether the structure of competition reflected in Fig. 4A.1 is real or simply an artifact of the form of this analysis.

Strategic group researchers have recognized the difficulties associated with this form of analysis and have adopted several approaches to try to solve these problems. Some researchers have tried to justify their results on the basis of "powerful" clustering algorithms—although this cannot be done in any statistically rigorous way (Hartigan, 1975). Others have used multiple clustering algorithms to discover a single set of groups in an industry—although using multiple algorithms still assumes that groups in an industry exist (Cool and Schendel, 1987).

Given the limitations of cluster analysis as a way to test the existence of strategic groups, one is forced to wonder whether strategic groups really exist or are an artifact of clustering analysis. The application of this method always finds groups. Harrigan (1985) found strategic groups in all eight industries she studied. Hergert (1983) found strategic groups in all fifty industries he studied. Indeed, in all the twenty-seven studies listed in Barney and Hoskisson (1990), no industry is found that does not contain strategic groups. Does this evidence suggest that strategic groups do exist, or does it suggest that clustering algorithms, when applied to a data set, always generate clusters?

THE INTUITIVE APPEAL OF CLUSTERING RESULTS

Since researchers have only limited ability to refer to the "power" of single or multiple clustering algorithms to avoid the circularity discussed above, many have adopted a second approach to demonstrating the existence of groups. This approach relies on the "intuitive appeal" of the group structure to individuals with an "intimate knowledge" of the industry being studied.

Reliance on the intuitive appeal of a set of strategic groups to demonstrate that groups exist does help researchers resolve the circularity problems noted earlier, for no longer is the existence of clusters taken as an indication that groups exist. Thus, in principle at least, it would be possible for researchers to apply one clustering algorithm or a set of clustering algorithms to a data set and generate a group structure that was not "intuitively appealing" and in this way fail to reject the null hypothesis that strategic groups do not exist.

However, the practical implications of this intuitive appeal approach to evaluate a group's analysis are less obvious. If management's intuitive understanding of the structure of competition in an industry is the ultimate criterion for judging the validity of a cluster analysis, one must ask, "Why go through all the trouble of a cluster analysis?" If the objective of a strategic group analysis is to inform managerial decision making, and if the ability of managers to make internal judgments about the structure of competition in an industry is critical to the analysis of the strategic group, the practical importance of such an analysis is no longer obvious.

STRATEGIC GROUP MEMBERSHIP AND FIRM PERFORMANCE

A third way that researchers have tried to demonstrate the existence of strategic groups—besides choosing "powerful" algorithms and pointing to the intuitive appeal of the group structure they have found—is based on the assertion that group membership affects, to some extent, the performance of individual firms (Caves and Porter, 1977). This assertion depends on the existence of mobility barriers. With mobility barriers in place, firms in a group earning higher-than-normal economic profits are protected from the profit-reducing entry of other firms changing their strategies and entering this group.

Caves and Porter (1977) define a mobility barrier as a structural attribute of a strategic group that makes it difficult (very costly) for firms not already in that group to move into it. This definition is supplemented by a list of examples, including scale economies and access to distribution channels. Although this definition is an important first step, it does not provide researchers much guidance in defining mobility barriers in a particular industry. As before, researchers have often had to rely on intimate knowledge of an industry to specify its possible mobility barriers (Harrigan, 1985).

To overcome the problem of discovering which (if any) mobility barriers exist in an industry, group researchers have adopted the following logic. If, in a given industry, a set of firm attributes, when clustered, yields groups of firms, and if firm performance varies between these groups, then the attributes that were used as the basis of the clustering analysis must be acting as mobility barriers in this industry. As McGee and Thomas (1986:155) note: "The existing literature appears to justify the existence of group structures by their contribution to explaining differences in profit rates." Thus the observed relationship between group membership and firm performance is taken as evidence of the existence of mobility barriers.

The primary limitation of this research logic is that different clusters of the same set of firms can all yield significant differences in firm performance by group. Thus the existence of performance differences between groups is no assurance that the operative set of mobility barriers (assuming they exist at all) in an industry have been found. This is shown in Barney and Hoskisson (1990). These authors conduct two strategic groups analyses on a single set of firms, generate two different group structures, and show how both of these group structures are correlated with firm performance.

Despite these problems, it is nevertheless the case that analysis of such a strategic group can be helpful in characterizing the structure of threats and opportunities facing firms in an industry. As Cool and Dierickx (1993) have shown, strategic groups analysis can enable managers to gain a rich understanding of how different firms in an industry compete, with whom they compete, and how that competition evolves over time.

REVIEW QUESTIONS

1. What are the major strategic groups in the worldwide automobile industry? What mobility barriers exist in this industry, and how are firms arrayed along these mobility barriers?

2. Evaluate the following statement: "The only reason we need the concept of strategic groups is that we do not have a good definition of what constitutes an industry."

CHAPTER 5

Evaluating Firm Strengths and Weaknesses: Resources and Capabilities

Consider the performance of Crown Cork & Seal, Inc. (CC&S). CC&S is in the metal container industry, with 1994 sales of $4.5 billion (266th in the 1994 Fortune 500). An analysis of the environment of metal container firms reveals numerous threats and relatively few opportunities. The level of rivalry in this industry is very high; over one hundred firms manufacture cans. Fierce price competition has consistently eroded margins, and efforts by industry incumbents to create price stability have been unsuccessful. Buyers have always been a significant threat in can manufacturing, and many have engaged in backward vertical integration. Indeed, Campbell Soup Company and PepsiCo. are some of the largest manufacturers of cans in the United States. Finally, numerous packaging substitutes for metal cans have been introduced over the last few years, including plastic bottles, glass bottles, and fiber foil containers. Only the threat of suppliers (steel and aluminum firms) and the threat of new entrants have not been significant in the industry. The threat of steel firms as suppliers has been checked by the existence of aluminum as an alternative raw material, and vice versa. Entry has not been a significant threat because there were few profits in this industry to motivate entry. Indeed, the largest firms in metal-can manufacturing during the 1970s (Continental, American, and National

Can) have all shifted their businesses away from cans and toward financial services, alternative forms of packaging, and a range of other unrelated businesses (Hamermesh and Rosenbloom, 1989).

In the face of what can only be described as a very competitive environment, Crown Cork & Seal has consistently earned very high levels of profitability. In 1994 CC&S profits were $131 million, up 32.2 percent from 1993, with an ROA of 2.7 percent and an ROE of 9.6 percent, considerably higher than the returns of its competitors in the metal can industry. CC&S seems to have developed and maintained this high level of performance through a combination of quality customer service, product focus, and efficient management ("The Fortune 500," 1995).

Crown Cork & Seal is not the only firm that has been able to obtain high levels of economic performance, despite conducting business in a very competitive industry. Wal-Mart stores, for example, operates in the highly competitive discount retail sales industry, an industry that has consistently experienced price competition and margin erosion since it was created in the mid-1960s. Indeed, several discount retail store chains have declared bankruptcy over the years. Despite these challenges, Wal-Mart has consistently earned a return on sales over twice the industry average (Ghemawat, 1986). The airline business is another industry racked by profit-destroying competition. But while total losses among U.S. airlines totaled over $10 billion in the early 1990s, Southwest Airlines' profits continued to grow. Indeed, Southwest Airlines has been one of the few consistently profitable airline firms in the world (Heskett and Hallowell, 1993). In the highly competitive steel industry, the market value of almost all vertically integrated steel producers in the United States has fallen for fifteen consecutive years. Despite these results, the market value of Nucor Steel has continued to soar, giving its shareholders one of the consistently highest rates of return for any investment in publicly traded firms in the United States (Ghemawat and Stander, 1992).

The performance of Crown Cork & Seal, Wal-Mart, Southwest Airlines, and Nucor Steel in industries with so many threats and few opportunities reminds us that a firm's competitive environment is not the only determinant of a firm's profit potential. Some firms are able to develop and implement strategies that generate high levels of profit in competitively difficult industries. Other firms conduct business in industries with relatively few threats and enormous opportunities, only to choose and implement strategies that generate below-normal economic performance. To understand the performance of both kinds of firms, it is necessary to look beyond the analysis of threats and opportunities that exist in a firm's environment and examine the unique strengths and weaknesses that a firm might possess.

In this chapter we examine models for analyzing a firm's strengths and weaknesses. This chapter discusses economic and other theories underlying models of strengths and weaknesses, describes how these models have been used to develop a framework for analyzing strengths and weaknesses, and examines some of the limitations of this framework.

5.1   TRADITIONAL RESEARCH ON FIRM STRENGTHS AND WEAKNESSES

Whereas models of environmental threats and opportunities are grounded in a single approach to economic analysis—the structure-conduct-performance paradigm—the study of firm strengths and weaknesses draws on a wider variety of research traditions, some in economics and others in noneconomic disciplines. Among the most important of these are (1) traditional research on firm distinctive competencies, (2) Ricardian economics, and (3) the theory of firm growth.

THEORIES OF DISTINCTIVE COMPETENCE

The first of the research traditions that underpins the modern study of firm strengths and weaknesses is work on distinctive competencies.

General Managers as Strengths and Weaknesses

Research on the competitive implications of a firm's internal strengths and weaknesses has a long tradition. Much of this work was begun at the Harvard Business School as early as 1911 by A. W. Shaw, M. T. Copeland, George Albert Smith, Jr., and Edmund P. Learned with the analysis of the role of general managers in organizations (Learned et al., 1969). In this early work it was assumed that decisions made by general managers (that is, managers with significant profit-and-loss responsibility in an organization) had a very large impact on a firm's performance. General managers, it was argued, were the individuals in an organization that had the responsibility for analyzing the firm's environment, understanding a firm's internal strengths and weaknesses, and choosing strategies to maximize value. Although general managers might call on a variety of line and staff managers to assist in this strategy-making effort, the quality of general managers in a firm was thought to determine the performance of firms. High-quality general managers were thought of as organizational strengths, and low-quality general managers were thought of as weaknesses.

This general management approach to understanding firm strengths and weaknesses has a great deal of validity, but two problems limit its applicability. First, even if one accepts the notion that general management decisions are the most important determinants of firm performance, the qualities and characteristics that make up a "high-quality" general manager are ambiguous and difficult to specify. In fact, the qualities of a "good" general manager are just as ambiguous as the qualities of "good" leaders (Yukl, 1989). In the case literature, general managers with widely different skills and styles are shown to be quite effective. For example, John Connelly, former president of Crown Cork & Seal, was intensely involved in every aspect of his organization (Hamermesh and Rosenbloom, 1989). Other successful CEOs tend to delegate much of the day-to-day management of their firms (Stodgill, 1974). Yet both types of general managers can be very effective.

Second, general managers are an important possible strength (or weakness) for an organization, but they are not the only organizational strength or weakness. An exclusive emphasis on general managers as a source of competitive advantage ignores a wide variety of firm attributes that may be important for understanding firm performance. Such an emphasis leads to the use of a strict hierarchical definition of *strategy* (see Section 1.2) and all the limitations of this approach to strategy formulation and implementation. In the end, general managers in organizations are probably similar to baseball managers: They receive too much credit when things go well and too much blame when things go poorly.

The Study of Distinctive Competence

While faculty members at the Harvard Business School were studying the impact of general managers on firm performance, some sociologists led by Phillip Selznick were studying the internal characteristics of organizations from a completely different perspective. In a series of articles and books, culminating in his book *Leadership and Administration* (Selznick, 1957), Selznick examined the relationship between what he called institutional leadership and distinctive competence.

According to Selznick, institutional leaders in organizations do more than carry out the classic managerial activities of decision making and administration. In addition, they create and define an organization's purpose or mission. In more contemporary terms, institutional leaders help create for an organization a vision around which its members can rally (Selznick, 1957). Institutional leaders also organize and structure a firm so that it reflects this fundamental purpose and vision. With this organization in place, Selznick suggests, institutional leaders then focus their attention on safeguarding a firm's distinctive values and identity—the distinctive vision of a firm—from internal and external threats. This organizational vision, in combination with organizational structure, helps define a firm's distinctive competencies—those activities that a particular firm does better than any competing firms.

Selznick did not go on to analyze the competitive or performance implications of institutional leadership or distinctive competence in any detail. However, it is not difficult to see that firms with distinctive competencies have strengths that may enable them to obtain competitive advantages, and that leaders as visionaries and institution builders, rather than just as decision makers and administrators, may be an important source of this competitive advantage (Selznick, 1957). This form of reasoning is similar to the models of organizational strengths and weaknesses that are discussed later in this chapter.

Selznick's analysis of distinctive competence has much to recommend it, but it has limitations as well. Most important of these is that Selznick's analysis focuses only on senior managers (his institutional leaders) as the ultimate source of competitive advantage for a firm and on a single tool (the development of an organizational vision) that senior managers can use to create distinctive competencies. Although these are important possible strengths and weaknesses in a firm, they are not the only possible strengths and weaknesses.

RICARDIAN ECONOMICS

Research on general managers and institutional leaders as possible strengths and weaknesses focuses exclusively on top managers, but the next major influence on the study of organizational strengths and weaknesses—Ricardian economics—traditionally included little or no role for managers as possible strengths or weaknesses. Instead, David Ricardo was interested in the economic consequences of the "original, unaugmentable, and indestructible gifts of Nature" (Ricardo, 1817). Much of this early work focused on the economic consequences of owning land.

Unlike many factors of production, the total supply of land is relatively fixed and cannot be significantly increased in response to higher demand and prices. Such factors of production are perfectly inelastic, since their quantity of supply is fixed and does not respond to price changes. In these settings, it is possible for those that own higher-quality factors of production with inelastic supply to earn an economic rent. As mentioned in Section 2.2, an economic rent is a payment to an owner of a factor of production in excess of the minimum required to induce that factor into employment (Hirshleifer, 1980).

Ricardo's argument concerning land as a factor of production is summarized in Fig. 5.1. Imagine that there are many parcels of land

FIGURE 5.1
Ricardian Rents and the Economics of Land with Different Levels of Fertility

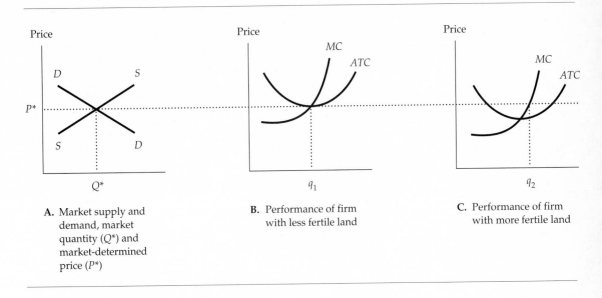

A. Market supply and demand, market quantity (Q^*) and market-determined price (P^*)

B. Performance of firm with less fertile land

C. Performance of firm with more fertile land

suitable for growing wheat. Also, suppose that the fertility of these different parcels varies from high fertility (low costs of production) to low fertility (high costs of production). The long-run supply curve for wheat in this market can be derived as follows: At low prices, only the most fertile land, will be cultivated; as prices rise, production continues on the very fertile land and additional crops are planted on less fertile land; at still higher prices, even less fertile land will be cultivated. This analysis leads to the simple market supply curve presented in panel A of Fig. 5.1. Given market demand, P^* is the market-determined price of wheat in this market.

Now consider the situation facing two different kinds of firms. Both of these firms follow traditional profit-maximizing logic by producing a quantity (q) such that marginal cost equals marginal revenue. However, this profit-maximizing decision for the firm with less fertile land (in panel B of Fig. 5.1) generates normal economic performance and zero economic profit. On the other hand, the firm with more fertile land (in panel C of Fig. 5.1) has average total costs less than the market-determined price and thus is able to earn an above-normal economic profit, or rent.

In traditional economic analysis, the economic profit earned by the firm with more fertile land should lead other firms to enter into this market, to obtain some land and begin production of wheat. However, all the land that can be used to produce wheat in a way that generates at least a normal return given the market price P^* is already in production. In particular, there is no more very fertile land left, and fertile land (by assumption) cannot be created. This is what is meant by land being inelastic in supply. Thus the firm with more fertile land and lower production costs has a sustained competitive advantage over firms with less fertile land and higher production costs and is able to earn an above-normal economic profit.

Of course, at least two events can threaten this sustained competitive advantage and economic rent. First, market demand may shift down and to the left. This would force firms with less fertile land to cease production, and it would also reduce the economic rent of the firm with more fertile land. If demand shifted far enough, this economic rent may disappear altogether.

Second, firms with less fertile land may discover low-cost ways of increasing their land's fertility, thereby reducing the competitive advantage of the firm with more fertile land. For example, firms with less fertile land may be able to use inexpensive fertilizers to increase their land's fertility, and they may be able to reduce their production costs to be closer to the costs of the firm that had the more fertile land initially. The existence of such low-cost fertilizers suggests that although *land* may be in fixed supply, *fertility* may not be. If enough firms can increase the fertility of their land, then the rents originally earned by the firm with the more fertile land will disappear, and this market will be closer to perfect competition. As discussed in Chapter 2, firms competing in conditions of perfect competition can expect to earn only normal economic profits, or zero economic rents.

Traditionally, most economists have implicitly assumed that relatively few factors of production have inelastic supply (Hirshleifer, 1980). Most economic models presume that if prices for a factor rise, more of that factor will be produced, increasing supply and ensuring that suppliers will earn only normal economic returns. However, more recently, there is a growing recognition that numerous resources used by firms are inelastic in supply and are possible sources of economic rents. Thus although labor per se is probably not inelastic in supply, highly skilled and creative laborers may be. Although individual managers are probably not inelastic in supply, managers who can work effectively in teams may be. And although top managers may not be inelastic in supply, top managers who are also institutional leaders (as suggested by Selznick and others) may be. Firms that own (or control) these kinds of resources may be able to earn economic rents—above-normal economic performance—by exploiting them. This observation is critical in the model of organizational strengths and weaknesses described in Section 5.2.

THE THEORY OF FIRM GROWTH

In 1959, Edith Penrose published a book titled *The Theory of the Growth of the Firm*. Penrose's objective was to understand the process through which firms grow and the limits of growth. Traditional economic models had analyzed firm growth using the assumptions and tools of neoclassical microeconomics (Penrose, 1959). Most important of these, for Penrose, was the assumption that firms could be appropriately modeled as if they were relatively simple production functions. In other words, traditional economic models assumed that firms simply observed supply and demand conditions and translated these conditions into levels of production that maximized firm profits (Nelson and Winter, 1982).

This abstract notion of what a firm is, had and continues to have utility in some circumstances. However, in attempting to understand constraints on the growth of firms, Penrose (1959) concluded that this abstraction was not helpful. Instead, she argued that firms should be understood, first, as an administrative framework that links and coordinates activities of numerous individuals and groups, and second, as a bundle of productive resources. The task facing managers was to exploit the bundle of productive resources controlled by a firm through the use of the administrative framework that had been created in a firm. According to Penrose, the growth of a firm is limited (1) by the productive opportunities that exist as a function of the bundle of productive resources controlled by a firm and (2) by the administrative framework used to coordinate the use of these resources.

Besides looking inside a firm to analyze the ability of firms to grow (in a way that parallels internal analyses in the SWOT framework), Penrose made several other contributions to the study of a firm's strengths and weaknesses. First, she observed that the bundles of productive resources controlled by firms can vary significantly by firm—that firms, in this sense, are fundamentally heterogeneous even if they are in the same industry. Second, Penrose adopted a very broad definition of what might be considered a productive resource. Where traditional economists (including Ricardo) focused on just a few resources that might be inelastic in supply (such as land), Penrose began to study the competitive implications of inelastic productive resources such as managerial teams, top management groups, and entrepreneurial skills. Finally, Penrose recognized that, even within this extended typology of productive resources, there still might be additional sources of firm heterogeneity. Thus in her analysis of entrepreneurial skills as a possible productive resource, Penrose observed that some entrepreneurs are more versatile than others, that some are more ingenious in fund raising, that some are more ambitious, and that some exercise better judgment.

5.2   ANALYZING ORGANIZATIONAL STRENGTHS AND WEAKNESSES

Research on the skills of general managers, institutional leaders, economic rents, and firm growth have recently been brought together to develop a rigorous model that can be used to analyze a firm's strengths and weaknesses. This general framework, usually called the *resource-based view of the firm* (Wernerfelt, 1984), focuses on the idiosyncratic, costly-to-copy resources controlled by a firm—resources whose exploitation may give a firm a competitive advantage. A growing number of authors are focusing their efforts on understanding the resource-based view, its implications for firm performance, and its relationship with the frameworks for studying environmental threats and opportunities discussed in Chapters 3 and 4 (Barney, 1986a, 1991; Conner, 1991; Mahoney and Pandian, 1992).

BASIC ASSUMPTIONS OF THE RESOURCE-BASED VIEW OF THE FIRM

This approach to studying a firm's internal strengths and weaknesses rests on two fundamental assumptions. First, building on Penrose (1959), this work assumes that firms can be thought of as bundles of productive resources and that different firms possess different bundles of these resources. This is the assumption of firm *resource heterogeneity*. Second, drawing from Selznick (1957) and Ricardo (1817), this approach assumes that some of these resources are either very costly to copy or inelastic in supply. This is the assumption of *resource immobility*. If (1) the resources that a firm possesses enable the firm to exploit opportunities or neutralize threats, (2) these resources are possessed by only a small number of competing firms, and (3) if they are costly to copy or inelastic in supply, then they may be firm strengths and thus potential sources of competitive advantage (Barney, 1991).

Resource Categories

Any of a wide range of firm attributes could be considered resources in this context. In general, firm resources are all assets, capabilities, competencies, organizational processes, firm attributes, information, knowledge, and so forth that are controlled by a firm and that enable the firm to conceive of and implement strategies that improve its efficiency and effectiveness (Daft, 1983).

Several authors have generated lists of firm attributes that may be thought of as resources (Hitt and Ireland, 1986; Thompson and Strickland, 1987). Generally, these resources can be conveniently divided into four categories: financial capital, physical capital, human capital, and organizational capital. *Financial capital* includes all the different money resources that firms can use to conceive of and implement strategies. Capital from entrepreneurs, from equity holders, from bond holders, and from banks is financial capital. Retained earnings is also an important type of financial capital.

Physical capital includes the physical technology used in a firm, a firm's plant and equipment, its geographic location, and its access to raw materials (Williamson, 1975). Specific examples of physical capital are a firm's computer hardware and software technology (Kirkpatrick, 1992), robots used in manufacturing (Badaracco and Hasegwa, 1988), and automated warehouses to control inventory costs (Ghemawat, 1986). Geographic location, as a type of physical capital, is an important resource for firms as diverse as Wal-Mart (Ghemawat, 1986) (with its operations in rural markets generating, on average, higher returns than its operations in more competitive urban markets), Gateway 2000 (a personal computer firm located in North Sioux City, North Dakota, where it has access to a relatively inexpensive, highly educated work force and is not subject to corporate income taxes) (Kupfer, 1991), and L. L. Bean (a catalogue retail firm that believes that its rural Maine location helps its employees identify with the outdoor lifestyle of many of its customers) (Holder, 1989).

Human capital includes the training, experience, judgment, intelligence, relationships, and insight of *individual* managers and workers in a firm (Becker, 1964). The importance of the human capital of well-known entrepreneurs such as Bill Gates (Microsoft) and Steve Jobs (formerly of Apple) is broadly understood (Deutschman, 1992; Kupfer, 1992). However, valuable human capital resources are not limited just to entrepreneurs or to senior managers. Several firms, including the Bell Labs division at AT&T and Du Pont, have invested heavily in training their engineering staffs to be more assertive and open to new technologies, thereby enhancing the human capital resources available to these firms (Rigdon, 1993; Alpert, 1992).

Whereas human capital is an attribute of single individuals, *organizational capital* is an attribute of collections of individuals. Organizational capital includes a firm's formal reporting structure (what Penrose called the "administrative framework"), its formal and informal planning, controlling, and coordinating systems, its culture and reputation, as well as informal relations among groups within a firm and between a firm and those in its environment (Tomer, 1987). Firms as diverse as Merck, Levi Strauss, Rubbermaid, and Harley Davidson use their positive management reputations as a type of organizational capital, to gain access to managerial labor markets, distribution networks, and customer groups (Caminiti, 1992). Hewlett-Packard relies on its organizational culture as an organizational resource, to help implement and manage change (Yoder, 1991).

Resources, Capabilities, and Competencies

As the resource-based view of the firm has developed, different authors have used different terms to describe strategically relevant financial, physical, individual, and organizational attributes. One of the earliest strategic management references to these organizational attributes was by Wernerfelt (1984), who called them "resources." Wernerfelt's terminology has been adopted by Barney (1991) and others. Prahalad and Bettis (1986), in their analysis of the implications of these kinds of organizational attributes for diversification strategies, called them a firm's "dominant logic." In more recent work on managing diversification, Prahalad and Hamel (1990) called these internal attributes of firms "core competencies." Stalk, Evans, and Shulman (1992), in some closely related work, call them "capabilities."

In practice, the differences among these various terms are subtle at best. Some have suggested that a firm's "resources" include its fundamental financial, physical, individual, and organizational capital attributes (Hill and Jones, 1992). "Capabilities," in contrast, include only those internal attributes that enable a firm to coordinate and exploit its other resources (Stalk, Evans, and Shulman, 1992). General practice seems to suggest that "core competencies" is restricted to firm attributes that enable managers to conceive of and implement certain corporate diversification strategies (Prahalad and Hamel, 1990).

Although these distinctions among resources, capabilities, and competencies can be drawn in theory, it is likely that they will become badly blurred in practice. In particular, it seems unlikely that a debate about whether a particular firm attribute is a "resource" and "capability" or a "competence" will be of much value to managers or firms. Given this state of affairs, the following conventions are adopted throughout the remainder of this book. First, the terms *resources* and *capabilities* are used interchangeably and often in parallel. Second, the term *core competence* is applied only in discussions of the conception or implementation of diversification strategies. Thus, *core competence* is largely restricted in use until Part 3.

A FRAMEWORK FOR ANALYSIS: VRIO

The definition of a firm's resources and capabilities, and the two assumptions of resource heterogeneity and resource immobility, are quite abstract and not directly amenable to the analysis of a firm's strengths and weaknesses. However, it is possible to develop a framework, based on this definition and on these two assumptions, that is more generally applicable. This framework is called the *VRIO framework*. It is structured in a series of four questions: (1) the question of value, (2) the question of rareness, (3) the question of imitability, and (4) the question of organization. The answers to these questions determine whether a particular firm resource or capability is a strength or a weakness. Table 5.1 summarizes the questions; each question is discussed in detail below.

The Question of Value

> *The Question of Value.* Do a firm's resources and capabilities enable the firm to respond to environmental threats or opportunities?

In order for resources and capabilities to be strengths, they must enable a firm to exploit environmental opportunities or neutralize environmental threats. Firm resources and capabilities that make it difficult for a firm to exploit opportunities or neutralize threats can be thought of as weaknesses. The question of value thus links internal analyses of strengths and weaknesses with external analyses of threats and opportunities. Throughout this book, the question of value will be addressed for different strategic options facing firms by applying the models of environmental threats and opportunities, developed in Chapters 3 and 4 and elsewhere. Thus, despite observations by some strategic management scholars, SCP-based models of environmental threats and

TABLE 5.1 **Questions Needed to Conduct a Resource-Based Analysis of a Firm's Internal Strengths and Weaknesses**	1. *The Question of Value:* Do a firm's resources and capabilities enable the firm to respond to environmental threats or opportunities? 2. *The Question of Rareness:* How may competing firms already possess particular valuable resources and capabilities? 3. *The Question of Imitability:* Do firms without a resource or capability face a cost disadvantage in obtaining it compared to firms that already possess it? 4. *The Question of Organization:* Is a firm organized to exploit the full competitive potential of its resources and capabilities?

opportunities are seen as complements to resource-based models of organizational strengths and weaknesses (Barney, 1991).

The answer to the question of value, for many firms, has been *yes*. For example, Sony has a great deal of experience in designing, manufacturing, and selling miniaturized electronic technology. Sony has used these resources and capabilities to exploit numerous market opportunities, including portable tape players, portable disc players, portable televisions, and easy-to-hold 8mm video cameras. 3M has used its resources and capabilities in substrates, coatings, and adhesives, along with an organizational culture that rewards risk taking and creativity, to exploit numerous market opportunities in office products, including invisible tape and Post-it notes. Sony's and 3M's resources and capabilities—including their specific technological skills and their creative organizational cultures—made it possible for these firms to respond to, and even create, new environmental opportunities (Schlender, 1992; Krogh, Praeger, Sorenson and Tomlinson, 1988).

Unfortunately, for other firms the answer to the question of value has been *no*. For example, long experience in traditional vertically integrated steel making made it almost impossible for USX to recognize or respond to fundamental changes in the structure of the steel industry. Unable to respond to these changes, USX decided to delay its investment in thin slab continuous casting steel-manufacturing technology. Nucor Steel, in contrast, was not shackled by its past, made these investments, and has become a major player in the international steel industry. In a similar way, Sears was unable to recognize and respond to changes in the retail market that had been created by Wal-Mart and specialty retail boutiques. In a sense, Sears's historical success, along with a commitment to stick with a traditional way of doing things, led it to miss some significant market opportunities. For both USX and Sears, resources and capabilities—in particular, their experience operating in an older competitive environment—were not valuable and prevented them from responding to competitive opportunities or threats (Rosenbloom and Christensen, 1990; Montgomery, 1989).

Changes in Resource Value.   Obviously, the fact that a firm's resources and capabilities have been valuable in the past does not necessarily imply that they will always be valuable. Changes in customer tastes, industry structure, or technology can render a firm's resources and capabilities less valuable. For example, General Electric's resources and capabilities in transistor manufacturing became much less valuable when semiconductors were invented. American Airlines' skills in managing its relationship with the Civil Aeronautics Board became much less valuable after airline deregulation. IBM's numerous resources and capabilities in the mainframe computing business became less valuable with the rise in power and reduction in price of personal and mini computers.

A firm that no longer possesses valuable resources and capabilities has two fundamental choices. One choice is to develop new and valuable resources and capabilities. When AT&T's skill in managing regulated telephone companies became less valuable after divestiture, AT&T began a concerted effort to develop new resources and capabilities. By entering into numerous strategic alliances, by engaging in applied research and development, and by facilitating communication and teamwork across its multiple business activities, AT&T has begun to develop the skills it will need to compete in the global computing and communications industry (Kirkpatrick, 1993).

The other choice is to attempt to apply traditional strengths in new ways, instead of developing new resources and capabilities. For example, the invention and diffusion of air conditioning in manufacturing plants significantly reduced the value of the electric fan manufacturing skills of the Hunter Fan Company, a traditional fan manufacturer. However, rather than abandoning its skills altogether, Hunter Fan exploited a new market where its traditional strengths would be valued: electric ceiling fans for homes and apartments. To address this new opportunity, Hunter Fan had to develop some additional resources and capabilities, including brass-plating skills and new distribution networks. But the resources and capabilities that had made Hunter successful in the industrial market were still valuable in the home market (personal communication).

Another firm that has sought to apply its traditional valuable resources in a new way is Okean Tribor, an acoustic equipment firm in St. Petersburg, Russia. Okean Tribor was a leading supplier of sonar devices that the Soviet navy used to track NATO submarines. With the breakup of the Soviet Union, Okean Tribor's traditional strengths were no longer valuable. Rather than abandoning these strengths, however, Okean Tribor has sought to apply them in the high-end audiophile market in the United States, where it is currently negotiating distribution agreements (Mendes, 1992).

Valuable Resources and Economic Performance.   The impact of valuable resources and capabilities on a firm's economic performance can be derived directly from the definition of *performance* presented in Chapter 2. In particular, a firm's resources and capabilities are valuable if, and only if, they reduce a firm's costs or increase its revenues compared to what would have been the case if this firm did not possess those resources. When exploiting firm resources and capabilities does not exploit opportunities or neutralize threats, strategies that use these resources and capabilities will not increase a firm's revenues or decrease a firm's costs. In fact, often the use of these resources and capabilities will actually reduce revenues or increase costs compared to what would have been the case if these nonvaluable resources had not been exploited (such resources and capabilities are *weaknesses*).

Of course, the resources and capabilities of different firms can be valuable in different ways. This can be true even if firms are competing in the same industry. For example, both Rolex and Timex manufacture watches but exploit very different valuable resources and capabilities. Rolex emphasizes its quality manufacturing, commitment to excellence, and high-status reputation in marketing its watches. Timex emphasizes its high volume, low-cost manufacturing skills and abilities. Rolex exploits its resources and capabilities in response to demand for very expensive watches. Timex exploits its resources and capabilities in response to demand for practical, reliable, low-cost time-keeping.

The Question of Rareness

Understanding the value of a firm's resources and capabilities is an important first consideration in understanding the firm's internal strengths and weaknesses. However, if a particular resource or capability is controlled by numerous competing firms, then that resource is unlikely to be a source of competitive advantage for any one of them. Instead, valuable but common (that is, not rare) resources and capabilities are sources of competitive parity. These observations lead to the second critical question for managers evaluating the competitive implications of their resources and capabilities: the question of rareness.

> *The Question of Rareness.* How many competing firms already possess particular valuable resources and capabilities?

Consider, for example, two firms competing in the global communications and computing industries: NEC and AT&T. Both are developing many of the same resources and capabilities that are likely to be needed in these industries over the next decade (Prahalad and Hamel, 1990; Kirkpatrick, 1993). These resources and capabilities are valuable, for they will enable these firms to respond to opportunities and threats in these industry environments. However, since at least two firms, and maybe others, are developing the same resources and capabilities, they may not be rare. If they are not rare, they cannot—by themselves—be sources of competitive advantage for either NEC or AT&T. If either of these firms is to gain a competitive advantage, it must exploit resources and capabilities that are different from the communication and computing skills that both firms are developing. These other resources might include relationships with current and potential customers and organizational culture.

To observe that common (not rare) resources or capabilities cannot generate a competitive advantage is not to dismiss them as unimportant for strategic managers. Instead, valuable but common resources and capabilities can help ensure a firm's survival when they are exploited to create competitive parity in an industry. Under conditions of competitive parity, though no one firm gains a competitive advantage, firms do increase their probability of survival.

Consider, for example, a telephone system as a resource or capability. Since telephone systems are widely available, and since virtually all organizations have access to telephone systems, these systems are not rare and thus are not a source of competitive advantage. However, firms that do not possess a telephone system are likely to give their competitors an important competitive advantage and place themselves at a competitive disadvantage. Unless firms with a competitive disadvantage change their activities, they are likely to earn below-normal economic returns. In the long run, the survival of these kinds of firms can be jeopardized.

How rare a valuable resource or capability must be in order to have the potential for generating a competitive advantage varies from situation to situation. It is not difficult to see that if a firm's valuable resources and capabilities are absolutely unique among a set of current and potential competitors, they can generate a competitive advantage. However, it may be possible for a small number of firms in an industry to possess a particular valuable resource or capability and still obtain a competitive advantage (Barney, 1991). In general, as long as the number of firms that possess a particular valuable resource or capability is less than the number of firms needed to generate perfect competition dynamics in an industry, that resource or capability can be considered rare and a potential source of competitive advantage (Barney, 1991).

Valuable but common resources and capabilities will be sources of only competitive parity, but valuable and rare resources and capabilities will be sources of at least temporary competitive advantage. For example, skills in developing and using point-of-purchase data collection to control inventory and product ordering have given Wal-Mart a competitive advantage over Kmart—a firm that, until recently, did not have access to this same timely information, and even when it did have access did not exploit the information as Wal-Mart has done. For many years, Wal-Mart's valuable point-of-purchase inventory control system was rare, at least relative to Kmart, its major U.S. competitor.

Managers at Kmart, however, are aware of these advantages possessed by Wal-Mart and have begun to develop similar technological skills and abilities (Steven, 1992). If Kmart is successful in developing these capabilities, they will no longer be rare for Wal-Mart and thus will not be a source of competitive advantage. In other words, Wal-Mart's competitive advantage based on these particular skills will have been only temporary. However, it may be that other Wal-Mart resources—including the geographic location of some of its stores—will be more difficult for Kmart to imitate. These resources may be sources of sustained competitive advantage (Ghemawat, 1986) for Wal-Mart.

The Question of Imitability

Valuable and rare organizational resources may be a source of competitive advantage. Indeed, firms with such resources are often strategic innovators, for they are able to conceive of and engage in strategies that other firms could not conceive of, could not implement, or both, because these other firms lacked the relevant resources and capabilities. These firms may gain the first-mover advantages discussed in Section 4.2 (Lieberman and Montgomery, 1988).

Valuable and rare organizational resources, however, can be sources of sustained competitive advantage only if firms that do not possess them face a cost disadvantage in obtaining them compared to firms that already possess them. In language developed by Lipman and Rumelt (1982) and Barney (1986a, 1986b), these kinds of resources are *imperfectly imitable*. These observations lead to the question of imitability.

> *The Question of Imitability.* Do firms without a resource or capability face a cost disadvantage in obtaining it compared to firms that already possess it?

Imagine an industry with five essentially identical firms. Each firm manufactures the same products, using the same raw materials, and sells the products to the same customers through the same distribution channels. It is not hard to see that firms in this kind of industry will earn normal economic performance (Barney, 1991). Now, suppose that one of these firms, for whatever reason, discovers or develops a heretofore unrecognized valuable resource and uses that resource either to exploit an environmental opportunity or to neutralize an environmental threat. Obviously, this one firm will gain a competitive advantage over its competitors and will probably experience an above-normal economic return.

This firm's competitors can respond to this competitive advantage in at least two ways. First, they can ignore the success of this one firm and continue as before. This action, of course, will put them at a competitive disadvantage, and they may earn below-normal economic profits. Second, these firms can attempt to understand why this one firm is able to be successful and then duplicate the resources of this one firm and implement a similar strategy. If competitors have no cost disadvantages in acquiring/developing the needed resources, then this imitative approach will generate competitive parity in the industry and normal economic performance.

However, sometimes, for reasons that are discussed below, competing firms may face an important cost disadvantage in duplicating a successful firm's valuable resources. If this is the case, this one innovative firm may gain a *sustained competitive advantage*—an advantage that is not competed away through strategic imitation. Firms that possess and exploit costly-to-imitate, rare, and valuable resources in choosing and implementing their strategies may enjoy a period of sustained competitive advantage and above-normal economic performance.

Forms of Imitation: Direct Duplication and Substitution.   In general, imitation occurs in one of two ways: direct duplication or substitution. Imitating firms can attempt to directly duplicate the resources possessed by the firm with a competitive advantage. Thus if a firm has a competitive advantage because of its research and development skills, imitating firms can attempt to develop their own research and development skills. If a firm has a competitive advantage because of its marketing expertise, imitating firms can attempt to develop their own marketing expertise. If the cost of direct duplication of a firm's resources or capabilities is greater than the cost of developing these resources and capabilities for the firm with the competitive advantage, then this advantage may be sustained. If direct duplication is no more costly than the original development of these resources or capabilities, then any competitive advantage will be only temporary.

The relative costs of direct duplication directly parallel the situation facing a firm with less fertile land competing with a firm with more fertile land studied by Ricardo and described in Fig. 5.1. Costly duplication suggests that the resources or capabilities in question are inelastic in supply and thus that firms that already possess these resources may earn an economic rent.

Imitating firms can attempt to substitute other resources for a costly-to-imitate resource possessed by a firm with a competitive advantage. For example, if one firm has a competitive advantage because of the interpersonal communication skills of its top management team, a competing firm may try to substitute a sophisticated management information system for interpersonal communication skills. If the effects of interpersonal communication skills and sophisticated management information systems are the same, then these resources can be thought of as substitutes. If substitute resources exist, and if imitating firms do not face a cost disadvantage in obtaining them, then the competitive advantage of other firms will be only temporary. However, if these resources have no substitutes, or if the cost of acquiring these substitutes is greater than the cost of obtaining the original resources, then competitive advantages can be sustained.

Again, the relative cost of substitutes in imitating the sources of a firm's competitive advantage directly parallels the role of substitutes in the analysis of Ricardian rents in Fig. 5.1. In that example, if less fertile land with low-cost fertilizer is strategically equivalent to more fertile land, then very fertile land is not likely to be a source of economic rents. However, if less fertile land with low-cost fertilizer is not a strategic substitute for very fertile land, or if fertilizer is very costly, then owning more valuable land can be a source of economic rents.

Sources of Cost Disadvantages in Imitating Resources.   Why might competing firms face a cost disadvantage in imitating a particular firm's resources? A variety of authors have studied a range of reasons why imitation might be costly (Dierickx and Cool, 1989; Barney, 1991; Mahoney and Pandian, 1992; Peteraf, 1993). Four of these reasons are discussed here.

1. Unique Historical Conditions—It may be the case that the low-cost acquisition or development of a resource for a particular firm depended on certain unique historical conditions. The ability of firms to acquire, develop, and exploit resources often depends on their place in time and space (Arthur, 1989; Barney, 1991). Once time and history pass, firms that do not have space-and-time-dependent resources face a significant cost disadvantage in obtaining and developing them, since doing so would require these other firms to re-create history. Dierickx and Cool (1989) suggest that these resources have important time compression diseconomies.

Consider, for example, Caterpillar, the heavy-duty construction equipment firm. During the months before the entry of the United States into the Second World War, the federal government decided that it would need a single supplier of construction equipment to build and maintain military bases and landing fields throughout the world. This single supplier not only would need to build high-quality construction equipment but also would need to develop an effective and efficient global service and supply network to support construction efforts throughout the world. At the time, no construction equipment firm in the world had this global service and supply network.

After a brief competition among several medium-size construction equipment firms, the federal government chose Caterpillar as its sole supplier. The government agreed to pay Caterpillar prices for its equipment high enough to enable Caterpillar to develop the required worldwide service and supply network. Caterpillar gladly accepted this opportunity and went about building high-quality construction equipment, along with a new worldwide service and supply network.

After the war, Caterpillar was the only firm in the world with a worldwide service and supply network. Indeed, Caterpillar still advertises its ability to deliver any part, for any piece of Caterpillar equipment, to any place in the world, in under two days. By using this valuable resource, Caterpillar was able to become the dominant firm in the heavy construction equipment industry. Even today, despite recessions and labor strife, Caterpillar remains the market share leader in virtually every category of heavy construction equipment (Rukstad and Horn, 1989).

Now consider the position of a firm trying to compete with Caterpillar by duplicating its worldwide service and supply network. In order to develop this network at the same cost as Caterpillar, this competing firm would have to receive the same kind of government support that Caterpillar received during the Second World War. This kind of support is not likely to be forthcoming. A firm might decide that, in order to build this network at low cost, it must simply re-create World War II. This would be, to say the least, difficult to do and very costly.

Interestingly, although no firm has ever been able to directly duplicate Caterpillar's global service and supply network, other firms have been successful in this industry by competing in ways that did not require this costly-to-imitate resource. These competitors have developed resources that are substitutes for Caterpillar's global service and supply network. In particular, Komatsu, the Japanese construction equipment firm, circumvented the need to have a highly developed global service and supply network by simply building construction equipment that broke down less frequently (Bartlett and Rangan, 1985).

There are at least two ways that unique historical circumstances can give a firm a sustained competitive advantage. First, it may be that a particular firm is the first in an industry to recognize and exploit an opportunity, and being first gives a firm one or more of the first-mover advantages discussed in Section 4.2. Thus although in principle other firms in an industry could have exploited an opportunity, that only one firm did so makes it more costly for other firms to imitate this original firm.

A second way that history can have an impact on a firm builds on the concept of path dependence (Arthur, 1989). A process is said to be path dependent when events early in the evolution of a process have significant effects on subsequent events. In the evolution of competitive advantage, path dependence suggests that a firm may gain a competitive advantage in the current period because of the acquisition and development of resources in earlier periods. In these earlier periods, it is often not clear what the full future value of particular resources will be. Because of this uncertainty, firms are able to acquire or develop resources for less than what will turn out to be their full value (Lipman and Rumelt, 1982; Barney, 1986a). However, once the full value of these resources is revealed, other firms seeking to acquire or develop these resources will need to pay their full known value, which (in general) will be greater than the costs incurred by the firm that acquired or developed the resources in some earlier period. The cost of acquiring both duplicate and substitute resources would rise once their full value became known (Hirshleifer, 1980).

Consider, for example, a firm that purchased land for ranching some time ago and discovered a rich supply of oil on this land in the current period. Just as Ricardo would suggest, the difference between the value of this land as a supplier of oil (high) and the value of this land for ranching (low) is economic rent for this firm. Moreover, other firms attempting to acquire this or adjacent land will now have to pay for the full value of the land in its use as a supply of oil (high) and thus will be at a cost disadvantage compared to the firm that acquired the land some time ago for ranching.

2. Causal Ambiguity—A second reason why a firm's resources and capabilities may be costly to imitate is that imitating firms may not understand the relationship between the resources and capabilities controlled by a firm and that firm's competitive advantage. In other words, the relationship between firm resources and capabilities and competitive advantage may be causally ambiguous (Dierickx and Cool, 1989).

At first, it seems unlikely that causal ambiguity about the sources of competitive advantage for a firm would ever exist. Managers in a firm seem likely to understand the sources of their own competitive advantage (Reed and DeFillippi, 1990). If managers in one firm understand the relationship between resources and competitive advantage, then it seems likely that managers in other firms would also be able to discover these relationships and thus would have a clear understanding of which resources and capabilities they should duplicate or seek substitutes for. If there are no other sources of cost disadvantage for imitating firms, imitation should lead to competitive parity and normal economic performance.

However, it is not always the case that managers in a particular firm fully understand the relationship between the resources and capabilities they control and competitive advantage. This lack of understanding could occur for at least three reasons. First, it may be that the resources and capabilities that generate competitive advantage are so taken for granted, so much a part of the day-to-day experience of managers in a firm, that these managers are unaware of them. Itami (1987) calls these kinds of taken-for-granted organizational characteristics "invisible assets." Organizational resources and capabilities such as teamwork among top managers (Barney and Tyler, 1990), organizational culture (Barney, 1986b), and relationships with customers and suppliers may be "invisible" in this sense. If managers in firms that have such capabilities do not understand their relationship to competitive advantage, managers in other firms face significant challenges in understanding which resources they should imitate.

Second, managers may have multiple hypotheses about which resources and capabilities enable their firm to gain a competitive advantage, but they may be unable to evaluate which of these resources and capabilities, alone or in combination, actually create the competitive advantage. For example, if one asks successful entrepreneurs what enabled them to be successful, they are likely to reply with several hypotheses such as "hard work, willingness to take risks, and a high-quality top management team." However, if one asks what happened to unsuccessful entrepreneurs, they too are likely to suggest that their firms were characterized by "hard work, willingness to take risks, and a high-quality top management team." It may be the case that "hard work, willingness to take risks, and a high-quality top management team" are important resources and capabilities for entrepreneurial firm success. However, other factors may also play a role. Without rigorous experiments, it is difficult to establish which of these resources have a causal relationship with competitive advantage and which do not.

Finally, it may be that not just a few resources and capabilities enable a firm to gain a competitive advantage but that literally thousands of these organizational attributes, bundled together, generate these advantages. Dierickx and Cool (1989) emphasize the importance of the interconnectedness of asset stocks and asset mass efficiencies as barriers to imitation. When the resources and capabilities that generate competitive advantage are complex networks of relationships between individuals, groups, and technology, imitation can be costly.

Historically, the field of strategic management has been enamored with the ability that some firms have to make correct "big decisions." This emphasis on "big" strategic decisions as the source of sustained competitive advantage reflects the original emphasis on general managers discussed in Section 5.1. The success of some organizations may be traceable to their ability to make correct "big" decisions (for example, IBM's big decision about the 360 series in the l960s, Boeing's big decision about the 747 in the 1970s). But in other cases, competitive advantage depends not on the ability to make a few big decisions well but on the ability to make numerous small decisions well. The ability to make numerous small decisions well is almost invisible to those outside the firm, for each of these decisions, by itself, is inconsequential. Collectively, however, they provide a firm a competitive advantage that is costly to imitate.

Consider, for example, The Mailbox, Inc., a very successful firm in the bulk mailing business in Dallas, Texas. If there ever was a business where it seems unlikely that a firm would have sustained competitive advantages, it is bulk mailing. Firms in this industry gather mail from customers, sort it by postal code, and then take it to the post office to be mailed. Where is the competitive advantage? Yet The Mailbox has enjoyed an enormous market share advantage in the Dallas–Fort Worth area for several years. Why?

When asked, senior managers at The Mailbox have some difficulty explaining their success. Indeed, they can point to no "big decisions" they have made to generate this advantage. However, as one examines their finance function, their operations, their human resource function, their marketing and sales function, as well as the way they treat their employees, it becomes clear that The Mailbox's success depends not on the ability to do one thing well but rather on the ability to do the hundreds of thousands of things needed to run a bulk mailing business well. Individually, each one of these resources and capabilities is not costly to imitate. Collectively, however, they are very costly to imitate. These hundreds of thousands of resources and capabilities are difficult to describe. Their relationship with this firm's overall competitive advantage is not clear. Firms seeking to imitate The Mailbox's success face significant challenges in even understanding what they might want to imitate, let alone how they should go about imitating this firm (personal communication).

3. *Social Complexity*—A third reason why a firm's resources and capabilities may be costly to imitate is that they may be socially complex phenomena, beyond the ability o.f firms to systematically manage and influence. When competitive advantages are based in such complex social phenomena, the ability of other firms to imitate these resources and capabilities either through direct duplication or through substitution is significantly constrained. Efforts to influence these kinds of phenomena are likely to be much more costly than they would be if these phenomena developed in a natural way over time in a firm (Porras and Berg, 1978).

A wide variety of firm resources and capabilities may be socially complex. Examples include the interpersonal relations among managers (Hambrick, 1987), a firm's culture (Barney, 1986b), and a firm's reputation among suppliers (Porter, 1980) and customers (Klein, Crawford, and Alchian, 1978; Klein and Leffler, 1981). Notice that in most of these cases it is possible to specify how these socially complex resources add value to a firm. Thus there is little or no causal ambiguity surrounding the link between these resources and capabilities and competitive advantage. But understanding that an organizational culture with certain attributes or that quality relations among managers can improve a firm's efficiency and effectiveness does not necessarily imply that firms lacking these attributes can engage in a systematic effort to create them, or that low-cost substitutes for them exist (Barney, 1986b, Dierickx and Cool, 1989). For the time being, such social engineering may be beyond the abilities of most firms (Barney, 1986b; Porras and Berg, 1978). At the very least, such social engineering is likely to be much more costly than it would be if socially complex resources evolved naturally within a firm.

This discussion does not mean to suggest that socially complex resources and capabilities do not change and evolve in an organization. They clearly do. Nor does this discussion mean to suggest that managers can never radically alter an organization's socially complex resources and capabilities. Such transformational leaders do seem to exist and do have an enormous impact on the socially complex resources and capabilities in a firm (Tichy and Devanna, 1986). Managers such as the late Mike Walsh at Tenneco, Lee Iacocca at Chrysler, and Jack Welch at General Electric are apparently such leaders. However, transformational leaders themselves are socially complex phenomena. The fact that a leader in one firm can transform the firm's socially complex resources and capabilities does not necessarily mean that other firms will be able to duplicate this feat at low cost. It may even be the case that although a particular leader may be able to transform the socially complex resources and capabilities in one firm, this same leader would be unable to transform the socially complex resources and capabilities in another firm (Tichy and Devanna, 1986).

Although the ability of socially complex resources and capabilities to generate sustained competitive advantages has been emphasized so far, *nonvaluable* socially complex resources and capabilities can create sustained competitive *disadvantages* for a firm. For example, large integrated steel firms, like USX, are saddled with organizational cultures, values, and management traditions that prevent them from adopting new technologies in a timely and efficient manner. These firms face significant competitive disadvantages compared to mini-mill producers such as Nucor, Florida Steel, North Star Steel, and Chaparral (Ghemawat and Stander, 1992).

It is interesting to note that firms seeking to imitate complex physical technology often do not face the cost disadvantages of imitating complex social phenomena. A great deal of physical technology (machine tools, robots, and so forth) can be purchased in supply markets (Barney, 1991). Even when a firm develops its own unique physical technology, reverse engineering tends to diffuse this technology among competing firms in a low-cost manner (Lieberman, 1987). Indeed, the costs of imitating a successful physical technology are often lower than the costs of developing a new technology (see Section 4.2).

Although physical technology is usually not costly to imitate, the application of this technology in a firm is likely to call for a wide variety of socially complex organizational resources and capabilities. These organizational resources may be costly to imitate, and, if they are valuable and rare, the combination of physical and socially complex resources may be a source of sustained competitive advantage.

For example, most medium-size and large firms own management information systems that provide information about accounting performance, personnel, and operations (Fuerst, Mata, and Barney, 1995). The computers, other hardware, and software that are used in these systems can usually be purchased. Even customized software developed in a firm can be imitated (by direct duplication or by a firm developing equivalent substitute software) without a significant cost disadvantage. However, in some firms, management information systems are tightly integrated with management decision making, information systems managers have close working relationships with line managers, and the management information system is a vital day-to-day tool in running the firm. These kinds of firms are likely to have a competitive advantage compared to firms that own a management information system but do not fully utilize it. Firms at a competitive disadvantage will be able to purchase the most up-to-date hardware and software. But these purchases by themselves will not generate competitive parity, because it is the socially complex link between the management information system and other parts of the organization that is the source of the advantage.

This interaction between physical resources and socially complex organizational resources is at the heart of many of the difficulties that U.S. firms have had imitating the manufacturing success of Japanese firms. Numerous firms, including Federal-Mogul Corporation (an auto parts manufacturer) and General Motors, have found that advanced physical technology, including computers and robots, by itself, does not assure high-quality, low-cost manufacturing. Rather, these physical resources must be part of a larger, socially complex manufacturing system. Thus despite investments in physical technology at five hundred leading U.S. manufacturing firms of over $800 billion, quality and costs are often still not comparable to those of competing Japanese firms (Naj, 1993).

4. Patents—At first glance, it might appear that a firm's patents would make it very costly for competitors to imitate a firm's products (Rumelt, 1984). Patents do have this effect in some industries. For example, patents in the pharmaceutical industry effectively foreclose other firms from attempting to develop competing drugs until a firm's patents expire (Porter, 1980). Patents raised the cost of imitation in the instant photography market as well.

However, from another point of view, a firm's patents may decrease, rather than increase, the costs of imitation. When a firm files for patent protection, it is forced to reveal a significant amount of information about its product. Governments require this information to ensure that the technology in question is patentable. By obtaining a patent, a firm may provide important information to competitors about how to imitate its technology (Lieberman and Montgomery, 1988).

Moreover, as suggested in Section 4.2, most technological developments in an industry are diffused throughout firms in that industry in a relatively brief period of time, even if the technology in question is patented. And patented technology is not immune from low-cost imitation. Patents may restrict direct duplication for a time, but they may actually increase the chances of substitution by functionally equivalent technologies.

Although patents may not be immune from low-cost imitation, the skills and abilities that enable a firm to develop numerous new products or services over time can be a source of sustained competitive advantage even though any one of these products or services may be imitated. Consider, for example, the performance of Sony. Most observers agree that Sony possesses special management and coordination skills that enable it to conceive, design, and manufacture high-quality miniaturized consumer electronics. However, virtually every time Sony brings out a new miniaturized product, several of its competitors quickly duplicate that product through reverse engineering, thereby reducing Sony's technological advantage. In what way can Sony's socially complex miniaturization resources and capabilities be a source of sustained competitive advantage when most of Sony's products are quickly imitated through direct duplication?

After Sony introduces each new product, it experiences a rapid increase in profits attributable to the new product's unique features. This increase, however, leads other firms to reverse-engineer the Sony product and introduce their own version. Increased competition results in a reduction in the profits associated with a new product. Thus at the level of individual products, Sony apparently enjoys only temporary competitive advantages. However, looking at the total returns earned by Sony across all of its new products over time makes clear the source of Sony's sustained competitive advantage: By exploiting its resources and capabilities in miniaturization, Sony is able to constantly introduce new and exciting personal electronics products. No one of these products generates a sustained competitive advantage. But over time, across several such product introductions, Sony's resource and capability advantages lead to sustained competitive advantages (Schlender, 1992).

The Question of Organization

A firm's potential for competitive advantage depends on the value, rareness, and imitability of its resources and capabilities. However, to fully realize this potential, a firm must be organized to exploit its resources and capabilities. These observations lead to the question of organization.

> *The Question of Organization.* Is a firm organized to exploit the full competitive potential of its resources and capabilities?

Numerous components of a firm's organization are relevant to the question of organization, including its formal reporting structure, its explicit management control systems, and its compensation policies. These components, often called *complementary* resources and capabilities, have limited ability to generate competitive advantage in isolation, but in combination with other resources and capabilities they can enable a firm to realize its full potential for competitive advantage (Amit and Schoemaker, 1993).

For example, it has already been suggested that much of Caterpillar's sustained competitive advantage in the heavy construction industry can be traced to its becoming the sole supplier of this equipment to Allied forces in the Second World War. However, if Caterpillar's management had not taken advantage of this opportunity by implementing a global formal reporting structure, global inventory and other control systems, and compensation policies that created incentives for employees to work around the world, then Caterpillar's potential for competitive advantage would not have been fully realized. By themselves, these attributes of Caterpillar's organization could not be a source of competitive advantage—that is, adopting a global organizational form was relevant for Caterpillar only because it was pursuing a global opportunity. However, this organization was essential for Caterpillar to realize its full competitive advantage potential.

In a similar way, much of Wal-Mart's continuing competitive advantage in the discount retailing industry can be attributed to its early entry into rural markets in the southern United States. However, to fully exploit this geographic advantage, Wal-Mart needed to implement appropriate reporting structures, control systems, and compensation policies. One component of Wal-Mart's organization—its point-of-purchase inventory control system—is being imitated by Kmart and thus by itself is not likely to be a source of sustained competitive advantage. But this inventory control system has enabled Wal-Mart to take full advantage of its rural locations by decreasing the probability of stockouts in those locations.

Having an appropriate organization in place has enabled Caterpillar and Wal-Mart to realize the full competitive advantage potential of their other resources and capabilities. Having an inappropriate organization in place prevented Xerox from taking full advantage of some of its most critical valuable, rare, and costly-to-imitate resources and capabilities.

Through the 1960s and early 1970s, Xerox invested in a series of very innovative technology development research efforts. Xerox managed this research effort by creating a stand-alone research center in Palo Alto, California (Xerox Palo Alto Research Center—PARC), and by assembling a large group of highly creative and innovative scientists and engineers to work there. Left to their own devices, the scientists and engineers at Xerox PARC developed an amazing array of technological innovations—the personal computer, the "mouse," windows-type software, the laser printer, the "paperless office," ethernet, and so forth. In retrospect, it is clear that the market potential of these technologies was enormous. Moreover, because they were developed at Xerox PARC, they were rare. Xerox might have been able to gain some important first-mover advantages if the organization had been able to translate these technologies into products, thereby increasing the cost to other firms of imitating these technologies.

Xerox possessed very valuable, rare, and costly-to-imitate resources and capabilities in the technologies developed at Xerox PARC, but Xerox did not have an organization in place to take advantage of these resources. No structure existed whereby Xerox PARC innovations could become known to managers elsewhere in the Xerox organization. Indeed, most Xerox managers—even many senior managers—were unaware of these technological developments through the mid-1970s. Once they finally became aware of them, very few of the technologies survived Xerox's highly bureaucratic product development process—a process in which product development projects were divided into hundreds of minute tasks and progress in each task was reviewed by dozens of large committees. Even innovations that survived the product development process were not exploited by Xerox managers, because management compensation at Xerox depended almost exclusively on maximizing current revenue. Short-term profitability was relatively less important in compensation calculations, and the development of markets for future sales and profitability was essentially irrelevant. Xerox's formal reporting structure, its explicit management control systems, and its compensation policies were all inconsistent with exploiting the valuable, rare, and costly-to-imitate resources developed at Xerox PARC. Not surprisingly, Xerox failed to exploit any of these potential sources of sustained competitive advantage (Kearns and Nadler, 1992; Smith and Alexander, 1988).

5.3   APPLYING THE VRIO FRAMEWORK

The questions of value, rareness, imitability, and organization can be brought together into a single framework to understand the return potential associated with exploiting any of a firm's resources or capabilities. This is done in Table 5.2. The relationship of the VRIO framework to traditional SWOT analysis of strengths and weaknesses is presented in Table 5.3.

If a resource or capability controlled by a firm is not valuable, that resource will not enable a firm to choose or implement strategies that exploit environmental opportunities or neutralize environmental threats. Organizing to exploit this resource will increase a firm's costs or decrease its revenues. These types of resources are weaknesses in a SWOT analysis. Firms will either have to fix these weaknesses or avoid using these resources when choosing and implementing strategies. If firms do exploit these kinds of resources and capabilities, they can expect to put themselves at a competitive disadvantage compared to firms that either do not possess these nonvaluable resources or do not use them in conceiving and implementing strategies. Firms at a competitive disadvantage are likely to earn below-normal economic profits.

If a resource or capability is valuable but not rare, exploiting this resource in conceiving and implementing strategies will generate competitive parity and normal economic performance. Exploiting these valuable-but-not-rare resources will generally not create above-normal economic performance for a firm, but failure to exploit them can put a firm at a competitive disadvantage. In this sense, valuable-but-not-rare resources can be thought of as strengths in a SWOT analysis.

If a resource or capability is valuable and rare but not costly to imitate, exploiting this resource will generate a temporary competitive advantage for a firm and above-normal economic profits. A firm that exploits this kind of resource is, in an important sense, gaining a first-mover advantage, since it is the first firm that is able to exploit a particular resource. However, once competing firms observe this competitive advantage, they will be able to acquire or develop the resources needed to implement this strategy through direct duplication or substitution at

TABLE 5.2
The VRIO Framework

Is a resource or capability . . .

Valuable?	Rare?	Costly to imitate?	Exploited by the organization?	Competitive implications	Economic performance
No	—	—	No	Competitive disadvantagel	Below normal
Yes	No	—	↑	Competitive parity	Normal
Yes	Yes	No	↓	Temporary competitive advantage	Above normal
Yes	Yes	Yes	Yes	Sustained competitive advantage	Above normal

no cost disadvantage compared to the first-moving firm. Over time, any competitive advantage that the first mover obtained would be competed away as other firms imitate the resources needed to compete. However, between the time a firm gains a competitive advantage by exploiting a valuable and rare but imitable resource or capability, and the time that competitive advantage is competed away through

TABLE 5.3
The Relationship Between the VRIO Framework and the Traditional SWOT Analysis of Strengths and Weaknesses

Is a resource or capability . . .

Valuable?	Rare?	Costly to imitate?	Exploited by the organization?	Strength or weakness
No	—	—	No	Weakness
Yes	No	—	↑	Strength
Yes	Yes	No	↓	Strength and distinctive competence
Yes	Yes	Yes	Yes	Strength and sustainable distinctive competence

imitation, the first-moving firm can earn above-normal economic performance. Consequently, this type of resource or capability can be thought of as an organizational strength and distinctive competence in a SWOT analysis.

If a resource or capability is valuable, rare, and costly to imitate, exploiting this resource will generate a sustained competitive advantage and above-normal economic profits. In this case, competing firms face a significant cost disadvantage in imitating a successful firm's resources and capabilities, and thus they cannot imitate this firm's strategies. As suggested in Section 5.2, this cost advantage may reflect the unique history of the successful firm, causal ambiguity about which resources to imitate, or the socially complex nature of these resources and capabilities. In any case, attempts to compete away the advantages of firms that exploit these resources will not generate above-normal or even normal performance for imitating firms. Even if these firms are able to acquire or develop the resources or capabilities in question, the very high costs of doing so would put them at a competitive disadvantage compared to the firm that already possessed the valuable, rare, and costly-to-imitate resources. These kinds of resources and capabilities are organizational strengths and sustainable distinctive competencies in a SWOT analysis.

The question of organization operates as an adjustment factor in the VRIO framework. For example, if a firm has a valuable, rare, and costly-to-imitate resource and capability but fails to organize itself to take full advantage of this resource, some of its potential above-normal return could be lost (this is the Xerox example). Extremely poor organization, in this case, could actually lead a firm that has the potential for above-normal performance to earn normal or even below-normal performance.

To examine how the VRIO framework can be applied in analyzing real strategic issues, consider the examples of the Macintosh computer, the "Pepsi Challenge," and the Polaroid SX-70 camera.

THE MACINTOSH COMPUTER

The development of personal computers has revolutionized the computing and information-processing businesses. As personal computers have moved rapidly through hardware and software generations, they have become easier to use and more versatile. However, this has not always been so. When IBM first introduced its personal computer, the PC, software was limited, as were training and documentation needed to assist owners in using their PCs. Indeed, it was not unusual for first-time computer users to spend thirty or forty hours to learn how to turn a PC on, bring the operating system on-line, and productively use the PC.

Apple Computer's approach to the development of its Macintosh was completely different from IBM's approach. The Macintosh was conceived as a user-friendly computer, one that would be easy for first-time computer users to operate, have simple forms of communication, and have powerful graphics capabilities. It took fifteen minutes (not thirty hours) to figure out how to use the Apple Macintosh. The IBM PC user manuals stacked several feet high; the Apple Macintosh user manual was two inches thick.

A variety of resources and capabilities were needed to develop the Macintosh computer at Apple. For example, engineers and senior managers at Apple needed to share the vision that a user-friendly computer could be developed. Moreover, they needed to possess this shared vision before other personal computer firms possessed it. Also needed were enormous coordination and teamwork between the hardware design team, the software design team, and the manufacturing design team so that the final computer would be easy to use and powerful and could be built in a way that made it affordable. There also had to be a willingness among Apple employees, in general, to experiment with new technologies and ideas (such as the mouse and windows-oriented software displays) and to take the risks associated with developing an alternative to the IBM standard. Apple also required the financial resources to engage in this bold experiment (it helped that Apple had over $100 million in cash from its successful Apple I and II lines of computers as it began the Macintosh project). Numerous other intangible, almost invisible assets, were also important in enabling Apple to conceive of and implement the Macintosh strategy.

Were these resources and capabilities valuable? In other words, did these resources and capabilities enable Apple to exploit environmental opportunities or neutralize environmental threats? The answer to these questions is apparently yes, since customers could save an enormous amount of time (and frustration) beginning with a Macintosh. Also a powerful graphics capability enabled Macintosh to be used in applications that were more difficult for IBM PC users. Notice, however, that asserting that these resources were valuable does not imply that the resources that led to the development of the IBM PC were not valuable. Rather, those resources—IBM's large market share in the mainframe industry, its established relationships with computer buyers in large corporations, and so forth—enabled IBM to develop a computer that became the de facto industry standard and the platform for which an enormous amount of software was written.

Were Apple's resources and capabilities rare? Apparently other firms in the computer industry were committing their time and energy to developing hardware and software for the IBM standard and were less willing to commit to the development of an entirely separate user-friendly system. Even those firms that developed their own standard (for example, Hewlett-Packard's 150 series) still built on IBM's original hardware and software decisions.

Were Apple's resources and capabilities costly to imitate? Right after the Macintosh was introduced, it seemed reasonable to expect that software engineers working on the IBM PC would soon be able to duplicate most, if not all, of the Macintosh's user-friendly characteristics. But this was not the case. Although the IBM PC has become more powerful, and software for the IBM PC (and its descendants) has become widely available, most observers agree that the Macintosh retained its user-friendly advantage for several years.

Only recently, with the development of Windows software by Microsoft, has true Mac-like user-friendliness come to the IBM PC. Even now, true Macintosh believers scoff at Windows. It is interesting to note, however, that with the introduction of Windows and increased competition in user-friendly computers, Apple has reduced the price of its Macintosh computers and entered into a variety of cooperative arrangements with IBM (Yoffie, 1992). Both actions are consistent with the observation that competition in user-friendly personal computers has increased.

Since the development of alternative approaches to user-friendly computers took so long, and apparently was so difficult, it is not unreasonable to conclude that at least some of the resources and capabilities that Apple used to develop the Macintosh were costly to imitate. For example, Apple managers' and engineers' belief that they could build a user-friendly computer before managers and engineers in other firms came to this conclusion seems to be an important path-dependent resource. Also, the close relationships between Apple hardware, software, and manufacturing engineers is a socially complex relationship. IBM has relied on arm's-length relationships with numerous independent software suppliers, including Microsoft. This choice may have delayed the interactive development of hardware and software needed for a user-friendly computer. If Apple was organized correctly to exploit these resources—not a totally realistic assumption given the highly publicized conflicts among top managers at Apple (Yoffie, 1992)—Apple should have earned above-normal economic returns on the use of these resources to develop and market the Macintosh computer. Most reports suggest that, in fact, the Macintosh computer has been a major profit producer for Apple.

However, as will be discussed in Section 5.4, sustained competitive advantages do not last forever. Apple now appears to be attempting to position itself to survive in a world in which the user-friendliness of its personal computer is no longer a competitive advantage.

THE "PEPSI CHALLENGE"

The cola wars between Pepsi and Coke in the United States and throughout the world are well known (Pearson and Irwin, 1988). However, Pepsi raised this competition to a new level during the mid-1970s with a new advertising campaign: the "Pepsi Challenge." It seems that numerous blind taste tests had indicated that consumers preferred the taste of Pepsi over the taste of Coke. To exploit this preference, Pepsi planned a new round of advertisements, celebrity endorsements, coupons, and retail discounts. The "Pepsi Challenge" was introduced in the Dallas–Fort Worth, Texas, market. At the time, there were three important soft drinks in that market: Coke, Pepsi, and Dr Pepper.

In implementing the "Pepsi Challenge," PepsiCo was attempting to acquire market share traditionally held by Coke and other firms in Dallas–Fort Worth. There is little doubt that adding market share has the potential to increase a firm's revenues in the soft-drink industry (Pearon and Irwin, 1988). Although Pepsi could reduce its costs by increasing the efficiency of the soft-drink bottlers that it owns, increasing revenues from the acquisition of market share is likely to have a much larger financial impact.

As Pepsi implemented the "Challenge" to acquire market share in Dallas–Fort Worth, the organization brought to bear an enormous wealth of resources and capabilities, including high-quality marketing and sales staffs, an excellent distribution system, and sufficient financial backing to do the job. All these resources were valuable, but were they also rare? Put another way, was there any resource or capability that Pepsi could use to implement the "Pepsi Challenge" that Coca-Cola could not use to defend its market share? The answer is *probably not*. Both firms possessed enormous marketing, sales, and distribution skills, and both had enormous financial strength. It seems likely that Coke could quickly imitate any action that Pepsi took. Assuming both firms were efficiently organized (a reasonable assumption in this case), the resources and capabilities that Pepsi brought to bear in the "Pepsi Challenge" were valuable but not rare (compared to Coke's resources and capabilities), and thus would generate only competitive parity and normal economic performance.

The situation was very different in the competition for market share between Pepsi and Dr Pepper. Resources and capabilities that would enable Pepsi to acquire share were still valuable. However, Pepsi had a broad range of resources that Dr Pepper (at the time, an independent soft-drink producer) did not have. Moreover, it would be very costly for Dr Pepper to acquire resources comparable to Pepsi's reputation in the market, huge advertising budget, and high-powered distribution network. Thus in the competition between Pepsi and Dr Pepper for market share, Pepsi possessed not only valuable but also rare and costly-to-imitate resources and capabilities. In this competitive battle, Pepsi seemed likely to earn above-normal economic performance.

The results of the "Pepsi Challenge" in Dallas–Fort Worth are quite interesting. After six months of intensive competition, including retail discounts, coupons, and increased advertising, Coke's market share increased from 33 percent to 37 percent, Pepsi's share doubled from 7 percent to 14 percent, and Dr Pepper's share went down "significantly." However, after six months of the "Pepsi Challenge," the retail price of soft drinks in this market was half of the prechallenge level. Pepsi doubled its market share but cut its revenue in half to do so. This outcome is very consistent with normal economic returns. Apparently, both Pepsi and Coke took market share away from Dr Pepper. However, the cost of acquiring that share increased so that the cost of acquiring share approximately equaled its value and thus was a source of normal economic returns for Pepsi (and Coke) in Dallas–Fort Worth.

Each of the firms in this competition learned some valuable lessons. Dr Pepper learned that if it wanted to be a major player in the soft-drink industry, then it would need to develop resources and capabilities that rivaled those of Pepsi and Coke. It was very unlikely that Dr Pepper could develop these resources on its own; thus Dr Pepper has gone through a series of acquisitions, joint ventures, and other cooperative activities to try to develop a resource base large enough to survive in this industry. Most recently, Dr Pepper and Seven-Up have joined forces in a merger (Pearson and Irwin, 1988).

PepsiCo and Coca-Cola learned that head-to-head competition for market share is not likely to be a source of competitive advantage for firms with equally matched resources and capabilities. Instead of continuing this head-to-head competition, PepsiCo and Coca-Cola have searched for alternative strategic directions. PepsiCo has diversified away from a sole reliance on soft drinks and has moved into non-cola drinks, the fast-food business, and the snack-food business. In its cola operations, Pepsi continues to seek out younger cola drinkers. Coca-Cola, after abandoning some unsuccessful diversification moves, remains focused on cola soft drinks but now emphasizes international sales. Indeed, over 60 percent of Coca-Cola's profits come from overseas sales, where Pepsi is not as strong a competitor (Pearson and

Irwin, 1988). In the domestic market, Coca-Cola has steered its marketing efforts more toward older cola drinkers. All this is not to suggest that Pepsi and Coca-Cola no longer compete in the soft-drink industry. They clearly do. However, both firms seem to have backed away from the intense rivalry of the cola wars.

THE POLAROID SX-70 CAMERA

Polaroid has historically been the leader in the instant photography market. Over the years, it has developed enormous research and development and product innovation capabilities. These resources, linked with Polaroid's strong patent position in instant photography, have been a source of above-normal performance for many years.

Although Polaroid enjoyed a strong position in this industry, its traditional products were difficult to use. The cameras were large and bulky, the development process required users to wait up to sixty seconds before using the camera again (users needed to time the development process, which made rapid use of the camera difficult), and its use left chemical-impregnated wastepaper. Polaroid needed a new approach to the instant photography market. This new approach became the SX-70 camera.

In developing the SX-70 camera, Polaroid had several objectives, including (1) a camera small enough to fit in a purse or pocket, (2) a single-lens reflex focusing system, (3) a development process that generated no waste, and (4) a development process that did not require users to wait before using the camera again. Polaroid mustered its impressive research capabilities and developed a camera that met all four objectives. Unfortunately, this development process, plus the costs of developing new manufacturing facilities, cost Polaroid over $3 billion. To recoup its costs, Polaroid needed to acquire over 80 percent of the worldwide market share for high-priced, high-performance cameras with the SX-70 (Berg and Merry, 1984). Thus the SX-70 found itself competing directly with Nikon, Cannon, and other well-respected cameras. Needless to say, Polaroid was unable to gain the required 80 percent share.

A VRIO analysis can be helpful in analyzing returns to the resources used to develop the SX-70 camera. Polaroid's research and development skills were *potentially* valuable in the instant photography market, but their use in developing a very expensive instant camera apparently did not meet customer needs or respond to other environmental opportunities in a timely manner. Thus exploiting these resources to develop the SX-70 camera had the effect of increasing costs without significantly increasing revenues. Because this application of these resources was not valuable, the fact that the resources were rare and costly to imitate did not enable the firm to earn normal or above-normal returns. Thus the exploitation of Polaroid's resources to develop the SX-70 camera should have generated below-normal economic performance.

After the lackluster market response to the SX-70 camera, Polaroid began stripping features from the camera to reduce its price. Over a period of several years, the price was reduced to as low as $19.95. At this price, Polaroid was able to sell a large number of instant cameras, although the profitability of this product was reduced by the high costs ($3 billion) of developing the original instant camera. Recently, Polaroid has reintroduced a modified version of the SX-70 camera under a different product name—the Spectra camera. This camera, plus the more careful application of Polaroid's enormous valuable, rare, and costly-to-imitate innovative resources, has enabled Polaroid to emerge from its SX-70 problems to become financially successful.

Ironically, the cost of imitating Polaroid's research and development skills has been reemphasized by a legal judgment against Kodak. The courts decided that Kodak had been unable to develop its own independent instant photography technology and had encroached on Polaroid's patents. Kodak was forced to pay a substantial penalty to Polaroid and leave the instant photography market. Polaroid's current performance reflects its resource-based control of the instant photography market (although the threat of electronic instant photography is certainly real).

5.4   LIMITATIONS OF THE VRIO FRAMEWORK

The resource-based view of the firm and the VRIO framework presented in Table 5.2 provide a powerful tool for analyzing a firm's internal organizational strengths and weaknesses. But this approach, like S-C-P-based models of the analysis of environmental threats and opportunities, has limitations. Three of the most important are discussed below.

SUSTAINED COMPETITIVE ADVANTAGE AND ENVIRONMENTAL UPHEAVAL

Earlier we suggested that a sustained competitive advantage does not last forever, even though it is founded on valuable, rare, and costly-to-imitate resources and capabilities. If the threats and opportunities that face a firm in its competitive environment remain relatively stable, then a firm with valuable, rare, and costly-to-imitate resources (if it is organized correctly) will be able to continue to exploit them to gain a competitive advantage. Also, if the types of threats and opportunities in a firm's environment evolve in predictable ways, a firm with these kinds of resources and capabilities will often be able to exploit and modify them to maintain a sustained competitive advantage. However, if a firm's threats and opportunities change in a rapid and *unpredictable* manner, the firm will often be unable to maintain a sustained competitive advantage.

These sudden and unpredictable changes in the threats and opportunities that face a firm are called *Schumpeterian revolutions* (Schumpeter, 1934), after Joseph Schumpeter, the economist who first described them and analyzed their economic consequences. Schumpeterian revolutions have the effect of drastically changing the value of a firm's resources by changing the threats and opportunities that face a firm. This may happen because of unanticipated changes in demand, radical new technological developments, violent political upheavals, and so forth.

Numerous industries are characterized by Schumpeterian revolutions. For example, the development of personal computers significantly altered the value of the manufacturing skills of typewriter companies. The development of electronic calculators significantly altered the value of the design and manufacturing skills of mechanical calculator firms. And the skills needed to manufacture high-quality vinyl long-playing records changed in value because of the introduction of compact disc technology.

The resource-based view of the firm can help managers choose strategies to gain sustained competitive advantage only as long as the rules of the game in an industry remain relatively fixed. But after a Schumpeterian revolution, what were weaknesses may become strengths and what were strengths may become weaknesses. Notice, however, that the competitive advantages of firms in this context are not competed away through imitation. Rather, they are replaced through a Schumpeterian revolution. Thus although sustained competitive advantages will not last forever, they are not competed away through imitation but can be displaced through revolutionary environmental changes.

MANAGERIAL INFLUENCE

A second limitation of the VRIO approach to studying organizational strengths and weaknesses is that it suggests that managers have a limited ability to create sustained competitive advantages. These limitations are summed up best, perhaps, by what might be called the *imitability paradox* (Barney, 1986b): The less costly it is for managers in a firm to develop or acquire resources that could generate competitive advantage, the less likely it is that these resources will be a source of sustained competitive advantage. In general, if any firm can develop or acquire a set of valuable resources at no cost disadvantage, then those resources will be imitable and a source of competitive parity in the long run.

What the imitability paradox suggests is that not all firms will be able to gain sustained competitive advantages. Managers in firms that have developed valuable, rare, and costly-to-imitate resources or capabilities over long periods of time (because of path dependence, causal ambiguity, or social complexity) may be able to help their firms gain sustained competitive advantages. But firms that do not have any of these special skills and capabilities, but attempt to acquire them without any cost advantages, will not gain sustained competitive advantages, because if one firm can acquire these resources, others will be able to as well.

Although the observation that not all firms will be able to obtain a sustained competitive advantage does suggest some limitations on managers' ability to affect firm performance, it is consistent with most research on the performance of firms in an industry (Jacobsen, 1988). In most industries, several firms (perhaps even the majority) apparently discover their own unique resources and capabilities and exploit them in ways that generate above-normal economic returns. However, there are often firms in an industry that are perpetually earning normal, and sometimes, below normal returns. These "perpetually failing" firms (Meyer and Zucker, 1989) simply have not developed valuable resources that would enable them to gain a sustained competitive advantage. Of course, at some point in the future, a Schumpeterian revolution may occur in these industries, making these perpetual losing firms suddenly able to gain competitive advantages and excel.

THE UNIT OF ANALYSIS

In S-C-P-based models of environmental opportunities and threats, the unit of analysis is the industry. This unit of analysis has several advantages for strategic analysts, not the least of which is access to data. Most government reports about firms are organized into industry categories, making information about the number of rivals, the power of suppliers and buyers, and so forth relatively accessible.

In resource-based models of organizational strengths and weaknesses, however, the unit of analysis shifts downward, inside the firm. The firm in this model is thought of as a bundle of resources and capabilities, and the analysis of the return potential of these resources must be conducted one resource at a time. Gaining access to this kind of intra-organizational information can be very difficult. These data problems are exacerbated when it is recognized that resources and capabilities can gain their ability to generate sustained competitive advantages precisely because they are difficult to describe and are invisible (Barney, 1991).

In the face of these challenges, it is tempting to raise the level of analysis of a firm's strengths and weaknesses to the level of the firm and analyze the value, rareness, imitability, and organization of a firm's products or services. This kind of analysis can be helpful, but it also can be misleading. Research on the diffusion of product technology cited in Section 4.2 (Lieberman and Montgomery, 1988) suggests that new products and services, with a few important exceptions, rapidly become diffused among a set of competing firms. However, as was suggested earlier for the Sony Corporation, a firm's particular product may be imitated and that firm still will have a sustained competitive advantage based on its underlying abilities to be innovative and creative.

Thus despite the significant challenges associated with firm resources as the unit of analysis in models of organizational strengths and weaknesses, a proper analysis seems to require an investigation of these intra-organizational phenomena. In the end, it is not surprising that understanding the implications of these intra-organizational resources will be critical in completing a SWOT analysis for a firm.

5.5   SUMMARY

This chapter develops a framework for analyzing a firm's organizational strengths and weaknesses. This framework is based on several literatures, including research on the impact of general managers in organizations, research on other types of distinctive competencies in a firm, work on Ricardian economics, and economic models of firm growth. The framework builds most directly on the resource-based view of the firm and on two critical assumptions: that firms have different resources and capabilities (the assumption of resource heterogeneity) and that these differences can persist over time (the assumption of resource immobility).

On the basis of these two assumptions, it is suggested that the answer to four questions can be used to determine the return potential of a firm's resources and capabilities. These four questions are the question of value, the question of rareness, the question of imitability, and the question of organization. This VRIO framework is applied to several real strategic situations. Three limitations of this approach—the impact of unanticipated changes in a firm's environment, limited managerial impact on performance, and data challenges associated with this unit of analysis—are also discussed.

REVIEW QUESTIONS

1. Which approach to strategy formulation is more likely to generate economic profits: (a) evaluating environmental opportunities and threats and then developing resources and capabilities to exploit these opportunities and neutralize these threats or (b) evaluating internal resources and capabilities and then searching for industries where they can be exploited? Why?

2. Which firm will have a higher level of economic performance: (a) a firm with valuable, rare, and costly-to-imitate resources and capabilities operating in a very attractive industry or (b) a firm with valuable, rare, and costly-to-imitate resources and capabilities operating in a very unattractive industry? Assume both these firms are appropriately organized. Explain your answer.

3. Which is more critical to sustaining human life—water or diamonds? Why do firms that provide water to customers generally earn lower economic profits than firms that provide diamonds?

4. Will a firm currently experiencing competitive parity be able to gain sustained competitive advantages by studying another firm that is currently experiencing sustained competitive advantage? Why or why not?

5. Your former college roommate calls you and asks to borrow $10,000 so that he can open a pizza restaurant in his hometown. He acknowledges that there is a high degree of rivalry in this market, that the cost of entry is low, and that there are numerous substitutes for pizza; but he believes that his pizza restaurant will have some sustained competitive advantages. For example, he is going to have sawdust on his floor, a variety of imported beers, and a late-night delivery service. Will you lend him the money? Why or why not?

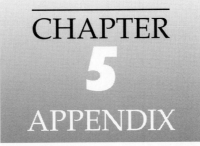

CHAPTER
5
APPENDIX

Value Chain Analysis and the Evaluation of Firm Strengths and Weaknesses

The VRIO framework can be used to evaluate the ability of internal organizational resources to generate a competitive advantage. The application of this framework, in combination with models of environmental threat and opportunity discussed in Chapters 3 and 4, enables a firm to engage in a rigorous SWOT analysis to choose strategies to implement.

Although the VRIO framework can be used to evaluate the return potential of a firm's resources, it does not provide a list of resources that should be subjected to analysis. Often, devising such a list is not a significant problem. Managers can, in an ad hoc way, suggest possible distinctive competencies that can be subjected to VRIO analysis. In some circumstances, however, the systematic study of internal capabilities can be facilitated by a more systematic approach to listing internal resources. Value chain analysis can be helpful in this context.

This appendix describes what a value chain is and shows how it can be applied, in conjunction with the VRIO framework, to evaluate the return potential of a firm's resources.

WHAT IS A VALUE CHAIN?

Most goods or services are produced by a series of vertical business activities—acquiring supplies of raw materials, manufacturing intermediate products, manufacturing of final products, sales and distribution, after-sales service, and so forth (Porter, 1985). For example, the sale of gasoline involves several vertically related business functions, including exploration for oil, drilling for oil, pumping and shipping oil, oil refining, shipping refined products, and retail sale of refined products. This set of vertically related activities is a product's value chain.

The total economic value that is created by this vertical chain of activities is split among them; some parts of the value chain may create more of the total value than other parts. Also, these activities can be undertaken by different firms, or they can be done in a single firm. A vertically integrated firm tends to have more activities in the value chain within the boundaries of the firm; a less vertically integrated firm tends to have fewer activities in the value chain under direct control. The activities in a value chain, and how they are linked to one another within and between firms, can be thought of as resources and capabilities that may be distinctive competencies and thus should be subjected to VRIO analyses.

Two different generic value chains have been proposed in the literature (Grant, 1991a). The first, proposed by the management consulting firm McKinsey and Company, is presented in Fig. 5A.l. This relatively simple model suggests that the creation of value almost always involves six distinct activities: technology development, product design, manufacturing, marketing, distribution, and service. Firms can develop valuable, rare, and costly-to-imitate capabilities in any one, or in any combination, of these activities. For example, many have suggested

FIGURE 5A.1
The Generic Value Chain Developed by McKinsey and Company

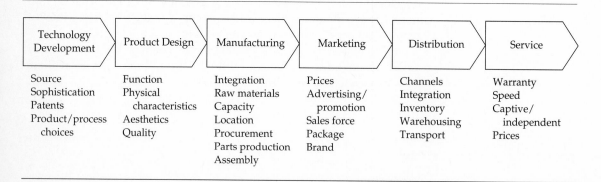

that Japanese firms have developed distinctive competencies in manufacturing and are now attempting to develop similar competencies in product design. One of the key questions facing Japanese firms concerns their ability to develop distinctive competencies in technology development, since until recently, most of the technology used by Japanese firms was developed elsewhere. Other firms may have no distinctive competencies in manufacturing but may have valuable, rare, and costly-to-imitate capabilities in product design, marketing, and distribution (such as The Limited in retail clothing).

A second generic value chain has been proposed by Porter (1985). This value chain, presented in Fig. 5A.2, divides value-creating activities into two large categories: primary activities and support activities. Primary activities include (1) inbound logistics (purchasing, inventory, and so forth), (2) production, (3) outbound logistics (warehousing and distribution), (4) sales and marketing, and (5) service (dealer support and customer service). Support activities include (1) infrastructure activities (planning, finance, information services, legal services), (2) technology development (research and development, product design), and (3) human resource management and development. Primary activities are directly associated with the manufacture and distribution of a product. Support activities assist a firm in accomplishing its primary activities. As is the case with the McKinsey value chain, a firm can develop distinctive competencies in any one, or in any combination, of the activities listed in Porter's value chain. These activities, and how they are linked to one another, are potential sources of distinctive competence and thus should be subjected to a VRIO analysis.

FIGURE 5A.2
The Generic Value Chain Developed by Porter. *Source:* Reprinted with permission of The Free Press, an imprint of Simon and Schuster, from *Competitive Advantage* by Michael E. Porter. Copyright © 1985 by The Free Press.

APPLYING THE VALUE CHAIN

The value chain, in conjunction with the VRIO framework, can be used to more completely explore sources of competitive advantage for any firm. Consider, again, the performance of Crown Cork & Seal, Inc. CC&S has earned consistently high rates of return in an industry (metal containers) characterized by high levels of threat and relatively low levels of opportunity. The value chain for metal containers (using a version of the McKinsey model) is presented in Fig. 5A.3. Notice that CC&S is not completely vertically integrated; it purchases raw materials (aluminum and steel) and sells its empty cans to food and beverage processors.

Although CC&S is not fully vertically integrated, it has developed distinctive competencies in some of the activities where it is vertically integrated. Consider, for example, sales activities. Other can companies' sales forces tend to adopt an arm's-length order-taking relationship with customers. CC&S, in contrast, aggressively seeks to satisfy customers, constantly searching for ways to decrease customer inventory, to develop new products that meet customer needs, and so forth. Over time, CC&S has developed close relationships with its customers. Those relationships are valuable (because they enable CC&S to meet its customers' needs, thereby increasing revenues). Those relationships are rare (few can-manufacturing firms have these kinds of relationships), and they are costly to imitate (because they are socially complex and would call for the changing of the entire culture of other can companies). CC&S's simple organizational structure enables the firm to exploit its sales activity competencies.

Another area where CC&S has a distinctive competence is in design and engineering activities (Hamermesh and Rosenbloom, 1989). Where most firms in this industry engage in research and development independent of specific customer needs, CC&S does R&D only to meet specific customer needs. This approach is valuable (since, as before, it enables CC&S to increase its revenues); it is rare (since few other firms have the relationships with customers needed to engage in this R&D); and it is costly to imitate (since the ability to engage in this type of R&D presumes close, cooperative relationships between a firm and its customers and such relationships are socially complex). Again, CC&S's organization, including reward systems that compensate R&D managers for solving customer problems instead of rewarding basic research, enables CC&S to exploit these capabilities.

Although CC&S has several distinctive competencies, not all of the activities it has integrated into are valuable, rare, and costly to imitate. For example, CC&S has adopted the industry standard in manufacturing, inventory holding, and distribution. These industry stan-

FIGURE 5A.3
Value Chain Analysis of Crown Cork & Seal. *Source:* From R. Grant, *Contemporary Strategy Analysis,* 1991. Basil Blackwell. Reprinted with permission.

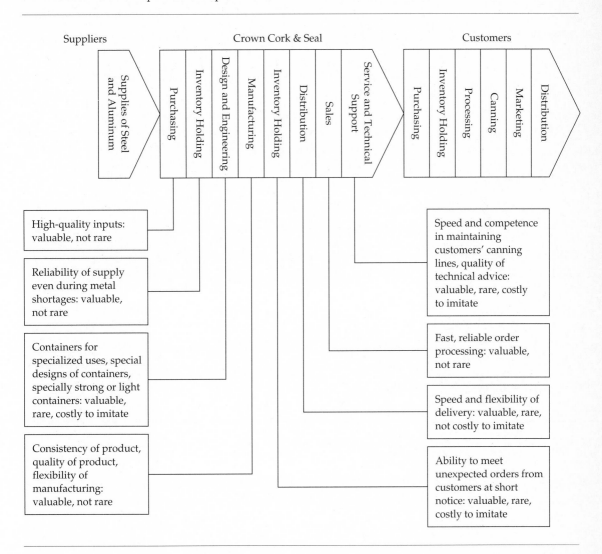

dards are valuable, but they are not rare and thus are not distinctive competencies for any firm in this industry, including CC&S. However, there seem to be few if any business activities where CC&S has adopted nonvaluable activities. Thus by exploiting those business activities where it has distinctive competencies, and by effectively managing its remaining activities, CC&S, overall, is able to obtain a sustained competitive advantage and above-normal economic profits despite an unfriendly competitive environment.

REVIEW QUESTIONS

1. Conduct a value chain analysis of writing a case analysis report for your strategic management professor.

2. How can you use value chain analysis to help your former college roommate learn how to earn economic profits from entering the fast-food pizza business in his hometown (see review question 1 in Chapter 3 and review question 5 in Chapter 5)?

PART II

BUSINESS STRATEGIES

CHAPTER 6

Competitive Strategies:
Cost Leadership

In Part 1 we examined the analytical tools needed to evaluate a firm's environmental threats and opportunities and its organizational strengths and weaknesses. Porter's (1980) five forces model was the major tool for analyzing threats. Opportunities associated with those threats, along with Porter's (1980) generic industry structures, were the major tools for analyzing opportunities. These tools all built on the structure-conduct-performance paradigm in industrial organizational economics. The VRIO framework was the major tool for analyzing organizational strengths and weaknesses. This framework built on the resource-based view of the firm.

An understanding of the threats and opportunities facing a firm, and of the strengths and weaknesses that a firm has, is an important precondition for strategic choice and action. However, the specific activities that firms can engage in to neutralize threats and exploit opportunities and strengths while avoiding or fixing weaknesses have yet to be specified in detail. These strategies are the subject of Parts 2 and 3. In Part 2 we examine specific strategies that firms can pursue within a particular market or industry. These types of strategies are usually called business strategies. In Part 3 we shift attention from actions firms take within a single market or industry and examine the strategies firms can pursue in leveraging their resources and capabilities across several markets or industries. These types of strategies are called corporate strategies.

6.1   GENERIC BUSINESS STRATEGIES

Firms in a single market or industry can pursue almost an infinite number of strategies. However, it is possible to divide these numerous specific strategies into two large categories: competitive strategies and cooperative strategies. Firms pursue competitive strategies when they seek to improve or maintain their performance through independent actions in a specific market or industry. Competitive strategies imagine independent firms trying to, in some sense, beat out other firms. These other firms could include a firm's rivals, substitutes, new entrants, suppliers, and buyers.

There are two major types of competitive business strategies: cost leadership and product differentiation (Porter, 1980). Firms pursuing cost-leadership strategies attempt to gain advantages by lowering their costs below those of competing firms. Firms pursuing product differentiation strategies attempt to gain advantages by increasing the perceived value of the products or services they provide to customers. Referring to the definition of *economic performance* in Chapter 2, we may say that cost-leadership strategies focus on reducing a firm's costs to enhance its performance and that product differentiation strategies focus on increasing a firm's revenues to enhance its performance. Cost-leadership strategies are discussed in detail in this chapter. Product differentiation strategies are discussed in Chapter 7.

Competitive business strategies are important strategic alternatives for many firms, but they are not the only business strategic alternatives. Over the last several years, more and more firms have begun to recognize that they can maintain or improve their economic performance not by competing with all the firms in their market or industry but by cooperating with at least some of them. Cooperative business strategies imagine collaborating firms working together to enhance their performance. Cooperation may develop between a firm and any of its competitors, including rivals, substitutes, new entrants, suppliers, or buyers.

Notice that although firms pursuing cooperative business strategies may be willing to collaborate with one another, this collaboration can have important competitive implications. Cooperating firms gain competitive advantages through their collaborative efforts. Instead of individual firms trying to beat out other individual firms (as is the case with competitive business strategies), competition unfolds among sets of cooperating firms trying to beat out other sets of cooperating firms as well as other individual firms in a market or industry.

As with competitive business strategies, there are two major types of cooperative business strategies: tacit collusion and strategic alliances. Firms pursuing tacit collusion strategies seek to enhance their performance by reducing the supply of products or services in a particular market or industry below the competitive level, thereby increasing prices above the competitive level. Thus firms pursuing this form of cooperative strategy focus primarily on revenues to enhance their performance. Firms pursuing strategic alliance strategies seek to enhance their performance by exploiting synergies with other firms in a market or industry. These synergies can reduce the costs of cooperating firms, increase their revenues, or do both. Tacit collusion cooperative strategies are discussed in Chapter 8; strategic alliance cooperative strategies are discussed in Chapter 9.

Both competitive and cooperative business strategies have been studied in the strategic management literature, but there is little doubt that competitive business strategies have received substantially more attention than cooperative ones. Competitive business strategies were first examined by Porter (1980). As Fig. 6.1 suggests, Porter argues that firms seeking to implement competitive strategies have three specific choices: cost leadership, product differentiation, and focus. Cost leadership and product differentiation are the competitive business strategy alternatives discussed in this and the next chapter.

According to Porter, a firm exploits the focus competitive alternative when it implements a cost-leadership or product differentiation strategy within a narrow market segment. Motel 6, with its national chain of low-price motels, has implemented a cost-leadership strategy. But La Quinta Inns, with its focus on the U.S. Southwest, has implemented a cost-leadership *focus* strategy. Macy's has implemented a product differentiation competitive strategy in retail clothing. But L. L. Bean has implemented a product differentiation *focus* strategy in catalogue sales of outdoors-oriented clothing. Because focus competitive

FIGURE 6.1
Generic Competitive Business Strategies Identified by Porter
Source: Reprinted with permission of The Free Press, an imprint of Simon and Schuster, from *Competitive Strategy: Techniques for Analyzing Industries and Competitors* by Michael E. Porter. Copyright © 1980 by The Free Press.

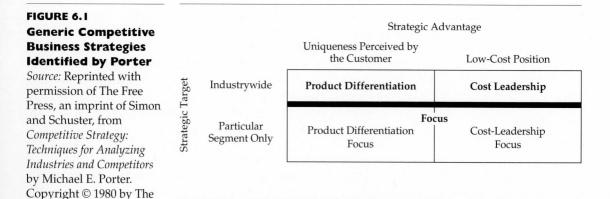

business strategies are special cases of either cost-leadership or product differentiation strategies, focus alternatives are discussed along with these other competitive strategy alternatives.

Cooperative business strategies are not as prominently featured in Porter's work, but they are important in the broader strategic management literature (Kogut, 1991; Hennart, 1989).

With this introduction, it is now possible to begin examining specific examples of each of these business strategic alternatives. We begin with cost-leadership strategies.

6.2 COST-LEADERSHIP COMPETITIVE BUSINESS STRATEGIES

DEFINING COST LEADERSHIP

A firm that chooses a cost-leadership strategy focuses on gaining advantages by reducing its economic costs below the cost of all of its competitors. This does not mean that the firm abandons alternative competitive strategies (such as product differentiation) or other generic strategic alternatives (such as cooperative or corporate generic strategies). Indeed, a single-minded focus on *just* independently reducing costs can lead a firm to make low-cost products that no one wants to buy. However, a firm pursuing a cost-leadership strategy focuses much of its effort on reducing its economic costs below those of competitors.

Numerous firms have pursued cost-leadership strategies. For example, Procter & Gamble has established Ivory soap as a cost leader in the home soap market. Ivory is packaged in plain paper wrappings and has avoided costly deodorants and fragrances. Many of Ivory's competitors (including Dial, Dove, and Irish Spring) are packaged in expensive foil wrappers and include deodorants and fragrances. Ivory is still advertised, but the advertisements tend to emphasize Ivory's low price, high value, and purity. Most of its competitors advertise their soaps' deodorizing effectiveness, ability to soften skin, sex appeal, and so forth. Ivory continues to be a successful product by keeping production costs low and providing solid value for customers (Lawrence and Sloan, 1992).

In automobiles, Hyundai has implemented a cost-leadership strategy with its emphasis on low-priced cars for basic transportation. Like Ivory soap, Hyundai spends a significant amount of money advertising its products, but the advertisements tend to emphasize Hyundai's sporty styling and high gas mileage. Hyundai is positioned as a fun and inexpensive car, not a high-performance sports car or a luxurious status symbol (Weiner, 1987). Hyundai's ability to sell these fun and inexpensive automobiles depends on its design choices (keep it simple) and low manufacturing costs.

Among watchmakers, Timex has very successfully implemented a cost-leadership strategy. Timex originally developed a low-cost replacement for expensive watch movements by substituting high-density steel pins ("pin levers") for jewels. However, with the development of more accurate and even less expensive electronic movements, Timex quickly moved to incorporate electronic movements into its watch line. Timex continues to advertise its low prices, its reliability ("Takes a lickin' and keeps on tickin'"), and overall value. A person wearing a Timex watch is unlikely to make any fashion statements but is likely to know what time it is (Roush, 1993).

SOURCES OF COST ADVANTAGE

There are many reasons why an individual firm may have a cost advantage over its competitors. A cost advantage is possible even when competing firms produce similar products. Some important sources of cost differences among firms are discussed below.

Size Differences and Economies of Scale

One of the most widely cited sources of cost advantage for a firm in a single business is its size (Scherer, 1980). When there are significant economies of scale in manufacturing, marketing, distribution, service, or other functions of a business, larger firms (up to some point) have a cost advantage over smaller firms. The relationship between firm size (measured in terms of volume of production) and costs (measured in terms of average costs per unit of production) when there are significant economies of scale is pictured in Fig. 6.2. As the volume of production increases, the average cost per unit decreases until some optimal volume of production (point X) is reached, after which the average costs per unit of production begin to rise because of diseconomies of scale. If the relationship between volume of production and average costs per unit of production depicted in Fig. 6.2 holds, and if a firm in an industry has the largest volume of production (but not greater than the optimal level, X), then that firm will have a cost advantage in that industry. There are various reasons why large volumes of production are often associated with lower average per unit costs. Important sources of economies of scale are listed in Table 6.1 and discussed below.

Volume of Production and Specialized Machines.   When a firm has high levels of production, it is typically able to purchase and use specialized manufacturing tools that cannot be kept in operation in

FIGURE 6.2
Economies of Scale

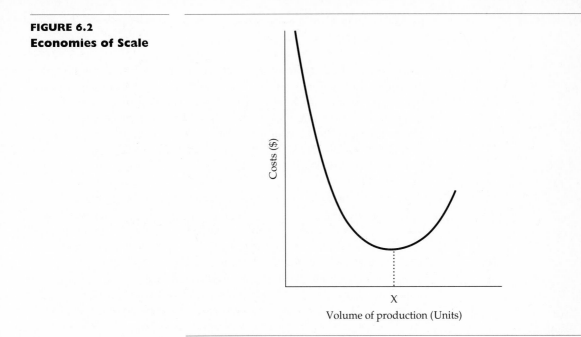

Volume of production (Units)

small firms. Manufacturing managers at BIC Corporation, for example, have emphasized this important advantage of high volumes of production. Mr. Charles Matjouranis, former director of manufacturing at BIC, once observed

> We are in the automation business. Because of our large volume, one tenth of 1 cent in savings turns out to be enormous . . . One advantage of the high-volume business is that you can get the best equipment and amortize it entirely over a short period of time (four to five months). I'm always looking for new equipment. If I see a cost-savings machine, I can buy it. I'm not constrained by money. (Christensen, Berg, and Salter, 1980:163).

TABLE 6.1
Major Sources of
Economies of Scale

1. Volume of production and specialized machines

2. Volume of production and cost of plant and equipment

3. Volume of production and employee specialization

4. Volume of production and overhead costs

Only firms with BIC's level of production in the pen industry have the ability to reduce their costs in this manner.

Volume of Production and the Cost of Plant and Equipment.   High volumes of production may allow a firm to build larger manufacturing operations. In some industries, the cost of building these manufacturing operations per unit of production is lower than the cost of building smaller manufacturing operations per unit of production. Thus large-volume firms, other factors being equal, will be able to build lower per unit cost manufacturing operations and will have lower average costs of production.

The link between volume of production and the cost of building manufacturing operations is particularly important in industries characterized by process manufacturing—chemical, oil refining, paper and pulp manufacturing, and so forth (Scherer, 1980). Because of the physical geometry of process manufacturing facilities, the costs of constructing a processing plant with increased capacity can be expected to rise as the two-thirds power of a plant's capacity (Moore, 1959; Lau and Tamura, 1972). The area of the surface of some three-dimensional containers (such as spheres and cylinders) increases at a slower rate than does the volume of these containers. Thus larger containers hold greater volumes and require less material per unit volume for the outside skins of these containers. Up to some point, increases in capacity come at a less-than-proportionate rise in the cost to build this capacity.

For example, it might cost a firm $100 to build a plant with a capacity of 1,000 units, for a per unit average cost of $.01. But, assuming the "two-thirds rule" applies, it might cost a firm $465 to build a plant with a capacity of 10,000 units ($465 = 10,000^{2/3}$), for a per unit average cost of $.0046. The difference between $.01 per unit and $.0046 per unit represents a cost advantage for a large-firm. Because it costs less per unit to build a large capacity plant, firms with large volumes of production that build large-capacity plants may have lower average per unit costs than firms with lower volumes of production and small-capacity plants.

Volume of Production and Employee Specialization.   High volumes of production are also associated with high levels of employee specialization (Scherer, 1980). As workers specialize in accomplishing a narrow task, they can become more and more efficient at this task, thereby reducing their firm's costs. This reasoning applies both in specialized manufacturing tasks (such as the highly specialized manufacturing functions in an assembly line) and in specialized management functions (such as the highly specialized managerial functions of accounting, finance, and sales). As Adam Smith first observed in 1776, cost advantages may be associated with the division of labor.

Smaller firms often do not possess the volume of production needed to justify this level of employee specialization. With smaller volumes of production, highly specialized employees may not have enough work to keep them busy an entire workday. This low volume of production is one reason why smaller firms often have employees who perform multiple business functions and often use outside contract employees and part-time workers to accomplish highly specialized functions like accounting, taxes, and human resource management.

Volume of Production and Overhead Costs.   A firm with high volumes of production has the luxury of spreading its overhead costs over more units and thereby reducing the overhead costs per unit. Suppose, in a particular industry, that the operation of a variety of accounting, control, and research and development functions, regardless of how large a firm is, is $100,000. Clearly, a firm that manufactures 1,000 units is imposing a cost of $100 per unit to cover overhead expenses. However, a firm that manufactures 10,000 units is imposing a cost of $10 per unit to cover overhead. Again, the larger-volume firm's average per unit costs are lower than the small-volume firm's average per unit costs.

Obviously, for a firm to generate a cost advantage in this manner, the firm's overhead costs cannot be highly and positively correlated with the firm's volume of production. If the overhead costs of a firm are highly and positively correlated with the firm's volume of production, then any increase in the volume of production will lead to a correspondingly large increase in the cost of overhead. A firm with overhead costs of $100,000 and a volume of production of 1,000 units will have an overhead cost of $1 million if it increases its volume of production to 10,000 units and if overhead costs are highly and positively correlated with the firm's volume of production. Obviously, the average overhead cost per unit ($100) is the same in each of these situations. However, as long as the volume of production and overhead costs are not correlated in this way, large-volume-of-production firms will have an advantage over low-volume-of-production firms in spreading overhead costs across units.

Size Differences and Diseconomies of Scale

Just as important economies of scale can generate cost advantages for larger firms, important diseconomies of scale can actually increase costs if they grow too large. As Fig. 6.2 shows, volumes of production beyond some optimal point (point X) actually lead to an increase in costs. If other firms in an industry have grown beyond the optimal size,

TABLE 6.2
Major Sources of
Diseconomies of Scale

1. Physical limits to efficient size

2. Managerial diseconomies

3. Worker motivation

4. Distance to markets and suppliers

a smaller firm (with a level of production closer to the optimal) may obtain a cost advantage even when all firms in the industry are producing very similar products. Sources of diseconomies of scale for a firm are listed in Table 6.2 and discussed below.

Physical Limits to Efficient Size.   Applying the "two-thirds rule" to the construction of manufacturing facilities seems to imply, for some industries at least, that larger is always better. However, there are some important physical limitations to the size of some manufacturing processes. Scherer (1980:84) notes that cement kilns develop unstable internal aerodynamics above 7 million barrels per year capacity. Perrow (1984) has suggested that scaling up nuclear reactors from small installations to huge facilities generates forces and physical processes that, though nondetectable in smaller facilities, can become significant in larger operations. These physical limitations on manufacturing processes reflect the underlying physics and engineering in a manufacturing process and suggest when the cost curve in Fig. 6.2 will begin to rise.

Managerial Diseconomies.   Although the underlying physics and engineering in a manufacturing process have an important impact on a firm's costs, managerial diseconomies are perhaps an even more important cause of these cost increases. As a firm increases in size, it often increases in complexity, and the ability of managers to control and operate it efficiently becomes limited.

One well-known example of a manufacturing plant that grew too large and thus became inefficient is Crown Cork & Seal's can-manufacturing plant in Philadelphia (Hamermesh and Rosenbloom, 1989). Through the early part of this century, this Philadelphia facility handled as many as seventy-five different can-manufacturing lines. The most efficient plants in the industry, however, were running from ten to fifteen lines simultaneously. The huge Philadelphia facility was simply too large to operate efficiently and was characterized by large numbers of breakdowns, a high percentage of idle lines, and poor quality products.

Worker Motivation.   A third source of diseconomies of scale depends on the relationship between firm size, employee specialization, and employee motivation. It has already been suggested that one of the advantages of increased volume of production is that it allows workers to specialize in smaller and more narrowly defined production tasks. With specialization, workers become more and more efficient at the particular task facing them.

However, a significant stream of research suggests that these types of very specialized jobs can be very demotivating for employees. Based in motivational theories taken from social psychology, this job design literature (Hackman and Oldham, 1980) suggests that as workers are removed further from the complete product that is the end result of a manufacturing process, the role that a worker's job plays in the overall manufacturing process becomes more and more obscure. As workers become mere "cogs in a manufacturing machine," worker motivation wanes, and productivity and quality both suffer.

Several manufacturing facilities in the U.S. automobile industry have experienced this worker demotivation and reduced quality due to worker overspecialization. Among others, Ford Motor Company has made significant efforts to help workers understand how their particular job contributes to the final product and to the success of the company. Ford has accomplished this by the use of a variety of employee participation schemes, including quality circles where each worker's point of view is sought (Maccoby, 1984). Some European automakers have been so concerned with the demotivating effects of highly specialized jobs that they have abandoned traditional assembly-line technology in favor of an assembly technology that lets a group of workers assemble an entire automobile (Taylor, 1994a).

Distance to Markets and Suppliers.   A final source of diseconomies of scale can be the distance between a large manufacturing facility and the place where the goods in question are to be sold, or the places where essential raw materials are purchased. Any reductions in cost attributable to the exploitation of economies of scale in manufacturing may be more than offset by large transportation costs associated with moving supplies and products to and from the manufacturing facility. Firms that build highly efficient plants without recognizing these significant transportation costs may put themselves in a competitive disadvantage compared to firms with slightly less efficient plants but plants that are located nearer suppliers and key markets.

One firm that tries to exploit its short distance from its key markets is Vans Shoes, Inc. Vans sells sneakers in the highly competitive U.S. market. However, instead of competing head to head with Nike, Reebok, and other high-priced shoe firms, Vans sells its basic shoes at prices that range from $29 to $50. Despite these relatively low prices, Vans has chosen to manufacturer its shoes in the United States. By doing so, Vans reduces the time it takes to bring new shoe designs to its customers. New Nike or Reebok designs, manufactured in the Far East, may take six months to reach the stores. Vans can deliver new models to stores in only nineteen days. Although Nike and Reebok may obtain substantial economies of scale (along with access to low-cost factors of production) by manufacturing their shoes in the Far East, they effectively create a niche for Vans's fast-delivery strategy. Vans's stock price almost doubled in the first six months after the company went public in 1991 (Neumeier, 1992).

Experience Differences and Learning-Curve Economies

A third possible source of cost advantages for firms in a particular business depends on their different cumulative levels of production. In some circumstances, firms with the greatest experience in manufacturing a product or service will have the lowest costs in an industry and thus will have a cost-based advantage. The link between cumulative volumes of production and cost has been formalized in the concept of the learning curve. This model is summarized in Fig. 6.3.

The Learning Curve and Economies of Scale.   As depicted in Fig. 6.3, the learning curve is very closely linked to economies of scale. Indeed, there are apparently only two differences between these concepts. First, where economies of scale focuses on the relationship between the volume of production at a given point in time and average unit costs, the learning curve focuses on the relationship between the *cumulative* volume of production and average unit costs. Second, where diseconomies

FIGURE 6.3
The Learning Curve and the Cost of Production

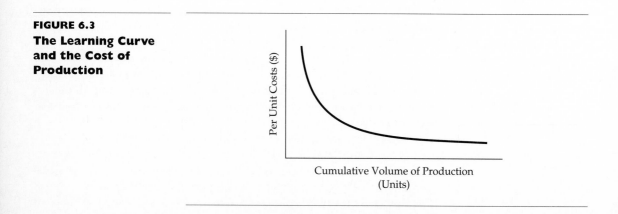

of scale are presumed to exist if a firm gets too large, there is no corresponding increase in costs in the learning-curve model as the cumulative volume of production grows. Rather, costs continue to fall until they approach the technologically possible lowest cost.

In general, the learning-curve model can be thought of as a dynamic generalization of the concept of economies of scale. Instead of simply examining the volume of production and costs at a given point in time, the learning-curve model attempts to relate the volume of production and costs over time.

The Learning Curve and Cost Advantages. The learning-curve model is based on the empirical observation that the costs of producing a unit of output fall as the cumulative volume of output increases. This outcome was first observed in the construction of aircraft during World War II. Research then showed that the labor costs per aircraft fell by 20 percent each time the cumulative volume of production doubled. A similar pattern has been observed in numerous industries, although the rate of cost reduction may vary. Some of these industries include the manufacture of ships, computers, spacecraft, and semiconductors (Moriarty and Allen, 1984; Scherer, 1980). In all these cases, increases in cumulative production have been associated with the improvement of work methods, a fine-tuning of the production operation, and detailed learning about how to make the production of products as efficient as possible.

However, learning-curve cost advantages are not restricted just to manufacturing. Learning can be associated with any business function, from purchasing raw materials through distribution and service. Also, there can be important learning effects in service industries as well. The learning curve is most often applied in the analysis of manufacturing costs, but it is important to recognize that the learning curve applies whenever the cost of accomplishing a business function falls as a function of the cumulative number of times a firm has engaged in that function.

The curve in Fig. 6.3 can be represented in equation form as

$$y = ax^{-\beta} \qquad\qquad Eq.\ 6.1$$

where a is the amount of time spent producing (that is, acquiring raw materials, manufacturing, distributing, and so forth) the first unit, x is the total number of units produced, β is a coefficient that describes the rate of learning in producing output, and y is the average time to produce all x units. In general, firms that produce the same products and services as their competitors, but do so in less time, will have an important cost advantage.

It is possible to use the learning-curve equation to anticipate the average time costs of producing a product. Suppose that it takes a team of workers 45 minutes to produce their first snipe trap. Given learning, it should take these same workers less time to produce their second snipe trap, say 27 minutes. With these two observations, it is possible to estimate the rate of learning for snipe trap manufacturing. The time to produce the first snipe trap, a, is 45 minutes. The total number of snipe traps produced, x, is 2. And the average time to produce these snipe traps, y, is 36 minutes: $(45 + 27)/2$. Plugging this information into the learning-curve equation, it is possible to calculate β, the rate of learning. (Fortunately, our calculators have logarithms built in.) In this example, β, the rate of learning in the production of snipe traps, is .3219. With this estimate of β, the learning curve for snipe trap production is

$$y = (45)(x)^{-.3219} \qquad\qquad Eq. \ 6.2$$

This equation can be used to anticipate the costs of producing products (snipe traps) in the future. It can also be used to compare the relative costs of producing for two different firms. Suppose there are two firms in the snipe trap business, Firm A and Firm B. Suppose that Firm A has just entered this business and has just produced its first snipe trap. It has already been shown that this first snipe trap will take approximately 45 minutes to produce. Firm B has been in the snipe trap business much longer than Firm A. Indeed, Firm B is building its sixth snipe trap. Using the learning-curve equation, the time costs of building this sixth trap can be estimated.

To estimate the cost of producing this sixth trap, one must first estimate the average time it takes to build each of six traps, multiply this average by 6 (to obtain the total time it takes to build six traps), estimate the average time it takes to build five traps, multiply this average by 5 (to obtain the total time it takes to build five traps), and then subtract the total time it takes to make five traps from the total time it takes to make six traps. This difference is the amount of time it takes to make just the sixth trap. These calculations are shown in Table 6.3 for snipe traps.

It turns out that the sixth trap will take approximately 17.8 minutes to produce. This compares with the 45 minutes that Firm A must take to produce its first snipe trap. The difference between 45 minutes and 17.8 minutes represents a significant cost advantage for Firm B over Firm A.

Learning Curve Names.   Different learning curves have different names. Unfortunately, the name of a learning curve does not appear in

TABLE 6.3
Application of the Learning Curve to Estimate Costs of Producing Snipe Traps for Two Firms: Firm A (Just Starting Production) and Firm B (Producing Its Sixth Snipe Trap)

Step 1:   Estimate learning-curve equation for production of snipe traps (done in text).

$$y = (45)(x)^{-.3219}$$

Step 2:   How long will it take Firm A to produce its first snipe trap?

45 minutes (same as for Firm B)

Step 3:   What is the average time it will take Firm B to produce six snipe traps?

$$y = (45)(6)^{-.3219}$$
$$= 25.3 \text{ minutes}$$

Step 4:   What is the total time it will take for Firm B to produce these six snipe traps?

$$151.8 \text{ minutes} = 6 \times 25.3 \text{ minutes}$$

Step 5:   What is the average time it took Firm B to produce five snipe traps?

$$y = (45)(5)^{-.3219}$$
$$= 26.8 \text{ minutes}$$

Step 6:   What is the total time it took Firm B to produce five snipe traps?

$$134 \text{ minutes} = 5 \times 26.8 \text{ minutes}$$

Step 7:   How much time will it take Firm B to produce only its sixth snipe trap?

total time to produce six	151.8 minutes
− total time to produce five	− 134.0 minutes
time to produce sixth trap	17.8 minutes

Therefore, it will take Firm A 45 minutes to make its snipe trap and Firm B only 17.8 minutes to make its sixth snipe trap.

the learning-curve equation but instead must be derived from that equation. The name of a learning curve is derived from the effect the learning has an average production costs when production is doubled. If it takes 10 hours to produce the first unit, and an average of 9 hours to produce the second unit (notice that total production has doubled from unit 1 to unit 2), this manufacturing process is said to have a 90 percent learning curve (9/10). If it averages 20 minutes to produce six products, and an average of 16 minutes to produce twelve products (production has doubled), this manufacturing process is said to have an 80 percent learning curve (16/20 = .80).

There is a mathematical relationship between the name of a learning curve and β in the learning-curve equation (Moriarty and Allen, 1984:111). However, for most purposes, the value of β and the learning curves listed in Table 6.4 are sufficient to calculate most learning-curve-based cost advantages.

**TABLE 6.4
Learning-Curve Names and β Values for Common Learning Curves**

Learning-Curve Name	Value of β
99%	.1044
98	.0291
97	.0439
96	.0589
95	.0740
94	.0893
93	.1047
92	.1203
91	.1361
90	.1520
89	.1681
88	.1844
87	.2009
86	.2176
85	.2345
84	.2515
83	.2688
82	.2863
81	.3040
80	.3219

The Learning Curve and Competitive Advantage. The learning-curve model summarized in Fig. 6.3 has been used to develop a model of cost-based competitive advantage that links learning with market share and average production costs. Perhaps the major proponents of the application of this learning-curve logic to create competitive advantage are Henderson (1974) and the Boston Consulting Group (1972).

The logic behind this application of the learning-curve model is straightforward. It seems clear that the first firm that successfully moves down the learning curve will obtain a cost advantage over rivals, just as Firm B in the snipe trap example has a cost advantage over Firm A. To move a production process down the learning curve, and thereby obtain costs lower than rivals' costs, a firm needs to have higher levels of cumulative volume of production. Of course, firms that are successful at producing high volumes of output need to sell that output to customers. Manufacturing to increase inventory may reduce a firm's manufacturing costs, but it will lead to disaster in the long run. In selling this output, firms are, in effect, increasing their market share. Thus to drive down the learning curve and obtain a cost advantage, firms must aggressively acquire market share.

This application of learning-curve logic has been criticized by a wide variety of authors (Hall and Howell, 1985). Two criticisms are particularly salient. First, although the acquisition of market share is likely to allow a firm to reduce its production costs, the acquisition of share itself is expensive. To acquire share, firms often must increase advertising and other marketing expenditures and reduce prices. Indeed, a significant amount of research suggests that the costs that firms will need to absorb in order to acquire market share often equal the value of that market share in lowering a firm's production costs (Montgomery and Wernerfelt, 1991). Thus efforts to move down the learning curve quickly, by acquiring market share, are likely to generate only normal economic profits.

The second major criticism of this application of the learning-curve model is that there is, according to this logic, no room for any product differentiation, cooperative business strategies, or corporate strategies (Hill, 1988). In other words, this application of the learning curve implicitly assumes that firms can compete only on the basis of their low costs and that any other strategies are not possible. Most industries, however, are characterized by opportunities for at least some of these other strategies, and thus this strict application of the learning-curve model can be misleading.

These criticisms aside, it is still the case that in many industries firms with larger cumulative levels of production, other things being equal, will have lower average production costs. Thus experience in all the facets of production can be a source of cost advantage even if the single-minded pursuit of market share to obtain these cost reductions may not give a firm above-normal economic returns.

Differential Low-Cost Access to Factors of Production

Besides economies of scale, diseconomies of scale, and learning-curve cost advantages, differential low-cost access to factors of production may create cost differences among firms producing similar products in an industry. Factors of production are any inputs used by a firm in conducting its business activities; they include labor, capital, land, and raw materials. A firm that has differential low-cost access to one or more of these factors is likely to have lower economic costs than its rivals.

Consider, for example, an oil company with fields in Saudi Arabia compared to an oil company with fields in the North Sea. The costs of obtaining crude oil for the first firm are considerably less than the cost of obtaining crude oil for the second. North Sea drilling involves the construction of giant offshore drilling platforms, housing workers on floating cities, and transporting oil across an often stormy sea. Drilling in Saudi Arabia requires only the simplest drilling technologies because the oil is found relatively close to the surface. It is not hard to believe that the costs of the Saudi-based firm will be lower than the costs of the North Sea–based firm.

Of course, in order to create a cost advantage, the cost of acquiring low-cost factors of production must be less than the cost savings generated by these factors. For example, even though it may be much less costly to drill for oil in Saudi Arabia than in the North Sea, if it is very expensive to purchase the rights to drill in Saudi compared to the costs of the rights to drill in the North Sea, the potential cost advantages of drilling in Saudi Arabia can be lost. As with all sources of cost advantages, firms must be careful to weigh the cost of acquiring that advantage against the value of that advantage for the firm.

Differential access to raw materials like oil, coal, and iron ore can be important determinants of a cost advantage. However, differential access to other factors of production can be just as important. For example, it may be easier (that is, less costly) to recruit highly trained electronics engineers for firms located near where these engineers receive their schooling than for firms located some distance away. This lower cost of recruiting is a partial explanation of the development of geographic technology centers like Silicon Valley in California, Route 128 in Massachusetts, and the Research Triangle in North Carolina. In all three cases, firms are located physically close to several universities that train the electronics engineers that are the lifeblood of high-technology companies.

Volume of production may also affect differential access to factors of production. A firm with very high volume of production may be able to use its market share as a lever to obtain discounts for raw materials and other supplies (Porter, 1980). These volume discounts may not be available to smaller firms. The search for volume discounts is one explanation for the recent development of hospital chains in the hospital industry. Chains of hospitals can purchase many of their supplies at a lower cost than can individual hospitals. Even individual hospitals are beginning to join together in purchasing consortia to reduce their cost of supply (Aguilar and Bhambri, 1983).

Technological Advantages Independent of Scale

Another possible source of cost advantage in an industry may be the different technologies that firms employ to manage their business. It has already been suggested that larger firms may have technology-based cost advantages reflecting their ability to exploit economies of scale (for example, the "two-thirds rule"). Here, technology-based cost advantages that do not depend on economies of scale are discussed.

Traditionally, discussion of technology-based cost advantages have focused on the machines, computers, and other physical tools that firms use to manage their business (Perrow, 1984). Clearly, in some industries, these physical technology differences between firms can create important cost differences—even when the firms in question are approximately the same size in terms of volume of production. In the steel industry, for example, technological advances can substantially reduce the cost of producing steel (Ghemawat and Stander, 1992). Firms with the latest steel-manufacturing technology will typically enjoy some cost advantage over similar-size firms without the latest technology. The same applies in the manufacturing of semiconductors (Shaffer, 1995b), automobiles (Treece, 1991), consumer electronics (McCormick and Stone, 1990), and a wide variety of other products.

These physical technology cost advantages occur in service firms, as well as in manufacturing firms. For example, early in its history, Charles Schwab, a leading discount brokerage, purchased a used IBM 360 computer that enabled Schwab to complete customer transactions more rapidly and at a lower cost compared to rivals (Schultz, 1989). The widespread use of computing technology in accounting firms has substantially reduced the costs of these service organizations as well.

However, the concept of technology can be easily broadened to include not just the physical tools that firms use to manage their business, but any processes within a firm used in this way (Perrow, 1970; Miles, 1980). This concept of firm technology includes not only the technological hardware of companies—the machines and robots—but also the technological software of firms—things like the quality of relations among labor and management, an organization's culture, and the quality of managerial controls (Tomer, 1987). All these characteristics of a firm can have an impact on a firm's economic costs.

Research in Japan, for example, suggests that while "hard technology," including automation and robots, is an important component of low-cost manufacturing, "soft technology" such as the use of quality circles on the manufacturing floor, a sense of loyalty from the worker to the firm (Ouchi, 1981), and an organizational culture that emphasizes cost control is just as important, if not more important, in explaining the cost position of some Japanese firms (Pascale and Athos, 1981). Work on so-called excellent U.S. firms also emphasizes the cost implications of these softer aspects of technology (Peters and Waterman, 1982). Firms that possess the right combination of technological hardware and software may enjoy lower costs even if they do not have scale or learning advantages over their rivals.

One firm that is currently learning about the limitations of technological hardware to reduce costs is General Motors. Through the 1980s, GM spent several billion dollars (one estimate has the figure as high as $40 billion) to install the most recent, up-to-date physical manufacturing technology, including robots, in many of its factories (Badaracco and Hasegawa, 1988). This massive investment in technological hardware, however, was not followed by a significant reduction in manufacturing costs. Indeed, the cost position of GM in the automobile industry has deteriorated over the last several years. More recently, GM seems to be investing in technological software as well as technological hardware to improve its manufacturing (Taylor, 1995). Whether these investments will actually reduce manufacturing costs at GM is still to be determined.

Policy Choices

Thus far this discussion has focused on reasons why a firm can gain a cost advantage despite producing products that are similar to competing firms' products. When firms produce essentially the same outputs, differences in economies of scale, learning-curve advantages, differential access to factors of production, and differences in technology can all create cost advantages (and disadvantages) for firms. However, firms can also make choices about the kinds of products and services they will sell—choices that have an impact on their relative cost position. In general, firms that are attempting to implement a cost-leadership strategy will choose to produce relatively simple standardized products that sell for relatively low prices compared to the products and prices of firms pursuing other business or corporate strategies (Porter, 1980). These kinds of products often tend to have high volumes of sales, which (if significant economies of scale exist) tend to reduce costs even further.

These kinds of product and price choices can be seen in a wide range of cost-leader firms. For example, Wal-Mart, a cost leader in retail sales, does not attempt to sell high-fashion clothing, the most sophisticated home electronics, or the highest-quality china. Nor is each Wal-Mart store cleverly designed to reflect the local culture. Although service is available at Wal-Mart, it is generally restricted to checking to see whether additional inventory exists in the store, managing returns and exchanges, and checking customers out. Instead of providing extra (expensive) services, Wal-Mart provides its customers with quality brand-name products at low prices. It can sell at these prices because of its high volume of sales, its efficient distribution network, and its low-cost store operations (Ghemawat, 1986).

BIC Corporation, a cost leader in the manufacture of pens, lighters, and razors, becomes involved in manufacturing a product only when the number and sophistication of the parts in the product can be dramatically simplified. BIC does not sell gold-filled pens with a lifetime warranty; it does not sell jeweled and crystal cigarette lighters; and it does not sell carefully balanced metal razors. Instead, BIC sells easy-to-manufacture, low-priced, disposable items and uses its huge volume of production to further reduce its costs (Christensen, Berg, and Salter, 1980).

These kinds of choices in product and pricing tend to have a very broad impact on a cost leader's operations. In these firms, the task of reducing costs is not delegated to a single function or to a special task force within the firm but is the responsibility of every manager and employee. Cost reduction sometimes becomes the central objective of the firm. Indeed, in this setting, management must be constantly alert to cost-cutting efforts that reduce the ability of the firm to meet customers' needs.

Some Japanese firms, including NEC, Sharp, Nissan, and Toyota, take the relationship between these policy choices and cost leadership to another level. These firms adopt what is called a target cost design system. This approach to product development begins by determining the price at which a new product is most likely to appeal to potential customers. This target price determines a product's target manufacturing costs, and all design, engineering, and supply decisions are made in an effort to meet or beat this target cost figure. These firms make policy choices about their product characteristics based on the implications of these choices for their manufacturing and other costs (Worthy, 1991).

This approach to product design stands in marked contrast to the product design process in many other firms. In these firms, product design and engineering may continue for some time before the cost of manufacturing a product is evaluated. The process of determining a product's manufacturing costs is often described as throwing the product "over the wall" between design engineers and the manufacturing function. If manufacturing costs are too high, products must go through a costly redesign process. Such redesign can delay product introduction and can force designers to make inappropriate design tradeoffs that would not have been made if the cost of manufacturing had been integrated into the design process earlier.

In this all-out effort to reduce costs, firms must avoid manufacturing or selling low-cost products that no one wants to buy. In the end, a firm's performance depends on the relationship between revenues and costs. However, if cutting costs threatens revenues, a low-cost firm may not remain profitable. One firm that has struggled in its cost-leadership strategy is Ikea, a Swedish home-furnishing retailer. Upon entering the U.S. market, Ikea had very low prices. However, some consumers found the level of its service to be even lower. Customers often had to wait an hour or more in line to purchase products. Ikea was distributing 7 million catalogues a year, but its telephone ordering system was inadequate. Ikea also had no way for customers to order products that were temporarily out of inventory. Underinvestment in service slowed Ikea's growth in North America (Trachtenberg, 1991), although the company has apparently responded to many of these service issues.

6.3   THE VALUE OF COST LEADERSHIP

COST LEADERSHIP AND ECONOMIC PERFORMANCE

There is little doubt that cost differences can exist among firms, even when those firms are manufacturing very similar products. Policy choices about the kinds of products that firms in an industry choose to produce can also create important cost differences. The impact of these cost differences on economic performance can be seen in Fig. 6.4.

The firms depicted in this figure are price takers—that is, the price of the products or services they sell is determined by market conditions and not by individual decisions of firms. This implies that there is effectively no product differentiation in this market and that no one firm's sales constitute a large percentage of this market. (Markets with product differentiation are discussed in Chapter 7; markets with dominant firms are discussed in Chapter 8.)

The price of goods or services in this type of market (P^*) is determined by aggregate industry supply and demand. This industry price determines the demand facing an individual firm in this market. Because these firms are price takers, the demand facing an individual

FIGURE 6.4
Cost Leadership and Economic Performance

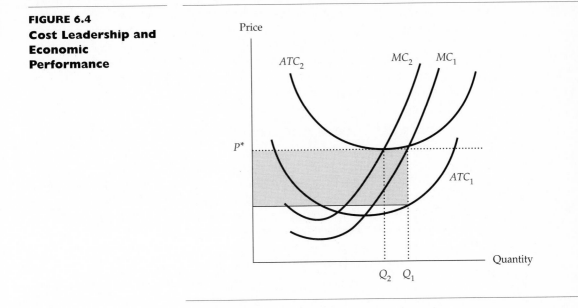

firm is horizontal—that is, firm decisions about levels of output have a negligible impact on overall industry supply and thus a negligible impact on the market determined price. As is well known, a firm in this setting maximizes its economic performance by producing a quantity of output (Q) so that marginal revenue equals marginal cost (MC). The ability of firms to earn economic profits in this setting depends on the relationship between the market-determined price (P^*) and the average total cost (ATC) of a firm at the quantity it chooses to produce.

Firms in the market depicted in Fig. 6.4 fall into two categories. All but one firm have the average-total-cost curve ATC_2 and marginal-cost curve MC_2. However, one firm in this industry has the average-total-cost curve ATC_1 and marginal-cost curve MC_1. Notice that ATC_1 is less than ATC_2 at the performance-maximizing quantities produced by these two kinds of firms (Q_1 and Q_2, respectively). In this particular example, firms with common average-total-cost curves are earning zero economic profits, while the low-cost firm is earning an economic profit (equal to the shaded area in Fig. 6.4). A variety of other examples could also be constructed: The cost-leader firm could be earning zero economic profits while other firms in the market are incurring economic losses; the cost-leader firm could be earning substantial economic profits while other firms are earning smaller economic profits;

the cost-leader firm could be incurring small economic losses while the other firms are incurring substantial economic losses, and so forth. However, in all these examples, the cost leader's economic performance is greater than the economic performance of other firms in the industry. Thus cost leadership can have an important impact on a firm's economic performance.

COST LEADERSHIP AND ENVIRONMENTAL THREATS

The value of cost leadership can also be analyzed relative to the models of environmental threats and opportunities presented in Chapters 3 and 4. How cost leadership reduces the threat of new entrants, rivalry, substitutes, buyers, and suppliers is discussed below. Describing the ways that cost leadership can enable a firm to exploit environmental opportunities is left as an exercise for the reader.

Cost Leadership and the Threat of Entry

A cost-leadership competitive strategy helps reduce the threat of new entrants by creating cost-based barriers to entry. Recall that many of the barriers to entry cited in Chapter 3, including economies of scale and cost advantages independent of scale, presume that incumbent firms have lower costs than potential entrants (Bain, 1956). If an incumbent firm is a cost leader, for any of the reasons listed above, then new entrants may have to invest heavily to reduce their costs prior to entry. Often, new entrants will enter using another business strategy (product differentiation or cooperative business strategies) or a corporate strategy rather than attempting to compete on costs.

The relationship between Caterpillar and Komatsu in the construction equipment industry (briefly described in Section 5.2) can be understood in these terms. Caterpillar obtained an important competitive advantage by gaining low-cost access to an important factor of production (a worldwide service and supply network). Komatsu has been unable to match Caterpillar's cost advantage in this area and thus has entered the worldwide construction equipment industry with high-quality machines that break down less frequently. Because Komatsu could not match Caterpillar's cost advantage in service and supply, the organization chose to differentiate its product on the basis of high reliability (Bartlett and Rangan, 1985).

Cost Leadership and the Threat of Rivalry

Firms with a low-cost position also reduce the threat of rivalry. The threat of rivalry is reduced through pricing strategies that low-cost firms can engage in and through their relative impact on the performance of a low-cost firm and its higher-cost rivals.

Cost-leader firms have two choices in pricing their products or services. First, these firms can set their prices equal to the prices of higher-cost competitors. Assuming that there are few opportunities for other firms to implement product differentiation competitive strategies, we can predict that customers will be indifferent about purchasing goods or services from the low-cost firm or from its high-cost rivals. However, at these competitive prices, high-cost firms are likely to earn a normal economic profit while the cost-leader firm is earning an above-normal profit.

Second, low-cost firms can price their goods or services slightly below the prices of their high-cost rivals. Again, assuming little product differentiation, we can predict that customers will no longer be indifferent about which firm they prefer to buy from. Obviously, the lower prices of the low-cost firm attract numerous customers, rapidly increasing the market share of the low-cost firm.

Each of these alternatives has strengths and weaknesses. Keeping prices equal to the competition's prices enables a low-cost firm to earn large margins on its sales. As important, this pricing approach at least partially conceals the fact that the low-cost firm has a cost advantage. Concealing this information reduces the chances that competitors will imitate the low-cost firm, thereby reducing its cost advantage (Barney, 1991). However, keeping prices equal to a competitor's prices does sacrifice market share and sales volume. Setting the low-cost firm's prices below the prices of competing firms has the opposite effects. Such a pricing strategy can significantly increase a firm's market share and total volume of sales, but at the cost of some of the profit margin of the low-cost firm. Also, setting prices to this lower level sends a signal to competitors that lower costs are possible. Such a signal may motivate competitors to try to reduce their costs, either through implementing their own cost-leadership competitive strategies or through implementing cooperative or corporate strategies that reduce costs.

In the end, the choice between these two pricing strategies depends on the ability of competing firms to respond to the cost advantages of cost leaders. If the potential responses of competing firms are likely to be very detrimental to the cost leader, then this firm should set its prices equal to competitors' prices, sacrificing some market share for increased profit margins and the release of less information. But if competitive reactions are not likely to threaten the cost leader, then dropping prices below competitors' prices should increase overall economic performance through increased volumes of profitable sales.

One firm that has chosen this second approach (setting prices lower than competitors' prices) is Arco Oil and Gas in its retail gasoline

sales. Starting in the early 1980s, Arco engaged in a series of restructurings, force reductions, and other efficiency moves to become a cost
leader in producing gasoline and related oil products in the United
States (Mack, 1990). Arco's goal was to have a cost structure such that
the organization could be profitable even if crude oil traded only for
$12 per barrel. As a result of these intense cost reductions, Arco has
been able to sell its gasoline at prices slightly lower than its competition's, while still being highly profitable. Arco executives apparently
felt that information about Arco cost advantages was already widely
available, that Arco cost advantages were relatively immune from imitation and were not likely to create incentives for other threatening
strategic moves by competitors, or both (Cook, 1988).

More generally, these strategic pricing options, and the potential
above-normal economic performance they hold, are available only to
cost leaders. These strategies enable a low-cost firm to earn above-
normal economic returns even if the industry within which this firm
operates is characterized by intense rivalry.

Cost Leadership and the Threat of Substitutes

As suggested in Section 3.2, substitutes become a threat to a firm when
their cost and performance, relative to the firm's current products or
services, become more attractive to customers. Thus when the price of
crude oil goes up, substitutes for crude oil become more attractive.
When the cost and performance of electronic calculators improve,
demand for mechanical adding machines disappears.

In this situation, cost leaders have the ability to keep their products and services attractive relative to substitutes. While high-cost
firms may have to charge high prices to cover their costs, thus making
substitutes more attractive, cost leaders can keep their prices low and
still earn normal or above-normal economic profits (Porter, 1980).

Cost Leadership and the Threat of Suppliers

Suppliers can become a threat to a firm by charging higher prices for
the goods or services they supply or by reducing the quality of those
goods or services. However, when a supplier sells to a cost leader, that
firm has greater flexibility in absorbing higher-cost supplies than does
a high-cost firm. Higher supply costs may destroy any above-normal
profits for high-cost firms but still allow a cost-leader firm to earn an
above-normal profit

Cost leadership based on large volumes of production and
economies of scale can also reduce the threat of suppliers. Large volumes of production imply large purchases of raw materials and other
supplies. Suppliers are not likely to jeopardize these sales by threaten-

ing their customers. Indeed, buyers are often able to use their purchasing volume to extract volume discounts from suppliers.

Cost Leadership and the Threat of Buyers

Cost leadership can also reduce the threat of buyers. Powerful buyers are a threat to firms when they insist on low prices or higher quality and service from their suppliers. Lower prices threaten firm revenues; higher quality can increase a firm's costs. Cost leaders can have their revenues reduced by buyer threats and still earn normal or above-normal profits. These firms can also absorb the greater costs of increased quality or service and may still have a cost advantage over their competition.

Buyers can also be a threat through backward vertical integration. Being a cost leader deters buyer backward vertical integration, since a buyer that vertically integrates backward will often not have costs as low as an incumbent cost leader (Porter, 1980). Rather than vertically integrating backward and increasing their cost of supplies, powerful buyers usually prefer to continue purchasing from their low-cost suppliers.

Finally, if cost leadership is based on large volumes of production, then the threat of buyers may be reduced, since buyers may depend on just a few firms for the goods or services they purchase. This dependence reduces the willingness of buyers to threaten a selling firm (Pfeffer and Salancik, 1978).

6.4   COST LEADERSHIP AND SUSTAINED COMPETITIVE ADVANTAGE

Given that cost leadership can be valuable, an important question becomes, Under what conditions will firms implementing this competitive strategy be able to maintain that leadership to obtain a sustained competitive advantage? If cost-leadership strategies can be implemented by numerous firms in an industry, or if no firms face a cost disadvantage in imitating a cost-leadership strategy, then being a cost leader does not generate a sustained competitive advantage for a firm. As was suggested in Chapter 5, the ability of a valuable cost-leadership competitive strategy to generate a sustained competitive advantage depends on that strategy being rare and costly to imitate, either through direct duplication or substitution. As suggested in Tables 6.5 and 6.6, the rareness and duplicability of a cost-leadership strategy depends, at least in part, on the sources of that cost advantage.

TABLE 6.5
The Rareness of Sources of Cost Advantage

Likely-to-be-rare sources of cost advantage	Less-likely-to-be-rare sources of cost advantage
Learning-curve economies of scale (especially in emerging industries)	Economies of scale (except when efficient plant size approximately equals total industry demand)
Differential low-cost access to factors of production	Diseconomies of scale
Technological software	Technological hardware (unless a firm has proprietary hardware development skills)
	Policy choices

TABLE 6.6
Cost Leadership and Sustained Competitive Advantage

	Source of cost advantage	Source of costly duplication		
		History	Uncertainty	Social Complexity
Low-cost duplication possible	1. Economies of scale	—	—	—
	2. Diseconomies of scale	—	—	—
May be costly to duplicate	3. Learning-curve economies	*	—	—
	4. Technological hardware	—	*	*
	5. Policy choices	*	—	—
Usually costly to duplicate	6. Differential low-cost access to factors of production	***	—	**
	7. Technological software	***	**	***

— = Not a source of costly imitation
 * = Somewhat likely to be a source of costly imitation
 ** = Likely to be a source of costly imitation
*** = Very likely to be a source of costly imitation

THE RARENESS OF SOURCES OF COST ADVANTAGE

Some of the sources of cost advantage listed in Table 6.5 are likely to be rare among a set of competing firms; others are less likely to be rare. Sources of cost advantage that are likely to be rare include (1) learning-curve economies (at least in emerging industries), (2) differential low-cost access to factors of production, and (3) technological "software." The remaining sources of cost advantage are less likely to be rare.

Rare Sources of Cost Advantage

Early in the evolution of an industry, substantial differences in the cumulative volume of production of different firms are not unusual. Indeed, this was one of the major benefits associated with first-mover advantages, discussed in Section 4.2. These differences in cumulative volume of production, in combination with substantial learning-curve economies, suggest that in some settings learning-curve advantages may be rare and thus a source of at least temporary competitive advantage.

The definition of differential access to factors of production implies that this access is often rare. Certainly, if large numbers of competing firms have this same access, then it cannot be a source of competitive advantage.

Technological software is also likely to be rare among a set of competing firms. These software attributes represent each firm's path through history. If these histories are unique, the technological software they create may also be rare. Of course, if several competing firms experience similar paths through history, the technological software in these firms is less likely to be rare.

Less Rare Sources of Cost Advantage

When the efficient size of a firm or plant is significantly smaller than the total size of an industry, there will usually be numerous efficient firms/plants in that industry, and a cost-leadership strategy based on economies of scale will not be rare. For example, if the efficient firm/plant size in an industry is 500 units, and the total size of the industry (measured in units produced) is 500,000 units, then there are likely to be numerous efficient firms/plants in this industry, and economies of scale are not likely to give any one firm a cost-based competitive advantage.

Cost advantages based on diseconomies of scale are also not likely to be rare. It is unusual for numerous firms to adopt levels of production in excess of optimal levels. If only a few firms are too large in this sense, then several competing firms in an industry that are *not* too large will have cost advantages over the firms that are too large. However, since several firms will enjoy these cost advantages, they are not rare.

One important exception to this generalization may be when changes in technology significantly reduce the most efficient scale of an operation. Given such changes in technology, several firms may be inefficiently large. If a small number of firms happens to be sized appropriately, then the cost advantages these firms obtain in this way may be rare. Such changes in technology have made large integrated steel producers "too big" relative to smaller mini-mills. Thus mini-mills have a cost advantage over larger integrated steel firms.

Technological hardware is also not likely to be rare, especially if it is developed by suppliers and sold on the open market. However, a firm that has developed proprietary technology development skills may be able to possess rare technological hardware that creates cost advantages.

Finally, policy choices by themselves are not likely to be a rare source of cost advantage, particularly if the product or service attributes in question are easy to describe and easy to imitate.

THE IMITABILITY OF SOURCES OF COST ADVANTAGE

Even when a particular source of cost advantage is rare, it must be costly to imitate in order to be a source of sustained competitive advantage. Both direct duplication and substitution, as forms of imitation, are important. Again, the imitability of a cost advantage depends, at least in part, on the source of that advantage.

Easy-to-Duplicate Sources of Cost Advantage

In general, economies of scale and diseconomies of scale are relatively easy-to-duplicate bases of cost leadership. As can be seen in Table 6.6, these sources of cost advantage do not build on history, uncertainty, or socially complex resources and capabilities and thus are not protected from duplication for these reasons.

For example, if a small number of firms does obtain a cost advantage based on economies of scale, and if the relationship between production scale and costs is widely understood among competing firms, then firms at a cost disadvantage will rapidly adjust their production to exploit these economies of scale. This can be done either by growing a firm's current operations to the point that the firm exploits economies or by combining previously separate operations to obtain these economies. Both actions enable a firm at a cost disadvantage to begin using specialized machines, reduce the cost of plant and equipment, increase employee specialization, and spread overhead costs more effectively.

Indeed, perhaps the only time economies of scale are not subject to low-cost duplication is when the efficient size of operations is a significant percentage of total demand in an industry. Of course, this is the situation described in Section 3.2's discussion of economies of scale as a barrier to entry. For example, as suggested earlier, BIC Corporation, with its dominant market share in the disposable pen market, has apparently been able to gain and retain an important cost advantage in that market based on economies of scale (Christensen, Berg, and Salter, 1980). BIC's ability to retain this advantage reflects the fact that the optimal plant size in the disposable pen market is a significant percentage of the pen market, and thus economies of scale act as a barrier to entry in that market.

Like economies of scale, in many settings diseconomies of scale will not be a source of sustained competitive advantage for firms that have *not* grown too large. In the short run, firms experiencing significant diseconomies can shrink the size of their operations to become more efficient. In the long run, firms that fail to adjust their size will earn below-normal economic profits and will cease operations.

Although in many ways reducing the size of operations to improve efficiency seems like a simple problem for managers in firms/plants, in practice it is often a difficult change to implement. Because of uncertainty, managers in a firm/plant that is too large may not understand that diseconomies of scale have increased their costs (Meyer and Zucker, 1989). Sometimes, managers conclude that the problem is that employees are not working hard enough, that problems in production can be fixed, and so forth. These firms/plants may continue their inefficient operations for some time, despite costs that are higher than the industry average.

Other psychological processes can also delay the abandonment of operations that are too large. Staw (1981) has described the psychological phenomenon known as escalation of commitment: Managers committed to an incorrect (cost-increasing or revenue-reducing) course of action *increase* their commitment to this action as its limitations become manifest. For example, a manager who believes that the optimal firm size in an industry is larger than the actual optimal size may remain committed to large operations despite costs that are higher than the industry average.

For all these reasons, firms suffering from diseconomies of scale must often turn to outside managers to assist in reducing costs (Hesterly, 1989). Outsiders bring a fresh view to the organization's problems and are not committed to the practices that generated the problems in the first place. One example of a firm turning to an outsider to reduce its costs is Campbell Soup Company. By hiring David Johnson, Campbell Soup got a no-nonsense manager who could cut through the managerial fiefdoms and foolishness that had led Campbell to lose market share, and market value, steadily throughout the 1980s. In his first eighteen months, Johnson closed twenty plants, laid off 364 employees at corporate headquarters, and began a new emphasis on earnings growth, return on equity, and return on invested cash. None of these actions was terribly novel, but it took an outsider to cut through the organizational red tape to make these changes happen. The results, so far, have been very positive for Campbell Soup (Saporito, 1991).

Of course, the results have been less positive for the firms that had a cost advantage based on Campbell Soup's inefficient organization. Johnson's moves had the effect of reducing those cost advantages. In the long run, firms suffering from high costs from diseconomies of scale either reduce their scale of operations (as Campbell did) or cease operation. Rarely will diseconomies of scale be a source of sustained competitive advantage for more efficiently organized firms.

Bases of Cost Leadership That May Be Costly to Duplicate

Although cost advantages based on learning-curve economies are rare (especially in emerging industries), they are usually not costly to duplicate. As suggested in Chapter 4, for learning-curve cost advantages to be a source of sustained competitive advantage, the learning obtained by a firm must be proprietary (Spence, 1981). Most recent empirical work suggests that in most industries learning is not proprietary and thus can be rapidly duplicated as competing firms move down the learning curve by increasing their cumulative volume of production (Mansfield, 1985; Lieberman, 1982, 1987).

However, the fact that in *most* industries learning is not costly to duplicate does not mean that learning is not costly to duplicate in all industries. In some industries the ability of firms to learn from their production experience may vary significantly. For example, some firms treat production errors as failures and systematically punish employees who make those errors. These firms effectively reduce risk taking among their production employees and thus reduce the chances of learning how to improve their production process. Alternatively, other firms treat production errors as opportunities to learn how to improve their production process. These firms are likely to move rapidly down the learning curve and retain cost advantages, despite the cumulative volume of production of competing firms. These different responses to production errors reflect the organizational cultures of these different firms. Since organizational cultures are socially complex, they can be very costly to duplicate (Barney, 1986b).

Because technological hardware can usually be purchased across supply markets, it is also not likely to be difficult to duplicate. However, sometimes technological hardware can be proprietary, or closely bundled with other unique, costly-to-duplicate resources controlled by a firm. In this case, technological hardware can be costly to duplicate.

It is unusual, but not impossible, for policy choices to be a source of sustained competitive cost advantages for a firm. As suggested earlier, if the policies in question focus on easy-to-describe and easy-to-imitate product characteristics, then duplication is likely, and cost advantages based on policy choices will be temporary. However, if policy choices reflect complex decision processes within a firm, teamwork among different parts of the design and manufacturing process, or any of the software commitments discussed previously, then policy choices can be a source of sustained competitive advantage, as long as only a few firms have the ability to make these choices. This was the case at Apple Computer, described in Section 5.3.

Costly-to-Duplicate Sources of Cost Advantage

Differential low-cost access to factors of production and technological software, because they build on historical, uncertain, and socially complex resources and capabilities, are usually costly-to-duplicate bases of cost leadership.

As suggested earlier, differential access to factors of production often depends on the location of a firm. Moreover, to be a source of economic profits, this valuable location must be obtained before its full value is widely understood.

Both these attributes of differential access to factors of production suggest that if, in fact, it is rare, it will often be costly to duplicate. First, some locations are effectively unique and cannot be duplicated. For example, most private golf clubs would like to own courses with the spectacular beauty of Pebble Beach in Monterey, California, but there is only one Pebble Beach—a course that runs parallel to some of the most beautiful ocean-front scenery in the world. Although "scenery" is an important factor of production in running and managing a golf course, the re-creation of Pebble Beach's scenery at some other location is simply beyond our technology.

Second, even if a location is not unique, once its value is revealed, acquisition of that location is not likely to generate economic profits. Thus, for example, although being located in Silicon Valley provides low-cost access to some important factors of production for electronics firms, firms that moved to this location after its value was revealed have substantially higher costs than firms that moved there before its full value was revealed. These higher costs effectively reduce the economic profit that otherwise could have been generated. Referring to the discussion in Chapter 5, these arguments suggest that gaining differential access to factors of production in a way that generates economic profits may reflect a firm's unique path through history (Barney, 1991).

Organizational Structure

The organizational structure required to fully implement a cost-leadership strategy is simple and lean. Cost-leading firms generally have relatively few layers in their reporting structure. Complicated reporting structures, including matrix structures where one employee reports to two or more people, are usually avoided (Davis and Lawrence, 1977). Corporate staff in these organizations is kept small. These firms do not vertically integrate into a wide range of business functions but instead focus on those few business functions where they have valuable, rare, and costly-to-imitate resources and capabilities (see Chapter 10).

One excellent example of a firm pursuing a cost-leadership strategy is Nucor Steel. A leader in the mini-mill industry, Nucor has only five layers in its reporting structure, compared to twelve to fifteen in its major higher-cost competitors. Most operating decisions at Nucor are delegated to plant managers, who have full profit-and-loss responsibility for their operations. Corporate staff at Nucor is small and focuses its efforts on accounting for revenues and costs and on exploring new manufacturing processes to further reduce Nucor's operating expenses and expand its business opportunities. Nucor's president, Ken Iverson, believes that Nucor does only two things well: building plants efficiently and running them effectively. Thus Nucor focuses its efforts in these areas and subcontracts many of its other business functions, including the purchase of its raw materials, to outside vendors (Ghemawat and Stander, 1992).

Even industries not traditionally populated by low-cost leaders are beginning to see the emergence of more efficient, lower-cost organizational structures. In the hospital industry, for example, Health Management Associates, a sixteen-hospital chain, is widely seen as a cost leader. It maintains this cost leadership by keeping corporate staff small (only thirty-two at corporate headquarters in 1993), by eliminating levels in the reporting structure (only one organizational layer between the CEO and hospital managers), by purchasing and improving used computer technology, and by giving each hospital it owns rigorous profit performance targets. The results of this organizational effort are impressive: Health Management Associates recently earned its thirty-third consecutive increase in quarterly earnings, operating profits are up an average of 23 percent per year since 1988, and net income increased 90 percent between 1991 and 1992 (Cooper, 1993).

Management Control Systems

Cost-leadership firms are typically characterized by very tight cost control systems; frequent and detailed cost control reports; an emphasis on quantitative cost goals and targets; and close supervision of labor, raw materials, inventory, and other costs (Porter, 1980). Again, Nucor is an example of a cost-leadership firm that has implemented these kinds of control systems. At Nucor, groups of employees are given weekly cost and productivity improvement goals. Groups that meet or exceed these goals receive extra compensation. Plant managers are held responsible for cost and profit performance. A plant manager who does not meet corporate performance expectations cannot expect a long career at Nucor (Ghemawat and Stander, 1992). Similar group-oriented cost reduction systems are in place at some of Nucor's major competitors, including Chaparral Steel (Ghemawat and Stander, 1992).

Less formal management control systems also drive a cost reduction philosophy at cost-leadership firms. For example, although Wal-Mart is one of the most successful retail operations in the world, Wal-Mart's Arkansas headquarters is plain and simple. Indeed, some have suggested that Wal-Mart's headquarters looks like one of Wal-Mart's warehouses. Its style of interior decoration was once described as "early bus station." Regional vice presidents at Wal-Mart travel every week, from Monday to Thursday, meet all day Friday, attend a companywide meeting on Saturday morning, and then have late Saturday and Sunday off, just in time to start traveling again on Monday. This schedule enables Wal-Mart to reduce its costs by 2 percent of sales by *not* opening independent regional offices. Wal-Mart even involves its customers in reducing costs by asking them to "help keep your costs low" by returning shopping carts to the designated areas in Wal-Mart's parking lots (Walton, 1992).

Compensation Policies

Compensation at cost-leadership firms is usually tied directly to cost-reducing efforts. Such firms often provide incentives for employees to work together to reduce costs and increase or maintain quality, and they expect *every* employee to take responsibility for both costs and quality.

As suggested earlier, Arco Oil and Gas has been very successful in exploiting its cost advantages. As the largest gasoline retailer in California, Arco enjoys substantial economy-of-scale advantages in oil refining. These cost advantages also reflect Arco's differential access to low-cost factors of production—that is, relatively inexpensive crude oil from its large Alaskan reserves. Under the leadership of Lodwrick Cook, Arco organized itself to exploit and extend its cost advantages. In the early 1980s, Arco eliminated credit purchases and passed the savings on to customers in the form of lower prices. In 1991 and 1992, Arco continued downsizing its organization—a process that was begun in the early 1980s—by reducing the number of its U.S. employees by

20,000, or 7 percent of its total work force. Through the 1980s and 1990s, Arco reduced the number of its service stations from 7,400 to 1,500, keeping only the best outlets. Arco service stations now sell almost 250,000 gallons a month, over twice the industry average. And overhead at Arco service stations averages only 5 cents per gallon—half of the industry average of 10 cents per gallon. As a result of these numerous actions, Arco has been able to sell gasoline for from 8 to 10 cents below the costs of its competitors and still earn a five-year average return on equity of 21.5 percent—over twice the industry average (Rose, 1991).

6.5   SUMMARY

After engaging in a complete SWOT analysis, firms must choose and implement strategies to generate competitive advantages. There are two broad categories of strategies: business and corporate. There are two types of business strategies: competitive and cooperative. Examples of competitive business strategies include cost leadership and product differentiation. Examples of cooperative business strategies include tacit collusion and strategic alliances. This chapter examines cost-leadership competitive business strategies.

There are several reasons why firms producing essentially the same products can have different economic costs. Some of the most important of these reasons are (1) size differences and economies of scale, (2) size differences and diseconomies of scale, (3) learning-curve economies, (4) differential access to factors of production, and (5) technological advantages independent of scale. In addition, firms competing in the same industry can make policy choices about the kinds of products and services to sell that will have an important impact on their relative cost position. Cost leadership in an industry can generate economic profits and can assist a firm in reducing the threat of each of the five forces in an industry outlined in Chapter 3.

Each of the sources of cost advantage discussed in this chapter can be a source of sustained competitive advantage if it is rare and costly to imitate. Overall, differential access to factors of production and technological software advantages independent of scale have the greatest potential to create cost-based sustained competitive advantages. The ability to take advantage of this potential depends on the firm organizing itself appropriately. Organizational structure, management control systems, and compensation policy all play an important role in this organizational question.

REVIEW QUESTIONS

1. Porter originally argued that there are *three* generic competitive strategies: cost leadership, product differentiation, and focus. Others have suggested that focus is just a special case of cost leadership or product differentiation and thus there are only *two* competitive strategies. It could also be argued that firms can choose from among numerous strategic alternatives, but whatever alternative they choose, the critical task is to implement that strategy efficiently. This suggests that there is *one* competitive strategy—efficiency. So, how many competitive strategies are there: three, two, or one? Does your answer affect the strategic decisions firms should make?

2. Ivory Soap, Hyundai, and Timex are all cited as examples of firms pursuing cost-leadership strategies, but these firms make substantial investments in advertising, which seems more likely to be associated with a product differentiation strategy. Are these firms really pursuing a cost-leadership strategy, or are they pursuing a product differentiation strategy by emphasizing their lower costs?

3. When economies of scale exist, firms with large volumes of production will have lower costs than will firms with smaller volumes of production. The realization of these economies of scale, however, is far from automatic. What actions can firms take to ensure that they realize whatever economies of sale are created by their volume of production?

4. Firms engage in forward pricing when they establish, during the early stages of the learning curve, a price for their products that is lower than their actual costs, in anticipation of lower costs later on, after significant learning has occurred. Under what conditions, if any, does forward pricing make sense? What risks, if any, do firms engaging in forward pricing face?

5. One way of thinking about organizing to implement cost-leadership strategies is that firms that pursue this strategy should be highly centralized, have high levels of direct supervision, and keep employee wages to an absolute minimum. Another approach is to decentralize decision-making authority—to ensure that individuals who know the most about reducing costs make decisions about how to reduce costs. This, in turn, would imply less direct supervision and somewhat higher levels of employee wages (why?). Which of these two approaches seems more reasonable? Under what conditions would these different approaches make more or less sense?

6. How can being a cost leader enable a firm to exploit the environmental opportunities discussed in Chapter 4?

CHAPTER 7

Competitive Strategies: Product Differentiation

7.1 PRODUCT DIFFERENTIATION STRATEGIES

Product differentiation is a competitive business strategy whereby firms attempt to gain a competitive advantage by increasing the perceived value of their products or services relative to the perceived value of other firms' products or services. These other firms can be either a particular firm's rivals or firms that provide substitute products or services.

Attempts to create differences in the relative perceived value of a firm's products or services often are made by altering the objective properties of those products or services (Porter, 1980). Rolex attempts to differentiate its watches from Timex watches by manufacturing them with solid gold cases. Mercedes attempts to differentiate its cars from Hyundai's cars through sophisticated engineering and high performance. McDonald's attempts to differentiate its fast food from the fast food sold by locally owned, single-outlet fast-food stands by selling the same food, at the same quality and prices, and in the same way at all of its thousands of outlets.

Firms often alter the objective properties of their products or services in order to implement a product differentiation strategy, but the existence of product differentiation, in the end, is *always* a matter of customer perception. Products sold by two different firms may be exactly the same, but if customers believe the first is more valuable than the second, then the first product has a differentiation advantage. For example, the original IBM personal computers were duplicated by a large number of other manufacturers (such as Compaq, Dell, and Hewlett-Packard). There were some minor differences in technology, but these machines were essentially identical. Yet for years corporate customers seemed to prefer IBM personal computers. Moreover, IBM was able to sell its personal computers at a higher price, even though IBM computers were essentially identical to these other firms' computers (Carroll, 1993).

When asked why they preferred purchasing IBM's personal computers, corporate customers often cited factors such as the service that IBM provided, the quality of IBM's machines, and the ability of IBM's personal computer to link up with IBM's mainframe computer software. These factors were cited even though published industry reports suggested that the service that other personal computer companies provided was as good as IBM's, that the quality of IBM's personal computers was not superior to the quality of other firms' personal computers, and that IBM's original personal computers had the same ability to link with mainframe software as other firms' original personal computers—none (Carroll, 1993). However, if products or services are *perceived* as being different, then product differentiation exists.

Just as perceptions can create product differentiation between products that are essentially identical, the lack of perceived differences between products with very different characteristics can prevent product differentiation. For example, many potential customers are likely to believe that Rolex watches (because they are so expensive) use state-of-the-art timekeeping technology and that watches manufactured by Casio (because they are less expensive) use less advanced technology. In fact, Rolex still uses an old timekeeping technology (a self-winding mainspring), and Casio uses the most sophisticated electronic timekeeping technology in the world (battery-driven quartz crystals). But because Casio is perceived to be less sophisticated than Rolex, Casio's potential technology-based product differentiation advantage over Rolex does not exist (Schnorbus, 1988).

Product differentiation is always a matter of customer perceptions, but firms can take a variety of actions to influence these perceptions. These actions can be thought of as bases of product differentiation. Research on bases of product differentiation falls into two broad categories: conceptual distinctions and empirical research.

CONCEPTUAL DISTINCTIONS AS BASES OF PRODUCT DIFFERENTIATION

A wide variety of authors, drawing on their personal experience and the research of others, have developed lists of ways in which firms can differentiate their products or services. One of the most important of these lists, developed by Porter (1980), is presented in Table 7.1. The seven conceptual bases of product differentiation that Porter identified are discussed below.

Product Features

Although the existence of product differentiation is always a matter of customer perception, one of the most obvious ways in which firms can attempt to influence those perceptions is to modify the objective properties of the products or services they sell. Changing product features is an attempt to do this.

In many industries firms try to modify product features to differentiate products. Bose and Yamaha attempt to differentiate their stereo equipment on the basis of sound quality, and Sony tends to focus on the physical size of the products it sells (Schlender, 1992). Ultra-Tide detergent (with bleach) emphasizes its ability to clean white clothes, and Spray 'n Wash emphasizes its ability to take out stains. Mercedes emphasizes engineering excellence and the performance of its cars, Toyota emphasizes quality and reliability, and Hyundai emphasizes sporty styling and price.

Linkages Between Functions

A less obvious but still important way in which a firm can attempt to differentiate its products is through linking different functions within the firm. For example, in selling mainframe computers, IBM has been very successful in linking the sales and service function. When a cus-

---

TABLE 7.1
Ways Firms Can Differentiate Their Products
Source: Porter (1980).

1. Product features

2. Linkages between functions

3. Timing

4. Location

5. Product mix

6. Links with other firms

7. Reputation

---

tomer purchases an IBM mainframe computer, it is not just buying a big blue box with electronic components. Instead, it is buying a relationship with IBM—a relationship that includes high levels of service and technical support. At IBM, the relationship with customers does not end with the purchase of a mainframe computer; it begins with this purchase (Carroll, 1993).

Another example of the importance of linking functions within a firm to help differentiate a product is described in Section 5.3: Apple Computer's ability to design and build a user-friendly personal computer, the Macintosh, depended critically on close relationships between teams of software engineers, hardware engineers, and production design engineers at Apple. Linking these functions enabled Apple to produce a highly differentiated product.

Timing

Introducing a product at the right time can help create product differentiation. As suggested in Section 4.2, in some industry settings (that is, in emerging industries) the critical issue is to be a first mover—to introduce a new product before all other firms. Being first in emerging industries can enable a firm to set important technological standards, preempt strategically valuable assets, and develop customer-switching costs. These possible results from first moving can create among customers a perception that the products or services of the first-moving firm are somehow more valuable than the products or services of other firms (Lieberman and Montgomery, 1988).

First moving has been an important determinant of perceived differences in the quality of education at universities in the United States and worldwide. In the United States, the first few universities founded (for example, Harvard and Yale) are seen as more prestigious than more recently founded state schools. In the United Kingdom, the oldest universities (including Oxford and Cambridge) are widely perceived to be superior to more recently founded universities. Regardless of whether the date of founding of a university has an impact on the quality of education one receives, if there is a *perceived* link between founding date and quality, founding date acts as a timing-based source of product differentiation (London, 1995).

Timing-based product differentiation, however, does not depend just on being a first mover. Sometimes, a firm can be a later mover in an industry but introduce products or services at just the right time and thereby gain a competitive advantage. This can happen when the ultimate success of a product or service depends on the availability of complementary products or technologies. For example, Head Ski's success in the 1960s depended not only on superior ski technology (metal) but also on the rapid growth of destination ski resorts, the development of technology for moving skiers up ski slopes rapidly, and the increase in consumer disposable income (Christensen and Stevenson, 1967). If Head had begun selling its skis before these other developments, it probably would not have been so successful.

In personal computers, the domination of Microsoft's MS-DOS operating system came only after the limitations of the CPM operating system and associated hardware became clear, and only after IBM introduced a personal computer that was able to exploit MS-DOS (Carroll, 1993). If MS-DOS had been marketed before these other events, Microsoft probably would not have enjoyed the rapid increase in size and performance that it has obtained (Wallace and Erickson, 1993).

Location

The physical location of a firm can also be a source of product differentiation. Consider two video rental stores. If these stores are approximately the same size, they probably will have the same current videos to rent, they probably will have the same "hot" titles from recent years, and they probably will have similar lists of classic movies. Thus if one focuses only on the videos available in these two stores, there appears to be no product differentiation. But these stores may differ in other ways. One of the most important is ease of customer access. If one store is located close to customers, or in a location that is easy for customers to get to, it may have a product differentiation advantage compared to the other store (if that other store is not also located in the same kind of way), even though the videos available in both stores are the same (Hotelling, 1929; Ricardo, 1817).

Product Mix

The mix of products or services sold by a firm can be a source of product differentiation. This is especially likely to be the case when those products or services are technologically linked or when a single set of customers purchases several of the firm's mix of products or services.

Hewlett-Packard (HP) is an example of the first kind of product linkage. HP has historically been a leader in the electronic instruments business. Through the 1940s, 1950s, and 1960s, the objective at HP was to design tools "for the engineer at the next bench." The idea was that if HP engineers required certain electronic measuring devices to do their jobs, then it was likely that other engineers in other companies would also need these instruments (Packard, 1995).

Beginning in the late 1960s, HP discovered that its engineer customers (both inside HP and at other firms) were purchasing HP instruments and attaching them with cables made by other firms to computers made by other firms. The value of these instruments, in combination with cables and computers, was greater than the value of instruments, cables, and computers sold separately. This realization was one of the major reasons why HP entered the computer business and began bundling its instruments and computers for certain customers (Packard, 1995).

Shopping malls are an example of the second kind of linkage among a mix of products. Many customers prefer to go to one location, to shop at several stores at once, rather than traveling to a series of locations to shop. This one-stop shopping reduces travel time and helps turn shopping into a social experience. Shopping is as much a social experience as an economic experience—especially among teenagers. Mall development companies have recognized that the value of several stores brought together in a particular location is greater than the value of those stores if they were isolated, and they have invested to help create this mix of retail shopping opportunities (Kotler, 1986).

Links with Other Firms

Another basis of product differentiation is linkages with other firms. Here, instead of differentiating products or services on the basis of linkages between functions within a single firm or linkages between different products, differentiation is based on explicit linkages between one firm's products and the products or services of other firms.

This form of product differentiation has increased in popularity over the last several years. For example, in the late 1980s, several credit card companies indicated that they would pay for extra automobile insurance if customers used these firms' credit cards to rent from specified car rental companies. These credit card companies attempted to use their links with car rental firms to differentiate their credit cards (Hansell, 1993). These linkages also made certain car rental companies (those with links to the credit card firms) more attractive than others.

More recently, movie studios have linked with fast-food restaurants to help differentiate certain movie productions, as well as to differentiate fast food. For example, Burger King sold its soft drinks in Teen-age Mutant Ninja Turtle cups and distributed Teen-age Mutant Ninja Turtle "action figures" with some meals (Gubernick, 1990). McDonald's has linked with the producers of the Batman movies to help market these movies while simultaneously making its own products more attractive. For several months, it was possible to buy McDonald's soft drinks in "bat cups" and to eat french fries from "bat containers" (Lipman, 1992).

In general, linkages between firms to differentiate their products are examples of cooperative strategic alliance strategies. The conditions under which cooperative strategic alliances add value and are sources of sustained competitive advantage are discussed in detail in Chapter 9.

Reputation

One of the most powerful bases of product differentiation is the reputation of a firm and of its products. Reputations are often very difficult to develop. However, once developed, they tend to last a long time, even if the basis for a firm's reputation no longer exists (Klein and Leffler, 1981).

For example, throughout the 1950s and 1960s, Chrysler Corporation had a reputation for high-quality engineering. In particular, Chrysler was known for its excellent transmissions. Whether there were product-based reasons for this reputation is not altogether clear—some have suggested that Chrysler introduced a water-cooled transmission that helped create the reputation. Nevertheless, once this reputation was in place, it remained fixed even though, over time, whatever technological advantages Chrysler transmissions might once have had were diffused throughout the automobile industry (Moritz and Seaman, 1984).

Reputations of firms continue to be important determinants of product differentiation. Although Mercedes and Nissan generally have reputations for producing high-quality cars, recent surveys of customer satisfaction show Mercedes slipping below several other automobile companies (such as Lexus, Infiniti, Honda, and Acura), and Nissan sometimes does not even make the top-10 customer satisfaction list (Armstrong, 1991a). Rolex continues to have a reputation for quality and status even though Rolex watches use outdated technology. Sony continues to have a reputation for excellence in stereo speakers even though most audiophiles argue that several U.S. firms make speakers that are better than any made by Japanese firms (Levine, 1995; Reed and Berlin, 1987).

The relative stability of firm and product reputations, despite reductions in overall quality, has led some economists to develop models of "optimal reputation cheating." These models attempt to describe the amount of reduced quality and performance that a firm with a reputation for high quality can engage in without significantly damaging that reputation (Rogerson, 1983; Allen, 1984). These models show that performing at a level lower than what customers expect, given a firm's reputation, apparently maximizes the economic performance of the firm (Klein and Leffler, 1981).

Although this kind of reasoning works well in abstract mathematical models, it is usually disastrous for real organizations. In the end, the ability of a firm to develop, nurture, and improve its reputation depends on customer experiences with that firm's products and services. If the actual performance of a firm's products or services is less than the expected level of performance, in the long run a firm's reputation will be reduced and no longer a source of product differentiation. Just as a positive reputation may provide a firm with a product differentiation advantage long after the quality of the firm's products or services has been reduced, so can a negative product reputation be a source of competitive disadvantage for a firm long after the quality of the firm's products or services is the same as, or even better than, the quality of other firms' products and services (Klein and Leffler, 1981). A firm with a positive reputation that engages in "optimal reputation cheating" may be creating a sustained competitive disadvantage for itself in some future period.

EMPIRICAL RESEARCH AND BASES OF PRODUCT DIFFERENTIATION

The conceptual work of Porter (1980) and others has gone a long way toward describing possible bases of product differentiation. However, although this conceptual approach describes a broad range of possible ways to differentiate products, it has little to say about how firms actually have differentiated their products. Empirical research can be used to describe the bases of product differentiation that have been used in a variety of industries. Two particularly important empirical techniques for studying the bases of product differentiation are multidimensional scaling and regression analysis of the determinants of product price.

Multidimensional Scaling

Multidimensional scaling is a mathematical technique for analyzing the perceived similarity of a set of products or services. This approach begins by asking a sample of customers to describe how similar several products sold in a single product market are to each other. For example, for the automobiles listed in Fig. 7.1, customers could be asked how similar a Ford Taurus is overall to a Chevrolet Lumina, a Honda Accord, a Mercedes 300E, and so forth. After numerous customers have been asked to characterize the similarity among these cars, an estimate of the perceived similarity of these cars, taken two at a time, can be developed. These measures of product similarity can be arranged in matrix form, as is done in Fig. 7.1.

This similarity matrix is used as input into a multidimensional scaling computer program. The object of the program is to discover a relatively small number (usually two or three) of underlying product dimensions that can be used to mathematically re-create the entire similarity matrix. If two or three underlying product dimensions allow the (reasonably) accurate re-creation of the entire similarity matrix, then those dimensions usually reflect the key bases of product differentiation used in a market. In Fig. 7.1, the hypothetical analysis of the automobile similarity matrix yields two interpretable dimensions: perceived performance and perceived reliability.

FIGURE 7.1
Hypothetical
Multidimensional
Scaling Analysis of
Ten Midsize
Automobiles

Measures of perceived similarity
(1.0 = cars are the same; 0.0 = cars are not similar at all)

	Taurus	Lumina	Accord	LeBaron	⋯	Mercedes
Taurus	1.0	.65	.76	.42	⋯	.54
Lumina	.65	1.0	.53	.47	⋯	.23
Accord	.76	.53	1.0	.65	⋯	.78
LeBaron	.42	.47	.65	1.0		.81
•	•	•	•	•	•	
•	•	•	•	•	•	
•	•	•	•	•	•	
Mercedes	.54	.23	.78	.81		1.0

Two dimensional analysis of this similarity matrix

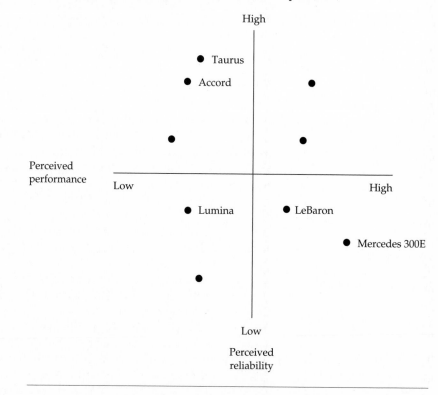

These dimensions can be used to analyze which products in a market compete directly against each other, which products are differentiated, and which segments of the market are not being exploited by currently available products. In Fig. 7.1, each of the automobiles is plotted on a two-dimensional surface in which the x-axis represents a product's dimension score on the perceived performance dimension and the y-axis represents a product's dimension score on the perceived reliability dimension. As can be seen in this figure, the Ford Taurus and Honda Accord compete against each other in the medium-performance/high-reliability segment of the market, the Chevrolet Lumina and Chrysler LeBaron compete in the medium-performance/medium-reliability segment, and Mercedes 300E is relatively isolated in the high-performance/medium-reliability segment.

Beyond revealing the bases of product differentiation that have been used in an industry, this type of analysis can also suggest new product differentiation opportunities. For example, a multidimensional scaling study of competing pain relievers revealed the pattern presented in Fig. 7.2. Notice that in this market, there seems to be room

FIGURE 7.2
Multidimensional Scaling of Perceived Differences Among Pain Relievers
Source: Urban and Hauser (1980:221); Row, Mason, Dickel, and Snyder (1989:125).

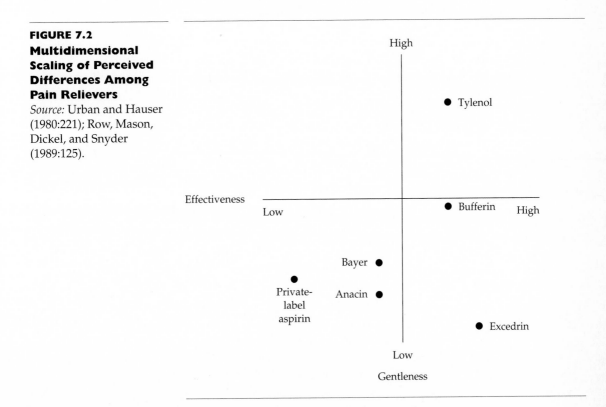

for products that are perceived to be very gentle and very effective (the upper-right quadrant of Fig. 7.2). Several firms have moved to fill this void with the development of extra-strength nonaspirin pain relievers (Rowe, Mason, and Dickel, 1982).

Regression Analysis

Multidimensional scaling is a pure inductive method for describing the bases of product differentiation in an industry. Analysts are not required to hypothesize which particular product attributes might be used as the basis of product differentiation but rather allow dimensions to emerge inductively from an analysis of perceived product similarities. Regression analysis of the determinants of product price is a more deductive approach to the empirical analysis of bases of product differentiation.

Consider the simple example presented in Table 7.2. Here once again the industry under consideration is automobiles. In this approach, however, the analyst proposes a wide range of characteristics that may have an impact on a car's price. In automobiles, product attributes such as engine displacement, passenger room, trunk size, perceived quality, acceleration, and braking capabilities may all have an impact on the price of a car. Each car being studied is measured relative to these possible bases of product differentiation. The product's price (in this case, the wholesale price of each automobile) is then taken as a dependent variable in a multiple regression analysis. The form of the equation is:

$$\text{Price}_i = b_0 + b_1 \text{ attribute}_1 + b_2 \text{ attribute}_2 + b_3 \text{ attribute}_3 + \ldots \; b_j \text{ attribute}_j$$

$$Eq. \; 7.1$$

where

Price_i = the price of product i

attribute_j = a measure of attribute j for product i

b_j = the regression coefficient measuring the impact of attribute j on the price of product i controlling for other product attributes

This regression model estimates the impact of each product attribute on the price of a product. A statistically significant regression coefficient in this equation suggests that a particular product attribute has a significant impact on a product's price and, by implication, can be thought of as a basis of product differentiation. In Table 7.2, it turns out

TABLE 7.2
Hypothetical Regression Analysis of Bases of Product Differentiation in Automobiles
Dependent variable: price

Independent Variables	Regression Coefficient	Statistical Significance
Constant	1.78	*
Engine displacement	.23	
Passenger room	2.89	
Trunk size	4.87	*
Perceived quality	.21	
Acceleration	21.34	**
Braking capabilities	.256	*

* = Significant at the .05 level
** = Significant at the .01 level

that acceleration, braking capabilities, and trunk size all have a significant impact on the price of cars and thus are likely to be bases of product differentiation in this market.

Application

Both multidimensional scaling and multiple regression have been applied to study the bases of product differentiation in a wide variety of industries. One particularly important study, by Caves and Williamson (1985), combined a statistical technique similar to multidimensional scaling (factor analysis) and a multiple regression approach to describe the bases of product differentiation for consumer and durable goods sold in the United States and Australia.

Caves and Williamson (1985) began by measuring a large number of attributes and characteristics of the products in their sample. Next, they analyzed these characteristics (using factor analysis) to discover a set of five underlying product attribute dimensions. These dimensions were then used as independent variables in a multiple regression analysis, with product price as a dependent variable. The results of these analyses are presented in Table 7.3.

Caves and Williamson (1985) found that the products in their sample were differentiated along five dimensions: the level of product customization, product complexity, emphasis on consumer marketing, distribution channels, and service and support. Each of these empirically derived bases of product differentiation is discussed below.

TABLE 7.3
Empirically Derived Bases of Product Differentiation
Source: Caves and Williamson (1985).

1. Products customized for specific customers

2. Product complexity

3. Emphasis on consumer marketing

4. Different distribution channels

5. Service and support

Product Customization.   Products are differentiated in the extent to which they are customized for particular customer applications. In the manufacturing tool industry, for example, Hurco Machine Tools of Indianapolis, Indiana, and other firms manufacture and sell general-purpose machine tools. These are stand-alone tools that can be used to mill steel into gears, panels, and other parts of machines. Germany's Trumpf Machine Tools and other firms manufacture semicustom machine tools—tools that are slightly more sophisticated and partially customized to a particular customer's manufacturing needs. Fanuc and other firms manufacture fully customized machine tools. These machine tools are actually a type of robot that is specifically designed to fit into a particular customer's unique manufacturing process (Badaracco and Hasegawa, 1988).

Product differentiation by level of customization is common in industries besides machine tools. For example, Hewlett-Packard and National Semiconductor specialize in designing general-purpose semiconductors. Other firms design semicustom semiconductors—devices that have some general-purpose components but also have some customer-specific attributes. And other firms, including Silicon Solutions of Palo Alto, California, design only fully customized chips. These chips are single purpose, are designed for a particular customer's need, and usually translate inefficient programming code into more efficient semiconductor hardware.

Product Complexity.   Products have been differentiated by their complexity. Compare, for example, BIC's crystal pen and a Cross pen. Both pens write, so writing per se is not a basis of differentiation. However, the standard BIC crystal ("writes first time, every time") has only seven parts, but the Cross pen has several dozen.

Consumer Marketing.   Differential emphasis on consumer marketing has been a basis for product differentiation. For example, hand soaps such as Lava and SoftSoap have received substantial consumer marketing support in the form of television advertisements, coupons, and so forth. In contrast, liquid and powder hand soaps for industrial uses receive little or no consumer marketing support. Again, both the highly marketed soaps and the industrial soaps help clean hands. Thus cleaning ability per se is not the basis of product differentiation. Rather, the extent to which consumer marketing is used to sell these different soaps is the basis for product differentiation.

Distribution Channels.   Products have been differentiated on the basis of alternative distribution channels. For example, in the soft-drink industry, Coca-Cola, Pepsi Co, and Seven-Up all distribute their drinks through a network of independent and company-owned bottlers. These firms manufacture key ingredients for their soft drinks and ship these ingredients to local bottlers, who add carbonated water, package the drinks in bottles or cans, and distribute the final product to soft-drink outlets in a given geographic area. Each local bottler has exclusive rights to distribute a particular brand in a geographic location (Porter and Wayland, 1991).

Canada Dry has adopted a completely different distribution network. Instead of relying on local bottlers, Canada Dry packages its final product in several locations and then ships its soft drinks directly to wholesale grocers, who distribute them to local grocery stores, convenience stores, and other retail outlets (Porter and Wayland, 1991).

One of the consequences of these alternative distribution strategies is that Canada Dry has a relatively strong presence in grocery stores but a relatively small presence in soft-drink vending machines. The vending machine market is dominated by Coca-Cola and Pepsi Co. These two firms have local distributors that maintain and stock vending machines. Canada Dry has no local distributors and is able to get its products into vending machines only when they are purchased by local Coca-Cola or Pepsi distributors. These local distributors are likely to purchase and stock Canada Dry products such as Canada Dry ginger ale, but they are contractually forbidden from purchasing Canada Dry's various cola products (Porter and Wayland, 1991).

Service and Support.   Products have been differentiated by the level of service and support associated with them. Some firms in the home appliance market, including General Electric, have not developed their own service and support network and instead rely on a network of independent service and support operations throughout the United States. Other firms in the same industry, including Sears, have developed their own service and support network (Ghemawat, 1993).

Differences in service and support have recently become a major point of competition in the automobile industry. Such firms as Lexus (a division of Toyota) and Saturn (a division of General Motors) compete not only on the basis of product quality but also on the basis of the level of service and support they provide. To emphasize Saturn's willingness to provide service and support, Saturn actually advertised a need that one of its customers had to replace a defective seat in a Saturn car. The customer lived in the Alaska wilderness, and Saturn sent a customer service representative there for just a single day to replace the defective seat.

PRODUCT DIFFERENTIATION AND CREATIVITY

The conceptual bases of product differentiation listed in Table 7.1 and the empirically derived bases of product differentiation listed in Table 7.3 together indicate a broad range of ways in which firms can differentiate their products and services. In the end, however, any effort to list all possible ways to differentiate products and services is doomed to failure. Product differentiation is ultimately an expression of the creativity of individuals and groups within firms and is limited only by the opportunities that exist in a particular industry and by the willingness and ability of firms to creatively explore ways to take advantage of those opportunities. It is not unreasonable to expect that the day some academic researcher claims to have developed the definitive list of bases of product differentiation, some creative engineer, marketing specialist, or manager will think of yet another way to differentiate his or her product.

7.2 THE VALUE OF PRODUCT DIFFERENTIATION

In order to have the potential for generating competitive advantages, the bases of product differentiation upon which a firm competes must be valuable. Economically valuable bases of product differentiation can enable a firm to increase its revenues, neutralize threats, and exploit opportunities.

PRODUCT DIFFERENTIATION AND ECONOMIC PERFORMANCE

Given the wide variety of ways in which firms can differentiate their products and services, it is not surprising that the impact of this particular strategy on firm performance and industry structure has received a great deal of attention in the economic literature. The two classic treatments of these relationships, developed independently and published at approximately the same time, are by Edward Chamberlin (1933) and Joan Robinson (1934).

Both Chamberlin and Robinson examine product differentiation and firm performance relative to perfect competition. Under perfect competition, there are assumed to be numerous firms in an industry, each controlling a small proportion of the market, and the products or services sold by these firms are assumed to be identical. Under these conditions, firms face a horizontal demand curve (since they have no control over the price they set for the products they sell), and they maximize their economic performance by producing and selling output such that marginal revenue equals marginal costs. The maximum economic performance a firm in a perfectly competitive market can obtain, assuming no cost differences across firms, is a normal economic profit.

When firms sell differentiated products, they gain some ability to adjust their prices. A firm can sell its output at very high prices and produce relatively smaller amounts of output, or it can sell its output at very low prices and produce relatively greater amounts of output. These tradeoffs between price and quantity produced suggest that firms selling differentiated products face a *downward-sloping* demand curve, rather than the horizontal demand curve for firms in a perfectly competitive market. Firms selling differentiated products and facing a downward-sloping demand curve are in an industry structure described as *monopolistic competition* by Chamberlin (1933). It is as if, within the market niche defined by a firm's differentiated product, a firm possesses a monopoly.

Monopolistically competitive firms still maximize their economic profit by producing and selling a quantity of products such that marginal revenue equals marginal cost. The price that firms can charge at this optimal point depends on the demand they face for their differentiated product. If demand is large, then the price that can be charged is greater; if demand is low, then the price that can be charged is lower. However, if a firm's average total cost is below the price it can charge (that is, if average total cost is less than the demand-determined price), then a firm selling a differentiated product can earn an above-normal economic profit (Calton and Perlott, 1994).

Consider the example presented in Fig. 7.3. Several curves are relevant in this figure. First, notice that the demand (*D*) facing a firm in this industry is downward sloping. This means that the industry is not perfectly competitive and that a firm has some control over the prices it will charge for its products. Also, the marginal-revenue curve (*MR*) is downward sloping and everywhere lower than the demand curve. Marginal revenue is downward sloping because in order to sell additional levels of output of a single product, a firm must be willing to

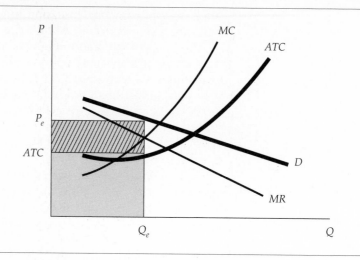

lower its price. The marginal-revenue curve is lower than the demand curve since this lower price applies to all the products sold by a firm, not just to any additional products the firm sells. The marginal-cost curve (*MC*) in Fig. 7.3 is upward sloping, indicating that in order to produce additional outputs, a firm must accept additional costs. The average-total-cost curve (*ATC*) can have a variety of shapes, depending on the economies of scale, the cost of factors of production, and other cost phenomena described in Chapter 6.

These four curves (demand, marginal revenue, marginal cost, and average total cost) can be used to determine the level of economic profit for a firm under monopolistic competition. In order to maximize profit, the firm produces an amount (Q_e) such that marginal costs equal marginal revenues. To determine the price of a firm's output at this level of production, a vertical line is drawn from the point where marginal costs equal marginal revenues. This line will intersect with the demand curve. Where this vertical line intersects demand, a horizontal line is drawn to the vertical (price) axis to determine the price a firm can charge. In Fig. 7.3, this price is P_e. At the point P_e, average total cost is less than the price. The total revenue obtained by the firm in this situation (price × quantity) is indicated by the shaded area in Fig. 7.3. The non-normal economic profit portion of this total revenue is indicated by the cross-hatched section of the shaded portion of the figure. Since this cross-hatched section is above average total costs in Fig. 7.3, it represents an above-normal economic profit. If this section were below average total costs, it would represent below-normal economic profits.

Chamberlin (1933) and Robinson (1934) go on to discuss the impact of entry into the market niche defined by a firm's differentiated product. As discussed in Section 3.1, a basic assumption of S-C-P models is that the existence of above-normal economic profits motivates entry into an industry or into a market niche within an industry. In monopolistically competitive industries, such entry means that the demand curve facing incumbent firms shifts downward and to the left. This implies that an incumbent firm's customers will buy less of its output if it maintains its prices or (equivalently) that a firm will have to lower its prices to maintain its current volume of sales. In the long run, entry into this market niche can lead to a situation where the price of goods or services sold when a firm produces output such that marginal cost equals marginal revenue is exactly equal to that firm's average total cost. At this point, a firm earns a normal economic return even if it still sells a differentiated product.

Much of Chamberlin and Robinson's analysis of competition and performance in monopolistically competitive industries has implications for a strategic analysis of product differentiation. The ability of a firm to market a differentiated product, and obtain above-normal economic profits, depends on that product either neutralizing threats or exploiting opportunities. The ability of a firm to maintain its competitive advantage depends, in turn, on the rareness and imitability of its organizational strengths and weaknesses.

PRODUCT DIFFERENTIATION AND ENVIRONMENTAL THREATS

Successful product differentiation helps a firm respond to each of the environmental threats that Porter identified. For example, product differentiation helps reduce the threat of new entry by forcing potential entrants to an industry to absorb not only the standard costs of beginning business but also the additional costs associated with overcoming incumbent firms' product differentiation advantages. The relationship between product differentiation and new entry has already been discussed in Section 3.2.

Product differentiation reduces the threat of rivalry, because each firm in an industry attempts to carve out its own unique product niche. Rivalry is not reduced to zero, for these products still compete with one another for a common set of customers, but it is somewhat attenuated, because the customers each firm seeks are different. For example, both a Rolls Royce and a Hyundai provide the same basic consumer need—transportation; but it is unlikely that potential customers of Rolls Royces will also be interested in purchasing a Hyundai, or vice versa.

Product differentiation also helps firms reduce the threat of substitutes by making a firm's current products appear more attractive than substitute products. For example, fresh food can be thought of as a substitute for frozen processed foods. In order to make its frozen processed foods more attractive than fresh foods, products like Stouffer's and Swanson are marketed heavily through television advertisements, newspaper ads, point-of-purchase displays, and coupons.

Product differentiation can also reduce the threat of suppliers. Powerful suppliers can raise the prices of the products or services they provide. Often, these increased supply costs must be passed on to a firm's customers in the form of higher prices. A firm without a highly differentiated product may find it difficult to pass its increased costs on to customers, since these customers will have numerous other ways to purchase similar products or services from a firm's competitors. However, a firm with a highly differentiated product may have loyal customers or customers who are unable to purchase similar products or services from other firms. These types of customers are more likely to accept increased prices due to a firm passing on increased costs caused by a powerful supplier. Thus a powerful supplier may be able to raise its prices, but these increases often do not reduce the profitability of a firm selling a highly differentiated product.

Of course, the ability of a firm selling a highly differentiated product to be somewhat immune from powerful suppliers may actually encourage suppliers to exercise their power. Since firms can pass increased costs on to customers, suppliers may decide to increase costs. At some point, even the most loyal customers of the most differentiated products or services may find a firm's prices too high. These price barriers suggest a limit to a firm's ability to raise prices. Any increase in supply costs once these barriers are reached results in reduced economic profits for a firm.

However, at these price and supply-cost levels, a firm may find it possible to obtain substitute supplies, or other firms may have entered into the supply market. The existence of substitute supplies or more suppliers both attenuates the power of suppliers and enables a firm selling a differentiated product to maintain positive economic profits.

The relationship between sugar suppliers and soft-drink manufacturers over the last twenty years has had many of these characteristics. In the 1970s, sugar was a major ingredient in soft drinks. However, in the early 1980s, sugar prices rose suddenly. At first, soft-drink companies were able to pass these increased costs on to customers in the form of increased prices. Customer loyalty to soft-drink brands, and dislike for soft-drink substitutes, kept customers purchasing soft drinks despite increased prices. However, as sugar prices continued to rise, several alternatives to sugar were developed. First, expensive sugar from sugar cane was supplemented by less expensive high-fructose corn syrup. Second, aspartame, a low-calorie sugar substitute (marketed under the brand name NutraSweet) was developed. Thus although soft-drink firms could raise their prices in response to increased sugar costs, ultimately these higher prices led to the development of sugar substitutes that reduced the power of sugar companies as suppliers to the soft drink industry (Casey, 1976).

Finally, product differentiation can reduce the threat of buyers. As both Chamberlin and Robinson observed, when a firm sells a highly differentiated product, it enjoys a quasi-monopoly in that segment of the market. Buyers interested in purchasing this particular product must buy it from a particular firm. Any potential buyer power is reduced by the ability of a firm to withhold highly valued products or services from a buyer.

PRODUCT DIFFERENTIATION AND ENVIRONMENTAL OPPORTUNITIES

Product differentiation can also help a firm take advantage of environmental opportunities. For example, in fragmented industries, firms with highly differentiated products or services may be able to use this product position to help consolidate the industry. In the highly fragmented commercial printing business, a national advertising campaign emphasizing quality printing and fast service has enabled Postal Instant Printing (PIP) to gain a large share of this fragmented market, although some recent management turmoil has created problems for this firm (Tannenbaum, 1993).

The role of product differentiation in emerging industries has been discussed in Section 4.2. By being a first mover in these industries, firms can gain product differentiation advantages based on perceived technological leadership, preemption of strategically valuable assets, and buyer loyalty due to high switching costs.

In mature industries, product differentiation efforts often switch from attempts to introduce radically new technologies to product refinement as a basis of product differentiation. For example, in the mature retail gasoline market, firms attempt to differentiate their products not by introducing radically new gasolines but rather by introducing slightly modified gasolines (cleaner-burning gasoline, gasoline that cleans fuel injectors, and so forth) and by altering the product mix (linking gasoline sales with convenience stores). Both Arco and Ashland Oil (through its SuperAmerica subsidiary) have attempted to differentiate their retail gasoline sales businesses in this manner (Wald, 1991).

Product differentiation can also be an important strategic option in a declining industry. Product differentiating firms may be able to become leaders in this kind of industry (based on their reputation, on unique product attributes, or on some other product differentiation basis). Alternatively, highly differentiated firms may be able to discover a viable market niche that will enable them to survive despite the overall decline in the market.

Finally, the decision to implement a product differentiation strategy can have a significant impact on how a firm acts in a global industry. In general, product differentiation requires a firm to be in close contact with its customers, to understand their idiosyncratic needs and how those needs can be addressed in a firm's products or services. Global strategies, where business functions are located in ways that minimize functional costs, may make it relatively difficult for a firm to differentiate its products or services in ways that are needed by different local markets. A multinational strategy, where different market segments throughout the world are serviced by quasi-independent operating divisions, may enable a firm to differentiate its products in ways that respond to local market needs (Bartlett and Ghoshal, 1989). The tradeoffs associated with global strategies for low costs and multinational strategies for local product differentiation are discussed in detail in Chapter 14.

7.3   PRODUCT DIFFERENTIATION AND SUSTAINED COMPETITIVE ADVANTAGE

Product differentiation strategies add value by enabling firms to charge for their products or services prices that are greater than a firm's average total cost. Firms that implement this strategy successfully can reduce a variety of environmental threats and exploit a variety of environmental opportunities. However, as discussed in Section 5.4, the ability of a strategy to add value to a firm must be linked with rare and costly-to-imitate organizational strengths and weaknesses in order to generate a sustained competitive advantage. Each of the bases of product differentiation listed earlier in this chapter varies with respect to how likely it is to be rare and how likely it is to be costly to imitate.

RARE BASES FOR PRODUCT DIFFERENTIATION

The concept of product differentiation generally assumes that the number of firms that have been able to differentiate their products in a particular way is, at some point in time, less than the number of firms needed to generate perfect competition dynamics (Calton and Perloff, 1994). When Chamberlin and Robinson suggest that highly differentiated firms can charge a price for their product that is greater than average total cost, they are asserting that these firms are implementing a rare competitive strategy.

Ultimately, the rareness of a product differentiation strategy depends on the ability of individual firms to be creative. As suggested earlier, highly creative firms will be able to discover or create new ways to differentiate their products or services. These kinds of firms will always be one step ahead of the competition, for rival firms will often be trying to imitate these firms' last product differentiation move while creative firms are working on their next product differentiation move.

THE IMITABILITY OF PRODUCT DIFFERENTIATION

Valuable and rare bases of product differentiation must be costly to imitate if they are to be sources of sustained competitive advantage. Both direct duplication and substitution, as approaches to imitation, are important.

Direct Duplication of Product Differentiation

Once a firm has discovered a new way to differentiate its product, it usually is forced to reveal that new source of product differentiation to its competitors when it begins selling its new products or services. For example, when Chrysler Corporation began selling its line of mini-vans—a new and creative way to differentiate Chrysler's station wagons from other firms' station wagons—Chrysler revealed minivans as a basis of product differentiation in this segment of the automobile market. When Seven-Up revealed its effort to differentiate its soft-drink product on the basis of its lack of caffeine, it revealed "caffeine-free" as a potential basis of product differentiation in that market. Also, when Procter & Gamble began selling concentrated laundry detergent in smaller boxes, it revealed concentration and container size as potential bases of product differentiation in the laundry detergent market. Thus although the rareness of product differentiation depends on the creativity of individual firms, the marketing of differentiated products or services often provides a road map to other firms seeking to duplicate a successful firm's differentiation efforts.

Bases of Product Differentiation That Are Easy to Duplicate.

Selling a differentiated product often reveals the basis of product differentiation, but such bases vary in the extent to which they are easy to duplicate and thus are subject to imitation. As can be seen in Table 7.4, easy-to-duplicate bases of product differentiation tend *not* to build on historical, uncertain, or socially complex firm resources or capabilities.

TABLE 7.4
Bases of Product Differentiation and the Cost of Duplication

	Basis of product differentiation	**Source of costly duplication**		
		History	Uncertainty	Social Complexity
Low-cost duplication possible	1. Product features	—	—	—
May be costly to duplicate	2. Product mix	*	*	*
	3. Links with other firms	*	—	**
	4. Product customization	*	—	**
	5. Product complexity	*	—	*
	6. Consumer marketing	—	**	—
Usually costly to duplicate	7. Links between functions	*	*	**
	8. Timing	***	*	—
	9. Location	***	—	—
	10. Reputation	***	**	***
	11. Distribution channels	**	*	**
	12. Service and support	*	*	**

— = Not likely to be a source of costly duplication
  * = Somewhat likely to be a source of costly duplication
 ** = Likely to be a source of costly duplication
*** = Very likely to be a source of costly duplication

For example, although many firms spend a great deal of time and energy trying to differentiate their products on the basis of product features, product features by themselves are usually relatively easy to duplicate. Rival firms can usually purchase the differentiated product and take it apart to discover the features that act as a basis of differentiation. Such reverse engineering has occurred for many products in numerous markets. For example, IBM's personal computer was reverse-engineered and duplicated by several firms. Kodak reverse-engineered several aspects of Polaroid's instant cameras. However, because these characteristics of Polaroid's cameras were patented, reverse engineering cost Kodak a great deal (Porter and Fuller, 1978).

Reverse engineering can even be applied to products that cannot be purchased and taken apart. For example, in the early 1990s, a new offensive football system, the run-and-shoot offense, began to become popular in the National Football League (Oates, 1992). This wide-open offensive system emphasizes quick play calling, multiple pass options, and a limited running attack. It was diffused throughout much of the league in at least two ways. Coaches who had experience working with the run-and-shoot offense began working at new teams, and teams that did not have an experienced run-and-shoot coach on their staffs spent hours watching videotape of run-and-shoot offenses to discover how the system worked. This "reconstruction" can be thought of as an example of reverse engineering.

Bases of Product Differentiation That May Be Costly to Duplicate. Some bases of product differentiation may be costly to duplicate, at least in some circumstances. A firm's product mix can be easy to duplicate if numerous competing firms possess the resources and capabilities that the firm uses to develop its product mix. The ability to offer both personal computers and printers to customers is not unique to Hewlett-Packard. IBM, Apple, Gateway 2000, and numerous other firms provide this similar product mix. But HP's ability to link its personal computers with its electronic instruments is unusual, since few (if any) firms have the same presence that HP has in both the personal computer business and the electronic instruments business (Packard, 1995).

Links with other firms may be easy to duplicate in some situations and costly to duplicate in others. For example, the first car rental firm that established a link with a credit card company, so that the credit card company would pay for a customer's extra insurance, may have obtained a brief product differentiation–based competitive advantage. However, as soon as the relationship was revealed (through advertising), numerous other credit card and car rental firms rapidly duplicated these linkages. Indeed, currently every major credit card firm has this type of relationship with at least one car rental firm. This suggests that these particular interfirm relations were not a source of sustained competitive advantage.

Some linkages between firms, however, can be very costly to imitate. This is especially likely when specific kinds of linkages can exist between only a few firms (that is, when only a few firms have the needed complementary resources and capabilities to link together), and when these linkages themselves are based on socially complex relationships (Barney, 1991). These kinds of cooperative interfirm relations are discussed in detail in Chapter 9.

In the same way, product customization and product complexity are often easy-to-duplicate bases of product differentiation. But sometimes the ability of a firm to customize its products for one of its customers depends on close relationships it has developed with those customers. Product customization of this sort depends on the willingness of a firm to share often proprietary details about its operations, products, research and development, or other characteristics with a supplying firm. Willingness to share this kind of information, in turn, depends on the ability of each firm to trust and rely on the other. The firm opening its operations to a supplier must trust that that supplier will not make this information broadly available to competing firms. The firm supplying the customized products must trust that its customer will not take unfair advantage by requiring the development of a customized product that has no other potential customers and then insisting on a lower-than-agreed-to price, higher-than-expected quality, and so forth (Barney and Hansen, 1994). If two firms have developed these kinds of socially complex relationships, and few other firms have them, then these links with other firms will be costly to duplicate and a source of sustained competitive advantage. These issues are discussed in detail in Chapter 9's discussion of cooperative strategic alliances and Chapter 10's discussion of vertical integration strategies.

Finally, consumer marketing, though a very common form of product differentiation, is often easy to duplicate. Many consumer marketing efforts seem to follow very tried-and-true paths, including advertising, point-of-purchase displays, and coupons. Rarely are these efforts difficult to duplicate. For example, in advertising beer, attractive bathing-suit-clad men and women engaging in some sporting contest (baseball, basketball, volleyball) or having a party are very common. Rarely will these characteristics of advertisements be difficult to duplicate, and thus rarely will they be a source of sustained competitive advantage.

However, periodically, an advertising campaign or slogan, a point-of-purchase display, or some other attribute of a consumer marketing campaign will unexpectedly catch on and create greater-than-expected product awareness. In marketing beer, slogans such as "Tastes great, less filling" and "Why ask why" and the "Spuds McKenzie" character have had these unusual effects. If a firm, in relation with its various consumer marketing agencies, is systematically able to develop superior consumer marketing campaigns, then this firm may be able to obtain a sustained competitive advantage. But if such campaigns are unpredictable and largely a matter of a firm's good luck, they cannot be expected to be a source of sustained competitive advantage (Barney, 1986a).

Bases of Product Differentiation That Are Costly to Duplicate.   The remaining bases of product differentiation listed in Table 7.4 are usually costly to duplicate. Firms that differentiate their products on these bases may be able to obtain sustained competitive advantages.

Linkages across functions within a single firm are usually a costly-to-duplicate basis of product differentiation. Where linkages with other firms can be either easy or costly to duplicate, depending on the nature of the relationship that exists between firms, linkages across functions within a single firm usually require socially complex, trusting relations. As will be described in detail in Chapters 10 and 12, there are numerous built-in conflicts between functions and divisions within a single firm. Organizations that have a history and culture that support cooperative relations among conflicting divisions may be able to set aside functional and divisional conflicts, to cooperate in delivering a differentiated product to the market (Porter, 1980). However, firms with a history of conflict across functional and divisional boundaries face a significant, and costly, challenge in altering these socially complex, historical patterns (Williamson, 1975; Barney, 1986b).

One firm that has been attempting to eliminate conflicts across its functions is Chrysler. Since its founding, different functions involved in design, engineering, and manufacturing at Chrysler have had adversarial relationships (Moritz and Seaman, 1984). Design engineers would develop body styles that conflicted with the requirements of engine designers; engine designers would develop power plants that were very costly to build, and so forth. The results of these adversarial relations were long delays in product development, product compromises, and lower quality. Recently, however, Chrysler has attempted to set aside traditional conflicts in developing automobile platforms (Taylor, 1994b). Reports suggest that this new cooperative approach has been successful, although it is still limited to a small group of engineers working on specific projects (Loeb, 1995a). Whether Chrysler will be able to develop these kinds of cooperative relations between other critical functions, and the costs of these attempts, are still not known.

Timing is also a difficult-to-duplicate basis of product differentiation. As suggested in Section 5.2, it is difficult (if not impossible) to re-create a firm's unique historical position. Rivals of a firm with a timing-based product differentiation advantage may need to seek alternative ways to differentiate their products.

Location is often a difficult-to-duplicate basis of product differentiation. This is especially the case when a firm's location is unique. For example, research on the hotel preferences of business travelers suggests that location is a major determinant of the decision to stay in a hotel. Hotels that are convenient to both major transportation and commercial centers in a city are preferred, other things being equal, to hotels in other types of locations. Indeed, location has been shown to be a more important decision criterion for business travelers than price. If only a few hotels in a city have these prime locations, and if no further hotel development is possible, then hotels with these locations can gain sustained competitive advantages.

Of all the bases of product differentiation listed in this chapter, perhaps none is more difficult to duplicate than a firm's reputation. A firm's reputation is actually a socially complex relationship between a firm and its customers, based on years of experience, commitment, and trust. Reputations are not built quickly, nor can they be bought and sold. Rather, they can only be developed over time by consistent investment in the relationship between a firm and its customers. A firm with a positive reputation can enjoy a significant competitive advantage, whereas a firm with a negative reputation, or no reputation, may have to invest significant amounts over long periods of time to match the differentiated firm.

Distribution channels can also be a costly-to-duplicate basis of product differentiation. This can be the case for at least two reasons. First, relations between a firm and its distribution channels are often socially complex and thus costly to duplicate. Second, the supply of distribution channels may not be completely elastic. Firms that already have access to these channels may be able to use them, but firms that do not have such access may be forced to create their own or develop new channels. Creating new channels, or developing entirely new means of distribution, can be difficult and costly undertakings (Hennart, 1988). These costs are one of the primary motivations underlying many international joint ventures (see Chapter 9).

Finally, level of service and support can be a costly-to-duplicate basis of product differentiation. In most industries, it is usually not too costly to provide a minimum level of service and support. In home electronics, this minimum level of service can be provided by a network of independent electronic repair shops. In automobiles, this level of service can be provided by service facilities associated with dealerships. In fast foods, this level of service can be provided by a minimum level of employee training.

However, moving beyond this minimum level of service and support can be difficult to duplicate for at least two reasons. First, increasing the quality of service and support may involve substantial amounts of costly training. McDonald's has created a sophisticated training facility (Hamburger University) to maintain its unusually high level of service in fast foods. General Electric has invested heavily in training for service and support over the last several years (Deutsch, 1991). Many Japanese automakers have spent millions on training employees to help support auto dealerships, before opening U.S. manufacturing facilities (Armstrong, 1991b).

More important than the direct costs of the training needed to provide high-quality service and support, these bases of product differentiation often reflect an attitude of a firm and its employees toward customers. In many firms throughout the world, the customer has become "the bad guy." This is, in many ways, understandable.

Employees tend to interact with their customers less frequently than they interact with other employees. When they do interact with customers, they are often the recipients of complaints directed at the firm. In these settings, hostility toward the customer can develop. Such hostility is, of course, inconsistent with a product differentiation strategy based on customer service and support.

In the end, high levels of customer service and support are based on socially complex relations between firms and customers. Firms that have conflicts with their customers may face some difficulty duplicating the high levels of service and support provided by competing firms.

Substitutes for Product Differentiation

The bases of product differentiation outlined in this chapter vary in how rare they are likely to be and in how difficult they are to duplicate. However, the ability of the bases of product differentiation to generate a sustained competitive advantage also depends on whether low-cost substitutes exist.

Substitutes for bases of product differentiation can take two forms. First, many of the bases of product differentiation listed in Table 7.4 can be substitutes for each other. For example, product features, product customization, and product complexity are all very similar bases of product differentiation and thus can act as substitutes for each other. A particular firm may try to develop a competitive advantage by differentiating its products on the basis of product customization only to find that its customization advantages are reduced as another firm alters the features of its products.

Thus, for example, there used to be personal computer word-processing software specifically designed for use in publishing. The level of customization of this publishing software was quite substantial. However, over the years, the addition of more features to standard word-processing packages narrowed the product differentiation gap between publishing-oriented word-processing software and general-use word-processing software.

In a similar way, linkages between functions, linkages between firms, and product mix, as bases of product differentiation, can also be substitutes for each other. IBM links its sales and service function to differentiate itself in the mainframe computer market. But other computer sales firms may develop close relationships with computer service companies to close this product differentiation advantage.

Second, other of the strategies discussed throughout this book can be substitutes for many of the bases of product differentiation listed in Table 7.4. For example, one firm may try to gain a competitive advantage through adjusting its product mix, and another firm may substitute strategic alliances to create the same type of product differentiation.

In the late 1980s, one firm in the travel services industry, Allegis Inc., attempted to implement a differentiation strategy by creating a unique mix of products that included an airline, a set of hotels, a car rental agency, and other travel-related services. Although Allegis was unique—no other firm *owned* all these components of the travel business—this product mix was easy to imitate by substituting alliances of many independent travel firms. Indeed, virtually any independent travel agent had at its disposal a much broader range of travel services than was ever owned by Allegis. Also, possible cross-subsidies in Allegis (deals in which the airline, for example, agreed to reduce its fare to make a hotel stay more attractive) were subject to substitution by independent providers of travel services. Since Allegis's product mix was easy to imitate, it did not give this firm a competitive advantage. Indeed, high operating costs and limited travel options gave Allegis a competitive disadvantage relative to cooperating independent travel services. Over time, this disadvantage led to the dissolution of Allegis (Ellis, 1987; Labich, 1987).

In contrast, some of the other bases of product differentiation discussed in this chapter have few obvious close substitutes. These include timing, location, distribution channels, and service and support. To the extent that these bases of product differentiation are also valuable, rare, and difficult to duplicate, they may be sources of sustained competitive advantage.

ORGANIZING FOR SUSTAINED PRODUCT DIFFERENTIATION ADVANTAGE

Organizational structure, management control systems, and compensation policies must be consistent with a firm's product differentiation efforts if a firm is to realize the full potential of those efforts. Whereas the organizational requirements for a cost-leadership strategy focus on reducing costs in developing and manufacturing products, the organizational requirements for a product differentiation strategy emphasize innovativeness, creative flair, and related marketing abilities (Porter, 1980). Some of these organizational requirements are listed in Table 7.5.

Tolerance for Creative Individuals

Many of the attributes listed in Table 7.5 are important for product-differentiating firms, but perhaps none is more important than a tolerance for creativity and failure (Woodman, Sawyer, and Griffin, 1993). Many organizations develop policies, procedures, and other control mechanisms to increase the predictability of managerial actions in a firm. However, this highly structured context can stifle creativity.

Some firms go to great lengths to protect creative individuals and teams from the stifling effects of organizational policies. At Texas

TABLE 7.5
Organizing to Realize the Full Potential of Product Differentiation Strategies

Organizational structure

1. Cross-divisional/cross-functional linkages
2. Willingness to explore new structures to exploit new opportunities
3. Isolated pockets of intense creative efforts

Management control systems

1. Flexibility in controlling activities
2. Tolerance for creative people
3. Ability to learn from innovative failures

Compensation policies

1. Rewards for risk taking, not punishment for failure
2. Rewards for creative flair
3. Subjective/qualitative performance measurement

Instruments (TI), for example, senior managers have both short-term profit responsibilities and longer-term strategic technology development responsibilities (Christensen et al., 1980). TI also has an internal venture-capital organization that will fund innovative ideas of employees. Together, these policies are designed to foster creativity and risk-taking at TI. To protect its newly formed creative teams, Chrysler has built a new design center where creative engineers can be protected from traditional organizational pressures (Taylor, 1994b). And to protect the independence and creativity of several of its recently acquired independent elevator service companies, Westinghouse's elevator division chose not to implement the full Westinghouse management control systems in these organizations (Applegate, Hertenstein, Wishart, and Addonizio, 1989).

Protecting creative individuals and teams from organizational policies and procedures does not mean that these individuals have no responsibilities and have free rein in a firm. However, product-differentiating firms must strike a balance between high levels of managerial control and high levels of creativity. This tradeoff is explored in detail in Chapter 12.

Failure as a Cost of Creativity

As important as protecting creativity from organizational bureaucracy and controls is, a product-differentiating firm must also be able to accept failure as a cost associated with innovation. Not all creative ways to differentiate products will turn out to be valuable (Woodman, Sawyer and Griffin, 1993). The history of business is strewn with examples of product differentiation failures. Failure is a natural consequence of attempts to implement product differentiation strategies. Indeed, a firm that experiences no product differentiation failures is probably not taking enough product differentiation risks.

7.4   IMPLEMENTING PRODUCT DIFFERENTIATION AND COST-LEADERSHIP STRATEGIES

The arguments developed in Chapter 6 and in this chapter suggest that cost-leadership and product differentiation competitive business strategies, under certain conditions, can create both sustained competitive advantages and above-normal economic profits. Given the beneficial impact of both strategies on a firm's competitive position, an important question becomes, Can a single firm simultaneously implement both strategies? After all, if each separately can improve a firm's performance, wouldn't it be better for a firm to implement both?

SIMULTANEOUS LOW-COST AND PRODUCT DIFFERENTIATION STRATEGIES WILL HURT FIRM PERFORMANCE

A quick comparison of the organizational requirements for the successful implementation of cost-leadership strategies (see Table 6.7) and product differentiation strategies (see Table 7.5) summarizes one perspective on the question of implementing these strategies simultaneously. In this view the organizational requirements of these strategies are essentially contradictory (Porter, 1980). Cost leadership requires simple reporting relationships, but product differentiation requires cross-divisional/cross-functional linkages. Cost leadership requires intense labor supervision, but product differentiation requires less intense supervision of creative employees. Cost leadership requires rewards for cost reduction, but product differentiation rewards for creative flair. It is reasonable to ask, Can a single firm combine these multiple contradictory skills and abilities?

Porter (1980) has argued that firms that attempt to implement both strategies will end up doing neither well. This logic leads to the curve pictured in Fig. 7.4. This figure suggests that there are two ways to earn superior economic performance within a single industry: (1) by selling high-priced products and gaining small market share (product differentiation) or (2) by selling low-priced products and gaining large market share (cost leadership). Firms that do not make this choice of strategies (medium price, medium market share) or that attempt to implement both strategies will fail. Porter calls these firms "stuck in the middle."

SIMULTANEOUS LOW-COST AND PRODUCT DIFFERENTIATION STRATEGIES WILL HELP FIRM PERFORMANCE

Recent work contradicts Porter's assertion about being "stuck in the middle." This work suggests that firms that are successful in both cost leadership and product differentiation can often expect to gain a sustained competitive advantage (Hill, 1988). This advantage reflects at least two processes.

Differentiation, Market Share, and Low-Cost Leadership

Firms that are able to successfully differentiate their products and services are likely to see an increase in their volume of sales. This is especially the case if the basis of product differentiation is attractive to a large number of potential customers (Hill, 1988). Thus product differentiation can lead to increased volumes of sales. It has already been established (in Chapter 6) that an increased volume of sales can lead to economies of scale, learning, and other forms of cost reduction. So, successful product differentiation can, in turn, lead to cost reductions and a cost-leadership position (Hill, 1988).

This is the situation that best describes McDonald's. McDonald's has traditionally followed a product differentiation strategy, emphasizing cleanliness, consistency, and fun in its fast-food outlets. Over time,

FIGURE 7.4
Simultaneous Implementation of Cost-Leadership and Product Differentiation Competitive Strategies: Being "Stuck in the Middle." *Source:* Porter (1980).

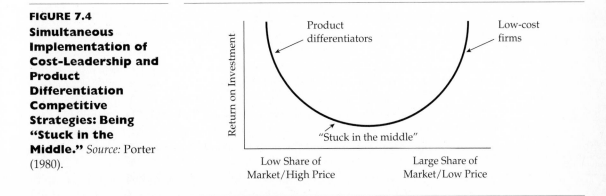

McDonald's has used its differentiated product to become the market share leader in the fast-food industry. This market position has enabled McDonald's to reduce its costs, so that McDonald's is now the cost leader in fast foods as well (Gibson, 1995). Thus McDonald's level of profitability depends both on its product differentiation strategy and its low-cost strategy. Even one of these two strategies by itself would be difficult to overcome; together they give McDonald's a very costly-to-imitate competitive advantage.

Managing Organizational Contradictions

Product differentiation can lead to high market share and low costs. It may also be the case that some firms develop special skills in managing the contradictions that are part of simultaneously implementing low-cost and product differentiation strategies. Some recent research on automobile manufacturing helps describe these special skills.

Traditional thinking in automotive manufacturing was that plants could either reduce manufacturing costs by speeding up the assembly line or increase the quality of the cars they made by slowing the line, emphasizing group production, and so forth. In general, it was thought that plants could not simultaneously build low-cost/high-quality (that is, low cost *and* highly differentiated) automobiles.

Several researchers at the Massachusetts Institute of Technology examined this traditional wisdom. They began by developing rigorous measures of the cost and quality performance of automobile plants and then applied these measures to over seventy auto plants throughout the world that assembled mid-sized sedans. What they discovered was six plants in the entire world that had, simultaneously, very low costs *and* very high quality (Womack, Jones and Roos, 1990).

In examining what made these six plants different from other auto plants, these researchers focused on a broad range of manufacturing policies, management practices, and cultural variables. Three important findings emerged. First, these six plants had the best manufacturing technology hardware available—robots, laser-guided paint machines, and so forth. However, manufacturing hardware by itself was not enough to make these plants special. In addition, policies and procedures at these plants implemented a range of highly participative, group-oriented management techniques, including participative management, quality circles, group production, and total quality management. As important, employees in these plants had a sense of loyalty and commitment toward the plant they worked for—a belief that they would be treated fairly by their plant managers (Womack, Jones, and Roos, 1990).

What this research shows is that firms *can* simultaneously implement cost-leadership and product differentiation strategies if they learn how to manage the contradictions inherent in these two strategies. And the management of these contradictions, in turn, depends on socially complex relations among employees, between employees and the technology they use, and between employees and the firm they work for. These relations are not only valuable (because they enable a firm to implement cost-leadership and differentiation strategies) but also socially complex and thus likely to be costly to imitate and a source of sustained competitive advantage (Womack, Jones, and Roos, 1990).

Recently, even Porter (1985) has backed off his original "stuck in the middle" arguments and now suggests that low-cost firms must have competitive levels of product differentiation to survive and that product differentiation firms must have competitive levels of cost to survive.

7.5   SUMMARY

Product differentiation exists when customers perceive a particular firm's products to be more valuable than other firms' products. Although differentiation can have several bases, it is, in the end, always a matter of customer perception.

Bases of product differentiation have been described in two ways: conceptually (including product features, linkage between functions, timing, location, product mix, links with other firms, and reputation) and empirically (including customization, product complexity, emphasis on consumer marketing, channels of distribution, and level of service and support). However, in the end, product differentiation is limited only by environmental opportunities and creativity in exploiting those opportunities.

The value of product differentiation has been studied by both Chamberlin and Robinson. Their work suggests that a firm with a differentiated product can set its prices greater than average total costs and thus obtain an above-normal profit. Each of the bases of product differentiation can be used to neutralize environmental threats and exploit environmental opportunities.

The rareness and imitability of bases of product differentiation vary. Highly imitable bases include product features. Somewhat imitable bases include product mix, links with other firms, product customization, and consumer marketing. Costly-to-imitate bases of product differentiation include linking business functions, timing, location, reputation, and service and support.

A variety of organizational attributes are required to successfully implement a product differentiation strategy. Porter argues that contradictions between these organizational characteristics and those required to implement a cost leadership strategy mean that firms that attempt to do both will perform poorly. More recent research notes the relationship between product differentiation, market share, and low costs and observes that some firms have learned to manage the contradictions between cost leadership and product differentiation.

REVIEW QUESTIONS

1. Although cost leadership is, perhaps, less relevant for firms pursuing product differentiation, costs are not totally irrelevant. What advice about costs would you give a firm pursuing a product differentiation strategy?

2. Product features are often the focus of product differentiation efforts. Yet product features are among the easiest-to-imitate bases of product differentiation and thus among the least likely bases of product differentiation to be a source of sustained competitive advantage. Does this seem paradoxical to you? If no, why not? If yes, how can you resolve this paradox?

3. What are the strengths and weaknesses of the different empirical approaches to describing the bases of product differentiation discussed in the chapter? What can these empirical approaches do for a manager that more conceptual approaches cannot do? What can the conceptual approaches do for a manager that the more empirical approaches cannot do?

4. "Monopolistic competition" is the term that Chamberlin developed to describe firms pursuing a product differentiation strategy in a competitive industry. In Chapter 4, it is suggested that one of the limitations of firms applying the S-C-P framework to make strategic choices is that, often, they can begin to behave as a monopolist, and monopolists generally are not able to maintain high levels of productive efficiency. Does this same problem exist for firms operating in a "monopolistic competition" context? Why or why not?

5. A firm with a highly differentiated product can increase the volume of its sales. Increased sales volumes can enable a firm to reduce its costs. High volumes with low costs can lead a firm to have very high profits, some of which the firm can use to invest in further differentiating its products. What advice would you give to a firm whose competition is enjoying this product differentiation and cost-leadership advantage?

CHAPTER
8

Cooperative Strategies: Tacit Collusion

As suggested in the previous two chapters, competitive strategies—cost leadership and product differentiation—are important generic strategic options for firms seeking business-level competitive advantages. Competitive strategies, however, are not the only business-level strategic options available. In this and the following chapter, we examine another class of business-level strategic options: cooperative strategies. In some situations, firms can obtain competitive advantages and above-normal profits not by contending with other firms but by cooperating with some of them. Cooperative strategies exist when firms work together to reach a common goal or objective.

There are numerous examples of cooperative strategies, including (illegal) explicit collusion, tacit collusion, joint ventures, licensing agreements, distribution agreements, and supply contracts. These different forms of cooperation can be organized into two broad categories: collusive strategies and strategic alliances. A collusive strategy exists when several firms in an industry cooperate to reduce industry output below the competitive level and raise prices above the competitive level (Scherer, 1980). There are two types of price/output collusion: explicit and tacit. A strategic alliance exists when several firms cooperate but industry output is not reduced (Kogut, 1988; Hennart, 1988). Examples include joint ventures, licensing agreements, and distribution agreements. Collusive strategies usually exist only among firms in a single industry, but strategic alliances can exist among firms within a single industry or between firms in different industries (Hennart, 1988).

In this chapter we examine the causes and consequences of collusive strategies as a form of interfirm cooperation (strategic alliances are the focus of Chapter 9). This chapter defines the so-called problem of cooperation and describes general solutions to this problem proposed in the literature; discusses incentives to cooperate through collusion, incentives to cheat on cooperative agreements, and the performance implications of different forms of cheating; and ends with an analysis of tacit collusion and sustained competitive advantage.

8.1   THE PROBLEM OF COOPERATION

The problem of cooperation can best be understood by analyzing a simple exchange game between two individuals.

A SIMPLE GAME

Imagine two individuals or organizations using the payoff matrix presented in Table 8.1 to choose between strategy A and strategy B. If both I and II choose strategy A, they each receive a payoff of $3,000. If I chooses strategy B, and II chooses strategy A, I receives a payoff of $5,000, and II receives nothing. If II chooses B, and I chooses A, II receives a payoff of $5,000, and I receives nothing. Finally, if both I and II choose strategy B, they both receive a payoff of $1,000. If I and II make a series of these strategic choices, what payoffs are associated with different patterns of choice, and what strategies are I and II likely to choose?

TABLE 8.1
Prisoner's Dilemma Game and Associated Payoff Matrix

		Firm One			
		Strategy A		Strategy B	
Firm Two	Strategy A	I.	$3,000	I:	$5,000
		II:	$3,000	II:	$0
	Strategy B	I:	$0	I:	$1,000
		II:	$5,000	II:	$1,000

This, of course, is a simple "prisoner's dilemma" game. At first, the answers to these questions seem simple enough. The maximum payoff that can be obtained in any one round of this game is $5,000. If the game is played five times, then the maximum payoff can be $25,000. This suggests that payoff-maximizing players should choose strategy B. However, if both choose strategy B over five rounds, each will obtain a total payoff of only $5,000.

Alternatively, each player may choose strategy A and receive a payoff of $3,000. If the game is played five times, both I and II will earn a total payoff of $15,000, less than the theoretically maximum (but very unlikely) payoff of $25,000, but greater than the $5,000 payoff if I and II choose strategy B on all five rounds.

Of course, various patterns of choice combine options A and B over several rounds. For example, if both players know that the game will be played for only five rounds, each may choose strategy A on the first four rounds (a $3,000 payoff per round) but then choose strategy B on the fifth round, hoping that the other player will stick with strategy A. This is an end-game strategy. If only one player chooses B in the fifth round, that player will earn a total payoff of $17,000, and the other player will earn a total payoff of only $12,000. However, if both players choose B in the fifth round, each will earn a total payoff of $13,000.

These patterns of choice represent decisions by players to compete, cooperate, or renege on a cooperative agreement. If both players in this simple game choose strategy B on all rounds, they are adopting a competitive strategy. Each time players choose strategy A, they are choosing to cooperate to maximize their payoff from the game. If players cooperate with each other on several rounds and then implement an end-game strategy, they are "cheating" on their (perhaps tacit) cooperative agreement (Fudenberg and Tirole, 1991). Ultimately, the payoff that one player obtains depends not just on that player's decisions but on decisions made by the other player as well.

Whether players in this kind of game choose to compete, cooperate, or cheat on a cooperative agreement depends on the broader context within which the game is played. For example, players are more likely to cooperate, and to continue cooperating, if (1) they can directly communicate with one another, (2) cheating does not lead to large payoffs, (3) cheating leads to costly sanctions, or (4) players are more interested in maximizing their payoffs than in beating the payoffs of other players (Fudenberg and Tirole, 1991). When these conditions do *not* exist, competition and cheating on cooperative agreements is more likely.

The simple game presented in Table 8.1 reflects the dilemmas facing all firms contemplating cooperative strategies. There are often strong incentives to engage in cooperative behavior. Such behavior can generate substantial economic profits (a five-round payoff of $15,000), especially compared with the profits of purely competitive actions (a five-round payoff of $5,000) (Scherer, 1980). But once cooperative agreements are in place, there are often strong incentives for firms that have agreed to cooperate to cheat on those agreements. In this game, a player that cheats in the fifth round can gain a total payoff of $17,000; if both players cheat in this round, each gains a total payoff of $13,000. In any case, the total payoffs to firms depend on decisions they make, as well as on decisions that other firms make. Whether firms will compete, cooperate, or cheat on cooperative agreements depends on the broader context within which cooperation occurs. The simultaneous incentives of firms to cooperate *and* to cheat on cooperative agreements is known as the "problem of cooperation" (Axelrod, 1984).

GENERAL SOLUTIONS TO THE PROBLEM OF COOPERATION

Several authors have examined ways to resolve the problem of cooperation. Thomas Hobbes (1952) suggested the most traditional explanation of how cooperation develops in society. Hobbes argued that, in the absence of some centralized authority, it is not possible to resolve the problem of cooperation and that cooperation will not emerge. According to Hobbes, cooperation develops only when a central authority (an individual or institution) forces other individuals or firms not to cheat on cooperative agreements. Put another way, the central authority implements sanctions (such as death, dismemberment, or banishment from the community) that make the cost of cheating very high.

Many authors have found Hobbes's analysis of cooperation unsatisfactory. For example, Granovetter (1985) observes that most economic exchanges occur within a context of social relations that have norms of expected behavior associated with them. When these social norms preclude cheating on cooperative relationships, their violation leads to the imposition of broad social sanctions. These sanctions, again, make cheating costly and help resolve the problem of cooperation. Notice that in Granovetter's solution, a central authority still exists and still acts to reduce cheating on cooperative agreements. However, this central authority is no longer an individual or institution but rather social norms of expected behavior.

Both Hobbes and Granovetter suggest that the problem of cooperation can be solved by central authorities imposing costly sanctions on cheating firms. However, firms may continue to cooperate even in the absence of these kinds of central authority, if both the returns to individual firms cooperating are high and the opportunity costs of individual firms cheating are high. This approach to the problem of cooperation is developed by Axelrod (1984).

Axelrod (1984) has observed that cooperation among firms is likely as long as (1) firms anticipate numerous interactions and (2) there are at least a few cooperative firms interacting with each other. Axelrod

(1984) established these conclusions in a novel way. He invited professional and amateur game theorists to submit a decision rule strategy to play a series of games with a payoff matrix similar to the one in Table 8.1. A wide range of strategies designed to maximize a player's payoffs were proposed. Some were very complicated, involving sophisticated tools for estimating the probability that another player would cooperate on a given round. Of all these strategies, however, none generated a higher total payoff than a simple cooperative strategy called "tit for tat." In the "tit for tat" strategy, a player cooperates until another player "cheats," at which time the first player adopts a noncooperative strategy as long as it is interacting with the cheating player.

According to Axelrod (1984), "tit for tat" works well as long as at least a few other players are also implementing this strategy. In this way, "tit for tat" gains very high payoffs when used in cooperation with other players using "tit for tat," and it minimizes losses experienced when other players play noncooperative strategies. Cooperation, according to Axelrod, is a good bet: If a firm cooperates with another cooperative firm, it does very well, and if it cooperates with a noncooperative firm, it does not do badly. Axelrod (1984) concludes that the high payoffs, and low costs, associated with cooperation effectively resolve the problem of cooperation, all without reliance on any form of central authority—individual, institutional, or social.

Thus despite the emphasis in the strategic management literature on independent firm action and competitive strategy, cooperative strategies may, in some circumstances, be sources of competitive advantage for firms. Indeed, the analysis of returns to cooperative strategies generally parallels the analysis of returns to any strategic options facing a firm. In particular, SWOT analysis, though originally developed for the analysis of competitive strategies, can be applied equally as well to cooperative strategies. Environmental opportunities depend on the ability of cooperation to enable a firm to reduce its costs or increase its revenues. Environmental threats are the incentives that cooperating firms have to "cheat" on cooperative agreements. Organizational strengths and weaknesses are the attributes of a firm that enable it to create and maintain cooperative relations with other firms. If those abilities are rare and costly to imitate, cooperative strategies can be sources of sustained competitive advantage.

8.2 THE VALUE OF COLLUSION AS A FORM OF ECONOMIC COOPERATION

In December 1994, William Christie, from Vanderbilt University, and Paul Schultz, from the Ohio State University, published an article in the *Journal of Finance* that brought into question certain trading practices at NASDAQ. NASDAQ is a multiple dealer stock market designed to produce narrow bid-ask price spreads through the competition for stock order flow among individual dealers. Despite this supposed competition, Christie and Schultz found that 70 of the 100 most frequently traded NASDAQ stocks did not trade in "odd eighths" (e.g., $18\frac{3}{8}$ or $23\frac{3}{8}$ or $45\frac{7}{8}$). Rather, these stocks only traded in "even eighths" (e.g., $18\frac{1}{4}$ or $23\frac{1}{2}$ or 46). By not trading in odd eighths, Christie and Schultz suggested that NASDAQ dealers were appropriating extra above-normal profits for themselves. Moreover, this lack of "odd eighths" quotes could not be explained by any competitive process. They therefore concluded that NASDAQ dealers were engaging in tacit collusion at the expense of those buying and selling stocks on this market.

The conclusions of this paper have had a sweeping effect in financial markets, in general, and at NASDAQ, in particular. Dozens of class action law suits have been filed against NASDAQ on behalf of those who lost money because of the lack of "odd eighths" quotes (Lux, 1995b; Cochran, 1995). The Department of Justice has opened an investigation of collusion at NASDAQ, and the Securities and Exchange Commission has begun investigating other trading practices at NASDAQ, including the late reporting of trades, and dealers backing away from quoted stock prices (Schroeder, 1995). In response, NASDAQ has hired various economists, including a Nobel prize winner, to demonstrate that Christie and Schultz's work was wrong (Lux, 1995a). Finally, a group of economists called the "Shadow SEC" met and debated the veracity of the collusion charges leveled at NASDAQ (Lux, 1995c). It is still uncertain how these law suits and debates will unfold over the next few years. At the very least, the NASDAQ story suggests that collusion, as a cooperative business strategy, is an important topic that practicing strategic managers must understand.

Collusion of any sort exists when firms in an industry agree to coordinate their output and pricing decisions. In some circumstances, such collusion can lead to above-normal economic profits. *Explicit* collusion exists when output and pricing decisions are coordinated directly, through direct communication and negotiation. This kind of collusion is illegal in most developed economies. *Tacit* collusion exists when output and pricing decisions are not coordinated through direct communication and negotiation but coordination develops nevertheless.

The case of "odd eighths" at NASDAQ is not the only recent example of firms possibly pursuing a collusion strategy. In 1990, major league baseball owners were found guilty of colluding in the market for baseball free agents, thereby trying to keep the price of hiring these free agents down (Bernstein, 1990). Archer Daniels Midland (ADM), a large agriculture products firm, has recently been accused of colluding with its competitors (Burton, Kilman, and Gibson, 1995). As of September 1995, at least eleven class action price-fixing lawsuits have been filed by ADM's customers against this firm's business practices (Behar, 1995). In 1991, MIT and Ivy League schools were accused of collusion by cooperating in the allocation of scholarships to needy applicants (Carlton, Bamberger, and Epstein, 1995). Recently, large appliance manufacturers (Patterson and Rose, 1994) and tire makers (Narisetti, 1995) have been investigated by the Department of Justice for collusive activities.

COLLUSION AND ECONOMIC PERFORMANCE

To examine the value of collusive forms of cooperation, consider a simple two-firm industry (a duopoly) where overall industry demand is expressed by the equation

$$P = 100 - Q \qquad\qquad Eq.\ 8.1$$

where P is the market-determined price and Q is industry output equal to the sum of the two firm outputs: $Q = q_1 + q_2$. For ease of exposition, assume that production costs are zero and that the two firms have agreed to divide any above-normal profits from collusion equally.

If the two firms in this industry collude and act as a "cooperative monopolist," they will want to produce a quantity, Q, such that *industry* marginal revenue equals *industry* marginal cost (Hirshliefer, 1980). Since each firm's production costs are zero, the firms' marginal costs are zero, and industry marginal costs are zero. When a demand curve is linear, it is easy to calculate the corresponding marginal-revenue curve (Hirshliefer, 1980:339), using the following relationship:

$$\text{If } P = A - BQ, \text{ then } MR = A - 2BQ \qquad\qquad Eq.\ 8.2$$

In this example, $A = 100$, and $B = 1$. Thus the marginal-revenue curve is $MR = 100 - 2Q$. Setting marginal costs equal to marginal revenue (to calculate the optimal level of production) leads to

$$MC = MR \qquad\qquad Eq.\ 8.3$$
$$0 = 100 - 2Q$$
$$Q = 50$$

Thus the profit-maximizing industry output in this example is 50 units. The profit-maximizing price on the demand curve can be calculated:

$$P = 100 - Q \qquad\qquad Eq.\ 8.4$$
$$= 100 - 50$$
$$= 50$$

along with total revenue:

$$R = P \times Q \qquad\qquad Eq.\ 8.5$$
$$= 50 \times 50$$
$$= 2{,}500$$

which, because production costs are zero, is also the industry total above-normal profit. Since these two firms agreed to divide this profit equally, each earns a profit of 1,250.

The profit potential of collusion in this example can be seen by comparing these profit results to the situation where each of these firms ignores the other in making price and output decisions. Instead of cooperating to set industry marginal cost equal to industry marginal revenue, purely competing firms act as price takers and set marginal costs equal to the market-determined price: $MC = P$.

By acting as a price taker, each firm sets marginal costs equal to price. However, marginal costs are still zero:

$$MC = P \qquad\qquad Eq.\ 8.6$$
$$0 = 100 - Q$$
$$Q = 100$$

Thus the total quantity produced in this industry will be 100 units. If $Q = 100$, then the equilibrium price on the demand curve equals zero ($P = 100 - Q \rightarrow P = 100 - 100$), total industry revenue equals zero ($R = P \times Q \rightarrow R = 0 \times 100$), and each firm earns zero economic profit—not nearly as attractive as the collusive result. More realistically, if marginal costs are positive, then prices and marginal revenue will be greater than zero. However, at this quantity and price level, economic profits will still be zero.

Put another way, a firm that successfully implements a collusive strategy is exploiting an opportunity to neutralize the threat of rivalry. As suggested in Chapter 4, one class of opportunities facing firms is the neutralization of environmental threats. One of those threats, rivalry, often takes the form of price competition. Left unchecked, rivalry can lead firms to gain zero economic profits, as is the case in this competitive duopoly. Collusion, on the other hand, enables a firm to neutralize the threat of rivalry and earn above-normal economic profits, as is the case in the cooperating duopoly. In this example, cooperating firms reduce output from the purely competitive level ($Q = 100$ in the competitive case, 50 in the cooperative case) and thereby earn above-normal returns (0 in the competitive case, 1,250 per firm in the cooperative case).

INCENTIVES TO CHEAT ON COLLUSIVE AGREEMENTS

Once firms collectively exploit the opportunity of neutralizing the threat of rivalry by colluding to restrict output and increase prices, individual firms have a strong incentive to cheat on this collusive agreement, especially if other firms stick to their agreements. This incentive to cheat on a collusive agreement is a major threat facing firms attempting to implement this type of cooperative strategy.

Consider, for example, an industry with six firms all selling undifferentiated products (this analysis can be generalized to differentiated products as well [Tirole, 1988]). If five firms stick with an agreement to sell 1,000 widgets for $10 apiece, but one firm breaks this agreement and sells 3,000 widgets for $9 apiece, each of the five firms will have revenues of $10,000 (1,000 × $10), but the cheating firm will have revenues of $27,000 (3,000 × $9). Assuming economic costs are constant (at $3 per widget), the five colluding firms will all have economic profits of $7,000 [1,000 × ($10 – $3)], but the cheating firm will have an economic profit of $18,000 [3,000 × ($9 – $3)]. By increasing its output and lowering its price by $1 per widget, the cheating firm is able to increase its economic profit substantially.

WAYS FIRMS CAN CHEAT ON COLLUSIVE AGREEMENTS

Firms can cheat on their collusive agreements in a wide variety of ways. These different forms of cheating are based on different assumptions about colluding partners' reactions to cheating, and they have different impacts on the performance of firms in an industry. Bertrand cheating and Cournot cheating—two of the most important forms of cheating in collusive agreements—and their performance consequences are presented in Table 8.2. These forms of cheating are compared first with fully collusive strategies and then with fully competitive price-taking strategies.

Bertrand Cheating

Economist and mathematician Joseph Bertrand examined what happens to profits when colluding firms begin cheating by lowering prices below the cooperative price. In his model, Bertrand makes the (unrealistic) assumption that each time cheating firms adjust their prices, they assume that other firms in the industry will continue cooperating. Bertrand's (1883) general conclusion is that, assuming little or no product differentiation among a small number of firms, if one firm decides to cheat on a collusive agreement through reducing its prices, others will as well and, in the long run, firms in this industry will earn normal economic profits.

To see how this happens, consider the simple example presented in Table 8.3. In this industry, there are only two firms (a duopoly) and

TABLE 8.2
Different Ways Firms Can Cheat on Collusive Agreements, Decision Variables, Behavioral Assumptions, and Equilibrium Performance Implications for Firms in a Duopoly Without Product Differentiation

Strategy	Decision variables	Behavioral assumptions	Performance implications
Cooperation	Price/quantity	Both firms maintain agreements	Share monopoly profits
Price taking	Price/quantity	Both firms ignore all interdependence	Normal profits
Bertrand cheating	Price	One firm assumes other firm will maintain price from previous period; no learning across periods	Normal profits
Cournot cheating	Quantity	One firm assumes other firm will maintain quantity from previous period; no learning across periods	Profits fall between shared monopoly and normal profits

TABLE 8.3
Bertrand Cheating in a Duopoly with Homogeneous Products

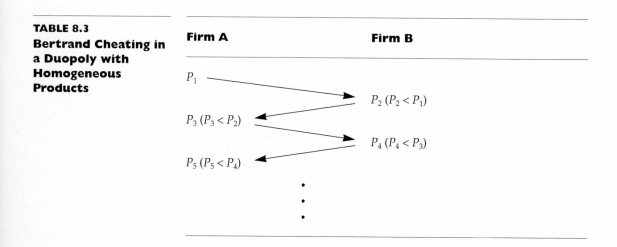

no product differentiation. Imagine that Firm A and Firm B have decided to restrict output such that the prices they charge for their products are P_1. Then Firm B decides to cheat on this agreement, increases its output, and sets its price equal to P_2. P_2 must be less than P_1, since any new price greater than or equal to P_1 will not increase Firm B's revenues. With the price equal to P_2, all customers switch to Firm B to buy its products. Firm A must respond and sets its new price at P_3 (where $P_3 < P_2$). Customers rapidly switch back to Firm A; Firm B responds, and so forth. This will continue until the prices charged by both firms generate revenues exactly equal to the firms' economic costs, at which point these firms will earn normal economic returns.

Cournot Cheating

Bertrand's analysis suggests that the above-normal returns that can be obtained by colluding firms are very fragile—that any price reductions by one firm will rapidly lead to normal economic profits for both firms. Antoine-Augustin Cournot took a slightly different approach to analyzing cheating in collusive arrangements. Instead of focusing on reductions in price, Cournot (1838) examined the performance consequences if colluding firms cheat by adjusting the quantity of their output and let market forces determine prices.

The performance implications of competing in quantity are examined in Table 8.4 for firms in a duopoly with the same demand and other characteristics as in Eq. (8.1). The intuition behind this table is straightforward. Like Bertrand, Cournot adopts the simplification that Firm A and Firm B will assume that decisions made in a previous period will continue unchanged. Where Bertrand focused on prices, Cournot focused on quantity produced.

Given this assumption, when Firms A and B decide on their own quantity of output, assuming the other firm's quantity is fixed from an earlier decision, they become monopolists over the part of industry demand that is not filled by the other firm. Each of these firms then chooses a profit-maximizing quantity. However, that quantity choice has an impact on the other firm, which adjusts the demand curve it faces to include demand not met by the first firm and chooses a new profit-maximizing quantity. This new quantity, of course, affects the first firm, which readjusts the demand curve it faces to include demand not met by the other firm, chooses a new profit-maximizing quantity, and so forth.

For example, in period 4 in Table 8.4, Firm B assumes that Firm A will produce the same quantity of output that it produced in period 3 ($q_1 = 37.5$), adjusts its demand curve to reflect Firm A's previous output [$P = 100 - Q \rightarrow P = 100 - (37.5 + q_2)$], chooses a profit-maximizing quantity

TABLE 8.4
The Performance Implications of Cournot Cheating in a Duopoly with Characteristics as in Eq. (8.1)

Demand curve: $P = 100 - Q$. Marginal revenue: $MR = 100 - 2Q$.
Marginal cost: $MC = ATC = 0$; $Q = q_1 + q_2$.
Since $MC = 0$, $R_t = \pi_t$.

Firm A	Firm B

1. Assumes that Firm B will produce quantity as in previous period (0) and then chooses profit-maximizing quantity

$$
\begin{aligned}
P &= 100 - Q \\
&= 100 - (q_1 + 0) \\
&= 100 - q_1 \\
MC &= MR \\
0 &= 100 - 2q_1 \\
q_1 &= 50 \\
P &= 50 \\
R_1 &= P \times q_1 \\
&= 2{,}500 \\
R_2 &= P \times q_2 \\
&= 0
\end{aligned}
$$

2. Assumes that Firm A will produce quantity as in previous period (50) and then choose profit-maximizing quantity

$$
\begin{aligned}
P &= 100 - Q \\
&= 100 - (50 + q_2) \\
&= 50 - q_2 \\
MC &= MR \\
0 &= 50 - 2q_2 \\
q_2 &= 25 \\
P &= 100 - Q \\
&= 100 - (50 + 25) \\
&= 25 \\
R_2 &= P \times q_2 \\
&= 625 \\
R_1 &= P \times q_2 \\
&= 1{,}250
\end{aligned}
$$

3. Assumes that Firm B will produce quantity as in previous period (25) and then chooses profit-maximizing quantity

$$
\begin{aligned}
P &= 100 - Q \\
&= 100 - (q_1 + 25) \\
&= 75 - q_1 \\
MC &= MR \\
0 &= 75 - 2q_1 \\
q_1 &= 37.5 \\
P &= 100 - Q \\
&= 100 - (37.5 + 25) \\
&= 37.5 \\
R_1 &= 37.5 \times 37.5 \\
&= 1{,}406.25 \\
R_2 &= 37.5 \times 25 \\
&= 937.5
\end{aligned}
$$

(continues)

TABLE 8.4
The Performance Implications of Cournot Cheating in a Duopoly with Characteristics as in Eq. (8.1) (continued)

4. Assumes that Firm A will produce quantity as in previous period (37.5) and then chooses profit-maximizing quantity

$$P = 100 - Q$$
$$= 100 - (37.5 + q_2)$$
$$= 62.5 - q_2$$
$$MC = MR$$
$$0 = 62.5 - 2q_2$$
$$q_2 = 31.25$$
$$P = 100 - Q$$
$$= 100 - (37.5 + 31.25)$$
$$= 31.25$$
$$R_2 = 31.25 \times 31.25$$
$$= 976.56$$
$$R_1 = 31.25 \times 37.5$$
$$= 1,171.875$$

5. Assumes that Firm B will produce quantity as in previous period (31.25) and then chooses profit-maximizing quantity

$$P = 100 - Q$$
$$= 100 - (q_1 + 31.25)$$
$$= 68.75 - q_1$$
$$MC = MR$$
$$0 = 68.75 - 2q_1$$
$$q_1 = 34.375$$
$$P = 100 - Q$$
$$= 100 - (34.375 + 31.25)$$
$$= 34.375$$
$$R_1 = 34.375 \times 34.375$$
$$= 1,181.64$$
$$R_2 = 34.375 \times 31.25$$
$$= 1,074.22$$

Equilibrium: Let $q_1 = 33.33$

$$P = 100 - Q$$
$$= 100 - (33.33 + q_2)$$
$$= 66.66 - q_2$$
$$MC = MR$$
$$0 = 66.66 - 2q_2$$
$$q_2 = 33.33$$
$$P = 100 - Q$$
$$= 100 - (33.33 + 33.33)$$
$$= 33.33$$
$$R_2 = 33.33 \times 33.33$$
$$= 1,110.88$$
$$R_1 = 33.33 \times 33.33$$
$$= 1,110.88$$

Pure competitive solution $< R_1 <$ Pure Cooperative Solution

$$0 < 1,11\ldots < 1,250$$

by setting marginal cost equal to marginal revenue ($MC = MR \rightarrow 0 = 62.5 - 2q_2 \rightarrow q_2 = 31.25$). The market price is then calculated [$P = 100 - Q \rightarrow P = 100 - (q_1 + q_2) \rightarrow P = 100 - (37.5 + 31.25) \rightarrow P = 31.25$], along with the revenues and total profit for Firm A ($R_1 = P \times q_1 \rightarrow R = 31.25 \times 37.5 = 1,171.875$) and for Firm B ($R_2 = P \times q_2 \rightarrow R = 31.25 \times 31.25 = 976.56$). This adjustment, and readjustment of quantities, with subsequent impacts on prices, continues until neither Firm A nor Firm B can improve its performance further.

It can be shown that, in the long run, competition in quantity will lead to the situation where one-third of total industry demand is provided by Firm A, one-third is provided by Firm B, and one-third is not produced, and thus prices will be higher than a competitive level. Firms that cheat in quantity produced earn greater-than-normal economic profits, but these profits are not as large as would be the case if firms completely cooperated in making production decisions.

Other Forms of Cheating

The performance results associated with both Bertrand cheating and Cournot cheating depend on assumptions that firms make about how other firms will respond to their own cheating. Both Bertrand and Cournot assume that firms take other firms' prices/outputs in the previous period as fixed, and that firms never learn that other firms adjust their prices/outputs in response to their own decisions. These assumptions seem very unrealistic.

In response to these unrealistic assumptions, other models of cheating on collusive arrangements have been developed. Edgeworth (1897), following Bertrand, examined price cheating. However, Edgeworth introduces capacity constraints in his model (based on the observation that firms can change their prices faster than they can change their quantity of output). Because of these capacity constraints, the market share of the firm with a higher price does not go to zero, and firms are able to avoid the perfect competition outcome of pure Bertrand cheating—that is, both firms make positive profits, though not as large as the profits in Cournot cheating.

Stackelberg (1934), following Cournot, focuses on quantity decisions but adopts the assumption that one firm (the so-called Stackelberg leader) accurately anticipates how other firms will respond to its output decision, adopts a profit-maximizing quantity, and holds that quantity constant over time. Other firms in this industry (Stackelberg followers) adjust their outputs accordingly. Firms in this kind of industry earn above-normal economic profits, but these profits are less than the above-normal returns earned by firms engaging in pure Cournot cheating.

Other authors adopt different assumptions about the behavior of rivals. Some authors have examined the profits associated with

Bertrand and Cournot cheating when firms sell differentiated products (Hall and Hitch, 1939; Sweezy, 1939; Hotelling, 1929); when there are time lags in discovering that a firm has cheated (Tirole, 1988); when different firms have different costs (Tirole, 1988); when firms simultaneously interact in several markets (Bernheim and Whinston, 1986); when other firms are unable to observe price or quantity cheating (Green and Porter, 1984); when prices cannot be adjusted quickly (Maskin and Tirole, 1988; Eaton and Engers, 1987); when firms have a reputation for not retaliating against cheaters (Ortega-Reichert, 1967), and so forth. Generally, long-run profits for firms that cheat on purely collusive agreements in these ways fall somewhere between the perfect competition, zero-economic-profit solution and the perfect cooperation, shared-monopoly-profit solution.

That the performance implications of cheating for colluding firms are so sensitive to assumptions that firms make about the motives and intentions of other firms is a significant limitation of this class of models. Many of these models represent very sophisticated applications of game theory (Fudenberg and Tirole, 1991). Although game theory can be used to test the performance implications of alternative sets of these behavioral assumptions, it cannot be used to specify which of these assumptions are most appropriate in different market and industry contexts. Indeed, there is no good reason to assume that all of a firm's rivals will have the same response to cheating on cooperative agreements, let alone good reason to know what these responses will be in different economic contexts. To develop a complete model of collusion strategies, a model that specifies which game-theoretic assumptions apply will need to be developed.

EXPLICIT AND TACIT COLLUSION

Since the performance implications of cheating on collusion depend so critically on the particular assumptions that firms have about how their rivals will respond to cheating, an important question becomes, How can a firm learn what its rivals' intentions are? The easiest way to answer this question is for firms to communicate directly with each other about their current price and output decisions and their future price and output decisions. This kind of direct communication will allow firms to judge the likely responses of others and enable them to negotiate price and output strategies that jointly maximize profits. In a sense, direct communication solves the problems associated with game-theoretic analyses of collusion by enabling firms to develop reasonably accurate ideas about how other firms will behave. Once a firm knows this information, it can choose the game-theoretic model that best fits, and it can perfectly anticipate the performance results of alternative actions.

Of course, this form of direct communication and negotiation—explicit collusion—is illegal in most developed economies. Managers in firms that explicitly collude may go to jail, and their firms may be subject to significant fines (Slade, 1990).

Instead of engaging in direct communication and explicit collusion, colluding firms seeking to choose joint profit-maximizing cooperative strategies must use tacit collusion. Instead of communicating directly, tacitly colluding firms send and interpret signals of intent to cooperate (or intent not to cooperate) sent by potential collusion partners (Scherer, 1980).

Sometimes, signals of intent to collude are very ambiguous. For example, when firms in an industry do not reduce their prices in response to a decrease in demand, they may be sending a signal that they want to collude, or they may be attempting to exploit their product differentiation to maintain high margins. When firms do not reduce their prices in response to reduced supply costs, they may be sending a signal that they want to collude, or they may be individually maximizing their economic performance. In both cases, the organizational intent implied by a firm's behavior is ambiguous at best.

Other signals of intent to collude are less ambiguous. For example, when General Electric wanted to slow price competition in the steam turbine industry, it widely advertised its prices to customers and publicly committed not to sell products below these prices. Moreover, GE provided customers with price guarantees: If GE reduced prices on its turbines at some time in the future, its customers would receive a refund equal to these price reductions. These actions sent to GE competitors a clear message that price reductions would be very costly to GE—a signal of an intent to collude on prices and one that helped reduce price competition in this industry. Both prices and margins in the steam turbine industry remained stable for approximately ten years as GE and its major competitor, Westinghouse, learned how to survive together in this industry (Porter, 1979b).

However, even tacit collusion, with no direct communication between cooperating firms, can be illegal. Firms that consciously make price and output decisions in order to reduce competition may be engaging in what the courts call "conscious parallelism" and thus be subject to antitrust laws and penalties (MacLeod, 1985). Indeed, the Department of Justice objected to the conscious parallelism engaged in by GE and Westinghouse in the steam turbine business and sued both firms in the late 1960s (Porter, 1979b). Firms contemplating tacit collusion as a form of interfirm cooperation should obtain competent legal counsel before proceeding, to see whether the signals of intent to cooperate that they plan to send are consistent with legal guidelines. This task is complicated by the fact that the probability of prosecution for tacit price/output collusion, at least in the United States, varies substantially, depending on the preferences and ideology of the administration in power in Washington D.C. (Sims and Lande, 1986).

TACIT COLLUSION: OPPORTUNITIES AND THREATS

Firms can use a variety of industry attributes to judge the likely intent of rivals and thus to determine the likelihood that tacit collusion will lead to above-normal economic profits. Put differently, these industry attributes can be used to evaluate the level of opportunity and threat associated with pursuing this cooperative strategy. Some of the most important of these industry attributes are listed in Table 8.5 and discussed below.

Small Number of Firms in an Industry

Tacit collusion is more likely to be successful if there are a small number of firms in an industry (Scherer, 1980). As suggested earlier, tacit collusion depends on the sending and interpreting of signals of intent to cooperate. Because direct communication about prices and output is forbidden, coordination must be indirect and implicit. Intense monitoring of other firms' behavior helps make this coordination possible. However, as the number of firms in an industry increases, the number of firms whose subtle signals must be monitored and interpreted also increases. Indeed, as the number of firms in an industry increases arithmetically, the number of relationships among those firms that must be monitored and nurtured increases geometrically (Williamson, 1975). As the number of relationships and subtle signals that must be interpreted increases, judging the intent of firms sending these signals becomes more problematic (and it is never easy), and maintaining tacit collusion agreements becomes more difficult.

TABLE 8.5
Industry Attributes That Facilitate the Development and Maintenance of Tacit Collusion

1. Small number of firms
2. Product homogeneity
3. Cost homogeneity
4. Price leaders
5. Industry social structure
6. High order frequency and small order size
7. Large inventories and order backlogs
8. Entry barriers

Having a large number of firms in an industry also reduces the impact of any one firm's cheating on the performance of other, still colluding, firms. If there are only two firms in an industry (a duopoly), and one reduces its prices (Bertrand cheating), then the increased sales of the cheating firm will significantly affect (reduce) the sales of the noncheating firm. To maintain its share, the noncheating firm will have to respond to the cheating firm, perhaps by reducing its prices, and the normal return equilibrium is not far away. Since cheating hurts both firms very much, it is less likely that either firm will want to cheat on a tacit agreement.

However, if there are fifty firms in an industry and one cheats by reducing its prices, that one firm will not have a significant impact on the sales of other firms, and cheating may create no response. If other firms are not likely to respond to isolated incidents of cheating, cheating is more likely. In the end, if the number of firms in an industry is very small, the interdependence among those firms is, on average, very clear to them, and tacit collusion is more likely. If the number of firms in an industry is large, the interdependence among those firms is less obvious, and tacit collusion is less likely.

Government regulators often use the number of firms competing in an industry as a signal that firms in an industry may decide to pursue collusive business strategies. For example, the charges leveled by former GE executive Edward J. Russell that GE and DeBeers were colluding to raise prices in the industrial diamond market were more believable because GE and DeBeers together dominate over 80 percent of this $600 million market (Schiller, 1992; 1994). The U.S. Department of Justice filed suit against GE for price fixing in this market. These charges were dismissed in 1995, however, when a federal judge concluded that there was insufficient evidence to bring GE to trial (Donoho, 1995).

Indeed, the relationship between the number of colluding firms and the ability to implement tacit collusion is so significant that most economists analyze collusion only under conditions of oligopoly (Tirole, 1988; Scherer, 1980). Research on government-sanctioned explicit price-fixing cartels in western Europe, where (presumably) direct communication between colluding firms can occur, indicates that over 80 percent of these cartels occurred in industries with ten or fewer firms (Edwards, 1964; Hay and Kelley, 1974). Thus even when explicit collusion is possible, a small number of firms seems to facilitate the implementation of this cooperative strategy. It is likely that small numbers are even more important for tacit collusion strategies. In general, having a small number of firms in an industry increases the probability that cheating firms will be discovered, and this likelihood reduces the payoffs associated with cheating.

Product Homogeneity

Tacit collusion is also more likely when firms produce and sell similar products or services (Scherer, 1980). In general, changes in prices are easier to monitor than are changes in product characteristics or features. A firm may cheat on a tacit collusion strategy by charging the agreed price but providing more features, higher quality, or better service. These efforts at product differentiation are somewhat more difficult to monitor and thus create strong incentives for cheating.

However, if differentiating the products or services of firms in an industry is very costly, potential competition must focus on price reductions, a relatively easy-to-monitor effort at cheating. Once spotted, price reductions (Bertrand cheating) have significant negative consequences for all firms (normal economic profits). Thus if firms in an industry produce homogeneous products or services, cheating on collusive agreements is more likely to be discovered, and this likelihood reduces the payoffs associated with cheating.

Product homogeneity may be a factor in the alleged collusive activities of Archer Daniels Midland (Burton, Kilman, and Gibson, 1995). The products that ADM sells are all agricultural commodities, or derived from agricultural commodities. There are limited opportunities to differentiate these kinds of products. Thus, any actions colluding firms take to "cheat" on their collusive agreements would have to focus on reducing prices. Because price reductions are so easy to observe, it is unlikely that colluding firms will cheat on their tacit agreements, since to do so would almost certainly jeopardize any above-normal economic profits that could have been obtained through collusion. Thus, the fact that ADM sells only commodities may have made collusion a more viable strategy for this firm than if it had sold non-commodity products as well.

Cost Homogeneity

Homogeneity of economic costs enhances the opportunities to implement tacit collusion. When firms have very different costs, their optimal level of output may be very different (Scherer, 1980). These differences make it difficult for firms to find a level of output that jointly maximizes profits. In this situation, any tacit collusion agreement is very unstable, since each firm has even stronger incentives to cheat.

Cost heterogeneity is widely cited as one of the major reasons why OPEC, an explicitly colluding cartel, has been unable to maintain output and price discipline (El Mallakh, 1982). Optimal levels of oil production vary sharply across members of OPEC, leading these countries to expand production beyond agreed-to collusive levels.

When cooperating firms have similar economic costs, it may be relatively easy for them to discover an output level that is mutually satisfactory. This facilitates tacit collusion.

Price Leaders

Another industry characteristic that creates opportunities for tacit collusion is the existence of industry price leaders. A price leader is a firm that sets "acceptable" industry prices or "acceptable" profit margins in an industry (Markham, 1951). A price leader is often a firm with the largest market share and helps create the order and discipline needed to make tacit collusion last over time. Also, a price leader can assist an industry to adjust to higher or lower prices, without jeopardizing an overall cooperative agreement, by defining industry standards for price or margin changes (Scherer, 1980). In general, price leaders can be thought of as Stackelberg leaders (Stackelberg, 1934).

Through the 1950s and 1960s, General Motors acted as a price leader in the U.S. automobile market. Each fall, with the introduction of new lines and models, GM publicized the percentage by which it planned to increase the price of its cars. Ford and Chrysler typically followed GM's lead, raising their prices by approximately the same percentage as announced by GM (White, 1971). Since the entry of Japanese and German firms to the automobile industry (and thus the violation of the small-numbers requirement listed earlier), GM no longer plays this price-leadership role.

Industry Social Structure

Industry social structure can create opportunities for tacit collusion. *Industry social structure* refers to accepted norms of behavior and competition that often evolve in industries. These norms are usually implicit and constitute what might be called an *industry culture.* Spender (1989) calls this collection of expectations and norms an "industry recipe" and emphasizes its pervasive impact on firm behavior. This industry recipe, in an important sense, defines the standard operating procedures, acceptable forms of competition, and norms of behavior for firms in an industry. Violation of these norms and expectations constitutes a major breech of "industrial etiquette."

Several factors may work together to help create an industry social structure. Some industries, when they first develop, are dominated by one or two firms with very large market share. Because of this dominance, most managers in the industry received their training and early experience in these dominant firms. In a sense, the culture within these dominant firms begins to define the culture in the industry as a whole, and expectations about acceptable forms of competition in the industry reflect expectations within the dominant firms. These industry expectations may continue long after dominant firms lose their share leadership. In the mainframe computer business, for example, IBM's dominance significantly affected the definition of acceptable competition. "White shirts and conservative ties" still dominate the mainframe business, despite IBM's well-known difficulties in the 1990s.

Managers in firms located in the same geographic area may come into contact at charity functions, in private clubs, and in other social settings. As suggested by Granovetter (1985), these social interactions may lead to the development of mutual expectations concerning acceptable competitive behavior and help create a sense of trustworthiness among firms contemplating collusion. Other social contacts among managers in an industry, including relationships developed at trade association meetings, can also help create an industry recipe.

However they evolve, these social expectations can facilitate tacit collusion by defining some forms of competition as unacceptable. If banned forms of competition would increase rivalry, an industry's culture can make tacit collusion easier to implement.

There is substantial evidence that industry social structure facilitated collusion among the owners of major league baseball franchises during the 1980s. Each major league baseball franchise in North America is independently owned. However, franchise owners must cooperate in leagues to establish playing schedules, a common set of rules, and other operating standards. While engaging in this legal cooperation, informal agreements not to bid aggressively on free agents were apparently struck. The effect of these agreements was to reduce payments to baseball players from 38 percent of team revenues to just 31 percent of team revenues by 1989 (Berstein, 1990). In 1990, an arbitrator found that major league baseball owners had behaved collusively and violated their labor agreement with the players union. The owners were subsequently fined $102.5 million, and players' salaries have risen to over 40 percent of team revenues.

High Order Frequency and Small Order Size

Firms may have incentives to cheat on cooperative agreements when maintaining a collusive agreement has high opportunity costs. Imagine, for example, that a firm that has agreed to tacit collusion is seeking a very large contract to supply product to an important customer. Also, suppose that this contract will last for several years. If this firm obtains this contract, it will have steady and profitable demand for its output for several years. If it does not obtain this contract, its profitability depends on uncertain industry demand and the willingness of other firms in the industry to maintain tacit collusion. Moreover, the opportunity to gain this secure supply contract happens infrequently, once every twenty years.

Given unanticipated changes in demand, linked with the vagaries of maintaining tacit collusion, the present value of the secure supply contract is likely to be greater than the present value of tacit collusion (Tirole, 1988). In other words, the opportunity costs of maintaining a tacit collusion strategy in this context are likely to be substantial, and firms are likely to abandon this strategy in favor of competing for the longer-term contract (Scherer, 1980). In this setting, a firm is likely to reduce prices below the collusive level in order to get the contract.

More generally, whenever firms in an industry gain sales opportunities through infrequent, large orders, the incentives to cheat on tacit collusion are usually stronger than the incentives to maintain tacit collusion. Conversely, when sales depend on numerous, small orders, firms have few incentives to cheat on tacit agreements to gain any one order, and thus tacit collusion is a more significant opportunity.

Numerous industries are characterized by infrequent, large orders. In military aircraft, the failure of McDonnell-Douglas (and its partners) to obtain the contract for the next generation of Stealth fighter from the Department of Defense is likely to affect this firm for ten to fifteen years (Schine, 1991). In commercial aircraft, AirBus's large order from United Airlines has had a significant effect on Boeing (Cole, 1992). It is unlikely that tacit collusion agreements could survive the rivalry created by these infrequent, large orders, even though the number of firms in these industries is quite small.

Large Inventories and Order Backlogs

The ability of firms to produce for inventory and to create order backlogs helps facilitate tacit collusion (Scherer, 1980). Inventory and order backlogs create buffers between a firm and its environment. With these buffers in place, firms do not have to react to every change in market conditions with changes in output and price. Instead of reducing prices when demand drops, firms can produce for inventory and store the products they sell. Instead of increasing prices when demand increases, firms can create an order backlog. These buffers help firms maintain consistency in their output and prices over time, thereby facilitating tacit collusion.

In some industries, inventories may be technologically infeasible, and order backlogs may not satisfy customers. For example, in the fresh fruit business, production for inventory is likely to lead to large spoilage costs. To avoid such costs, firms facing unanticipated reductions in demand, or greater-than-anticipated supply, are likely to have to reduce their prices. These rapid changes in prices can have a very destabilizing impact on an industry's price/output structure and make tacit collusion very difficult.

Entry Barriers

Each of the industry attributes listed in Table 8.5 has an impact on the level of opportunity for tacit collusion in an industry. None, however, is more important for this strategy than the existence of barriers to entry. Without barriers to entry, the above-normal profits associated with tacit collusion will create incentives for firms to enter into an industry (Bain, 1956). New entry into an industry reduces the collusion-enhancing attributes of each of the other industry characteristics listed in Table 8.5. New entry increases the number of firms in the industry. New entry is likely to create both product heterogeneity (as new firms introduce new products) and cost heterogeneity (new firms often have costs different from colluding incumbents'). New entrants are likely to ignore price leaders and often are not part of the industry social structure. New entrants are also likely to compete for all orders, small or large, to shrink order backlogs to satisfy customers, and to reduce inventories through stiff price competition. Overall, new entrants can be thought of as loose cannons in otherwise placid and calm industries (Spender, 1989). To reduce the threat of new entrants, tacitly colluding firms must be protected by barriers to entry.

In Section 3.2, we discuss five common barriers to entry (see Table 3.1). Each barrier can reduce the threat of entry. However, they can also create other problems for creating and sustaining tacit collusion agreements.

For example, each firm in an industry can deter entry by reducing its costs as much as it can through exploiting economies of scale (barrier 1 in Table 3.1) and cost advantages independent of scale (barrier 3). However, unless firms in an industry reduce their costs at the same rate, and to the same level, such cost reduction efforts are likely to lead to cost heterogeneity in an industry. If substantial cost heterogeneity exists, low-cost incumbent firms have a strong incentive to cheat on tacit collusion agreements to exploit their cost advantage. Thus cost heterogeneity created by firms attempting to establish cost-based barriers to entry may lead to the breakdown of tacit collusion agreements.

The same conclusion applies to firms in an industry that attempt to deter entry through product differentiation (barrier 2). Unless all (or most) firms in an industry differentiate their products in the same way, and to the same extent, efforts to deter entry though product differentiation are likely to lead to product heterogeneity, which, in turn, is likely to make tacit collusion more difficult to create and maintain).

The costs associated with erecting the remaining two barriers to entry (barrier 4, contrived deterrence, and barrier 5, government regulation of entry) can also create cost heterogeneity and reduce the opportunity for tacit collusion. This is especially the case if these costs are borne by one or by a small number of incumbent firms. If the costs of creating these barriers are borne by one or by a small number of incumbent firms, these firms' costs can be greater, thereby creating cost heterogeneity in the industry. Cost heterogeneity, as suggested earlier, can reduce the likelihood of successful tacit collusion.

Thus although the entry barriers listed in Table 3.1 are essential if firms in an industry seek to implement a tacit collusion strategy, the erection of these barriers can lead to the failure of this cooperative effort. In general, entry barriers will facilitate the implementation of a tacit collusion strategy only when they (1) successfully deter entry and (2) do not create significant levels of cost or product heterogeneity within an industry.

8.3 TACIT COLLUSION AND SUSTAINED COMPETITIVE ADVANTAGE

The analysis of tacit collusion, so far, specifies the conditions under which this strategy can be used to exploit the opportunity of neutralizing the threat of rivalry. However, for tacit collusion to be a source of sustained competitive advantage, it must also be rare and costly to imitate, and a firm must organize itself successfully to implement this strategy.

THE RARENESS OF TACIT COLLUSION

At first, it appears that tacit collusion strategies violate the rareness requirement of a sustained competitive advantage. After all, *rareness* in Chapters 6 and 7 implied that a small number of firms in an industry have the resources needed to implement a low-cost or product differentiation strategy. For tacit collusion to work, all or certainly the majority of firms in an industry must be involved. In what sense can a strategy implemented by all firms in an industry be considered rare?

The answer to this question depends on the first industry attribute listed in Table 8.5: the small-numbers requirement. From the perspective of firms currently in an industry, the tacit collusion strategy is not rare. But the development of tacit collusion requires a small number of industry incumbents, so from the point of view of both incumbents *and* potential entrants, the tacit collusion strategy is rare. It is very unlikely that numerous firms, including incumbents and potential entrants, could successfully implement a tacit collusion strategy. Thus, from this broader perspective, tacit collusion must be rare in order to generate above-normal economic profits.

THE IMITABILITY OF TACIT COLLUSION

As with the other business strategies discussed in this book, the imitability of tacit collusion depends both on the ability of firms to duplicate this strategy directly and their ability to implement substitutes for it.

Direct Duplication

Tacit collusion seems to violate the costly-to-duplicate requirement of sustained competitive advantage. For tacit collusion to work in an industry, incumbent firms that have not joined in the collusion must *not* face a cost disadvantage if they choose to do so. If it is very costly for noncolluding incumbents to begin colluding, then collusion will break down, and the above-normal profits associated with this strategy will be lost. Thus costly-to-duplicate strategies, in this context, appear to reduce the chance for sustained competitive advantage.

However, including potential entrants in the analysis resolves this apparent contradiction. Since all colluding incumbent firms are implementing the same strategy (tacit collusion), firm-level resources that are costly to duplicate are logically equivalent to industry-level barriers to entry. Industry barriers to entry are essential for the successful implementation of a tacit collusion strategy. Thus if not only incumbent firms but also potential entrants into an industry are included in an analysis, the VRIO framework developed in Chapter 5 can be extended to cooperative tacit collusion strategies. In this context, the small-numbers industry attribute is equivalent to the rareness requirement, and the barrier-to-entry industry attribute is equivalent to the costly-to-duplicate requirement.

Substitutes for Tacit Collusion

There are few obvious close substitutes for tacit collusion. Certainly, cost leadership and product differentiation, rather than being substitutes for tacit collusion, are likely to prevent firms from cooperating with one another. Strategic alliances (discussed in the next chapter) can sometimes be used to facilitate the development of collusive agreements. Put in this context, strategic alliances can help create the conditions necessary for collusion but are not substitutes for collusion. Moreover, most current research on alliances suggests that they are not usually associated with the development of collusive arrangements (Ordover and Willig, 1985).

Perhaps the closest substitute for tacit collusion is a particular form of diversification—horizontal diversification. A firm engaging in horizontal diversification acquires its rivals. If it does enough of this, it can begin acting as a monopolist in its industry. As we have seen, fully cooperating firms behave as if they were a "collective monopolist." But horizontal diversification that could lead to monopoly power is not allowed in most developed economies. Moreover, when monopolists do operate in these economies, they are usually subject to significant profit and activity regulations—regulations that limit their ability to earn monopoly profits. For these reasons, horizontal diversification is usually not a close substitute for tacit collusion.

TACIT COLLUSION AND ORGANIZATION

As with all strategies, the return potential of tacit collusion depends on the ability of firms to organize themselves to implement this strategy. In the implementing of tacit collusion strategies, two organizational issues are particularly important: maintaining organizational efficiency and organizational self-discipline.

Organizational Efficiency

One of the most significant organizational issues facing tacitly colluding firms concerns the efficiency of their organization. Under competitive conditions, firms are forced to keep their head count and their overhead expenditures low and to cut out strategically unimportant spending. Thus competitive pressures tend to lead to lean and efficient organizations. Firms that do not meet these criteria either change or are forced out of business by more efficient firms.

Under tacit collusion, competitive pressures toward organizational efficiency are not as pronounced. Indeed, the above-normal profits associated with tacit collusion often depend on a firm *not* driving its cost to the lowest possible level, *not* differentiating products as quickly as possible, and so forth. Such competitive actions are likely to upset tacit collusion, especially if they create cost or product heterogeneity, rivalry, and price competition. In restraining these competitive tendencies, colluding firms may decrease their overall efficiency and effectiveness. This may not be a problem, as long as tacit collusion continues, and as long as barriers to entry are in place. However, if collusion breaks down, or if entry occurs, inefficient organizations may be subject to intense competitive pressures.

Given the fragile character of tacit collusion, and the threat of potential entrants, colluding firms would be well advised to maintain an efficient organization—to act *as if* they were facing a competitive environment even though they are not. Of course, maintaining this efficiency is likely to be difficult, given the constraints that tacit collusion places on a firm. Moreover, such efficiency may be costly in the face of current collusion and may reduce (somewhat) a firm's current economic profit. However, if tacit collusion might break down sometime in the future, the ability to move quickly toward a more efficient organization may be worthwhile.

Research on tacitly colluding, explicitly colluding, and monopolistic firms suggests that most of these firms are unable to maintain high levels of organizational efficiency. They tend to become top-heavy with management, highly bureaucratic, risk averse, overinvested in luxurious office buildings, and so forth. For these reasons, tacit collusion strategies appear to sow the seeds of their own destruction. As tacitly colluding firms become progressively more inefficient in their organization, they become more tempting prey for more efficient new entrants. At some point, the low cost of displacing inefficient incumbent firms may attract new entrants into an industry, despite substantial barriers to entry.

Organizational Self-Discipline

The other significant organizational challenge facing colluding firms concerns the maintenance of self-discipline. Once a firm has committed itself to a tacit collusion strategy, its willingness to stick to that strategy will almost certainly be tested. Thus, for example, once General Electric signaled that it would not engage in price competition in the steam turbine industry, Westinghouse (its major competitor) announced price reductions. In a sense, Westinghouse was testing GE's resolve to stick with its tacit collusion strategy. GE did reduce its prices but gave its customers substantial rebates on previously purchased products. This action indicated that GE would stick by its commitment to price stability. Shortly thereafter, Westinghouse increased its prices to match GE's original prices, and price stability continued in the industry for almost fifteen years (Porter, 1979b).

Since tacitly colluding firms will almost certainly be tested in their resolve to maintain price and output stability, the ability to successfully implement this strategy depends on an unusual level of organizational self-discipline. Only when a tacitly colluding firm knows exactly what it is about, and is able to refrain from competitive actions in response to tests by its competitors, is this strategy likely to be successful. This self-discipline will need to be reinforced by appropriate management control systems and compensation policies.

8.4   SUMMARY

The problem of cooperation exists because firms, simultaneously, have strong incentives to cooperate and strong incentives to cheat on cooperative agreements. Traditional solutions to the problem of cooperation emphasize the role of some central authority, in the form of an individual or institution, in forcing cooperation (the Hobbesian solution). More recent solutions to this problem suggest that this central authority may be social norms (Granovetter's solution). Alternatively, the benefits of cooperation, compared to the costs of cheating, may enable a firm to remain in cooperative agreements without any form of central authority (Axelrod's solution).

The traditional way of examining cooperation in economic models focuses on explicit and tacit collusion. The primary benefit of collusion is that firms can establish prices and outputs that jointly maximize their profits. In some circumstances, such joint maximization is a much higher profit alternative than competing, acting as price takers, and earning normal economic profits. Put another way, explicit collusion and tacit collusion enable a firm to exploit the environmental opportunity of avoiding rivalry.

Although explicit and tacit collusion can present an important opportunity to firms, there are threats to this strategy as well. The threats depend on the incentives that cooperating firms have to cheat on collusive agreements. Colluding firms can cheat on their agreements in a variety of ways, including altering their prices (Bertrand cheating) and altering their output (Cournot cheating). Each of these alternative forms of cheating leads to long-run firm performance that falls somewhere between the zero economic profits of perfect competition and the shared monopoly profits of perfect cooperation. Which particular performance outcome occurs depends on the specific behaviors that cooperating firms engage in if others cheat.

If firms could communicate directly, they could judge the motives and intentions of other firms with reasonable accuracy. However, such explicit collusion is illegal. Instead, firms must rely on signals and other indicators of other firms' motives and intentions. Cooperation in this context is called tacit collusion. Firms can use a variety of industry attributes to judge the likelihood that other firms will cheat on collusion agreements, thereby estimating the likelihood that tacit collusion is a viable strategic option.

Tacit collusion can also be examined for its ability to generate sustained competitive advantages. If both incumbent firms and potential entrants into an industry are considered, standard VRIO analysis can be applied to tacit collusion. The rareness criterion can be thought of as equivalent to the small-numbers requirement, and the costly-to-imitate criterion can be thought of as equivalent to the barriers-to-entry requirement. Two critical organizational issues for firms implementing tacit collusion are the need for (1) organizational efficiency and (2) self-discipline in the face of other firms' testing of a firm's commitment to tacit collusion.

REVIEW QUESTIONS

1. Axelrod (1984) has shown that cooperation is likely as long as firms anticipate numerous interactions and as long as at least a few potentially interacting firms are willing to cooperate with each other. Others have argued that cooperation is likely to emerge in prisoner's dilemma games (a) as long as players can directly communicate, (b) if cheating does not lead to large payoffs, (c) if cheating leads to costly sanctions, and (d) if players are interested more in maximizing their payoffs than in beating the payoffs of other players. How are these two lists of the preconditions of cooperation related?

2. Both Granovetter (1985) and Axelrod (1984) argue that cooperation can emerge between firms, even in the absence of some central organizing institution. Does that mean that these authors believe that firms are somehow "altruistic"? Is there any room for altruism in these models of cooperation?

3. Firms that engage in Cournot cheating will earn higher levels of performance than will firms that engage in Bertrand cheating. Why then would firms ever engage in Bertrand cheating?

4. Both cost homogeneity and product homogeneity enhance the ability of firms in an industry to implement tacit collusion strategies. Under what conditions, if any, would a firm be able to simultaneously pursue a cost-leadership strategy or a product differentiation strategy while simultaneously trying to implement a tacit collusion strategy? Are these sets of strategies mutually exclusive?

5. At one level, the requirement that all firms in an industry be involved in a tacit collusion strategy in order for that strategy to be viable seems to contradict the rareness and imitability requirements for sustained competitive advantage, first discussed in Chapter 5. Is it possible to rationalize this apparent contradiction? If yes, how? If no, why not?

6. Some have argued that the implementation of a tacit collusion strategy will lead a firm to be relatively inefficient. Others have argued that the implementation of a tacit collusion strategy requires firms to be very efficient—at implementing this strategy. Which is it? Do firms implementing a tacit collusion strategy become less efficient or more efficient? Justify your answer.

CHAPTER
9

Cooperative Strategies: Strategic Alliances

As described in Chapter 8, interfirm cooperation that takes the form of tacit collusion is a difficult strategy to develop and maintain. Firms often have strong economic incentives to collude tacitly, but there are also strong incentives to cheat on these cooperative agreements once they are established. Moreover, because explicit collusion is typically illegal, the ability of firms to collude depends on some rather special industry characteristics—such as small numbers of competing firms, homogeneous costs, homogeneous products, and entry barriers— together with some highly developed organizational skills in reading and interpreting signals that may indicate a willingness to collude. In the end, it becomes clear that although tacit collusion is not impossible, it is also probably not widely implemented. Other forms of cooperation are more common. Among these is a wide class of cooperative strategies called strategic alliances, the subject of this chapter (Kogut, 1988; Hennart, 1988).

9.1 TYPES OF STRATEGIC ALLIANCE

A strategic alliance exists whenever two or more independent organizations cooperate in the development, manufacture, or sale of products

FIGURE 9.1
Types of Strategic Alliance

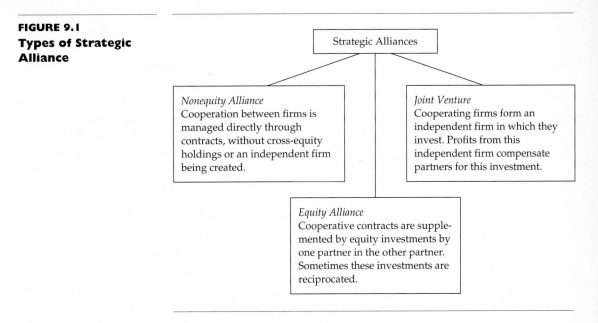

or services (Kogut, 1988; Hennart, 1988). Strategic alliances can be grouped into three broad categories: nonequity alliances, equity alliances, and joint ventures (see Fig. 9.1). In a nonequity alliance, cooperating firms agree to work together to develop, manufacture, or sell products or services, but they do not take equity positions in each other or form an independent organizational unit to manage their cooperative efforts. Rather, these cooperative relations are managed through the use of various forms of contracts. Licensing agreements (where one firm allows others to use its brand name to sell products), supply agreements (where one firm agrees to supply others), and distribution agreements (where one firm agrees to distribute the products of others) are examples of nonequity strategic alliances.

In an equity alliance, cooperating firms supplement contracts with equity holdings in alliance partners. For example, when General Motors began importing small cars manufactured by Isuzu, not only did these partners have supply contracts in place, but GM purchased 34.2 percent of Isuzu's stock (Badaracco and Hasegawa, 1988).

In a joint venture, cooperating firms create a legally independent firm in which they invest and from which they share any profits that are created (Hennart, 1988).

9.2   THE ECONOMIC VALUE OF STRATEGIC ALLIANCES

The use of nonequity alliances, equity alliances, and joint ventures has grown substantially over the last several years (Ernst and Bleeke, 1993). For example, by 1992, IBM had over four hundred strategic alliances with various companies in the United States and overseas. Corning has developed several hundred strategic alliances with numerous firms. One of these alliances, Dow Corning (a joint venture with Dow Chemical) is listed in the Fortune 500 (Bartlett and Ghoshal, 1993). Overall, the rate of joint-venture formation between U.S. and international firms has been growing at an annual rate of 27 percent since 1985 (Ernst and Bleeke, 1992).

STRATEGIC ALLIANCES AND ECONOMIC PERFORMANCE

In general, firms have an incentive to cooperate in strategic alliances when the value of their resources and assets combined is greater than the value of their resources and assets separately. This notion of resource complementarity is a definition of *synergy* and exists as long as the inequality in Eq. (9.1) holds:

$$NPV(A + B) > NPV(A) + NPV(B) \qquad \text{Eq. 9.1}$$

where,

$NPV(A + B)$ = the net present value of Firm A's and Firm B's assets combined

$NPV(A)$ = the net present value of Firm A's assets alone

$NPV(B)$ = the net present value of Firm B's assets alone

ALLIANCE OPPORTUNITIES

Several sources of interfirm synergy in strategic alliances have been discussed in the literature. Some of the most important are listed in Table 9.1 and discussed below. These interfirm synergies represent opportunities that can be exploited through strategic alliances (Harrigan, 1988; Hagedoorn, 1993).

Exploiting Economies of Scale

One of the most often cited reasons for the development of strategic alliances is the exploitation of economies of scale by firms that, if acting independently, would not be large enough to obtain these cost advantages (Kogut, 1988). In this context, the complementary resources and assets that alliance partners possess are their development, manufac-

**TABLE 9.1
Sources of Interfirm
Synergies That Can
Motivate Strategic
Alliances**

1. Exploiting economies of scale

2. Learning from competitors

3. Managing risk and sharing costs

4. Facilitating tacit collusion

5. Low-cost entry into new markets

6. Low-cost entry into new industries and new industry segments

7. Managing uncertainty

turing, or distribution activities. The cost of these activities, when combined in a strategic alliance, can be less than the cost of the activities separately.

An example of a strategic alliance to exploit economies of scale can be found in the aluminum industry. The efficient scale of a bauxite mine is substantially larger than the efficient scale of an aluminum smelter (Stuckey, 1983). A single firm operating an efficient bauxite mine is likely to generate many times more bauxite than it can process in its efficient aluminum smelters. To run its smelters efficiently, this single firm would have to mine bauxite in a less efficient, smaller-scale way or sell its excess bauxite on the open market. For reasons to be described later in this chapter and in Chapter 10, selling excess bauxite on the open market is difficult. Thus to obtain all the economies of scale associated with bauxite mining while keeping their smelters efficiently small, many aluminum firms have joined in joint-venture mining operations. Indeed, joint ventures currently account for over half of the world's bauxite-mining capacity (Hennart, 1988).

Learning from Competitors

Firms can also use strategic alliances to learn important skills and abilities from their competitors (Shan, Walker, and Kogut, 1994). These otherwise competing firms may have an incentive to cooperate even though cooperation may help a firm compete in all of its business activities, not just in the strategic alliance.

The joint venture between General Motors and Toyota has been widely cited for its potential to help GM learn about manufacturing high-quality small cars at a profit from Toyota (Badaracco and Hasegawa, 1988). To take advantage of this learning potential, GM rotates managers from its other manufacturing facilities to the joint venture and then back out to GM plants. Of course, Toyota would not be willing to become associated with GM in this strategic alliance (and risk sharing its knowledge about manufacturing small cars) unless it also gained from this relationship. From Toyota's point of view, this joint venture enables Toyota to gain a stronger foothold in the U.S. market by providing access to GM's impressive U.S. distribution network and by reducing the political liabilities associated with importing numerous cars into the U.S. market (by facilitating Toyota's continued entry into the U.S. market). Moreover, Toyota may believe that GM's ability to learn about manufacturing small cars is limited, for much of this ability is tacit, socially complex, and difficult to imitate (Teece, 1977).

Although learning from competitors through strategic alliances can be an important opportunity, at least two risks are associated with this type of alliance. First, as suggested above, this form of alliance can allow a competing firm to develop the skills and abilities it needs to compete more effectively in all segments of its business. This development, in the long run, can hurt the alliance partner who is being learned from. Some have argued that strategic alliances between U.S. and Japanese firms have given the Japanese firms access to critical technologies that have generated important competitive advantages (Reich, 1986). According to this line of thought, by cooperating with Japanese firms, U.S. firms transferred their skills and abilities to these Japanese firms, which then used these abilities to compete against their former partners. Of course, U.S. firms have gained some access to closed Japanese markets through their strategic alliances with local Japanese partners. The question facing all firms contemplating alliances with firms in their industry is, Is the value of learning obtained through such an alliance greater than the competitive threat that may be created through this form of cooperation?

A second risk of this form of strategic alliance is that competing firms seeking to learn from each other may appear to be violating antitrust laws. Indeed, as will be discussed below, the traditional way of analyzing the benefits of strategic alliances with competitors has been to assume that such alliances are created to facilitate tacit collusion (Pfeffer and Nowak, 1976). Government regulators may conclude that strategic alliances designed to facilitate learning from competitors are actually forms of tacit or even explicit collusion, and they may subject these alliances to intense legal scrutiny. This was the case in GM's alliance with Toyota (Badaracco and Hasegawa, 1988).

Managing Risk and Sharing Costs

Strategic alliances can also help a firm manage the risks and share the costs associated with new business investments. Sometimes, the investment required to exploit an opportunity can be very large. Acting alone, a firm making this investment may be "betting the company," substantially increasing the probability of bankruptcy. Even when failure will not bankrupt a firm, the downside risks of some costly investments can be substantial.

In this context, forming strategic alliances spreads the risk of failure by sharing the costs among several firms. Reports from the semiconductor-manufacturing industry suggest that the sheer size of the investment required to build a full-service, vertically integrated semiconductor fabrication plant is so large that few, if any, single-firm plants will be built in the future. Instead, several firms are likely to form joint ventures to fund and manage these facilities (personal communication). The high risk of offshore oil drilling has led most firms in this industry to join in drilling consortia when exploiting possible sites (Hennart, 1988).

Risk management and cost sharing seem to be at the heart of new alliances created in the automobile industry. The Big Three auto companies continue to compete in product markets but have alliances to invest in risky but high-potential research efforts. Such research and development alliances include a cooperative effort to develop composite materials, cleaner-burning engine technologies, and at least four other joint efforts (Stertz, 1991; Suris, 1993). Risk management and cost sharing have also led the British Broadcasting Company to develop an alliance with Capital Cities/ABC to share news-gathering networks throughout the world (Jensen, 1993a).

Alliances to manage risk and share costs can also be important in industries where industrywide technology and communication standards are important. As these industries emerge, several competing standards may exist. These multiple standards can be allowed to compete until the standard that will predominate in the industry emerges. Alternatively, firms in an industry can cooperate to create a standard that meets the needs of cooperating firms. By cooperating, firms manage the risks and reduce the costs associated with going it alone. The cooperative approach to standard setting was used in the emerging high-density television industry to create a technology standard acceptable to many of the key players (Carnevale, 1993).

Facilitating Tacit Collusion

Another incentive for cooperating in strategic alliances is that such activities may facilitate the development of tacit collusion. Recall that tacit collusion is made more difficult by legal restrictions on communication between firms. However, separate firms, even if they are in the same industry, can form strategic alliances. Although communication between these firms cannot legally include sharing information about prices and costs for products or services that are produced outside the alliance, such interaction does help create the social setting within which tacit collusion may develop (Burgers, Hill, and Kim, 1993).

As suggested earlier, most research on strategic alliances has focused on the implications of these actions for tacit collusion. Several authors have concluded that joint ventures, as a form of alliance, do increase the probability of tacit collusion. For example, Fusfeld (1958) found that joint ventures created two industrial groups, besides U.S. Steel, in the U.S. iron and steel industry in the early 1900s. In this sense, joint ventures in the steel industry were a substitute for U.S. Steel's vertical integration and had the effect of creating an oligopoly in what (without joint ventures) would have been a more competitive market. Pate (1969) and Boyle (1968) found that over 50 percent of joint-venture parents belong to the same industry. Mead (1967), after examining 885 joint-venture bids for oil and gas leases, found only 16 instances where joint-venture partners competed on another tract in the same sale. These results suggest that joint ventures might encourage subsequent tacit collusion among firms in the same industry (Kent, 1991; Bloch, 1995).

Also, Pfeffer and Nowak (1976) found that joint ventures were most likely in industries of moderate concentration. These authors argued that in highly concentrated industries joint ventures were not needed to create conditions conducive to collusion (that is, the small-numbers condition discussed in Chapter 8 already holds), and in nonconcentrated industries these conditions could not be created by joint ventures. Only when joint-venturing activity could effectively create concentrated industries—under conditions of moderate concentration—were joint ventures seen as likely.

More recent work, however, disputes these findings (Kent, 1991). Joint ventures between firms in the same industry may be valuable for a variety of reasons that have little or nothing to do with collusion (Kogut, 1988; Hennart, 1988). Moreover, by using a lower level of aggregation than Pfeffer and Nowak's (1976), Duncan (1982) disputed Pfeffer and Nowak's conclusions. Pfeffer and Nowak defined industries by using two-digit SIC codes; by using three-digit SIC-code industry definitions, Duncan found that 73 percent of the joint ventures in his sample had parent firms coming from different industries. Although joint ventures between firms in the same industry (defined at this lower level of aggregation) may have collusive implications, Duncan has shown that these kinds of joint ventures are relatively rare.

Low-Cost Entry into New Markets

Another motivation for strategic alliances cited in the literature is the impact of these relationships on the cost of entry into new markets, especially entry into foreign markets (Kogut, 1988; Hennart, 1988). In this context, one partner typically brings products or services (as resources) to the alliance, and the other partner brings local knowledge, local distribution networks, and local political influence (as resources) to the relationship. Low-cost entry into new markets is the primary motivation behind the numerous international alliances in the telecommunications industry (Keller, 1993).

Even in the absence of government regulations on entry, the development of local distribution networks can be a costly and difficult process. Such actions generally require a great deal of knowledge about local conditions. Local alliance partners may already possess this knowledge. By cooperating with local partners, firms can substantially reduce the cost of entry into these markets. Alliances can be even more important when government regulations favor local firms over firms from other countries. In this context, alliances with local partners may be the only economically viable means of entry into a market (Tomlinson, 1970; Friedman and Kalmanoff, 1961).

Some empirical results support these observations. For example, Stopford and Wells (1972) found that when entry into a foreign market was based on a product differentiation strategy (a strategy that presumably requires a great deal of local knowledge), joint ventures with local partners (presumably to obtain local knowledge) were more likely, compared with entry into foreign markets based on a low-cost or other strategy. Also, when the culture of a firm's country of origin is very different from the culture of the country it is seeking to enter, Kogut and Singh (1986) found that entering firms are more likely to use joint ventures to enter, thereby obtaining the cultural expertise of the local partner.

A strategic alliance with a local partner is almost the only way to enter into some new markets. For example, virtually all entry by U.S. firms into the Japanese domestic market has been with Japanese alliance partners (Pope and Hamilton, 1993). The possible creation of trade barriers to protect European and other markets has made strategic alliances between North American firms and local partners in these protected markets much more important and frequent. Government restrictions on entry into India has *required* foreign firms, in many circumstances, to obtain local strategic alliance partners (Jacob, 1992a), as does the increased use of local-content laws in several European countries and the United States. Overall, the increased globalization of the world's industry, linked with heterogeneous cultures and political systems and barriers to free trade, makes international strategic alliances more valuable and common (Hennart, 1988).

Low-Cost Entry into New Industries and New Industry Segments

Strategic alliances can also facilitate a firm's entry into a new industry or into new segments of an industry. Entry into an industry can require skills, abilities, and products that a potential entrant does not possess.

Strategic alliances can help a firm enter a new industry, by avoiding the high costs of creating these skills, abilities, and products (Kogut, 1988).

For example, recently, Du Pont wanted to enter into the electronics industry. However, building the skills and abilities need to develop competitive products in this industry can be very difficult and costly (Freedman and Hudson, 1986). Rather than absorbing these costs, Du Pont developed a strategic alliance (Du Pont/Phillips Optical) with an established electronics firm, Phillips, to distribute some of Phillips's products in the United States. In this way Du Pont was able to enter into a new industry (electronics) without having to absorb all the costs of creating electronics resources and abilities from the ground up.

Of course, for this joint venture to succeed, Phillips must have had an incentive to cooperate with Du Pont. Where Du Pont was looking to reduce its cost of entry into a new industry, Phillips was looking to reduce its cost of continued entry into a new market: the United States. Phillips used its alliance with Du Pont to sell in the United States the compact discs it already was selling in Europe (Freedman and Hudson, 1986).

Just as Du Pont used an alliance with Phillips to facilitate entry into the electronics industry, IBM is using an alliance with the producers of the "Terminator" movies (James Cameron, Stan Winston, and Scott Ross) to begin entry into the entertainment industry (Turner and Hooper, 1993). Indeed, the potential of multimedia interactive video and other forms of entertainment has led to a large number of alliances between traditional computer firms and movie producers.

Notice that alliance partners do not have to obtain the same advantages from cooperation in order for the complementary resources and assets condition described in Eq. (9.1) to hold. All that is required is that the present value of the combined resources and assets is greater than the present value of each of these resources and assets separately. The sources of this increased value to alliance partners may or may not be the same.

Alliances to facilitate entry into new industries can be valuable even when the skills needed in these industries are not as complex and difficult to learn as skills in the electronics or movie industries. For example, rather than developing their own frozen novelty foods, Welch Foods Inc. and Leaf Inc. (maker of Heath candy bars) asked Eskimo Pie to formulate products for this industry. Eskimo Pie developed Welch's frozen grape-juice bar and the Heath toffee ice-cream bar. These firms then split the profits derived from these products (Teitelbaum, 1992). As long as the cost of using an alliance to enter a new industry is less than the cost of learning new skills and capabilities, an alliance can be a valuable strategic opportunity.

Entry facilitated by alliances need not be restricted to entry into new industries. Often, firms will cooperate in order to facilitate entry into a new segment of an industry. For example, Coca-Cola and Nestlé recently formed a joint venture to begin manufacturing and distributing coffee in aluminum cans in the Korean market (Darlin, 1991). This represents a new industry segment for both firms.

Managing Uncertainty

Finally, firms may use strategic alliances to manage uncertainty. Under conditions of high uncertainty, firms may not be able to tell, at a particular point in time, which of several different strategies they should pursue (Knight, 1965). In this context, firms have an incentive to retain the flexibility to move quickly into a particular market or industry once the full value of that strategy is revealed (Kogut, 1991; Burgers, Hill, and Kim, 1993). In this sense, strategic alliances enable a firm to maintain a point of entry into a market or industry, without incurring the costs associated with full-scale entry.

Based on this logic, Kogut (1991) has analyzed joint ventures as real options, using option-pricing theory (Black and Scholes, 1972, 1973). In this sense, a joint venture is an option that a firm buys, under conditions of uncertainty, to retain the ability to move quickly into a market or industry if valuable opportunities present themselves. One way in which firms can move quickly into a market is simply to buy out their partner(s) in the joint venture. Moreover, by investing in a joint venture, a firm may gain access to the information it needs to evaluate full-scale entry into a market (Balakrishnan and Koza, 1993).

According to Kogut (1991), firms that invest in joint ventures as options will acquire their alliance partners only after the market signals an unexpected increase in value of the venture—that is, only after uncertainty is reduced and the true, positive value of entering into a market is known. Kogut's (1991) empirical findings are consistent with these expectations.

Given these observations, it is not surprising to see firms in newly uncertain environments develop numerous strategic alliances. For example, AT&T, just after the divestiture of the regional operating companies, was suddenly in a new and highly competitive environment. Although there were many opportunities, which of these held the highest value for AT&T was unclear. In this context, AT&T developed several hundred strategic alliances (Keller, 1993; Kogut, 1991; Sankar et al., 1995). Only after AT&T examined opportunities in several industries did it begin to resolve some of its uncertainty by full-scale entry into some of them, including the computer business through its acquisition of NCR. The recent spin-off of AT&T's computer operations suggests that its synergies with the computer industry either did not exist, or were not fully realized. In the same way, as IBM faced increasingly uncertain fortunes in the late 1980s and early 1990s, it began to invest in more strategic alliances to learn about new strategic alternatives and to retain strategic flexibility (Zachary and Yoder, 1991; Hooper, 1993).

STRATEGIC ALLIANCES AND GENERIC INDUSTRY STRUCTURES

Some of the incentives to cooperate in strategic alliances listed in Table 9.1 exist only when cooperating firms have similar strategic goals and objectives. For example, firms seeking economies of scale through strategic alliances must find partners that are also searching for economies of scale and have production or distribution processes that can be conveniently linked within a strategic alliance to obtain cost reductions. Also, firms seeking to develop tacit collusion through strategic alliances must find partners with whom collusion is likely to develop, and with whom collusion is likely to have the effect of reducing industry output and increasing industry prices. A strategic alliance in which all parties are seeking the same advantages from the alliance is called a *symmetric* alliance (Hennart, 1988).

Some of the other incentives to cooperate in strategic alliances can be realized only when cooperating firms have different strategic goals and abilities. For example, an alliance that facilitates entry into new markets or into new industries and new industry segments presumes that at least one partner in the alliance is operating in a market or industry segment that another firm in the alliance is not operating in. Also, strategic alliances designed to facilitate learning presume that cooperating firms differ. If they did not differ along some strategically relevant dimension, one firm could not learn from another. These kinds of strategic alliance are called *asymmetric* alliances (Hennart, 1988).

Other incentives to cooperate in strategic alliances can exist whether firms are similar to or different from one another. When alliances are used to manage uncertainty, that uncertainty can stem from factors within a firm's current market or industry or from factors associated with entering new markets or industries. The same can be said of alliances to manage risk. When uncertainty/risk exists within a single industry, partnering with other firms in that industry can help manage that uncertainty/risk. Such strategic alliances are likely to be symmetric. When managing uncertainty/risk requires partnerships across market or industry boundaries, asymmetric alliances are formed. Alliances in which firm interests can be similar to or different from one another are called *mixed* alliances.

The distinction between symmetric, asymmetric, and mixed strategic alliances helps clarify which kinds of strategic alliance are likely to be opportunities in different generic industry structures (discussed in Section 4.2) (Nielsen, 1988). These relationships are summarized in Table 9.2.

TABLE 9.2
Types of Strategic Alliance and Generic Industry Structures

Types of Alliance	Generic Industry Structure

Symmetric alliances
   Economies of scale
   Tacit collusion
	Mature industries
	Fragmented industries
	   (with strategic groups)

Asymmetric alliances
   Low-cost entry into new markets
   Low-cost entry into new industries
      and new industry segments
   Learning from competitors
	Emerging industries
	Fragmented industries
	   (with no strategic groups)
	Declining industries
	Global industries

Mixed alliances
   Managing uncertainty
   Managing risks and sharing costs
	All generic industry structures

Since symmetric alliances can exist only among similar firms, these kinds of alliance are most likely to generate advantages for firms in very mature industries (where firms have similar products, technologies, customers, and so forth) or in fragmented industries with large groups of similar firms (where firms within each group are similar to each other). In these industry settings, symmetric strategic alliances that are designed to exploit economies of scale or lead to the development of tacit collusion are most likely.

Asymmetric strategic alliances are most likely when cooperating firms are different from each other. Thus asymmetric alliances are most likely in emerging industries (before industry standards create firm homogeneity), in fragmented industries without strategic groups, in declining industries (where firms pursue several different strategies), and in global industries (where cultural and political heterogeneity exists). In these industry settings, asymmetric alliances to gain entry into new markets or industries and alliances to facilitate learning are most likely to be important strategic opportunities.

Mixed strategic alliances can exist in any industry setting. Thus alliances to manage risk and uncertainty can be opportunities in any generic industry structure.

ALLIANCE THREATS: INCENTIVES TO CHEAT ON STRATEGIC ALLIANCE AGREEMENTS

Just as there are incentives to cooperate in strategic alliances, there are also incentives to cheat on these cooperative agreements. Cheating can

TABLE 9.3	Adverse selection	Potential partners misrepresent the value of the skills and abilities they bring to the alliance
Ways to Cheat in Strategic Alliance	Moral hazard	Partners provide to the alliance skills and abilities of lower quality than they promised
	Holdup	Partners exploit the transaction-specific investments made by others in the alliance

occur in at least three different ways: adverse selection, moral hazard, and holdup (see Table 9.3).

Adverse Selection

Potential cooperative partners can misrepresent the skills, abilities, and other resources that they will bring to an alliance. This form of cheating, called *adverse selection* (Barney and Ouchi, 1986), exists when an alliance partner promises to bring to an alliance certain resources that it either does not control or cannot acquire. For example, a local firm engages in adverse selection when it promises to make available to alliance partners a local distribution network that does not currently exist. Firms engaging in adverse selection are *not* competent alliance partners.

Adverse selection in a strategic alliance is likely only when it is difficult or costly to observe the skills or resources that a partner brings to an alliance. If potential partners can easily see that a firm is misrepresenting the skills and resources it possesses, they will not create a strategic alliance with that firm. Armed with such understanding, they will seek a different alliance partner, develop the needed skills and resources internally, or perhaps forgo this particular business opportunity.

However, evaluating the veracity of the claims of potential alliance partners is often not easy. The ability to evaluate these claims depends on information that a firm may not possess. To fully evaluate claims about a potential partner's political contacts, for example, a firm needs its own political contacts; to fully evaluate claims about potential partners' market knowledge, a firm needs significant market knowledge. A firm that can completely, and at low cost, evaluate the resources and abilities of potential alliance partners probably does not really need that strategic alliance. The fact that a firm is seeking an alliance partner is in some sense an indication that the firm has limited abilities to evaluate potential partners.

In general, the less tangible the resources and skills that are to be brought to a strategic alliance, the more costly it will be to estimate their value before an alliance is created, and the more likely is adverse selection to occur. Firms considering alliances with partners bringing intangible resources such as "knowledge of local conditions" or "contacts with key political figures" will need to guard against this form of cheating (Barney and Ouchi, 1986).

Even when the resources and capabilities that a potential partner alleges that it will bring to an alliance are *not* intangible, adverse selection can occur. For example, over thirty franchisees at Postal Instant Press (PIP) have alleged that the firm failed to fully inform them of the financial situation that led to a leveraged buyout of PIP in 1989. By omitting this and related financial information from sales pitches to potential franchisees, PIP is alleged to have induced individuals to purchase franchise outlets. PIP denies the allegations, and court action is still pending (Tannenbaum, 1993). If PIP is found guilty of misleading potential franchisees about its financial resources and capabilities, it will have been guilty of adverse selection.

Moral Hazard

Partners in an alliance may possess high-quality resources and capabilities of significant value in an alliance but fail to make those resources and capabilities available to alliance partners. This form of cheating is called *moral hazard* (Barney and Ouchi, 1986; Holmström, 1979). For example, a partner in an engineering strategic alliance may agree to send only its most talented and best trained engineers to work in the alliance but then actually send less talented, poorly trained engineers. These less qualified engineers may not be able to contribute substantially to making the alliance successful, but they may be able to learn a great deal from the highly qualified engineers provided by other alliance partners. In this way, the less qualified engineers effectively transfer wealth from other alliance partners to their own firm (Ouchi, 1984; Bresser, 1988).

Often both parties in a failed alliance accuse each other of moral hazard. For example, in the late 1980s, Boston Ventures, a New England investment firm, purchased Motown Records. Boston Ventures then entered into an alliance with MCA to distribute Motown's records. Unfortunately, sales of Motown's recordings through MCA's distribution networks never met expectations. Motown blamed MCA for failing to aggressively promote the recordings; MCA accused Motown of producing records that simply were not popular hits. After just a few years, this alliance crumbled, and Motown signed a distribution agreement with Polygram Records (Turner, 1991). The responsibility of each party in this alliance for its collapse will be determined in a court of law.

The existence of moral hazard in a strategic alliance does not necessarily mean that one or more parties to that alliance are malicious or dishonest. Rather, what often happens is that market conditions change after an alliance is formed, requiring one or more partners to an alliance to change their strategies.

For example, in the early days of the personal computer industry, Compaq Computer Corporation relied on a network of independent distributors to sell its computers. However, as competition in the personal industry increased, mail order and so-called computer superstores became much more valuable distribution networks, and alliances between Compaq and its traditional distributors became strained. By the early 1990s, Compaq's traditional distributors were unable to obtain in a timely manner all the inventory they wanted. Indeed, to satisfy the needs of large accounts, some traditional distributors actually purchased Compaq computers from local computer superstores and then shipped them to their customers (Pope, 1993). Compaq's shift from independent dealers to alternative distributors looked like moral hazard—at least from the point of view of the independent dealers. But from Compaq's perspective, this change simply reflected economic realities in the personal computer industry.

Holdup

Even if alliance partners engage in neither adverse selection nor moral hazard, another form of cheating may evolve. Once a strategic alliance has been created, partner firms may make investments that have value only in the context of that alliance and in no other economic exchanges. For example, managers from one alliance partner may have to develop close, trusting relationships with managers from other alliance partners. These close relationships are very valuable in the context of the alliance but have limited economic value in other economic exchanges. Also, one partner may have to customize its manufacturing equipment, distribution network, and key organizational policies to cooperate with other partners. These modifications have significant value in the context of the alliance but do not help the firm, and may even hurt it, in economic exchanges outside the alliance. Whenever an investment's value in its first best use (in this case, within the alliance) is much greater than its value in its second best use (in this case, outside the alliance), that investment is said to be transaction-specific (Williamson, 1975; Klein, Crawford, and Alchian, 1978).

When one firm makes more transaction-specific investments in a strategic alliance than partner firms make, that firm may be subject to the form of cheating called *holdup* (Barney and Ouchi, 1986). Holdup occurs when a firm that has not made significant transaction-specific investments demands from an alliance returns that are higher than what the partners agreed to when they created the alliance.

For example, two alliance partners agree to a fifty-fifty split of the costs and profits associated with the alliance. To make the alliance work, Firm A has to customize its production process. Firm B, however, does not have to modify itself to cooperate with Firm A. The value to Firm A of this customized production process, *if it is used in the strategic alliance,* is $5,000. But outside the alliance, this customized process is only worth $200 (as scrap).

Obviously, Firm A has made a transaction-specific investment in this alliance, and Firm B has not. Thus Firm A may be subject to holdup by Firm B. In particular, Firm B may threaten to leave the alliance unless Firm A agrees to give Firm B part of the $5,000 value that Firm A obtains by using the modified production process in the alliance. Rather than lose all the value that could be generated by its investment, Firm A may be willing to give up some of its $5,000 to avoid gaining only $200. Indeed, if Firm B extracts up to the value of Firm A's production process in its next best use (here, only $200), Firm A will still be better off continuing in this relationship rather than dissolving it. Thus even though Firm A and Firm B agree on a fifty-fifty split from this strategic alliance, the agreement may be modified if one party to the alliance makes significant transaction-specific investments (Klein, Crawford, and Alchian, 1978). Research on international joint ventures suggests that the existence of transaction-specific investments in these relationships often leads to holdup problems (Yan and Gray, 1994).

Although holdup is a form of cheating in strategic alliances, the threat of holdup can be a motivation for creating an alliance. Bauxite-smelting companies often join in joint ventures with mining companies in order to exploit economies of scale in mining. However, these firms have another option: They could choose to operate large and efficient mines by themselves and then sell the excess bauxite (over and above their needs for their own smelters) on the open market. Unfortunately, however, bauxite is not a homogeneous commodity. Moreover, different kinds of bauxite require different smelting technologies. In order for one firm to sell its excess bauxite on the market, other smelting firms would have to make enormous investments, the sole purpose of which would be to refine that particular firm's bauxite. These investments would be transaction-specific and subject these other smelters to holdup problems.

In this context, a strategic alliance can be thought of as a way of reducing the threat of holdup by creating an explicit management framework for resolving holdup problems. In other words, although holdup problems might still exist in these strategic alliances, the alliance framework may still be a better way to manage these problems than attempts to manage them in arm's-length market relationships

(Williamson, 1985). (These issues are discussed in more detail in Chapter 10's analysis of vertical integration strategies.)

In all three forms of cheating in a strategic alliance, the cheating firm effectively extracts wealth from its partners and transfers this wealth to itself. How these forms of cheating can be controlled is discussed later in this chapter.

9.3   STRATEGIC ALLIANCES AND SUSTAINED COMPETITIVE ADVANTAGE

The ability of strategic alliances, like all the other strategies discussed in this book, to be sources of sustained competitive advantage can be analyzed by using the VRIO framework developed in Chapter 5. An alliance is economically valuable when the inequality in Eq. (9.1) is greater than the costs imposed in an alliance if one or more partners cheat. In addition, for a strategic alliance to be a source of *sustained* competitive advantage, it must be rare and costly to imitate, and the firm must be organized to fully exploit the alliance. These issues are considered below.

THE RARENESS OF STRATEGIC ALLIANCES

The rareness of strategic alliances depends on the number of competing firms that have already implemented an alliance. But the rareness of a strategic alliance also depends on the benefits that firms obtain from their alliances and not just on the frequency with which alliances exist.

Consider, for example, the automobile industry in the United States. Over the last several years, strategic alliances have become very common in this industry, especially with Japanese auto firms. Ford has developed an alliance with Mazda, Chrysler has developed an alliance with Mitsubishi, and GM has developed an alliance with Toyota. Given the frequency with which alliances have developed in this industry, it is tempting to conclude that strategic alliances are not rare and thus not a source of competitive advantage.

Closer examination, however, suggests that these alliances may have been created for different reasons. For example, GM and Toyota have cooperated only in building a single line of cars, the Chevrolet Nova. GM has been less interested in learning design skills from Toyota and has been more interested in learning about manufacturing high-quality small cars profitably (Badaracco and Hasegawa, 1988). Ford and Mazda, in contrast, have worked closely together in designing new cars and have contemplated joint manufacturing operations

(Patterson, 1991; Williams and Kanabayaski, 1993). Mitsubishi has acted primarily as a supplier to Chrysler, and (until recently) there has been relatively little joint development or manufacturing (Ennis, 1991). Thus although all three U.S. firms have strategic alliances, the alliances serve different purposes, and thus each may be rare.

One of the reasons why the benefits that accrue from a particular strategic alliance may be rare is that relatively few firms may have the complementary resources and abilities needed to form an alliance. This is particularly likely when an alliance is formed to enter into a new market and especially a new *foreign* market. In many less developed economies, only one local firm or a very few local firms may exist with the local knowledge, contacts, and distribution network needed to facilitate entry into that market. Moreover, sometimes the government acts to limit the number of these local firms. Although several firms may seek entry into this market, only a very small number will be able to form a strategic alliance with the local entity, and therefore the benefits that accrue to the allied firms will likely be rare.

THE IMITABILITY OF STRATEGIC ALLIANCES

As discussed in Section 5.2, the resources and capabilities that enable firms to conceive of and implement valuable strategies may be imitated in two ways: direct duplication and substitution. Both duplication and substitution are important considerations in analyzing the imitability of strategic alliances.

Direct Duplication of Strategic Alliances

Recent research suggests that successful strategic alliances are based on socially complex relations among alliance partners (Ernst and Bleeke, 1993; Barney and Hansen, 1994). In this sense, successful strategic alliances often go well beyond simple legal contracts and are characterized by socially complex phenomena such as a trusting relationship between alliance partners, friendship, and even (perhaps) a willingness to suspend narrow self-interest for the longer-term good of the relationship.

Ernst and Bleeke (1993) argue that the development of trusting relationships between alliance partners is both difficult to do and essential to the success of strategic alliances. Approximately one-third of the forty-nine alliances these authors studied failed to meet the expectations of partner firms. The most common cause of failure was the partners' inability to trust one another. Interpersonal communication, tolerance for cultural differences, patience, and willingness to sacrifice short-term profits for longer-term success were all important determinants of the level of trust among alliance partners (Ernst and Bleeke, 1993).

Of course, not all firms in an industry are likely to have the organizational and relation-building skills required for successful alliance building. If these skills and abilities are rare among a set of competing firms and costly to develop, then firms that are able to exploit these abilities by creating alliances may gain competitive advantages. Examples of firms that have developed these specialized skills include Corning, a firm with several hundred strategic alliances (Bartlett and Ghoshal, 1993).

Substitutes for Strategic Alliances

Even if the purpose and objectives of a strategic alliance are valuable and rare, and even if the relationships on which an alliance is created are socially complex and costly to imitate, that alliance will still not generate a sustained competitive advantage if low-cost substitutes are available. At least two possible substitutes for strategic alliances exist: internal development and acquisitions.

Internal Development. In some situations, the cost of realizing a particular synergy through internal development efforts may approximately equal the cost of realizing this same synergy through a strategic alliance. When this is the case, internal development will be a substitute for a strategic alliance. In other situations, the cost of realizing this synergy through internal development may be greater than the cost of realizing it through an alliance, in which case internal development is not a substitute for a strategic alliance. The relative costs of using internal development and using strategic alliances to realize a particular synergy depend on the cost of gaining access to the resources and capabilities needed to create this synergy and on the costs of managing the links between these resources to realize this synergy.

Hennart (1988) has shown that in some circumstances alliances will be a less costly way of gaining access to resources and capabilities than will internal development. This will be the case when the marginal cost of using another firm's resources and capabilities through an alliance is almost zero. For example, if one firm already has a distribution network in place, and if that network could be used to distribute another firm's products or services, then the marginal cost of using that network to distribute the additional product or service is almost zero. In this context, even if a firm could develop its own distribution network at relatively low cost, the extremely low cost of using the established network makes a strategic alliance preferred over internal development, and internal development is not a substitute for a strategic alliance. It is not surprising to see relatively recent entrants into the

U.S. automobile market, for example, use alliances with established GM, Ford, and Chrysler dealers to distribute their products (Patterson, 1991). Nor is it surprising that as U.S. telecommunications firms have expanded operations overseas, they have formed alliances with firms that already possess distribution networks in these markets (Keller, 1993). In these cases, the cost of gaining access to distribution capabilities is much lower through an alliance than it would be if these firms developed their own distribution network.

More generally, when the internal realization of a synergy requires the development of resources or capabilities that are path dependent, uncertain, or socially complex, it is often less costly to gain access to these resources through an alliance with a firm that already possesses them rather than attempting to develop these resources independently. In this situation, internal development efforts are not a substitute for strategic alliances. But when the realization of a synergy does not require the development of such resources, internal development and strategic alliances can be strategic substitutes.

However, the relative costs of gaining access to resources and capabilities through internal development and strategic alliances are not the only relevant issue in evaluating these as strategic substitutes. The relative costs of managing the links needed to realize a particular synergy in these different ways are also important. For example, it might be the case that it would be much less costly for a particular firm to use an alliance to gain access to another firm's distribution network, instead of developing such a network from scratch. But if the cost of managing this alliance is very high, internal development might be preferred over the strategic alliance, despite the low cost of gaining access to another firm's resources or capabilities through an alliance (Shortell and Zajac, 1988).

There is a significant amount of research on the ability of firms to develop cooperative and synergistic relationships within their boundaries (Hoskisson and Hitt, 1990), and there is an ever-increasing amount of research on the importance of cooperative relationships in strategic alliances (Ernst and Bleeke, 1993). But there is little consensus about the cost of cooperating within a firm to realize a synergy, compared to the cost of managing links between firms in a strategic alliance to realize a synergy.

On the one hand, economists like Williamson (1975) and Teece (1977) have assumed that cooperation is probably less costly to develop within a firm than between firms. The fact that managers within a firm report within a single hierarchy suggests, for these authors at least, that formal authority can be used to ensure low-cost cooperation. This suggests that even when gaining access to the resources and capabilities needed to create a synergy is more costly through internal development than it is through a strategic alliance, the additional costs may be more than offset by the lower cost of managing the links between these resources to realize these synergies internally.

On the other hand, others have criticized the assumption that cooperation within a firm is less costly to create than is cooperation between firms. Grossman and Hart (1986) suggest that bringing a transaction within the boundaries of a firm does not "magically" reduce the cost of developing cooperation. This argument suggests that developing cooperative relations between firms and developing cooperative relations between units within a firm are about equally costly, and thus that the choice between internal development and strategic alliances should depend only on the relative cost of gaining access to the relevant resources and capabilities through these mechanisms. If internal development and strategic alliances do not differ in the cost of gaining access to the resources needed to create synergies, then they will be strategic substitutes.

Whether the costs of managing the links between the resources in order to create synergies vary between internal development and strategic alliances probably depends on the cooperative capabilities of firms. Some firms may be very skilled at developing high levels of intraorganizational cooperation and thus pursue this as a low-cost approach to exploiting potential synergies. The well-known cooperative cultures at Hewlett-Packard and several Japanese firms may make internal cooperation to exploit synergies a preferred approach for these firms (see Chapter 12). Other firms may have become very skilled at developing interorganizational cooperation and thus pursue strategic alliances as a low-cost approach to exploiting potential synergies. The success of Corning and Dow Chemical in developing and nurturing strategic alliances with numerous partners suggests that these firms may prefer this approach to exploiting potential synergies (Bartlett and Ghoshal, 1993).

If these different types of relationship-building skills enable several firms to exploit the same potential synergies at equally low cost, then internal development and strategic alliances are likely to be close strategic substitutes. However, if different firms have very different costs in exploiting the same kinds of strategic synergies, then these two approaches are not likely to be strategic substitutes.

Acquisitions.   The acquisition of other firms can also be a substitute for alliances (Kogut, 1988; 1991). In this case, rather than developing a strategic alliance or attempting to develop and exploit the relevant resources internally, a firm seeking the synergies listed in Table 9.1 may simply acquire another firm that already possesses the relevant resources and capabilities and attempt to exploit the potential synergies in that way. Such acquisitions have the effect of diversifying the portfolio of businesses in which a firm is operating. However, diversifying acquisitions have three characteristics that often limit the extent to which they can act as substitutes for strategic alliances.

First, there may be legal constraints on acquisitions. These are especially likely if firms are seeking advantages by combining with other firms in their own industry (Hennart, 1988). Thus, for example, using acquisitions as a substitute for strategic alliances in the aluminum industry would lead to a very concentrated industry and subject some of these firms to serious antitrust liabilities (Scherer, 1980). These firms have acquisitions foreclosed to them and must look elsewhere to gain the advantages from cooperation.

Second, strategic alliances enable a firm to retain its flexibility either to enter or not to enter into a new business. Acquisitions limit that flexibility, since they represent a strong commitment to engage in a certain business activity. Thus, following Kogut (1991), under conditions of high uncertainty, firms may choose strategic alliances over acquisitions as a way to obtain synergies from complementary resources while maintaining the flexibility that alliances create.

Finally, firms may choose strategic alliances over acquisitions because of the unwanted organizational baggage that often comes with an acquisition (Hennart, 1988). Sometimes, synergies between firms depend on the combining of particular functions, divisions, or other assets in the firms. A strategic alliance can focus on exploiting synergies just between the related parts of the firms. Acquisitions, in contrast, generally include the entire organization, both the parts of a firm where a synergy exists and the parts where synergies do not exist.

From the point of view of the acquiring firm, parts of a firm where synergies do not exist are essentially unwanted baggage. These parts of the firm may be sold off subsequent to an acquisition. However, this selloff may be costly and time-consuming. If enough baggage exists, firms may determine that an acquisition is not a viable option, even though important synergies exist between a firm and a potential acquisition target. To gain these synergies, an alternative approach—a strategic alliance—will be required.

One firm that chose to acquire a firm to gain access to some special resources, rather than develop a strategic alliance to exploit these links, was Turner Broadcasting (Pearl and Landro, 1993). Turner Broadcasting was looking to establish a new cable network but needed access to a large library of older films. MGM possessed such a library. In an attempt to gain access to MGM's film library, Turner Broadcasting acquired all of MGM. Upon acquisition, Turner Broadcasting began selling off all the unwanted parts of MGM until all that remained was MGM's film library. Although Turner Broadcasting has been able to create a new cable network with the MGM library acquisition (the TNT network), the process of acquiring MGM and selling off unwanted assets was very expensive and tapped Turner's financial resources to the maximum. One wonders whether Turner Broadcasting would not have been better off negotiating a strategic alliance with MGM (or with some other firm with an extensive film library), thereby avoiding the substantial costs of an acquisition.

ORGANIZING FOR STRATEGIC ALLIANCES

One of the most important determinants of the success of strategic alliances is their organization. The primary purpose of organizing a strategic alliance is to enable partners in the alliance to gain all the benefits associated with cooperation while minimizing the probability that cooperating firms will cheat on their cooperative agreements.

The organizing skills required in managing alliances are, in many ways, unique. It often takes some time for firms to learn these skills and thus to realize the full potential of their alliances. This is why Apple Computer, as it anticipated a large and complex alliance with IBM and Motorola to develop a new personal computer architecture, began first developing less elaborate and complex alliances. By cooperating, for example, with Sony in the development of the PowerBook, Apple began to learn the organizational skills it would need to make its more complex alliance with IBM and Motorola successful (Schlender, 1991; Corcoran, 1993).

A variety of tools and mechanisms can be used to minimize the probability of cheating in inter-firm exchanges: nonequity alliances, equity alliances, firm reputations, joint ventures, and trust.

Nonequity Alliances: Explicit Contracts and Legal Sanctions

One way to avoid cheating in strategic alliances is for parties to an alliance to anticipate the ways in which cheating may occur (including adverse selection, moral hazard, and holdup) and to write explicit contracts that define legal liability if cheating does occur. Writing these contracts, together with the close monitoring of contractual compliance and the threat of legal sanctions, can reduce the probability of cheating (Williamson, 1975). In Section 9.1 such strategic alliances were called nonequity alliances.

However, as will be discussed in detail in Chapter 10, contracts sometimes fail to anticipate all forms of cheating that might occur. And firms may cheat on cooperative agreements in subtle ways that are difficult to evaluate in terms of contractual requirements. Thus, for example, a contract may require parties in a strategic alliance to make available to the alliance certain proprietary technologies or processes. However, it may be very difficult to communicate the subtleties of these technologies or processes to alliance partners. Does this failure in communication represent a clear violation of contractual requirements, or does it represent a good-faith effort by alliance partners? Moreover, how can one partner tell whether it is obtaining all the necessary information about a technology or process when it is unaware of all the information that exists in another firm? Thus although contracts are an important component of most strategic alliances, they do not resolve all the problems associated with cheating.

Equity Alliances: Contracts and Equity Investments

If contracts do help resolve the threat of cheating to some extent, the control power of contracts can be enhanced by having partners in an alliance make equity investments in each other. When Firm A buys a substantial equity position in its alliance partner, Firm B, the market value of Firm A now depends, to some extent, on the economic performance of that partner. The incentive of Firm A to cheat Firm B falls, for to do so would be to reduce the economic performance of Firm B and thus the value of Firm A's investment in its partner. In Section 9.1 these kinds of strategic alliances were called equity alliances.

Many firms use cross-equity investments to help manage their strategic alliances. These arrangements are particularly common in Japan, where a firm's largest equity holders often include several of its suppliers, including its main banks (Ouchi, 1984). Barney (1990) has shown that such equity investments, because they reduce the threat of cheating in alliances with suppliers, can reduce these firms' supply costs. In turn, not only do firms have equity positions in their suppliers, but suppliers often have substantial equity positions in the firms they sell to.

Firm Reputations

A third constraint on incentives to cheat in strategic alliances exists in the effect that a reputation for cheating has on a firm's future opportunities (Barney and Hansen, 1994; Weigelt and Camerer, 1988). Although it is often difficult to anticipate all the different ways in which an alliance partner may cheat, it is often easy to describe after the fact how an alliance partner has cheated. Information about an alliance partner that has cheated is likely to become widely known (Granovetter, 1985). A firm with a reputation as a cheater is not likely to be able to develop strategic alliances with other partners in the future, despite any special resources or abilities that it might be able to bring to an alliance. In this way, cheating in a current alliance may foreclose opportunities for developing valuable alliances (Barney and Hansen, 1994). For this reason, firms may decide not to cheat in their current alliances.

There is substantial evidence that the effect of reputation on future business opportunities is important (Eichenseher and Shields, 1985; Beatty and Ritter, 1986). Firms go to great lengths to make sure that they do not develop this negative reputation. Nevertheless, this reputational control of cheating in strategic alliances does have several limitations.

First, subtle cheating in a strategic alliance may not become public; and if it does become public, the responsibility for the failure of the strategic alliance may not be totally unambiguous. In one equity joint venture attempting to perfect the design of a new turbine for power generation, financial troubles made one partner considerably more anxious than the other partner to complete product development (personal communication). The financially healthy and thus patient partner believed that if the alliance required an additional infusion of capital, the financially troubled partner would have to abandon the alliance and would have to sell its part of the alliance at a relatively low price. The patient partner thus encouraged alliance engineers to work slowly and carefully in the guise of developing the technology to reach its full potential. The financially troubled and thus impatient partner encouraged alliance engineers to work quickly, perhaps sacrificing some quality to develop the technology sooner. Eventually, the impatient partner ran out of money, sold its share of the alliance to the patient partner at a reduced price, and accused the patient partner of not acting in good faith to facilitate the rapid development of the new technology. The patient partner accused the other firm of pushing the technology too quickly, thereby sacrificing quality and, perhaps, worker safety. In some sense, both firms were cheating on their agreement to develop the new technology cooperatively. However, this cheating was subtle and difficult to spot and had relatively little impact on the reputation of either firm or on the ability of either firm to establish alliances in the future. It is likely that most observers would simply conclude that the patient partner obtained a windfall because of the impatient partner's bad luck.

Second, although one partner to an alliance may be unambiguously cheating on the relationship, one or both of the firms may not be sufficiently connected into a network with other firms to make this information public. When information about cheating remains private, public reputations are not tarnished and future opportunities are not forgone. This is especially likely to happen if one or both alliance partners operate in less developed economies where information about partner behavior may not be rapidly diffused to other firms or to other countries.

Finally, the effect of a tarnished reputation, as long as cheating in an alliance is unambiguous and publicly known, may foreclose future opportunities for a firm, but it does little to address the current losses experienced by the firm that was cheated. Moreover, any of the forms of cheating discussed earlier—adverse selection, moral hazard, or holdup—can result in substantial losses for a firm currently in an alliance. Indeed, the wealth created by cheating in a current alliance may be large enough to make a firm willing to forgo future alliances. This would be the case if the present value of cheating in the current alliance is greater than the present value of engaging in future alliances. In this case, a tarnished reputation may be of minor consequence to a cheating firm (Tirole, 1988).

Joint Ventures

A fourth way to reduce the threat of cheating is for partners in a strategic alliance to invest in a joint venture. Creating a separate legal entity, in which alliance partners invest and from whose profits they earn returns on their investments, reduces some of the risks of cheating in strategic alliances. When a joint venture is created, the ability of partners to earn returns on their investments depends on the economic success of the joint venture. Partners in joint ventures have limited interests in behaving in ways that hurt the performance of the joint venture, because such behaviors end up hurting themselves. Moreover, unlike reputational consequences of cheating, cheating in a joint venture does not just foreclose future alliance opportunities; it can hurt the cheating firm in the current period as well.

Given the advantages of joint ventures in controlling cheating, it is not surprising that when the probability of cheating in a cooperative relationship is greatest, a joint venture is usually the preferred form of cooperation (Williamson, 1985; Kogut, 1988; Hennart, 1988). There are some clear economies of scale in bauxite mining, for example. However, transaction-specific investments would lead to significant holdup problems in selling excess bauxite in the open market, and legal constraints prevent the acquisition of other smelter companies to create an intraorganizational demand for excess bauxite. Holdup problems would continue to exist in any mining strategic alliances that might be created. Nonequity alliances, equity alliances, and reputational effects are not likely to restrain cheating in this situation, as the returns to holdup, once transaction-specific investments are in place, can be very large. Thus most of the strategic alliances created to mine bauxite take the form of joint ventures (Scherer, 1980). Only this form of strategic alliance is likely to create incentives strong enough to reduce the probability of cheating significantly.

Despite these strengths, joint ventures are not able to costlessly reduce all cheating in an alliance. Sometimes the present value of cheating in a joint venture is sufficiently large that a firm cheats even though doing so hurts the joint venture and forecloses future opportunities. For example, through a joint venture, a particular firm may gain access to a technology that would be valuable if used in another of its lines of business. This firm may be tempted to transfer this technology to this other line of business even if it has agreed not to do so and even if doing so would limit the performance of its joint venture. Because the above-normal returns earned in this other line of business may have a greater present value than the returns that could have been earned in the joint venture and the returns that could have been earned in the future with other strategic alliances, cheating may occur in a joint venture.

Trust

It is sometimes the case that alliance partners rely only on legalistic and narrowly economic approaches to manage their alliance. However, recent work seems to suggest that although successful alliance partners do not ignore legal and economic disincentives to cheating, they strongly support these narrower linkages with a rich set of interpersonal relations and trust (Ernst and Bleeke, 1993; Barney and Hansen, 1994). These "relational contracts" (discussed generally in Chapter 10) help reduce the threat of cheating (Williamson, 1983). More important, trust may enable partners to explore exchange opportunities that they could not explore if only legal and economic organizing mechanisms were in place.

At first glance, this argument may seem far-fetched. However, both theory and research offer support for this approach to managing strategic alliances. In theory, a firm investing in a large number of strategic alliances over time can be thought of as playing a large number of prisoner's dilemma games of the sort described in Section 8.1. As discussed there, Axelrod (1984) has shown that a cooperative "tit for tat" strategy has the highest total payoffs in this situation. As applied to strategic alliances, "tit for tat" would take the following form: Firms entering into alliances continue in them as long as their partners behave in a trustworthy manner; if a partner behaves in an untrustworthy manner, the alliance is severed. As long as at least a few potential alliance partners are also using "tit for tat" strategies, the benefits gained from long-lasting and valuable alliances more than compensate for the short-lived costs endured by a firm that is cheated by an alliance partner (Ring and Van de Ven, 1992).

Empirically, work by Ernst and Bleeke (1993) suggests that successful alliance partners typically *do not* specify all the terms and conditions in their relationship in a legal contract and *do not* specify all possible forms of cheating and their consequences. Moreover, when joint ventures are formed, partners do not always insist on simple fifty-fifty splits of equity ownership and profit sharing. Rather, successful alliances involve trust, a willingness to be flexible, a willingness to learn, and a willingness to let the alliance develop in ways that the partners could not have anticipated.

Mohr and Spekman (1994) also find that commitment, coordination, and trust are all important determinants of alliance success. Put another way, a strategic alliance is a relationship that evolves over time. Allowing the lawyers and economists to too-rigorously define, a priori, the boundaries of that relationship may limit it and may stunt its development (Zaheer and Venkatraman, 1995; Barney and Hansen, 1994).

This "trust" approach also has implications for the extent to which strategic alliances may be sources of sustained competitive advantage for firms. The ability to move into strategic alliances in this trusting way may be very valuable over the long run. There is strong reason to believe that this ability is not uniformly distributed across all firms that might have an interest in forming strategic alliances, and that this ability may be history-dependent and socially complex and thus costly to imitate. Firms with these skills may be able to gain sustained competitive advantages from their alliance relationships. The observation that just a few firms, including Corning, are well known for their strategic alliance successes is consistent with the observation that these alliance management skills may be valuable, rare, and costly to imitate (Barney and Hansen, 1994).

9.4 SUMMARY

Tacit collusion, as a form of interfirm cooperation, is difficult to create and maintain. Strategic alliances, in contrast, are much more common and growing in frequency. Strategic alliances exist whenever two or more organizations cooperate in the development, manufacture, or sale of products or services. Strategic alliances can be grouped into three large categories: nonequity alliances, equity alliances, and joint ventures.

There are many reasons to join in strategic alliances: exploiting economies of scale, learning from competitors, managing risk and sharing costs, facilitating tacit collusion, low-cost entry into new markets, low-cost entry into new industries and industry segments, and managing uncertainty. In all these cases, a strategic alliance is an attempt to exploit a potential synergy between independent firms.

Just as there are incentives to cooperate in strategic alliances, there are also incentives to cheat. Cheating generally takes one or a combination of three forms: adverse selection, moral hazard, or holdup.

The value of strategic alliances can be analyzed by using the model of generic industry structures discussed in Chapter 4. Symmetric alliances are most common in mature industries and in fragmented industries with large strategic groups of firms. Asymmetric alliances are most common in emerging industries, in fragmented industries without strategic groups, and in global industries. Mixed alliances can exist in any industry structure.

Strategic alliances can be a source of sustained competitive advantage. The rareness of alliances depends not only on the number of competing firms that have developed an alliance but also on the benefits that firms gain through their alliances.

Imitation through direct duplication of an alliance may be costly because of the socially complex relations that underlie an alliance. However, imitation through substitution is possible. Two substitutes for alliances may be internal development, where firms develop and exploit the relevant sets of resources and capabilities on their own, and diversifying acquisitions. Internal development is a substitute for a strategic alliance only when it is no more costly to develop the required resources inside a firm, compared to cooperating to use another firm's resources, and when it is no more costly to develop cooperative relations inside the firm, compared to the cost of developing cooperative relations with other firms. Diversifying acquisitions may be a substitute for strategic alliances when (1) there are no legal constraints in acquisitions, (2) strategic flexibility is not an important consideration, and (3) the acquired firm has relatively little unwanted organizational baggage.

The key issue facing firms in organizing their alliances is to facilitate cooperation while avoiding the threat of cheating. Nonequity alliances, equity alliances, firm reputations, joint ventures, and trust can reduce the threat of cheating.

REVIEW QUESTIONS

1. One reason why firms might want to pursue a strategic alliance strategy is to exploit economies of scale. Exploiting economies of scale should reduce a firm's costs. Does this mean that a firm pursuing an alliance strategy to exploit economies of scale is actually pursuing a cost-leadership strategy? Why or why not?

2. Consider the joint venture between General Motors and Toyota. GM has been interested in learning how to manufacture profitably high-quality small cars from its alliance with Toyota. Toyota has been

interested in gaining access to GM's U.S. distribution network and in reducing the political liability associated with local content laws. Which of these firms do you think is more likely to accomplish its objectives, and why?

3. Some have argued that strategic alliances are one way in which firms can help facilitate the development of a tacit collusion strategy. In your view, what are the critical differences between tacit collusion strategies and strategic alliance strategies? How can one tell whether two firms are engaging in alliances to facilitate collusion or are engaging in an alliance for other purposes?

4. Some have argued that alliances can be used to help firms evaluate the economic potential of entering into a new industry or market. Under what conditions will a firm seeking to evaluate these opportunities need to invest in an alliance to accomplish this evaluation? Why couldn't such a firm simply hire some smart managers, consultants, and industry experts to evaluate the economic potential of entering into a new industry? What, if anything, about an alliance makes this a better way to evaluate entry opportunities than alternatives?

5. If adverse selection, moral hazard, and holdup are such significant problems for firms pursuing alliance strategies, why do firms even bother with alliances? Why don't they instead adopt an internal devlopment strategy to replace strategic alliances?

PART III

CORPORATE STRATEGIES

CHAPTER 10

Vertical Integration Strategies

Most of the strategies discussed in Part II focus on how firms can use their resources and capabilities to gain competitive advantages in a particular market or an industry. Firms implementing cost-leadership or product differentiation do so by exploiting their resources and capabilities to gain competitive advantages over other firms competing in their market or industry. In a similar way, tacit collusion cooperative strategies seek to gain economic profits by creating cooperation among firms in a single business or industry. And many of the motivations for engaging in strategic alliance cooperative strategies focus on firms gaining or extending competitive advantages within their current market and within their current business or industry. These motivations include exploiting economies of scale, learning from competitors, managing risk, and facilitating tacit collusion.

However, the last three motivations for exploring strategic alliance discussed in Chapter 9—to enter new markets, to enter new industries or industry segments, and to manage uncertainty—raise the possibility that firms can use strategic alliances to leverage their resources and capabilities to explore economic opportunities outside their traditional market and outside their traditional industry. When firms are motivated to create alliances in order to enter new markets, new industries, or new industry segments, they are moving away from business-level strategies and toward exploring opportunities for leveraging their resources and capabilities in new markets or industries. And when firms are motivated to create alliances to manage uncertainty, often that uncertainty reflects changes in a firm's competitive environment, changes that require the firm to begin to explore economic opportunities in new markets or industries.

Part III examines this class of leveraging strategies. Whereas Part II examines the conditions under which firms can use their resources and capabilities to gain competitive advantages in a single business or industry (i.e., business strategies), Part III examines the conditions under which firms can leverage their traditional resources to gain competitive advantage and economic profits by entering new markets and industries. These leveraging strategies are often called corporate strategies. There are numerous examples of corporate strategies, beyond the three motivations for strategic alliances already discussed. In Chapter 10 we examine vertical integration corporate strategies, where firms extend their business activities across different stages of the value chain that exists in a particular market or industry. In Chapters 11 and 12 we examine diversification strategies, where firms leverage their resources and capabilities by entering into new markets or industries. Chapter 11 explores the economic value of engaging in a diversification strategy; Chapter 12 examines the complex organizational requirements of implementing a diversification strategy. Chapter 13 discusses the strategic implications of mergers and acquisitions, a common method for leveraging a firm's resources in new markets or industries. Chapter 14 analyzes global strategies as an example of efforts by firms to leverage their resources and capabilities in an increasingly global economy.

10.1 DEFINING VERTICAL INTEGRATION

In the appendix to Chapter 5, the concept of the value chain was introduced. A value chain is the set of discrete activities that must be accomplished to design, build, sell, and distribute a product or service. Each of the activities listed in a product's or service's value chain must be accomplished in order for that product or service to be sold to customers. Different firms, however, can make different decisions about which of those activities they would like to engage in on their own and which they would like other firms to engage in. The number of stages in a product's or service's value chain that a particular firm engages in defines that firm's level of vertical integration. The greater this number, the more vertically integrated a firm is; the smaller this number, the less vertically integrated a firm is.

THE LEVEL AND DIRECTION OF VERTICAL INTEGRATION

The number of stages in the value chain that a firm engages in does not have to remain constant over time. Firms can become more vertically integrated by engaging in more stages of the value chain, and they can become less vertically integrated by engaging in fewer stages of the value chain. Whenever firms increase the number of value chain stages that they engage in, and those new stages bring them closer to direct interaction with a product's or service's ultimate customer, they are said to be engaging in *forward vertical integration.* When Coca-Cola began buying its previously franchised independent bottlers, it was engaging in forward vertical integration (Porter and Wayland, 1991). Whenever firms increase the number of value chain stages that they engage in, and those new stages move them farther away from a product's or service's ultimate customer, they are said to be engaging in *backward vertical integration.* When Home Box Office, Inc., began producing its own movies for screening on the HBO cable channel, it was engaging in backward vertical integration (Brown, 1994).

MEASURING THE DEGREE OF VERTICAL INTEGRATION

As suggested in the appendix to Chapter 5, it is sometimes possible to directly observe which stages of the value chain a firm is engaging in and thus the level of that firm's vertical integration. This was the case with Crown Cork & Seal, as revealed in Fig. 5A.3. Sometimes, however, it is more difficult to directly observe a firm's level of vertical integration. This is especially the case when a firm believes that its level of vertical integration is a potential source of competitive advantage and thus is not likely to reveal this information freely to competitors. In this situation, it is possible to get a sense of the degree of a firm's vertical integration—though not a complete list of the steps in the value chain integrated by the firm—from a close examination of the firm's value added as a percentage of sales (Adelman, 1955; Gort, 1962). This measure of vertical integration can be computed directly from a firm's accounting performance numbers, which are widely available if a firm is publicly traded. Value added as a percentage of sales measures that portion of a firm's sales that are generated by activities conducted within the boundaries of the firm. A firm with a high ratio between value added and sales has brought many of the value-creating activities associated with its business inside its boundaries, consistent with a high level of vertical integration. A firm with a low ratio between value added and sales does not have, on average, as high a level of vertical integration (Laffer, 1969; Tucker and Wilder, 1977; Harrigan, 1986). Maddigan (1979) has shown that value added as a percentage of sales is an appropriate approach to measuring the level of vertical integration of a firm in a wide range of situations.

Value added as a percentage of sales is computed as in Eq. (10.1):

$$\text{vertical integration}_i = \frac{\text{value added}_i - (\text{net income}_i + \text{income taxes}_i)}{\text{sales}_i - (\text{net income}_i + \text{income taxes}_i)}$$

Eq. 10.1

where,

vertical integration$_i$ = the level of vertical integration for firm$_i$

value added$_i$ = the level of value added for firm$_i$

net income$_i$ = the level of net income for firm$_i$

income taxes$_i$ = firm$_i$'s income taxes

sales$_i$ = firm$_i$'s sales

The sum of net income and income taxes is subtracted in both the numerator and the denominator in Eq. (10.1) to control for inflation and changes in the tax code over time (Maddigan, 1979). Net income, income taxes, and sales can all be taken directly from a firm's profit-and-loss statement. Value added can be calculated as in Eq. (10.2) (Tucker and Wilder, 1978):

value added = depreciation + amortization + fixed charges +
             interest expense + labor and related expenses +
             pension and retirement expenses + income
             taxes + net income (after taxes) + rental expense   *Eq. 10.2*

Again, most of the accounting numbers for calculating value added can be found either in a firm's profit-and-loss statement or in its balance sheet.

10.2   THE ECONOMIC VALUE OF VERTICAL INTEGRATION

Vertical integration decisions can be understood as a particular example of governance choices that firms make in managing their economic exchanges. In all governance decisions, the question facing managers is, Given a potentially valuable economic exchange, what is the most efficient way of managing or governing that exchange? Vertical integration is a valuable form of governance when its benefits outweigh its

FIGURE 10.1
The Range of Exchange Management Devices

Market Governance — Intermediate Governance — Hierarchical Governance (Vertical Integration)

costs. The benefits and costs of vertical integration as a governance strategy are discussed below.

Vertical integration is an important way in which firms can govern their economic exchanges, but it is only one of a wide variety of governance choices available to managers. The broad range of possible governance mechanisms that managers can use to efficiently engage in potentially valuable exchanges is represented in Fig. 10.1. At one extreme, parties to an exchange may interact across a faceless and nameless market and rely entirely on market-determined prices to manage an exchange. This approach is often called *market governance* (Williamson, 1975). We saw in Chapter 9 that parties to an exchange can use a variety of strategic alliances—including nonequity alliances, equity alliances, and joint ventures—to manage an exchange. Strategic alliances are an example of a broad class of approaches to managing exchanges that are not quite market governance but are also not quite vertical integration. This class of governance mechanisms is often called *intermediate governance* (Williamson, 1975). At the other extreme, an exchange may be managed within a single firm. When such an exchange involves different stages in a product's or service's value chain, this form of governance is called *vertical integration*. More generally, the use of the firm to manage economic exchanges is often called *hierarchical governance* (Williamson, 1975).

THE THREAT OF OPPORTUNISM AND THE COST OF GOVERNANCE

If a particular exchange is seen as being potentially valuable, the purposes of governance mechanisms—whether market, intermediate, or hierarchical—are to minimize the threat that exchange partners will be unfairly exploited in an exchange and to do so at the lowest cost possible. We have already seen, in the case of cooperative strategic alliances, that despite strong incentives to cooperate, there can also exist strong incentives to cheat. This threat can exist in any economic exchange, including those managed through market and hierarchical forms of governance. Williamson (1975) calls this threat the threat of opportunism. Opportunism exists whenever parties to an exchange exploit the vulnerabilities of exchange partners (Sabel, 1993). In this sense, adverse selection, moral hazard, and holdup (discussed in Section 9.2) are specific examples of opportunistic behavior.

The purpose of governance is to create an institutional framework where opportunistic behaviors can be discovered and appropriate remedies can be imposed on the parties to an exchange behaving opportunistically. If the creation of exchange governance is done well, then parties to an exchange will find it in their rational self-interest not to behave opportunistically, for their opportunistic behaviors will be discovered and appropriately sanctioned. In this setting, parties to an exchange will find it too costly to engage in opportunistic behavior, and an exchange can go forward with little risk of opportunistic behavior.

In general, the more elaborate a governance device, the broader is the range of potential opportunistic behavior that it can discover, and the broader is the range of exchanges within which it can be used to manage opportunism. These observations suggest that intermediate forms of governance (see Fig. 10.1) will be able to manage a broader range of potential opportunistic behaviors than will market forms of governance and that hierarchical forms of governance will be able to manage a broader range of potential opportunistic behaviors than will intermediate forms of governance. If all exchange partners had to worry about was minimizing the threat of opportunism, they would choose more elaborate forms of governance over less elaborate forms of governance, and vertical integration would be the most common form of exchange governance (Barney and Ouchi, 1986).

But minimizing the threat of opportunism is not the only thing that exchange partners need to consider. They must also concern themselves with the cost of managing opportunism. Governance is not costless. In general, the more elaborate the form of governance, the greater is the direct cost of governance (D'Aveni and Ravenscraft, 1994). Most agree that the direct costs of market forms of governance are less than the direct costs of intermediate forms of governance, and that the direct costs of intermediate forms of governance are less than the direct costs of hierarchical forms of governance. If all exchange partners had to concern themselves with was minimizing the cost of governance in managing their economic exchanges, they would always choose market forms of governance.

But exchange partners need to concern themselves with both minimizing the threat of opportunism *and* minimizing the cost of governance. Thus rational economic actors will choose just the level of governance needed to minimize the threat of opportunism in a particular exchange.

DETERMINANTS OF THE THREAT OF OPPORTUNISM

The appropriate form of governance for a particular economic exchange depends on the threat of opportunism in that exchange. Thus an important question is, What are the determinants of the threat of opportunism in a particular economic exchange? A great deal of theoretical and empirical research has addressed this question (Barney and Hesterly, 1996). This work has identified two primary determinants of the threat of opportunistic behavior in an economic exchange: the level of transaction-specific investment in an exchange and the level of uncertainty and complexity in an exchange.

Transaction-Specific Investment and Opportunism

The concept of transaction-specific investment was introduced in Section 9.2, in the discussion of the threat of holdup in strategic alliances. An investment is said to be transaction-specific when its value in a particular exchange is much greater than its value in any alternative exchanges. Thus if Firm A invests in a special technology that can be used only in an exchange with Firm B, Firm A has made a transaction-specific investment. If Firm B has not made a similar investment, then Firm B can exploit the specific investment made by Firm A. The economic value of this exploitation can be as much as the difference between the value of this investment in its first best use and its value in its second best use. If the value of this investment in its highest-valued use (that is, in the exchange between Firm A and Firm B) is $10,000, and its value in its next-highest-valued use (that is, in any exchange not between Firm A and Firm B) is only $500, then the firm that has not made this investment can appropriate economic value from the firm that has made this investment up to $9,500. As long as the value of the appropriation is less then $9,500, it is still better for Firm A, which made the specific investment, to continue in this exchange, rather than canceling the exchange and thereby gaining only $500.

One of the implications of this threat of opportunistic behavior is that exchanges that require high levels of transaction-specific investment by parties to an exchange are more likely to be governed by elaborate forms of exchange governance, including vertically integrated hierarchical governance, than are transactions that do not require this high level of specific investment. Presumably, hierarchical forms of governance have more elaborate mechanisms in place to discover and control opportunism, in the face of specific investment, than do non-hierarchical forms of governance. Thus, for example, *market* forms of governance must rely primarily on prices and simple contracts to discover and control the threat of opportunism, and *intermediate* forms of governance must rely on more elaborate forms of contract and cross-equity investments, but *hierarchical* forms of governance can employ not only prices (e.g., transfer prices) and contracts but also managerial hierarchies to discover and control opportunism.

Williamson (1975) argues that managerial hierarchies control the threat of opportunism through "managerial fiat." If one or more parties to an exchange behave in ways that put the exchange at risk, managers in this hierarchy can ensure that the exchange will continue by engaging in close monitoring and by using their hierarchical authority to punish opportunistic parties. In the extreme, individuals who engage in such behaviors, within a hierarchical governance framework, can be fired and replaced by individuals who are less likely to engage in such activities.

Uncertainty, Complexity, and Opportunism

The level of uncertainty and complexity can also be an important determinant of the extent to which opportunism is a threat in an economic exchange. When parties to an exchange can anticipate, before the exchange actually occurs, how that exchange will unfold, in all its detail, they will be able to anticipate all the different ways in which exchange partners can behave opportunistically. In this setting, it is usually possible to write a relatively complete contract that specifies all the ways in which the exchange will evolve and the rights and responsibilities of all parties in this relationship over time. In such certain and relatively simple exchanges, opportunism is not a significant threat, for there can be no unpleasant surprises.

But when an exchange is characterized by high levels of uncertainty and complexity, it may be very difficult, if not impossible, for exchange partners to anticipate all possible ways in which an exchange might evolve. In particular, it may not be possible to anticipate how an exchange's evolution will affect the ability of different parties in the exchange to behave opportunistically. When possible sources of opportunistic behavior cannot be anticipated, the threat of opportunistic behavior may be greater than it is when all possible sources of opportunistic behavior in an exchange can be anticipated.

When the level of uncertainty and complexity in an exchange is great, the threat of opportunism may also be great, and more elaborate forms of costly governance—including vertically integrated hierarchical governance—may be appropriate. Vertical integration can be used to manage the problem of exchange uncertainty and complexity over time. Thus although it may not be possible to anticipate all possible sources of opportunism when an exchange is begun, over time these sources of opportunistic threat can be revealed. Hierarchical governance creates a setting in which these sources of opportunism can be discovered and, once discovered, managed in a way that avoids the liabilities normally associated with opportunistic behavior.

A TYPOLOGY OF GOVERNANCE MECHANISMS

Thus far, the simple three-part governance typology presented in Fig. 10.1 has been used to describe a firm's governance options. In reality, firms have a much broader range of governance choices besides market governance, intermediate governance, and hierarchical governance. The most important of these options are listed in Table 10.1 and discussed below. Notice that vertically integrated hierarchical governance has been expanded into governance by internal markets, by bureaucracy, and by clans.

Spot-Market Contracts

When there are large numbers of equally qualified buyers and sellers in a market, and when the quality of the goods or services that are being exchanged in this market can be determined at a very low cost, the most appropriate form of exchange governance is a spot-market contract. A spot-market contract is a simple agreement between a buyer and a seller that specifies the amount of a good or service that is to be purchased, the price at which this exchange is to occur, and the timing of this exchange. Examples of markets where spot-market contracts are effective tools for managing exchanges include the spot market for crude oil, most farm commodity markets, and the New York Stock Exchange. In these highly competitive settings, the price of the good or service that is being exchanged reflects fully and accurately the expected economic value of that good or service (Hirshleifer, 1980).

Spot-market contracts control opportunism because buyers and sellers can always switch to alternative exchange partners—and can do so at very low cost—if their current exchange partners begin to behave

TABLE 10.1
A Typology of Governance Devices

Devices Not Vertically Integrated	Vertically Integrated Devices
Spot-market contracts	Internal markets
Complete contingent claims contracts	Bureaucracy
Sequential contracting	Clan governance
Relational contracting	

opportunistically. The switch is easy to make because there are large numbers of equally qualified buyers and sellers. Moreover, exchange partners will be able to spot such opportunistic behavior—and can do so at very low cost—because evaluating the quality of the products or services being exchanged is easy. In this setting, parties to exchanges have little interest in behaving opportunistically because to do so would be very costly for them.

Consider, for example, the spot market for crude oil. Suppose that one firm wants to purchase 10,000 barrels of high-grade crude from a supplier, that this buyer and seller agree to a price and delivery date, but that the supplier tries to take unfair advantage of this customer by substituting low-grade crude. First, it is very likely that the customer will discover the opportunistic behavior of the supplier, since it is relatively easy to distinguish between low-grade crude and high-grade crude. Second, once this opportunistic behavior is discovered, the buyer always has the option of purchasing crude from numerous other suppliers and so is not constrained to continue purchasing from the opportunistic supplier. Finally, the buyer that has been cheated can sue the opportunistic supplier and demonstrate to all of its potential customers that this supplier cannot be trusted. Thus, not only is this exchange between a particular buyer and this supplier put at risk, but so are all the future exchanges in which this supplier might want to engage in the future. Given the high probability of being discovered and the value of the opportunities forgone if opportunistic behavior is discovered, it simply is not in the rational self-interest of those buying and selling in these types of markets to behave opportunistically. Therefore, they don't.

Moreover, in these spot markets the threat of opportunism is essentially eliminated, at very low cost. Complex contracts do not have to be written and enforced, legions of attorneys and accountants do not have to be hired, and a costly bureaucracy does not have to be created in order to minimize the threat of opportunism. Rather, this threat is minimized by means of a relatively simple contractual relationship, in the context of large numbers of equally qualified buyers and sellers and the low-cost ability to ascertain the quality of the goods or services being transferred. The presence of large numbers of equally qualified buyers and sellers suggests that no transaction-specific investments are necessary to complete these transactions. The ability to ascertain the quality of the goods or services being exchanged at low cost implies that there is low uncertainty and complexity in these exchanges. Low specific investment plus low transaction uncertainty and complexity implies a low threat of opportunistic behavior.

Of course, simple spot-market contracts work only in these very special conditions. In particular, if transaction-specific investments must be made to enable an exchange to go through, once these invest-ments are made, there are no longer numerous equally qualified buy-ers and sellers, and the risk of opportunistic behavior increases. Also, if it is costly to determine the quality of the good or service being exchanged, then the threat of opportunism also increases.

Complete Contingent Claims Contracts

When spot-market contracts cannot be used to efficiently control the threat of opportunism in an exchange, a more elaborate contract—a complete contingent claims contract—may be required. A complete contingent claims contract is a contract between exchange partners that specifies all possible future states in an exchange and the associated rights and responsibilities of parties to that exchange in all these differ-ent states. Complete contingent claims contracts imagine the possibil-ity that a particular exchange might evolve in several different ways. However, this contract also anticipates these different future states and specifies all rights and responsibilities of exchange partners in them (Nöldeke and Schmidt, 1995).

Complete contingent claims contracts control the threat of oppor-tunism through the close monitoring of the contract and through the threat of legal or other sanctions that can be imposed if parties to an exchange violate their contractual obligations. If the parties develop a truly complete, complete contingent claims contract, then they will all know their rights and responsibilities in all future states of their rela-tionship, and they can use the contract to ensure that other parties to the exchange fulfill their sides of the bargain.

Most people who purchase a new car enter into a complete con-tingent claims contract with the dealer and manufacturer. This contract is called a guarantee. Most guarantees say that if, for whatever reason, a new car breaks down, the dealer/manufacturer will repair the car as long as the breakdown occurs within a defined time period or before a certain number of miles are put on the car. Typically only a few contin-gencies are added to these complete contracts. For example, if the new car is used in a car race, the guarantee is null and void; and if the car is subjected to unusual stress and strain, the guarantee is null and void. These guarantees also generally do not cover batteries and tires (although they may be guaranteed by their own manufacturers).

Why is this complete contingent claims contract or guarantee so important to new car buyers? At the time they purchase a car, they can-not determine its quality. They can determine the car's quality only after purchasing the car and driving it for some time. Since the level of uncertainty in this exchange is higher than in a spot market, car buyers usually insist on some sort of complete contingent claims contract or guarantee. It is possible to purchase cars without such guarantees. In this case, however, a different kind of complete contingent claims contract is written between the buyer and seller. This contract states that the car is being sold "as is" and the buyer is responsible for maintaining and fixing it no matter what happens to it.

Complete contingent claims contracts are like the rules that govern a sporting contest. If these rules are complete and well written, referees instantly know whether a particular play violates the rules of the game. This is the case in the game of baseball. Hundreds of thousands—maybe even millions—of baseball games are played each year throughout the world. Moreover, the basic rules of baseball have remained largely unchanged since late last century. Virtually every bizarre and weird play that could happen in baseball has already happened and is covered by the complete contingent claims contract rules that govern the game.

For example, suppose an outfielder fields a base hit and throws the ball toward home plate, and the ball hits a bird flying over the field. What is the right call? This actually happened to Dave Winfield in the old Toronto stadium when he was playing for the New York Yankees. When the ball hit the bird, umpires working the game knew instantly what the appropriate call was and made it without hesitation: The bird was defined as a hazard of the field, the ball was to be played as it bounced off the bird, and runners could advance at their own risk. In another game, a third baseman who wanted a slowly bunted ground ball to go foul got down on his hands and knees and literally blew the ball over the foul line. What is the right call? The rules state that fielders cannot use any artificial means whatsoever (including their breath) to make a ball go foul. Thus this was actually a fair ball, and runners could advance at their own risk. Again, the umpires instantly knew what the right call was and made it, because baseball is governed by a very complete, complete contingent claims contract.

American football, in contrast, does not have as nearly a complete, complete contingent claims contract set of rules. Far fewer games of American football are played each year, and many of the key rules and regulations have evolved dramatically over the last several decades, suggesting that experience in games played in earlier eras cannot be used to anticipate unusual plays in the modern era. In this situation, it is not uncommon for a play to occur that is not anticipated by the rules and for which the "right call" is ambiguous at best.

For example, several years ago, the New England Patriots were playing the Miami Dolphins in a playoff game in New England. This game occurred in a blinding snowstorm—an inconvenient but not infrequent situation. Neither team had been terribly successful in scoring under these conditions. In particular, Miami had missed several field-goal attempts (where a team kicks the ball through the goal at the end of the field to score three points). As the game wound down, New England found itself in the position to try for its own field goal. Kicking field goals on a snow-covered field is very difficult—as Miami had already discovered. To alleviate these difficulties, the New England coach called a timeout and then had a stadium worker drive a snow blower onto the field and clear off the snow from the point where the field goal was to be attempted. The referees looked at each other in amazement, unsure about whether this action was legal. During their indecision, the field goal was attempted and made, and New England won the game. Of course, the following year, the rules of American football were altered to outlaw this kind of activity. However, before this change in the rules, the complete contingent claims contract that had been used to govern American football was less complete than it should have been.

This American football example points to some important limitations of complete contingent claims contracts as a governance device. Certainly, if parties to an exchange can unambiguously define all future states in an exchange relationship, they can write a complete contingent claims contract that can be used to minimize the threat of opportunism. However, when all future possible states in an exchange cannot be anticipated, or when it is difficult to unambiguously define these future states, a threat of opportunism remains.

Consider, for example, the apparently simple task of purchasing wheat. Wheat is a commodity for which there are numerous buyers and sellers, and for which spot-market contracts can often be used to manage the threat of opportunism. However, suppose that the quality of a particular type of wheat varies significantly, depending on whether rain falls during the week before the wheat is harvested. If it does rain during the week before harvest, the moisture content of the wheat will increase, as will the probability that the wheat will rot more quickly. Because of these issues, imagine that a buyer and seller of this type of wheat write a complete contingent claims contract that specifies one price for the wheat if it does not rain in the week prior to harvest and a second lower price if it does rain in the week prior to harvest. This seems like an unambiguous complete contingent claims contract that will minimize the probability of opportunistic behavior in this exchange.

However, some ambiguities might exist and might allow for some opportunistic behavior in this contract. For example, what is a week? Is a week five days; is it seven days? How one answers this question determines the price of this wheat if it happens to rain on day six or day seven. Also, what is rain? The buyer of this wheat has a strong incentive to define *rain* as broadly as possible: A heavy fog is really rain; high humidity can be thought of as rain; a farmer spitting in the field can also be thought of as rain. By adopting this broad definition, the buyer can reduce the price paid for the wheat. In contrast, the seller has a strong incentive to adopt a very narrow definition of *rain*: Sure, it might have sprinkled a bit on the wheatfield during the relevant week, but an inch of sprinkle can hardly be considered rain. Last year, it rained—the river overflowed, the town was flooded, and the fields were under five feet of water. Compared to last year, a one-inch drizzle certainly cannot be considered rain.

When it is difficult to anticipate all future states in an exchange relationship, and when it is difficult to unambiguously define these future states, the use of complete contingent claims contracts to manage the threat of opportunism can be costly and ineffective. Disagreements about these contracts often can be resolved in the courts, but litigation is costly and time-consuming. On the other hand, if it is possible to anticipate all future states in an exchange and to unambiguously define those states, a complete contingent claims contract can be a very effective mechanism for controlling the threat of opportunism in an exchange at low cost.

Sequential Contracting

In many exchanges, it may not be possible to completely and unambiguously define all possible future states of a relationship for all time. But it might be possible to specify all future states of an exchange, and unambiguously define them, for a defined period of time. After this period of time is over, parties to the exchange can engage in a renegotiation process to develop another time-limited complete contingent claims contract. This contracting/recontracting process is called sequential contracting (Williamson, 1979).

Sequential contracting enables parties to an exchange to economize on the difficulty of unambiguously defining all possible future states of an exchange, for all time, when an exchange begins. Thus, for example, although a newly graduated 28-year-old MBA may want to work for a particular firm, it is difficult for that new hire to anticipate the kinds of challenges that will energize her when she is 45 or 50 years old. However, she might be able to anticipate the kinds of challenges that will energize her for five years. In the same way, a firm might have some difficulty anticipating how it will be able to generate economic value with this newly graduated MBA twenty or so years in the future, but the firm is likely to know how she could generate economic value for the next five years. In this setting, this MBA and the firm may be able to sign a complete contingent claims contract for five years and then at the end of that period renegotiate to either develop a new time-limited complete contingent claims contract or decide to explore exchange opportunities with different partners.

Sequential contracting helps reduce the threat of opportunism through the contracting and recontracting process, together with the close monitoring of the actions of both parties during the time periods when the contract is in force. Most employment contracts, many supply contracts, and most licensing agreements have this sequential contracting structure.

Sequential contracting has several strengths, but it can have one significant liability—a liability that subjects it to potentially high levels of opportunistic behavior. The contracting/recontracting process assumes that once a contract's time period has expired, competition for the next contract period will be open to numerous different exchange partners. Partially, it is the threat that parties to an exchange may look elsewhere for exchange partners that helps keep the threat of opportunism to a minimum during that period of time when a contract is in force. However, it is often the case that, in the recontracting process, exchange partners that have already been engaging in an exchange have an important competitive advantage over those that have not been engaging in this exchange. Williamson (1975) describes this process as "learning by doing."

After parties to an exchange have worked with each other for a period of time, their experience in this relationship can make them a more attractive partner in the renegotiating process than partners without that experience. Of course, this kind of experience is an example of a transaction-specific investment: It can be quite valuable if this relationship continues; it has limited value in alternative uses.

Consider, for example, the relationship between a firm that owns and operates an oil refinery and a firm that owns and operates oil pipelines, as depicted in Fig. 10.2. Assume that this oil refinery is built on the edge of a deep-water bay and that it has been receiving supplies of crude oil from large tanker ships. Also, suppose that an oil field exists several miles distant from the refinery location but the only way to transport crude oil from the oil field to the refinery is with trucks—a more costly means of transport than the tanker ships. Suppose too that an oil pipeline company approaches the refinery and indicates that it would be willing to build a pipeline from the oil field to the refinery if, in turn, the oil refinery would agree to pump a defined number of barrels of crude at an agreed-to price for some period of time—say five years—through the pipeline. If reasonable prices can be negotiated, the oil refinery is likely to find this offer attractive, for the cost of crude oil carried by the pipeline is likely to be lower than the cost of crude oil delivered by ship or by truck. Based on this analysis, the refinery and the oil pipeline firm are likely to explore this exchange opportunity.

However, look at this exchange from the point of view of the pipeline company. Suppose a contract is signed and that things go

FIGURE 10.2
The Exchange Between an Oil Refinery and an Oil Pipeline Company

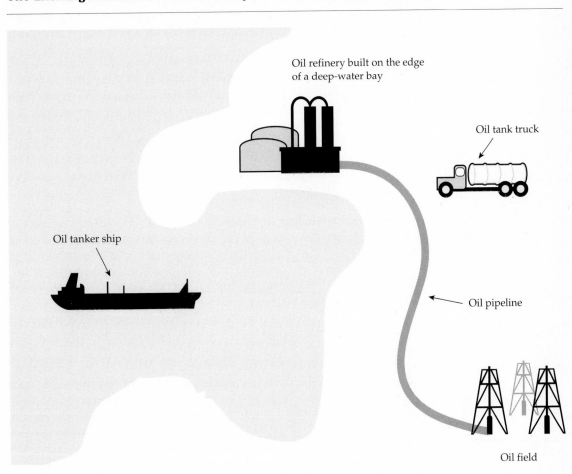

Oil refinery built on the edge
of a deep-water bay

Oil tank truck

Oil tanker ship

Oil pipeline

Oil field

along well for five years—most reasonable contingencies during this
five-year period were anticipated, and appropriate contractual guarantees were in place. Now, however, it is time to renegotiate the supply
contract. Who is at risk in this renegotiation? If the value of the refinery,
with its pipeline supply in place, is $1 million but drops to $900,000 if it
has to start using oil supplied by tanker ships and trucks, the refiner
has made some transaction-specific investments. But the specific
investment made by the pipeline firm is substantially larger. The
pipeline might be worth $750,000 as long as it is pumping oil to the

refinery. But if it is not pumping oil, it has very limited value—either as scrap or (perhaps) as the world's largest enclosed water slide. If the value of the pipeline is only $10,000 if it is not pumping oil to the refinery, the pipeline firm faces a significant risk of holdup in the renegotiation process.

Of course, the pipeline firm is not likely to be managed by stupid people. These managers will have anticipated these holdup problems in the renegotiation process and will have insisted on prices high enough on the crude oil pumped during the first contract period that the pipeline would be a profitable venture even if it had to be closed because of holdup problems during renegotiation. Of course, this tactic would have had the effect of driving up the price of crude oil carried by the pipeline, perhaps to the point where piped crude was no longer less costly than oil delivered to the refinery by tanker ships and trucks.

Thus on the one hand, this sequential contracting process is likely to put the pipeline firm at significant risk of holdup during renegotiation, after it has made its transaction-specific investments. On the other hand, efforts by the pipeline company to protect itself from this holdup are likely to drive the price of crude pumped through the pipeline up, and the pipeline might not be built in the first place. When sequential contracting has the effect of creating asymmetric transaction-specific investment, the contracting/recontracting process is not likely to reduce the threat of opportunism that all parties to an exchange find acceptable.

One option that the oil refinery and the pipeline firm can explore to manage this difficult situation is some sort of strategic alliance, even perhaps a joint venture in which each of these firms owns equity positions in an independent entity that, in turn, owns and operates the oil pipeline and the refinery. However, as suggested in Chapter 9, the threat of adverse selection, moral hazard, and holdup can continue even if an alliance is created. If an alliance cannot be used to solve the opportunism problems in this exchange, then these firms may have to opt for hierarchical governance and vertical integration. Correctly designed, hierarchical governance could enable the pipeline to be built and simultaneously could minimize the threat of opportunism in this exchange.

Relational Contracting

It is important to recognize that each of the market and intermediate forms of governance discussed so far can be supplemented and supported by what Williamson (1979) calls relational contracts. Relational contracts can be thought of as the interpersonal relationships that make it possible for the traditional forms of contract discussed earlier to operate efficiently.

As discussed in Chapter 8, Granovetter (1985) and many other authors have observed that narrow, highly economic exchanges often occur within a broader, more social context. This social context can act as a partial substitute for each of the governance mechanisms discussed thus far in this chapter. For example, although a complete contingent claims contract has many positive features as a governance mechanism, the difficulty of accurately anticipating all future states in an exchange relationship can limit the range of exchanges in which this form of contract can be used. However, if parties to an exchange can believe that exchange partners will not engage in certain classes of unnamed and unanticipated forms of opportunism—despite the fact that these contingencies are not written into the explicit contract—the range of exchanges in which complete contingent claims contracts can be applied can be increased substantially.

In the end, virtually all economic exchanges are based on relational contracts to some extent. Certainly, even the simplest contract, if it has to include clauses that specify *all* potential contingencies, would be very difficult to write and execute. In this context, interpersonal attributes such as trust, friendship, and a commitment to ethical behavior can be important in enabling an exchange to go through. The extent to which these relationships can enable firms to gain sustained competitive advantages is discussed later in this chapter.

Internal Markets

If exchange partners have determined that, in order to efficiently avoid opportunism problems, some form of hierarchical governance is necessary, several governance options are available. Internal markets are the first of these options. In internal-market governance, many of the attributes of vertically nonintegrated governance, including the use of contracts and prices to govern exchange relationships, are re-created within a hierarchical structure. Of course, if it were possible to perfectly reconstruct market forms of governance within a hierarchy, it would not have been necessary to manage this exchange through a hierarchy in the first place.

Rather than perfectly re-creating market forms of governance within a hierarchy, internal markets rely on hierarchical analogies to the attributes of market governance. For example, whereas freely negotiated contracts between independent economic actors are used to manage exchanges in market forms of governance, contracts mediated by a "boss" who has some level of command authority are used to manage these relations in an internal market. Also, whereas prices are important in external markets, transfer prices are important in internal markets.

Internal markets are most often used to manage the relationships among diversified businesses in a diversified firm and less frequently used to manage the relationships among vertically integrated businesses. For this reason, a more detailed discussion of governance by means of internal markets is postponed until Chapter 12's discussion of organizing to implement a diversification strategy.

Bureaucracy

External forms of governance use contracts and prices to govern economic exchanges, and internal markets use mediated contracts and transfer prices to govern economic exchanges. Bureaucratic forms of hierarchical governance use policies, procedures, rules, and regulations to govern these exchanges (Ouchi, 1980). Bureaucracy has a bad reputation. But bureaucracy, appropriately applied, can be used to manage exchanges in an efficient manner and in a manner that reduces the threat of opportunistic behavior.

By using bureaucracy, parties to an exchange can refer to rules and procedures to understand their responsibilities in an exchange with other functions in the firm. In an important sense, these bureaucratic rules and regulations act as a complete contingent claims contract or a sequential contract inside a firm. However, within a hierarchy, the problems normally associated with complete contingent claims contracts and sequential contracts can be obviated by a manager with command authority who judiciously applies and modifies the rules and procedures to meet the specific needs in an exchange.

Put differently, if it were possible to write a set of bureaucratic rules that could be perfectly applied in mediating all exchanges in a firm, then those rules should be written, and the exchange should be managed not through hierarchical forms of governance but rather through nonhierarchical forms of market governance. The fact that no bureaucracy can be applied perfectly to govern a hierarchical exchange suggests that managers within a firm need to modify and apply rules—using their experience and judgment—in ways that minimize, at the lowest cost possible, the threat of opportunism in these internal exchanges. A manager to whom both exchange partners report and who has command authority over those exchange partners, is well positioned to manage exchanges in this manner.

Clans

Sometimes, the level of specific investment and uncertainty in an exchange is so great that even bureaucratic forms of governance—even applied with wisdom and judgment—cannot be used to efficiently manage an exchange. In this most extreme setting, Ouchi (1980) suggests the use of another form of governance, a form he calls "clan governance." Whereas bureaucratic forms of hierarchical governance rely on rules and regulations to govern exchanges, clan governance relies on common values, beliefs, trust, and friendship to reduce the threat of opportunism in an exchange. Just as bureaucracy can be thought of as the hierarchical equivalent of different types of market contracts, clans can be thought of as the hierarchical equivalent of relational contracts.

The logic of governance discussed to this point suggests that clan forms of governance should be used to manage only those exchanges that are characterized by very high levels of transaction-specific investment, uncertainty, and complexity. Clan governance is far from a panacea, to be used to manage all exchanges within a vertically integrated firm. Rather, clan governance is a specific tool to manage a narrow range of hierarchical exchanges. Exchanges that involve less specific investment and are less uncertain and less complex should be governed by other means, including internal markets and bureaucracy.

Although clan governance is a special governance tool to be used in very specific situations, it is interesting to note that intraorganizational clans are socially complex forms of governance. Because they are socially complex, clan forms of governance, if applied in an economically valuable way, may be a source of sustained competitive advantage for a firm. These issues are discussed in detail below.

EMPIRICAL TESTS OF THE TRANSACTIONS-COST MODEL OF VERTICAL INTEGRATION

The logic that firms can use to determine which business functions to manage through market forms of governance, which through intermediate forms of governance, and which through hierarchical forms of governance is known as transactions-cost economics. Transactions-cost economics has been the object of a great deal of empirical research in economics, organization theory, and strategic management. Much of this empirical work supports the essential elements of transactions-cost theory, including the notion that the threat of opportunism to a large extent determines the form of economic governance and that exchange partners will adopt the form of governance that, at the lowest possible cost, minimizes the threat of opportunism.

For example, MacDonald (1985), MacMillan, Hambrick, and Pennings (1986), and Caves and Bradburd (1988) show that when firms need to make transaction-specific *capital* investments (such as investments in plant and equipment) in order to engage in a particular economic exchange, the exchange is more likely to be vertically integrated than an exchange not requiring these kinds of investments would be. Armour and Teece (1980), Anderson and Schmittlein (1984), Anderson (1985), John and Weitz (1988), and Masten, Meehan, and Snyder (1991) examine the impact of transaction-specific *human capital* investments on vertical integration decisions and find that the more transaction-specific human capital investments are, the more likely are these exchanges to be managed through hierarchical forms of governance. Stuckey (1983) and Joskow (1985) have examined the impact of making site specific investments, similar to the oil refinery/oil pipeline example described earlier, on vertical integration decisions, and they have found that the greater the level of site specificity in an investment is, the more likely is an exchange to be managed through hierarchical governance. Levy (1985), MacDonald (1985), and Caves and Bradburd (1988) have shown that when only a small number of qualified buyers and sellers exist for a particular exchange (a situation that often reflects the existence of transaction-specific investments), vertically integrated hierarchical forms of governance are more likely to be used than either intermediate or market forms of governance.

Most of this research examines the impact of various forms of transaction-specific investment on vertical integration decisions. The preponderance of evidence suggests that, on average, the higher the required level of transaction-specific investment is, the more likely it is that vertically integrated hierarchical forms of governance will be employed. The impact that uncertainty and complexity in an exchange have on vertical integration decisions has also been examined, although these results are not as consistent as is research on transaction-specific investment (Joskow, 1988; Mahoney, 1992). Sometimes, high levels of uncertainty and complexity lead exchange partners to choose vertical integration in order to minimize the threat of opportunism. On the other hand, some researchers have shown that under conditions of high uncertainty and complexity, exchange partners may want to retain a great deal of flexibility in how they manage their exchanges. Vertically integrated hierarchical governance is usually less flexible than intermediate or market forms of governance. Firms that choose vertical integration to control the threat of opportunism in uncertain and complex exchanges may find it more costly to abandon those exchanges in the future, compared to firms that opt for intermediate or market forms of governance (Walker and Weber, 1984; Kogut, 1991; Balakrishnan and Koza, 1993). The conditions under which the need to reduce the threat of opportunism in uncertain and complex exchanges outweighs the need to retain flexibility in these kinds of exchanges has not yet been articulated in the literature.

VERTICAL INTEGRATION, TRANSACTIONS-COST ECONOMICS, AND OUTSOURCING

One of the critical messages of a transactions-cost economics approach to vertical integration is that virtually every business function and activity can be managed through market, intermediate, or hierarchical forms of governance. Hierarchical governance and vertical integration should be applied to only those transactions where the value of the extra control associated with hierarchical governance is greater than the extra costs associated with this form of governance. This extra control is relevant only when the threat of opportunism in an exchange is high. Thus vertical integration and hierarchical governance are valuable only when the threat of opportunism is substantial.

Recently, this logic has been applied (and some say misapplied) to questions of outsourcing. Without an explicit consideration of the costs and benefits of vertical integration, managers in firms are often tempted to vertically integrate too many business transactions. As long as the product markets in which firms compete are not terribly competitive, it is possible for firms to absorb the extra costs of too much vertical integration and still survive. However, as competitive pressures increase, managers are forced to examine, transaction by transaction, the most efficient form of governance. In recent years, this has led to relatively high levels of outsourcing, where firms replace hierarchical forms of governance with intermediate or market forms of governance (Tully, 1994).

Much of this outsourcing is probably quite reasonable and consistent with transactions-cost logic. However, in their zeal for outsourcing, some firms may have gone too far and outsourced too many business activities. According to transactions-cost logic, firms should not outsource exchanges characterized by high levels of transaction-specific investment, uncertainty, and complexity. Interestingly, exchanges characterized by high levels of transaction-specific investment, uncertainty, and complexity are precisely the exchanges that are most likely to create valuable, rare, and costly-to-imitate resources and capabilities for a firm. Outsourcing the exchanges that are most likely to generate competitive advantages for a firm puts those competitive advantages at risk.

In Chapter 5, it was suggested that costly-to-imitate resources and capabilities can be a source of sustained competitive advantage for a firm, and that resources built up over long periods of time that are causally ambiguous and socially complex are likely to be immune from imitation, compared to other types of resources and capabilities. The links between transaction-specific investment, uncertainty, and complexity, on the one hand, and history, causal ambiguity, and social complexity, on the other hand, are clear. Resources and capabilities that build up over long periods of time (history) are likely to be characterized by high levels of transaction-specific investment; the creation of causally ambiguous resources and capabilities is uncertain; and socially complex resources are the result of complex exchanges within firms. Thus the exchanges that transactions-cost economics suggests should be vertically integrated are the same kinds of exchanges that are likely to generate sustained competitive advantages for firms. Firms that adopt inappropriate intermediate or market forms of governance for these exchanges not only are exposing themselves to higher-than-necessary levels of opportunistic threat but also may be forfeiting current and future sources of competitive advantage.

A firm that outsources exchanges that have the potential to create valuable, rare, and costly-to-imitate resources risks becoming what might be called an "empty corporation" (Postin, 1988; Jones, 1986): a firm that has outsourced the development of all of its strategically important resources and capabilities and thus is not likely to be able to develop and appropriate those resources and capabilities for its future. Although much of the current trend in outsourcing is probably efficient and thus appropriate, firms must always guard against the risk of outsourcing exchanges that are going to enable it to gain and sustain competitive advantages. Applying transactions cost logic to vertical integration decisions helps address this problem.

10.3   VERTICAL INTEGRATION AND SUSTAINED COMPETITIVE ADVANTAGE

Transactions-cost economics provides a powerful set of tools that firms can use to decide their level of vertical integration. However, thus far, this analysis has adopted the assumption that the potential economic value of a particular exchange is independent of the form of governance used to manage that exchange. Put differently, transactions-cost economics assumes that the economic value of an exchange is a given, and that the task facing managers is simply to choose the form of governance that minimizes the threat of opportunism in extracting this value at the lowest cost possible (Williamson, 1991). Traditional transactions-cost analyses do not recognize the possibility that the way in which an exchange is governed can have a direct impact on the value that an exchange can create—that is, that governance itself can be a source of economic rents.

Consider the following examples. Suppose that two firms are evaluating the same transaction. Traditional logic suggests that these two firms will come to similar conclusions about the level of threat of opportunism in this exchange and thus will adopt the same, or at least substitute, forms of governance. In this situation, governance per se cannot be a source of economic profits. But if these two firms come to different conclusions about the level of threat in this exchange, they may come to different conclusions about the appropriate form of governance for this transaction. The identification of different governance mechanisms suggests that these firms will have different costs of governing this exchange, face different residual threats from opportunism, and, perhaps, even come to different conclusions about the economic potential of this exchange. All these differences are potential sources of competitive advantage for these firms—advantages that derive from the differential ability of firms to make governance decisions.

RARENESS AND IMITABILITY IN VERTICAL INTEGRATION STRATEGIES

To derive competitive advantages from governance choices, it is necessary to introduce more heterogeneity into transactions-cost economics than has traditionally been introduced. Heterogeneity can be introduced by recognizing that economic actors may differ in (1) their ability to analyze uncertain and complex economic transactions, (2) their ability to conceive of and implement different governance mechanisms, and (3) their propensity to behave opportunistically. If these differences in governance skills are valuable, rare, and costly to imitate, the vertical integration decisions they imply can be a source of sustained competitive advantage—if a firm is organized to exploit the full competitive potential of its special vertical integration skills.

Differences in the Ability to Analyze Uncertain and Complex Transactions

It is widely recognized that individuals can vary in their ability to analyze different economic exchange opportunities. What is complex and uncertain to one person may be simple and obvious to another (Barney, 1994). Differences in analysis skills can exist in firms as well. One firm may conclude that a potential economic exchange is very complex and uncertain; another may conclude that the same economic exchange is actually quite simple and obvious (Tyler and Steensma, 1995).

Differences in the ability to analyze uncertain and complex economic exchanges reflect numerous differences between individuals and between firms. Differences in native intelligence, training, and experience may lead individuals to come to very different conclusions about the complexity and uncertainty of an exchange. Analogies exist in the firm for each of these individual-level phenomena. For example, firms may differ in their ability to tap into the intelligence of their employees. As a result, some firms may behave as if they are more intelligent than others. Also, firms may vary with respect to the training of their employees and their experience in analyzing certain types of economic exchanges. For all these reasons, firms may come to very different conclusions about the level of uncertainty and complexity in a particular exchange.

Of course, these differences among individuals and firms are competitively relevant only to the extent that they have some implications for how firms make governance decisions. For example, suppose that two firms are contemplating the same economic transaction. The "objective" properties of this transaction are constant across these two firms. However, if these firms differ in their ability to analyze these "objective" properties, they are likely to come to different conclusions about the level of uncertainty and complexity in these exchanges and thus to different conclusions about what the optimal level of governance for these exchanges is likely to be. Suppose that the actual (but difficult-to-observe) level of uncertainty in this exchange is quite low, that one firm comes to this conclusion, but that the second, less skilled firm concludes that the level of uncertainty in this exchange is actually quite high. The first (more accurate) firm will be able to choose a less elaborate and less costly form of governance and still be assured about reducing the threat of opportunism, compared to the second, less skilled firm. The ability to use less costly governance to manage an exchange will give the more skilled firm at least a temporary competitive advantage since, relative to the only other firm in this simple example, these highly developed exchange analysis skills are rare.

For these analysis skills to be a source of sustained competitive advantage, they must be immune from imitation, either through direct duplication or substitution. The imitability of these skills seems likely to depend on their source. For example, innate individual intelligence is probably a relatively fixed attribute and thus not subject to low-cost duplication, although individuals not endowed with high levels of intelligence might still be able to behave as if they were by surrounding themselves with highly skilled individuals, sophisticated databases, and related technologies. Organizational abilities to tap into the intelligence of employees seem likely to depend on the organizational culture and related attributes of a firm—attributes already shown to be usually not subject to low-cost duplication or easy substitution (Barney, 1994). Individual and organizational training and experience can only accumulate over time and thus may not be subject to low-cost duplication or substitution. On the other hand, if there are decreasing returns to training and experience, in the long run competing firms will develop strategically equivalent levels of training and experience.

Differences in the Ability to Conceive of and Implement Governance Mechanisms

Another potentially important difference between economic actors is the ability of individuals and firms to conceive of and implement different governance mechanisms. In a particular exchange, different economic actors may all come to exactly the same conclusion about the threat of opportunism but differ in their abilities to build governance mechanisms to address this threat. If more skilled individuals and firms can develop less costly governance mechanisms to address the opportunism threats in an exchange, compared to less skilled individuals and firms that have to develop more costly governance mechanisms to address these same opportunism threats, the more skilled individuals and firms can gain competitive advantages from their governance choices.

Differences in governance ability are not restricted to the ability that different economic actors might possess in building different governance mechanisms. (e.g., when one firm might be more skilled at using complete contingent claims contracts to manage exchanges while another might be more skilled at using sequential contracting.) Economic actors might also vary with respect to their ability to use the same governance mechanism. Thus, for example, suppose two competing firms decide to govern the same type of exchange by using a combination of a complete contingent claims contract and a relational contract. However, suppose that one of these firms is able to write and administer this form of governance at much lower cost, compared to the other firm. Here, despite the fact that both firms have (apparently) come to the same conclusion about the nature of a particular transaction, and despite the fact that both have implemented the same governance mechanisms to manage this relationship, the fact that one firm is more skilled in implementing these governance mechanisms than the other suggests that a competitive advantage might exist.

The possibility that firms may vary in their ability to conceive of and implement governance devices was briefly discussed, for the case of strategic alliances, in Chapter 9. In that chapter, it was acknowledged that most U.S. automakers have developed strategic alliances with Japanese automakers and that if one asked only whether these U.S. firms have alliances with Japanese firms, one could conclude that these alliances are not rare and thus not a source of competitive advantage. However, when it is recognized that different U.S. automakers get different things out of their alliances with Japanese automakers, it is clear that these alliances can be rare and thus a source of at least a temporary competitive advantage. These observations can be generalized by observing that, even when competing individuals and firms all choose the same governance devices for a transaction, differences in the ability to implement these devices can create important competitive advantages.

As was the case with different skills in analyzing uncertain economic exchanges, whether different skills in conceiving of and implementing governance devices will be a source of sustained competitive advantage depends on the sources of those skill differences. If those sources reflect an economic actor's unique history, if they reflect numerous "little" decisions in these actors, and if they are socially complex, they are likely to be immune from low-cost imitation and thus possible sources of sustained competitive advantage.

Differences in the Propensity to Behave Opportunistically

The first two ways in which governance choices can be sources of competitive advantage—differences in exchange analysis skills and differences in the ability to conceive of and implement governance mechanisms—focus primarily on the uncertainty and complexity of transactions-cost analyses of vertical integration. Although the "objective" level of uncertainty and complexity in an exchange may be a constant property of that exchange, the perceived uncertainty and complexity of the exchange are likely to vary both with the exchange analysis skills of different actors and with the ability of these different actors to conceive of and implement governance devices. However, in addition to differences in the perceived level of uncertainty in an exchange, there may also be important differences in the propensity of different economic actors to behave opportunistically. If these differences exist and can be discovered at low cost, then those exchanging with less opportunistically inclined exchange partners will be able to invest in less costly governance than will those exchanging with more opportunistically inclined exchange partners. This lower-cost governance can be a source of competitive advantage vis-à-vis firms that interact with opportunistically inclined exchange partners and thus require greater levels of costly governance to reduce the threat of opportunism.

Traditional transactions-cost logic does not deny the possibility that different economic actors might vary in their propensity to behave opportunistically. However, this logic also suggests that it is very difficult to distinguish between individuals and firms that are actually less likely to engage in opportunistic behavior and those that only claim that they are less likely to engage in opportunistic behavior (Williamson, 1975). Claiming that one is not opportunistic when one actually is, is an example of adverse selection. Thus to gain the lower governance cost advantages associated with engaging in exchanges with less opportunistic exchange partners, it must be possible to reliably—and at low cost—distinguish between exchange partners who are actually less inclined to behave opportunistically and those who only claim to be less inclined to behave opportunistically.

If it were possible to directly observe the opportunistic tendencies of possible exchange partners, these adverse selection problems would not exist. However, since degree of willingness to behave opportunistically is not tattooed on exchange partners' foreheads, exchange partners must rely on market signals of a partner's intentions (Spence,

1973). Market signals are actions taken by an individual or firm that indicate the level of some attribute of that individual or firm that cannot be directly observed, such as willingness to behave opportunistically. For such an action to be a signal, two conditions must hold: (1) The action must be correlated with the underlying but unobservable attribute, and (2) investing in this signal must be less costly for those that possess this attribute than for those that do not possess it.

A variety of behaviors can be used as market signals to indicate that a potential exchange partner is not likely to behave opportunistically. For example, such exchange partners are likely to be more willing to be open to outside auditors and more willing to commit themselves to transaction-specific investments in an exchange (Barney and Hansen, 1994). Such activities eliminate opportunistic behavior as an option for those individuals or firms that engage in them. Exchange partners that would not have engaged in opportunistic behavior anyway—that is, those with a low propensity to behave opportunistically—do not give up any options by engaging in these behaviors. On the other hand, exchange partners that might have behaved opportunistically forfeit this opportunity when they open themselves up to outside auditors and commit themselves to an exchange by making transaction-specific investments to that exchange. Thus the opportunity cost to exchange partners that might have behaved opportunistically is higher than the opportunity cost to exchange partners that would not have behaved opportunistically, and willingness to be open to outside auditors and to commit to an exchange by making transaction-specific investments can be thought of as signals of a low level of opportunism in a potential exchange partner. Engaging in exchanges with partners who are not likely to behave opportunistically will require less elaborate forms of governance—and thus less costly forms of governance—than engaging in exchanges with partners who may behave opportunistically.

Advantages from Reducing Costs and from Increasing Opportunity Sets

Thus far, the discussion of variance in the tendency of exchange partners to behave opportunistically has focused on the lower-cost governance that is possible if less opportunistic exchange partners are found. However, exchanges with these types of partners can also have an impact on the opportunity set facing a firm.

Traditional transactions-cost logic suggests that the form (and thus cost) of governance varies with the level of transaction-specific investment, uncertainty, and complexity in an exchange. Ultimately, for exchanges with very high levels of transaction-specific investment, uncertainty, and complexity, very costly hierarchical forms of governance may have to be implemented. In some circumstances, it may be the case that the cost of this hierarchical governance could be greater than the anticipated return from an exchange. For example, it might be the case that if a research and development function and a sales function are able to cooperate in the development and distribution of a new product or service, this new product or service could be worth $500,000. However, given the level of transaction-specific investment, uncertainty, and complexity in this relationship, the cost of managing this relationship through a hierarchy might be $600,000—that is, the number of managers, accountants, lawyers, and others that would have to be retained in a hierarchy to manage the relationship between R&D and sales would cost about $600,000. In this setting, a potentially valuable transaction (worth $500,000) will have to be abandoned because of the high cost of managing this transaction ($600,000).

On the other hand, suppose that both the R&D function and the sales function are populated by managers who are unlikely to engage in opportunistic behavior despite the fact that their exchange is characterized by high levels of transaction-specific investment, uncertainty, and complexity. If these two functions can reliably signal their low opportunistic tendencies to each other, they may be able to cooperate in a less costly intermediate or market form of governance. Suppose that the cost of signaling low opportunistic tendencies is $10,000 for the R&D function and $10,000 for the sales function, and that the cost of the intermediate governance form they choose is only $50,000. Obviously, the total cost of forming this governance device in this setting ($70,000) is less than the potential value of this exchange ($500,000), and this exchange will go forward.

Put differently, engaging in exchanges with less opportunistic exchange partners not only can directly reduce the cost of governance that otherwise would have to be absorbed to manage these exchanges but also can increase the range of exchange opportunities that these exchange partners can explore. Thus these exchange partners can gain governance cost advantages over those who engage in exchanges with partners who are more likely to behave opportunistically, and they can obtain revenue opportunities not available to others.

THE QUESTION OF ORGANIZATION: U-FORM DESIGN

Suppose a firm has conducted a transactions cost analysis of all the exchanges it engages in, has chosen the optimal form of governance for each of these transactions, and has concluded that only five business activities should be managed through hierarchical forms of governance: manufacturing, sales, research and development, human resources, and legal. This means that all the other activities in this firm's value chain—finance, marketing, and so forth—are managed through nonhierarchical means (for example, through complete contingent claims or other contracts with outside vendors and through strategic alliances or joint ventures). Given this level of vertical integration, an important question is, How should these activities be organized to take advantage of their full competitive potential?

The fact that this firm has decided to vertically integrate into these five activities and no others suggests that it has concluded that the level of transaction-specific investment, uncertainty, and complexity that exists in the relationship among these activities is such that the efficient management of their interaction will require direct supervision by a manager with some command authority, as well as a high level of direct cooperation among activities. Research has shown that the best way to manage this type of firm is through what is called a U-form design (Williamson, 1975; Barney and Ouchi, 1986). A U-form organization has structural, control, and compensation components.

U-Form Organizational Structure

The U-form structure for a firm that has vertically integrated manufacturing, sales, research and development, human resource, and legal activities is presented in Fig. 10.3. This organizational structure is also called a functional organizational structure, since each of the vertically integrated business activities can also be called business functions. The *U* in the expression *U-form structure* stands for the word *unitary*: Only one person in a U-form organization has a firmwide perspective—the president or chief executive officer (CEO). Every other employee is a functional specialist—in the case of the organization depicted in Fig. 10.3, a functional specialist in manufacturing, sales, R&D, human resources, or legal issues. The CEO in a U-form organization has two basic responsibilities: (1) to formulate the strategy of the firm and (2) to coordinate the activities of the functional specialists in the firm to facilitate the implementation of the strategy.

**FIGURE 10.3
An Example of U-form Organizational Structure**

Strategy Formulation.   The CEO in a U-form organization engages in strategy formulation by applying the models and tools discussed throughout this book. CEOs must evaluate environmental threats and opportunities, understand their firms' strengths and weaknesses, and then choose one or more of the strategic options discussed in this book. In addition, CEOs must decide which business functions to include within the boundaries of the firm and which to keep outside the boundaries of the firm.

Although the responsibility for strategy formulation in a U-form organization ultimately rests with the CEO, this individual needs to draw on the insights, analysis, and involvement of functional managers throughout the firm. CEOs who refuse to involve functional managers in strategy formulation run two risks. First, strategic decisions made in isolation from functional managers may be made without complete information. The fact that a function has been integrated within the organizational hierarchy suggests that managers in that function are likely to possess information, insights, and a point of view that are important for the long-run success of the firm. Failure to incorporate that information, those insights, and that point of view can jeopardize the quality of the strategy that is formulated. Second, limiting the involvement of functional managers in strategy formulation can limit their understanding of, and commitment to, the chosen strategy. This can severely limit their ability, and willingness, to implement any strategy that is formulated (Floyd and Wooldridge, 1992).

Coordinating Functions for Strategy Implementation.   Even the best formulated strategy is competitively irrelevant if it is not implemented. The CEO must work closely with functional managers to implement whatever strategy has been chosen.

From the CEO's perspective, coordinating functional specialists to implement a strategy almost always involves conflict resolution. Conflicts among functional managers in a U-form organization are both expected and normal. Indeed, if there is no conflict among certain functional managers in a U-form organization, then some of these managers probably are not doing their jobs. The task facing the CEO is not to pretend conflict does not exist, or to ignore it, but to manage it in a way that facilitates strategy implementation.

Consider, for example, the relationship between manufacturing and sales managers. Typically, manufacturing managers prefer to manufacture a single product with long production runs. Sales managers, however, generally prefer to sell numerous customized products. Manufacturing managers generally do not like large inventories of finished products; sales managers prefer large inventories of finished products because they facilitate rapid deliveries to customers. If these various interests of manufacturing and sales managers do not, at least sometimes, come into conflict in a U-form organization, then the manufacturing manager is not focusing enough on cost reduction and quality improvement in manufacturing, or the sales manager is not focusing enough on meeting customer needs in a timely way, or both.

Numerous other conflicts arise among functional managers in a U-form organization. Accountants often focus on maximizing managerial accountability and close analysis of costs; R&D managers may fear that such accounting practices will interfere with innovation and creativity. Finance managers often focus on the relationship between a firm and its external capital markets; human resource managers are more concerned with the relationship between a firm and external labor markets. Corporate attorneys may object to certain human resource management practices that enable other functional managers to do their jobs.

In this context, the CEO's job is to help resolve conflicts in ways that facilitate the implementation of the firm's strategy. Functional managers do not have to "like" each other. However, if the vertical integration analysis has been done correctly, the functions that have been included within a firm's boundary are essential for its competitive success. Allowing functional conflicts to prevent the cooperation that is needed to implement a firm's strategy can undermine a firm's performance in a significant way.

Management Control Systems in a U-Form Organization

The CEO in a U-form organization can use a variety of management controls to help resolve functional conflicts and implement a firm's strategy. Among the most important are the internal budgeting process and management committees and task forces.

The Budgeting Process. Budgeting is one of the most important control mechanisms available to CEOs in U-form organizations. Indeed, in most U-form companies, enormous management effort goes into the creation of budgets and the evaluation of performance relative to budgets. Budgets are developed for costs, revenues, and a variety of other activities performed by a firm's functional managers. Often, managerial compensation and promotion opportunities depend on the ability of a manager to meet budget expectations.

Although budgets are an important control tool, they can have unintended negative consequences. For example, the use of budgets can lead functional managers to overemphasize short-term behavior that is easy to measure and underemphasize longer-term behavior that is more difficult to measure. Thus, for example, the strategically correct thing for a functional manager to do might be to increase expenditures for maintenance and management training, thereby ensuring that the function will have both the technology and the skilled people needed to do the job in the future. An overemphasis on meeting current budget requirements, however, might lead this manager to delay maintenance and training expenditures. By meeting short-term budgetary demands, this manager may be sacrificing the long-term viability of this function and thereby compromising the long-term viability of the firm.

The tendency of budgets to lead managers to underinvest in the future and overinvest in the short term reflects the fact that many budgets rely solely on accounting numbers of performance to set targets for functional managers. As discussed in Chapter 2, accounting numbers count investments that pay off only in future periods as costs in the current period. Shifting the emphasis from accounting-based budgets to budgets that address the net present value of the activities pursued by a function helps to address this short-term problem. This use of economic-performance-based budgets is discussed in detail in Chapter 12.

Besides moving from accounting-based budgets to economic-performance-based budgets, managers in U-form organizations can do several other things to make full use of budgets as a management control device. Various researchers suggest that evaluating a functional manager's performance relative to budgets can be an effective control device when the process used in developing budgets is open and participative and reflects the economic reality facing functional managers and the firm, and when quantitative evaluations of a functional manager's performance are augmented by qualitative evaluations of that performance (Ouchi, 1982; Gupta, 1987). Adopting an open and participative process for setting budgets helps ensure that budgeted targets are realistic and that functional managers understand and accept them. Including qualitative criteria for evaluation reduces the chances that functional managers will engage in behaviors that are very harmful in the long run but enable them to make budget in the short run.

Management Committees.   In addition to budgets, the CEO of a U-form organization can use various internal management committees as management control devices. Two particularly common types are the executive committee and the operations committee (these committees have different names in different organizations).

The executive committee in a U-form organization typically consists of the CEO and two or three key functional senior managers. It normally meets weekly and reviews the performance of the firm on a weekly basis. Functions represented on this committee generally include accounting, legal, and other functions (such as manufacturing or sales) that are most central to the firm's short-term business success.

The fundamental purpose of the executive committee is to track the short-term performance of the firm, to note and correct any budget variances for functional managers, and to respond to any crises that might emerge.

In addition to the executive committee, another group of managers meets regularly to help control the operations of the firm. Often called the operations committee, this committee typically meets monthly and usually consists of the CEO and each of the heads of the functional areas included in the firm. The executive committee is a subset of the operations committee.

The primary objective of the operations committee is to track firm performance over time intervals slightly longer than the weekly interval of primary interest to the executive committee, and to monitor longer-term strategic investments and activities. Such investments might include plant expansions, the introduction of new products, and the implementation of cost reduction or quality improvement programs. The operations committee provides a forum in which senior functional managers can come together to share concerns and opportunities and to coordinate efforts to implement strategies.

In addition to these two standing committees, various other committees and task forces can be organized within the U-form organization to manage specific projects and tasks. These additional groups are typically chaired by a member of the executive or operations committee and report to one or both of these standing committees as warranted.

Compensation Policy in a U-Form Organization

Another tool that a CEO can use to help manage a U-form organization efficiently is compensation policy (Balkin and Gomez-Mejia, 1990). Historically, the compensation of functional managers and of the CEO in a U-form organization has been only loosely tied to the economic performance of the organization. Indeed, as long as this type of firm was profitable, employees continued to work and continued to be paid. However, over the last several years, more firms have begun to tie the compensation for both the CEO and functional managers to the firm's performance.

The simplest form of these pay-for-performance schemes makes management compensation depend, at least in part, on the firm's meeting some specified performance targets—such as market share, accounting profitability, or leverage. This approach relates firm performance to management compensation, but it can have some unintended consequences. In particular, performance targets that are based on various accounting measures of firm performance can lead managers to underinvest in longer-term strategies and in intangible resources and capabilities. These are the limitations associated with accounting measures of performance, as discussed in Chapter 2.

For example, in the 1980s Archie McCardell, president of International Harvester (IH), was given a pay-for-performance contract that granted a substantial bonus if IH's profitability ratios were greater than or equal to industry average ratios by a prespecified year (Hamermesh and Christensen, 1981). There are some data to suggest that McCardell put off investing in plant and equipment and delayed divesting certain businesses in an effort to meet these objectives. Both investing in plant and equipment and divesting certain businesses would have been very costly in the short run but were essential for the continued success of IH. McCardell obtained his bonus, but International Harvester was soon bankrupt (Hamermesh and Christensen, 1981).

In response to these kinds of problems, many firms are moving away from accounting-based pay-for-performance compensation schemes and instead are moving toward economic-based pay for performance. Some of the main tools of this form of compensation are stock and stock options. The idea is to give managers in U-form organizations incentives to behave as if they were owners of the firm by making them owners. Equity in a firm, if it becomes a significant percentage of a manager's net worth, can provide such incentives. Stock options, which can be exercised in some future time period, have provided longer-term incentives for U-form managers.

In 1991, 86 percent of the median income of the 19 highest-paid CEOs in the United States came in the form of stock grants and other stock options (Tully, 1992b) worth almost $8.8 million per CEO. Most of these highly paid CEOs headed up firms with impressive economic performance numbers. For example, Coca-Cola's return to shareholders had averaged 35 percent a year from 1981 to 1991 and 43 percent per year from 1987 to 1991. In 1991 Roberto C. Goizueta, CEO of Coca-Cola, received as compensation a restricted stock grant worth $56 million. Goizueta, however, will not be able to sell any of these shares until later in the 1990s. Stanley Gault, former CEO at Rubbermaid, took over as CEO at Goodyear in 1991 and promptly received stock grants worth $21.8 million. Then, in his first year, Gault implemented strategies that increased Goodyear's stock price from $30 per share to over $73 per share (Tully, 1992b).

Of course, questions remain about these substantial pay-for-performance compensation schemes. How much compensation in the form of stock do CEOs need to be paid in order to appropriately motivate their behavior? Does the CEO, as a single manager, really have that much impact on the overall performance of a firm (see the discussion of the hierarchical definition of strategy in Section 1.2)? How far down in the organization should these pay-for-performance compensation schemes go—to the CEO only, to the CEO and senior functional managers, to all employees? What signal does this very high level of compensation send to employees throughout a firm? Whatever the specific answers to this question, the general trend to tie management compensation more closely to the economic performance of firms is unlikely to stop (Crystal, 1991).

Symptoms of a "Sick" U-Form Organization

In combination, U-form structure, management control systems, and compensation polices can be used effectively to manage a firm that has vertically integrated just the functions that it needs to be successful in a single primary business. If numerous nonessential functions are also included within a firm's boundaries, the efficiency of the U-form design can begin to deteriorate. And if a firm begins to move beyond vertically integrating functions in a single primary business and begins to enter into multiple businesses, the U-form design will no longer be an effective management tool. These limitations reveal themselves in what can be called symptoms of a "sick" U-form. Common symptoms of a "sick" U-form organization are listed in Table 10.2 and discussed below.

Tyranny of the Day to Day. As a firm begins operating in numerous unnecessary functions or in numerous businesses, the level of conflict among functional managers begins to increase. This increased conflict reflects the increased level of functional work that must be accomplished in a firm that has vertically integrated too broadly or expanded into multiple businesses. As these conflicts increase in frequency, more and more of the CEO's time and energy must be focused on resolving them in ways that facilitate strategy implementation. As the CEO's attention becomes more focused on resolving functional conflicts, less attention can be paid to formulating the firm's strategy. In a sense, the day-to-day demands of conflict resolution force the formulation of longer-term strategy off the CEO's agenda. When this occurs, CEOs are accomplishing only one of their major responsibilities, strategy implementation, and failing to accomplish the other, strategy formulation.

TABLE 10.2 **Symptoms of a "Sick"** **U-Form Organization**	1. Tyranny of the day to day
	2. Strategy formulation by organizational autobiography
	3. The ivory tower syndrome
	4. Fort Apache disease

Strategy Formulation by Organizational Autobiography.   After some period of time, most CEOs come to realize the risks they run by not focusing enough on strategy formulation. The demand for resolving interfunctional conflicts does not go away, however, especially if the firm continues to be vertically integrated into too many functions or continues to expand into multiple businesses. One apparent solution to this dilemma is for CEOs to narrow the focus of their strategy formulation efforts while continuing to manage interfunctional conflicts.

One way this narrowing of the task of strategy formulation can be accomplished is by emphasizing strategy formulation from a single functional perspective, such as a focus on financial strategy, marketing strategy, research and development strategy, or sales strategy. Of all the functions that CEOs could choose to emphasize in their efforts to focus strategy formulation, the most likely choice is the function with which they are most familiar. Since most CEOs, at one time in their career, were functional managers, it is natural for them to emphasize their previous functional responsibility in their strategy formulation efforts. This can be thought of as strategy formulation by organizational autobiography.

Obviously, such a limited focus in strategy formulation is not viable in the long run. No one function in this type of firm can, by itself, guarantee economic success. This is why multiple functions are usually integrated within a firm's boundary. The nature of multifunctional firms assumes that several functions must work together for a firm to be successful. Moreover, an inappropriate emphasis on a single business function in strategy formulation is likely to lead to increased cross-functional conflicts, as underemphasized functions battle for an increasingly scarce commodity—CEO attention.

The Ivory Tower Syndrome.   Beleaguered by the tyranny of the day to day and the problems associated with organizational autobiography, CEOs often fall victim to another organizational pathology—the ivory tower syndrome. The afflicted CEO abandons all efforts at strategy implementation and focuses instead only on strategy formulation. In a sense, such CEOs banish themselves to a pristine ivory tower to consider the long-term strategies of the firm.

Ivory tower syndrome is not problematic if the CEO delegates strategy implementation to someone else in the firm. Often this delegation leads to splitting the CEO's job into two parts: strategy formulation (often done by the CEO) and strategy implementation (often delegated to a newly appointed chief operating officer, or COO). As long as the CEO and COO are able to work together effectively, this division of labor can be effective and can enable the functional organization to continue.

If strategy implementation is not delegated to a COO, ivory tower syndrome can be disastrous for a firm. The firm may possess a clearly articulated strategy and vision, but the day-to-day activities needed to implement the strategy are ignored, and strategy implementation deteriorates into cross-functional wars.

Fort Apache Disease.   A highly problematic organizational pathology for U-form organizations that have integrated too broadly or are operating in multiple businesses is Fort Apache disease. Afflicted CEOs work closely with two or three associates whom they trust completely, and they view the rest of the managers in the firm—those not in this close-knit top management group—as the "enemy." Just as in the old movie *Fort Apache*, or its modern version, *Fort Apache, The Bronx*, battle lines are clearly drawn, trust is nonexistent, and the ability of the firm to formulate and implement strategy vanishes. Managers among the trusted few blame everyone else for the firm's problems; managers outside this small group perceive the CEO to be paranoid, dictatorial, and arbitrary.

Solutions for a "Sick" U-Form Organization

Each symptom of U-form "sickness" can seriously reduce the effectiveness of a multifunctional firm. Failure to diagnose and resolve these problems is likely to put the firm's long-term survival at risk. Fortunately, solutions for these pathologies can be derived from an understanding of their causes: Either the firm has integrated too many inappropriate functions within its boundaries, or it has begun operating in multiple businesses.

If the cause of the problems is that a firm has integrated inappropriate functions within its boundary, the task facing management is to apply the tools discussed in this chapter to redraw the boundaries of the firm. Transactions-cost logic suggests that only business activities characterized by high levels of transaction-specific investment, uncertainty, and complexity should be vertically integrated into the firm. These are the kinds of activities that are most likely to generate valuable, rare, and costly-to-imitate resources and capabilities. By carefully refocusing the firm on its strategically most important functions, management can avoid or cure many of the symptoms of a "sick" U-form.

If the cause of the problems is that a firm is operating in multiple businesses, management needs to recognize that it has begun to implement a new corporate strategy—diversification. The vertical integration strategies described in this chapter are used by firms seeking to leverage their skills across stages of the value chain in a single market or industry. When these leveraging efforts begin to move a firm out of a single market or industry to leverage its skills in new markets or industries, the firm moves from a vertical integration strategy to a diversification strategy.

Diversification strategies are the subject of the next two chapters. In Chapter 11 we discuss the conditions under which a diversification strategy is economically viable. In Chapter 12 we examine ways to organize to implement this strategy.

10.4   SUMMARY

The number of stages in a product's or service's value chain that a firm engages in defines the firm's level of vertical integration. Sometimes a firm's level of vertical integration can be observed directly. At other times it must be inferred from a firm's ratio of value added to sales.

Vertical integration is one governance option that firms can use to manage economic exchanges. Governance options can be grouped into three broad categories: market governance, intermediate governance, and hierarchical governance (vertical integration). Managers should choose the form of governance that, at the lowest cost possible, minimizes the threat of opportunistic behavior in an exchange. The threat of opportunism in an exchange depends, in turn, on the level of transaction-specific investment, uncertainty, and complexity in the exchange. In general the direct costs of governance increase as managers move from market forms of governance to hierarchical forms of governance.

The simple three-way distinction between market, intermediate, and hierarchical governance can be expanded. Some common specific mechanisms of governance available to managers are spot-market contracts, complete contingent claims contracts, sequential contracting, relational contracting, internal markets, bureaucracy, and clans. The economic value of each of these governance devices is discussed, along with the implications of this analysis for outsourcing decisions.

For governance decisions to be a source of competitive advantage, there must be (1) differences in firms' ability to analyze uncertain and complex transactions, (2) differences in firms' ability to conceive of and implement governance devices, or (3) differences in firms' propensity to behave opportunistically.

The most efficient organizational design for implementing a vertical integration strategy is the U-form design. A variety of management techniques can be used to help a U-form organization work efficiently. However, if a firm has vertically integrated into inappropriate business activities or is operating in multiple businesses, U-form performance will begin to deteriorate. Particular examples of this U-form deterioration are discussed.

REVIEW QUESTIONS

1. Some firms have engaged in backward vertical integration strategies in order to appropriate the economic profits that would have been earned by suppliers selling to them. How is this motivation for backward vertical integration related to the transactions-cost logic for vertical integration described in this chapter? (*Hint:* Compare the competitive conditions under which firms may earn economic profits to the competitive conditions under which firms will be motivated to minimize transactions cost through vertical integration.)

2. Traditional transactions-cost logic assumes that gains from trade in an exchange are unrelated to the form of governance that is used to manage an exchange. Do you agree with this assumption? For example, might it ever be the case that gains from trade between two exchange partners will be greater if these partners adopt a complete contingent claims contract approach to governance instead of a vertically integrated hierarchical approach to governance?

3. Another popular explanation of vertical integration decisions made by firms is called "resource dependence theory." In this explanation, firms are assumed to pursue vertical integration strategies whenever the acquisition of a critical resource is uncertain or threatened. How is this theory of vertical integration related to the transactions-cost theory developed in this chapter?

4. You are about to purchase a home. What kinds of opportunistic threats do you face in this purchase? What governance mechanisms can you put into place to minimize these threats?

5. According to transactions-cost logic, clan governance is a very costly form of hierarchical governance that should be used only to manage transactions with very high transactions cost. Yet the popular business press seems to extol the virtues of clan-like forms of management and suggests that clan governance should be used to manage many, if not all, hierarchical exchanges. Which of these points of view do you accept and why?

CHAPTER

11

Diversification Strategies

In Section 10.3 we discussed some of the limitations of the U-form organization for implementing vertical integration strategies. Many of these limitations are signs that a firm has moved away from being vertically integrated in a single market or industry and has begun operations in multiple markets or multiple industries. Firms that operate in multiple markets or multiple industries at the same time have begun to implement a diversification strategy.

In this chapter we examine the economic value of diversification strategies and the conditions under which they can be expected to generate competitive advantages for a firm. Chapter 12 focuses on organizing to implement a diversification strategy.

11.1 TYPES OF DIVERSIFICATION

Firms vary in the extent to which they have diversified the mix of businesses they pursue. Perhaps the simplest way of characterizing differences in the level of diversification focuses on the relatedness of the businesses pursued by a firm. Firms can pursue a strategy of *limited* diversification, of *related* diversification, or of *unrelated* diversification (see Fig. 11.1).

FIGURE 11.1
Levels and Types of
Diversification

A. Limited Diversification

■ **Single-business:** 95 percent or more of firm revenues comes from a single business

■ **Dominant-business:** between 70 and 95 percent of firm revenues comes from a single business

B. Related Diversification

■ **Related-constrained:** less than 70 percent of firm revenues comes from a single business, and different businesses share numerous links and common attributes

■ **Related-linked:** less than 70 percent of firm revenues comes from a single business, and different businesses share only a few links and common attributes or different links and common attributes

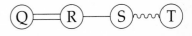

C. Unrelated Diversification

■ Less than 70 percent of firm revenues comes from a single business, and there are few, if any, links or common attributes among business

LIMITED DIVERSIFICATION

A firm has implemented a strategy of limited diversification when all or most of its business activities fall within a single industry (see Fig. 11.1A). Rumelt (1974) includes two kinds of firms in this diversification category: *single-business* firms (firms with greater than 95 percent of their total sales in a single industry) and *dominant-business* firms (firms with between 70 percent and 95 percent of their total sales in a single industry). Differences between single-business and dominant-business firms are represented in Fig. 11.1A. Single-business Firm A pursues a single-business strategy. Dominant-business Firm E is linked with the smaller Firm F in a dominant-business strategy.

In an important sense, firms pursuing a strategy of limited diversification are not leveraging their resources and capabilities beyond a single market or industry. Thus the analysis of limited diversification is logically equivalent to the analysis of business-level strategies (discussed in Part II) and to the analysis of vertical integration strategies (discussed in Chapter 10). Since these kinds of strategies have already been discussed, the remainder of this chapter focuses on leveraging strategies that involve higher levels of diversification.

RELATED DIVERSIFICATION

As a firm begins to engage in businesses in more than one market or industry, it moves away from being a single-business or dominant-business firm and begins to adopt higher levels of diversification. Rumelt (1974) suggests that when less than 70 percent of a firm's revenues comes from a single line of business and these multiple lines of business are linked in some ways, the firm has implemented a strategy of related diversification.

Rumelt (1974) identifies two ways in which the businesses that a diversified firm pursues can be related (see Fig. 11.1B). If all the businesses in which a firm operates share a significant number of inputs, production technologies, distribution channels, similar customers, and so forth, the diversification strategy is called *related-constrained*. The strategy is said to be constrained because corporate managers pursue business opportunities in new markets or industries only if those markets or industries share numerous resource and capability requirements with the businesses the firm is currently pursuing. Commonalities across businesses in a strategy of related-constrained diversification are represented by the linkages among Businesses K, L, M, and N in the "related-constrained" section of Fig. 11.1B.

If the different businesses that a single firm pursues are linked on only a couple of dimensions, or if different sets of businesses are linked along very different dimensions, the diversification strategy is called *related-linked*. For example, Business Q and Business R may share similar production technology, Business R and Business S may share similar customers, Business S and Business T may share similar suppliers, and Business Q and Business T may have no common attributes. This strategy is represented in the "related-linked" section of Fig. 11.1B by businesses with relatively few links between them and with different links between them (i.e., straight lines and curved lines).

UNRELATED DIVERSIFICATION

Firms that pursue a strategy of related diversification have some type of linkages among most, if not all, the different businesses they pursue. However, it is possible for firms to pursue numerous different businesses and for there to be no linkages among these businesses (see Fig.

11.1C). When less than 70 percent of a firm's revenues is generated by a single business, and when a firm's businesses share few, if any, common attributes, then according to Rumelt (1974) that firm is pursuing a strategy of unrelated diversification.

11.2   THE VALUE OF DIVERSIFICATION

In order for a diversification strategy—related, or unrelated—to add economic value to a firm, two conditions must be met. First, some synergy must exist among the businesses pursued by the diversified firm. Formally, this synergy requirement can be expressed as

$$NPV \sum_{t=1}^{n} B_t > NPV(B_1) + NPV(B_2) + \ldots + NPV(B_n) \qquad Eq.\ 11.1$$

where,

$$NPV(B_t) = \text{the present value at Business } t.$$

This is a generalization of the definition of *synergy* in a strategic alliance, discussed in Section 9.2. Without synergies coming from some source, there can be no economic reason to combine several businesses into a single enterprise.

If the inequality in Eq. (11.1) holds, a firm is said to be exploiting an economy of scope. Economies of scope exist because of the cost savings or revenue enhancements that a firm experiences because of the mix of businesses that it is operating in. (Economies of *scope* are not to be confused with economies of *scale*—cost advantages due to a firm's volume of production in a particular business.)

Second, not only must some synergy or economy of scope exist, but it must be less costly for a diversified firm to realize this synergy than for outside equity holders to realize this synergy. Outside equity investors can gain many of the economies of scope associated with diversification on their own, without the involvement of a firm. They do this by investing in a diversified portfolio of stocks. Moreover, investors can realize some of these synergies at almost zero cost. In these situations, it makes little economic sense for investors to "hire" managers in a firm to manage diversification for them, especially since organizing the diversified firm can be very costly (see Chapter 12). Rather, firms should implement a diversification strategy only to obtain synergies that outside investors find too costly to create on their own.

Several motivations for pursuing a diversification strategy exist. Some of the most important are listed in Table 11.1 and discussed below.

TABLE 11.1
Motivations for Implementing a Diversification Strategy

1. Operational economies of scope
   - Shared activities
   - Core competencies
2. Financial economies of scope
   - Internal capital allocation
   - Risk reduction
   - Tax advantages
3. Anticompetitive economies of scope
   - Multipoint competition
   - Exploiting market power
4. Employee incentives for diversification
   - Diversifying employees' human capital investments
   - Maximizing management compensation

These motivations for diversification vary in how they meet the two value-creating criteria. Some of these motivations are based on real synergies, but outside investors can create them at low cost on their own. Some cannot be created by outside investors, but whether or not the inequality in Eq. (11.1) is met is less clear. And some meet both criteria.

DIVERSIFICATION TO EXPLOIT OPERATIONAL ECONOMIES OF SCOPE

Sometimes, economies of scope may reflect operational links among the businesses a firm engages in. Operational economies of scope typically take one of two forms: shared activities and shared core competencies.

Shared Activities

In the appendix to Chapter 5, it was suggested that value chain analysis can be used to describe the specific business activities of a firm. This same value chain analysis can also be used to describe the business activities that may be shared across several different businesses within a diversified firm. These shared activities are potential sources of operational economies of scope for diversified firms.

Consider, for example, the hypothetical firm presented in Fig. 11.2. This diversified firm engages in three businesses: A, B, and C. How-

FIGURE 11.2
A Hypothetical Firm
Sharing Activities
Among Three
Businesses

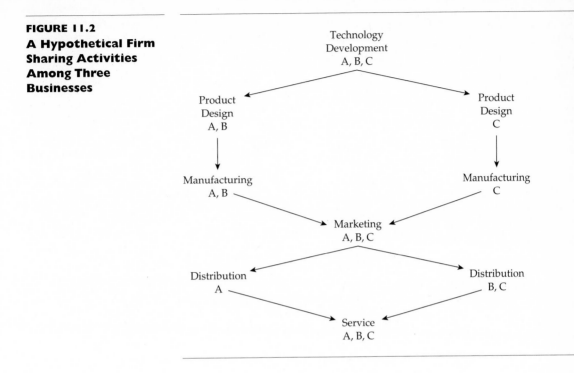

ever, these three businesses share a variety of activities throughout their value chains. For example, all three draw on the same technology development operation. Product design and manufacturing are shared in Businesses A and B and separate for Business C. All three businesses share a common marketing and service operation. Business A has its own distribution system.

These kinds of shared activities are quite common among both related-constrained and related-linked diversified firms. At Texas Instruments, for example, the defense electronics, semi-conductor, and computer businesses share some research and development activities and often share common manufacturing locations (Burrows, 1995; Rogers, 1992). The operating systems and applications software businesses at Microsoft operate in the same location and have overlapping distribution networks (Wallace and Erickson, 1993). Procter & Gamble's numerous different consumer products businesses often share common manufacturing locations and rely on a common distribution network (through retail grocery stores) (Porter, 1981b).

Porter (1985), Rumelt (1974), and Ansoff (1965) have developed lists of ways in which activities can link different businesses in a firm.

Some of the most important of these activity linkages, and their position in a business's value chain, are summarized in Table 11.2. Shared activities can add value to a firm by reducing costs or increasing revenues.

Shared Activities and Cost Reduction.　In Section 6.2 sources of cost advantage for firms were described. Some of these sources of cost advantage may be obtained through activity sharing across businesses in a diversified firm. For example, if several businesses in a diversified firm manufacture similar products and services, and if there are important economies of scale in this manufacturing process, then a diversified firm may be able to capture the cost advantages associated with these economies of scale by sharing these manufacturing activities among its different businesses. Each business, then, could enjoy cost advantages that would otherwise be possible only if the business were large enough, as an independent entity, to exploit these economies of scale. Such savings are not restricted to manufacturing businesses. Columbia Hospital Corporation uses shared activities across its numerous hospital operations to reduce costs (Tomsho, 1992).

Activity sharing can also enable a diversified firm to obtain cost reductions based on learning-curve economies. It may be the case that each business in a diversified firm, acting independently, does not have a sufficiently high level of cumulative volume of production to exploit learning and reduce costs. But if these businesses are able to share critical activities, the cumulative volume in these activities will rise more quickly, accelerating any learning opportunities that might exist and thereby reducing the costs of each business in the diversified firm.

Activity sharing may also enable a firm that has developed low-cost production technology in one of its businesses, or in a common technology development laboratory, to reduce the direct production costs of each of the firm's businesses. Moreover, each business is spared the high costs associated with developing this production technology on its own.

Finally, it may be the case that one business in a diversified firm has obtained differential access to certain factors of production—raw materials, employees, managerial talent, technology. If several of this firm's businesses draw on these same factors of production, then activity sharing can have the effect of reducing the supply costs of all these businesses. Again, these businesses will have lower costs than they would have had if they were not part of this diversified firm and thus did not have differential access to the factors of production through shared activities.

Failure to exploit shared activities across businesses can lead to out-of-control costs. For example, the Kentucky Fried Chicken division

**TABLE 11.2
Possible Shared
Activities and Their
Place in the Value
Chain**
Source: Porter (1985),
Rumelt (1974), and Ansoff
(1965)

Value Chain Activity	Shared Activities
Input activities	Common purchasing
	Common inventory control system
	Common warehousing facilities
	Common inventory delivery system
	Common quality assurance
	Common input requirements system
	Common suppliers
Production activities	Common product components
	Common product components manufacturing
	Common assembly facilities
	Common quality control system
	Common maintenance operation
	Common inventory control system
Warehousing and distribution	Common product delivery system
	Common warehouse facilities
Sales and marketing	Common advertising efforts
	Common promotional activities
	Cross-selling of products
	Common pricing systems
	Common marketing departments
	Common distribution channels
	Common sales forces
	Common sales offices
	Common order processing services
Dealer support and service	Common service network
	Common guarantees and warranties
	Common accounts receivable management systems
	Common dealer training
	Common dealer support services

of PepsiCo encouraged each of its regional business operations in North American to develop its own quality improvement plans. The result was enormous redundancy and at least three conflicting quality efforts—all leading to higher-than-necessary cost. In a similar way, Levi Strauss's unwillingness to centralize and coordinate order processing led to a situation where six separate order-processing computer systems operated simultaneously. This costly redundancy was replaced by a single, integrated ordering system (Fuchsberg, 1992).

Shared Activities and Revenue Enhancement.   Lower costs are often central to obtaining economies of scope through shared activities, but such sharing can also increase the revenues in diversified firms' businesses. This can happen in at least two ways.

First, it may be the case that shared product development and sales activities may enable two or more businesses in a diversified firm to offer a bundled set of products to customers. Sometimes, the value of these "product bundles" to customers is greater than the value of each product separately. This greater customer value can generate for each business revenues greater than what would have been the case if the businesses were not together and sharing activities in a diversified firm.

In the telecommunications industry, for example, separate firms sell telephones, access to telephone lines, equipment to route calls in an office, mobile telephones, and paging services. A customer that requires all these services could contact five different companies. Each of these five different firms would likely possess its own unique technological standards and software, making the development of an integrated telecommunications system for the customer difficult at best. Alternatively, a single diversified firm sharing sales activities across these businesses could significantly reduce the search costs of potential customers. This one-stop shopping is likely to be valuable to customers, who might be willing to pay for this convenience a slightly higher price than they would pay if they purchased these services from five separate firms. Moreover, if this diversified firm also shares some technology development activities across its businesses, it might be able to offer an integrated telecommunications network to potential customers. The extra value of this integrated network for customers is very likely to be reflected in prices that are higher than the prices that would have been possible if each of these businesses were independent or if activities among these businesses were not shared. Most of the regional telephone operating companies in the United States—including Bell South, Southwestern Bell, and Pacific Telesis—are attempting to gain these economies of scope (Carnevale, 1993).

Such "product bundles" are important in other firms as well. Many grocery stores now sell prepared foods alongside traditional grocery products in the belief that busy customers want access to all kinds of food products—in the same location (de Lisser, 1993).

Second, shared activities can enhance business revenues by exploiting the strong, positive reputations of some of a firm's businesses in other of its businesses. For example, if one business has a strong positive reputation for high-quality manufacturing, other businesses sharing this manufacturing activity will gain some of the advantages of this reputation. And, if one business has a strong positive reputation for selling high-performance products, other businesses sharing sales and marketing activities with this business will gain some of the advantages of this reputation. In both cases, businesses that draw on another business's strong reputation through shared activities with that business will have larger revenues than would be the case if these businesses were operating on their own.

Hewlett-Packard has used shared activities to enhance revenues in some of its businesses (Yoder, 1991). Through the 1970s and early 1980s, hardware and software development in each of HP's businesses was conducted independently, without shared activities. Although HP was able to market some of the highest-quality printers, plotters, and computers through each of these independent businesses, each of these systems adopted very different hardware and software conventions. These differences made it very difficult for HP customers to build an integrated HP computing system. Beginning in the late 1980s, hardware and software development activities at HP began to be shared, although each business retained significant levels of design autonomy. The results of this increased design-activity sharing are easier-to-integrate products and significant increases in revenues and performance for many of HP's businesses.

Shared Activities and Outside Investors. If shared activities in a diversified firm reduce the firm's costs or increase its revenues compared to the costs or revenues of a nondiversified firm, then the inequality in Eq. (11.1) holds—that is, shared activities are an operational economy of scope. However, for shared activities to be valuable, generating this synergy must be more costly for outside investors than for the diversified firm.

In general, outside investors have limited ability to exploit shared activities among businesses. Such activity sharing typically requires a level of organizational control and integration that cannot be duplicated in a diversified portfolio of stocks.

The Limits of Activity Sharing. Despite the potential of activity sharing to generate valuable economies of scope, this approach has three important limits (Davis et al., 1992). First, substantial organizational issues are often associated with a diversified firm's learning how to manage cross-business relationships. Managing these relationships effectively can be very difficult, and failure can lead to excess bureaucracy, inefficiency, and organizational gridlock (these organizational issues are discussed in Chapter 12).

Second, sharing activities may limit the ability of a particular business to meet its specific customers' needs. For example, if two businesses share manufacturing activities, they may reduce their manufacturing costs through exploiting economies of scale. However, to exploit these economies of scale, these businesses may need to build products using somewhat standardized components that do not fully meet their customers' needs. Businesses that share distribution activities may have lower overall distribution costs but be unable to distribute their products to all their customers. Businesses that share sales activities may have lower overall sales costs but be unable to provide the specialized selling required in each business.

One diversified firm that has struggled with the ability to meet the specialized needs of customers in its different divisions is General Motors (Loomis, 1993). To exploit economies of scale in the design of new automobiles, GM shared design across its several automobile divisions. The result, through the 1980s, was cookie-cutter cars—the traditional distinctiveness of several GM divisions, including Oldsmobile and Cadillac, was all but lost.

Third, activity sharing that exploits the reputation of one business in other firm businesses can go both ways. If one business in a diversified firm has a poor reputation, sharing activities with that business can reduce the quality of the reputation of other businesses in the firm.

Taken together, these limits on activity sharing can more than offset any possible gains. Indeed, over the last decade, more and more diversified firms have been abandoning efforts at activity sharing in favor of managing each business's activities independently (Rapoport, 1992). For example, ABB Inc. (a Swiss engineering firm) and CIBA-Geigy (a Swiss chemicals firm) have adopted explicit corporate policies that restrict almost all activity sharing across businesses. Other diversified firms, including Nestlé, Westinghouse, and General Electric, restrict activity sharing to just one or two activities (such as research and development or management training). However, to the extent that a diversified firm can exploit shared activities while avoiding these problems, shared activities can add value to a firm.

Core Competencies

Recently, a second operational linkage among the businesses of a diversified firm has been described. Unlike shared activities, this linkage is based on different businesses in a diversified firm sharing less tangible resources such as managerial and technical know-how, experience, and wisdom (Grant, 1988). Prahalad and Hamel (1990) call this source of operational economy of scope a firm's "core competence." They define core competence as "the collective learning in the organization, especially how to coordinate diverse production skills and integrate multiple streams of technologies" (1990:82). Core competencies are complex sets of resources and capabilities that link different businesses in a diversified firm through managerial and technical know-how, experience, and wisdom (Chatterjee and Wernerfelt, 1991).

For example, according to Prahalad and Hamel (1990), 3M has a core competence in substrates, adhesives, and coatings. Collectively, employees at 3M know more about applying adhesives and coatings on different kinds of substrates than do managers in any other organization. Over the years, 3M has applied these resources and capabilities in a wide variety of products, including Post-it notes, magnetic tape, photographic film, pressure-sensitive tape, and coated abrasives. At first glance, this widely diversified set of products seems to have little or nothing in common. Certainly these different businesses share few, if any, specific business activities. Yet they all draw on a single core set of resources and capabilities in substrates, adhesives, and coatings.

Honda also manufactures and sells a wide range of products—luxury automobiles, motorcycles, lawn mowers, portable electric generators. These numerous products all draw on a single core competence in the manufacturing of engines and power trains (Prahalad and Hamel, 1990). Some of these common resources and capabilities are exploited at Honda through shared activities among businesses. But most of these businesses share few, if any, activities but are nevertheless linked by a core competence.

When a diversified firm exploits a core competence, the operations within each of its different businesses are significantly affected by the accumulated knowledge, experience, and wisdom gained from the firm's previous business activities (Markides and Williamson, 1994). These different businesses may all exploit similar technologies, they may address similar kinds of customers, or they may adopt similar management principles. Although these businesses may differ in important ways, managers moving from one of these businesses to another will experience many common elements, despite the firm's diversification strategy.

Core Competencies and Shared Activities.   Core competencies may or may not exist in parallel with shared activities. For example, most observers would agree that Hanson Trust, PLC, has a well-defined core competence in the acquisition and management of businesses in mature markets (Hill and Jones, 1992). Indeed, the essential elements of this core competence can be described in a series of guiding principles (see Table 11.3). Over the years, Hanson Trust has developed certain management principles and has applied them to the managing of each of the mature businesses it has acquired. Despite the clear core competence that exists at Hanson Trust, the different businesses share virtually no activities. Indeed, the lack of activity sharing among Hanson businesses is a manifestation of Hanson's core competence in acquiring and managing businesses in mature markets.

TABLE 11.3

Core Competencies at Hanson Trust—a Seemingly Unrelated Diversified Firm

Source: Summarized from Charles Hill, "Hanson PLC," in Charles Hill and Gareth Jones (1992). *Strategic Management*, 2d ed. Boston: Houghton Mifflin, pp. 764–783.

When considering a potential acquisition . . .

1. Focus on mature, low-technology industries with low current performance where current management has made some progress toward improving performance

2. Engage in intensive research, summarized on a single page, into a firm's performance and prospects, especially for firms contemplating a leveraged buyout

3. Evaluate the size and likelihood of the downside risk of an acquisition—the implications for Hanson if everything goes wrong

4. Evaluate the possibility of using the target's assets to secure debt for the acquisition effort

5. Evaluate the ability of disposing of some of the target's current businesses to pay down the debt from the acquisition

6. Evaluate how much excess overhead in a potential target can be eliminated after an acquisition

After an acquisition has occurred . . .

1. Eliminate excess overhead, sell off unwanted businesses, and reduce debt

2. Delegate to business managers all day-to-day operational decisions below capital expenditure limits set by Hanson

3. Exercise tight financial controls through operating budgets and capital spending limits

4. Create incentives, including bonuses, for business managers to meet their operating budget targets within their capital spending limits

5. Do not appoint business managers to Hanson's board of directors

6. Deemphasize any possible operating economies of scope among Hanson businesses

It would be easy to conclude that a firm like Hanson Trust, which does not share activities among its businesses, is pursuing a strategy of unrelated diversification (Hill and Jones, 1992). However, the existence of a well-defined core competence at Hanson suggests that this seemingly unrelated diversification is in fact a type of related diversification. Indeed, since all of Hanson's businesses must meet all of the criteria enumerated in Table 11.3, from this core competence perspective Hanson is actually pursuing a strategy of related-constrained diversification (Montgomery and Wernerfelt, 1988).

Other firms use shared activities to support or even create core competencies. For example, AT&T is currently developing the core competencies it will need to excel in the integrated computers and telecommunications industry of the near future (Kirkpatrick, 1993). To develop these competencies, AT&T has created several cross-business teams to develop technology (shared research and development), to analyze markets (shared marketing), and to facilitate product design (shared product design). Bell Labs continues to provide a shared research and development activity for all of AT&T's businesses. Other aspects of this new core competence at AT&T, including a new openness in management and a new organizational culture that supports individual creativity, are not directly supported by specific shared activities across AT&T businesses.

Core Competencies as an Economy of Scope. To understand how core competencies can reduce a firm's costs or increase revenues, it is necessary to understand how core competencies emerge over time. Most firms begin operations in a single business (Barney, 1990). Imagine that a firm has carefully evaluated all of its current business opportunities and has fully funded all of those with a positive net present value. Any of the above-normal returns that this firm has left over after fully funding all its current positive net present value opportunities can be thought of as free cash flow (Jensen, 1986). Firms can spend this free cash in a variety of ways: They can spend it on managerial perquisites; they can give it to shareholders; they can use it to invest in new businesses.

Suppose a firm chooses to use this cash to invest in a new business. In other words, suppose a firm chooses to implement a diversification strategy. If this firm is seeking to maximize the return from implementing this diversification strategy, which of all the possible businesses that it could invest in should it invest in? Obviously, a profit-maximizing firm will choose to begin operations in a business where it has a competitive advantage. What kind of business is likely to generate this competitive advantage for this firm? The obvious answer is a business where the same underlying resources and capabilities that gave this firm an advantage in its original business are still valuable, rare, and costly to imitate. Thus this first diversification move sees the firm investing in a business that is closely related to its original business, in that both businesses draw on a common set of underlying resources and capabilities where the firm already has a competitive advantage.

Put another way, a firm that diversifies by exploiting its resource and capability advantages in its original business will have lower costs than firms that begin a new business without these resource and capability advantages, or without higher revenues than firms lacking these advantages, or both. As long as this firm organizes itself to take advantage of these resources and capability advantages in its new business, it should earn an above-normal economic profit in its new business, along with the above-normal profit it will still be earning in its original business (Nayyar, 1990; Robins and Wiersma, 1995).

Of course, over time, this diversified firm is likely to develop new resources and capabilities through its operations in the new business. These new resources and capabilities enhance the entire set of skills that a firm might be able to bring to still another business. Using the above-normal profits it has obtained in its previous businesses, this firm is likely to enter another new business. Again, choosing from among all the new businesses it could enter, it is likely to begin operations in a business where it can exploit its now-expanded resource and capability advantages to obtain a competitive advantage, and so forth.

After a firm has engaged in this diversification strategy several times, the resources and capabilities that enable it to operate successfully in several businesses are its core competencies (Prahalad and Hamel, 1990). A firm develops these core competencies by transferring the technical and management knowledge, experience, and wisdom it developed in earlier businesses to its new diversified businesses. A firm that has just begun this diversification process has implemented a dominant-business strategy. If all of a firm's businesses share the same core competencies, then that firm has implemented a strategy of related-constrained diversification. If different businesses exploit different groups of resources and capabilities, that firm has implemented a strategy of related-linked diversification. In any case, these core competencies enable firms to have lower costs or higher revenues as they include more businesses in their diversified portfolio, compared to firms without these competencies.

Compare, for example, the performance of GTE and NEC (Prahalad and Hamel, 1990). In 1980, GTE was a large ($9.98 billion in sales) and successful telecommunications firm with business operations in telephones, telephone operations, communication-switching devices, semiconductors, and color display technologies (including color televisions). NEC was a much smaller firm ($3.8 billion in sales) with a similar technological base but no experience in managing telephone operations. However, by 1988, NEC had reversed positions with GTE, with sales of $21.89 billion compared to GTE sales of $16.46 billion.

Prahalad and Hamel (1990) attribute this difference in growth rates to NEC's willingness to invest in and leverage its core competencies. Early in the 1980s, NEC managers concluded that success in the worldwide telecommunications market would depend on unique resources and capabilities in the design, manufacture, and application of semiconductor technology. These resources and capabilities, NEC managers concluded, were the core competencies that would link NEC's diverse business operations. To develop these core competencies, NEC expanded its semiconductor operations and developed strategic alliances with several firms in the computer and telecommunications industries.

GTE, in contrast, managed each of its businesses as a separate operating unit and failed to develop any economies of scope to link them. Through the 1980s, GTE divested most of the businesses that could have helped it develop core competencies for the computing and communications industries, including the semiconductor and communication-switching devices businesses. By divesting these businesses, GTE was increasing its cost of operating in the computing and communications industries and forgoing revenues it could have obtained in these industries.

What is the result of these different strategies? NEC is well positioned to exploit the growing computing and communications industries, and GTE is essentially a regulated telephone operating company. By developing the resources and capabilities it would need to compete in the computing and communications industries, NEC put itself in a position where it could obtain lower costs and higher revenues from operations in these industries, compared to firms without these core competencies.

Of course, not all firms develop core competencies in this logical and rational manner. As was the case with emergent strategies (discussed in Chapter 1), some core competencies emerge over time as firms attempt to rationalize their diversification moves. However, no matter how a firm develops core competencies, to the extent that they enable a diversified firm to have lower costs or larger revenues in its business operations, these competencies can be thought of as sources of economies of scope.

Core Competencies and Outside Investors.   As is the case with shared activities, outside investors have little ability to create or exploit core competence links between businesses on their own. Rather, they must "hire" firms to create and exploit these operational economies of scale for them. Thus if core competencies do create synergies, they are likely to be economically valuable for firms pursuing a diversification strategy.

If core competencies do not create synergies, however, they will not be economically valuable even though outside investors cannot exploit them on their own. For example, PepsiCo has tried to leverage its marketing skills learned in the soft drink industry by entering the fast-food industry through its acquisition of Pizza Hut, Taco Bell, and Kentucky Fried Chicken. Thus far, PepsiCo has experienced only moderate success in these diversification moves (Sellers, 1995). Kodak has had similar difficulties leveraging its imaging skills in the emerging digital-imaging industry (Nulty, 1995), as has PolyGram in leveraging its entertainment expertise in the movie industry (Tracht-enberg and Pope, 1995). In all these cases, core competence-based economies of scope may prove illusory.

The Limits of Core Competencies.   Just as there are limits to the value of shared activities as sources of economies of scope, so there are limits on core competencies as sources of these economies. The first of these limitations stems from important organizational issues to be discussed in Chapter 12. The way that a diversified firm is organized can either facilitate the exploitation of core competencies or prevent this exploitation from occurring.

A second limitation of core competencies is a result of the intangible nature of these economies of scope. Whereas shared activities are reflected in tangible operations in a diversified firm, core competencies may be reflected only in shared knowledge, experience, and wisdom across businesses. Prahalad and Bettis (1986) emphasize the intangible character of these relationships when they describe them as a "dominant logic," or a common way of thinking about strategy across different businesses.

The intangibility of core competencies can lead diversified firms to make two kinds of errors in managing relatedness (Porter, 1985; Prahalad and Hamel, 1990). First, intangible core competencies can be illusory inventions by creative managers to justify poor diversification moves. Managers can always find some intangible core competencies to link even the most completely unrelated businesses and thereby justify their diversification strategy. A firm that manufactures airplanes and running shoes can rationalize this diversification by claiming to have a core competence in managing transportation businesses. A firm operating in the professional football business and the movie business can rationalize this diversification by claiming to have a core competence in managing entertainment businesses. Such "invented competencies" are not real sources of economies of scope.

Second, a diversified firm's businesses may be linked by a core competence, but this competence may affect these businesses' costs or revenues in a trivial way. Thus, for example, all of a firm's businesses may be affected by government actions, but the impact of these actions on costs and revenues in each business may be quite small. A firm may have a core competence in managing relationships with the government, but this core competence will not reduce costs or enhance revenues for these particular businesses very much. Also, each of a diversified firm's businesses may use some advertising. However, if advertising does not have a major impact on revenues for these businesses, core competencies in advertising are not likely to significantly reduce a firm's costs or increase its revenues. In this case, a core competence may be a source of economies of scope, but the value of those economies may be very small.

If a firm possesses core competencies and is able to avoid the limitations of this type of operational synergy, core competencies can be valuable economies of scope for a diversified firm.

DIVERSIFICATION TO EXPLOIT FINANCIAL ECONOMIES OF SCOPE

A second class of motivations for diversification shifts attention away from operational linkages among a firm's businesses and toward financial advantages associated with diversification. Three financial implications of diversification have been studied: diversification and capital allocation, diversification and risk reduction, and tax advantages of diversification.

Diversification and Capital Allocation

Capital can be allocated to businesses in one of two ways. First, businesses operating as independent entities can compete for capital in the external capital market. They do this by providing a sufficiently high return to induce investors to purchase shares of their equity, by having a sufficiently high cash flow to repay principal and interest on debt, and in other ways (Williamson, 1975). Alternatively, a business can be part of a diversified firm. That diversified firm competes in the external capital market and allocates capital among its various businesses. In a sense, diversification creates an internal capital market in which businesses in a diversified firm compete for corporate capital (Williamson, 1975).

Internal Capital Allocation as an Economy of Scope.   For an internal capital market to create value for a diversified firm, it must offer some efficiency advantages over an external capital market. Williamson (1975) has suggested that a potential efficiency gain from internal capital markets depends on the greater amount and quality of information that a diversified firm possesses about the businesses it owns, compared with the information that external suppliers of capital possess. Owning a business gives a diversified firm access to detailed and accurate information about the actual performance of the business, its true future prospects, and thus the actual amount of capital that should be allocated to it. External sources of capital, in contrast, have relatively limited access to information and thus have a limited ability to judge the actual performance and future prospects of a business (Williamson, 1975).

Some have questioned whether a diversified firm, as a source of capital, actually has more and better information about a business it owns, compared to external sources of capital. After all, independent businesses seeking capital have a strong incentive to provide sufficient information to external suppliers of capital to obtain required funds. However, a firm that owns a business may have at least two informational advantages over external sources of capital.

First, although an independent business has an incentive to provide information to external sources of capital, it also has an incentive to downplay or even not report any negative information about its performance and prospects (recall the discussion of the limits of accounting measures of performance in Section 2.3). Such negative information would raise an independent firm's cost of capital (Copeland and Weston, 1983). External sources of capital have limited ability to force a business to reveal all information about its performance and prospects and thus may provide capital at a lower cost than would be the case if they had full information. Ownership gives a firm the right to compel more complete disclosure, although even here full disclosure is not guaranteed (Williamson, 1975). With this more complete information, a diversified firm can allocate just the right amount of capital, at the appropriate cost, to each business.

Second, an independent business may have an incentive not to reveal all the positive information about its performance and prospects. In Chapter 5, the ability of a firm to earn above-normal profits was shown to depend on the imitability of a firm's resources and capabilities. An independent business that informs external sources of capital about all of its sources of competitive advantage is also informing its potential competitors about these sources of advantage. This information sharing increases the probability that these sources of advantage will be imitated (Barney, 1991). Because of the competitive implications of sharing this information, firms may choose not to share it, and external sources of capital may underestimate the true performance and prospects of a business.

A diversified firm, however, may gain access to this additional positive information about its businesses without revealing it to potential competitors. This information enables the diversified firm to make more informed decisions about how much capital to allocate to a business and about the cost of that capital, compared to the external capital market (Williamson, 1975).

Over time, there should be fewer errors in funding businesses through internal capital markets, compared to funding businesses through external capital markets. Fewer funding errors, over time, suggest a slight capital allocation advantage for a diversified firm, compared to an external capital market. This advantage should be reflected in somewhat higher rates of return on invested capital for the diversified firm, compared to the rates of return on invested capital for external sources of capital (Williamson, 1975).

The businesses within a diversified firm do not necessarily gain cost-of-capital advantages by being part of a diversified firm's portfolio. Several authors have argued that since a diversified firm has lower overall risk (see discussion below), it will have a lower cost of capital, which it can pass along to the businesses within its portfolio. Although the lower risks associated with a diversified firm may lower the firm's cost of capital, the appropriate cost of capital of businesses within the firm depends on the performance and prospects of those businesses. The firm's advantages in evaluating its businesses' performance and prospects result in more appropriate capital allocation, not just in lower cost of capital for those businesses. Indeed, a business's cost of capital may be lower than what it could have obtained in the external capital market (because the firm is able to more fully evaluate the positive aspects of that business), or it may be greater than what it could have obtained in the external capital market (because the firm is able to more fully evaluate the negative aspects of that business) (Williamson, 1975).

Of course, if these businesses also have lower cost or higher revenue expectations because they are part of a diversified firm, then those cost/revenue advantages will be reflected in the appropriate cost of capital for these businesses. In this sense, any operational economies of scope for businesses in a diversified firm may be recognized by a diversified firm exploiting financial economies of scope.

Capital Allocation and Outside Investors. If diversified firms possess capital allocation advantages over external capital markets, then outside investors will typically be unable to duplicate this advantage. Generally, outside investors have no more information than external capital markets have about the prospects of a business. Thus to gain the benefits of these capital allocation economies of scope, outside investors will have to rely on the manager of a diversified firm.

An obvious exception to this generalization exists if an outside investor happens to possess the same type and quality of information about the prospects of a business as the managers of a diversified firm possess. Armed with such information, such investors could duplicate the advantages of internal capital markets on their own.

Limits on Internal Capital Markets.　Although internal capital allocation has several potential advantages for a diversified firm, several limits of this process also exist. First, the level and type of diversification that a firm pursues can affect the efficiency of this allocation process. A firm that implements a strategy of unrelated diversification, where managers have to evaluate the performance and prospects of numerous very different businesses, puts a greater strain on the capital allocation skills of its managers than does a firm that implements related diversification (Barney and Ouchi, 1986). Indeed, in the extreme, the capital allocation efficiency of a firm pursuing broad-based unrelated diversification will probably not be superior to the capital allocation efficiency of the external capital market.

Second, the increased efficiency of internal capital allocation depends on managers in a diversified firm having better information for capital allocation than the information available to external sources of capital. However, this higher-quality information is not guaranteed. The incentives that can lead managers to exaggerate their performance and prospects to external capital sources can also lead to this behavior within a diversified firm. Indeed, several examples of business managers falsifying performance records to gain access to more internal capital have been reported (Perry and Barney, 1981). Research suggests that capital allocation requests by managers are routinely discounted in diversified firms in order to correct for these managers' inflated estimates of the performance and prospects of their businesses (Bethel, 1990).

Finally, not only do business managers have an incentive to inflate the performance and prospects of their business in a diversified firm, but managers in charge of capital allocation in these firms may have an incentive to continue investing in a business despite its poor performance and prospects. The reputation and status of these managers often depend on the success of these business investments, since they often initially approved them (Staw, 1981). These managers often continue throwing good money at these businesses in hope that they will someday improve, thereby justifying their original decision. Staw calls this process "escalation of commitment" and has presented numerous examples of managers' becoming irrationally committed to a particular investment (Staw, 1981).

Research on the value of internal capital markets in diversified firms suggests that, on average, the limitations of these markets often outweigh their advantages. For example, even controlling for firm size, excessive investment in poorly performing businesses in a diversified firm reduces the market value of the average diversified firm (Comment and Jarrell, 1995). However, the fact that many firms do not gain the advantages associated with internal capital markets does not necessarily imply that no firms gain these advantages. If only a few firms are able to obtain the advantages of internal capital markets while successfully avoiding their limitations, this financial economy of scope may be a source of at least a temporary competitive advantage.

Diversification and Risk Reduction

Another possible financial economy of scope for a diversified firm has already been briefly mentioned—that is, the risk of diversified firms is lower than the risk of undiversified firms. Consider, for example, the risk of two businesses operating separately, compared to the risk of a diversified firm operating in those same two businesses simultaneously. If the risk of returns in Business I (measured by the standard deviation of those returns over time) is sd_I, and the risk of returns in Business II (measured by the standard deviation of those returns over time) is sd_{II}, and if these two returns are distributed normally, then the risk of a diversified firm operating in both businesses simultaneously is given by

$$sd_{I,II} = \sqrt{w^2 sd_I^2 + (1-w)^2 sd_{II} + 2w(1-w)COV_{I,II}} \qquad Eq.\ 11.2$$

where,

$sd_{I,II}$ = the riskiness of the combined businesses

w = the percentage of the total investment in this diversified firm invested in Business I

$(1-w)$ = the percentage of the total investment in this diversified firm invested in Business II

$COV_{I,II}$ = the correlation of the returns of Business I and Business II times the standard deviation of returns in Business I and Business II

or

$$COV_{I,II} = r_{I,II} sd_I sd_{II} \qquad Eq.\ 11.3$$

where,

$r_{I,II}$ = the correlation of returns of Business I and Business II

If $sd_I = .8$, $sd_{II} = 1.3$, $w = .4$, and $r_{I,II} = -.8$, then Eq. (11.2) becomes

$$sd_{I,II} = \sqrt{(.4)^2(.8)^2 + (1 - .4)^2(1.3)^2 + 2(.4)(1 - .4)[(-.8)(.8)(1.3)]}$$

$$= .558 \qquad\qquad\qquad\qquad Eq.\ 11.4$$

Notice that the risk of engaging in Business I and Business II simultaneously (.558) is less than the risk of engaging either in Business I by itself (.8) or in Business II by itself (1.3). This risk of engaging in both businesses simultaneously will be lower, compared to engaging in at least one of these businesses, as long as the returns from Business I and Business II are not perfectly and positively correlated—that is, as long as $r_{I,II} < 1.0$. For example, if $r_{I,II} = -.2$, then $sd_{I,II} = .782$ (the diversified firm is still less risky than either business operated separately); if $r_{I,II} = .7$, then $sd_{I,II} = 1.0296$ (the diversified firm is riskier than Business I by itself but less risky than Business II by itself).

Of course, this analysis can be generalized to firms pursuing more than two businesses simultaneously. It can also be generalized to multiple businesses whose returns are not normally distributed (Copeland and Weston, 1983). The fundamental conclusion of this analysis remains unchanged: Firms can reduce their overall risk by engaging in multiple businesses with imperfectly correlated returns over time.

Although a firm can reduce its overall risk by engaging in a set of diversified businesses, such risk-reducing strategies are generally not valuable to a firm's investors (Chang and Thomas, 1989). These investors, including equity holders and debt holders, have lower-cost ways to reduce their risk (Williamson, 1975; Golbe, 1981).

Equity and debt holders can reduce their risk by investing, either directly or through mutual funds, in a fully diversified portfolio of stocks and bonds. The cost of creating and maintaining this diversified portfolio (that is, commissions to brokers or management fees to mutual funds) is much less than the cost of conceiving and implementing a corporate diversification strategy (that is, salaries and bonuses for corporate managers). Moreover, equity and debt holders can modify their portfolios at very low cost. Modifying a diversified firm's portfolio of businesses, through mergers and acquisitions, internal development, or other means, is likely to be much more costly. For these reasons, equity and debt holders prefer to diversify their portfolios to reduce risk themselves, rather than have firm managers diversify to reduce risk for them (Jensen, 1986; Jensen and Meckling, 1976). Empirical research in several industries suggests that when firms pursue diversification strategies solely to reduce risk, these strategies reduce the economic performance of these firms (Hill and Hansen, 1991; Amit and Livnat, 1988b).

This analysis does not necessarily imply that equity and debt holders will object to all forms of firm diversification. For example, diversification that enables a firm to exploit operational economies of scope (either through shared activities or core competencies) can increase the expected rate of return for these investors. Also, diversification that enables a firm to exploit capital allocation efficiencies can be valuable to these stakeholders. Rather, equity and debt holders will object to diversification whose *sole* purpose is risk reduction.

Tax Advantages of Diversification

Another financial economy of scope from diversification stems from possible tax advantages of this corporate strategy. These possible tax advantages reflect one or a combination of two effects. First, a diversified firm can use losses in some of its businesses to offset profits in others, thereby reducing its overall tax liability (Scott, 1977). Of course, substantial losses in some of its businesses may overwhelm profits in other businesses, forcing businesses that would have remained solvent if they were independent to cease operation. However, as long as business losses are not too large, a diversified firm's tax liability can be reduced. Empirical research suggests that diversified firms do, sometimes, offset profits in some businesses with losses in others, although the tax savings of these activities are quite small (Copeland and Weston, 1983).

Second, Brennan (1979), Cox, Ross, and Rubinstein (1979), and Stapleton (1982) show that diversification can increase a firm's debt capacity. This effect on debt capacity is greatest when the cash flows of a diversified firm's businesses are perfectly and negatively correlated (Copeland and Weston, 1983). However, even when these cash flows are perfectly and positively correlated, there can still be a (modest) increase in debt capacity.

Debt capacity is important in tax environments when interest payments on debt are tax deductible. In this context, diversified firms can increase their leverage up to their debt capacity and reduce their tax liability accordingly. Of course, if interest payments are not tax deductible, or if the marginal corporate tax rate is relatively small, then the tax advantages of diversification can be quite small (Galai and Masulis, 1976). Recent empirical work suggests that diversified firms do have greater debt capacity than undiversified firms. However, low marginal corporate tax rates, at least in the United States, make the accompanying tax savings quite small (Copeland and Weston, 1983).

DIVERSIFICATION TO EXPLOIT ANTICOMPETITIVE ECONOMIES OF SCOPE

A third group of motivations for diversification is based on the relationship between diversification strategies and various anticompetitive activities by firms. Two specific examples of these activities are (1) multipoint competition to facilitate mutual forbearance and tacit collusion and (2) exploiting market power.

Multipoint Competition

Multipoint competition exists when two or more diversified firms simultaneously compete in multiple markets. For example, Hewlett-Packard and IBM compete in both the minicomputer market and the market for computer printers. Michelin and Goodyear compete in both the U.S. automobile tire market and the European automobile tire market. Ford and General Motors compete in both the automobile market and the defense electronics market (Karnani and Wernerfelt, 1985).

Multipoint competition can serve to facilitate a particular type of tacit collusion called *mutual forbearance.* Consider the situation facing two diversified firms, A and B. These two firms operate in the same businesses, I, II, III, and IV (see Fig. 11.3). In this context, any decisions that Firm A might make to compete aggressively in Businesses I and III must take into account the possibility that Firm B will respond by competing aggressively in Businesses II and IV, and vice versa.

The potential loss that each of these firms may experience in some of its businesses must be compared to the potential gain that each might obtain if it exploits competitive advantages in other of its businesses (Bernheim and Whinston, 1990). If the present value of gains does not outweigh the present value of losses from retaliation, then both firms will avoid competitive activity. Refraining from competition is mutual forbearance (Tirole, 1988; Edwards, 1955; Bernheim and Whinston, 1990).

Mutual forbearance as a result of multipoint competition has occurred in several industries. Karnani and Wernerfelt (1985) describe this form of tacit collusion between Michelin and Goodyear, Maxwell House and Folger's, Caterpillar and John Deere, and BIC and Gillette. Another clear example of such cooperation can be found in the airline industry (Gimeno, 1994). In November 1989, America West began service into the Houston Intercontinental Airport with very low introductory fairs. Continental Airlines, the dominant firm at Houston Intercontinental, rapidly responded to America West's low Houston fares by reducing the price of its flights from Phoenix, Arizona, to several cities in the United States. Phoenix is the home airport of America West. Within just a few weeks, America West withdrew its low intro-

FIGURE 11.3
Multipoint
Competition Between
Hypothetical Firms A
and B

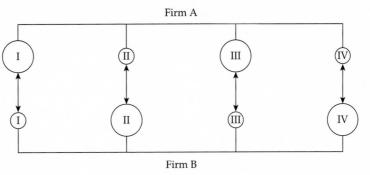

ductory fares in the Houston market, and Continental withdrew its reduced prices in the Phoenix market. The threat of retaliation across markets apparently led America West and Continental to tacitly collude on prices.

However, sometimes multipoint competition does not lead to mutual forbearance. Consider, for example, the conflict between Walt Disney Company and Time Warner (Landro, Reilly, and Turner, 1993). Disney operates in the theme park, movie and television production, and television broadcasting industries. Time Warner operates in the theme park and movie and television production industries and also operates a very large magazine business (*Time, People, Sports Illustrated,* and so forth). From 1988 through 1993, Disney spent over $40 million in advertising its theme parks in Time Warner magazines. Despite this substantial revenue, Time Warner began an aggressive advertising campaign aimed at wooing customers away from Disney theme parks to its own. Disney retaliated by canceling all of its advertising in Time Warner magazines. Time Warner responded to Disney's actions by canceling a corporate meeting to be held in Florida at Disney World. Disney responded to Time Warner's meeting cancellation by refusing to broadcast Time Warner theme park advertisements on its Los Angeles television station (Reilly and Turner, 1993).

Some recent research investigates the conditions under which mutual forbearance strategies are pursued, as well as conditions under which multipoint competition does not lead to mutual forbearance (Gimeno, 1994). In general, the value of the threat of retaliation must be substantial for multipoint competition to lead to mutual forbearance. However, not only must the payoffs to mutual forbearance be substantial, but the firms pursuing this strategy must have strong strategic linkages among their diversified businesses (smith and Wilson, 1995). Bernheim and Whinston (1990) recognize this strategic linkage requirement when they model mutual forbearance, assuming that firms choose optimal price/quantity levels across all the diversified businesses they invest in, simultaneously. This suggests that firms pursuing mutual forbearance strategies based on multipoint competition are pursuing a form of related diversification.

To the extent that diversified firms use multipoint competition to implement mutual forbearance strategies, and to the extent that these strategies enable these firms to have lower costs or higher revenues than would be the case otherwise, this type of tacit collusion can be valuable for a diversified firm. Moreover, outside investors cannot generally create these synergies on their own. In this sense, mutual forbearance can be a source of valuable economies of scope.

Diversification and Market Power

Internal allocations of capital among a diversified firm's businesses may enable a firm to exploit in some of its businesses the market power advantages it enjoys in other of its businesses. For example, suppose that a firm is earning monopoly profits in a particular business. This firm can use some of these monopoly profits to subsidize the operations of another of its businesses. This cross-subsidization can take several forms, including predatory pricing—that is, setting prices so that they are less than the subsidized business's costs (Tirole, 1988). The effect of this cross-subsidy may be to drive competitors out of the subsidized business and then to obtain monopoly profits in that subsidized business. In a sense, diversification enables a firm to apply its monopoly power in several different businesses. Economists call this a "deep pockets" model of diversification (Tirole, 1988).

Diversified firms with operations in regulated monopolies have been criticized for this kind of cross-subsidization. For example, most of the regional telephone companies in the United States are engaging in diversification strategies. The consent decree that forced the breakup of AT&T expressly forbids cross-subsidies between these regional companies' telephone monopolies and other business activities, under the assumption that such subsidies would give these firms an unfair competitive advantage in their diversified business activities (Carnevale, 1993).

The distinction between cross-subsidies to exploit market power as an economy of scope and other economies of scope is subtle at best. For other economies of scope, especially operating economies and capital allocation economies, the objective of diversification is to reduce a firm's costs or increase its revenues. For market power economies of scope, the objective is to enable a business to sustain losses caused by predatory pricing long enough to force competitors out of business. For all these economies of scope, competing independent firms may be at a competitive disadvantage. However, in the case of operating economies of scope and capital allocation economies of scope, that competitive disadvantage reflects a diversified firm's increased efficiency. In the anticompetitive case, that disadvantage reflects a diversified firm's market power (Gimeno, 1994).

Although these market power economies of scope, in principle, may exist, relatively little empirical work documents their existence (Grant, 1991). Indeed, research on regulated utilities diversifying into nonregulated businesses suggests not that these firms use monopoly profits in their regulated businesses to unfairly subsidize nonregulated businesses but that the poor management skills developed in the regulated businesses tend to make diversification less profitable rather than more profitable (Russo, 1992). Thus it has yet to be established that the inequality in Eq. (11.1) holds for diversification strategies designed to exploit market power.

EMPLOYEE INCENTIVES TO DIVERSIFY

Employees may have incentives to diversify that are independent of any benefits from other sources of economies of scope. This is especially the case for employees in senior management positions and employees with long tenure in a particular firm. These employee incentives reflect the interest of employees to diversify their human capital investments and the relationship between firm size and management compensation. Both motivations are examples of agency problems associated with diversification (Jensen and Meckling, 1976)—that is, they are examples of conflicts of interest between employees and other stakeholders of a firm.

Diversifying Human Capital Investments

An employee with long tenure in a particular firm has made substantial firm-specific human capital investments (Amihud and Lev, 1981). These are investments in understanding an organization's culture, policies, and procedures, knowing the "right" people to contact to complete a task, and so forth. Such investments have significant value in the firm where they were developed but almost no value in other firms. If a firm were to cease operations, employees would instantly lose almost all of this firm-specific human capital investment. To reduce this risk, employees can diversify their human capital investments. A low-cost way to accomplish this diversification is for a firm to implement a corporate diversification strategy. Thus the reduced risk of bankruptcy stemming from corporate diversification is a direct benefit to employees, especially employees with long tenure.

Research suggests that some corporate diversification strategies are pursued so managers can diversify their firm-specific human capital investments. For example, Amihud and Lev (1981) show that manager-controlled firms (firms whose equity is widely held by numerous small investors) are more diversified than owner-controlled firms (firms whose equity is closely held by a small number of large investors). Thus managers who are left to pursue their own interests in manager-controlled firms opt for higher levels of diversification.

Although diversification of human capital investments is in the self-interest of managers with substantial firm-specific human capital investments, such diversification by itself is not an economy of scope—that is, the inequality in Eq. (11.1) does not hold. However, it will be the case that a firm pursuing a diversification strategy for any of the valuable motivations discussed previously will also have the effect of diversifying the human capital investments of its managers.

Firm Size and Management Compensation

A second agency motivation for diversification depends on the relationship between firm size and managerial compensation. Research over the years demonstrates conclusively that the primary determinant of the compensation of top managers in a firm is not the economic performance of the firm but the size of the firm, usually measured in sales. Thus managers seeking to maximize their income should attempt to grow their firm (Finkelstein and Hambrick, 1989). One of the easiest ways to grow a firm is through diversification, especially unrelated diversification through mergers and acquisitions. By making large acquisitions, a diversified firm can grow substantially in a short period of time, leading senior managers to earn higher incomes (Finkelstein and Hambrick, 1989). All of this is independent of any economic profit that diversification may or may not generate. Senior managers need only worry about economic profit if the level of that profit is so low that unfriendly takeovers are a threat or so low that the board of directors may be forced to replace management (Jensen and Meckling, 1976).

Recently, the traditional relationship between firm size and management compensation has begun to break down. As suggested in Section 10.3, more and more, the compensation of senior managers is being tied to economic performance of firms. In particular, the use of stock options and other forms of deferred compensation makes it in management's self-interest to be concerned with economic performance.

These changes in compensation do not necessarily imply that firms will abandon all forms of diversification. They do suggest that firms will abandon those forms of diversification that do not generate real economies of scope.

MOTIVES FOR DIVERSIFICATION AND TYPES OF DIVERSIFICATION

The different motives for diversification listed in Table 11.1 have implications for the type of diversification strategy a firm pursues. The relationship between motives for diversification and type of diversification are summarized in Table 11.4.

Operating economies of scope, including shared activities and core competencies, can be realized only under conditions of related diversification. Indeed, operational links among a related-diversified firm's businesses are the sources of these economies of scope. If all the businesses in a diversified firm share the same activities or build on the

TABLE 11.4 **Relationship Between** **Motivation for** **Diversification and** **Type of** **Diversification**	Motivation	Related Diversification	Unrelated Diversification
	Operating economies of scope		
	■ Shared activities	X	
	■ Core competencies	X	
	Financial economies of scope		
	■ Internal capital allocation	X	
	■ Risk reduction		X
	■ Tax advantages		X
	Anticompetitive economies of scope		
	■ Multipoint competition	X	
	■ Exploiting market share	X	X
	Employee incentives for diversification		
	■ Diversifying employees' human capital investments		X
	■ Maximizing management compensation	X	X

same core competencies, that firm is pursuing related-constrained diversification. If different businesses share different activities or different core competencies, that firm is pursuing a related-linked diversification.

Capital allocation, as a financial economy of scope, can usually be realized only when a firm implements a strategy of related diversification, either related-constrained or related-linked. For internal capital markets to have a capital allocation advantage over external capital markets, firm managers must have access to better information than the information available to external sources of capital. Moreover, internal managers must be able to evaluate and interpret this information in a more subtle and complex way, to understand a business's performance and prospects more completely than external sources of capital (Williamson, 1975). These information-processing requirements are most likely to be met when a firm's multiple businesses are related along several important dimensions. In this case, evaluation experience developed in one business can be used in evaluating other businesses.

On the other hand, risk reduction, as a financial economy of scope, is accomplished most effectively through a strategy of unrelated diversification. Recall that firm risk is reduced most completely when the expected rates of return among a firm's businesses are perfectly and negatively correlated. This implies that these businesses are in very different industries, with very different changes in demand over time. Both characteristics are consistent with unrelated diversification. Of course, this is not to suggest that related diversification does not reduce a firm's risk. As long as a firm's businesses' cash flows are not perfectly and positively correlated, any form of diversification will reduce firm risk to some degree.

The same arguments apply to tax savings as a form of financial economy of scope. The chance that losses in some businesses will offset profits in other businesses is greater if those businesses' cash flows are not positively correlated over time—that is, if a firm is pursuing unrelated diversification. Debt capacity and the ability to deduct interest payments are also greatest in the unrelated case, although even in the case where businesses' cash flows are perfectly and positively correlated, diversification can have a small positive impact on debt capacity.

Multipoint competition leading to mutual forbearance is most likely to operate in conditions of related diversification. Recall that mutual forbearance requires firm managers to set price and output levels across all their diversified businesses simultaneously. This joint price/output determination process is a form of related diversification.

Exploiting market power as an anticompetitive economy of scope, on the other hand, can operate in either related or unrelated diversification strategies. Managers in a diversified firm seeking to exploit market power advantages may adopt the joint price/output determination process described for multipoint competition. Alternatively, firms exploiting their market power advantages may simply allocate monopoly profits from one business to support price competition in another business. This simple reallocation process assumes fewer linkages between firms than does joint price/output determination in mutual forbearance strategies.

Employees' efforts to diversify human capital investments are most likely to succeed when a firm pursues unrelated diversification. The negative or zero correlation among these businesses' cash flows has the effect of reducing the firm's risk, which in turn diversifies the human capital investments of employees. On the other hand, managerial objectives to grow a firm, in order to maximize compensation, can be accomplished through either related or unrelated diversification. Both strategies can lead to rapid growth in firm sales, although related diversification that exploits valuable economies of scope may, in the long run, generate profits more effectively than unrelated diversification.

THE LIMITS OF UNRELATED DIVERSIFICATION

One of the interesting implications of Table 11.4 concerns important limits to the ability of unrelated diversification to add value to a firm. Each of the diversification motives that seem to hold the greatest potential for adding value to a firm (shared activities, core competencies, efficient internal capital allocation, and mutual forbearance strategies) are most likely to be realized under conditions of related diversification. Motives for diversification that have small positive, or even negative, effects on firm value (risk reduction, tax motivations, exploiting market power, human capital diversification, and employee compensation) are most likely to be realized under conditions of unrelated diversification or can operate in either unrelated or related diversification. The general conclusion is that unrelated diversification is less likely than related diversification to add value to a firm (Chatterjee and Wernerfelt, 1991).

This observation is consistent with a very large literature that examines the relationship between diversification and firm performance. This literature, summarized in Table 11.5, generally shows that related diversified firms outperform unrelated diversified firms. Much of the corporate restructuring that occurred in the 1980s and 1990s can be understood as an effort by unrelated diversified firms to rationalize their portfolio of businesses (Williams, Paez, Sanders, 1988).

Specific examples of how unrelated diversification has hurt firm performance are legion. For example, Kinder Care Learning Centers, a day-care management firm, once entered the savings and loan business. Within a short period of time, Kinder Care had to file for bankruptcy

TABLE 11.5
Empirical Research Examining the Value of Related and Unrelated Diversification

Authors	Findings	Comments
Weston and Mansinghka, 1971	Diversification outperforms no diversification	Differences are not statistically significant
Rumelt, 1974	Related diversification outperforms unrelated	Early application of definitions in Fig. 11.1
Berry, 1975	Related diversification outperforms unrelated	Diversification defined through SIC code industries
Levitt, 1975	Diversification outperforms no diversification	Compares alternative ways of diversifying
Salter and Weinhold, 1979	Unrelated diversification underperforms industry averages	
Jacquemin and Berry, 1979	Related diversification outperforms unrelated	SIC code industries
Christensen and Montgomery, 1981	Related diversification outperforms unrelated	Most of performance difference due to R&D, risk, and capital intensity
Bettis, 1981	Related diversification outperforms unrelated	Economies in marketing, R&D, risk, and capital intensity important
Bettis and Hall, 1982	No difference between related and unrelated	Rumelt's findings due to biased sample
Rumelt, 1982	Related diversification outperforms unrelated	Controls for market structure
Backaitis et al., 1984	Related diversification outperforms unrelated	Focuses on role of market power
Michel and Shaked, 1984	Unrelated diversification outperforms related	Reverses traditional finding
Lecraw, 1984	Related diversification outperforms unrelated	Return on equity; Canadian sample
Montgomery and Singh, 1984	Unrelated diversifiers have higher systematic risk	Debt and market position lead to this risk increase
Bettis and Mahajan, 1985	Related diversification outperforms unrelated	Relatedness necessary but not sufficient for high performance; control for industry growth

(continues)

TABLE 11.5
Empirical Research Examining the Value of Related and Unrelated Diversification *(continued)*

Authors	Findings	Comments
Palepu, 1985	Related diversification outperforms unrelated	
Varadarajan, 1986	Related diversification outperforms unrelated	
Jose, Nichols, and Stevens, 1986	Related diversification outperforms unrelated	Focuses on market value of firm; control for R&D and promotional activities
Grant et al., 1986	Related diversification outperforms unrelated	Both product and international diversification are important
Galbraith et al., 1986	Unrelated diversification most valuable in uncertain settings	
Varadarajan and Ramanujam, 1987	Related diversification outperforms unrelated	Focuses on return on equity and invested capital
Dubofsky and Varadarajan, 1987	Related diversification outperforms unrelated	Risk-adjusted return on equity
Grant et al., 1988	Related diversification outperforms unrelated	United Kingdom sample
Amit and Livnat, 1988a	Related diversification outperforms unrelated	Unrelated does lead to stable cash flows, and high leverage
Amit and Livnat, 1988b	Unrelated diversification is associated with lower risk	
Simmods, 1990	Related diversification does not outperform unrelated	Controls for effects of mergers and acquisitions on firm performance
Nguyen and Devinney, 1990	Technologically related activities do generate economies of scope	Canadian sample
Grant and Jammine, 1988	Related diversification does not outperform unrelated	Control for industry effects, United Kingdom sample
Robins and Wiersma, 1995	Related diversification outperforms unrelated	Relatedness measured by focusing on core competencies across businesses

protection (Jereski, 1993). Tenneco, a much larger unrelated diversified firm, suffered relatively low performance until Mike Walsh began rationalizing this firm's portfolio of business (Field, 1991). Unrelated diversification at Beatrice (Bailey, 1990), ITT (Sherman, 1995), and numerous other firms has been associated with the relatively low performance cited in Table 11.5. This is why fewer and fewer firms are implementing a strategy of pure unrelated diversification.

11.3   DIVERSIFICATION AND SUSTAINED COMPETITIVE ADVANTAGE

The research summarized in Table 11.5 suggests that related diversification can be valuable and unrelated diversification is usually not valuable. However, as we have seen with all the other strategies discussed in this book, the fact that a strategy is valuable does not necessarily imply that it will be a source of sustained competitive advantage. In order for diversification to be a source of sustained competitive advantage, it must be not only valuable but also rare and costly to imitate, and a firm must be organized to implement this strategy. The rareness and imitability of diversification are discussed in this section; organizational questions are deferred until Chapter 12.

THE RARENESS OF DIVERSIFICATION

At first glance, it seems clear that diversification per se is usually not a rare firm strategy. Most large firms have adopted some form of diversification, if only the limited diversification of a dominant-business firm. Even many small and medium-size firms have adopted different levels of diversification strategy.

However, the rareness of diversification depends not on diversification per se but on how rare the particular economy of scope associated with that diversification is. For example, it has already been suggested that NEC has been developing core competencies that will enable it to compete successfully in an integrated computing and communications industry (Prahalad and Hamel, 1990). However, recent reports suggest that AT&T is developing similar core competencies (Kirkpatrick, 1993). If both reports are accurate, then when businesses within NEC and AT&T begin competing, the economies of scope obtained from these firms' core competencies will be less rare than would be the case if they had not both developed these competencies. Returns to these economies of scope will be reduced.

The shared software development activities described at Hewlett-Packard (Yoder, 1991) may be a more rare economy of scope. Several computer firms share software development activities, but few firms share these activities across the same set of businesses as Hewlett-Packard (that is, across plotters, printers, personal computers, and minicomputers). This rare shared activity may give HP businesses an economy of scope that competing firms do not possess.

THE IMITABILITY OF DIVERSIFICATION

Both forms of imitation—direct duplication and substitution—are relevant in evaluating the ability of diversification strategies to generate sustained competitive advantages even if the economies of scope that they create are rare.

Direct Duplication of Diversification

Although a particular diversified firm may not currently enjoy certain economies of scope, it may act to gain those economies. However, as will be seen in Chapter 12, developing the cooperative relations among the businesses in a diversified firm that are needed to gain these economies is often not easy. These relationships are socially complex, requiring time to develop and nurture. Research suggests that even firms dedicated to developing these economies of scope may not be able to do so, given a history of competitive relations among businesses. For this reason, firms seeking economies of scope to support the operations of their businesses may opt for substitutes for diversification.

Substitutes for Diversification

Two obvious substitutes for diversification exist. First, instead of obtaining cost or revenue advantages from exploiting economies of scope across businesses, a firm may decide to simply grow and develop each of its businesses separately. In this sense, a firm that successfully implements a cost-leadership strategy in a business or a product differentiation strategy in a business can obtain the cost or revenue advantages of economies of scope, but without developing cross-business relations. Growing independent businesses in a diversified firm can be a substitute for exploiting economies of scope in a diversification strategy.

One firm that has chosen this course is Nestlé. Nestlé exploits few, if any, economies of scope among its different businesses. Rather, Nestlé has focused its efforts on growing each of its international operations to the point that they obtain cost or revenue advantages that could have been obtained in some form of related diversification. Thus, for example, Nestlé's operation in the United States is sufficiently large to exploit economies of scale in production, sales, and marketing, without reliance on economies of scope between U.S. operations and operations in other countries (Templeman, 1993).

A second substitute for exploiting economies of scope in diversification can be found in strategic alliances. By using a strategic alliance, firms can gain the economies of scope they could have obtained if they had carefully developed relations across businesses they owned. Thus, for example, instead of a firm exploiting research and development economies between two businesses, it might form a strategic alliance with a different firm and form a joint research and development lab. Instead of a firm exploiting sales economies by linking its businesses through a common sales force, it might develop a sales agreement with another firm and obtain cost or revenue advantages in this way. A well-publicized alliance between MCI and British Telecom can be understood as a partial substitute for AT&T's diversification strategy for offering international communication services to corporate customers (Keller and Carnevale, 1993).

Teece (1980) has developed an argument suggesting conditions under which obtaining economies of scope through diversification will be less costly than obtaining economies of scope through strategic alliances. In general, the cost of exploiting economies of scope internally, through diversification, will be lower when the threat of opportunistic action by potential alliance partners is greatest. When the probability of adverse selection, moral hazard, or holdup is significant in a strategic alliance, internal cooperation among diversified businesses may be a low-cost alternative for firms.

However, even when the threat of opportunism is not high, strategic alliances may still not be a low-cost substitute for diversification. As suggested in Section 9.3, the cooperative relations in strategic alliances are socially complex, often difficult to develop. Thus a firm that is unable to develop cooperative relations among its diversified businesses to exploit economies of scope may face significant challenges in developing cooperative relations with strategic alliance partners to exploit similar economies.

RESEARCH ON DIVERSIFICATION AND SUSTAINED COMPETITIVE ADVANTAGE

Most research on diversification fails to consider the rareness and imitability of the economies of scope that diversification seeks to create (Markides and Williamson, 1994). Most of this work implicitly compares the economic performance of firms that have diversified in a valuable way to the economic performance of firms that have not diversified in a valuable way, either by remaining a single-business firm or by implementing a strategy of unrelated diversification (Ramanujam and Varadarajan, 1989). Not surprisingly, most of this research—as summarized in Table 11.5—suggests that firms that have implemented a valuable dominant-business, related-constrained, or related-linked diversification strategy outperform firms that have implemented only a single-business or an unrelated diversification strategy.

However, this empirical research tends to misrepresent the actual competition that related-diversified firms face. Sometimes businesses in a diversified firm compete against single-business firms or against businesses in an unrelated diversified firm. However, often businesses in a diversified firm compete against other businesses in diversified firms. In this context, the kinds of economies of scope that these different diversified firms pursue—how rare and costly to imitate they are— can have a significant impact on the competitive position of a business. Even businesses in a diversified firm that compete against single-business firms or against businesses in unrelated diversified firms need to consider whether these businesses have obtained the same economies of scope they have through strategic substitutes.

For example, if Business A in Firm I competes against Business B in Firm II, and Firm I and Firm II exploit exactly the same economies of scope through their diversification strategies, then that diversification strategy will not be a source of competitive advantage for Business A or Business B. But if Business A in Firm I competes against Business C in Firm III, and Firm I exploits a valuable economy of scope through its diversification strategy while Firm III does not exploit a valuable economy of scope through its diversification strategy, then Business A may gain a competitive advantage from Firm I's diversification strategy, if Firm III has not found a strategic substitute for the economy of scope exploited by Firm I.

In both cases, all competing firms (I, II, and III) were implementing a diversification strategy. However, when that diversification strategy was valuable but not rare, diversification was *not* a source of competitive advantage. When that valuable diversification strategy was rare and costly to imitate, it could be a source of competitive advantage. Research that examines only the relationship between the level and type of diversification and a firm's competitive position fails to recognize the importance of the rareness and imitability of diversification strategies.

11.4   SUMMARY

Firms implement diversification strategies that range from limited diversification (single business, dominant business) to related diversification (related-constrained, related-linked) to unrelated diversification. In order to be valuable, diversification strategies must create economies of scope that individual investors find too costly to create or exploit.

Several motivations for implementing diversification strategies exist, including (1) exploiting operational economies of scope (shared activities, core competencies), (2) exploiting financial economies of scope (internal capital allocation, risk reduction, obtaining tax advantages), (3) exploiting anticompetitive economies of scope (multipoint competition, market power advantages), and (4) employee incentives to diversify (diversifying employees' human capital investments, maximizing management compensation). These different motivations for diversification vary in their value. They also are associated with different types of diversification. Motivations that lead to related diversification are most likely to add value to a firm. Motivations that lead to unrelated diversification are less likely to add value to a firm.

The ability of a diversification strategy to create sustained competitive advantages depends not only on the value of that strategy but also on its rareness and imitability. The rareness of a diversification strategy depends on the number of competing firms that are exploiting the same economies of scope through diversification. Imitation can occur either through direct duplication or through substitutes. Direct duplication can be costly, since exploiting most economies of scope requires cooperative, socially complex, relations among a firm's businesses. Important substitutes for diversification are (1) relevant economies obtained through independent actions of businesses within a firm and (2) relevant economies obtained through strategic alliances. Most research on diversification has failed to examine the rareness and imitability questions.

This discussion set aside important organizational issues in implementing diversification strategies (Nayyar, 1992). These issues are examined in detail in the next chapter.

REVIEW QUESTIONS

1. One simple way to think about relatedness is to look at the products or services a firm manufactures. The more similar these products or services are, the more related is the firm's diversification strategy. However, will firms that exploit core competencies in their diversification strategies always produce similar products or services? Why or why not?

2. A firm implementing a diversification strategy has just acquired what it claims is a strategically related target firm but announces that it is not going to change this recently acquired firm in any way. Will this type of diversifying acquisition enable the firm to realize any valuable economies of scope that could not be duplicated by outside investors on their own? Why or why not?

3. One of the reasons why internal capital markets may be more efficient than external capital markets is that firms may not want to reveal full information about their sources of competitive advantage to external capital markets, in order to reduce the threat of competitive imitation. This suggests that external capital markets may systematically undervalue firms with competitive advantages that are subject to imitation. Do you agree with this analysis? If yes, how could you trade on this information in your own investment activities? If no, why not?

4. A particular firm is owned by members of a single family; most of the wealth of this family is derived from the operations of this firm; and the family does not want to "go public" with the firm by selling its equity position to outside investors. Will this firm pursue a highly related diversification strategy or a somewhat less related diversification strategy? Why?

5. Under what conditions will a related diversification strategy *not* be a source of competitive advantage for a firm?

CHAPTER
12

Organizing to Implement Diversification Strategies

The arguments developed in Chapter 11 specify the conditions under which a diversification strategy can (1) add value to a firm (when it exploits a real economy of scope that cannot be easily duplicated by outside investors) and (2) be a source of temporary and sustained competitive advantage (when this economy of scope is valuable, rare, and costly to imitate). Throughout that discussion, the importance of efficiently organizing to implement a diversification strategy was emphasized. A firm may choose a diversification strategy for appropriate value-added and competitive reasons. However, if a firm does not organize itself to implement this strategy efficiently, this potential can be squandered, and the firm will lose some of its above-normal profits, or it will earn only normal or below-normal profits on its diversification strategy. Organizing issues are discussed in this chapter. We examine first the agency-cost-reducing objectives of this organizing effort and then the organizational structure, management control systems, and compensation policies that can be used to implement a diversification strategy.

12.1 AGENCY COSTS

One of the criteria, described in Chapter 11, for evaluating whether a particular economy of scope should be used as a basis of a diversification strategy is whether a firm's outside investors, at low cost, could duplicate that economy of scope. If independent investors, acting in their own behalf, could duplicate all the benefits of a particular economy of scope at very low cost, why would they want to "hire" managers in a firm to create this economy of scope for them? After all, hiring managers to create this economy of scope is a much more costly way of obtaining any benefits of this economy than investors' obtaining these benefits on their own would be.

When investors cannot realize an economy of scope on their own, however, it is in their self-interest to delegate to managers the day-to-day management of their financial investment in a firm. As a result, managers can use the investors' financial capital to exploit these economies of scope. Any economic profits generated from these economies of scope can be transferred back to the investors in the form of dividends or capital gains on the value of the investment.

Jensen and Meckling (1976) suggest that whenever one party to an exchange delegates decision-making authority to a second party, an agency relationship exists between these parties. The party delegating this decision-making authority is the *principal;* the party to whom this authority is delegated is the *agent.* In the context of diversification leveraging strategies, an agency relationship exists between a firm's outside stockholders (as principals) and its managers (as agents) to the extent that stockholders delegate the day-to-day management of their investment to those managers.

AGENCY RELATIONSHIPS AND AGENCY COSTS

The agency relationship between stockholders and managers can be very effective as long as managers make investment decisions in ways that are consistent with stockholders' interests. Thus, if stockholders are interested in maximizing the rate of return on their investment in a firm, and if managers make their investment decisions with the objective of maximizing the rate of return on those investments, then stockholders will have few concerns about delegating the day-to-day management of their investments to managers.

Unfortunately, in numerous situations the interests of a firm's outside stockholders and its managers do not coincide (Hill and Snell, 1988). When parties in an agency relationship differ in their decision-making objectives, agency problems arise. Parties in an agency relationship can engage in a variety of actions to reduce these problems, but such actions are costly. Moreover, despite these actions, it may not be possible to completely resolve agency problems, and unresolved agency problems can also be costly. The cost of actions taken to reduce agency problems, and the cost of unresolved agency problems, are *agency costs*. Agency costs can substantially reduce the economic benefits that could have been created through an agency relationship.

SOURCES OF AGENCY COSTS

Stockholders are residual claimants to a firm's cash flow (Alchian and Demsetz, 1972). These investors have a claim to a firm's cash flow after all other claims to that cash flow are satisfied. Other claimants include employees (through their wages and other forms of compensation), management (through their salaries and other forms of compensation), suppliers of raw materials (through cash payments), sources of debt capital (through principal and interest payments on bank debt, bonds, and other forms of debt), and the government (through taxes). Given their status as residual claimants, stockholders have a strong interest in managers' making decisions that maximize the present value of the cash flow that a firm generates. By maximizing the present value of a firm's cash flow, managers maximize the amount of cash available to stockholders as residual claimants. As long as managers attempt to maximize the present value of their firm's cash flow, agency problems do not arise between managers and stockholders. But managers can make numerous decisions that have the effect of reducing the present value of a firm's cash flow, thereby reducing the wealth of outside stockholders and creating agency problems between a firm's managers and stockholders. Sources of these agency costs include managerial perquisites and aversion to risk.

Managerial Perquisites

Managers can decide to take some of a firm's capital and invest it in perquisites that do not add economic value to the firm but do directly benefit those managers (Lambert, 1986). Examples of such investments include lavish offices, fleets of corporate jets, and corporate vacation homes. To the extent that such investments directly benefit managers and divert capital from positive present-value investment opportunities, they create agency problems between a firm and its outside stockholders (Jensen and Meckling, 1976).

Of course, not all payments from a firm's cash flow to managers create agency problems. As a supplier of managerial talent to a firm, managers can claim some of a firm's cash flow. Moreover, sometimes lavish offices, corporate jets, corporate vacation homes, and similar perquisites can be positive present-value investments for a firm. Lavish offices can send to customers a signal of a firm's profitability and thus its reliability (Klein and Leffler, 1981). Corporate jets can be used to transport critical decision makers to the right place at the right time. Corporate vacation homes can be made available to customers as part of a firm's marketing efforts. In order for these investments to be sources of agency costs, they must both directly benefit managers and have a negative present value.

Managerial Risk Aversion

Through negative present-value investments in managerial perquisites, managers can reduce the residual cash flow available to stockholders. Managers may also be more risk averse in their decision making than stockholders would prefer them to be. These different risk preferences can create agency problems.

As discussed in Chapter 11, stockholders can diversify their portfolio of investments at very low cost. Through their diversification efforts, they can eliminate all firm-specific risk in their portfolios. In this setting, stockholders are indifferent to the riskiness per se of investments made by individual firms. Rather, their interest is solely in the discounted present value of the cash flows created by these investments.

Managers, in contrast, have limited ability to diversify their human capital investments in their firm (Amihud and Lev, 1981). Some portion of these investments are specific to a particular firm and have limited value in alternative uses (Williamson, 1975). The value of a manager's human capital investment in a firm depends critically on the continued existence of the firm. Thus managers are *not* indifferent to the riskiness of investment opportunities in a firm. Very risky investments may jeopardize a firm's survival and thus eliminate the value of a manager's human capital investments (Tomer, 1987). These incentives can lead managers to be more risk averse in their decision making than stockholders would prefer them to be (Marcus, 1982).

Consider, for example, two mutually exclusive investment opportunities being evaluated by a firm. The first investment has a very attractive cash flow pattern, although it is very risky (as reflected in a high discount rate of 35 percent applied to this investment). The present value of this first investment, despite its riskiness, is $500. The second investment has a less attractive cash flow pattern than the first, although this investment is considerably less risky than the first (as reflected in the relatively low discount rate of 15 percent applied to this investment). Despite the less attractive pattern of cash flow, the present value of the second investment is $400. Since these investments are mutually exclusive, managers must choose one of them.

Given the interest of stockholders to maximize the present value of a firm's cash flow, stockholders would prefer managers to choose the first investment, because its present value is greater than the present value of the second investment. However, because managers cannot diversify their human capital investments as efficiently as stockholders can diversify their investment portfolios, managers are concerned about the relative riskiness of these alternative investments. Managers may choose the second investment, despite its lower present value, because it does not put their human capital investments at risk to the same extent as the first investment. To the extent that managers are more risk averse in their decision making than outside stockholders would prefer, agency problems can arise between a firm and its stock-holders (Jensen and Meckling, 1976).

MONITORING, BONDING, AND RESIDUAL AGENCY COSTS

Managers could safely ignore agency problems with stockholders if these conflicts did not adversely affect their ability to manage a firm's assets. However, Jensen and Meckling (1976) show that, as long as capital markets are semistrong efficient, the cost of agency problems with stockholders will be reflected in the cost of equity capital for firms. In the face of significant agency problems, firms will find their cost of capital rising, and their ability to take advantage of profitable opportunities will be limited.

Jensen and Meckling's (1976) logic is straightforward. If capital markets are at least semistrong efficient (Fama, 1970), then all public information about the value of investing in a firm's equity will be reflected in the cost of that firm's equity. Information about the divergence of managers' interests and stockholders' interests in the managing of a firm's assets is often public information. If managerial interests significantly vary from the interests of outside investors, those investors will require a greater rate of return on investing in that firm, compared to the case where managerial interests do not diverge from the interests of outside investors. This higher required rate of return is the higher cost of equity capital for the firm with significant agency problems.

Jensen and Meckling's (1976) analysis suggests that managers seeking to reduce their firm's cost of capital have an incentive to reduce agency problems between themselves and their firm's outside stock-holders. By doing so, managers can lower their firm's cost of capital and can explore a wider range of valuable economic opportunities. However, managers cannot reduce these agency problems by simply "assuring" outside investors that their interests will be considered during decision making. Outside stockholders will find it difficult to distinguish between managerial assertions that are sincere and those that are examples of adverse selection or moral hazard (Williamson, 1975; Barney and Ouchi, 1986). In reducing agency conflicts, talk is cheap and without value unless it is backed up by actions.

Agency conflicts between managers and stockholders can be partially resolved in at least two ways: through the use of monitoring mechanisms or bonding mechanisms (Jensen and Meckling, 1976). *Monitoring mechanisms* are institutional devices through which a firm's stockholders can observe, measure, evaluate, and control managerial behavior. The purpose of monitoring mechanisms is not to enable outside investors to replace managers in their decision-making role, but rather to ensure that when managers engage in decision making, they do so in a way consistent with stockholders' interests. *Bonding mechanisms* are investments or policies that managers adopt to reassure outside stockholders that they will behave in ways consistent with stockholders' interests when making decisions.

Of course, monitoring and bonding are not costless. Nor are they completely effective in eliminating all conflicts of interest between managers and outside stockholders. In semistrong efficient capital markets, the costs of monitoring, the costs of bonding, and any residual agency costs will be reflected in a firm's cost of capital. Thus managers seeking to gain access to low-cost capital have a strong incentive to choose and implement low-cost monitoring and bonding mechanisms.

In the context of agency problems between managers and outside stockholders, organizing to implement diversification strategies can be seen as the creation of monitoring and bonding devices to reassure outside stockholders that decisions being made throughout the firm are consistent with the interests of outside stockholders. Effective organizing efforts reduce perceived conflicts of interest between a firm's managers and outside investors, and do so at the lowest possible cost. *A firm's organizational structure, management control systems, and compensation policies can all have important monitoring and bonding attributes.*

12.2   ORGANIZATIONAL STRUCTURE

The most common organizational structure for implementing a diversification strategy is the M-form, or multidivisional, structure. A typical M-form structure, as it would appear in a firm's annual report, is presented in Fig. 12.1. This same structure is redrawn in Fig. 12.2 to emphasize the roles and responsibilities of each of the major components of the M-form organization.

In the multidivisional structure, each business that the firm engages in is managed through one or several divisions. Different firms have different names for these divisions—strategic business units (SBUs), business groups, companies. But whatever their name, the divisions in an M-form organization are true profit-and-loss centers: Profits and losses are calculated at the level of the division in these firms.

FIGURE 12.1

An Example of M-Form Organizational Structure as Depicted in a Firm's Annual Report

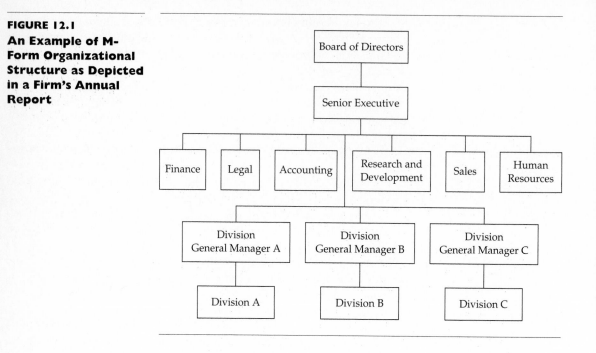

Different firms use different criteria for defining the boundaries of profit-and-loss centers. For example, General Electric defines its divisions in terms of the types of products that each division manufactures and sells (for example, Consumer Electronics, Nuclear, Medical Imaging, and so forth). Nestlé defines its divisions with reference to the geographic scope of each of its businesses (North America, South America, and so forth). General Motors defines its divisions in terms of the brand names of its products (Pontiac, Cadillac, Oldsmobile, Saturn, and so forth). However they are defined, divisions in an M-form organization should be large enough to represent identifiable business activities but small enough so that a division general manager can effectively manage each one. Indeed, each division in an M-form organization typically adopts a U-form structure (see Fig. 10.3), and the division general manager takes on the role of a U-form senior executive for his or her division.

As suggested in Section 12.1, the M-form organizational structure can be understood as a monitoring and bonding device. Each of the major components of this structure enables outside stockholders to observe the decision-making activities of managers (and thus facilitates monitoring), reassures outside stockholders that decision-making activities are consistent with their interests (and thus facilitates bond-

**FIGURE 12.2
An M-Form Structure
Redrawn to
Emphasize Roles and
Responsibilities**

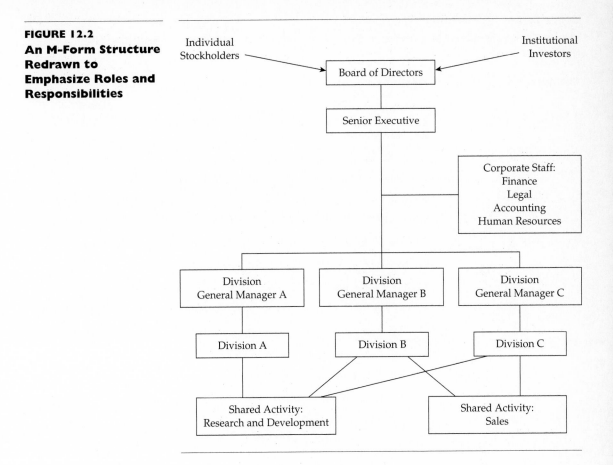

ing), or both. The monitoring and bonding activities of the major components of the M-form structure—the board of directors, institutional investors, the senior executive, corporate staff, division general managers, and shared activity managers—are summarized in Table 12.1 and discussed below.

BOARD OF DIRECTORS

One of the major monitoring devices present in an M-form organization is the firm's board of directors. In principle, all of a firm's senior managers report to the board. The board's primary responsibility is to monitor decision making in the firm, to ensure that it is consistent with the interests of outside equity holders.

A board of directors typically consists of from ten to fifteen individuals drawn from a firm's top management group and from

TABLE 12.1
Major Components of the M-Form Structure and Their Monitoring and Bonding Activities

Component	Activity
Board of directors	Evaluates the firm's decision making to ensure that it is consistent with the interests of equity holders (monitoring)
Institutional investors	Evaluates the firm's decision making to ensure that it is consistent with the interests of major institutional equity investors (monitoring)
Senior executive	Formulates corporate strategies consistent with equity holder's interests (bonding) and assures strategy implementation (monitoring) Strategy formulation: ■ Decides what business the firm should operate in ■ Decides how the firm should compete in those businesses ■ Specifies the economies of scope around which the diversified firm will operate Strategy implementation: ■ Encourages cooperation across divisions to exploit economies of scope ■ Evaluates performance of divisions ■ Allocates capital across divisions
Corporate staff	Provides information to the senior executive about internal and external environments for strategy formulation and implementation (monitoring and bonding)
Division general managers	Formulates divisional strategies consistent with corporate strategies (bonding) and assures strategy implementation (bonding) Strategy formulation: ■ Decide how the division will compete in its business, given the corporate strategy Strategy implementation: ■ Coordinate decisions and actions of functional managers reporting to the division general manager to implement divisional strategy ■ Compete for corporate capital allocations ■ Cooperate with other divisions to exploit corporate economies of scope
Shared activity managers	Support the operations of multiple divisions (bonding)

individuals outside the firm. A firm's senior executive (often identified by the title "President" or "Chief Executive Officer"), its chief financial officer (CFO), and a few other senior managers are usually on the board—although managers on the board are typically outnumbered by outsiders. The firm's senior executive is often but not always the chairman of the board (a term used here to denote both female and male executives). The task of managerial board members—including the board chair—is to provide other board members information and insights about critical decisions being made in the firm and the effect those decisions are likely to have on a firm's equity holders (Finkelstein and D'Aveni, 1994). The task of outsiders on the board is to evaluate the past, current, and future performance of the firm, and of its senior managers, to ensure that the actions taken in the firm are consistent with shareholders' interests.

Boards of directors are typically organized into several subcommittees. An audit committee is responsible for ensuring the accuracy of accounting and financial statements. A finance committee maintains the relationship between the firm and external capital markets. A nominating committee nominates new board members. A personnel and compensation committee evaluates and compensates the performance of a firm's senior executive and other senior managers. Often, membership on these standing committees is reserved for external board members. Other standing committees reflect specific issues for a particular firm and are typically open to external and internal board members (Kesner, 1988; Zahra and Pearce, 1989).

Passive Versus Active Boards

For many years, the boards of major firms were relatively passive and would take dramatic action, such as firing the senior executive, only if a firm's performance was significantly below expectations for long periods of time (Magnet, 1993). However, in the 1990s, boards have become more active proponents of equity holders' interests (Kesner and Johnson, 1990). In the early 1990s, senior executives from American Express (James D. Robinson III), General Motors (Robert C. Stempel), Digital Equipment (Kenneth H. Olsen), Compaq Computer (Rod Canion), Tenneco (James L. Ketelsen), Time Warner (Nicholas J. Nicholas Jr.), Goodyear (Tom H. Barrett), IBM (John Akers), and Kmart (Joseph Antonini) were forced to retire or were stripped of some of their managerial responsibilities by active boards (Loomis, 1993; Schonfeld, 1995). This recent surge in board activity reflects a new economic reality in the 1980s and 1990s: If a board does not become more active in monitoring firm performance, then other monitoring mechanisms will. Thus the board of directors has become progressively more influential in representing the interests of a firm's equity holders (Kosnik, 1990; Lublin and Duff, 1995).

This new activity, however, can go too far. If boards begin actively managing a firm on a day-to-day basis, the efficiency advantages of the separation of ownership and control begin to break down. Recall that a firm that has appropriately chosen its diversification leveraging strategy will be pursuing a strategy that outside investors cannot pursue on their own. This suggests that outside investors, or their representatives on a firm's board, will be limited in their ability to manage a firm's diversification strategy from day to day. To the extent that a board attempts to manage a firm from day to day, rather than simply monitoring the firm's actions and performance, it is unlikely that the full value of a diversification strategy will be realized.

Fama and Jensen (1983) have suggested one way to think about the roles and responsibilities of a firm's board of directors, as opposed to the roles and responsibilities of a firm's management. These authors observe that most business decision making involves four distinct activities (see Fig. 12.3). Two of these activities, initiation and implementation of strategies, are thought to be the exclusive province of managers. The other two, ratification and monitoring, are the responsibility of boards of directors representing equity holders' interests. As long as board activity focuses on ratifying and monitoring strategic decisions, such activity is likely to reduce potential agency conflicts in ways that preserve the efficiency benefits of the separation of ownership and control.

FIGURE 12.3
The Responsibilities of Management and the Board of Directors in the Decision-Making Process.
Source: Fama and Jensen (1983).

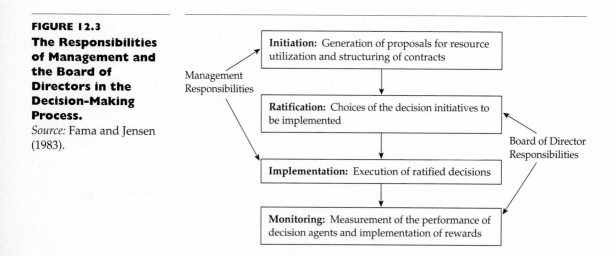

Insiders and Outsiders on the Board

Recent increases in board activity have refocused attention on the advantages and disadvantages of insiders (that is, managers) versus outsiders on the board. In one way, this seems like a simple problem. Since the primary role of the board of directors is to monitor managerial decisions to ensure that they are consistent with the interests of equity holders, it follows that the board should consist primarily of outsiders, for they face no conflict of interest in evaluating managerial performance. Obviously, managers, as inside members of the board, face significant conflicts of interest in evaluating their own performance (Lorsch, 1989; Weidenbaum, 1986).

Research on outsider members of boards of directors tends to support this point of view (Boyd, 1990). Outside directors, as compared to insiders, tend to focus more on monitoring a firm's economic performance rather than other measures of firm performance (recall from Section 2.3 the discussion of the multiple stakeholders approach to defining firm performance) (Johnson, Hoskisson, and Hitt, 1993). Obviously, a firm's economic performance is most relevant to its equity investors (Fama and Jensen, 1983). Outside board members are more likely than inside members to dismiss CEOs following poor performance (Coughlan and Schmidt, 1985; Warner, Watts, and Wruck, 1988; Weisbach, 1988). Also, outside board members have a stronger incentive than inside members have to maintain their reputation as effective monitors. This incentive by itself can lead to more effective monitoring by outside board members (Fama and Jensen, 1983). Moreover, the monitoring effectiveness of outside board members seems to be substantially enhanced when they personally own a substantial amount of a firm's equity (Baysinger and Butler, 1985; Shleifer and Vishny, 1986).

For example, William Agee was only dismissed as CEO of Morrison-Knudsen Corporation *after* several new outsiders were added to the board—despite unexpected losses, the resignation of other board members, a letter from senior managers at Morrison-Knudsen detailing numerous operational, financial, and strategic problems that had been created by Agee, and warnings from the firm's banks about potential loan covenant defaults (Rigdon and Lublin, 1995). Even with outside board members, most boards of directors proceed very slowly when dismissing a firm's senior executives (Lublin and Duff, 1995).

However, just because outside members face fewer conflicts of interest in evaluating managerial performance compared to management insiders on the board, it is not the case that they face no conflicts of interest. Directors can receive substantial compensation for their service on a board, often as much as $100,000 per year. And the size of this cash compensation often has little relationship to the performance of a firm.

In response to the conflicts of interest created by these fees, a recent report from the Association of Corporate Boards has recommended, among other changes, that outside directors receive virtually all their board-related compensation in the form of stock and that other noncash benefits programs for board members be eliminated (Lublin, 1995).

But even if all conflicts of interest could be eliminated for outside board members, it would still be the case that boards of directors should include some inside/managerial members (Zajac and West-phal, 1994). Managers bring something to the board that cannot be easily duplicated by outsiders—detailed information about the decision-making activities inside the firm. This is precisely the information that outsiders need to effectively monitor the activities of a firm, and it is information available to them only if they work closely with insiders (managers). One way to gain access to this information is to include managers as members of the board of directors (Baysinger and Hoskisson, 1990; Hoskisson and Turk, 1990; Cochran, Wood, and Jones, 1985; Vance, 1964). Thus, while most work suggests that a board of directors should be composed primarily of outsiders, there is an important role for insiders/managers to play as members of a firm's board.

INSTITUTIONAL OWNERS

One of the reasons why boards of directors have become more active over the last several years is the growth of large institutional investors (Rediker and Seth, 1995; Magnet, 1993). Large institutional investors have very strong incentives to monitor the behavior of firms, to ensure that decisions are made in ways that enhance the value of their investment. So large investors have begun to exercise more direct influence on a firm's board of directors, and thus on the decision-making processes in a firm (Allen, 1993; Lipin, 1995). Several U.S. firms have recently been targeted by large institutional investors, including Kmart, ITT, Baxter International, US Air, and United States Shoe (Schonfeld, 1995). Moreover, this activism is not limited to the United States. In 1995, for example, institutional investors played an important role in ousting senior managers in several French firms, including Cie. de Suez, Cie. de Navigation Mixte, and Alcatel-Alsthom (Kamm, 1995).

Institutional owners are usually pension funds, mutual funds, or other groups of individual investors that have joined together to manage their investments. As is seen in Fig. 12.4, institutional investors have grown from being a relatively small factor in the investment community in the early 1960s to be a very large factor in the 1990s. Currently, institutional investors own over 50 percent of the outstanding equity of U.S. firms (Stewart, 1993).

FIGURE 12.4
Growth in Holdings of Institutional Investors in Publicly Traded U.S. Firms.
Source: Stewart (1993:36).

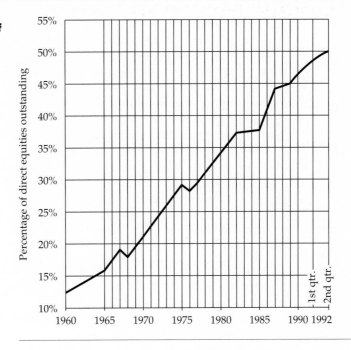

Are Institutional Investors Myopic?

Institutional investors can use their investment clout to insist that a firm's management behaves in ways consistent with the interests of equity holders. Researchers who assume that institutional investors are interested more in maximizing the short-term value of their portfolios than in the long-term performance of firms in those portfolios fear that such power will force firms to make only short-term investments (Hill, Hitt, and Hoskisson, 1988; Choate and Linger, 1986; Graves and Waddock, 1990). Recent research in the United States and Japan, however, suggests that institutional investors are not unduly myopic (Hansen and Hill, 1991). Rather, as suggested earlier, equity investors apply standard discounted present-value logic in valuing the performance of a firm. If the present value of a firm's activities is positive, these activities will be consistent with the interests of equity investors, even institutional investors, despite any short-term costs or losses associated with these activities.

For example, Hansen and Hill (1991) examined the impact of institutional ownership on research and development investments in

R&D-intensive industries. R&D investments tend to be longer-term in orientation. If institutional investors are myopic, they should influence firms to invest in relatively less R&D, in favor of investments that generate shorter-term profits. Hansen and Hill (1991) were able to show that high levels of institutional ownership did not adversely affect the level of R&D in a firm. These findings are consistent with the notion that institutional investors are not inappropriately concerned with the short term in their monitoring activities.

More generally, Bergh (1995) has shown that high levels of institutional ownership lead firms to sell strategically unrelated businesses. This effect of institutional investors is enhanced if, in addition, outside directors on a firm's board have substantial equity investments in the firm. Given the discussion of the value of unrelated diversification in Chapter 11, it seems clear that these divestment actions are consistent with maximizing the present value of a firm (Bethel and Liebeskind, 1993).

THE SENIOR EXECUTIVE

The senior executive (the president or chief executive officer) in an M-form organization has the same two responsibilities as a senior executive in a U-form organization (see Section 10.3): strategy formulation and strategy implementation. The focus of these activities, however, is not the same. In a U-form organization, strategy formulation focuses on deciding how a firm should compete in its primary business. In an M-form organization, strategy formulation focuses on which businesses a firm should compete in and how the firm should compete in those businesses. In other words, in an M-form organization, the senior executive's primary strategy formulation task is to specify the economies of scope around which the diversified firm should operate. In a U-form organization, strategy implementation focuses on coordinating functions to implement strategy. In an M-form organization, strategy implementation focuses on encouraging appropriate cooperation among divisions, in order to exploit valuable economies of scope. Senior executives in M-form organizations have several tools to assist in strategy implementation efforts, including processes for evaluating divisional performance and for allocating capital.

From the perspective of agency problems in a diversified firm, the senior executive's strategy formulation responsibilities can be understood as assuring outside investors that a firm is exploiting economies of scope that have the potential to reduce a firm's costs or increase its revenues in ways that cannot be duplicated by outside investors acting on their own (i.e., as a bonding mechanism). The senior executive's strategy implementation responsibilities can be understood as an effort to assure that this potential is realized through a firm's operations and activities (i.e., as a monitoring mechanism).

Strategy Formulation

At the broadest level, deciding which businesses a diversified firm should operate in is equivalent to discovering and developing valuable economies of scope among a firm's current and potential businesses. If these economies of scope are also rare and costly to imitate, they can be a source of sustained competitive advantage for a diversified firm.

The senior executive is uniquely positioned to discover, develop, and nurture valuable economies of scope in a diversified firm. Every other manager in this kind of firm either has a divisional point of view (for example, division general managers and shared activity managers) or is a functional specialist (for example, corporate staff and functional managers within divisions). Only the senior executive has a truly corporate perspective. However, like the senior executive in a U-form organization, the senior executive in an M-form organization should involve numerous other divisional and functional managers in strategy formulation, to ensure complete and accurate information as input to the process and a broad understanding of and commitment to that strategy once it has been formulated.

Strategy Implementation

As is the case for senior executives in a U-form structure, strategy implementation in an M-form almost always involves resolving conflicts among groups of managers. However, instead of simply resolving conflicts between functional managers (as is the case in a U-form), senior executives in M-form organizations must resolve conflicts within and between each of the major managerial components of the M-form structure: corporate staff, division general managers, and shared activity managers. Various corporate staff managers may disagree about the economic relevance of their staff functions; corporate staff may come into conflict with division general managers over various corporate programs and activities; division general managers may disagree with how capital is allocated across divisions; division general managers may come into conflict with shared activity managers about how shared activities should be managed; shared activity managers may disagree with corporate staff about their mutual roles and responsibilities, and so forth.

Obviously, the numerous and often conflicting relationships among groups of managers in an M-form organization can place significant strategy implementation burdens on the senior executive (Westley and Mintzberg, 1989). While resolving these numerous conflicts, however, the senior executive needs to keep in mind the reasons why the firm began pursuing a diversification strategy in the first place: to exploit real economies of scope that outside investors cannot realize on their own. Any strategy implementation decisions that jeopardize the realization of these real economies of scope is inconsistent with the underlying strategic objectives of a diversified firm. These issues are analyzed in detail in the discussion of management control systems in the M-form organization (Section 12.3).

The Office of the President: Chairman, CEO, and COO

It is often the case that the roles and responsibilities of the senior executive in an M-form organization are greater than what can be reasonably managed by a single individual. This is especially likely if a firm is broadly diversified across numerous complex products and complex markets. In this situation, it is not uncommon for the tasks of the senior executive to be divided among two or three people: the chairman of the board, the chief executive officer, and the chief operating officer. The primary responsibilities of each of these roles in an M-form organization are listed in Table 12.2. Together, these roles are known as the "office of the president." In general, as the tasks facing the office of the president become more demanding and complex, the more likely it is that the roles and responsibilities of this office will be divided among two or three people.

There is currently some debate about whether the roles of board chair and CEO should be combined or separated, and if separated, what kinds of people should occupy these positions (Finkelstein and D'Aveni, 1994). Some have argued that the role of CEO and chairman of the board should definitely be separated and that the role of the chairman should be filled by an outside (nonmanagerial) member of the board of directors (Neff, 1990). These arguments are based on the assumption that only an outside member of the board of directors can ensure the independent monitoring required to resolve agency conflicts in the modern diversified corporation (Lorsch, 1989; Dobrzynski, 1991; Rechner and Dalton, 1989). Others have argued that effective monitoring often requires more information than what would be avail-

TABLE 12.2 **Responsibilities of** **Three Different Roles** **in the Office of the** **President**	Chairman of the board	Supervision of the board of directors in its monitoring role
	Chief executive officer	Strategy formulation
	Chief operating officer	Strategy implementation

able to outsiders, and thus that the roles of board chair and CEO should be combined (Donaldson, 1990; Fama and Jensen, 1983:314–315) and filled by a firm's senior manager.

Empirical research on this question suggests that whether these roles of CEO and chairman should be combined or not depends on the complexity of the information analysis and monitoring task facing the CEO and chairman (Rechner and Dalton, 1991). Boyd (1995) found that combining the roles of CEO and chairman is positively correlated with firm performance when firms operate in slow-growth and simple competitive environments—environments that do not overtax the cognitive capability of a single individual. This finding suggests that combining these roles does not necessarily increase agency conflicts between a firm and its equity holders. Boyd (1995) also found that separating the roles of CEO and board chair is positively correlated with firm performance when firms operate in high-growth and very complex environments. In such environments, a single individual cannot fulfill all the responsibilities of both CEO and chairman, and thus the two roles need to be held by separate individuals. Other research on the effects of combining the roles of CEO and chairman indicates that such a combination can reduce agency costs in some settings and raise it in others (Finkelstein and D'Aveni, 1994).

CORPORATE STAFF

The primary responsibility of corporate staff is to provide information about the firm's external and internal environments to the firm's senior executive. This information is vital for both the strategy formulation and the strategy implementation responsibilities of the senior executive and makes effective monitoring and bonding possible. Corporate staff functions that provide information about a firm's external environment include finance, investor relations, legal affairs, regulatory affairs, and corporate advertising. Corporate staff functions that provide information about a firm's internal environment include accounting and corporate human resources. These corporate staff functions report directly to a firm's senior executive and are a conduit of information to that executive.

Corporate and Divisional Staff

Many organizations re-create some corporate staff functions within each division of the organization. This is particularly true for internally oriented corporate staff functions such as accounting and human resources. At the division level, divisional staff managers usually have a direct "solid-line" reporting relationship to their respective corporate staff functional managers and a less formal "dotted-line" reporting relationship to their division general manager. The reporting relationship between the divisional staff manager and the corporate staff manager is the link that enables the corporate staff manager to collect the information that the senior executive requires for strategy formulation, strategy implementation, monitoring, and bonding. The senior executive can also use this corporate staff—division staff relationship to communicate corporate policies and procedures to the divisions, although these policies can also be communicated directly by the senior executive to division general managers.

Although divisional staff managers usually have a less formal relationship with their division general managers, in practice division general managers can have an important influence on the activities of divisional staff. After all, divisional staff managers may formally report to corporate staff managers, but they spend virtually all their time interacting with their division general managers and with the other functional managers who report to their division general managers. These divided loyalties can sometimes affect the timeliness and accuracy of the information transmitted from divisional staff managers to corporate staff managers and thus affect the timeliness and accuracy of the information the senior executive uses for strategy formulation, strategy implementation, monitoring, and bonding.

Nowhere are these divided loyalties potentially more problematic than in accounting staff functions. Obviously, it is vitally important for the senior executive in an M-form organization to receive timely and accurate information about divisional performance. If the timeliness and accuracy of that information are inappropriately affected by division general managers, the effectiveness of senior management can be adversely affected. Moreover, in some situations, division general managers can have very strong incentives to affect the timeliness and accuracy of divisional performance information, especially if a division general manager's compensation depends on this information, or if the capital allocated to a division depends on this information.

Efficient monitoring by the senior executive requires that corporate staff, and especially the accounting corporate staff function, remain organizationally independent of division general managers—thus the importance of the solid-line relationship between divisional staff managers and corporate staff managers. Nevertheless, the ability of corporate staff to obtain accurate performance information from divisions also depends on close cooperative working relationships between corporate staff, divisional staff, and division general managers—thus the importance of the dotted-line relationship between divisional staff managers and division general managers. Maintaining the balance between, on the one hand, the distance and objectivity needed to evaluate a division's performance and, on the other hand, the cooperation and teamwork needed to gain access to the information needed to evaluate a division's performance distinguishes excellent from mediocre corporate staff managers.

Overinvolvement in Managing Division Operations

Over and above the failure to maintain a balance between objectivity and cooperation in evaluating divisional performance, the one sure way that corporate staff can fail in a multidivisional firm is to become too involved in the day-to-day operations of divisions. In an M-form structure, the management of such day-to-day operations is delegated to division general managers and to functional managers who report to division general managers. Corporate staff managers collect and transmit information; they do not manage divisional operations.

One way to ensure that corporate staff does not become too involved in managing the day-to-day operations of divisions is to keep corporate staff small. This is certainly true for some of the best-managed diversified firms in the world. For example, just 1.5 percent of Johnson & Johnson's 82,700 employees work at the firm's headquarters, and only some of those individuals are members of the corporate staff. Hanson Industries has in its U.S. headquarters 120 people who help manage a diversified firm with $8 billion in revenues. Clayton, Dubilier and Rice, a management buyout firm, has only 11 headquarters staff managers overseeing eight businesses with collective sales of over $6 billion (Dumaine, 1992).

Numerous examples of corporate staff managers having an inappropriate influence on divisional operations can be cited. In many firms, corporate human resource departments specify wage and compensation schemes that, though appropriate in some divisions, make it impossible to attract labor or management in other divisions. It is not surprising that corporate human resource departments are often called the "antipersonnel" department in these types of firms. In other firms, staff accounting practices can lead division general managers to make decisions that are quite inconsistent with the long-term economic success of a division.

All of this is not to suggest that corporate staff managers never possess expertise that could benefit the operations of divisions. Obviously, they sometimes do. But when corporate staff begins to significantly influence day-to-day divisional activities, it ceases to be corporate staff and instead should be thought of as a shared activity. As described below, the management challenge facing a shared activity is quite different from the management challenge facing a corporate staff function. For shared activity managers, the primary task is to engage in activities that satisfy the needs and requirements of division general managers. For corporate staff, the primary task is to engage in activities that satisfy the needs and requirements of the senior executive. Confusion between these two tasks often leads to difficulties for corporate staff managers.

DIVISION GENERAL MANAGERS

Division general managers in an M-form organization have primary responsibility for managing a firm's businesses from day to day. Division general managers have full profit-and-loss responsibility and typically have multiple functional managers reporting to them. As general managers, they have both strategy formulation and strategy implementation responsibilities. On the strategy formulation side, division general managers choose strategies for their divisions, within the broader strategic context established by the senior executive of the firm. Many of the analytical tools described in Chapters 1 through 10 of this book can be used by division general managers to make these strategy formulation decisions.

The strategy implementation responsibilities of division general managers in an M-form organization parallel the strategy implementation responsibilities of senior executives in U-form organizations. In particular, division general managers must be able to coordinate the activities of often conflicting functional managers in order to implement a division's strategies. Each of the symptoms of a sick U-form organization (see Section 10.3) can also exist within a division of an M-form organization.

In addition to their responsibilities as a U-form senior executive, division general managers in an M-form organization have two additional responsibilities: to compete for corporate capital and to cooperate with other divisions to exploit corporate economies of scope. Division general managers compete for corporate capital by obtaining high rates of return on capital invested in previous periods by the corporation in their business. In most firms, divisions that have demonstrated the ability to generate high rates of return on earlier capital investments gain access to more capital, or to lower-cost capital, compared to divisions that have not demonstrated a history of such performance.

Division general managers cooperate to exploit economies of scope by working with shared activity managers, corporate staff managers, and the senior executive in the firm to isolate, understand, and use the economies of scope around which the diversified firm was originally organized. Division general managers can even become involved in discovering new economies of scope that were not anticipated when the firm's diversification strategy was originally implemented but nevertheless may be both valuable and costly for outside investors to create on their own.

A careful reader will recognize a fundamental conflict between the last two responsibilities of division general managers in an M-form organization. These managers are required to compete for corporate capital and to cooperate to exploit economies of scope at the same time. Competition is important, for it leads division general managers to focus on generating high levels of economic performance from their divisions. If each division is generating high levels of economic performance, then the diversified firm as a whole is likely to do well also. But cooperation is important to exploit economies of scope that are the economic justification for implementing a diversification strategy in the first place. If divisions do not cooperate in exploiting these economies, there are few, if any, justifications for implementing a diversification strategy, and the diversified firm should be split into multiple independent entities.

The need to simultaneously compete and cooperate puts significant managerial burdens on division general managers (Golden, 1992). It is likely that this ability is both rare across most diversified firms and costly to imitate. This special managerial skill probably goes a long way in explaining both why most diversified firms do not earn above-normal profits from their diversification efforts and why a few such firms may (Berger and Otek, 1995; Lang and Stulz, 1994; Rumelt, 1991).

SHARED ACTIVITY MANAGERS

One of the potential diversification economies of scope identified in Chapter 11 is shared activities. Divisions in an M-form organization exploit this economy of scope when one or more of the stages in their value chains are managed in common. Typical examples of activities shared across two or more divisions in a multidivisional firm include common sales forces, common distribution systems, common manufacturing facilities, and common research and development efforts (also see Table 11.2). The primary responsibility of the individuals who manage shared activities is to support the operations of the divisions that share the activity.

The way in which M-form structure is often depicted in company annual reports (as in Fig. 12.1) tends to obscure the operational role of shared activities. In this version of the M-form organizational chart, no distinction is made between corporate staff functions and shared activity functions. Moreover, it appears that managers of shared activities report directly to a firm's senior executive, just like corporate staff. These ambiguities are resolved by redrawing the M-form organizational chart to emphasize the roles and responsibilities of different units within the M-form (as in Fig. 12.2). In this more accurate representation of how an M-form actually functions, corporate staff groups are separated from shared activity managers, and each is shown reporting to its primary internal "customer"—the senior executive for corporate staff groups, two or more division general managers for shared activity managers.

Shared Activities as Cost Centers

Shared activities are often managed as cost centers in an M-form structure. When that is the case, shared activity managers do not attempt to create profits when they provide services to the divisions they support. Rather, these services are priced to internal customers in such a way that the shared activity just covers its cost of operating.

Because cost center shared activities do not have to generate profits from their operations, the cost of the services they provide to divisions can be less than the cost of similar services provided either by a division itself or by outside suppliers. Well-managed cost center shared activities will provide lower-cost comparable services unless either of these situations exists: (1) The services needed by a division require the managers of shared activities to acquire or develop costly resources and capabilities already possessed by that division or by an outside supplier, or (2) The cost of providing services is highly sensitive to economies of scale, and shared activities do not enjoy the scale of outside suppliers.

If a shared activity is managed as a cost center, and the cost of services from this shared activity is *greater than* the cost of similar services provided by alternative sources, then either this shared activity is not being well managed, or it was not a real economy of scope in the first place. However, when the cost of services from a shared activity is *less than* the cost of comparable services provided by a division itself or by an outside supplier, then division general managers have a strong incentive to use the services of shared activities, thereby exploiting an economy of scope that may have been one of the original reasons why a firm implemented a diversification strategy.

Although managing shared activities as cost centers can give division managers incentives to exploit an economy of scope in a diversified firm, this management approach can create problems as well. In particular, since cost center shared activities can often undercut the price of alternative sources of service available to divisions, the managers of shared activities have only limited incentives to compete for their internal customers (the divisions) with these other sources of service. This situation can lead the service center to supply the division with lower-quality services than the division could obtain on its own, either internally or from an outside supplier. It is not uncommon for division general managers to complain about poor service, shoddy quality, and indifferent responses from shared activities in a diversified firm.

These management difficulties are worsened when a firm's senior executive, in order to ensure that shared activity economies of scope are exploited in a diversified firm, *requires* division general managers to use the services of shared activities, no matter what. In effect, the senior executive, in a desire to ensure that economies of scope are exploited, creates an internal monopoly for shared activities in the firm. In this monopoly setting, it is not uncommon for both the cost of services provided to divisions from a shared activity to rise and the quality of those services to fall.

Shared Activities as Profit Centers

In the face of these challenges, some diversified firms are beginning to manage shared activities as profit centers, rather than as cost centers. Moreover, rather than requiring divisions to use the services of shared activities, divisions retain the right to purchase services from internal shared activities or from outside suppliers or to provide services for themselves (Halal, 1994). In this setting, managers of shared activities are required to compete for their internal customers on the basis of the price and quality of the services they provide.

One firm that has taken this profit center approach to managing shared activities is ABB Inc., a Swiss engineering firm. ABB eliminated almost all of its corporate staff and reorganized its remaining staff functions into shared activities. Shared activities in ABB compete to provide services to ABB divisions. Not only do some traditional shared activities—such as research and development and sales—compete for internal customers, but many traditional staff functions—such as human resources, marketing, and finance—do as well. ABB's approach to managing shared activities has resulted in a relatively small corporate staff and in increasingly specialized and customized shared activities (Bartlett and Ghoshal, 1993).

Of course, the greatest risk associated with treating shared activities as profit centers and letting them compete for divisional customers is that divisions may choose to obtain no services or support from shared activities. Although this course of action may be in the self-interest of each division, it is not in the best interest of the corporation if, in fact, shared activities are an important economy of scope around which the diversified firm is organized.

In the end, whether a shared activity is managed as a cost center or as a profit center, the task facing the managers of shared activities is the same: to provide such highly customized and high-quality services to divisional customers at a reasonable cost that those internal customers will not want to seek alternative suppliers outside the firm or provide those services themselves. In an M-form organization, the best way to ensure that shared activity economies of scope are realized is for shared activity managers to satisfy their internal customers.

12.4   MANAGEMENT CONTROL SYSTEMS

The M-form structure presented in Figs. 12.1 and 12.2 is complex and multifaceted. No organizational structure by itself, however, is able to fully implement a diversification leveraging strategy. The M-form structure must be supplemented with a variety of management control systems (Simons, 1994). Three of the most important—systems for evaluating divisional performance, for allocating capital across divisions, and for transferring intermediate products between divisions— are discussed in this section. Each of these systems is an additional monitoring and bonding mechanism that firms can use to help reduce agency problems.

EVALUATING DIVISIONAL PERFORMANCE

Since divisions in an M-form structure are profit-and-loss centers, evaluating divisional performance should, in principle, be straightforward: Divisions that are very profitable should be evaluated more positively than divisions that are less profitable. In practice, this seemingly simple task is surprisingly complex. Two problems typically arise: (1) How should division profitability be measured, and (2) how should economy-of-scope linkages between divisions be factored into divisional performance?

Measuring Divisional Performance with Accounting Numbers

The most traditional approach to measuring and evaluating divisional profitability uses divisional versions of the accounting measures of performance first introduced in Section 2.3. In Chapter 2, such ratios as return on total assets (ROA), return on equity (ROE), gross profit margin, inventory turnover, and accounts receivable turnover were all calculated for the firm (see Table 2.3). These same ratios can also be calculated for divisions within a diversified firm.

Divisional performance can also be evaluated along numerous other accounting dimensions that the senior executive and the corporate staff think are important. For example, in addition to using traditional accounting ratios, General Electric evaluates its divisions in terms of market share and sales growth. Apparently, senior management at GE believes that GE divisions are most likely to be successful in businesses where they are a market-share leader in a growing industry (Tichy and Sherman, 1993).

Setting Accounting Performance Standards.   Of course, accounting-based measures of performance do not, by themselves, indicate whether a division has performed well. To reach this conclusion, a division's accounting performance must be compared to some standard. Diversified firms typically use one of two standards to evaluate divisional accounting measures of performance.

Some firms simply require all their divisions to meet or exceed a common hurdle rate for the measures of performance that they designate as important. For example, in order to meet corporate expectations, all divisions in a firm might be expected to generate an ROI of at least 10 percent, or an ROS of at least 12 percent. GE requires that each of its divisions be either first or second in market share in a market growing at a specified rate if those divisions are to remain part of the diversified portfolio at GE (Loeb, 1995).

The great advantage of the common hurdle rate approach to evaluating divisional accounting performance is its simplicity. Every division general manager knows exactly what the performance standards are and exactly what the consequences are if those standards are not met. This simplicity, however, can be quite deceiving.

Suppose, for example, that a division is able to obtain an ROI of 125 percent. This huge ROI is almost certainly larger than whatever the common hurdle rate in this firm might be. But simply because a division earned an ROI greater than the common hurdle rate—even if it earned an ROI of 125 percent—it does not follow that this division was managed well. It may be the case that, given changes in a division's industry structure or some other favorable economic circumstances, other businesses in this industry earned an ROI of 250 percent. In this context, an ROI of 125 percent represents management failure, even though it is well above the common hurdle rate in that firm.

In the same way, if a division was able to earn an ROI of only 1.5 percent, well below the common hurdle rate in this firm, it does not necessarily follow that this division was managed poorly. If all the other businesses in this industry earned an average ROI of –45 percent, then an ROI of 1.5 percent can be thought of as an enormous accomplishment.

Those observations lead to consideration of the second set of standards used to evaluate divisional accounting performance. In this second approach, the expected level of performance is adjusted across divisions to reflect the particular industry and economic conditions of different divisions. For example, some divisions may be expected to earn an ROI of 10 percent, others an ROI of 14 percent, and still others an ROI of 17 percent. Divisional performance expectations are established in a negotiation process that typically involves the division general manager, the senior executive in the firm, and various corporate staff functions.

The performance expectations of different divisions can reflect the unique circumstances of each division's business environment. But it is nevertheless the case that if the performance expectations of a business fall below some level for a sustained period of time, most diversified firms will take steps either to change the way business is conducted by that division or to divest themselves of that division.

Establishing Budgets.   Whether the first or second approach is used in establishing standards for evaluating the performance of a division, those standards are usually reflected in a division's budget. A division's budget is usually negotiated among division general managers, the senior executive, and corporate staff. This budget reflects a division's expected revenues and costs over the next budgeting period and is a division's operating plan for this time period.

In most diversified firms, enormous time and energy are dedicated to budgeting. This process, when it works well, forces division managers to become explicit about their short- and long-term strategies and about the implications of those strategies for their division's revenues, costs, and profits. More often than not, division general managers are held accountable for the level of performance specified in their division's budget.

The budgeting process is not without pitfalls (Duffy, 1989). Managers throughout an M-form organization can "game" the budgeting process, to establish performance guidelines that favor them. For example, division general managers might understate a division's expected performance in order to make it easier to meet or exceed budgeted expectations. Alternatively, divisions seeking additional capital may overstate a division's expected performance and thereby shift capital away from higher-return projects to their own lower-return projects.

Gaming the budgeting system is, apparently, quite common in diversified firms. Bethel (1990) studied the budget negotiation process between division general managers, a firm's senior executives, and corporate staff for a large sample of diversified firms in the United States. She concluded that senior executives and corporate staff routinely discount division sales projections, profitability projections, and capital requests. Some of this discounting reflects the belief that division general managers are systematically overly optimistic when they make budget requests. However, some of this discounting reflects the belief that division general managers, anticipating discounting, inflate their budget requests.

Limits of Accounting Measures of Divisional Performance

Aside from the budgeting process—which can create bizarre incentives inside a diversified firm—there are some additional limitations of accounting measures of divisional performance. Most reflect the limitations of accounting measures of firm performance described in Section 2.3.

Managerial Discretion.   Just as managers often have some discretion in how they choose accounting methods in reporting a firm's performance, so too do division general managers often have some discretion in how they choose accounting methods in reporting a division's performance. Thus accounting measures of divisional performance reflect, to some degree at least, the interests and preferences of division general managers. For example, when a division general manager's compensation depends on a division's reported accounting performance, division general managers can engage in a variety of activities to increase the reported performance of their division in a particular year (Watts and Zimmerman, 1986; Healy, 1985; Bowen, Noreen, and Lacey, 1981).

This managerial discretion is one reason why it is important for division-level accounting managers to have a solid-line relationship with the corporate accounting staff function but only a dotted-line relationship with the division general manager. This dual reporting relationship brings more objectivity to the process of accounting for a division's performance. However, even when this reporting relationship is in place, accounting abuses can go on. In one firm, division general managers simply lied about the level of performance in their division. Indeed, the size of this lying was so large that, once it was discovered, the firm's overall accounting performance had to be restated (Perry and Barney, 1981). At Daiwa Bank, one manager was able to hide $1.1 billion in trading losses by overstating the bank's deposits (Sapsford, Sesit, and O'Brien, 1995). This abuse of internal accounting reports led to the expulsion of Daiwa Bank from the U.S. market. Similar accounting abuses have been reported at Solomon, Inc., Kidder Peabody and Co., and Barings PLC.

Short-Term Bias.   A second limitation of accounting measures of divisional performance is that they often have a short-term bias. The reason for this bias is that longer-term, multiple-year investments in a division are usually treated, for accounting purposes, as costs in the years in which they do not generate revenues that exceed costs. In this context, division general managers have limited incentives to invest in the longer-term health of their division—especially if division general managers can get promoted out of their division because of the (artificially) high accounting performance they report.

This short-term bias in accounting measures of divisional performance can manifest itself in a variety of ways. For example, divisions may delay or forgo maintenance on plant and equipment to prop up short-term accounting profitability. Divisions may systematically underinvest in developing new customers—customers that might not generate sales revenues for several years. Also, divisions may not invest in research and development, managerial training, and other capabilities in a division—capabilities that may be vital to the long-run success and viability of a division's business (Hoskisson and Hitt, 1988). An overreliance on accounting-based measures of divisional performance can lead a diversified firm to systematically underinvest in its long-run success and profitability.

Agency Problems.   In the end, the fundamental problem with using accounting measures of performance to evaluate divisions is that these measures can give division general managers incentives that are inconsistent with the interests of stockholders. As discussed above, stockholders in a firm would like to see the firm managed in such a way that the present value of its future cash flow is maximized. As described in Chapter 2, there is surprisingly little relationship between accounting measures of performance—whether they are applied at the firm or the divisional level—and maximizing the present value of a firm's or division's cash flow.

 To the extent that divisions are evaluated by means of accounting measures of performance, a diversified firm is contributing to, not eliminating, agency problems between itself and its stockholders. Far from reassuring stockholders that their interests are being cared for, reliance on accounting measures of performance assures stockholders that their interests are *not* paramount in the strategies or operations of a diversified firm's divisions. As suggested earlier in this chapter, these agency problems will be reflected in a firm's cost of capital.

Measuring Divisional Economic Performance

Given the numerous limitations of accounting measures of divisional performance, several firms have begun adopting alternative methods of evaluating this performance. These alternatives focus directly on the present value of the cash flow generated by a division and thus do not create the same agency problems as accounting-based approaches.

 Perhaps the most popular of these economically oriented measures of division performance is economic value added (EVA) (Stern, Stewart, and Chew, 1995; Tully, 1993). EVA is calculated by subtracting the cost of capital employed in a division from that division's earnings:

$$EVA = \text{adjusted accounting earnings} - (\text{weighted average cost of capital} \times \text{total capital employed by a division}) \qquad Eq.\ 12.1$$

 Several of the terms in the EVA formula require some discussion.

For example, the calculation of economic value added begins with a division's "adjusted" accounting earnings. These are a division's traditional accounting earnings, adjusted so that they approximate what would be a division's economic earnings.

Given the discussion of accounting and economic performance in Chapter 2, it is clear that numerous adjustments will have to be applied to accounting earnings to make them more closely approximate economic earnings. For example, traditional accounting practices require R&D spending to be deducted each year from a division's earnings. As described earlier, this can lead division general managers to underinvest in longer-term R&D efforts. In the EVA measure of divisional performance, R&D spending is added back into a division's performance, and R&D is then treated as an asset and depreciated over some period of time.

One consulting firm (Stern Stewart) that specializes in implementing EVA-based divisional evaluation systems in multidivisional firms makes up to forty "adjustments" to a division's standard accounting earnings so that they more closely approximate economic earnings (*Journal of Applied Corporate Finance,* 1994). Many of these adjustments are proprietary to this consulting firm.

The terms in parentheses in Eq. (12.1) reflect the cost of investing in a division. Rather than using some accounting-based measure of the value of this investment, EVA applies financial theory and multiplies the amount of money invested in a division by a firm's weighted average cost of capital (that is, the cost of its equity × the percentage of its capital that takes the form of equity plus the cost of its debt × the percentage of its capital that takes the form of debt). This number can be thought of as the opportunity cost of investing in a particular division, as opposed to investing in any other division in the firm.

By adjusting a division's earnings, and accounting for the cost of investing in a division, economic value added is a much more accurate estimate of a division's economic performance than are traditional accounting measures of performance. The number of diversified firms evaluating their divisions with EVA-based measures of divisional performance is impressive and growing. These firms include AT&T, Coca-Cola, Quaker Oats, CSX, Briggs and Stratton, and Allied Signal (Tully, 1993). At Allied Signal, divisions that do not earn their cost of capital are awarded the infamous "leaky bucket" award. If this performance is not improved, division general managers are replaced (Tully, 1995a). The use of EVA has been touted as the key to creating economic wealth in a diversified corporation (Tully, 1993). Even the U.S. Postal Service is exploring the application of EVA to its operations (Tully, 1995b).

The Ambiguity of Divisional Performance

Whether a firm uses accounting measures to evaluate the performance of a division or uses economic measures of performance like EVA, divisional performance in a well-managed diversified firm can never be evaluated unambiguously. Consider a simple example.

Suppose that in a particular multidivisional firm there are only two divisions (Division A and Division B) and one shared activity (research and development). Also, suppose that the two divisions are managed as profit-and-loss centers and that the R&D shared activity is managed as a cost center. To support this R&D effort, each division pays $10 million per year and has been doing so for ten years. Finally, suppose that after ten years of effort (and investment) the R&D group develops a valuable new technology that perfectly addresses Division A's business needs.

Obviously, no matter how divisional performance is measured, it is likely to be the case that Division A's performance will rise in relation to Division B's performance. In this situation, what percentage of Division A's improved performance should be allocated to Division A, what percentage should be allocated to the R&D group, and what percentage should be allocated to Division B? The managers in each part of this diversified firm can make compelling arguments in their favor. Division general manager A can reasonably argue that without Division A's efforts to exploit the new technology, the full value of the technology would never have been realized. The R&D manager can reasonably argue that without the R&D effort, there would not have been a technology to exploit in the first place. And division general manager B can reasonably argue that without the dedicated long-term investment of Division B in R&D, there would have been no new technology and no performance increase for Division A.

That all three of these arguments can be made suggests that, to the extent that a firm exploits real economies of scope in implementing a diversification strategy, it will not be possible to unambiguously evaluate the performance of individual divisions in that firm. The fact that there are economies of scope in a diversified firm means that all of the businesses a firm operates in are more valuable bundled together than they would be if kept separate from one another. Efforts to unambiguously evaluate the performance of these businesses as if they were separate from one another are futile.

One solution to this problem is to force businesses in a diversified firm to operate independently of each other. If each business operates independently, then it will be possible to unambiguously evaluate its performance. Of course, to the extent that this independence is enforced, the diversified firm is unlikely to be able to realize the very economies of scope that were the justification of the diversification strategy in the first place.

Divisional performance ambiguity is bad enough when shared activities are the primary economy of scope that a diversified firm is trying to exploit. This ambiguity increases dramatically when the economy of scope is based on intangible core competencies. In this situation, it is shared learning and experience that justify a firm's diversification efforts. The intangible nature of these economies of scope multiplies the difficulty of the divisional evaluation task.

Even firms that apply rigorous EVA measures of divisional performance are unable to fully resolve these performance ambiguity difficulties. For example, the Coca-Cola division of Coca-Cola Company has made enormous investments in the Coke brand name over the years, and the Diet Coke division has exploited some of that brand-name capital in its own marketing efforts. Of course, it is not clear that all of Diet Coke's success can be attributed to the Coke brand name. After all, Diet Coke has developed its own creative advertising, has developed its own loyal group of customers, and so forth. How much of Diet Coke's success—as measured through that division's economic value added—should be allocated to the Coke brand name (an investment made long before Diet Coke was even conceived), and how much should be allocated to the Diet Coke division's efforts? EVA measures of divisional performance do not resolve ambiguities created when economies of scope exist across divisions (*Journal of Applied Corporate Finance*, 1994).

In the end, the quantitative evaluation of divisional performance—with either accounting or economic measures—must be supplemented by the experience and judgment of senior executives in a diversified firm. Only by evaluating a division's performance numbers in the context of a broader, more subjective, evaluation of the division's performance can a true picture of divisional performance be developed. Dell Computer has recognized the importance of using experience and judgment in evaluating its business operations. Dell's president, Michael Dell, has recently hired several experienced senior managers to work with him in expanding his computer company. The youngest of these new managers is ten years older than Dell (Jacob, 1995b). Since this new management team was created, Dell Computer's stock price grew from $16 per share in July 1993 to $74.25 per share in July 1995.

ALLOCATING CORPORATE CAPITAL

Another potentially valuable economy of scope outlined in Chapter 11 (besides shared activities and core competencies) is internal capital allocation. In that discussion (see Section 11.2), it was suggested that for internal capital allocation to be a justification for diversification, the information made available to senior executives allocating capital in a diversified firm must be superior, in both amount and quality, to the information available to external sources of capital in the external capital market. Both the quality and the quantity of the information available in an internal capital market depend on the organization of the diversified firm.

As suggested in Chapter 11, one of the primary limitations of internal capital markets is that division general managers have a strong incentive to overstate their division's prospects and understate its problems, in order to gain access to more capital at lower costs. Having an independent accounting function in a diversified firm can help address this problem. However, given the ambiguities inherent in evaluating divisional performance in a well-managed diversified firm, independent accountants do not resolve all these informational problems.

Zero-Based Capital Budgeting

One process for allocating capital in this corporate context is for the senior executives to create a list of all capital allocation requests from divisions in a firm, rank them from "most important" to "least important," and then fund all the projects a firm can afford, given the amount of capital it has available. This is zero-based budgeting. In principle, with zero-based budgeting, no project will receive funding for the future simply because it received funding in the past. Rather, each project has to stand on its own merits each year by being included among the important projects the firm can afford to fund.

Zero-based budgeting has some attractive features, but it has some important limitations as well. First, evaluating and ranking all projects in a diversified firm from "most important" to "least important" is a very difficult task. It not only puts unrealistic analysis and decision-making demands on the senior managers but also can be fraught with political intrigue and "backroom" capital allocation deals.

Second, even if such a ranking could be developed, the assumption that the amount of capital available for allocation is fixed can lead either to investing in projects that do *not* have a positive present value or not investing in projects that do have a positive present value. Zero-based budgeting leads to investing in projects that do *not* have a positive present value when the sum of all capital requests with a positive present value is less than the total (fixed) amount of capital available. In this situation, negative present-value projects are funded simply because a firm has sufficient capital to make this investment (Jensen, 1986, 1988). Zero-based budgeting leads to a failure to invest in projects that have a positive present value when the sum of all positive net-present-value projects in a firm is greater than the total (fixed) amount of capital available. In this situation, positive present-value projects are not funded, simply because a firm assumes it has insufficient capital to make this investment. In both cases, the internal market for capital allocation will be less efficient than an external capital market where the amount of capital available for allocation to positive present-value projects is not fixed (Copeland and Westen, 1983).

Cross-Divisional Capital Allocation

To avoid the problems of zero-based budgeting, some firms manage capital allocation as a cross-divisional process. Rather than requiring a senior executive to rank all of a firm's capital projects from "most important" to "least important," some firms bring their division general managers (with their staffs) together with the senior executive (with the corporate staff) and the shared activity managers, to collectively decide how capital should be allocated. In this setting, division general managers take turns summarizing their division's performance, prospects, and capital requests. After each presentation, the senior executive, corporate staff, shared activity managers, and other division general managers have an opportunity to ask difficult, pointed questions in an attempt to fully understand a division's capital needs. In this context, it is difficult for "backroom" capital allocation deals to remain intact. Moreover, the strengths and weaknesses of each division's performance and prospects can be revealed.

With this more accurate information in place, managers in a diversified firm can apply present-value criteria and choose to invest in just those activities that have positive present value and not to invest in projects with negative present value. If this process is managed well, the amount of capital to be allocated across divisions is not fixed. Rather, the amount of capital to be allocated depends entirely on the sum of the positive present-value investments available in a firm.

This type of cross-divisional meeting requires a fair amount of cooperation, trust, and teamwork among the different parts of a diversified organization (Priem, 1990; Wooldridge and Floyd, 1990). This is a high standard for managing the capital allocation process. The difficulty of managing this process effectively may be one of the reasons why internal capital allocation often fails to qualify as a valuable economy of scope in diversified firms (Westley, 1990).

TRANSFERRING INTERMEDIATE PRODUCTS

The existence of economies of scope across multiple divisions in a diversified firm often means that products or services produced in one division are used as inputs for products or services produced by a second division. Intermediate products or services can be transferred between any of the units in an M-form organization. This transfer is, perhaps, most important and problematic when it occurs between profit center divisions. The transfer of intermediate products or services among divisions is managed through a transfer pricing system: One division "sells" its product or service to a second division for a transfer price.

Setting Optimal Transfer Prices

From an economic point of view, the rule for establishing the optimal transfer price in a diversified firm is quite simple: The transfer price should be the value of the opportunities forgone when one division's product or service is transferred to another division. Consider the following example (Brickley, Smith, and Zimmermann, 1996). Division A's marginal cost of production is $5 per unit, but Division A can sell all of its output to outside customers for $6 per unit. If Division A can sell all of its output to outside customers for $6 per unit, the value of the opportunity forgone of transferring a unit of production from Division A to Division B is $6—the amount of money that Division A forgoes by transferring its production to Division B instead of selling it to the market.

But if Division A is selling all the units it can to external customers for $6 per unit but still has some excess manufacturing capacity, the value of the opportunity forgone in transferring the product from Division A to Division B is only $5 per unit—Division A's marginal cost of production. Since the external market cannot absorb any more of Division A's product at $6 per unit, the value of the opportunity forgone when Division A transfers units of production to Division B is not $6 per unit (Division A can't get that price) but only $5 per unit.

When transfer prices are set equal to opportunity costs, selling divisions will produce output up to the point that the marginal cost of the last unit produced equals the transfer price. Moreover, buying divisions will buy units from other divisions in the firm as long as the net revenues from doing so just cover the transfer price. If there are no interdependencies between divisions, these transfer prices will lead profit-maximizing divisions to optimize the diversified firm's profits (Eccles, 1985).

Difficulties in Setting Optimal Transfer Prices

Setting transfer prices equal to opportunity costs sounds simple enough, but it is very difficult to do in real diversified firms. Establishing optimal transfer prices requires information about the value of the opportunities forgone by the "selling" division. This, in turn, requires information about this division's marginal costs, its manufacturing capacity, external demand for its products, and so forth. Much of this information is difficult to calculate. Moreover, it is rarely stable. As market conditions change, demand for a division's products can change, marginal costs can change, and the value of opportunities forgone can change. Also, to the extent that a selling division customizes the products or services it transfers to other divisions in a diversified firm, the value of the opportunities forgone by this selling division become even more difficult to calculate.

Even if this information could be obtained and updated rapidly, division general managers in selling divisions have strong incentives to manipulate the information in ways that increase the perceived value of the opportunities forgone by their division. These division general managers can thus increase the transfer price for the products or services they sell to internal customers and thereby appropriate for themselves profits that should have been allocated to buying divisions.

Setting Transfer Prices in Practice

Since it is rarely possible for firms to establish an optimal transfer pricing scheme, most diversified firms must adopt some form of transfer pricing that attempts to approximate optimal prices. Several of these transfer pricing schemes are described in Table 12.3. However, no matter what particular schemes a firm uses, the transfer prices it generates

TABLE 12.3 **Alternative Transfer Pricing Schemes** *Source:* Eccles (1985)	Exchange autonomy	■ Buying and selling division general managers are free to negotiate transfer price without corporate involvement.
		■ Transfer price is set equal to the selling division's price to external customers.
	Mandated full cost	■ Transfer price is set equal to the selling division's actual cost of production.
		■ Transfer price is set equal to the selling division's standard cost (that is, the cost of production if the selling division were operating at maximum efficiency).
	Mandated market based	■ Transfer price is set equal to the market price in the selling division's market.
	Dual pricing	■ Transfer price for the buying division is set equal to the selling division's actual or standard costs.
		■ Transfer price for the selling division is set equal to the price to external customers or to the market price in the selling division's market.

will, at times, create inefficiencies and conflicts in a diversified firm (Cyert and March, 1963; Swieringa and Waterhouse, 1982). Some of these inefficiencies and conflicts are described in Table 12.4.

The inefficiencies and conflicts created by transfer pricing schemes that only approximate optimal transfer prices mean that few

---

TABLE 12.4
Weaknesses of Alternative Transfer Pricing Schemes

1. Buying and selling divisions negotiate transfer price.
   - What about the negotiating and haggling costs?
   - The corporation risks not exploiting economies of scope if the right transfer price cannot be negotiated.

2. Transfer price is set equal to the selling division's price to external customers.
   - Which customers? Different selling division customers may get different prices.
   - Shouldn't the volume created by the buying division for a selling division be reflected in a lower transfer price?
   - The selling division doesn't have marketing expenses when selling to another division. Shouldn't that be reflected in a lower transfer price?

3. Transfer price is set equal to the selling division's actual costs.
   - What are those actual costs, and who gets to determine them?
   - *All* the selling division's costs, or only the costs relevant to the products being purchased by the buying division?

4. Transfer price is set equal to the selling division's standard costs.
   - Standard costs are the costs the selling division would incur if it were running at maximum efficiency. This hypothetical capacity subsidizes the buying division.

5. Transfer price is set equal to the market price.
   - If the product in question is highly differentiated, there is no simple "market price."
   - Shouldn't the volume created by the buying division for a selling division be reflected in a lower transfer price?
   - The selling division doesn't have marketing expenses when selling to a buying division. Shouldn't that be reflected in a lower transfer price?

6. Transfer price is set equal to actual costs for the selling division and to market price for the buying division.
   - This combination of schemes simply combines the problems of setting transfer price.

---

diversified firms are ever fully satisfied with how they set transfer prices. Indeed, Gupta and Govindarajan (1986) found that as the level of resource sharing in a diversified firm increases (thereby increasing the importance of transfer pricing mechanisms), the level of job satisfaction for division general managers decreases.

It is not unusual for a diversified firm to change its transfer pricing mechanisms every few years in an attempt to find the "right" transfer pricing mechanism. Economic theory tells us what the "right" transfer pricing mechanism is: Transfer prices should equal opportunity cost. However, this "correct" transfer price mechanism cannot be implemented in most firms. Firms that continually change their transfer pricing mechanisms generally find that all these systems have some weaknesses. In choosing which system to use, a firm should be less concerned about finding the "right" transfer pricing mechanism and more concerned about choosing a transfer pricing policy that creates the fewest management problems—or at least the kinds of problems that the firm can manage effectively. Indeed, Swieringa and Waterhouse (1982) suggest that the search for optimal transfer pricing should be abandoned in favor of treating transfer pricing as a conflict resolution process. Viewed in this way, transfer pricing highlights differences between divisions and thus makes it possible to begin to resolve those differences in a mutually beneficial way.

12.4 COMPENSATION POLICIES

A firm's compensation policies constitute a final set of monitoring and bonding mechanisms for implementing a diversification strategy. Many of the compensation issues raised in Chapter 10's discussion of U-form organizational structures apply equally as well to compensation in M-form organizations.

Traditionally, the compensation of senior managers in a diversified firm has been only loosely connected to the firm's economic performance. Jensen and Murphy (1990) examined the relationship between executive compensation and firm performance, and found that differences in CEO cash compensation (salary plus cash bonus) are not very responsive to differences in firm performance. In particular, Jensen and Murphy (1990) showed that a CEO whose shareholders lost, collectively, $400 million in a year earned average cash compensation worth $800,000, while a CEO whose shareholders gained, collectively, $400 million in a year earned average cash compensation worth $1,040,000. Thus an $800 million difference in the performance of a firm only had, on average, a $204,000 impact on the size of a CEO's salary and cash bonus.

However, Jensen and Murphy (1990) were able to show that if a substantial percentage of a CEO's compensation came in the form of stock and stock options in the firm, changes in compensation would be closely linked with changes in firm performance. In particular, the $800 million difference in firm performance described above would be associated with a $1.2 million difference in the value of CEO compensation, if CEO compensation included stock and stock options in addition to cash compensation.

These and similar findings reported elsewhere have led more and more diversified firms to include stock and stock options as part of the compensation package for the CEO. As important, many firms now extend this noncash compensation to other senior managers in a diversified firm, including division general managers. For example, the top thirteen hundred managers at General Dynamics receive stock and stock options as part of their compensation package. Moreover, the cash bonuses of these managers also depend on General Dynamics' stock market performance (Dial and Murphy, 1995). At Johnson & Johnson, all division general managers receive a five-component compensation package. The level of only one of those components, salary, does not depend on the economic profitability of the business over which a division general manager presides. The level of the other four components—a cash bonus, stock grants, stock options, and a deferred income package—varies with the economic performance of a particular division. Moreover, the value of some of these variable components of compensation also depends on Johnson & Johnson's long-term economic performance (Aguilar and Bhambri, 1983).

As reported in Section 10.3, by 1991, 86 percent of the compensation of the 19 highest-paid CEOs in the United States came in the form of stock grants and other stock options. Only 47 of the 200 highest-paid CEOs in 1991 did not receive at least some of their compensation in the form of stock (Tully, 1992b). Less complete information exists about the compensation package of division general managers and other senior managers in diversified firms, but it is very likely that much of the compensation of these managers also comes in the form of stock and stock options.

To the extent that compensation in diversified firms gives managers incentives to make decisions consistent with stockholders' interests, these policies can be thought of as bonding mechanisms that reduce agency problems (Finkelstein and Hambrick, 1988). Certainly, making the value of top management compensation depend, to some extent, on the value of a firm's stock gives managers incentives to maximize the value of their firm's stock, thereby reducing agency costs (Rosen, 1982).

12.5 SUMMARY

To be valuable, diversification strategies must exploit, at low cost, economies of scope that are not available to outside investors. One implication of this requirement is that outside investors must delegate the day-to-day management of their investments in a firm to the firm's managers. This practice creates an agency relationship between a firm's outside investors (and principals) and its managers (as agents). As long as managers make decisions in ways that are consistent with investors' interests, no agency problems arise. However, it is not uncommon for conflicts of interest between these two parties to emerge and thus for agency problems to exist.

Both managers and outside investors can engage in a variety of activities to minimize agency problems. In general, these activities can be described as either monitoring activities or bonding activities. Organizing to implement a diversification strategy can be understood as an effort to create low-cost and effective monitoring and bonding mechanisms.

A diversified firm's organizational structure is a particularly important monitoring and bonding device. The best organizational structure for implementing a diversification leveraging strategy is the multidivisional, or M-form, structure. The M-form structure has several critical components that have both monitoring and bonding responsibilities. These components include the board of directors, institutional investors, the senior executive, corporate staff, division general managers, and shared activity managers. This organizational structure is supported by a variety of management control processes. Three critical processes for firms implementing diversification leveraging strategies are (1) evaluating the performance of divisions, (2) allocating capital across divisions, and (3) transferring intermediate products between divisions. The existence of economies of scope in firms implementing diversification strategies significantly complicates the management of these processes in ways that facilitate monitoring and bonding.

Finally, a firm's compensation policies can also act as monitoring and bonding mechanisms for implementing a diversification leveraging strategy. Historically, management compensation has been only loosely connected to a firm's economic performance, but the last few years have seen the increased popularity of using stock and stock options to help compensate managers. Such compensation schemes act as bonding mechanisms and help reduce agency conflicts between managers and outside investors.

REVIEW QUESTIONS

1. Agency theory has been criticized for assuming that managers, left on their own, will behave in ways that reduce the wealth of outside equity holders when, in fact, most managers are highly responsible stewards of the assets they control. This alternative view of managers has been called "stewardship theory." Do you agree with this criticism of agency theory? Why or why not?

2. Suppose that stewardship theory is correct and that most managers, most of the time, behave responsibly and make decisions that maximize the present value of the assets they control. What implications, if any, would this supposition have for organizing to implement diversification strategies?

3. The M-form structure enables firms to pursue complex diversification strategies by delegating different management responsibilities to different individuals and groups within a firm. Will there come a time when a firm becomes too large and too complex to be managed even through an M-form structure? In other words, is there a natural limit to the efficient size of a firm?

4. Most observers agree that centrally planned economies fail because it is impossible for bureaucrats in large government hierarchies to coordinate different sectors of an economy as efficiently as market mechanisms do. Many diversified firms, however, are as large as some economies and use private sector hierarchies to coordinate diverse business activities in a firm. Are these large private sector hierarchies somehow different from the government hierarchies of centrally planned economies? If yes, in what way? If no, why do these large private sector hierarchies continue to exist?

5. Suppose that the optimal transfer price between one business and all other business activities in a firm is the market price. What does this condition say about whether this firm should own this business?

CHAPTER 13

Merger and Acquisition Strategies

13.1 MERGERS AND ACQUISITIONS AND CORPORATE STRATEGY

Thus far, we have focused on the economic consequences of corporate strategies once they have been implemented. It has been shown that, in some circumstances, both vertical integration and diversification can be sources of competitive advantage. Less attention has been focused on the performance implications of the process through which firms become vertically integrated or diversified. This is the primary topic of Chapter 13.

That merger and acquisition strategies are an important strategic option open to firms pursuing vertical integration or diversification strategies can hardly be disputed. The number of firms that have used merger and acquisition strategies to become vertically integrated or diversified over the last few years is staggering. In the first three quarters of 1994, there were 5,800 mergers or acquisitions involving at least one firm with headquarters in the United States—roughly one such merger and acquisition transaction per hour during this time period (Pare, 1994). The economic value of merger and acquisition corporate strategies is even more staggering. The total value of mergers and acquisitions involving a U.S. firm in 1994 was $344 billion, beating the previous record of $336 billion in 1988. The value of such mergers and acquisitions in the first half of 1995 was $164.4 billion, the biggest first half of the year ever in mergers and acquisitions (Lipin, 1995).

The list of firms involved in mergers and acquisitions is long and varied, although most seem focused either on changing their level of vertical integration or modifying their diversification strategies. For example, IBM's $3.5 billion acquisition of Lotus Development Corporation can be understood as an attempt by IBM to vertically integrate into the personal computer software industry. Seagram's $5.7 billion acquisition of 85 percent of Matsushita Electric Industrial's share in media giant MCA can be seen as a diversification move by Seagram. And Disney's almost $20 billion acquisition of Capital Cities/ABC can be seen as a vertical integration move by Disney into the entertainment distribution business (Lipin, 1995).

Moreover, merger and acquisition activities are not limited to just a few industries. Merger and acquisitions have been important in the entertainment industry (Disney/Capital Cities; Seagram/MCA), in banking and financial services (First Union/First Fidelity Bancorporation; Fleet Financial Group/Shawmut National), in construction (Ingersoll-Rand/Clark Equipment), and in packaging (Crown Cork & Seal/CarnaudMetalbox). In the first half of 1995, merger and acquisition activity in basic industries, such as chemicals and paper, totaled $16.8 billion, up from $8.1 billion during the same time period in 1994 (Lipin, 1995).

That mergers and acquisitions are a very common, and economically important, corporate strategy is clear. What is less clear is that these strategies create above-normal economic profits for the firms that pursue them. The purpose of this chapter is to highlight the conditions under which merger and acquisition strategies will, and will not, be a source of economic profits for firms pursuing them.

13.2 THE VALUE OF MERGER AND ACQUISITION STRATEGIES

Like the value of all the other strategies discussed in this book, the value of merger and acquisition strategies depends on the context within which these strategies are implemented. To the extent that a merger or acquisition enables a firm to exploit competitive opportunities or neutralize threats, that merger or acquisition will enable the firm to reduce its costs or increase its revenues, and that strategy will be economically valuable. In this section, two merger and acquisition contexts are discussed: mergers and acquisitions between strategically unrelated firms and mergers and acquisitions between strategically related firms.

MERGERS AND ACQUISITIONS: THE UNRELATED CASE

Imagine the following scenario: One firm (the target) is the object of an acquisition effort, and ten firms (the bidders) are interested in making this acquisition. The current market value of the target firm is $10,000, the current market value of the bidding firms is $15,000, and the capital market within which the bidding firms operate is semi-strong efficient (Fama, 1970). There is no strategic relatedness between these bidding firms and the target. This means that the value of any one of these bidding firms when combined with the target firm exactly equals the sum of the value of these firms as separate entities—that is,

$$NPV(A + B) = NPV(A) + NPV(B) \qquad Eq.\ 13.1$$

where,

$NPV(A)$ = net present value of Firm A as a stand-alone entity

$NPV(B)$ = net present value of Firm B as a stand-alone entity

$NPV(A + B)$ = net present value of Firms A and B as a combined entity

At what price will this target firm be acquired, and what are the economic performance implications for bidding and target firms at this price?

In this, and all acquisition situations, bidding firms will be willing to pay a price for a target up to the value that the target firm adds to the bidder once it is acquired. This price, P, is

$$P = NPV(A + B) - NPV(A) \qquad Eq.\ 13.2$$

Notice that P does not depend on the value of the target firm acting as an independent business but, rather, depends on the value that the target firm creates when it is combined with the bidding firm. Any price for a target less than P will be a source of an above-normal economic profit for a bidding firm; any price equal to P will be a source of normal economic profits; and any price greater than P will be a source of below-normal economic profits for the bidding firm that acquires the target.

In this specific scenario, the present value of each bidding firm is $15,000, and the present value of the bidding firms combined with the target firm is $25,000 ($15,000 from the bidding firm plus $10,000 from the target firm, assuming that the bidding and target firms are not strategically related). The maximum price that a bidding firm will be willing to pay for this target is $10,000 ($25,000 – $15,000). Any price greater than $10,000 will lead to below-normal profits for a bidder; a price less than $10,000 will generate above-normal profits.

It is not hard to see that the price of this acquisition will quickly rise to $10,000 and that at this price the bidding firm that acquires the target will earn only normal economic performance. The price of this acquisition will quickly rise to $10,000 because any bid less than $10,000 will generate above-normal profits for a successful bidder. These potential above-normal profits, in turn, will generate entry into the bidding war for a target. Moreover, because the capital market for bidding firms is semi-strong efficient, these firms will be able to gain access to any capital they might need to make investments that have a positive net present value (Copeland and Weston, 1983). Because entry into the acquisition contest is assured, the price of the acquisition will quickly rise to its value, and economic profits will not be created.

Moreover, at this $10,000 price, the target firm's shareholders will also gain only normal economic profits. Indeed, for them, all that has occurred is that the market value of the target firm has been capitalized in the form of a cash payment from the bidder to the target. The target was worth $10,000, and that is exactly what these shareholders will receive.

MERGERS AND ACQUISITIONS: THE RELATED CASE

The conclusion that the acquisition of strategically unrelated targets will generate only normal economic profits for both the bidding and the target firms is not surprising. It is very consistent with the discussion of the economic consequences of unrelated diversification in Chapter 11. There, it is argued that there is no economic justification for a corporate diversification strategy that does not build on some type of economy of scope across the businesses within which a firm operates, and thus that unrelated diversification is not an economically viable corporate strategy. Thus, as was the case in the analysis of strategic alliances in Chapter 9, vertical integration in Chapter 10, and diversification in Chapter 11, some sort of strategic synergy must be at the core of a merger and acquisition strategy if that strategy is to have the potential of generating economic profits (Seth, 1990).

Types of Strategic Relatedness

The literature describes a wide variety of ways in which bidding and target firms can be strategically related (Trautwein, 1990; Walter and Barney, 1990). Three particularly important lists of these potential linkages have been developed by the Federal Trade Commission (FTC), by Lubatkin (1983), and by Jensen and Ruback (1983).

The FTC Categories.   Because mergers and acquisitions can have the effect of increasing (or decreasing) the level of concentration in an industry, the Federal Trade Commission is charged with the responsibility of evaluating the competitive implications of proposed mergers or acquisitions. In principle, the FTC will disallow any acquisition involving firms with headquarters in the United States that could have the potential for generating monopoly (or oligopoly) profits in an industry. To help in this regulatory effort, the FTC has developed a typology of mergers and acquisitions (see Table 13.1). Each category in this typology can be thought of as a different way in which a bidding firm and a target firm can be related in a merger or acquisition.

According to the FTC, a firm engages in a *vertical merger* when it vertically integrates, either forward or backward, through its acquisition efforts. Vertical mergers could include a firm purchasing critical suppliers of raw materials (backward vertical integration) or acquiring customers and distribution networks (forward vertical integration). Disney's acquisition of Capital Cities/ABC can be understood as an attempt by Disney to forward vertically integrate into the entertainment distribution industry (Huey, 1995).

A firm engages in a *horizontal merger* when it acquires a former competitor. Obviously, the FTC is particularly concerned with the competitive implications of horizontal mergers, since these strategies can have the most direct and obvious anticompetitive implications in an industry (see Chapter 8's discussion of tacit collusion in oligopolies). For example, several years ago, Coca-Cola Company tried to acquire the Dr. Pepper Company. The FTC concluded that such a merger would generate very high levels of concentration in the soft-drink industry—levels of concentration that could have led to monopoly power for Coca-Cola. Thus the FTC disallowed this acquisition effort (Prince, 1994). More recently, regulatory concern forced Microsoft to abandon its horizontal merger effort with Intuit, the leading firm in personal finance software (Shaffer, 1995b).

TABLE 13.1 **FTC Categories of** **Mergers and** **Acquisitions**	Vertical merger	A firm acquires former suppliers or customers.
	Horizontal merger	A firm acquires a former competitor.
	Product extension merger	A firm gains access to complementary products through an acquisition.
	Market extension merger	A firm gains access to complementary markets through an acquisition.
	Conglomerate merger	There is no strategic relatedness between a bidding and a target firm.

The third type of merger identified by the FTC is a *product extension merger*. In a product extension merger, firms acquire complementary products through their merger and acquisition activities. Examples include Philip Morris's acquisition of Kraft (to extend Philip Morris's presence in consumer food products), Novell's acquisition of WordPerfect (to extend Novell's presence in the personal computer software applications market), AT&T's acquisition of McCaw Cellular telephone (to extend AT&T's presence in the mobile telephone business) (Kupfer, 1994), and Johnson & Johnson's effort to take over the Cordis Corporation (to gain access to a full line of angioplasty medical technology to complement some J & J technologies) (Winslow, 1995).

The fourth type of merger identified by the FTC is a *market extension merger*. Here, the primary objective is to gain access to new geographic markets. Examples include Crown Cork & Seal's acquisition of CarnaudMetalbox (to gain access to the French packaging market), and Burlington Northern's merger with Santa Fe Pacific (to gain access to Santa Fe Pacific's rail network) (Pare, 1994).

The final type of merger or acquisition identified by the FTC is a *conglomerate merger*. For the FTC, conglomerate mergers are a residual category. If there are no vertical, horizontal, product extension, or market extension links between firms, the FTC defines the merger or acquisition activity between firms as a conglomerate merger.

Given our earlier conclusion that mergers or acquisitions between strategically *unrelated* firms will not generate above-normal profits for either bidders or targets, it should not be surprising that there are currently relatively few examples of conglomerate mergers or acquisitions. However, at various times in history, conglomerate mergers and acquisitions have been relatively common. In the 1960s, for example, most acquisitions took the form of conglomerate mergers. Rumelt (1974) found that the fraction of single-business firms in the Fortune 500 dropped from 22.8 percent in 1959 to 14.8 percent in 1969, while the fraction of firms in the Fortune 500 pursuing unrelated diversification strategies rose from 7.3 percent to 18.7 percent during the same time period. These findings are consistent with an increase in the number of conglomerate mergers and acquisitions during the 1960s.

Despite the popularity of conglomerate mergers in the 1960s, most strategically unrelated mergers or acquisitions are divested shortly after they are completed. Ravenscraft and Scherer (1987) have shown that over one-third of the conglomerate mergers of the 1960s were divested by the early 1980s. Using a longer time series of data, Porter (1987) showed that over 50 percent of these acquisitions were subsequently divested. These results are all consistent with our earlier conclusion that strategically unrelated mergers or acquisitions are not a source of economic profits.

Because firms can be strategically related in multiple ways, it is often the case that a particular merger or acquisition can be simultaneously categorized in two or more of the FTC merger and acquisition categories. For example, Crown Cork & Seal's acquisition of Carnaud-Metalbox is a market extension merger (it provided CC&S access to a new geographic market), but it also is a product extension merger (it provided CC&S access to some unique CarnaudMetalbox packaging technology). National Australia Bank's acquisition of Michigan National is a market extension merger (it provided National Australia access to the United States financial market), but it also is a product extension merger (it provided National Australia access to some financial products that the bank did not previously possess) (Grant, 1995).

Other Types of Strategic Relatedness.   Although the FTC categories of mergers and acquisitions provide some information about possible motives underlying these corporate strategies, they do not capture the full range of possible links that might exist between bidding and target firms. Several authors have attempted to develop more complete lists of possible sources of relatedness between bidding and target firms. Two of these lists are particularly important. The first, developed by Lubatkin (1983) and summarized in Table 13.2, includes technical economies (in marketing, production, and similar forms of relatedness), pecuniary economies (market power), and diversification economies (in portfolio management and risk reduction) as possible bases of strategic relatedness between bidding and target firms.

TABLE 13.2 **Lubatkin's (1983) List** **of Potential Sources** **of Strategic** **Relatedness Between** **Bidding and Target** **Firms**	Technical economies	Scale economies that occur when the physical processes inside a firm are altered so that the same amounts of input produce higher quantity of outputs. Sources of technical economies include marketing, production, experience, scheduling, banking, and compensation.
	Pecuniary economies	Economies achieved by the ability of firms to dictate prices by exerting market power.
	Diversification economies	Economies achieved by improving a firm's performance relative to its risk attributes or lowering its risk attributes relative to its performance. Sources of diversification economies include portfolio management and risk reduction.

The second important list of possible sources of strategic related-ness between bidding and target firms was developed by Jensen and Ruback (1983) in their comprehensive review of empirical research on the economic returns to mergers and acquisitions. This list is summa-rized in Table 13.3 and includes the following factors as possible sources of economic gains in mergers and acquisitions: potential reduc-tions in production or distribution costs (from economies of scale, ver-tical integration, reduction in agency costs, and so forth), the realiza-tion of financial opportunities (such as gaining access to underutilized tax shields, avoiding bankruptcy costs), the creation of market power, and the ability to eliminate inefficient management in the target firm.

To be economically valuable, links between bidding and target firms must meet the same criteria as diversification strategies (see Chapter 11). First, these links must build on real synergies between bid-ding and target firms. If real synergies exist between these firms, then the equality in Eq. (13.1) becomes an inequality:

$$NPV(A + B) > NPV(A) + NPV(B) \qquad Eq.\ 13.3$$

If this inequality holds, these two firms are more valuable merged together than they are as separate entities. This additional value can

---

TABLE 13.3
Jensen and Ruback's (1983) List of Reasons Why Bidding Firms Might Want to Engage in Merger and Acquisition Strategies

To reduce production or distribution costs

1. Through economies of scale
2. Through vertical integration
3. Through the adoption of more efficient production or organizational technology
4. Through the increased utilization of the bidder's management team
5. Through a reduction of agency costs by bringing organization-specific assets under common ownership

Financial motivations

1. To gain access to underutilized tax shields
2. To avoid bankruptcy costs
3. To increase leverage opportunities
4. To gain other tax advantages

To gain market power in product markets

To eliminate inefficient target management

reflect either cost savings or revenue enhancements that are created by merging these two firms. Second, not only must this synergy exist, but it must be less costly for the merged firm to realize this synergy than for outside equity holders to realize it on their own. As is the case with diversification strategies, by investing in a diversified portfolio of stocks, outside equity investors can gain many of the synergies associated with a merger or acquisition on their own. Moreover, investors can realize some of these synergies at almost zero cost. In this situation, it makes little sense for investors to "hire" managers in firms to realize these synergies for them through a merger or acquisition. Rather, firms should pursue merger and acquisition strategies only to obtain synergies that outside investors find too costly to create on their own.

Economic Profits in Related Acquisitions

If bidding and target firms are strategically related, then the economic value of these two firms combined is greater than the economic value of these two firms as separate entities. To see how the inequality in Eq. (13.3) affects returns to merger and acquisition strategies, consider the following scenario: There is one target firm and ten bidding firms. The market value of the target firm as a stand-alone entity is $10,000, and the market value of the bidding firms as stand-alone entities is $15,000. The bidding and target firms are strategically related. Any of the types of relatedness identified by the FTC, by Lubatkin (1983), or by Jensen and Ruback (1983) could be the source of these synergies. These synergies imply that when any of the bidding firms and the target are combined, the market value of this combined entity will be $32,000—note that $32,000 is greater than the sum of $15,000 plus $10,000, and thus the inequality in Eq. (13.3) holds. Assuming the capital market within which the bidding firms are operating is semistrong efficient, at what price will this target firm be acquired, and what are the economic profit implications for bidding and target firms at this price?

As before, bidding firms will be willing to pay a price for a target up to the value that a target firm adds once it is acquired. Thus the formula for determining the maximum price, P, that bidding firms are willing to pay for a target—Eq. (13.2)—remains unchanged. Applying that formula to this strategically related scenario implies that bidding firms will be willing to pay up to $17,000 ($P$ = $32,000 – $15,000) to acquire this target.

As was the case for the strategically unrelated acquisition, it is not hard to see that the price for actually acquiring the target firm in this scenario will rapidly rise to $17,000. The price will quickly rise to $17,000 because any bid less than $17,000 has the potential for generating above-normal profits for a bidding firm. Suppose that one bidding firm offers $13,000 for the target. For this $13,000, the bidding firm gains access to a target that will generate $17,000 of value once it is acquired. Thus, to this bidding firm, the target is worth $17,000, and a bid of $13,000 will generate a $4,000 economic profit. Of course, these potential profits will motivate entry into the competitive bidding process. Entry will be possible since each of the ten bidding firms can realize the same synergy with this target, and since capital markets are semistrong efficient.

At this $17,000 price, the successful bidding firm earns normal economic profits. After all, this firm has acquired an asset that will generate $17,000 of value and has paid $17,000 to do so. However, the owners of the target firm will earn an economic profit worth $7,000. As a stand-alone firm, the target is worth $10,000; when combined with a bidding firm, it is worth $17,000. The difference between the value of the target as a stand-alone entity and its value in combination with a bidding firm is the value of the above-normal economic profit that can be appropriated by the owners of the target firm.

Thus the existence of strategic relatedness between bidding and target firms, as defined in Eq. (13.3), is not a sufficient condition for the shareholders of bidding firms to earn above-normal profits from their acquisition strategies. If the economic potential of acquiring a particular target firm is widely known, if several potential bidding firms can all obtain this value by acquiring a target, and if semistrong capital market efficiency holds (Fama, 1970), then shareholders of bidding firms will, at best, earn only normal economic profits from implementing an acquisition strategy. In this setting, a "strategically related" merger or acquisition will create economic value, but this value will be distributed in the form of above-normal economic profits to the shareholders of acquired target firms.

Note that the fact that a particular target is not the object of multiple bids does not necessarily imply that a bidding firm will be able to earn above-normal economic performance from its acquisition of a target. A bidding firm, in anticipation of other potential bidders, may make an initial bid equal to the full synergistic value of the target. With such a bid, this bidding firm will be able to acquire the target but will earn only normal economic profits from doing so. In this case, the threat of anticipated competition for a target leads to normal economic profits for a bidding firm.

Also, different bidding firms may have different types of strategic relatedness with target firms, and these performance implications of mergers and acquisitions will still be unchanged. All that is required is that the different bidding firms value targets at the same level. When this is the case, bidding firms will earn normal economic profits and targets will earn above-normal profits. However, in real merger and acquisition situations, it seems likely that when different bidding firms value the acquisition of targets at the same level, the type of relatedness that exists between one bidder and targets is likely to be quite similar to the type of relatedness that exists between other bidders and targets. This homogeneity in relatedness leads to a homogeneity in the valuation of targets, which in turn leads to zero economic profits for bidders upon acquisition.

EMPIRICAL RESEARCH ON THE PERFORMANCE IMPLICATIONS OF MERGERS AND ACQUISITIONS

Our discussion of returns to bidding and target firms in strategically related and strategically unrelated mergers and acquisitions leads to a variety of important empirical questions. Several of these questions—including whether most acquisitions occur between strategically related or strategically unrelated firms, and the return implications of these different acquisition contexts on returns to bidding and target firms—have been addressed in the empirical literature.

For example, Jensen and Ruback (1983) reviewed over forty empirical merger and acquisition studies in the finance literature. They examined acquisitions that were negotiated between a bidding firm's management and a target firm's management, and they examined offers to buy a target firm's shares made directly to the target firm's shareholders. Jensen and Ruback concluded that the completion of the first type of acquisition, on average, increases the market value of target firms by 20 percent, and leaves the market value of bidding firms unchanged. In contrast, acquisition offers made directly to a target firm's shareholders, on average, increase the market value of a target firm by 30 percent and have a small positive impact (4 percent) on the value of the successful bidding firm. Judging from the empirical evidence in finance, Jensen and Ruback (1983:47) concluded that "corporate takeovers generate positive gains, . . . target firm shareholders benefit, and . . . bidding firm shareholders do not lose."

However, Jensen and Ruback (1983) are less confident about the sources of value creation in mergers and acquisitions. Although they cite numerous potential synergies between bidding and target firms in mergers and acquisitions (see Table 13.3), most of the research they review examines only how much value mergers and acquisitions create and who appropriates that value, not the sources of that value. The only two studies they review that examine potential sources of value creation (Eckbo, 1983; Stillman, 1983) focused only on the ability of horizontal acquisitions to generate above-normal profits through the creation of market power (see Chapter 8's discussion of industry concentration and tacit collusion). However, both Eckbo (1983) and Stillman (1983) conclude that horizontal mergers do not create market power or

$4,000 for their targets. At this price, these bidding firms will all earn normal economic profits, except for Firm A, which will earn an economic profit equal to $2,000.

In order for Firm A to obtain this above-normal economic profit, the value of Firm A's synergy with target firms must be greater than the value of any other bidding firms with that target. This special value will generally reflect unusual resources and capabilities possessed by Firm A—resources and capabilities that are more valuable in combination with target firms than are the resources and capabilities that other bidding firms possess. Put differently, to be a source of economic profits and competitive advantage, Firm A's link with targets must be based on firm resources and capabilities that are rare among those firms competing in this market for corporate control.

However, not only does Firm A have to possess valuable and rare links with bidding firms to gain economic profits and competitive advantages from its acquisition strategies, but information about these special synergies must not be known by other firms. If other bidding firms know about the additional value associated with acquiring a target, they are likely to try to duplicate this value for themselves. Typically, they would accomplish this by imitating the type of relatedness that exists between Firm A and targets, by acquiring the resources and capabilities that enabled Firm A to have its valuable synergy with targets. Once other bidders acquired the resources and capabilities necessary to obtain this more valuable synergy, they would be able to enter into bidding, thereby increasing the likelihood that the shareholders of successful bidding firms would earn normal economic profits.

The acquisition or development of these resources and capabilities would not even have to be completed before bidding for target firms began, because bidding firms could anticipate that they would be able to acquire or develop these resources and capabilities at some point in the future, and thus the present value of acquiring these targets for these bidders would be the same as for Firm A. In this setting, the price of an acquisition will rise to equal its full value for Firm A and for those bidders who anticipate the ability to acquire the resources and capabilities controlled by Firm A. Firm A can be shielded from this competition only if other bidding firms are unaware of the higher-valued strategic relatedness available to Firm A and the sources of this higher-valued strategic relatedness.

Target firms must also be unaware of Firm A's special resources and capabilities if Firm A is to obtain above-normal profits from an acquisition. If target firms were aware of this extra value available to Firm A, along with the sources of this value, they could inform other bidding firms. These bidding firms could then adjust their bids to reflect this higher value, and competitive bidding would reduce above-normal profits to bidders to a normal level. Target firms are likely to inform bidding firms in this way because increasing the number of bidders with more valuable synergies increases the likelihood that target firms will extract all the economic value created in a merger or acquisition (Turk, 1987). Though there may be many different managerial motives behind target firms' seeking out "white knights" as alternative merger partners after an acquisition attempt has been made, the effect of such actions is to increase the number of fully informed bidders for a target. This, in turn, reduces the economic profit that bidding firms obtain.

Thus far, it has been assumed that only one firm has a more valuable source of strategic relatedness with targets (in this example, worth $12,000 compared to all other bidding firms' strategic relatedness worth only $10,000). However, the argument also applies to the more complex case where several bidding firms have more valuable synergies with targets than are the synergies whose value is publicly known. As long as the number of targets is greater than, or equal to, the number of firms with these more valuable sources of strategic relatedness, each of the bidding firms can complete an acquisition, and each can earn varying amounts of economic profits—depending on the value of each of these bidding firms' synergies with specific targets.

The impact of valuable, rare, and private synergies on above-normal profits for the shareholders of bidding firms even holds when different bidding firms all have different values as stand-alone entities and in combination with different targets—that is, when each bidding firm acting in a market for corporate control is unique. Consider the example in Table 13.5. The present value of the four firms in this table (A, B, C, and D) as stand-alone entities ranges from $2,000 to $5,000, and the present value of these firms when combined with targets ranges from $9,000 to $12,000. From Eq. (13.2) it is clear that Firm A must pay less than $9,000 for a target in order to gain economic profits, Firm B less than $6,000, Firm C less than $7,000, and Firm D less than $7,000.

If publicly available information suggests that firms with the right resources and capabilities can obtain, from acquiring a target, an

TABLE 13.5 **Present Value of** **Strategic Relatedness** **Between Four Firms** **and Targets**	**Firm A**	**Firm B**	**Firm C**	**Firm D**
Present value of strategic relatedness with targets	$12,000	$11,000	$10,000	$9,000
Present value of firm as a stand-alone entity	3,000	5,000	3,000	2,000

incremental growth in their economic value worth $7,000, then several things are likely to occur. First, Firm B is likely to acquire or develop the resources and capabilities that enable Firms C and D to obtain a $7,000 present-value increase from acquiring a target. Next, the price of a target is likely to rise to $7,000. If several target firms are available, all the firms in Table 13.5 will be able to acquire a target, but only Firm A will make an above-normal economic profit from doing so (worth $2,000). If only one target is available, only Firm A will complete the acquisition or merger, and its above-normal profit, though still positive, will be slightly smaller ($2,000 less some small amount). If there are not enough targets for all bidding firms, then which firms (B, C, or D) will complete an acquisition is indeterminate, although whichever of these firms does so will not obtain an above-normal profit. Also, Firm A will complete an acquisition and still earn an abnormal return for its shareholders equal to $2,000 (minus some small amount).

Adding a firm (Firm E) that is identical to Firm A in Table 13.5 highlights the requirement that the number of firms with a more valuable synergy with targets must be less than, or equal to, the number of targets in order for these bidding firms to earn economic profits. If there are two or more targets, then both Firm A and Firm E can execute an acquisition for above-normal profits. However, if there is only one target, then Firms A and E are likely to engage in competitive bidding, perhaps driving the price of this target up to the point that acquiring it will no longer be a source of economic profits (that is, setting P equal to $9,000). In this process, Firms A and E will be ensuring that the shareholders of this acquired firm earn substantial above-normal profits.

VALUABLE, RARE, AND COSTLY-TO-IMITATE SYNERGIES BETWEEN BIDDING AND TARGET FIRMS

The existence of firms that have valuable, rare, and private synergies with targets is not the only factor that can result in an imperfectly competitive market for corporate control. If other bidders cannot imitate one bidder's valuable and rare synergies with targets, then competition in this market for corporate control will be imperfect, and the shareholders of this special bidding firm will earn economic profits. In this case, the existence of valuable and rare synergies does not need to be private, for other bidding firms cannot imitate these synergies, and therefore bids that substantially reduce the above-normal profits for the shareholders of the special bidding firm are not forthcoming.

Typically, bidding firms will be unable to imitate one bidder's valuable and rare synergies with targets when the strategic relatedness between the special bidder and the targets stems from some rare and costly-to-imitate resources or capabilities controlled by the special bidding firm. Any of the costly-to-imitate resources and capabilities discussed in Section 5.2 could create costly-to-imitate synergies between a firm and a target. If, in addition, these synergies are valuable and rare, they can be a source of above-normal profits to the shareholders of the special bidding firm. This can happen even if all firms in this market for corporate control are aware of the more valuable synergies controlled by this firm and its sources. Although information about this special synergy is publicly available, shareholders of special bidding firms will earn an above-normal profit when acquisition occurs. The shareholders of target firms will not obtain this profit, because competitive bidding dynamics cannot unfold when the sources of a more valuable synergy are costly to imitate.

As before, the number of firms with this special synergy must be less than the number of targets, in order for the shareholders of these firms to obtain above-normal profits. If there are more of these special bidders than there are targets, then these firms are likely to engage in competitive bidding for targets, once again shifting above-normal profits from bidding to target firm shareholders.

If the number of bidding firms with these special attributes is less than the number of target firms, then the level of economic profit they obtain will be approximately the same as for bidding firms with valuable, rare, and private synergies with targets. However, if the number of special bidders and number of targets are the same, the market for corporate control takes on many of the attributes of a bilateral monopoly. In this setting, the level of above-normal profits that the shareholders of bidding firms obtain depends on their negotiating skills and is somewhat indeterminate. When all bidders and targets know the value of a target for a particular bidder that has valuable, rare, and costly-to-imitate synergies with targets, the negotiated price is likely to fall somewhere between the value of targets for firms that have the high-value synergy and the value of targets for other bidding firms.

Of course, it may be possible for a valuable, rare, and costly-to-imitate synergy between a bidding and a target firm to also be private. Indeed, it is often the case that those attributes of a firm that are costly to imitate are also difficult to describe (Barney, 1988) and thus can be held as proprietary information. In that case, the analysis of above-normal profits associated with valuable, rare, and private synergies presented earlier applies.

UNEXPECTED VALUABLE SYNERGIES BETWEEN BIDDING AND TARGET FIRMS

The discussion of above-normal profits to bidding firms implementing merger and acquisition strategies has adopted, for convenience, the strong assumption that the present value of the strategic relatedness between bidders and targets is known with certainty by individual bidders. This is, in principle, possible but certainly not likely. Most modern acquisitions and mergers are massively complex, involving numerous unknown and complicated relationships between firms. In these settings, unexpected events after an acquisition has been completed may make the synergy from an acquisition or merger more valuable than bidders and targets anticipated it would be. The price that bidding firms will pay to acquire a target will equal the expected value of the target only when the target is combined with the bidder. The difference between the unexpected value of an acquisition actually obtained by a bidder and the price the bidder paid for the acquisition is an above-normal profit for the shareholders of the bidding firm.

Of course, by definition, bidding firms cannot expect to obtain unexpected value from an acquisition. Unexpected value, in this context, is a surprise, a manifestation of a bidding firm's good luck, not its skill in acquiring targets (Barney, 1988).

IMPLICATIONS FOR BIDDING FIRM MANAGERS

The existence of valuable, rare, and private synergies between bidding and target firms, and of valuable, rare, and costly-to-imitate synergies between bidding and target firms, suggests that although, on average, most bidding firms do not generate above-normal economic profits from their acquisition strategies, in some special circumstances it may be possible for bidding firms to create such profits. Thus the task facing managers in firms contemplating merger and acquisition strategies is to choose merger and acquisition strategies that have the greatest likelihood of being able to generate above-normal returns for their shareholders. Several important managerial prescriptions can be derived from this discussion. These "rules" for bidding firm managers are summarized in Table 13.6 and discussed below.

TABLE 13.6
Rules for Bidding Firm Managers

1. Search for valuable and rare synergies.

2. Keep information away from other bidders.

3. Keep information away from targets.

4. Avoid winning bidding wars.

5. Close the deal quickly.

Search for Rare Synergies

One of the main reasons why bidding firms do not obtain above-normal performance from acquiring strategically related target firms is that several other bidding firms value the target firm in the same way. When multiple bidders all value a target in the same way, competitive bidding is likely. Competitive bidding, in turn, drives out the potential for superior performance. To avoid this problem, bidding firms should seek to acquire targets with which they enjoy valuable and rare synergies.

Operationally, the search for rare synergies suggests that managers in bidding firms need to consider not only the value of a target firm when combined with their own company, but also the value of a target firm when combined with other potential bidders. For it is the difference between the value of a particular bidding firm's relationship with a target and the value of other bidding firms' relationships with that target that defines the size of the potential economic profits from an acquisition.

In practice, the search for valuable and rare synergies is likely to become a search for valuable and rare resources already controlled by a firm that are synergistically related to a target. For example, if a bidding firm has a unique reputation in its product market, and if the target firm's products could benefit by association with that reputation, then the target firm may be more valuable to this particular bidder than to other bidders (firms that do not possess this special reputation). Also, if a particular bidder possesses the largest market share in its industry, the best distribution system, or restricted access to certain key raw materials, and if the target firm would benefit from being associated with these valuable and rare resources, then the acquisition of this target may be a source of economic profits.

The search for valuable and rare synergies as a basis of mergers and acquisitions tends to rule out certain synergies as sources of economic profits. For example, most acquisitions can lead to a reduction in overhead costs, since much of the corporate overhead associated with the target firm can be eliminated subsequent to acquisition. However, the ability to eliminate these overhead costs is not unique to any one bidder, and thus the value created by these reduced costs will usually be captured by the shareholders of the target firm.

Keep Information Away from Other Bidders

One of the keys to earning superior performance in an acquisition strategy is to avoid multiple bidders for a single target. One way to accomplish this is to keep information about the bidding process, and about the sources of synergies between a bidder and target that underlie this bidding process, as private as possible. To become involved in bidding for a target, other firms must be aware of the value of the synergies between themselves and that target. If only one bidding firm knows this information, and if this bidding firm can close the deal before the full value of the target is known, then this bidding firm may earn above-normal economic profits from completing this acquisition.

Of course, in many circumstances, keeping all this information private is difficult. Often, it is illegal. For example, when seeking to acquire a publicly traded firm, potential bidders must meet disclosure requirements that effectively reduce the amount of private information a bidder can retain. In these circumstances, unless a bidding firm has some valuable, rare, and costly-to-imitate synergy with a target firm, the possibility of economic profits coming from an acquisition is very low. It is not surprising that the research conducted on mergers and acquisitions of firms traded on public stock exchanges governed by SEC disclosure rules suggests that, most of the time, bidding firms do not earn economic profits from implementing their acquisition strategies (Jensen and Ruback, 1983).

But not all potential targets are publicly traded. Privately held firms may be acquired in an information environment that can create opportunities for above-normal performance for bidding firms. Moreover, even when acquiring a publicly traded firm, a bidder does not have to release all the information it has about the potential value of that target in combination with itself. Indeed, if some of this value reflects a bidding firm's taken-for-granted "invisible" assets, it may not be possible to communicate this information. In this case, as well, there may be opportunities for above-normal profits to bidding firms.

Keep Information Away from Targets

Not only should bidding firms keep information about the value of their synergy with a target away from other bidders, but they also should keep this information away from target firms. Suppose that the value of a target firm to a bidding firm is $8,000 but the bidding firm, in an attempt to earn economic profits, has bid only $5,000 for the target. If the target knows that it is actually worth $8,000, it is very likely to hold out for a higher bid. In fact, the target may contact other potential bidding firms and tell them of the opportunity created by the $5,000 bid. As the number of bidders goes up, the possibility of superior economic performance for bidders goes down. Therefore, to keep the possibility of these profits alive, bidding firms must not fully reveal the value of their synergies with a target firm.

Again, in some circumstances, it is very difficult, or even illegal, to attempt to limit the flow of information to target firms. In these settings, superior economic performance for bidding firms is very unlikely.

Limiting the amount of information that flows to the target firm may have some other consequences as well. For example, it has been shown that a complete sharing of information, insights, and perspectives before an acquisition is completed increases the probability that synergies will actually be realized once an acquisition is completed (Jemison and Sitkin, 1986). By limiting the flow of information between itself and a target, a bidding firm may actually be increasing the cost of integrating the target into its ongoing business, thereby jeopardizing at least some of the superior economic performance that limiting information flow is designed to create. Bidding firms will need to carefully balance the economic consequences of limiting the information they share with the target firm in order to generate superior economic performance against the costs that limiting information flow may create.

Avoid Winning Bidding Wars

It should be reasonably clear that if a number of firms bid for the same target, the probability that the firm that successfully acquires the target will earn above-normal profits is very low. Indeed, to ensure that competitive bidding occurs, target firms can actively encourage other bidding firms to enter into the bidding process. The implications of these arguments are clear: Bidding firms should generally avoid winning a bidding war. To "win" a bidding war, a bidding firm will often have to pay a price at least equal to the full value of the target. Many times, given the emotions of an intense bidding contest, the winning bid may actually be larger than the true value of the target. Completing this type of acquisition will certainly reduce the economic performance of the bidding firm.

The only time it might make sense to "win" a bidding war is when the winning firm possesses a rare and private, or rare and costly-to-imitate, synergy with a target that is more valuable than the strategic relatedness that exists between any other bidders and that target. In this setting, the winning firm may be able to earn an above-normal profit if it is able to fully realize the value of its synergy.

Close the Deal Quickly

A final rule of thumb to obtain superior performance from implementing merger and acquisition strategies is to close the deal quickly. All the economic processes that make it difficult for bidding firms to earn economic profits from acquiring a strategically related target take time to unfold. It takes time for other bidders to become aware of the economic value associated with acquiring a target; it takes time for the target to recruit other bidders; information leakage becomes more of a problem over time, and so forth. A bidding firm that begins and ends the bidding process quickly may forestall some of these processes and thereby retain some superior performance for itself from an acquisition.

The admonition to close the deal quickly should not be taken to mean that bidding firms need to make their acquisition decisions quickly. Indeed, the search for valuable and rare synergies should be undertaken with great care. There should be little rush in isolating and evaluating acquisition candidates. However, once a target firm has been located and valued, bidding firms have a strong incentive to reduce the period of time between the first bid and the completion of the deal. The longer this period of negotiation is, the less likely is the bidding firm to earn economic profits from the acquisition.

Service Corporation International: An Example

Empirical research on mergers and acquisitions suggests that it is not easy for bidding firms to earn economic profits from these strategies. However, it may be possible for some bidding firms, some of the time, to do so. One firm that has seemed to be successful in earning above-normal profits from its merger and acquisition strategies is Service Corporation International (SCI). SCI is in the funeral home and cemetery business. It has grown from a collection of five funeral homes in 1967 to being the largest owner of cemeteries and funeral homes in the United States today. It has done this through an aggressive and highly profitable acquisitions program in this historically fragmented industry (see the discussion of consolidation strategies in fragmented industries in Section 4.2).

The valuable and rare synergy that SCI has brought to the funeral home industry is the application of traditional business practices in a highly fragmented and not professionally managed industry. SCI-owned funeral homes operate with gross margins approaching 30 percent, nearly three times the gross margins of independently owned funeral homes. These increased margins reflect savings from centralized purchasing services, centralized embalming and professional services, and the sharing of underutilized resources (including hearses) among funeral homes within geographic regions. SCI's scale advantages make a particular funeral home more valuable to SCI than to one of SCI's competitors, and more valuable than if a particular funeral home was left as a stand-alone business.

Moreover, the funeral homes that SCI targets for acquisition are, typically, family owned and lack heirs to continue the business. Many of the owner/operators of these funeral homes are not fully aware of the value of their operations to SCI (they are morticians more than business managers), nor are they just interested in maximizing the sale price of their funeral homes. Rather, they are often looking to maintain continuity of service in a community, secure employment for their loyal employees, and ensure a comfortable (if not lavish) retirement for themselves. Being acquired by SCI is likely to be the only alternative to closing the funeral home once an owner/operator retires. Extracting less than the full value of the home when selling to SCI often seems preferable to other alternatives.

Because SCI's acquisition of funeral homes exploits real and valuable synergies, this strategy has the potential for generating superior economic performance. Because SCI has been the only firm implementing this strategy in the funeral home industry, because the funeral homes that SCI acquires are generally not publicly traded, and because the owner/operators of these funeral homes often have interests besides simply maximizing the price of their operation when they sell it, it seems likely that SCI's acquisition strategy has generated superior economic performance (Jacob, 1992c).

IMPLICATIONS FOR TARGET FIRM MANAGERS

Although bidding firm managers can do several things to attempt to maximize the probability of earning economic profits from their merger and acquisition strategies, target firm managers can attempt to counter these efforts, to ensure that the owners of target firms appropriate whatever value is created by a merger or acquisition. These "rules" for target firm managers are summarized in Table 13.7 and discussed below.

Seek Information from Bidders

One way in which a bidder can attempt to obtain superior performance from implementing an acquisition strategy is by keeping private the information about the source and value of the strategic relatedness that exists between the bidder and target. If that synergy is actually worth $12,000 but targets believe it is only worth $8,000, then a target might be willing to settle for a bid of $8,000 and thereby forgo the extra $4,000 it could have extracted from the bidder. Once the target knows that its true value to the bidder is $12,000, it is in a much better position to obtain this full value when the acquisition is completed.

TABLE 13.7 **Rules for Target Firm Managers**	1. Seek information from bidders. 2. Invite other bidders to join the bidding competition. 3. Delay but do not stop the acquisition.

It is well known that bidding firms must fully inform themselves about the resources and capabilities of potential acquisition targets to ensure that they price those targets appropriately. However, what is not as well known is that target firms must also inform themselves about the resources and capabilities of current and potential bidders. In this way, target firms can become fully aware of the value that they hold for bidders, and they are more likely to be able to extract this full value in the acquisition process.

Invite Other Bidders to Join the Bidding Competition

Once a target firm is fully aware of the nature and value of the synergies that exist between it and current bidding firms, it can exploit this information by seeking other firms that may have the same synergy with it and then informing these firms of a potential acquisition opportunity. By inviting other firms into the bidding process, the target firm increases the competitiveness of the market for corporate control, thereby increasing the probability that the value created by an acquisition will be fully captured by the target firm.

Delay But Do Not Stop the Acquisition

As suggested earlier, bidding firms have a strong incentive to expedite the acquisition process, to prevent other bidders from becoming involved in an acquisition. Of course, the target firm wants other bidding firms to enter the process. To increase the probability of receiving more than one bid, target firms have a strong incentive to delay an acquisition.

The objective, however, should be to delay an acquisition to create a more competitive market for corporate control, not to stop an acquisition. If a valuable synergy exists between a bidding and a target firm, the merger of these two firms will create economic value. If the market for corporate control within which this merger occurs is competitive, then the shareholders of the target firm will appropriate the full value of this synergy. Preventing an acquisition in this setting can be very costly to the shareholders of the target firm.

Target firm managers can engage in a wide variety of activities to delay the completion of an acquisition. Some of these actions have the effect of reducing the wealth of target firm shareholders, some have no impact on the wealth of target firm shareholders, and some increase the wealth of target firm shareholders. Some common responses of target firm management to takeover efforts, along with their economic implications for the shareholders of target firms, are summarized in Table 13.8 and discussed below.

**TABLE 13.8
The Wealth Effects of
Target Firm
Management
Responses to
Acquisition Efforts**

1. Responses that reduce the wealth of target firm shareholders
   - Greenmail
   - Stand-still agreements
   - Poison pills
2. Responses that do not affect the wealth of target firm shareholders
   - Shark repellents
   - Pac Man defense
   - Crown jewel sale
   - Law suits
3. Responses that increase the wealth of target firm shareholders
   - Search for white knights
   - Creation of bidding auctions
   - Golden parachutes

Responses That Reduce the Wealth of Target Firm Shareholders.
Greenmail, stand-still agreements, and "poison pills" are antitakeover
actions that target firm managers take that reduce the wealth of target
firm shareholders (Walkling and Long, 1984). Greenmail is a maneuver
in which a target firm's management purchases any of the target firm's
stock owned by a bidder, and does so for a price that is greater than the
current market value of that stock (Kosnik, 1987). Greenmail effectively
ends a bidding firm's effort to acquire a particular target, and does so
in a way that can greatly reduce the wealth of a target firm's shareholders. Not only do these shareholders not appropriate any economic
value that could have been created if an acquisition had been completed, but they have to bear the cost of the premium price that management pays to buy its stock back from the bidding firm (Walsh, 1989).

   Not surprisingly, target firms that resort to greenmail substantially reduce the economic wealth of their shareholders (Kosnik, 1987;
Turk, 1992). Dann and DeAngelo (1983) found that the value of target
firms paying greenmail drops, on average, 1.76 percent; Bradley and
Wakeman (1983) report a 2.85 percent drop in the value of such firms.
These reductions in value increase if greenmail leads to the cancellation
of a takeover effort. Bradley and Wakeman (1983) found that such
episodes led to a 5.50 percent reduction in the value of target firms.

These reductions in the value of target firms as a response to their greenmail activities stands in marked contrast to the generally positive market response to efforts by a firm to repurchase its own shares in nongreenmail situations (Masulis, 1980; Dann, 1981).

Stand-still agreements are often negotiated in conjunction with greenmail. A stand-still agreement is a contract between a target and a bidding firm wherein the bidding firm agrees not to attempt to take over the target for some period of time. When a target firm negotiates a stand-still agreement, it prevents the current acquisition effort from being completed, and it reduces the number of bidders that might become involved in future acquisition efforts. Thus the shareholders of this target firm forgo any value that could have been created if the current acquisition had occurred, and they also lose some of the value that they could have appropriated in future acquisition episodes by the target's inviting multiple bidders into a market for corporate control.

Stand-still agreements, either alone or in conjunction with greenmail, reduce the economic value of a target firm. Dann and DeAngelo (1983) found that stand-still agreements that were unaccompanied by stock repurchase agreements reduced the value of a target firm by 4.05 percent. Such agreements, in combination with stock repurchases, reduced the value of a target firm by 4.52 percent.

So-called poison pills include any of a variety of actions that target firm managers can take to make the acquisition of the target prohibitively expensive (Turk, 1987). In one common poison pill maneuver a target firm issues rights to its current stockholders indicating that if the firm is acquired in an unfriendly takeover, it will distribute a special cash dividend to stockholders (Lamphier, 1980). This cash dividend effectively increases the cost of acquiring the target and can discourage otherwise interested bidding firms from attempting to acquire this target. Another poison pill tactic substitutes the distribution of additional shares of a target firm's stock, at very low prices, for the special cash dividend. Issuing this low-price stock to current stockholders effectively undermines the value of a bidding firm's equity investment in a target and thus increases the cost of the acquisition. Other poison pills involve granting current stockholders other rights—rights that effectively increase the cost of an unfriendly takeover (Metz, 1988).

Although poison pills are creative devices that target firms can use to prevent an acquisition, they generally have not been very effective. If a bidding firm and a target firm are strategically related, the value that can be created in an acquisition can be substantial, and most of this value will be appropriated by the stockholders of the target firm. Thus target firm stockholders have a strong incentive to have the target firm be acquired, and they are amenable to direct offers made by a bidding firm to them, as individual investors. These direct offers to purchase a publicly traded firm's stock directly from stockholders are called *tender offers* (Jensen and Ruback, 1983). To the extent that poison pills actually do prevent mergers or acquisitions, they are usually bad for the shareholders of target firms.

Responses That Do Not Affect the Wealth of Target Firm Shareholders. Target firm management can engage in a wide variety of additional actions to try to delay their acquisition by a bidding firm. Many of these actions do not significantly delay or stop the completion of an acquisition. Since they do not significantly extend the duration of an acquisition effort, and since they do not stop this effort, they have little impact on the wealth of a target firm's shareholders.

One class of these responses is known as "shark repellents." Shark repellents include a variety of relatively minor corporate governance changes that, in principle, are supposed to make it somewhat more difficult to acquire a target firm. Common examples of shark repellents include supermajority voting rules (which specify that more than 50 percent of the target firm's board of directors must approve a takeover) and state incorporation laws (in some states incorporation laws make it difficult to acquire a firm incorporated in that state). However, if the value created by an acquisition is sufficiently large, these shark repellents will neither slow an acquisition attempt significantly nor prevent it from being completed.

Another response that does not affect the wealth of target firm shareholders is known as the "Pac Man defense." Targets using this tactic fend off an acquisition by taking over the firm or firms bidding for them. Just as in the old video game, the hunted becomes the hunter; the target turns the tables on current and potential bidders. One firm that successfully employed the Pac Man defense was American Brands, a diversified tobacco products company (Freedman and Burrough, 1988). In 1987, American Brands fought off an acquisition by acquiring its suitor, E II Holdings, Inc. However, in 1988, the Liggett Group launched an unfriendly takeover bid for American Brands. At the time, it was speculated that the owners of the Liggett Group really wanted to sell Liggett and that their bid to acquire American Brands was designed to spur American Brands into implementing its Pac Man defense to acquire the Liggett Group.

It should not be too surprising that the Pac Man defense does not, on average, either hurt or help the stockholders of target firms. In this defense, targets become bidders, and we know from the empirical literature that, on average, bidding firms earn only normal economic profits from their acquisition efforts. Thus one would expect that, on average, the Pac Man defense would generate only normal economic profits for the stockholders of target firms implementing it.

Another ineffective and inconsequential response is called a "crown jewel sale." The idea behind a crown jewel sale is that, sometimes, a bidding firm is interested in just a few of the businesses currently being operated by the target firm. These businesses are the target firm's "crown jewels." To prevent an acquisition, the target firm can sell off these crown jewels, either directly to the bidding firm or by setting up a separate company to own and operate these businesses. In this way, the bidding firm is likely to be less interested in acquiring the target.

Perhaps one of the most famous crown-jewel-sale defenses was employed by Pillsbury in its attempt to stave off an unfriendly takeover by Grand Met (Gibson, Lublin, and Allen, 1988). At the time, the general belief was that Grand Met was particularly interested in acquiring Pillsbury's Burger King business. By setting up Burger King as a separate business entity, management at Pillsbury apparently believed that the full value of its Burger King operating unit would be revealed to the stock market and Grand Met's ability to earn economic profits from the acquisition of Burger King would fall. Moreover, Pillsbury management also apparently believed that Grand Met would no longer be interested in acquiring the rest of Pillsbury. Pillsbury was wrong on both counts, as Grand Met completed its acquisition of Pillsbury shortly after Pillsbury announced its crown-jewel-sale defense (Helyar and Burrough, 1988a).

A final relatively ineffective defense that most target firm managers pursue is filing lawsuits against bidding firms. Indeed, at least in the United States, the filing of a lawsuit is almost inevitable as soon as an acquisition effort is announced. These suits, however, usually do not delay or stop an acquisition or merger.

Responses That Increase the Wealth of Target Firm Shareholders. As suggested in Table 13.7, some of the actions that the management of target firms can take to delay (but not stop) an acquisition actually benefit target firm shareholders. The first of these is the search for a "white knight"—another bidding firm that agrees to acquire a particular target in the place of the original bidding firm. Target firm management may prefer to be acquired by some bidding firms more than by others. For example, it may be the case that some bidding firms possess much more valuable synergies with a target firm than other bidding firms. It may also be the case that some bidding firms will take a longer-term view in managing a target firm's assets than other bidding firms. In both cases, target firm managers are likely to prefer some bidding firms over other bidding firms.

As suggested earlier, whatever the motivation a target firm's management has, inviting a white knight to bid on a target firm has the effect of increasing by at least one the number of firms bidding for a target. If there is currently only one bidder, inviting a white knight into the bidding competition doubles the number of firms actually bidding for a target. As the number of bidders increases, the competitiveness of the market for corporate control and the likelihood that the shareholders of the target firm will appropriate all the value created by an acquisition also increase. On average, the entrance of a white knight into a competitive bidding contest for a target firm increases the wealth of target firm shareholders by 17 percent (Turk, 1987).

If adding one firm to the competitive bidding process increases the wealth of target firm shareholders some, then adding more firms to the process is likely to increase this wealth even more. Target firms can accomplish this outcome by creating an auction among bidding firms. RJR-Nabisco accomplished this in 1988 when it orchestrated a series of competitive bids from several potential bidders (Helyar and Burrough, 1988b). In the end, the competition for RJR-Nabisco came down to a group led by the firm's top management team (including President Ross Johnson) and the leveraged buyout firm Kohlberg Kravis and Roberts (KKR). At one point in this auction, KKR increased its bid by $12 per share, to a final offer of over $25 billion.

In March 1995, KKR ended its investment in RJR-Nabisco. KKR's acquisition of RJR-Nabisco created a great deal of value (one estimate puts the value created through this acquisition equal to $51 billion, over $15 billion more than the value that would have been created if KKR had not acquired and aggressively managed RJR-Nabisco), but investors in KKR were unable to appropriate much of this value. KKR investors apparently earned on their investment in RJR-Nabisco a return much lower than the return they would have received if they had invested in a fully diversified portfolio of stocks (Kaplan, 1995). Much of KKR's inability to appropriate the value it helped create is traceable to the auction among multiple bidders that RJR-Nabisco created when it was acquired in 1988. On average, the creation of an auction among multiple bidders increases the wealth of target firm shareholders by 20 percent (Turk, 1987).

A third action that the managers of a target firm can take to increase the wealth of their shareholders from an acquisition effort is the institution of "golden parachutes." A golden parachute is a compensation arrangement between a firm and its senior management team that promises these individuals a substantial cash payment if their firm is acquired and they lose their jobs in the process. These cash payments can appear to be very large but are actually quite small in comparison to the total value that can be created if a merger or acquisition is completed. In this sense, golden parachutes are a small price to pay to give a potential target firm's top managers incentives not to stand in the way of completing a takeover of their firm (Singh and Harianto, 1989). Put differently, golden parachutes reduce agency problems for the shareholders of a potential target firm by aligning the interests of top managers with the interests of that firm's stockholders. On average, when a firm announces golden-parachute compensation packages for its top management team, the value of this potential target firm's equity increases by 7 percent (Turk, 1987).

Overall, there is substantial evidence that delaying an acquisition long enough to ensure that a competitive market for corporate control emerges can significantly benefit the shareholders of target firms. Turk (1987) found that when target firms did not delay the completion of an acquisition, their shareholders experienced, on average, a 36 percent increase in the value of their stock once the acquisition was complete. If, on the other hand, target firms did delay the completion of the acquisition, this average increase in value jumped to 65 percent.

Of course, target firm managers can delay too long. Delaying too long can create opportunity costs of their firm's shareholders, for these individuals do not actually realize the gain from an acquisition until it is completed. Also, long delays can jeopardize the completion of an acquisition, in which case the shareholders of the target firm do not realize any gains from the acquisition.

ORGANIZING TO IMPLEMENT A MERGER OR ACQUISITION

To realize the full value of any strategic relatedness that exists between a bidding and a target firm, the merged organizations must be appropriately organized. The realization of each of the types of strategic relatedness discussed earlier in this chapter requires at least some coordination and integration between the bidding and target firms after an acquisition has occurred. For example, to realize economies of scale from an acquisition, bidding and target firms must coordinate in the combined firm the functions that are sensitive to economies of scale. To realize the value of any technology that a bidding firm acquires from a target firm, the combined firm must use this technology in developing, manufacturing, or selling its products. To exploit underutilized leverage capacity in the target firm, the balance sheets of the bidding and target firms must be merged, and the resulting firm must then seek additional debt funding. To realize the opportunity of replacing the target firm's inefficient management with more efficient management from the bidding firm, these management changes must actually take place.

Postacquisition coordination and integration is essential if bidding and target firms are to realize the full potential of the strategic relatedness that drove the acquisition in the first place. If a bidding firm decides not to coordinate or integrate any of its business activities with the activities of a target firm, then why was this target firm acquired? Just as vertical integration and diversification require the active management of linkages among different parts of a firm, mergers and acquisitions (as one way in which vertical integration and diversification strategies can be created) require the active management of linkages between a bidding and a target firm.

Given that most merger and acquisition strategies are used to create either vertical integration or diversification strategies, the organizational approaches previously described for implementing these two strategies are relevant for implementing merger and acquisition strategies as well. Thus mergers and acquisitions designed to create vertical integration should be managed through the U-form structure, and those designed to create diversification strategies should be managed through the M-form structure. The management control systems and compensation policies associated with implementing vertical integration and diversification strategies should also be applied in organizing to implement merger and acquisition strategies.

Although, in general, organizing to implement merger and acquisition strategies can be seen as a special case of organizing to implement vertical integration or diversification strategies, implementing merger and acquisition strategies can create special problems. Most of these problems reflect the fact that operational, functional, strategic, and cultural differences between bidding and target firms involved in a merger or acquisition are likely to be much greater than these same differences between the different parts of a business that were brought together through vertical integration and diversification strategies. The reason for this difference is that the firms involved in a merger or acquisition have had a separate existence, separate histories, separate management philosophies, and separate strategies.

Differences between bidding and target firms can manifest themselves in a wide variety of ways. For example, bidding and target firms may own and operate different computer systems, different telephone systems, and other conflicting technologies. These firms might have very different human resource policies and practices. One firm might have a very generous retirement and health care program; the other, a less generous program. One firm's compensation system might focus on high salaries; the other firm's compensation system might focus on large cash bonuses and stock options. Also, these firms might have very different relationships with customers. At one firm, customers might be thought of as business partners; in another, the relationship with customers might be more arm's length in character. Integrating bidding and target firms may require the resolution of numerous differences.

Perhaps the most significant challenge in integrating bidding and target firms has to do with cultural differences (Cartwright and Cooper, 1993). In Chapter 5, we discussed the difficulty of changing a firm's organizational culture. Simply because a firm has been acquired does not mean that the culture in that firm will rapidly change, to become more like the culture of the bidding firm. Indeed, cultural conflicts can last for very long periods of time (Chatterjee et al., 1992).

For example, the Douglas Aircraft Company was acquired by the McDonnell Company (to form McDonnell-Douglas Corporation) in 1967, and cultural conflicts between these two parts of the business persist. Members of the Douglas family accuse McDonnell-Douglas of failing to maintain their commitment to former Douglas Aircraft workers by terminating health care benefits for retired nonunion employees. Members of the McDonnell family argue that they have a fiduciary responsibility to keep the firm solvent. These different views about the roles and responsibilities of management reflect deep-seated cultural differences between the two firms: Douglas Aircraft was an entrepreneurial southern California start-up, founded by Donald Douglas, Sr., an engineer who was always interested more in his employees and products than in his own personal wealth. The McDonnell Company was founded by James McDonnell, a no-nonsense midwestern manager renowned for his autocratic management style and emphasis on profitability (Harris, 1994). These cultural conflicts continue almost thirty years after the merger occurred.

Operational, functional, strategic, and cultural differences between bidding and target firms can all be compounded by the merger and acquisition process—especially if that process was unfriendly. Unfriendly takeovers can generate in target firm management anger and animosity toward the management of the bidding firm. For example, when the Bank of New York took over Irving Bank in a 1988 unfriendly acquisition, the chairman of Irving Bank, Joseph Rice, was almost immediately dismissed. This action reflected the fact that the takeover fight between the Bank of New York and Irving Bank had looked like a personal duel between Rice and Carter Bacot, Bank of New York chairman (Guenther, 1988). Such personal animosities obviously make coordination and integration all the more difficult—though no less important (Gutknecht and Keys, 1993). Research has shown that top management turnover is much higher in firms that have been taken over compared to firms not subject to takeovers, reflecting one approach to resolving these management conflicts (Walsh and Ellwood, 1991; Walsh, 1988).

The difficulties often associated with organizing to implement a merger and acquisition strategy can be thought of as an additional cost of the acquisition process. Bidding firms, in addition to estimating the value of the strategic relatedness between themselves and a target firm, also need to estimate the cost of organizing to implement an acquisition. The value that a target firm brings to a bidding firm through an acquisition should be discounted by the cost of organizing to implement this strategy. In some circumstances, it may be the case that the cost of organizing to realize the value of strategic relatedness between a bidding firm and a target may be greater than the value of that strategic relatedness, in which case the acquisition should not occur.

Many observers argue that potential synergies between bidding and target firms are often not fully realized. For example, despite the numerous multimedia mergers in the 1990s (Time Warner and Turner Broadcasting, Walt Disney and Capital Cities/ABC, GE and NBC, Westinghouse and CBS), only Viacom and News Corporation seem to have been able to realize any important synergies (Landro, 1995).

Although organizing to implement mergers and acquisitions can be a source of significant cost, it can also be a source of value and opportunity (Shanley and Collea, 1992). Haspeslagh and Jemison (1987) argue that value creation can continue to occur in a merger or acquisition long after the formal acquisition is complete. As bidding and target firms continue to coordinate and integrate their operations, unanticipated opportunities for value creation can be discovered. These sources of value could not have been anticipated at the time a firm was originally acquired (and thus are, at least partially, a manifestation of a bidding firm's good luck), but bidding firms can influence the probability of discovering these unanticipated sources of value by learning to cooperate effectively with bidding firms while organizing to implement a merger or acquisition strategy.

13.4   SUMMARY

Firms can use mergers and acquisitions to create their vertical integration or diversification corporate strategies. Mergers or acquisitions between strategically unrelated firms can be expected to generate only normal profits for both bidders and targets. Thus firms contemplating merger and acquisition strategies must search for strategically related targets.

Several sources of strategic relatedness have been discussed in the literature. On average, the acquisition of strategically related targets does create economic value, but most of that value is captured by the shareholders of target firms. The shareholders of bidding firms generally earn normal economic profits even when bidding firms acquire strategically related targets. Empirical research on mergers and acquisitions is consistent with these expectations. As Jensen and Ruback (1983) observe, acquisitions do create value, that value is captured by target firms, and acquisitions do not hurt bidding firms.

Given that most mergers and acquisitions generate only normal economic profits for bidding firms, an important question becomes, Why are there so many mergers and acquisitions? Explanations of the number of firms pursuing these strategies include (1) the desire to ensure firm survival, (2) the existence of free cash flow, (3) agency problems between bidding firm managers and shareholders, (4) managerial hubris, and (5) the possibility that some bidding firms might earn economic profits from implementing merger and acquisition strategies.

To gain competitive advantages and economic profits from mergers or acquisitions, these strategies must be either valuable, rare, and private, or valuable, rare, and costly to imitate. In addition, a bidding firm may exploit unanticipated sources of strategic relatedness with a target. These unanticipated sources of relatedness can also be a source of economic profits for a bidding firm. These observations have several implications for the managers of bidding and target firms.

Organizing to implement a merger or acquisition strategy can be seen as a special case of organizing to implement either a vertical integration strategy or a diversification strategy. However, operational, functional, strategic, and cultural differences between bidding and target firms may make the coordination and integration of bidding and target firms more difficult than the integration of different parts of a firm in a vertical integration or diversification context not created through a merger or acquisition. Cultural differences between bidding and target firms are particularly problematic. Bidding firms need to estimate the cost of organizing to implement a merger or acquisition strategy and discount the value of a target by that cost. However, organizing to implement a merger or acquisition can also be a way in which bidding and target firms discover unanticipated synergies.

REVIEW QUESTIONS

1. Consider the following scenario: A firm acquires a strategically related target after successfully fending off four other bidding firms. Under what conditions, if any, can the firm that acquired this target expect to earn an economic profit from doing so?

2. Consider this scenario: A firm acquires a strategically related target; there were no other bidding firms. Is this acquisition situation necessarily different from the situation described in question 1? Under what conditions, if any, can the firm that acquired this target expect to earn an economic profit from doing so?

3. Some researchers have argued that the existence of free cash flow can lead managers in a firm to make inappropriate acquisition decisions. To avoid these problems, these authors have argued, firms should increase their debt-to-equity ratio and "soak up" free cash flow through interest and principal payments. Is free cash flow a significant problem for many firms? What are the strengths and weaknesses of increased leverage as a response to free cash flow problems in a firm?

4. The hubris hypothesis suggests that managers continue to engage in acquisitions, even though on average they do not generate economic profits, because of the unrealistic belief on the part of these managers that they can manage a target firm's assets more efficiently than can that firm's current management. This type of systematic nonrationality usually does not last too long in competitive market conditions: Firms led by managers with these unrealistic beliefs change, are acquired, or go bankrupt in the long run. Are there any attributes of the market for corporate control that suggest that managerial hubris could exist in this market, despite its performance-reducing implications for bidding firms? If yes, what are these attributes? If no, can the hubris hypothesis be a legitimate explanation of continuing acquisition activity?

5. It has been shown that so-called poison pills rarely prevent a takeover from occurring. In fact, sometimes when a firm announces that it is instituting a poison pill, its stock price goes up. Why could that happen?

CHAPTER 14

Global Strategies

Vertical integration, diversification, and merger and acquisition are different strategies that firms can use to leverage their resource and capability advantages in one business activity to gain advantages in other strategically related business activities. Some strategic alliance strategies can have this same leveraging implication for firms as well. Thus far, most of our discussion of these leveraging opportunities has focused on how firms can leverage their resources and capabilities across different businesses in different industries. This is what Hewlett-Packard accomplished when it leveraged its resources and capabilities in electrical engineering and management, developed in the electronic instruments business, by entering the personal computer and printer businesses (Packard, 1995). In a similar way, PepsiCo has attempted to leverage its management and marketing skills, developed in the soft-drink industry, by entering into the snack-foods and fast-food restaurant businesses (Sellers, 1995).

However, firms can also leverage their resources and capabilities by engaging in business activities in new markets. This possibility has already been discussed at various points in this book. One of the environmental opportunities described in Section 4.2 is the ability that some firms might have to engage in international business operations (Porter, 1980). Such operations necessarily require a firm to operate in multiple distinct geographic markets. One of the motivations for engaging in strategic alliances, discussed in Section 9.2, is to facilitate a firm's entry into a new geographic market (Kogut, 1988; Hennart,

1988). Finally, one of the FTC merger and acquisition categories discussed in Section 13.2 is market extension acquisitions, where bidding firms acquire targets to gain access to new geographic markets within which they can operate.

This chapter focuses on leveraging a firm's resources and capabilities across multiple distinct markets. In particular, we examine the performance and competitive implications of these strategies when they lead a firm to operate across country borders. Firms that operate in multiple countries are implementing global strategies.

At some level, global strategies have existed since before the beginning of recorded time. Certainly, trade across country borders has been an important determinant of the wealth of individuals, companies, and countries throughout history. The search for trading opportunities and trade routes was a primary motivation for the exploration of the Western Hemisphere. Thus it would be inappropriate to argue that global strategies are an invention of the late twentieth century.

In the past, however, the implementation of global strategies was limited to relatively small numbers of risk-taking individuals and firms. Today these strategies are becoming remarkably common. In 1994, total revenue of the 500 largest firms in the world was $10,245.3 billion (over $10 trillion), and growing at a rate slightly lower than 10 percent a year (Jacob, 1995a). The vast majority of these firms operate in multiple countries and thus are implementing global strategies. These same 500 firms had assets of $30,848.2 billion in 1994, and 34,515,427 employees (Jacob, 1995a). Nearly 20 percent of the 1994 pre-tax profits of U.S. firms operating in multiple country markets came from sales in nondomestic operations (Richman, 1995). For example, Boeing (1994 revenues of $21.9 billion) sold 70 percent of its planes in 1994 in overseas markets; one-seventh of these planes were sold to Chinese airlines. These global strategies are not just restricted to developed economies. For example, Citicorp made 44 percent of its 1994 profits in developing countries (Jacob, 1995a).

Global leveraging strategies are increasingly important not just to large corporations. Smaller firms are also pursuing these kinds of international business opportunities. Arby's (a U.S. fast-food restaurant), Domino's Pizza, DryClean USA, and Page Boy Maternity have all recently begun operations in Mexico and are attempting to expand their international operations, despite currency fluctuations and political risks (Moffett, 1993). In 1993, Sean Nguyen, president of NEI Electronics (1992 sales of $4 million), announced plans to build and operate an electronics manufacturing plant in Vietnam (Leinster, 1993). Indeed, after the U.S. embargo on investment in Vietnam was lifted on February 3, 1994, numerous U.S. firms began operations there, including Caterpillar, Briggs and Stratton, Otis Elevator, Motorola, Citibank, IBM, and General Electric (Glinow and Clarke, 1995). Logitech, the world's leading manufacturer of personal computer mouses, had headquarters in California and Switzerland when it was first founded in 1982, and R&D and manufacturing operations in Taiwan and Ireland just a couple of years later (Oviatt and McDougall, 1995). In an important sense, Logitech began operations pursuing a global leveraging strategy. Momenta Corporation (a firm in the pen-based computer industry), Oxford Instruments (a firm supplying high field magnets to physics laboratories), SPEA (a firm in the graphics software business), and Technomed (a medical products firm) were all very small, and very new, companies when they began pursuing business opportunities in multiple country markets (Oviatt and McDougall, 1995).

The increased use of global strategies by both large and small firms suggests that the economic opportunities associated with operating in multiple geographic markets can be substantial. But to generate economic profits for firms, these opportunities must exploit a firms' valuable, rare, and costly-to-imitate resources and capabilities. Moreover, a firm must be appropriately organized to realize the full competitive potential of these resources and capabilities. This chapter examines the conditions under which global strategies can create economic value, as well as the conditions under which they can be sources of sustained competitive advantages.

14.1 THE VALUE OF GLOBAL STRATEGIES

Global strategies are leveraging strategies. So to be economically valuable, they must meet the two value criteria originally introduced in Chapter 11's discussion of diversification strategies: (1) They must exploit real economies of scope, and (2) It must be costly for outside investors to realize these economies of scope on their own. Many of the economies of scope that we discussed in the context of strategic alliances, vertical integration, diversification, and merger and acquisition strategies can be created when firms operate across multiple businesses. These same economies can also be created when firms operate across multiple geographic markets.

More generally, like all the strategies discussed in this book, to be valuable, global strategies must enable a firm to exploit environmental opportunities or neutralize environmental threats. To the extent that global strategies enable a firm to respond to its environment, they will also enable a firm to reduce its costs or increase its revenues compared to what would have been the case if that firm did not pursue these strategies. Several potentially valuable economies of scope particularly

TABLE 14.1
Potential Sources of Economies of Scope for Firms Pursuing Global Strategies

1. To gain access to new customers for current products or services
2. To gain access to low-cost factors of production
3. To develop new core competencies
4. To leverage current core competencies in new ways
5. To manage corporate risk

relevant for firms pursuing global strategies are summarized in Table 14.1 and discussed below.

TO GAIN ACCESS TO NEW CUSTOMERS FOR CURRENT PRODUCTS OR SERVICES

The most obvious economy of scope that may motivate firms to pursue a global strategy is the potential new customers for a firm's current products or services that such a strategy might generate. To the extent that customers outside a firm's domestic market are willing and able to buy a firm's current products or services, implementing a global strategy can directly increase a firm's revenues. Gaining access to these customers can also help a firm manage changes in domestic demand as its products or services evolve through different stages of their life cycle. Finally, gaining access to these new customers can increase a firm's volume of production. If production processes are subject to economies of scale, global strategies can also have the effect of decreasing a firm's costs.

Globalization and Firm Revenues

If customers outside a firm's domestic market are willing and able to purchase its products or services, then selling into these markets will increase the firm's revenues. However, it is not always clear that the products and services that a firm sells in its domestic market will also sell in foreign markets.

Are Nondomestic Customers Willing to Buy?   It may be the case that customer preferences vary significantly in a firm's domestic and foreign markets. These different preferences may require firms seeking to globalize their operations to substantially change their current products or services before nondomestic customers are willing to purchase them.

This challenge faced many U.S. home appliance manufacturers as they looked to expand their operations into Europe and Asia. In the United States, the physical size of most home appliances (washing machines, dryers, refrigerators, dishwashers, and so forth) has become standardized, and these standard sizes are built into new homes, condominiums, and apartments. Standard sizes have also emerged in Europe and Asia. But these non-U.S. standard sizes are much smaller than the U.S. sizes, requiring U.S. manufacturers to substantially retool their manufacturing operations in order to build products that might be attractive to Asian and European customers (Yoshino, Hall, and Malnight, 1991).

Different physical standards can require a globalizing firm to change its current products or services to sell them into a nondomestic market. Physical standards, however, can easily be measured and described. Differences in tastes can be much more challenging for firms looking to sell their products or services outside the domestic market.

Disney discovered the challenges associated with differences in tastes across nondomestic markets in two of its globalization efforts—Disneyland Tokyo and Euro-Disney. When Disneyland Tokyo opened in April 1983, several adjustments to the theme park formula that had been so successful in California and Florida were apparent. For example, the main entrance-way into the Tokyo park did not adopt a turn-of-the-century "Main Street USA" theme; instead the Tokyo park features cultural and other exhibits from around the world. Nevertheless, Disneyland Tokyo featured Disney's traditional cartoon characters (Mickey Mouse, Goofy, Donald Duck) along with its movie-based fairy-tale characters (Pinocchio, Snow White, Cinderella) and many rides and attractions originally developed for its U.S. operations. Although Disneyland Tokyo turned out to be a financial success almost since the day it opened, the Walt Disney Company at the outset limited its financial stake in this venture. Disney licensed the use of its characters and technologies to a group of Japanese investors in return for 10 percent of the park's gate receipts and 5 percent of its other receipts (Jones, 1991). These financial arrangements have severely limited Disney's profits from Disneyland Tokyo.

The Walt Disney Company was determined to not lose these profit opportunities when it began theme park operations in Europe. Buoyed by its success with one Disney-based theme park outside the United States, Disney approached its entry into the European theme park market with confidence. Again, efforts were made to modify the traditional Disney formula to be consistent with European tastes (Greenhouse, 1991). But this time the Walt Disney Company took a 49 percent ownership stake in its foreign venture (as large a stake as French law would allow). In return, Disney was to receive 10 percent of Euro-Disney's admission fees, 5 percent of Euro-Disney's food and merchandise revenues, management fees, incentive fees, and 49 percent of Euro-Disney's profits. Unfortunately, the kinds of modifications to the traditional Disney formula that worked so well in Japan have not generated the demand for Euro-Disney that was anticipated when the theme park opened (Toy and Dwyer, 1994). The largely American themes in Euro-Disney are offensive to some European visitors. Hotel rooms near Euro-Disney are different from (and more expensive than) the kinds of hotel rooms that Europeans generally prefer. As a result, Disney had to restructure the financial operations of Euro-Disney in an attempt to enhance its profit potential (Solomon, 1994).

The unwillingness of customers in nondomestic markets to purchase a firm's current products or services is not limited to attempts by U.S. firms to begin operations in non-U.S. markets. Yugo had difficulty selling its automobile products in the United States. Apparently, U.S. consumers were unwilling to accept poor-performing, poor-quality automobiles, despite their low price. Sony, despite its success in Japan, was unable to carve out significant market share in the U.S. video market with its Betamax technology. Most observers blame Sony's reluctance to license this technology to other manufacturers, together with the shorter recording time available on Betamax, for this product failure (Perry, 1991). Apparently, U.S. customers wanted a broad choice of manufacturers and longer recording capabilities than Betamax could provide. Marks and Spencer's efforts to enter the Canadian retail market with its traditional mix of clothing and food stores—a mix that has been extremely successful in the United Kingdom—also met with stiff consumer resistance (Montgomery, 1993).

In the end, in order for access to new customers for a firm's current products or services to be an economy of scope for a firm implementing a global strategy, those products or services must address the needs, wants, and preferences of customers in foreign markets at least as well as, if not better than, alternatives. Globalizing firms may have to pursue many of the cost-leadership and product differentiation business strategies discussed in Chapters 6 and 7, modified to address the specific market needs in a non domestic market. Only in this situation will customers in nondomestic markets be willing to buy a firm's current products or services.

Are Nondomestic Customers Able to Buy?   Customers in foreign markets might be willing to buy a firm's current products or services but be unable to buy them. This can occur for at least three reasons: (1) inadequate distribution channels, (2) trade barriers, and (3) insufficient wealth to make purchases.

Inadequate distribution channels make it difficult, if not impossible, for a firm to make its products or services available to customers outside its domestic market. In some nondomestic markets, adequate distribution networks exist but are tied up by firms already operating in these markets. Many European firms face this situation as they try to enter the U.S. market. In such a situation, globalizing firms must either build their own distribution networks from scratch (a very costly endeavor) or work with a local partner to utilize the networks that are already in place. As was suggested in Chapter 9, the marginal cost of using already established distribution networks in a new market is almost zero. Thus, cooperating, through strategic alliances, with firms that already have access to distribution networks is often preferable to building networks from scratch.

However, the problem facing some globalizing firms is not that distribution networks are tied up by firms already operating in a market. Rather, the problem is that distribution networks do not exist or operate in ways that are very different from the operation of distribution networks in a firm's domestic market. This problem can be serious when firms seek to expand their global operations into developing economies. Inadequate transportation, warehousing, and retail facilities can make it difficult to distribute a firm's products or services into a new geographic market. These kinds of problems have hampered investment in Russia since the breakup of the Soviet Union, as well as in China. For example, when Nestlé entered the Chinese dairy market, it had to build a network of gravel roads connecting the villages where dairy farmers produce milk and factory collection points. Obtaining the right to build this network of roads took thirteen years of negotiation with Chinese government officials. Nestlé management expects its Chinese dairy business to generate significant profits by the turn of the century (Rapoport, 1994).

Such distribution problems are not limited to developing economies. For example, Japanese retail distribution is much more fragmented, and much less efficient, than the system that exists in either the United States or western Europe. Rather than being dominated by large grocery stores, discount retail operations, and retail superstores, the Japanese retail distribution network is dominated by numerous small, mom-and-pop operations (Yoshino and Stoneham, 1992). Many Western firms find this distribution network difficult to use, because its operating principles are so different from what they have seen in their domestic markets. However, Procter & Gamble and a few other firms have been able to crack open this Japanese distribution system and exploit significant sales opportunities in Japan.

Even if distribution networks exist in nondomestic markets, and even if globalizing firms can operate through those networks if they

TABLE 14.2
Tariff and Nontariff Trade Barriers

Tariffs: taxes levied on imported goods or services	Quotas: quantity limits on the number of products or services that can be imported	Nontariff barriers: rules, regulations, and policies that increase the cost of importing products or services
Import duties	Voluntary quotas	Government policies
Supplemental duties	Involuntary quotas	Government procurement policies
Variable levies	Restricted import licenses	Government-sponsored export subsidies
Border levies	Minimum import limits	Domestic assistance programs
Countervailing duties	Embargoes	Custom policies
		Valuation systems
		Tariff classifications
		Documentation requirements
		Fees
		Quality standards
		Packaging standards
		Labeling standards

have access to them, it still might be the case that entry into these markets can be restricted by various tariff and nontariff trade barriers. A list of such trade barriers is presented in Table 14.2. Trade barriers, no matter what their specific form, have the effect of increasing the cost of selling a firm's current products or services in a new nondomestic market and thus make it difficult for a firm to realize this economy of scope from its global strategy.

Despite a worldwide movement toward free trade and reduction in trade barriers, trade barriers are still an important economic phenomenon for many firms seeking to implement a global strategy. Japanese automobile manufacturers have faced voluntary quotas and various other trade barriers as they have sought to expand their presence in the U.S. market; U.S. automobile firms have argued that Japan has used a series of tariff and nontariff trade barriers to restrict their entry into in the Japanese market (Davis, 1995). Kodak recently asked the U.S. government to begin negotiations to facilitate Kodak's entry into the Japanese photography market—a market that Kodak argues is controlled, through a government-sanctioned monopoly, by Fuji (Bounds and Davis, 1995). Historically, beginning operations in India was hampered by a variety of tariff and nontariff trade barriers. Tariffs in India have averaged more than 80 percent; foreign firms have been restricted to a 40 percent ownership stake in their operations in India; and foreign imports have required government approvals and licenses that could take up to three years to obtain (Jacob, 1992a). Over the last several years, many of these trade barriers in India have been reduced but not eliminated. The same is true for the United States. The tariff on imported goods and services imposed by the U.S. government reached an all-time high of 60 percent in 1932. It averaged from 12 to 15 percent after the Second World War and now averages about 5 percent for most imports into the United States. Thus U.S. trade barriers have been reduced but not eliminated (Rugman and Hodgetts, 1995).

Governments create trade barriers for a wide variety of reasons: to protect local employment, to encourage local production to replace imports, to protect new industries from competition, to encourage foreign direct investment, and to promote export activity. However, for firms seeking to implement globalization strategies, trade barriers, no matter why they are erected, have the effect of increasing the cost of implementing these strategies. Indeed, trade barriers can be thought of as a special case of artificial barriers to entry, as discussed in Section 3.2. Such barriers to entry can turn what could have been economically viable strategies into nonviable strategies.

Finally, customers may be willing but unable to purchase a firm's current products or services even if distribution networks are in place and trade barriers are not making globalization efforts too costly. If these customers lack the wealth, or sufficient hard currency, to make these purchases, then the potential value of this economy of scope can go unrealized.

Insufficient consumer wealth limits the ability of firms to sell products or services into a variety of markets. For example, per capita income is $450 per year in the Sudan, $200 per year in Bangladesh, and $190 per year in Chad. In these countries, it is unlikely that there will be significant demand for many products or services originally designed for affluent Western economies. This situation also exists in India. The middle class in India is large and growing (300 million people in 1991), but the income of this middle class is considerably lower than the income of middle classes in other economies. In 1992 in India, annual incomes greater than $700 per year were considered middle-class incomes (Jacob, 1992a). These income levels are sufficient to create demand for some consumer products. For example, Gillette estimates the market in India for its shaving products to include 240 million consumers, and Nestlé believes that the market in India for its noodles, ketchup, and instant coffee products includes over 100 million people. However, the potential market for higher-end products in India is somewhat smaller. For example, Bausch & Lomb believes that only about 30 million consumers in India can afford to purchase its high-end sunglasses and soft contact lenses (Jacob, 1992a). The level of consumer wealth is such an important determinant of the economic potential of beginning operations in a new country that McDonald's adjusts the number of restaurants it expects to build in a new market by the per capita income of people in that market (Serwer, 1994).

Even if there is sufficient wealth in a country to create market demand, lack of hard currency can hamper globalization efforts. Hard currencies are currencies that are traded, and thus have value, on international money markets. When a global firm does business in a country with hard currency, the firm can take whatever after-tax profits it earns in that country and translate those profits into other hard currencies—including the currency of the country in which the firm has headquarters. Moreover, since the value of hard currencies can fluctuate in the world economy, firms can also manage their currency risk by engaging in various hedging strategies in world money markets. Some firms move beyond simply hedging their currency risk and attempt to generate profits from their currency-trading activities. For example, Nestlé Swiss food operations make up less than 5 percent of this firm's worldwide sales, but the Swiss-based currency-trading operation at Nestlé often generates more than 5 percent of the company's worldwide profits (Rapoport, 1994).

When globalizing firms begin operations in countries without hard currency, they are able to obtain few of these advantages. Indeed, without hard currency, cash payments to global firms are made with a currency that has essentially no value outside the country where the payments are made. Although these payments can be used for additional investment inside that country, a global firm has limited ability to extract profits from countries without hard currencies and even less ability to hedge currency fluctuation risks in this context. The lack of hard currency has discouraged firms from entering a wide variety of countries—India, Russia, China—despite the substantial demand for products and services in those countries (Jacob, 1992a; Ignatius, 1993; Kraar, 1995).

The most common solution to the lack of hard currency in a non-domestic market is called *countertrade*. When global firms engage in countertrade, they receive payment for the products or services they sell into a country, but not in the form of currency. They receive payment in the form of other products or services that they can sell on the world market. Countertrade has been a particularly important way by which firms have tried to gain access to the markets in the former Soviet Union.

For example, in 1993, Marc Rich and Company (a Swiss commodity-trading firm) put together the following deal: Marc Rich purchased 70,000 tons of raw sugar from Brazil on the open market; shipped this sugar to Ukraine, where it was refined; then transported 30,000 tons of refined sugar (after using some to pay the refineries) to Siberia, where it was sold for 130,000 tons of oil products that, in turn, were shipped to Mongolia in exchange for 35,000 tons of copper concentrate, which was moved to Kazakhstan, where it was refined into copper, and, finally, sold on the world market to obtain hard currency (Ignatius, 1993). This complicated countertrade deal is typical of the kinds of actions that global firms must take if they are to engage in business in countries without hard currency and if they desire to extract their profits out of those countries. Indeed, countertrade in various forms is actually quite common. One estimate suggests that countertrade accounts for between 10 and 20 percent of world trade (Marin, 1990).

Although countertrade can enable a firm to begin operations in countries without hard currency, it can create difficulties as well. In particular, in order to do business, a firm must be willing to accept payment in the form of some good or commodity that it must sell in order to obtain hard currency. This is not likely to be a problem for a firm like Marc Rich that specializes in buying and selling commodities. However, a firm that does not have this expertise might find itself taking possession of natural gas, sesame seeds, or rattan in order to sell its products or services in a country. If this firm has limited expertise in these kinds of commodities, it may have to use brokers and other advisers to complete these transactions. This, of course, increases the cost of using countertrade as a way to facilitate global operations.

Globalization and Product Life Cycles

Gaining access to new customers not only can directly increase a firm's revenues but also can enable a firm to manage its products or services through their life cycle. A typical product life cycle is depicted in Fig. 14.1. Different stages in this life cycle are defined by different growth rates in demand for a product. Thus, in the first emerging stage (called "introduction" in the figure), relatively few firms are producing a product, there are relatively few customers, and the rate of growth in demand for the product is relatively low. In the second stage ("growth") of the product life cycle, demand increases rapidly, and many new firms enter to begin producing the product or service. In the third phase of the product life cycle ("maturity"), the number of firms producing a product or service remains stable, demand growth levels off, and firms direct their investment efforts toward refining the process by which a product or service is created and away from developing entirely new products. In the final phase of the product life cycle ("decline"), demand drops off

**FIGURE 14.1
The Product Life
Cycle**

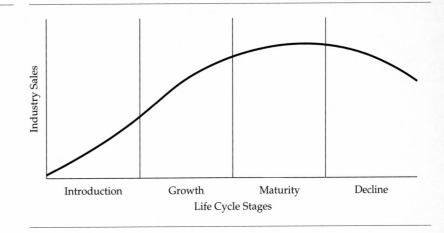

when a technologically superior product or service is introduced (Abernathy and Utterback, 1978; Utterback and Abernathy, 1975). As described in Section 4.2, the product life cycle has a direct impact on the structure of opportunities in an industry (Grant, 1991).

From a global strategy perspective, the critical observation about product life cycles is that a product or service can be at different stages of its life cycle in different countries. Thus a firm can use the resources and capabilities it developed during a particular stage of the life cycle in its domestic market during that same stage of the life cycle in a nondomestic market. This can substantially enhance a firm's economic performance.

One firm that has been very successful in managing its product life cycles through globalization efforts is Crown Cork & Seal. This firm had a traditional strength in the manufacturing of three-piece metal containers, when the introduction of two-piece metal cans into the U.S. market rapidly made three-piece cans obsolete. However, rather than abandoning its three-piece manufacturing technology, Crown Cork & Seal moved many of its three-piece manufacturing operations overseas into developing countries where demand for three-piece cans was just emerging. In this way, Crown Cork & Seal was able to extend the effective life of its three-piece manufacturing operations and substantially enhance its economic performance (Bradley and Cavanaugh, 1994; Hamermesh and Rosenbloom, 1989).

Globalization and Cost Reduction

Gaining access to new customers for a firm's current products or services can increase a firm's volume of sales. If aspects of a firm's production process are sensitive to economies of scale, this increased volume of sales can reduce the firm's costs and enable the firm to gain cost advantages in both its nondomestic and its domestic markets (see Chapter 6).

Many scholars, over many years, have pointed out the potential of international operations to generate economies of scale (Fayerweather, 1969; Fayerweather and Kapoor, 1975; Fayerweather, 1982; Hout, Porter, and Rudden, 1982). Most of these authors recognize that the realization of economies of scale from global operations requires a high degree of integration across firm borders. Integration must focus on those aspects of a firm's operations where economies of scale can be realized. For example, McDonald's attempts to generate training-based economies of scale through the operation of a single management training center for all of its global operations (Serwer, 1994). AT&T attempts to generate research and development economies of scale with its Bell Laboratories subsidiary (Kirkpatrick, 1993). Firms in the float glass, color television, and chemical industries have all attempted to exploit manufacturing economies of scope through their global operations (Prahalad and Doz, 1987; Bartlett and Goshal, 1989).

Many firms in the worldwide automobile industry have attempted to realize manufacturing economies of scale through their global operations. According to one estimate, the minimum efficient scale of a single compact-car manufacturing plant is 400,000 units per year (Porter, 1986:43; Ghoshal, 1987:436). Such a plant would produce approximately 20 percent of all the automobiles sold in Britain, Italy, or France in 1987. Obviously, to exploit this 400,000 cars per year manufacturing efficiency, European automobile firms have had to sell cars in more than just a single country market (Kobrin, 1991). Thus the implementation of a global strategy has enabled these firms to realize an important manufacturing economy of scale.

Although there are numerous potential sources of economies of scale from global operations, some recent empirical research suggests the most likely sources of these economies. Kobrin (1991) found that exploiting global economies of scale in research and development and in marketing was very important in the sample of fifty-six global industries that he studied. Kobrin also found that, as technological change has made it possible to efficiently operate smaller plants, manufacturing economies of scale have become less important sources of economic value in these same industries. Overall, Kobrin (1991) found that exploiting economies of scale, no matter what their source, is becoming a more important source of economic value in most global industries.

TO GAIN ACCESS TO LOW-COST FACTORS OF PRODUCTION

Just as gaining access to new customers can be an important economy of scope for globalizing firms, so is gaining access to low-cost factors of production such as raw materials, labor, and technology.

Raw Materials

Gaining access to low-cost raw materials is, perhaps, the most traditional reason why firms begin global operations. For example, in 1600, the British East India Company was formed with an initial investment of $70,000 to manage trade between England and the Far East, including India. In 1601, the third British East India Company fleet sailed for the Indies to buy cloves, pepper, silk, coffee, saltpeter, and other products. This fleet generated a return on investment of 234 percent (Trager, 1992). These profits led to the formation of the Dutch East India Company in 1602 and the French East India Company in 1664. Similar firms were organized to manage trade in the New World. Hudsons Bay Company was chartered in 1670 to manage the fur trade, and the rival North West Company was organized in 1784 for the same purpose. All these organizations were created to gain access to low-cost raw materials that were available in nondomestic markets.

Gaining access to low-cost raw materials is still an important reason why some firms engage in global enterprise. In some industries, including the oil and gas industries, virtually the only reason why firms have begun international operations is to gain access to low-cost raw materials. For example, oil companies from thirteen countries have begun buying rights to explore oil reserves in Vietnam (Leinster, 1993).

Labor

In addition to gaining access to low-cost raw materials, firms also begin global operations in order to gain access to low-cost labor. After the Second World War, Japan had some of the lowest labor costs, and highest labor productivity, in the world. Over time, however, the improving Japanese economy and the increased value of the yen had the effect of increasing labor costs in Japan, and South Korea, Taiwan, Singapore, and Malaysia all emerged as geographic areas with inexpensive and highly productive labor. In the last few years, China, Mexico, and Vietnam have taken this role in the world economy (Kraar, 1992).

Numerous firms have attempted to gain the advantages of low labor costs by moving their manufacturing operations. Consider, for example, Mineba, a Japanese ball-bearing and semiconductor manufacturer. To exploit low labor costs, Mineba manufactured ball bearings in Japan in the 1950s and early 1960s and in Singapore in the 1970s and since 1980 has been manufacturing them in Thailand. Currently, 60 percent of Mineba's ball-bearing output is manufactured in Thailand (Collis, 1991). Hewlett-Packard operates manufacturing and assembly operations in Malaysia and Mexico, Japan's Mitsubishi Motors recently opened an automobile assembly plant in Vietnam, General Motors operates assembly plants in Mexico, and Motorola has begun operations in China. All these investments were motivated, at least partly, by the availability of low-cost labor in these countries (Engardio, 1993).

While gaining access to low-cost labor can be an important determinant of a firm's globalization efforts, this access by itself is usually not sufficient to motivate entry into particular countries. After all, relative labor costs can change over time. For example, South Korea used to be the country in which most sports shoes were manufactured. In 1990, Korean shoe manufacturers employed 130,000 workers in 302 factories. However, by 1993, only 80,000 Koreans were employed in the shoe industry, and only 244 factories (most employing fewer than 100 people) remained. A significant portion of the shoe-manufacturing industry had moved from Korea to China because of the labor cost advantages of China (approximately $40 per employee per month) compared to Korea (approximately $800 per employee per month) (Gain, 1993).

Moreover, low labor costs are not beneficial if a country's work force is not able to produce high-quality products efficiently. In the sport shoe industry, China still does not have access to some of the manufacturing technology and supporting industries (for example, synthetic fabrics) to efficiently produce high-end sports shoes and high-technology hiking boots available in Korea. As a result, Korea has been able to maintain a presence in the shoe-manufacturing industry (Gain, 1993). However, when a country's labor force is highly educated and highly motivated, and when supporting technology and industries are in place, relatively low-cost labor can lead firms to begin operations in that country (Porter, 1990).

One interesting example of firms gaining access to low-cost labor through their global strategies is *maquiladoras*—manufacturing plants that are owned by non-Mexican international companies and operated in Mexico near the U.S. border. The primary driver behind maquiladora investments is low labor costs. Labor costs in maquiladoras are about 20 percent less than the labor costs of similar plants located in the United States. In addition, firms exporting from maquiladoras to the United States have to pay duties only on the value added that was created in Mexico; maquiladoras do not have to pay Mexican taxes on the goods processed in Mexico; and the cost of land on which plants are built in Mexico is substantially lower than what would be the case in the United States (Reibstein et al., 1991). However, a recent study by the Banco de Mexico suggests that without the 20 percent cost-of-labor advantage, most maquiladoras would not be profitable operations (de Forest, 1994).

Given the cost advantages in operating maquiladoras, it is not surprising that investment in this global strategy has increased substantially over time. In 1965, there were only 12 maquiladora plants. By 1990, approximately 1,700 of them were in operation, and over 55 percent of them resulted from investments made by U.S. firms. For example, TRW has a maquiladora plant that assembles seat belts, and Mattel has a maquiladora plant that assembles toys. Currently, only oil generates more foreign currency for Mexico than maquiladoras (DePalma, 1994).

Technology

Another factor of production that firms can gain low-cost access to through international operations is technology. Historically, Japanese firms have tried to gain access to technology by partnering with non-Japanese firms. While the non-Japanese firms have often been looking to gain access to new customers for their current products or services by operating in Japan, the Japanese firms have used this entry into the Japanese market to gain access to foreign technology (Zimmerman, 1985; Osborn and Baughn, 1987).

Recently, however, some Japanese firms have begun to use entry into various U.S. markets as a way to gain access to additional technology. For example, in 1986, the Sumitomo Corporation announced investments in two venture-capital firms operating in the United States (Grace Venture Partnership and Hambro International Venture Fund) in order "to obtain new technologies and new business opportunities" (Nihon Kezai Shimbun, cited in Hurry, Miller, and Bowman, 1992). By 1992, approximately fifty Japanese firms were engaged in venture-capital investments in new technology in the United States. Hurry, Miller, and Bowman (1992) have been able to show that the primary goal of these investments in the United States has been to gain access to new technologies that Japanese firms could use in other products or services. This objective stands in marked contrast to U.S. venture-capital firms, whose primary goal in making new venture investments, according to these authors, was to maximize their current performance.

Of course, the use of global strategies to gain low-cost access to technology is not limited to Japanese firms. Hamel (1991:86) cites one Japanese manager's comments about his European strategic alliance partner: "The only motivation for [our European partner] is to get mass manufacturing technology. They see [the alliance] as a short circuit. As soon as they have this they'll lose interest [in the alliance]."

TO DEVELOP NEW CORE COMPETENCIES

One of the most compelling reasons for firms to begin operations outside their domestic markets is to refine their current core competencies and to develop new core competencies. By beginning operations outside their domestic markets, firms can gain a greater understanding of the strengths and weaknesses of their core competencies. By exposing these competencies to new competitive contexts, traditional competencies can be modified, and new competencies can be developed.

Of course, for global operations to affect a firm's core competencies, firms must learn from their experiences in nondomestic markets. Moreover, once these new core competencies are developed, they must be exploited in a firm's other operations in order to realize their full economic potential.

Learning from Global Operations

Learning from global operations is anything but automatic. Many firms that begin operations in a nondomestic market encounter challenges and difficulties and then immediately withdraw from their globalization efforts. Other firms continue to try to operate globally but are unable to learn how to modify and change their core competencies.

Hamel (1991) studied several international strategic alliances in an effort to understand why some firms in these alliances were able to learn from their global operations, modify their core competencies, and develop new core competencies, while others were not. Hamel identified the intent to learn, the transparency of business partners, and receptivity to learning as determinants of a firm's ability to learn from its global operations (see Table 14.3).

The Intent to Learn.   Hamel (1991) found that a firm had to have a strong intent to learn from its global operations if those operations were to have an effect on the firm's core competencies. Moreover, this intent had to be communicated to all those who worked in a firm's global activities. Compare, for example, a quote from a manager whose firm failed to learn from its global operations with a quote from a manager whose firm was able to learn from these operations (Hamel, 1991:91):

> Our engineers were just as good as [our partner's]. In fact, theirs were narrower technically, but they had a much better understanding of what the company was trying to accomplish. They knew they were there to learn; our people didn't.

**TABLE 14.3
Determinants of the Ability of a Firm to Learn from Its Global Operations**
Source: Hamel (1991).

1. The intent to learn

2. The transparency of business partners

3. Receptivity to learning

> We wanted to make learning an automatic discipline. We asked the staff every day, "What did you learn from [our partner] today?" Learning was carefully monitored and recorded.

Obviously, the second firm was in a much better position than the first to learn from its global operations and to modify its current core competencies and develop new core competencies. According to Hamel (1991), learning from global operations takes place by design, not by default.

Transparency and Learning.   Hamel (1991) found that firms were more likely to learn from their global operations when they interacted with what he calls "transparent" business partners. Some global business partners are more open and accessible than others. This variance in accessibility can reflect different organizational philosophies, practices, and procedures, as well as differences in the culture of a firm's home country. For example, knowledge in Japanese and most other Asian cultures tends to be context specific and deeply embedded in the broader social system (Benedict, 1946; Terpstra and David, 1985). This makes it difficult for many Western managers to understand and appreciate the subtlety of Japanese business practices and Japanese culture (Peterson and Schwind, 1977; Peterson and Shimada, 1978). This, in turn, limits the ability of Western managers to learn from their operations in the Japanese market or from their Japanese partners (Hamel, 1991).

In contrast, knowledge in most Western cultures tends to be less context specific, less deeply embedded in the broader social system. Such knowledge can be written down, can be taught in classes, and can be transmitted, all at a relatively low cost. Japanese managers working in Western economies are more likely to be able to appreciate and understand Western business practices and thus more able to learn from their operations in the West and from their Western partners.

Receptivity to Learning.   Firms also vary in their receptiveness to learning. A firm's receptiveness to learning is affected by its culture, its operating procedures, and its history. Research on organizational learning suggests that, before firms can learn from their global operations, they must be prepared to unlearn (Burgleman, 1983b; Hedberg, 1981; Nystrom and Starbuck, 1984). Unlearning requires a firm to modify or abandon traditional ways of engaging in business. Unlearning can be difficult, especially if a firm has a long history of success using old patterns of behavior and if those old patterns of behavior are reflected in a firm's organizational structure, its management control systems, and its compensation policies (Argyris and Schon, 1978).

Even if unlearning is possible, a firm may not have the resources it needs to learn. If a firm is using all of its available managerial time and talent, capital, and technology just to compete on a day-to-day business, the additional task of learning from international operations can go undone. This is a special form of the tyranny of the day to day discussed in Section 10.3. Although managers in this situation often acknowledge the importance of learning from their global operations in order to modify their current core competencies or build new ones, they simply may not have the time or energy to do so (Burgleman, 1983a).

The ability to learn from international operations can also be hampered if managers perceive that there is a great deal to be learned. It is often difficult for a firm to understand how it can evolve from its current state to a position where it operates with new and more valuable core competencies. This difficulty is exacerbated when the distance between where a firm is and where it needs to be is large. Hamel (1991:97) quotes one Western manager who perceived this large learning gap after visiting a state-of-the-art manufacturing facility operated by a Japanese partner:

> It's no good for us to simply observe where they are today, what we have to find out is how they got from where we are to where they are. We need to experiment and learn with intermediate technologies before duplicating what they've done.

Leveraging New Core Competencies in Additional Markets

Once a firm has been able to learn from its global operations and modify its traditional core competencies or develop new core competencies, it must then leverage those competencies across all of its operations, both domestic and global, in order to realize their full value. Firms that have a history of leveraging their core competencies across multiple businesses, by implementing the organizational structures, control systems, and compensation policies discussed in Chapter 12, will be able to exploit numerous environmental opportunities and neutralize numerous environmental threats (Hamel, 1991).

TO LEVERAGE CURRENT CORE COMPETENCIES IN NEW WAYS

Global operations can also create opportunities for firms to leverage their traditional core competencies in new ways. This capability is related to, though different from, using global operations to gain access to new customers for a firm's current products or services. When firms gain access to new customers for their current products, they often leverage their domestic core competencies across country boundaries. When they leverage core competencies in new ways, they not only extend operations across country boundaries but also leverage their competencies across products and services in ways that would not be economically viable in their domestic market.

Consider, for example, Honda. There is widespread agreement that Honda has developed core competencies in the design and manufacture of power trains. Honda has used this core competence to facilitate entry into a variety of product markets—including motorcycles, automobiles, and snow blowers—both in its domestic Japanese market and in nondomestic markets such as the United States (Prahalad and Hamel, 1990). However, Honda has begun to explore in the U.S. market some competence-leverage opportunities that are not available in the Japanese market. In particular, Honda has begun to design and manufacture lawn mowers of various sizes for the home in the U.S. market. Lawn mowers clearly build on Honda's traditional power train competence. Given the crowded living conditions in Japan, consumer demand for lawn mowers in that country has never been very great. Lawns in the United States, however, can be very large, and consumer demand for high-quality lawn mowers in that market is substantial. The opportunity for Honda to begin to leverage its power train competencies in the sale of lawn mowers to U.S. homeowners exists only because Honda operates outside its Japanese home market.

TO MANAGE CORPORATE RISK

The value of risk reduction for firms pursuing a diversification strategy was evaluated in Section 11.2. There it was suggested that although diversified operations across businesses with imperfectly correlated cash flows can reduce a firm's risk, outside stockholders can manage this risk more efficiently on their own by investing in a diversified portfolio of stocks. Thus stockholders have little interest in hiring managers to operate a diversified portfolio of businesses, the sole purpose of which is risk diversification.

Similar conclusions apply to firms pursuing global strategies—with one qualification. Certainly, firms that pursue business opportunities with imperfectly correlated cash flows across multiple markets in order to reduce their risk, where stockholders could reduce that risk more efficiently on their own, are not pursuing a valuable strategy. However, in some circumstances it may be difficult for stockholders in one market to diversify their portfolio of investments across multiple markets. To the extent that such barriers to diversification exist for individual stockholders but not for firms pursuing global strategies, risk reduction can be a viable motivation for pursuing a global strategy. In general, whenever barriers to international capital flows exist, individual investors may not be able to diversify their portfolios across country boundaries optimally. In this context, individual investors can indirectly diversify their portfolio of investments by purchasing shares in diversified multinationals (Agmon and Lessard, 1977).

There is empirical evidence that suggests that barriers to international capital flows, in fact, exist for at least some countries (Adler and Dumas, 1983). These have the effect of increasing the cost to individual investors of investing in a nondomestic capital market, and they include different tax structures across countries, different accounting standards, different securities regulations, and different political and economic systems. These barriers to capital flow lead investors to hold more domestic stocks in their portfolio than they would hold if they were able, at low cost, to hold a worldwide market portfolio of stocks (Lessard, 1976; Senback and Beedles, 1980).

There is also empirical evidence suggesting that pursuing a global diversification strategy when barriers to capital flow exist can benefit shareholders (Severn, 1974). The stock prices of firms pursuing these strategies in this situation are higher, controlling for other factors, than the stock prices of firms not providing this service to their investors (Adler and Dumas, 1983; Errunza and Senbet, 1981, 1984; Logue, 1982; Rugman, 1979; Severn, 1974).

However, firms pursuing global strategies should approach this risk reduction motivation with caution. Barriers to capital flows across countries are not stable. Over time, it seems reasonable to expect that these barriers will be reduced as the level of economic integration in the world economy increases. It is already the case that various international monetary markets exist and that individual investors can gain access to these markets at low cost (either directly or indirectly through mutual funds). When barriers to capital flow disappear, risk reduction per se will no longer be a viable motivation for pursuing a global strategy. This suggests that globalization strategies primarily designed to reduce the level of a firm's risk are not likely in the long run to add significant economic value to a firm. However, as was the case with risk-reducing diversification motives described in Chapter 11, if a firm is pursuing a globalization strategy in order to exploit another valuable economy of scope, the pursuit of that strategy will also have the effect of reducing the firm's level of risk.

THE LOCAL RESPONSIVENESS/GLOBAL INTEGRATION TRADEOFF

As firms pursue the economies of scope listed in Table 14.1, they constantly face a tradeoff between the advantages of being responsive to market conditions in their nondomestic markets and the advantages of integrating their operations across the multiple markets in which they operate. This tradeoff was originally discussed in Chapter 4.

On the one hand, local responsiveness can help firms be successful in addressing the local needs of nondomestic customers, thereby increasing demand for a firm's current products or services. Moreover, local responsiveness enables a firm to expose its traditional core competencies to new competitive situations, thereby increasing the chances that those core competencies will be improved or will be augmented by new core competencies. Finally, detailed local knowledge is essential if firms are going to leverage their traditional competencies in new ways in their nondomestic markets. Honda was able to begin exploiting its power train competencies in the U.S. lawn mower market only because of its detailed knowledge of, and responsiveness to, that market.

On the other hand, the full exploitation of the economies of scale that can be created by selling a firm's current products or services in a nondomestic market can occur only if there is tight integration across all the markets in which a firm operates. Gaining access to low-cost factors of production can not only help a firm succeed in a nondomestic market but also help it succeed in all its markets—as long as those factors of production are used by many parts of the global firm. Developing new core competencies and using traditional core competencies in new ways can certainly be beneficial in a particular nondomestic market. However, the full value of these economies of scope is realized only when they are transferred from a particular domestic market into the operations of a firm in all its other markets.

Traditionally, it has been thought that firms have to choose between local responsiveness and global integration. For example, firms like CIBA-Geigy (a Swiss chemical company), Nestlé (a Swiss food company), and Phillips (a Dutch consumer electronics firm) have chosen to emphasize local responsiveness. Nestlé, for example, owns nearly 8,000 brand names worldwide. However, of those 8,000 brands, only 750 are registered in more than one country, and only 80 are registered in more than 10 countries (Rapoport, 1994).

Nestlé adjusts its product attributes to the needs of local consumers, adopts brand names that resonate with those consumers, and builds its brands for long-run profitability. For example, in the United States, Nestlé's condensed milk carries the brand name "Carnation" (obtained through the acquisition of the Carnation Company); in Asia, this same product carries the brand name "Bear Brand." Nestlé delegates brand management authority to country managers, who can (and do) adjust traditional marketing and manufacturing strategies in accordance with local tastes and preferences. For example, Nestlé's Thailand management group dropped traditional coffee-marketing efforts that focused on taste, aroma, and stimulation and instead began selling coffee as a drink that promotes relaxation and romance. This marketing strategy resonated with Thais experiencing urban stress, and it prompted Nestlé coffee sales in Thailand to jump from $25 million in 1987 to $100 million in 1994 (Rapoport, 1994).

Of course, all this local responsiveness comes at a cost. Firms that emphasize local responsiveness are often unable to realize the full value of the economies of scope and scale that they could realize if their operations across country borders were more integrated. Numerous firms have focused on appropriating this economic value and have pursued a more integrated global strategy. Examples of such firms include IBM, General Electric, Toyota Motor Corporation, and most major pharmaceutical firms, to name just a few.

Globally integrated firms locate business functions and activities in countries that have a comparative advantage in these functions or activities. For example, the production of components for most consumer electronics is research intensive, capital intensive, and subject to significant economies of scale. To manage component *manufacturing* successfully, most globally integrated consumer electronics firms have located their component operations in technologically advanced countries like the United States and Japan. Because the *assembly* of these components into consumer products is labor intensive, most globally integrated consumer electronics firms have located their assembly operations in countries with relatively low labor costs, including Mexico and China.

Of course, one of the costs of locating different business functions and activities in different locations is that these different functions and activities must be coordinated and integrated. Operations in one country might very efficiently manufacture certain components. However, if the wrong components are shipped to the assembly location, or if the right components are shipped at the wrong time, any advantages that could have been obtained from exploiting the comparative advantages of different countries can be lost. Shipping costs can also reduce the return to global integration.

To ensure that the different operations in a globally integrated firm are appropriately coordinated, these firms typically manufacture more standardized products, using more standardized components, than do locally responsive firms. Standardization enables these firms to realize substantial economies of scale and scope, but it can limit their ability to respond to the specific needs of individual markets. When global product standards exist, as in the personal computer industry and the semiconductor chip industry, such standardization is not problematic. Also, when local responsiveness requires only a few modifications of a standardized product (for example, changing the shape of the electric plug or changing the color of a product), global integration can be very effective. However, when local responsiveness requires a great deal of local knowledge and product modifications, global integration can create problems for a firm pursuing a global strategy.

THE TRANSNATIONAL STRATEGY

Recently, two authors (Bartlett and Ghoshal, 1989) have argued that the traditional tradeoff between global integration and local responsiveness can be replaced by a *transnational strategy* that exploits all the advantages of both global integration and local responsiveness. According to Bartlett and Ghoshal (1989), firms implementing a transnational strategy treat their global operations as an integrated network of distributed and interdependent resources and capabilities. In this context, a firm's operations in each country are not simply independent activities attempting to respond to local market needs; they are also repositories of ideas, technologies, and management approaches that the firm might be able to use and apply in its other global operations. Put differently, operations in different countries can be thought of as "experiments" in the creation of new core competencies. Some of these experiments will work and generate important new core competencies; others will fail to have such benefits for a firm.

When a particular country operation develops a competence in manufacturing a particular product, providing a particular service, or engaging in a particular activity that can be used by other country operations, the country operation with this competence can achieve global economies of scale by becoming the firm's primary supplier of this product, service, or activity. In this way, local responsiveness is retained as country managers constantly search for new competencies that enable them to maximize profits in their particular markets, and global integration and economies are realized as country operations that have developed unique competencies become suppliers for all other country operations.

Managing a firm that is attempting to be both locally responsive and globally integrated is not an easy task. Some of these organizational challenges are discussed in Section 14.2.

FINANCIAL AND POLITICAL RISKS IN PURSUING GLOBAL STRATEGIES

There is little doubt that the realization of the economies of scope listed in Table 14.1 can be a source of economic value for firms pursuing global strategies. However, the nature of global strategies can create significant risks that these economies of scope will never be realized. Beyond the implementation problems (to be discussed later in this chapter), both financial circumstances and political events can significantly reduce the value of global strategies.

Financial Risks: Currency Fluctuation and Inflation

As firms begin to pursue global strategies, they may begin to expose themselves to financial risks that are less obvious within a single domestic market. In particular, currency fluctuations can significantly affect the value of a firm's global investments. Such fluctuations can turn what had been a losing investment into a profitable investment (this is the good news). They can also turn what had been a profitable investment into a losing investment (this is the bad news). In addition to currency fluctuations, different rates of inflation across countries can require very different managerial approaches, business strategies, and accounting practices. Certainly, when a firm first begins global operations, these financial risks can seem daunting.

Fortunately, it is now possible for firms to hedge most of these risks, through the use of a variety of financial instruments and strategies. The development of international money markets, together with growing experience in operating in high-inflation economies, has substantially reduced the threat of these financial risks for firms pursuing global strategies. Of course, the benefits of these financial tools and experience in high-inflation environments do not accrue to firms automatically. Firms seeking to implement global strategies must develop the resources and capabilities they will need to manage these financial risks. Moreover, these hedging strategies can do nothing to reduce the business risks that firms assume when they enter into nondomestic markets. For example, it may be the case that consumers in a nondomestic market simply do not want to purchase a firm's products or services, in which case this economy of scope cannot be realized. Moreover, these financial strategies cannot manage political risks that can exist for firms pursuing a global strategy.

Political Risks

The political environment is an important consideration in all strategic decisions. Changes in the political rules of the game can have the effect of increasing some environmental threats, reducing others, and thereby changing the value of a firm's resources and capabilities (Porter, 1980). However, the political environment can be even more problematic as firms pursue global strategies.

Types of Political Risks.   Politics can affect the value of a firm's global strategies at the macro and micro levels. At the macro level, broad changes in the political situation in a country can change the value of an investment. For example, after the Second World War, nationalist governments came to power in many countries in the Middle East. These governments expropriated for little or no compensation many of the assets of international oil and gas companies located in their countries. Expropriation of foreign company assets also occurred when the Shah of Iran was overthrown, when a communist government was elected in Chile, and when new governments came to power in Angola, Ethiopia, Peru, and Zambia (Rugman and Hodgetts, 1995).

Government upheaval and the attendant risks to global firms are facts of life in some countries. Consider, for example, oil-rich Nigeria. Since its independence in 1960, Nigeria has experienced several successful coups d'états, two failed coup d'états, one civil war, two civil governments, and six military regimes (Glynn, 1993). The prudent course of action for firms engaging in global business activities in Nigeria is to expect the current government to change and to plan accordingly.

Of course, government changes are not always bad for global firms. The fall of the Soviet Union and the introduction of capitalism into eastern Europe have created enormous opportunities for firms pursuing global strategies. For example, Volkswagen recently invested $6 billion in a Czech automobile firm; Opel (General Motors' European division) recently invested $680 million in a car-manufacturing facility in the former East Germany; and General Electric has invested $150 million in a light-bulb manufacturing operation in Hungary (Roth, 1990; "GM's Opel Unit to Build Plant in East Germany," 1990; Tully, 1990).

At the micro level, politics in a country can affect the fortunes of particular firms in particular industries. For example, the success of Japanese automobile companies in the U.S. market has subjected these firms to a variety of political challenges, including local-content legislation and voluntary import quotas (Ring, Lenway, and Govekar, 1990). These political risks exist even though there have been no major macro changes in the political system in the United States.

Quantifying Political Risks. Political scientists have attempted to quantify the political risk that firms seeking to implement global strategies are likely to face in different countries. Although different studies vary in detail, the country attributes listed in Table 14.4 summarize most of the important determinants of political risk for firms pursuing global strategies (Dichtl and Koeglmayr, 1986). Firms can apply the criteria listed in the table by evaluating the political and economic conditions in a country and by adding up the scores associated with these conditions. For example, a country that has a very unstable political system (14 points), a great deal of control of the economic system (9 points), and significant import restrictions (10 points) represents more political risk than a country that does not have these attributes.

TABLE 14.4
Quantifying Political Risks from Global Operations
Source: From E. Dichtl and H. G. Koeglmayr, "Country Risk Ratings," *Management International Review,* 26(4), (1986), pp. 2–10. Reprinted with permission.

	Increments to Country Risk If Risk Factor Is . . .	
	Low	High
The Political Economic Environment		
1. Stability of the political system	3	14
2. Imminent internal conflicts	0	14
3. External threats to stability	0	12
4. Degree of control of the economic system	5	9
5. Reliability of country as a trade partner	4	12
6. Constitutional guarantees	2	12
7. Effectiveness of public administration	3	12
8. Labor relations and social peace	3	15
Domestic Economic Conditions		
1. Size of the population	4	8
2. Per capita income	2	10
3. Economic growth over the last 5 years	2	7
4. Potential growth over the next 3 years	3	10
5. Inflation over the last 2 years	2	10
6. Availability of domestic capital markets to outsiders	3	7
7. Availability of high-quality local labor force	2	8
8. Possibility of employing foreign nationals	2	8
9. Availability of energy resources	2	14
10. Environmental pollution legal requirements	4	8
11. Transportation and communication infrastructure	2	14
External Economic Relations		
1. Import restrictions	2	10
2. Export restrictions	2	10
3. Restrictions on foreign investments	3	9
4. Freedom to set up or engage in partnerships	3	9

(continues)

TABLE 14.4
Quantifying Political Risks from Global Operations
(continued)

	Increments to Country Risk If Risk Factor Is . . .	
	Low	**High**
5. Legal protection for brands and products	3	9
6. Restrictions on monetary transfers	2	8
7. Revaluation of currency in the last 5 years	2	7
8. Balance-of-payments situation	2	9
9. Drain on hard currency through energy imports	3	14
10. International financial standing	3	8
11. Restrictions of the exchange of local and foreign currencies	2	8

Managing Political Risk.   Unlike financial risks, there are relatively few tools for managing the political risks associated with pursuing a global strategy. Obviously, one option would be to pursue global opportunities only in countries where political risk is very small. However, it is often the case that significant business opportunities exist in politically risky countries precisely because they are politically risky. Alternatively, firms can limit their investment in politically risky environments. However, these limited investments may not enable a firm to take full advantage of whatever economies of scope might exist by engaging in business in that country.

A final generic approach to managing political risk is to see each of the determinants of political risk, listed in Table 14.4, as negotiation points as a firm enters into a new country market. In many circumstances, those in a nondomestic market have just as much an interest in seeing a firm begin doing business in a new market as does the firm contemplating entry. Global firms can sometimes use this bargaining power to negotiate entry conditions that reduce, or even neutralize, some of the sources of political risk in a country. Of course, no matter how skilled a firm is in negotiating these entry conditions, a change of government or changes in laws can quickly nullify any agreements.

A final approach to managing political risk is to turn this risk from a threat into an opportunity. One firm that has been successful in this way is Schlumberger, an international oil service company. Schlumberger has headquarters in New York, Paris, and the Caribbean; it is a truly international company. Schlumberger management has adopted a policy of strict neutrality in interactions with governments in the developing world. Because of this policy, Schlumberger has been able to avoid political entanglements and continues to do business where many firms find the political risks too great. Put differently, Schlumberger has developed valuable, rare, and costly-to-imitate resources and capabilities in managing political risks and is using these resources to generate high levels of economic performance (Auletta, 1983).

THE VALUE OF GLOBAL STRATEGIES: THE EMPIRICAL EVIDENCE

Overall, research on the economic consequences of implementing global strategies is mixed. Leftwich (1974), Dunning (1973), Errunza and Senbet (1981), Grant (1987), and Rugman (1979) all found that the performance of firms pursuing global strategies is superior to the performance of firms operating only in domestic markets. However, most of this work has not examined the particular economies of scope that a firm is attempting to realize through its globalization effort. Moreover, several of these studies have attempted to evaluate the impact of global strategies on firm performance by using accounting measures of performance. More recently, work by Brewer (1981) and Michel and Shaked (1986) has found that the risk-adjusted performance of firms pursuing a global strategy is not different from the risk-adjusted performance of firms pursuing purely domestic strategies.

These ambivalent findings are not surprising, since the economic value of global strategies depends on whether a firm pursues valuable economies of scope when implementing this strategy. Most of this empirical work fails to examine the economies of scope that a firm's global strategy might be based on. Moreover, even if a firm is able to realize real economies of scope from its global strategies, to be a source of sustained competitive advantage, this economy of scope must also be rare and costly to imitate, and the firm must be organized to fully realize it.

14.2   GLOBAL STRATEGIES AND SUSTAINED COMPETITIVE ADVANTAGE

Much of the discussion of rareness and imitability in vertical integration, diversification, and merger and acquisition strategies also applies to global strategies. However, some aspects of rareness and imitability are unique to global strategies.

THE RARENESS OF GLOBAL STRATEGIES

In many ways, it seems likely that global strategies are becoming less rare among most competing firms. Consider, for example, the increasingly global activities of many U.S. telephone companies.

The government breakup of AT&T created seven regional telephone companies in the United States. For the first few years of their existence, these regional telephone companies concentrated on the regulated telephone business in their geographic regions. However, as restrictions on their business activities were reduced, these telephone companies began to explore nonregulated telephone business opportunities, including cellular telephone services, telephone equipment, and communications consulting. It seemed to be only a matter of time before these U.S. telephone companies began to explore global business opportunities.

Indeed, the globalization of these firms is now occurring. Ameritech and Bell Atlantic have formed a partnership to purchase New Zealand's telephone system for $2.4 billion. Ameritech owns a German publisher of specialized telephone directories. Bell Atlantic has an alliance with U.S. West and the government of the Czech Republic to build a cellular phone system there. Bell South owns paging systems in Britain and Australia, has an ownership interest in French cellular and cable television companies, and has cellular franchises in Argentina, Mexico, New Zealand, and Uruguay. NYNEX owns part of eleven British cable systems, and Pacific Telesis owns 26 percent of a consortium that is building a cellular system in Germany. Southwestern Bell is participating in a consortium that has purchased 51 percent of Mexico's state-owned telephone system; Southwestern Bell also has interests in cable television systems in Britain and Israel. U.S. West has formed joint ventures with the governments of Hungary and Russia to build cellular telephone systems there (Kirkpatrick, 1993). It is apparently the case that global strategies are no longer rare among U.S. regional telephone companies.

There are, of course, several reasons for the increased popularity of global strategies among U.S. regional telephone companies and in other industries as well. Not the least of them are the substantial economies of scope that globalizing firms can realize. In addition, several changes in the organization of the global economy have facilitated the growth in popularity of global strategies. For example, the recently negotiated General Agreement on Tariff and Trade (GATT) treaty, in conjunction with the development of the European Community (EC), the Andean Common Market (ANCOM), the Association of Southeast Asian Nations (ASEAN), the North American Free Trade Agreement (NAFTA), and other free-trade zones, has substantially reduced both tariff and nontariff barriers to trade. These changes have helped facilitate trade among countries included in an agreement; they have also spurred firms that wish to take advantage of these opportunities to expand their operations into these countries.

Improvements in the technological infrastructure of international business is also an important contributor to the growth in the number of firms pursuing global strategies. Transportation (especially air travel) and communication (via computers, fax, telephones, pagers, cellular telephones, and so forth) have evolved to the point where it is now much easier for firms to monitor and integrate their global operations than it was just a few years ago. This infrastructure helps reduce the cost of implementing a global strategy and thus increases the probability that firms will pursue these opportunities.

Finally, the emergence of various communication, technical, and accounting standards is facilitating global strategies. For example, there is currently a de facto world standard in personal computers. Moreover, most of the software that runs off these computers is flexible and interchangeable. Someone can write a report on a PC in India and print that report out on a PC in France with no real difficulties. There is also a world de factor standard business language—English. Although fully understanding a non-English-speaking culture requires managers to learn the native tongue, it is nevertheless possible to manage global business operations by using English.

Even though it seems that more and more firms are pursuing global strategies, it does not follow that these strategies will never be rare among a set of competing firms. Despite the increased popularity of these strategies, rare global strategies can exist in at least two ways. Given the enormous range of business opportunities that exist around the globe, it may very well be the case that huge numbers of firms can implement global strategies and still not compete head to head when implementing these strategies. Recall that the rareness requirement is that the resources and capabilities that a firm brings to implementing a strategy must be rare among competing firms. If, for a particular global opportunity, there happen to be few direct competitors, this rareness criterion can be met.

Even if several firms are competing to exploit the same global opportunity, the rareness criterion can still be met if the resources and capabilities that a particular firm brings to this global competition are rare (Caves, 1971; Dunning, 1973; Hymer, 1976). Examples of these rare resources and capabilities might include unusual marketing skills, highly differentiated products, special technology, superior management talent, and economies of scale (Errunza and Senbet, 1981). To the extent that a firm pursues one of the economies of scope listed in Table 14.1 using resources and capabilities that are rare among competing firms, that firm can gain at least a temporary competitive advantage from its global strategy.

THE IMITABILITY OF GLOBAL STRATEGIES

Like all the strategies discussed in this book, both the direct duplication of global strategies and substitutes for global strategies are important in evaluating the imitability of these actions.

Direct Duplication of Global Strategies

In evaluating the possibility of the direct duplication of global strategies, two questions must be asked: (1) Will firms try to duplicate valuable and rare global strategies? (2) Will firms be able to duplicate these valuable and rare strategies?

There seems little doubt that, in the absence of artificial barriers, the profits generated by one firm's valuable and rare global strategies will motivate other firms to try to imitate the resources and capabilities required to implement these strategies. This is what occurred among the regional telephone companies. Once Ameritech and Bell Atlantic demonstrated that there was economic value to be had by engaging in a global strategy, most of the other regional telephone companies quickly tried to follow their lead. This rush to globalization has occurred in numerous other industries as well. For example, the processed-food industry at one time had a strong home-market orientation. But because of the success of Nestlé and Procter & Gamble worldwide, most processed-food companies now engage in at least some global operations (Rapoport, 1994).

However, simply because competing firms often try to duplicate a successful firm's global strategy does not mean that they are always able to do so. To the extent that a successful firm exploits resources or capabilities that are path dependent, uncertain, or socially complex in its globalization efforts, direct duplication may be too costly, and thus globalization can be a source of sustained competitive advantage. Indeed, there is some reason to believe that at least some of the resources and capabilities that enable a firm to pursue a global strategy are likely to be costly to imitate.

For example, the ability to develop detailed local knowledge of nondomestic markets may require firms to have management teams with a great deal of foreign experience. Some firms may have this kind of experience in their top management teams; other firms may not. In a recent survey of 433 chief executive officers from around the world, Anders (1989) reported that 14 percent of U.S. CEOs had no foreign experience and that the foreign experience of 56 percent of U.S. CEOs was limited to vacation travel. Of course, it can take a great deal of time for a firm that does not have much foreign experience in its management team to develop that experience. Firms that lack this kind of experience will have to bring managers in from outside the organization, invest in developing this experience internally, or both. Of course, these activities are costly. The cost of creating this experience base in a firm's management team can be thought of as the cost of direct duplication.

Substitutes for Global Strategies

Even if direct duplication of a firm's global strategies is costly, there might still exist substitutes that limit the ability of that strategy to generate sustained competitive advantages. In particular, because global strategies are just a special case of leveraging strategies, any of the other leveraging strategies discussed in this book—including some types of strategic alliances, vertical integration, diversification, and mergers and acquisitions—can be at least partial substitutes for global strategies.

For example, it may be possible for a firm to gain at least some of the economies of scope listed in Table 14.1 by implementing a diversification strategy within a single country market, especially if that market is large and geographically diverse. One such market, of course, is the United States. A firm that originally conducted business in the northeastern United States can gain many of the benefits of globalization by beginning business operations in the southern United States, on the West Coast, or in the Pacific Northwest. In this sense, geographic diversification within the United States is at least a partial substitute for globalization and is one reason why many U.S. firms have lagged behind European and Asian firms in their globalization efforts.

There are, however, some economies of scope listed in Table 14.1 that can be gained only through global operations. For example, since there are usually few limits on capital flows within most countries, risk management is a valuable economy of scope only for firms pursuing business opportunities across countries where barriers to capital flow exist. Moreover, the potential value of some of the economies listed in Table 14.1 is substantially greater in a global context, compared to the value of those economies in a substitute context. For example, the ability to develop new core competencies is, on average, much greater for globalizing firms than for firms pursuing a substitute strategy.

THE ORGANIZATION OF GLOBAL STRATEGIES

To realize the full economic potential of a valuable, rare, and costly-to-imitate global strategy, firms must be appropriately organized.

Becoming Globalized: Organizational Options

A firm implements a global strategy when it diversifies its business operations across country boundaries. However, firms can organize their global business operations in a wide variety of ways. Some of the most common, ranging from simple export operations to managing a wholly owned foreign subsidiary, are listed in Table 14.5. These options can be thought of as different levels of vertical integration into global activities available to a firm. As firms become more vertically integrated into global operations, their level of direct investment in nondomestic markets increases. This investment is called *foreign direct investment*.

Market Governance, Exporting, and Global Strategies. Firms can maintain traditional arm's-length market relationships between themselves and their nondomestic customers and still implement global strategies. They do this by simply exporting their products or services to nondomestic markets and limiting any foreign direct investment into non domestic markets. Of course, exporting firms generally have to work with some partner or partners to receive, market, and distribute their products in a nondomestic setting. However, it is possible for exporting firms to use complete contingent claims contracts to manage their relationship with these foreign partners and thereby maintain arm's-length relationships with them (see the discussion of complete contingent claims contracts in Section 10.2)—all the time limiting foreign direct investment.

The advantages of adopting exporting as a way to manage a global strategy include its relatively low cost and the limited risk exposure that firms that pursue globalization in this manner face. Firms that are just beginning to consider global strategies can use market-based exporting to test the global waters—to find out if there is demand for

TABLE 14.5 **Organizing Options for Firms Pursuing Global Strategies**	Market Governance	Intermediate Market Governance	Hierarchical Governance
	Exporting	Licensing	Mergers
		Nonequity alliances	Acquisitions
		Equity alliances	Wholly owned subsidiaries
		Joint ventures	

their current products or services, to develop some experience operating in nondomestic markets, to begin to develop relationships that could be valuable in subsequent global strategy efforts. If firms discover that there is not much demand for their products or services in a nondomestic market, or if they discover that they do not have the resources and capabilities to effectively compete in those markets, they can simply cease their exporting operations. The direct cost of ceasing export operations can be quite low, especially if a firm's volume of exports is small and the firm has not invested in plant and equipment designed to facilitate exporting. Certainly, if a firm has limited its foreign direct investment, it does not risk losing this investment if it ceases export operations.

However, the opportunity costs associated with restricting a firm's global operations to exporting can be significant. Of the economies of scope listed in Table 14.1, only gaining access to new customers for a firm's current products or services can be realized through exporting. Other economies of scope that hold some potential for firms exploring global business operations are out of the reach of firms that restrict their global operations to exporting. For some firms, realizing economies from gaining access to new customers is sufficient, and exporting is a long-run viable strategy. However, to the extent that other economies of scope might exist for a firm, limiting global operations to exporting can limit the firm's economic profit.

Intermediate Market Governance, Strategic Alliances, and Global Strategies.   If a firm decides to move beyond market governance and exporting in pursuing global strategies, a wide range of intermediate market governance devices—called *strategic alliances* in Chapters 9 and 10—are available. These alliances range from simple licensing arrangements, where a domestic firm grants a firm in a nondomestic market the right to use its products and brand names to sell products in that nondomestic market, to full-blown joint ventures, where a domestic firm and a nondomestic firm create an independent organizational entity to manage globalization efforts. As suggested in Chapter 9, the recent growth in the number of firms pursuing strategic alliance strategies is a direct result of the growth in popularity of global strategies. Strategic alliances are one of the most common ways that firms manage their globalization efforts.

Most of Chapter 9's discussion of the value, rareness, imitability, and organization of strategic alliances applies to the analysis of strategic alliances to implement a global strategy. However, many of the opportunities and challenges of managing strategic alliances as cooperative strategies, discussed in Chapter 9, are exaggerated in the context of global strategic alliances.

For example, it was suggested that opportunistic behavior (in the form of adverse selection, moral hazard, or holdup) can threaten the stability of strategic alliances. Opportunistic behavior is a problem because partners in a strategic alliance find it costly to observe and evaluate the performance of alliance partners. Obviously, the costs and difficulty of evaluating the performance of an alliance partner in a global alliance are greater than the costs and difficulty of evaluating the performance of an alliance partner in a purely domestic alliance. Geographic distance, differences in traditional business practices, language barriers, and cultural differences can make it very difficult for firms to accurately evaluate the performance and intentions of global alliance partners.

These challenges can manifest themselves at multiple levels in a global strategic alliance. For example, Adler, Brahm, and Graham (1992) have shown that managers in U.S. organizations, on average, have a negotiation style very different from that of managers in Chinese organizations. Chinese managers tend to interrupt each other and ask many more questions during negotiations than do U.S. managers. As U.S. and Chinese firms begin to negotiate collaborative agreements, it will be difficult for U.S. managers to judge whether the Chinese negotiation style reflects Chinese managers' fundamental distrust of U.S. managers or is simply a manifestation of traditional Chinese business practices and culture.

Similar management style differences have been noted between Western and Japanese managers. Hamel (1991:95) quotes one Western manager:

> Whenever I made a presentation [to our partner], I was one person against ten or twelve. They'd put me in front of a flip chart, and then stop me while they went into a conversation in Japanese for ten minutes. If I asked them a question they would break into Japanese to first decide what I wanted to know, and then would discuss options in terms of what they might tell me, and finally would come back with an answer.

During those ten-minute breaks in the conversation, it would be very difficult for this manager to know whether the Japanese managers were trying to develop a complete and accurate answer to his question or scheming to provide an incomplete and misleading answer. In this ambiguous setting, to prevent potential opportunism, Western managers might demand greater levels of governance than were actually necessary. In fact, Shane (1994) has shown that differences in the perceived trustworthiness of international partners has an impact on the kind of governance mechanisms that are put into place when firms begin global operations. If partners are not perceived as being trustworthy, then elaborate governance devices, including joint ventures, are created—even if the partners are in fact trustworthy.

Cultural and style conflicts leading to perceived opportunism problems are not restricted to alliances between Asian and Western organizations. U.S. firms operating with Mexican partners often discover numerous subtle and complex cultural differences. A U.S. firm operating a steel conveyor plant in Puebla, Mexico, implemented a three-stage employee grievance policy. An employee who had a grievance first went to the immediate supervisor and then continued up the chain of command until the grievance was resolved one way or another. U.S. managers were satisfied with this system and pleased that no grievances had been registered—until the day the entire plant walked out on strike. It turns out that there had been numerous grievances, but Mexican workers had felt uncomfortable directly confronting their supervisors with these problems. Such confrontations are considered antisocial in Mexican culture (de Forest, 1994).

Although significant challenges are associated with managing strategic alliances across country boundaries, there are significant opportunities as well. Strategic alliances can enable a firm pursuing a global strategy to realize any of the economies of scope listed in Table 14.1. Moreover, if a firm is able to develop valuable, rare, and costly-to-imitate resources and capabilities in managing strategic alliances, the use of alliances in a global context can be a source of sustained competitive advantage.

Hierarchical Governance, Vertical Integration, and Global Strategies.
Firms may decide to vertically integrate in their global operations by acquiring a firm in a nondomestic market or by forming a new wholly owned subsidiary to manage their operations in a nondomestic market. Obviously, both of these global investments involve substantial direct foreign investment by a firm over long periods of time. These investments are subject to both political and economic risks and should be undertaken only if the economy of scope that can be realized through global operations is significant and other ways of realizing this economy of scope are not effective or efficient.

Although hierarchical governance and vertical integration in global operations can be expensive and risky, they can have some important advantages for globalizing firms. First, like strategic alliances, this approach to globalization can enable a firm to realize any of the economies of scope listed in Table 14.1. Moreover, vertical integration enables managers to use a wider range of organizational controls to limit the threat of opportunism than are normally available in market forms of global governance or intermediate market forms of global governance. Finally, unlike strategic alliances, where any profits from global operations must be shared with global partners, vertically integrating into global operations enables firms to capture all the economic profits from their global operations.

Managing the Globally Diversified Firm

In many ways, the management of global operations can be thought of as a special case of managing the diversified firm. Thus many of the issues discussed in Chapter 12 apply here. However, managing a globally diversified firm does create some unique challenges and opportunities.

Organizational Structure.   Firms pursuing a global strategy have four basic organizational structural alternatives, listed in Table 14.6 and discussed below. Although each of these structures has some special features, they are all special cases of the multidivisional structure first introduced in Chapter 12.

Some firms organize their international operations as a *decentralized federation*. In this organizational structure, each country in which a firm operates is organized as a full profit-and-loss division headed by a division general manager who is typically the president of the company in a particular country (Bartlett and Ghoshal, 1989; Bartlett, 1986). In a decentralized federation, there are very few shared activities or other synergies among different divisions/country companies, and corporate headquarters plays a limited strategic role. Corporate staff functions are generally limited to the collection of accounting and other performance information from divisions/country companies and to

TABLE 14.6 **Structural Options** **for Firms Pursuing** **Global Strategies** *Source:* Bartlett and Ghoshal (1989).	Decentralized federation	Strategic and operational decisions are delegated to divisions/country companies.
	Coordinated federation	Operational decisions are delegated to divisions/country companies; strategic decisions are retained at corporate headquarters.
	Centralized hub	Strategic and operational decisions are retained at corporate headquarters.
	Transnational structure	Strategic and operational decisions are delegated to those organizational entities that maximize responsiveness to local conditions and global integration.

reporting this aggregate information to appropriate government officials and to the financial markets. Most employees within the divisions/country companies in a decentralized federation may not even be aware that they are part of a larger globally diversified firm. Both strategic and operational decision making are delegated to division general managers/country company presidents in a decentralized federation organizational structure. There are relatively few examples of pure decentralized federations in today's world economy, but firms like Nestlé, CIBA-Geigy, and Electrolux have many of the attributes of this type of structure (Baden-Fuller and Stopford, 1991).

A second structural option for global firms is the *coordinated federation*. In a coordinated federation, each country operation is organized as a full profit-and-loss center, and division general managers can be presidents of country companies. However, unlike the case in a decentralized federation, strategic and operational decisions are not fully delegated to division general managers. Operational decisions are delegated to division general managers/country presidents, but broader strategic decisions are made at corporate headquarters. Moreover, coordinated federations attempt to exploit various shared activities and other synergies among their divisions/country companies. It is not uncommon for coordinated federations to have corporately sponsored central research and development laboratories, corporately sponsored manufacturing and technology development initiatives, and corporately sponsored management training and development operations (Bartlett, 1986). There are numerous examples of coordinated federations in today's world economy, including General Electric, General Motors, IBM, and Coca-Cola.

A third structural option for globally operating firms is the *centralized hub*. In centralized hubs, operations in different companies may be organized into profit-and-loss centers, and division general managers may be country company presidents. However, most of the strategic and operational decision making in these firms takes place at the corporate center. The role of divisions/country companies in centralized hubs is simply to implement the strategies, tactics, and policies that have been chosen at headquarters. Of course, divisions/country companies are also a source of information for headquarters staff when these decisions are being made. However, in centralized hubs, strategic and operational decision rights are retained at the corporate center (Bartlett, 1986). Many Japanese and Korean firms are managed as centralized hubs, including Toyota, Mitsubishi, and NEC (in Japan) and Goldstar, Daewoo, and Hyundai (in Korea) (Kraar, 1992).

A fourth structural option for globalizing firms is the *transnational structure* (Bartlett and Ghoshal, 1989). This structure is most appropriate for implementing the transnational strategy described in Section

14.1. In many ways, the transnational structure is similar to the coordinated federation. In both, strategic decision-making responsibility is largely retained at the corporate center, and operational decision making is largely delegated to division general managers/country presidents. However, important differences also exist.

In a coordinated federation structure, shared activities and other cross-divisional/cross-country synergies are managed by the corporate center. Thus, for many of these firms, if research and development is seen as a potentially valuable synergy, a central research and development laboratory is created and managed by the corporate center. In the transnational structure, these centers of corporate synergy may be managed by the corporate center. However, they are more likely to be managed by specific divisions/country companies within the corporation. Thus, for example, if one division/country company develops valuable, rare, and costly to imitate research and development capabilities in its ongoing business activities in a particular country, that division/country company could become the center of research and development activity for the entire corporation. If one division/country company develops valuable, rare, and costly-to-imitate manufacturing technology development skills in its ongoing business activities in a particular country, that division/country company could become the center for manufacturing technology development for the entire corporation.

The role of corporate headquarters in a transnational structure is to constantly scan business operations across different countries for resources and capabilities that might be a source of competitive advantage for other divisions/country companies in the firm. Once these special skills are located, corporate staff must then determine the best way to exploit these potential synergies—whether they should be developed within a single division/country company (to gain economies of scale) and then transferred to other divisions/country companies, or developed through an alliance between two or more divisions/country companies (to gain economies of scale) and then transferred to other divisions/country companies, or developed for the entire firm at corporate headquarters. These options are not available to decentralized federations (which always must let individual divisions/country companies develop their own competencies), coordinated federations, or centralized hubs (which always develop corporatewide synergies at the corporate level). Firms that have been successful in adopting this transnational structure include Ford (Ford Europe has become a leader for automobile design in all of the Ford Motor Company) and Ericson (Ericson's Australian subsidiary developed this Swedish company's first electronic telecommunication switch, and corporate headquarters was able to help transfer this technology to other Ericson subsidiaries) (Bartlett and Ghoshal, 1989; Grant, 1991a).

Organizational Structure, Local Responsiveness, and Global Integration.   It should be clear that the choice among those four organizational approaches to managing global strategies depends on the trade-offs that firms are willing to make between local responsiveness and global integration (see Fig. 14.2). Firms that seek to maximize their local responsiveness will tend to choose a decentralized federation structure. Firms that seek to maximize global integration in their operations will typically opt for centralized hub structures. Firms that seek to balance the need for local responsiveness and global integration will typically choose centralized federations. Firms that attempt to optimize both local responsiveness and global integration will choose a transnational organizational structure.

Management Control Systems and Compensation Policies.   Like the multidivisional structure discussed in Chapter 12, none of the organizational structures described in Table 14.5 can stand alone, without the support of a variety of management control systems and management compensation policies. All the management control processes discussed in Chapter 12, including evaluating the performance of divisions, allocating capital, and managing the exchange of intermediate products among divisions, also are important for firms organizing to implement a global strategy. Moreover, the same management compensation challenges and opportunities discussed in that chapter apply in the organization of global strategies as well.

However, as is often the case when organizing processes originally developed to manage diversification within a domestic market are extended to the management of global diversification, many of the

FIGURE 14.2
Local Responsiveness, Global Integration, and Organizational Structure
Source: From R. Grant, *Contemporary Strategy Analysis*, 1991, Basil Blackwell. Reprinted with permission.

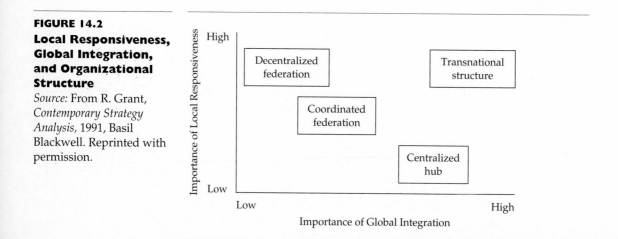

management challenges highlighted in Chapter 12 are exacerbated in a global context. This puts an even greater burden on senior managers in a globally diversified firm to choose control systems and compensation policies that create incentives for division general managers/country presidents to appropriately cooperate to realize the economies of scope that originally motivated the implementation of a global strategy.

14.3   SUMMARY

Global strategies can be seen as a special case of a broader leveraging strategy. Firms implement global strategies when they pursue business opportunities that cross country borders. Like all leveraging strategies, global strategies must exploit real economies of scope that outside investors find too costly to exploit on their own in order to be valuable. Five potentially valuable economies of scope in global strategies are (1) to gain access to new customers for a firm's current products or services, (2) to gain access to low-cost factors of production, (3) to develop new core competencies, (4) to leverage current core competencies in new ways, and (5) to manage corporate risk.

As firms pursue these economies of scope, they must evaluate the extent to which they can be responsive to local market needs and obtain the advantages of global integration. Firms that attempt to accomplish both these objectives are said to be implementing a transnational strategy. Both economic and political risks can affect the value of a firm's global strategies.

To be a source of sustained competitive advantages, a firm's global strategies must be valuable, rare, and costly to imitate, and the firm must be organized to realize the full potential of its global strategies. Even though more and more firms are pursuing global strategies, these strategies can still be rare, for at least two reasons: (1) Given the broad range of global opportunities, firms may not compete head to head with other firms pursuing the same global strategies that they are pursuing. (2) Firms may bring valuable and rare resources and capabilities to the global strategies they pursue. Both direct duplication and substitution can affect the imitability of a firm's global strategy. Direct duplication is not likely when firms bring valuable, rare, and costly-to-imitate resources and capabilities to bear in their global strategies. Several substitutes for global strategies exist, including some strategic alliances, vertical integration, diversification, and mergers and acquisitions, especially if these strategies are pursued in a large and diverse market. However, some potential economies of scope from global strategies can be exploited only by operating across country borders.

Firms have several organizational options as they pursue global strategies, including market forms of governance (for example, exports), intermediate forms of governance (for example, strategic alliances), and hierarchical forms of governance (for example, wholly owned subsidiaries). Four alternative structures, all special cases of the multidivisional structure introduced in Chapter 12, can be used to manage these global operations: a decentralized federation structure, a coordinated federation structure, a centralized hub structure, and a transnational structure. These structures need to be consistent with a firm's emphasis on being responsive to local markets, on exploiting global integration opportunities, or both.

REVIEW QUESTIONS

1. Are global strategies always just a special case of diversification strategies that a firm might pursue? What, if anything, is different about global strategies and diversification strategies?

2. In your view, is gaining access to low-cost labor a sufficient reason for a firm to pursue a global strategy? Why or why not? In your view, is gaining access to special tax breaks a sufficient reason for a firm to pursue a global strategy? Why or why not?

3. The transnational strategy is often seen as one way in which firms can avoid the limitations inherent in the local responsiveness/global integration tradeoff. However, given the obvious advantages of being both locally responsive and globally integrated, why are apparently only a relatively few firms implementing a transnational strategy? What implications does your analysis have for the ability of a transnational strategy to be a source of sustained competitive advantage for a firm?

4. On average, is the threat of adverse selection and moral hazard in strategic alliances greater for firms pursuing a global strategy or a domestic strategy? Why?

5. How are the organizational options for implementing a global strategy, listed in Table 14.6, related to the M-form structure described in Chapter 12? Are these global organizational options just special cases of the M-form structure, with slightly different emphases, or are these global organizational options fundamentally different from the M-form structure?

References

Abernathy, W. J., and J. M. Utterback (1978). "Patterns of technological innovation." *Technology Review*, 80, pp. 40–47.

Adelman, M. A. (1955). "Concept and statistical measurement of vertical integration." In National Bureau for Economic Research (eds.), *Business Concentration and Price Policy*. (pp. 281–322). Princeton, NJ: Princeton University Press.

Adler, M., and B. Dumas (1983). "International portfolio choice and corporate finance: A synthesis." *Journal of Finance*, 38, pp. 925–984.

Adler, N. J., R. Brahm, and J. L. Graham (1992). "Strategy implementation: A comparison of face-to-face negotiations in the People's Republic of China and the United States." *Strategic Management Journal*, 13, pp. 449–466.

Agmon, T., and D. R. Lessard (1977). "Investor recognition of corporate international diversification." *Journal of Finance*, 32, pp. 1049–1056.

Aguilar, F. J., and A. Bhambri (1983). "Johnson & Johnson (A)." Harvard Business School, Case no. 9-384-053.

Aguilar, F. J., J. L. Bower, and B. Gomes-Casseres (1985). "Restructuring European Petrochemicals: Imperial Chemical Industries, P. L. C." Harvard Business School, Case No. 9-385-203.

Alchian, A. (1950). "Uncertainty, evolution, and economic theory." *Journal of Political Economy*, 58, pp. 211–222.

Alchian, A., and H. Demsetz (1972). "Production, information costs, and economic organization." *American Economic Review*, 62, pp. 777–795.

Allen, F. (1984). "Reputation and product quality." *Rand Journal of Economics*, 15(3), pp. 3311–3327.

Allen, F. (1993). "Strategic management and financial markets." *Strategic Management Journal*, 14, pp. 11–22.

Allen, M., and M. Siconolfi (1993). "Dell computer drops planned share offering." *Wall Street Journal*, February 25, p. A3.

Alpert, M. (1992). "The care and feeding of engineers." *Fortune*, September 21, pp. 86–95.

Altman, E. I. (1968). "Financial ratios, discriminant analysis and the prediction of corporate bankruptcy." *Journal of Finance*, 23, pp. 589–609.

Altman, E. I., R. G. Haldeman, and P. Narayanan (1977). "Zeta analysis: A new model to identify bankruptcy risk of corporations." *Journal of Banking and Finance*, 1, pp. 29–54.

Amihud, Y., and B. Lev (1981). "Risk reduction as managerial motive for conglomerate mergers." *Bell Journal of Economics*, 12, pp. 605–617.

Amit, R., and J. Livnat (1988a). "Diversification strategies, business cycles and economic performance." *Strategic Management Journal*, 9, pp. 99–110.

Amit, R., and J. Livnat (1988b). "Diversification and the risk-return trade-off." *Academy of Management Journal*, 31, pp. 154–166.

Amit, R., and J. Livnat (1988c). "Diversification strategies, business cycles, and economic performance." *Strategic Management Journal*, 9, pp. 99–110.

Amit, R., and P. J. H. Schoemaker (1993). "Strategic assets and organizational rent." *Strategic Management Journal*, 14(1), pp. 33–45.

Anders, G. (1989). "Going global: Vision vs. reality." *Wall Street Journal*, September 22, p. R21.

Anderson, E. (1985). "The salesperson as outside agent or employee." *Marketing Science*, 4, pp. 234–254.

Anderson, E., and D. Schmittlein (1984). "Integration of sales force: An empirical examination." *Rand Journal of Economics*, 15, pp. 385–395.

Andrews, K. R. (1971). *The Concept of Corporate Strategy*. Homewood, IL: Irwin.

Ansoff, H. I. (1965). *Corporate Strategy*. New York: McGraw-Hill.

Applegate, L. M., J. H. Hertenstein, N. Wishart, and M. Addonizio (1989). "Westinghouse Electric Corp.: Automating the capital budgeting process (A)." Harvard Business School, Case no. 9-189-119.

Aragon, G. A. (1982). *A Manager's Complete Guide to Financial Techniques*. New York: Free Press.

Argyris, C., and D. A. Schon (1978). *Organizational Learning*. Reading, MA: Addison-Wesley.

Armour, H. O., and D. J. Teece (1980). "Vertical integration and technological innovation." *Review of Economics and Statistics*, 60, pp. 470–474.

Armstrong, J. S. (1982). "The value of formal planning for strategic decisions: Review of empirical research." *Strategic Management Journal*, 3, pp. 197–211.

Armstrong, L. (1991a). "Who's the most pampered motorist of all?" *Business Week*, June 10, pp. 90–92.

Armstrong, L. (1991b). "Services: The customer as 'Honored Guest.'" *Business Week*, October 25, p. 104.

Arthur, W. B. (1989). "Competing technologies, increasing returns, and lock-in by historical events." *Economic Journal*, 99, pp. 116–131.

Auletta, K. (1983). "A certain poetry—Parts I and II." *The New Yorker*, June 6, pp. 46–109, June 13, pp. 50–91.

Axelrod, R. M. (1984). *The Evolution of Cooperation*. New York: Basic Books.

Backaitis, N. T., R. Balakrishnan, and K. R. Harrigan (1984). *The dimensions of diversification posture, market power, and performance: The continuing debate.* Working paper, Columbia University.

Badaracco, J. L., and N. Hasegawa (1988). "General Motors' Asian alliances." Harvard Business School, Case no. 9-388-094.

Baden-Fuller, C. W. F., and J. M. Stopford (1991). "Globalization frustrated: The case of white goods." *Strategic Management Journal*, 12, pp. 493–507.

Bailey, J. (1990). "Move to buy Beatrice fits ConAgra pattern: Aggressive expansion." *Wall Street Journal*, June 13, p. A1.

Bain, J. S. (1956). *Barriers to New Competition.* Cambridge, MA: Harvard University Press.

Bain, J. S. (1968). *Industrial Organization.* New York: Wiley.

Balakrishnan, S., and M. Koza (1993). "Information asymmetry, adverse selection and joint-ventures." *Journal of Economic Behavior & Organization*, 20, pp. 99-117.

Balkin, D., and L. Gomez-Mejia (1990). "Matching compensation and organizational strategies." *Strategic Management Journal*, 11, pp. 153–169.

Ball, R., and P. Brown (1968). "An empirical examination of accounting income numbers." *Journal of Accounting Research*, 6, pp. 159–178.

Banz, R. W. (1981). "The relationship between return and market value of common stocks." *Journal of Financial Economics*, 9, pp. 3–18.

Barney, J. B. (1986a). "Strategic factor markets: Expectations, luck and business strategy." *Management Science*, 32, pp. 1512–1514.

Barney, J. B. (1986b). "Organizational culture: Can it be a source of sustained competitive advantage?" *Academy of Management Review*, 11, pp. 656–665.

Barney, J. B. (1986c). "Types of competition and the theory of strategy: Toward an integrative framework." *Academy of Management Review*, 11, pp. 791–800.

Barney, J. B. (1988). "Returns to bidding firms in mergers and acquisitions: Reconsidering the relatedness hypothesis." *Strategic Management Journal*, 9, pp. 71–78.

Barney, J. B. (1990). "Profit sharing bonuses and the cost of debt: Business finance and compensation policy in Japanese electronics firms." *Asia Pacific Journal of Management*, 7, pp. 49–64.

Barney, J. B. (1991). "Firm resources and sustained competitive advantage." *Journal of Management*, 17, pp. 99–120.

Barney, J. B. (1994). "Bringing managers back in: A resource-based analysis of the role of managers in creating and sustaining competitive advantages for firms." In *Does Management Matter?* (pp. 3–36). Lund, Sweden: Institute of Economic Research, Lund University.

Barney, J. B., and M. H. Hansen (1994). "Trustworthiness as a source of competitive advantage." *Strategic Management Journal*, 15 (Winter Special Issue), pp. 175–190.

Barney, J. B. and W. Hesterly (1996). "Organizational economics: Understanding the relationship between organizations and economic analysis." In S. Clegg, C. Hardy, and W. Nord (eds.), *Handbook of Organization Theory*, forthcoming.

Barney, J. B., and R. E. Hoskisson (1990). "Strategic groups: Untested assertions and research proposals." *Managerial and Decision Economics*, 11, pp. 187–198.

Barney, J. B., and W. G. Ouchi (1986). *Organizational Economics.* San Francisco: Jossey-Bass.

Barney, J. B., and B. Tyler (1990). "The attributes of top management teams and sustained competitive advantage." In M. Lawless and L. Gomez-Mejia (eds.), *Managing the High Technology Firm* (pp. 33–48). Greenwich, CT: JAI Press.

Bartlett, C. A. (1986). "Building and managing the transnational: The new organizational challenge." In M. E. Porter (ed.), *Competition in Global Industries* (pp. 367–401). Boston: Harvard Business School Press.

Bartlett, C. A. and S. Ghoshal (1989). *Managing Across Borders: The Transnational Solution.* Boston: Harvard Business School Press.

Bartlett, C. A., and S. Ghoshal (1993). "Beyond the M-form: Toward a managerial theory of the firm." *Strategic Management Journal,* 14, pp. 23–46.

Bartlett, C. A., and A. Nanda (1993). "Corning Incorporated: A network of alliances." Harvard Business School, Case no. 5-394-018.

Bartlett, C. A., and U. S. Rangan (1985). "Komatsu Ltd." Harvard Business School, Case no. 9-385-277.

Basu, S. (1977). "Investment performance of common stocks in relation to their price-earnings ratios: A test of the efficient markets hypothesis." *Journal of Finance,* 24, pp. 663–682.

Baumol, W. J., J. C. Panzar, and R. P. Willig (1982). *Contestable Markets and the Theory of Industry Structure.* New York: Harcourt, Brace, Jovanovich.

Baysinger, B. D., and H. N. Butler (1985). "The role of corporate law in the theory of the firm." *Journal of Law & Economics,* 28(1), pp. 179–191.

Baysinger, B. D., and R. E. Hoskisson (1990). "The composition of boards of directors and strategic control: Effects on corporate strategy."*Academy of Management Review,* 15, pp. 72–87.

Beatty, R., and R. Ritter (1986). "Investment banking, reputation, and the underpricing of initial public offerings." *Journal of Financial Economics,* 15, pp. 213–232.

Becker, G. S. (1964). *Human Capital.* New York: Columbia University Press.

Behar, R. (1995). "ADM watch: Price fixing lawsuits are piling up." *Fortune,* September 18, p. 20.

Benedict, R. (1946). *The Chrysanthemum and the Sword.* New York: New American Library.

Berg, N. A., and G. W. Merry (1984). "Polaroid-Kodak." Harvard Business School, Case no. 9-378-165.

Berger, P., and E. Otek (1995). "Diversification effect on firm value." *Journal of Financial Economics,* 37, pp. 36–65.

Bergh, D. (1995). "Size and relatedness of units sold: An agency theory and resource-based perspective." *Strategic Management Journal,* 16, pp. 221–239.

Bernheim, R. D., and M. D. Whinston (1990). "Multimarket contact and collusive behavior." *Rand Journal of Economics,* 12, pp. 605–617.

Berry, C. H. (1975). *Corporate Growth and Diversification.* Princeton, NJ: Princeton University Press.

Berstein, A. (1990). "The baseball owners get beaned." *Business Week,* October 15, p. 122.

Bertrand, J. (1883). "Théorie mathématique de la richesse sociale." *Journal des Savants,* pp. 499–508.

Bethel, J. E. (1990). *The capital allocation process and managerial mobility: A theoretical and empirical investigation.* Unpublished doctoral dissertation, University of California, Los Angeles.

Bethel, J. E. and J. Liebeskind (1993). "The effects of ownership structure on corporate restructuring." *Strategic Management Journal,* 14, pp. 15–31.

Bettis, R. A. (1981). "Performance differences in related and unrelated diversified firms." *Strategic Management Journal,* 2, pp. 379–393.

Bettis, R. A. (1983). "Modern financial theory, corporate strategy and public policy: Three conundrums." *Academy of Management Review*, 8(3), pp. 406–415.

Bettis, R. A., and W. K. Hall (1982). "Diversification strategy, accounting determined risk, and accounting determined return." *Academy of Management Journal*, 25, pp. 254–264.

Bettis, R. A.. and V. Mahajan (1985). "Risk/return performance of diversified firms." *Management Science*, 31, pp. 785–799.

Birnbaum, J. H., and M. Waldholz (1993). "Harsh medicine: Attack on drug prices opens Clinton's fight for health-care plan." *Wall Street Journal*, February 16, p. A1.

Black, F., and M. Scholes (1972). "The valuation of option contracts and a test of market efficiency." *Journal of Finance*, 27, pp. 399–418.

Black, F., and M. Scholes (1973). "The pricing of options and corporate liabilities." *Journal of Political Economy*, 81, pp. 637–659.

Blackman, A. (1990). "Moscow's Big Mac attack." *Time*, February 5, p. 51.

Bloch, F. (1995). "Endogenous structures of association in oligopolies." *Rand Journal of Economics*, 26, pp. 537–556.

Blume, M. E. (1975). "Betas and their regression tendencies." *Journal of Finance*, 30, pp. 785–795.

Bond, R. S., and D. F. Lean (1977). *Sales, Promotion, and Product Differentiation in Two Prescription Drug Markets*. Washington, DC: U.S. Federal Trade Commission.

Boston Consulting Group (1972). *Perspectives on Experience*. Boston: Author.

Bounds, W., and B. Davis (1995). "U.S. to launch new case against Japan over Kodak." *Wall Street Journal*, June 30, p. A3.

Bowen, R. M., E. W. Noreen, and J. M. Lacey (1981). "Determinants of the corporate decision to capitalize interest." *Journal of Accounting & Economics*, Vol. 3 (2), pp. 151–179.

Bowers, B. (1993). "Government watch: Support of textile firms has seeds of an 'America Inc.'" *Wall Street Journal*, July 28, p. B2.

Boyd, B. K. (1990). "Corporate linkages and organizational environment: A test of the resource dependence model." *Strategic Management Journal*, 11, pp. 419–430.

Boyd, B. K. (1995). "CEO duality and firm performance: A contingency model." *Strategic Management Journal*, 16, pp. 301–312.

Boyle, S. E. (1968). "Estimate of the number and size distribution of domestic joint subsidiaries." *Antitrust Law and Economics Review*, 1, pp. 81–92.

Bradley, M., and L. Wakeman (1983). "The wealth effects of targeted share repurchases." *Journal of Financial Economics*, 11, pp. 301–328.

Bradley, S. P. and Cavanaugh, S. (1994). "Crown Cork and Seal in 1989." Harvard Business School, Case, 9-793-035.

Brennan, M. (1979). "The pricing of contingent claims in discrete time models." *Journal of Finance*, 34, pp. 53–68.

Bresnahan, T. F. (1985). "Post-entry competition in the plain paper copier market." *American Economic Review*, 75, pp. 15–19.

Bresser, R. K. (1988). "Cooperative strategy." *Strategic Management Journal*, 9, pp. 475–492.

Brewer, H. L. (1981). "Investor benefits from corporate international diversification." *Journal of Financial and Quantitative Analysis*, 16, pp. 113–126.

Brickley, J., C. Smith, and J. Zimmerman (1996). *Organizational Architecture: A Managerial Economics Approach*. Homewood, IL: Irwin.

Bright, A. A. (1949). *The Electric Lamp Industry*. New York: Macmillan.

Bromiley, P., M. Govekar, and A. Marcus (1988). "On using event-study methodology in strategic management research." *Technovation*, 8, pp. 25–40.

Brown, R. (1994). "Original programming comes to life on cable." *Broadcasting & Cable*, April 4, p. 24.

Brown, S. J., and J. B. Warner (1980). "Measuring security price performance." *Journal of Financial Economics*, 8, pp. 205–258.

Brown, S. J., and J. B. Warner (1985). "Using daily stock returns: The case of event studies." *Journal of Financial Economics*, 14(1), pp. 3–31.

Burgleman, R. A. (1983a). "A model of the interaction of strategic behavior, corporate context and the concept of strategy." *Academy of Management Review*, 8(1), pp. 61–70.

Burgleman, R. A. (1983b). "A process model of internal corporate venturing in the diversified major firm." *Administrative Science Quarterly*, 28(2), pp. 223–244.

Burgers, W. P., C. W. L. Hill, and W. C. Kim (1993). "A theory of global strategic alliances: The case of the global auto industry." *Strategic Management Journal*, 14, pp. 419–432.

Burrows, P. (1995). "Now, TI means 'taking initiative.'" *Business Week*, May 15, pp. 120–121.

Burten, T., S. Kilman, and R. Gibson (1995). "Investigators suspect a global conspiracy in Archer-Daniels case." *Wall Street Journal*, July 28, pp. A1+.

Business Week (1983). "A dogfight could nick the F-18." February 14, pp. 64–68.

Business Week (1990). "Sizing up the outstanding mergers and acquisitions of the decade." January 15, p. 57.

Calton, D. W., and J. M. Perloff (1994). *Modern Industrial Organization*. 2d ed. New York: HarperCollins.

Cameron, K. (1978). "Measuring organizational effectiveness in institutions of higher education." *Administrative Science Quarterly*, 23, pp. 604–632.

Cameron, K. (1981). "Perceptions of organizational effectiveness over organizational life cycles." *Administrative Science Quarterly*, 26(4), pp. 525–544.

Cameron, K. (1986). "Effectiveness as paradox: Consensus and conflict in conceptions of organizational effectiveness." *Management Science*, 32, pp. 539–553.

Caminiti, S. (1992). "The payoff from a good reputation." *Fortune*, February 10, pp. 74–77.

Carey, S. (1993). "USAir declares war over fares in California." *Wall Street Journal*, June 9, p. B1.

Carlton, D. W., G. Bamberger, and R. Epstein (1995). "Antitrust and higher education: Was there a conspiracy to restrict financial aid?." *Rand Journal of Economics*, 26, pp. 131–147.

Carnevale, M. L. (1993a). "HDTV bidders agree to merge their systems." *Wall Street Journal*, May 24, p. B1+.

Carnevale, M. L. (1993b). "Ring in the new: Telephone service seems on the brink of huge innovations." *Wall Street Journal*, Feburary 10, p. A1.

Carroll, G. R., and J. Delacroix (1982). "Organizational mortality in the newspaper industries of Argentina and Ireland: An ecological approach." *Administrative Science Quarterly*, 27, pp. 169–198.

Carroll, P. (1993). *Big Blues: The Unmaking of IBM*. New York: Crown.

Cartwright, S. and C. Cooper (1993). "The role of culture compatibility in successful organizational marriage." *Academy of Management Executive*, 7(2), pp. 57–70.

Casey, J. (1976). "High fructose corn syrup." *Research Management*, 19, pp. 27–32.

Caves, R. E. (1971). "International corporations: The industrial economics of foreign investment." *Economica*, 38, February pp. 1–28.

Caves, R. E., and R. M. Bradburd (1988). "The empirical determinants of vertical integration." *Journal of Economic Behavior and Organization*, 9, pp. 265–279.

Caves, R. E., and M. E. Porter (1977). "From entry barriers to mobility barriers: Conjectural decisions and contrived deterrence to new competition." *Quarterly Journal of Economics*, 91, pp. 241–262.

Caves, R. E., and P. Williamson (1985). "What is product differentiation, really?" *Journal of Industrial Economics*, 34, pp. 113–132.

Chamberlin, E. H. (1933). *The Theory of Monopolistic Competition*. Cambridge, MA: Harvard University Press.

Chandler, A. (1962). *Strategy and Structure: Chapters in the History of the Industrial Enterprise*. Cambridge, MA: MIT Press.

Chang, Y., and H. Thomas (1989). "The impact of diversification strategy on risk-return performance." *Strategic Management Journal*, 10, pp. 271–284.

Chappell, H. W., and D. C. Cheng (1984). Firms' acquisition decisions and Tobin's q ratio." *Journal of Economics & Business*, 36(1), pp. 29–42.

Chatterjee, S., M. Lubatkin, D. Schweiger, and Y. Weber (1992). "Cultural differences and shareholder value in related mergers: Linking equity and human capital." *Strategic Management Journal*, 13, pp. 319–334.

Chatterjee, S. and B. Wernerfelt (1991). "The link between resources and type of diversification: Theory and evidence." *Strategic Management Journal*, 12, pp. 33–48.

Choate, P., and J. K. Linger (1986). *The High-Flex Society: Shaping America's Economic Future*. New York: Knopf.

Christensen, C. R., K. R. Andrews, J. L. Bower, G. Hamermesh, and M. E. Porter (1980). *Business Policy: Text and Cases*. Homewood, IL: Irwin.

Christensen, C. R., N. A. Berg, and M. S. Salter (1980). *Policy Formulation and Administration: A Casebook of Senior Management Problems in Business*. 8th ed. Homewood, IL: Irwin.

Christensen, C. R., and H. H. Stevenson (1967). "Head Ski Co." Harvard Business School, Case no. 9-313-120.

Christensen, H. K., and C. A. Montgomery (1981). "Corporate economic performance: Diversification strategy vs. market structure." *Strategic Management Journal*, 2, pp. 327–343.

Christie, W. G. and P. Schultz (1994). "Why do NASDAQ market makers avoid odd-eighth quotes?." *Journal of Finance*, 49, pp. 1813–1840.

Churchman, C. W. (1971). *The Design of Inquiring Systems: Basic Concepts of Systems and Organizations.* New York: Basic Books.

Coase, R. H. (1937). "The nature of the firm." *Economica*, 4, pp. 386–405.

Cochran, P. L., R. A. Wood, and T. B. Jones (1985). "The composition of board of directors and incidence of golden parachutes." *Academy of Management Journal*, 28, pp. 664–671.

Cochran, T. N. (1995). "Spreading the wealth." *Barron's*, 75, June 19, p. 18.

Cole, J. (1992). "Rising turbulence: Boeing's dominance of aircraft industry is beginning to erode." *Wall Street Journal*, July 10, p. A1.

Collis, D. J. (1991). "A resource-based analysis of global competition: The case of the bearing industry." *Strategic Management Journal*, 12 (Summer Special Issue), pp. 49–68.

Comment, R. and G. Jarrell (1995). "Corporate focus and stock returns," *Journal of Financial Economics*, 37, pp. 67–87.

Conner, K. R. (1991). "A historical comparison of resource-based theory and five schools of thought within industrial organization economics: Do we have a new theory of the firm?." *Journal of Management*, 17(1), pp. 121–154.

Conner, K. R., and R. P. Rumelt (1991). "Software piracy: An analysis of protection strategies." *Management Science*, 37(2), pp. 125–139.

Connolly, T., E. J. Conlon, and S. J. Deutsch (1980). "Organizational effectiveness: A multiple-constituency approach." *Academy of Management Review*, 5(2), pp. 211–217.

Cook, J. (1988). "$30 a barrel profits in an $18 world." *Forbes*, March 21, pp. 110–114.

Cool, K. O., and I. Dierickx (1993). "Rivalry, strategic groups and firm profitability." *Strategic Management Journal*, 14, pp. 47–59.

Cool, K. O., and D. Schendel (1987). "Strategic group formation and performance: The case of the U.S. pharmaceutical industry, 1963–1982." *Management Science*, 33, pp. 1102–1124.

Cooper, H. (1993). "Health management associates thrives as others falter." *Wall Street Journal*, May 4, p. B4.

Copeland, T. E., and J. F. Weston (1983). *Financial Theory and Corporate Policy.* Reading, MA: Addison-Wesley.

Corcoran, C. (1993). "At last, users can inspect IBM's PowerPC systems." *Infoworld*, November 15, pp. 1, 6.

Cosier, R. A. (1978). "An evaluation of the effectiveness of dialectical inquiry systems." *Management Science*, 24(14), pp. 1483–1490.

Cosier, R. A. (1981). "Dialectical inquiry in strategic planning: A case of premature acceptance?" *Academy of Management Review*, 6(4), pp. 643–648.

Coughlan, A. T., and R. M. Schmidt (1985). "Executive compensation, managerial turnover, and firm performance." *Journal of Accounting & Economics*, 7, pp. 43–66.

Cournot, A. (1838). *Recherches sur les Principes Mathématiques de la Théorie des Richesses.* English edition: *Researches into the Mathematical Principles of the Theory of Wealth*, ed. N. Bacon (London: Macmillan, 1897).

Cox, J., S. Ross, and M. Rubinstein (1979). "Option pricing: A simplified approach." *Journal of Financial Economics*, 7, pp. 229–263.

Cox, M. (1993). "Electronic campus: Technology threatens to shatter the world of college textbooks." , June 1, p. A1.

Crystal, G. (1991). "How much CEOs really make." *Fortune*, June 17, pp. 72–80.

Cummings, L. L. (1978). "Organizational participation—A critique and model." *Academy of Management Review*, 2(4), pp. 586–601.

Cyert, R., and J. G. March (1963). *A Behavioral Theory of the Firm*. Englewood Cliffs, NJ: Prentice-Hall.

Daft, R. (1983). *Organization Theory and Design*, New York: West.

Dahl, J. (1993). "Travel agents' fare share soars as airlines log losses." *Wall Street Journal*, February 23, p. B1.

Dambolena, I. G., and S. J. Khoury (1980). "Ratio stability and corporate failure." *Journal of Finance*, 35(4), pp. 1017–1026.

Dann, L. Y. (1981). "Common stock repurchases: An analysis of returns to bondholders and stockholders." *Journal of Financial Economics*, 9, pp. 113–138.

Dann, L. Y., and H. DeAngelo (1983). "Standstill agreements, privately negotiated stock repurchases, and the market for corporate control." *Journal of Financial Economics*, 11, pp. 275–300.

Darlin, D. (1991). "Coke and Nestlé launch first coffee drink." *Wall Street Journal*, October 1, p. B1+.

D'Aveni, R., and D. Ravenscraft (1994). "Economics of integration versus bureaucracy costs: Does vertical integration improve performance?" *Academy of Management Journal*, 37, 1167–1206.

Davidson, J. H. (1976). "Why most new consumer brands fail." *Harvard Business Review*, March–April, pp. 117–122.

Davis, B. (1995). "U.S. expects goals in pact with Japan to be met even without overt backing." *Wall Street Journal*, June 30, p. A3.

Davis, P., R. Robinson, J. Pearce, and S. Park (1992). "Business unit relatedness and performance: A look at the pulp and paper industry." *Strategic Management Journal*, 13, pp. 349–361.

Davis, S. M., and P. R. Lawrence (1977). *Matrix*. Reading, MA: Addison-Wesley.

de Forest, M. E. (1994). "Thinking of a plant in Mexico?" *Academy of Management Executive*, 8(1), pp. 33–40.

DeGeorge, G. (1994). "Someone woke the elephants." *Business Week*, April 4, p. 52.

de Lisser, E. (1993). "Catering to cooking-phobic customers, supermarkets stress carryout." *Wall Street Journal*, April 5, p. B1.

Demetrakakes, P. (1994). "Household-chemical makers concentrate on downsizing." *Packaging*, 39(1), p. 41.

Demsetz, H. (1973). "Industry structure, market rivalry, and public policy." *Journal of Law & Economics*, 16, pp. 1–9.

DePalma, A. (1994). "Trade pact is spurring Mexican deals in the U.S." *New York Times*, March 17, pp. C1, C3.

Deutsch, C. H. (1991). "How is it done? For a small fee . . ." *New York Times*, October 27, p. 25.

Deutschman, A. (1992). "Bill Gates' next challenge." *Fortune*, December 28, pp. 30–41.

Deveny, K. (1992). "Marketscan: Antacid makers find holiday season is a gas." *Wall Street Journal*, December 31, p. B1.

Dial, J., and K. J. Murphy (1995). "Incentives, downsizing, and value creation at General Dynamics." *Journal of Financial Economics*, 37, pp. 261–314.

Dichtl, E., and H. G. Koeglmayr (1986). "Country risk ratings." *Management International Review*, 26(4), pp. 2–10.

Dierickx, I., and K. Cool (1989). "Asset stock accumulation and sustainability of competitive advantage." *Management Science*, 35, pp. 1504–1511.

Dixit, A. K. (1982). "Recent developments in oligopoly theory." *Papers and Proceedings of the American Economic Association* (94th annual meeting), 72(2), pp. 12–17.

Dobrzynski, J. (1991). "How America can get the 'patient' capital it needs," *Business Week*, October, 21, p. 112.

Dodd, P. (1980). "Merger proposals, managerial discretion and stockholder wealth." *Journal of Financial Economics*, 8, pp. 105–138.

Donaldson, L. (1990). "The ethereal hand: Organizational economics and management theory." *Academy of Management Review*, 15, pp. 369–381.

Donoho, R. (1995). "GE off hook in price-fix case." *Sales and Marketing Management*, 147, p. 11.

Dubofsky, P., and P. Varadarajan (1987). "Diversification and measures of performance: Additional empirical evidence." *Academy of Management Journal*, 30, pp. 597–608.

Duffy, M. (1989). "ZBB, MBO, PPB, and their effectiveness within the planning/marketing process." *Strategic Management Journal*, 12, pp. 155–160.

Duke, J., and H. Hunt (1990). "An empirical examination of debt covenant restrictions and accounting-related debt proxies." *Journal of Accounting & Economics*, 12, pp. 45–63.

Dumaine, B. (1992). "Is big still good?" *Fortune*, April 20, pp. 50–60.

Dumaine, B. (1994). "A knockout year for CEO pay." *Fortune*, July 25, pp. 94–103.

Duncan, L. (1982). "Impacts of new entry and horizontal joint ventures on industrial rates of return." *Review of Economics and Statistics*, 64, pp. 120–125.

Dunning, J. H. (1973). "The determinants of international production." *Oxford Economic Papers*, 25, pp. 289–336.

Eaton, J., and M. Engers (1987). "International price competition." *Mimeo*, University of Virginia.

Eccles, R. (1985). *The Transfer Pricing Problem: A Theory for Practice*. Lexington, MA: Lexington Books.

Eckbo, B. E. (1983). "Horizontal mergers, collusion, and stockholder wealth." *Journal of Financial Economics*, 11, pp. 241–273.

Economist (1993). "Thailand: How cheap can you get?" August 21, pp. 29–30.

Edgeworth, F. (1897). "La Teoria Pura del Monopolio." *Giornale degli Economisti*, 40, pp. 13–31. In English: "The pure theory of monopoly," in *Papers Relating to Political Economy*, vol. 1, ed. F. Edgeworth (London: Macmillan, 1925).

Edwards, C. D. (1955). "Conglomerate bigness as a source of power." In *Business Concentration and Price Policy*, NBER Conference Report. Princeton, NJ: Princeton University Press.

Edwards, C. D. (1964). *Cartelization in Western Europe.* Washington, DC: U.S. Department of State, Government Printing Office.

Eger, C. E. (1983). "An empirical test of the redistribution effect in pure exchange mergers." *Journal of Financial and Quantitative Analysis*, 18, pp. 547–572.

Eichenseher, J., and D. Shields (1985). "Reputation and corporate strategy: A review of recent theory and applications." *Strategic Management Journal*, 9, pp. 443–454.

Ellis, J. (1987). "The unraveling of an idea: How Dick Ferris' grand plan for Allegis collapsed." *Business Week*, June 22, pp. 42–43.

El Mallakh, R. (1982). *OPEC: Twenty Years and Beyond.* Boulder, CO: Westview Press.

Engardio, P. (1993). "Motorola in China: A great leap forward." *Business Week*, May 17, pp. 58–59.

Engel, P. G. (1984). "Bankruptcy: A refuge for all reasons?" *Industry Week*, March 5, pp. 63–68.

Ennis, P. (1991). "Mitsubishi group wary of deeper ties to Chrysler." *Tokyo Business Today*, July, p. 10.

Ernst, D., and J. Bleeke (1993). *Collaborating to Compete: Using Strategic Alliances and Acquisitions in the Global Marketplace.* New York: Wiley.

Errunza, V., and L. W. Senbet (1981). "The effects of international operations on the market value of the firm: Theory and evidence." *Journal of Finance*, 36, pp. 401–418.

Errunza, V., and L. W. Senbet (1984). "International corporate diversification, market valuation and size-adjusted evidence." *Journal of Finance*, 39, pp. 727–745.

Fama, E. F. (1970). "Efficient capital markets: A review of theory and empirical work." *Journal of Finance*, 25, pp. 383–417.

Fama, E. F., L. Fisher, M. C. Jensen, and R. Roll (1969). "The adjustment of stock prices to new information." *International Economic Review*, 10(1), pp. 1–21.

Fama, E. F., and M. C. Jensen (1983). "Separation of ownership and control." *Journal of Law & Economics*, 26, pp. 301–325.

Fayerweather, J. (1969). *International Business Management: Conceptual Framework.* New York: McGraw-Hill.

Fayerweather, J. (1982). *International Business Strategy and Administration.* Cambridge, MA: Ballinger.

Fayerweather, J., and A. Kapoor (1975). *Strategy and Negotiation for the International Company.* Cambridge, MA: Ballinger.

Field, N. W. (1991). "Success depends on leadership." *Fortune*, November 18, pp. 153–154.

Finkelstein, S., and R. D'Aveni (1994). "CEO duality as a double-edged sword: How boards of directors balance entrenchment avoidance and unity of command." *Academy of Management Journal*, 37, pp. 1079–1108.

Finkelstein, S., and D. Hambrick (1988). "Chief executive compensation: A synthesis and reconciliation." *Strategic Management Journal*, 9, pp. 543–558.

Finkelstein, S., and D. C. Hambrick (1989). "Chief executive compensation: A study of the intersection of markets and political processes." *Strategic Management Journal*, 10, pp. 121–134.

Finn, E. A. (1987). "General Eclectic." *Forbes*, March 23, pp. 74–80.

Firth, M. (1980). "Takeovers, shareholder returns and the theory of the firm." *Quarterly Journal of Economics*, 94, pp. 235–260.

Fisher, F. M. (1979). "Diagnosing monopoly." *Quarterly Review of Economics & Business*, 19, pp. 7–33.

Fisher, F. M., and J. J. McGowan (1983). "On the misuse of accounting rates of return to infer monopoly profits." *American Economic Review*, 73, pp. 82–97.

Floyd, S. W., and B. Wooldridge (1992). "Middle management involvement in strategy and its association with strategic type: A research note." *Strategic Management Journal*, 13 (Special Issue), pp. 153–167.

Fortune. (1995). "The Fortune 500." May 15, pp. F1–F22.

Freedman, A. M., and B. Burrough (1988). "American Brands rejects 'Pac-Man' ploy." *Wall Street Journal*, September 19, p. A3.

Freedman, A., and R. Hudson (1980). "Du Pont and Phillips plan joint venture to make, market laser disc products." *Wall Street Journal*, December 22, p. 10.

Freeman, J., G. R. Carroll, and M. T. Hannan (1983). "The liability of newness: Age dependence in organizational death rates." *American Sociological Review*, 48, pp. 692–710.

Friedman, W., and G. Kalmanoff (1961). *Joint International Business Ventures*. New York: Columbia University Press.

Fuchsberg, G. (1992). "Decentralized management can have its drawbacks." *Wall Street Journal*, December 9, p. B1.

Fudenberg, D., and J. Tirole (1991). *Game Theory*. Cambridge, MA: MIT Press.

Fuerst, B., F. Mata, and J. Barney (1995). "Information technology and sustained competitive advantage: Reason-based analysis." *MIS Quarterly*, Forthcoming.

Fusfeld, D. (1958). "Joint subsidiaries in the iron and steel industry." *American Economic Review*, 48, pp. 578–587.

Gain, S. (1993). "Korea is overthrown as sneaker champ." *Wall Street Journal*, October 7, p. A14.

Galai, D., and R. W. Masulis (1976). "The option pricing model and the risk factor of stock." *Journal of Financial Economics*, 3, pp. 53–82.

Galbraith, C., B. Samuelson, C. Stiles, and G. Merrill (1986). "Diversification, industry research and development and performance." *Academy of Management Proceedings*, 46th annual meeting, Academy of Management, pp. 17–20.

Gatling, R. (1993). "McDonald's: A recipe for success in Central Europe." *Business Eastern Europe*, 22, pp. 6–7.

Ghemawat, P. (1984). "Du Pont in titanium dioxide (A)." Harvard Business School, Case no. 9-385-140.

Ghemawat, P. (1986). "Wal-Mart stores' discount operations." Harvard Business School, Case no. 9-387-018.

Ghemawat, P. (1993). "Sears, Roebuck and Company: The merchandise group." Harvard Business School, Case no. 9-794-039.

Ghemawat, P., and H. J. Stander, III (1992). "Nucor at a crossroads." Harvard Business School, Case no. 9-793-039.

Ghoshal, S. (1987). "Global strategy: An organizing framework." *Strategic Management Journal*, 8, pp. 425–440.

Gibson, R. (1991). "McDonald's insiders increase their sales of company's stock." *Wall Street Journal*, June 14, p. A1.

Gibson, R. (1995). "Food: At McDonald's, new recipes for buns, eggs." *Wall Street Journal*, June 13, p. B1.

Gibson, R., J. S. Lublin, and M. Allen (1988). "Proposal to stave off bid by Grand Met criticized; defense plan is upheld." *Wall Street Journal*, November 5, p. A3.

Gilbert, R. J., and D. M. Newbery (1982). "Preemptive patenting and the persistence of monopoly." *American Economic Review*, 72(3), pp. 514–526.

Gimeno, J. (1994). *Multipoint competition, market rivalry and firm performance: A test of the mutual forbearance hypothesis in the United States airline industry, 1984–1988*. Unpublished doctoral dissertation, Purdue University.

Glinow, M., and Clarke, L. (1995). "Vietnam: Tiger or kitten?" *Academy of Management Executive*, 9, pp. 34–47.

Glueck, W. F. (1980). *Business Policy and Strategic Management*. New York: McGraw-Hill.

Glynn, M. A. (1993). "Strategic planning in Nigeria versus U.S.: A case of anticipating the (next) coup." *Academy of Management Executive*, 7(3), pp. 82–83.

Golbe, D. L. (1981). "The effects of imminent bankruptcy on stockholder risk preferences and behavior." *Bell Journal of Economics*, 12(1), pp. 321–328.

Golden, B. (1992). "SBU strategy and performance: The moderating effects of the corporate-SBU relationship." *Strategic Mangement Journal*, 13, pp. 145–158.

Goodman, P. S., R. S. Atkin, and F. D. Schoorman (1983). "On the demise of organizational effectiveness studies". In K. Cameron and D. Whetten (eds.), *Organizational Effectiveness: A Comparison of Multiple Models*. New York: Academic Press.

Gordon, R. A., and J. E. Howell (1959). *Higher Education for Business*. New York: Columbia University Press.

Gort, M. (1962). *Diversification and Integration in American Industry*. Princeton, NJ: Princeton University Press.

Granovetter, M. (1985). "Economic action and social structure: The problem of embeddedness." *American Journal of Sociology*, 91, pp. 481–510.

Grant, L. (1995). "Here comes Hugh." *Fortune*, August 21, pp. 43–52.

Grant, R. M. (1988). "On 'dominant logic' relatedness and the link between diversity and performance." *Strategic Management Journal*, 9, pp. 639–642.

Grant, R. M. (1987). "Multinationality and performance among British manufacturing companies." *Journal of International Business Studies*, 18, pp. 78–89.

Grant, R. M. (1991a). *Contemporary Strategy Analysis*. Cambridge, MA: Basil Blackwell.

Grant, R. M. (1991b). "Porter's 'Competitive Advantage of Nations': An assessment," *Strategic Management Journal*, 12, pp. 535–548.

Grant, R. M., and A. Jammine (1988). "Performance differences between the Wrigley/Rumelt strategic categories." *Strategic Management Journal*, 9, pp. 333–346.

Grant, R. M., A. Jammine, and H. Thomas (1986). "The impact of diversification strategy upon the profitability of British manufacturing firms." *Academy of Management Proceedings*, 46th Annual Meeting, Academy of Management, pp. 26–30.

Grant, R. M., A. Jammine, and H. Thomas (1988). "Diversity, diversification, and profitability among British manufacturing companies, 1974–1984." *Academy of Management Journal*, 31, pp. 771–801.

Graves, S., and S. Waddock (1990). "Institutional ownership and control: Implications for long-term corporate strategy." *Academy of Management Executive*, 4(1), pp. 75–83.

Green, E. J., and R. H. Porter (1984). "Noncooperative collusion under imperfect price information." *Econometrica*, 52, pp. 87–100.

Greenhouse, S. (1991). "Playing Disney in the Parisian fields." *New York Times*, February 17, Section 3, pp. 1, 6.

Gross, N. (1995). "The technology paradox." *Business Week*, March 6, pp. 76–84.

Grossman, S., and O. Hart (1986). "The costs and benefits of ownership: A theory of vertical and lateral integration." *Journal of Political Economy*, 94, pp. 691–719.

Gubernick, L. (1990). "Turtle power." *Forbes*, May 28, pp. 52–58.

Guenther, R. (1988). "Bank of New York faces daunting task." *Wall Street Journal*, October 7, A4.

Gupta, A. K., and V. Govindarajan (1986). "Resource sharing among SBUs: Strategic antecedents and administrative implications." *Academy of Management Journal*, 29, pp. 695–714.

Gutknecht, J., and J. Keys (1993). "Mergers, acquisitions and takeovers: Maintaining morale of survivors and protecting employees." *Academy of Management Executive*, 7(3), pp. 26–36.

Hackman, J. R., and G. R. Oldham (1980). *Work Redesign*. Reading, MA: Addison-Wesley.

Hagedoorn, J. (1993). "Understanding the rationale of strategic technology partnering: Interorganizational modes of cooperation and sectoral differences." *Strategic Management Journal*, 14, pp. 371–385.

Halal, W. (1994). "From hierarchy to enterprise: Internal markets are the new foundation of management." *Academy of Management Executive*, 8(4), pp. 69–83.

Hall, G., and S. Howell (1985). "The experience curve from the economist's perspective." *Strategic Management Journal*, 6, pp. 197–212.

Hall, R. L., and C. J. Hitch (1939). "Price theory and business behavior." *Oxford Economic Papers*, 2, pp. 12–45.

Hambrick, D. (1987). "Top management teams: Key to strategic success." *California Management Review*, 30, pp. 88–108.

Hamel, G. (1991) "Competition for competence and inter-partner learning within international strategic alliances." *Strategic Management Journal*, 12, pp. 83–103.

Hamermesh, R. G., and E. T. Christensen (1981). "International Harvester (A)." Harvard Business School, Case no. 9-381-052.

Hamermesh, R. G., and R. S. Rosenbloom (1989). "Crown Cork and Seal Co., Inc." Harvard Business School, Case no. 9-388-096.

Hamilton, A. (1983). "Alternative to oil." *Banker*, 133(683), pp. 105–109.

Hannan, M. T., and J. Freeman (1977). "The population ecology of organizations." *American Journal of Sociology*, 72, pp. 267–272.

Hansell, S. (1993). "American Express skids in shift on car insurance." *New York Times*, July 27, p. D4.

Hansen, G. S., and C. W. L. Hill (1991). "Are institutional investors myopic? A time-series study of four technology-driven industries." *Strategic Management Journal*, 12, pp. 1–16.

Harari, O. (1994). "Colluding with competitors is a dead end." *Management Review*, 83(10), pp. 53–55.

Harrigan, K. R. (1980). *Strategies for Declining Businesses*, Lexington, MA: Lexington Books.

Harrigan, K. R. (1985). "An application of clustering for strategic group analysis." *Strategic Management Journal*, 6, pp. 55–74.

Harrigan, K. R. (1986). "Matching vertical integration strategies to competitive conditions." *Strategic Management Journal*, 7, pp. 535–555.

Harrigan, K. R. (1988). "Joint ventures and competitive strategy." *Strategic Management Journal*, 9, pp. 141–158.

Harris, R. J. (1994). "McDonnell, Douglas: Two families living on different planes." *Wall Street Journal*, December 2, p. A1.

Hartigan, J. A. (1975). *Clustering Algorithms*. New York: Wiley.

Hartley, R. F. (1991). *Management Mistakes & Successes*. 3d ed. New York: Wiley.

Haspeslagh, P. C., and D. B. Jemison (1987). "Acquisitions—Myths and reality." *Sloan Management Review*, 28, pp. 53–58.

Hatten, K. J. (1974). *Strategic models in the brewing industries*. Unpublished doctoral dissertation, Purdue University.

Hatten, K. J., and M. L. Hatten (1988). *Effective Strategic Management*. Englewood Cliffs, NJ: Prentice-Hall.

Hatten, K. J., and D. E. Schendel (1977). "Heterogeneity within an industry." *Journal of Industrial Economics*, 26(2), pp. 592–610.

Hatten, K. J., D. E. Schendel, and A. C. Cooper (1978). "A strategic model of the U.S. brewing industry: 1952–1971." *Academy of Management Journal*, 21, pp. 592–610.

Hay, G. A., and D. Kelly (1974). "An empirical survey of price fixing conspiracies." *Journal of Law & Economics*, 17, pp. 13–38.

Hayes, R., and W. Abernathy (1980). "Managing our way to economic decline." *Harvard Business Review*, July–August, pp. 67–77.

Hayes, R. H., and S. G. Wheelwright (1979). "The dynamics of process-product life cycles." *Harvard Business Review*, March–April, pp. 127–136.

Healy, P. M. (1985). "The effect of bonus schemes on accounting decisions." *Journal of Accounting & Economics*, 7, pp. 85–107.

Hedberg, B. L. T. (1981). "How organizations learn and unlearn". In P. C. Nystrom and W. H. Starbuck (eds.), *Handbook of Organizational Design*, London: Oxford University Press.

Helyar, J. (1991). "Race tracks try new marketing tricks." *Wall Street Journal*, June 7, p. B1.

Helyar, J., and B. Burrough (1988a). "RJR Nabisco board throws open bidding process; Pillsbury says it plans to spin off Burger King unit." *Wall Street Journal*, November 8, p. A3.

Helyar, J., and B. Burrough (1988b). "Buy-out bluff: How underdog KKR won RJR Nabisco without highest bid." *Wall Street Journal*, December 2, p. A1.

Henderson, B. (1974). *The Experience Curve Reviewed III—How Does It Work?* Boston: Boston Consulting Group.

Hennart, J. F. (1988). "A transaction cost theory of equity joint ventures." *Strategic Management Journal*, 9, pp. 361–374.

Hergert, M. (1983). *The incidence and implications of strategic groupings in U.S. manufacturing industries.* Unpublished doctoral dissertation, Harvard University.

Heskett, J. L., and R. H. Hallowell (1993). "Southwest Airlines: 1993 (A)." Harvard Business School, Case no. 9-694-023.

Hesterly, W. S. (1989). *Top management succession as a determinant of firm performance and de-escalation: An agency problem.* Unpublished doctoral dissertation, University of California, Los Angeles.

Higgins, J. M. (1983). *Organizational Policy and Strategic Management: Text and Cases.* 2d ed. Chicago: Dryden Press.

Hill, C. W. L. (1988). "Differentiation versus low cost or differentiation and low cost: A contingency framework." *Academy of Management Review*, 13(3), pp. 401–412.

Hill, C. W. L., and G. Hansen (1991). "A longitudinal study of the cause and consequence of changes in diversification in the U.S. pharmaceutical industry, 1977–1986." *Strategic Management Journal*, 12, pp. 187–199.

Hill, C. W. L., M. A. Hitt, and R. E. Hoskisson (1988). "Declining U.S. competitiveness: Reflections on a crisis." *Academy of Management Executive*, 2(1), pp. 51–60.

Hill, C. W. L., and G. R. Jones (1992). *Strategic Management Theory: An Integrated Approach.* Boston: Houghton Mifflin.

Hill, C. W. L., and S. Snell (1988). "External control, corporate strategy, and firm performance in research intensive industries." *Strategic Management Journal*, 9, pp. 577–590.

Hirshleifer, J. (1980). *Price Theory and Applications.* Englewood Cliffs, NJ: Prentice-Hall.

Hitt, M. A., and R. D. Ireland (1986). "Relationships among corporate-level distinct competencies, diversification strategy, corporate strategy and performance." *Journal of Management Studies*, 23, pp. 401–416.

Hitt, M. A., R. D. Ireland, and K. A. Palia (1982). "Industrial firms, grand strategy and functional performance: Moderating effects of technology and uncertainty." *Academy of Management Journal*, 25, pp. 265–298.

Hobbes, T. (1952). *Leviathan.* London: Oxford University Press.

Hofer, C. W., and D. Schendel (1978). *Strategy Formulation: Analytical Concepts.* St. Paul, MN: West Publishing.

Holder, D. (1989). "L. L. Bean, Inc.—1974." Harvard Business School, Case no. 9-676-014.

Holmström, B. (1979). "Moral hazard and observability." *Bell Journal of Economics*, 10(1), pp. 74–91.

Hooper, L. (1993). "CD ventures planned by IBM, Blockbuster." *Wall Street Journal*, May 11, pp. 8, B1+.

Hoskisson R., and M. Hitt (1988). "Strategic control systems and relative R&D investment in large multiproduct firms." *Strategic Management Journal*, 9, pp. 605–621.

Hoskisson, R., and M. Hitt (1990). "Antecedents and performance outcomes of diversification: Review and critique of theoretical perspectives." *Journal of Management*, 16, pp. 461–509.

Hoskisson, R. E., M. A. Hitt, R. A. Johnson, and D. D. Moesel (1993). "Construct validity of an objective (entropy) categorical measure of diversification strategy." *Strategic Management Journal*, 14, pp. 215–235.

Hoskisson, R. E., and T. A. Turk (1990). "Corporate restructuring: Governance and control limits of the internal capital market." *Academy of Management Review*, 15, pp. 459–477.

Hotelling, H. (1929). "Stability in competition." *Economic Journal*, 39, pp. 41–57.

Hout, T., M. E. Porter, and E. Rudden (1982). "How global companies win out." *Harvard Business Review*, September-October, pp. 98–108.

Huey, J. (1991). "Nothing is impossible." *Fortune*, September 23, pp. 134–140.

Huey, J. (1993). "The world's best brand." *Fortune*, May 31, pp. 44–54.

Huey, J. (1995). "Eisner explains everything." *Fortune*, April 17, pp. 44–68.

Hunt, M. S. (1972). *Competition in the major home appliance industry, 1960–1970*. Unpublished doctoral dissertation, Harvard University.

Hurry, D., A. T. Miller, and E. H. Bowman (1992). "Calls on high-technology: Japanese exploration of venture capital investments in the United States." *Strategic Management Journal*, 13, pp. 85–101.

Hylton, R. (1995). "Merger mania and fat profits make the big banks look good." *Fortune*, August 7, pp. 259–260.

Hymer, S. (1976). *The International Operations of National Firms: A Study of Direct Foreign Investment*. Cambridge, MA: MIT Press.

Ignatius, A. (1993). "Commodity giant: Marc Rich & Co. does big deals at big risk in former U.S.S.R." *Wall Street Journal*, May 13, p. A1.

Ingrassia, P., and A. Q. Nomani (1993). "Second thoughts: Some fear a backlash as Detroit prepares charges against Japan." *Wall Street Journal*, February 8, p. A1.

Ijiri, Y. (1980). "Recovery rate and cash flow accounting." *Financial Executive*, 48(3), pp. 54–60.

Itami, H. (1987). *Mobilizing Invisible Assets*. Cambridge, MA: Harvard University Press.

Jacob, R. (1992a). "India is opening for business." *Fortune*, November 16, pp. 128–130.

Jacob, R. (1992b). "Thriving in a lame economy." *Fortune*, October 5, pp. 44–54.

Jacob, R. (1992c). "Service Corp. International: Acquisitions done the right way." *Fortune*, November 16, p. 96.

Jacob, R. (1995a). "Global 500." *Fortune*, August 7, pp. 130–136.

Jacob, R. (1995b). "The resurrection of Michael Dell." *Fortune*, September 18, pp. 117–128.

Jacobsen, R. (1988). "The persistence of abnormal returns." *Strategic Management Journal*, 9(5), pp. 415–430.

Jacquemin, A. P., and C. H. Berry (1979). "Entropy measure of diversification and corporate growth." *Journal of Industrial Economics*, 27, pp. 359–369.

Jemison, D. B., and S. B. Sitkin (1986). "Corporate acquisitions: A process perspective." *Academy of Management Review*, 11, pp. 145–163.

Jensen, E. (1993a). "ABC and BBC pool their radio-TV news coverage." *Wall Street Journal*, March 26, p. B1+.

Jensen, E. (1993b). "Tales are oft told as TV talk shows fill up air time." *Wall Street Journal*, May 25, p. A1.

Jensen, E., and M. Robichaux (1993). "Fifth network sparks interest of TV industry." *Wall Street Journal*, June 28, p. B1.

Jensen, M. C. (1968). "The performance of mutual funds in the period 1945–64." *Journal of Finance*, 23(2), pp. 389–416.

Jensen, M. C. (1986). "Agency costs of free cash flow, corporate finance, and takeovers." *American Economic Review*, 76, pp. 323–329.

Jensen, M. (1988). "Takeovers: Their causes and consequences." *Journal of Economic Perspectives*, 2(1), pp. 21–48.

Jensen, M. C., and W. H. Meckling (1976). "Theory of the firm: Managerial behavior, agency costs, and ownership structure." *Journal of Financial Economics*, 3, pp. 305–360.

Jensen, M. C., and K. J. Murphy (1990). "Performance pay and top management incentives." *Journal of Political Economy*, 98, pp. 225–264.

Jensen, M. C., and R. S. Ruback (1983). "The market for corporate control: The scientific evidence." *Journal of Financial Economics*, 11, pp. 5–50.

Jereski, L. (1993). "Kinder-Care is a new toy for the bulls." *Wall Street Journal*, April 20, p. C1.

John, G., and B. A. Weitz (1988). "Forward integration into distribution: An empirical test of the transaction cost analysis." *Journal of Law, Economics and Organization*, 4, pp. 337–355.

Johnson, R. A., R. E. Hoskisson, and M. A. Hitt (1993). "Board of director involvement in restructuring: The effects of board versus managerial controls and characteristics." *Strategic Management Journal*, 14, pp. 33–50.

Jones, G. (1991). "Michael Eisner's Disney Company." In C. W. L. Hill and G. Jones, *Strategic Management* (pp. 784–805). Boston: Houghton-Mifflin.

Jones, N. (1986). "The hollow corporation." *Business Week*, March 3, pp. 56–59.

Jose, M. L., L. M. Nichols, and J. L. Stevens (1986). "Contribution of diversification, promotion, and R&D to the value of multiproduct firms: A Tobin's q approach." *Financial Management*, 14(4), pp. 33–42.

Joskow, P. L. (1985). "Vertical integration and long-term contracts: The case of coal-burning electric generating plants." *Journal of Law, Economics and Organization*, 1, pp. 33–80.

Joskow, P. L. (1988). "Asset specificity and the structure of vertical relationships." *Journal of Law, Economics and Organization*, 4, pp. 95–117.

Journal of Applied Corporate Finance (1994). "Stern Stewart EVA Roundtable." 7, pp. 46–70.

Kalay, A. (1982). "Stockholder-bondholder conflict and dividend constraints." *Journal of Financial Economics*, 10, pp. 211–233.

Kamm, T. (1995). "Another head rolls in French revolution." *Wall Street Journal*, July 10, p. 8.

Kanter, R. M., and D. Brinkerhoff (1981). "Organizational performance: Recent developments in measurement." *Annual Review of Sociology*, 7, pp. 321–349.

Kaplan, S. N. (1995). "Taking stock of the RJR Nabisco buyout." *Wall Street Journal*, March 30, p. A16.

Karnani, A., and B. Wernerfelt (1985). "Multiple point competition." *Strategic Management Journal*, 6, pp. 87–96.

Kearns, D. T., and D. A. Nadler (1992). *Prophets in the Dark*. New York: Harper-Collins.

Keller, J. J. (1993). "Sprint hangs back as its rivals forge global alliances." *Wall Street Journal*, June 4, p. B4.

Keller, J. J., and M. L. Carnevale (1993). "Clear message: MCI-BT tie is seen setting off a battle in communications." *Wall Street Journal*, June 3, p. A1.

Kent, D. H. (1991). "Joint ventures vs. non-joint ventures: An empirical investigation." *Strategic Management Journal*, 12, pp. 387–393.

Kesner, I. F. (1988). "Director's characteristics and committee membership: An investigation of type, occupation tenure and gender." *Academy of Management Journal*, 31, pp. 66–84.

Kesner, I. F., and R. B. Johnson (1990). "An investigation of the relationship between board composition and stockholder suits." *Strategic Management Journal*, 11, pp. 327–336.

Kessel, R. (1971). "A study of the effects of competition in the tax-exempt bond market." *Journal of Political Economy*, 79, pp. 706–738.

Kestin, H. (1986). "Nothing like a Dane." *Forbes*, November 3, pp. 145–148.

Khoury, S. J. (1983). *Investment Management: Theory and Application*. New York: Macmillan.

Kirkpatrick, D. (1992). "The revolution at Compaq Computer." *Fortune*, December 14, pp. 80–88.

Kirkpatrick, D. (1993). "Could AT&T rule the world?" *Fortune*, May 17, pp. 54–56.

Kirkpatrick, D. (1995). "IBM moves to fix its Microsoft problem." *Fortune*, July 10, pp. 102–113.

Klebnikov, P. (1991). "The powerhouse." *Forbes*, September 2, pp. 46–52.

Klein, B., R. Crawford, and A. Alchian (1978). "Vertical integration, appropriable rents, and the competitive contracting process." *Journal of Law & Economics*, 21, pp. 297–326.

Klein, B., and K. Leffler (1981). "The role of market forces in assuring contractual performance." *Journal of Political Economy*, 89, pp. 615–641.

Klemperer, P. (1986). *Markets with consumer switching costs*. Unpublished doctoral dissertation, Graduate School of Business, Stanford University.

Knight, F. H. (1965). *Risk, Uncertainty, and Profit*. New York: Wiley.

Kobrin, S. (1991). "An empirical analysis of the determinants of global integration." *Strategic Management Journal*, 12, pp. 17–31.

Kogut, B. (1988) "Joint ventures: Theoretical and empirical perspectives." *Strategic Management Journal*, 9, pp. 319–332.

Kogut, B. (1991). "Joint ventures and the option to expand and acquire." *Management Science*, 37, pp. 19–33.

Kogut, B., and H. Singh (1986). *Entering the United States by acquisition or joint venture: Country patterns, and cultural characteristics*. Working paper, Department of Management, Wharton School of Business, University of Pennsylvania.

Kogut, B., and U. Zander (1992). "Knowledge of the firm, combinative capabilities, and the replication of technology." *Organization Science*, 3, pp. 383–397.

Kosnik, R. D. (1987). "Greenmail: A study of board performance in corporate governance." *Administrative Science Quarterly*, 32, pp. 163–185.

Kosnik, R. D. (1990). "Effects of board demography and directors' incentives on corporate greenmail decisions." *Academy of Management Journal*, 33, pp. 129–150.

Kotler, P. (1986). *Principles of Marketing*. Englewood Cliffs, NJ: Prentice-Hall.

Kraar, L. (1992). "Korea's tigers keep roaring." *Fortune*, May 4, pp. 108–110.

Kraar, L. (1995). "The risks are rising in China." *Fortune*, March 6, pp. 179–180.

Krafcik, J. K., and J. P. MacDuffie (1989). *Explaining High Performance Manufacturing: The International Automotive Assembly Plant Study*. Cambridge, MA: International Motor Vehicle Program, MIT.

Krogh, L., J. Praeger, D. Sorenson, and J. Tomlinson (1988). "How 3M evaluates its R&D programs." *Research Technology Management*, 31, pp. 10–14.

Kupfer, A. (1991). "The champion of cheap clones." *Fortune,* September 23, pp. 115–120.

Kupfer, A. (1992). "Who's winning the PC price wars?" *Fortune*, September 21, pp. 80–82.

Kupfer, A. (1994). "The future of the phone companies." *Fortune*, October 3, pp. 95–106.

Labich, K. (1987). "How Dick Ferris blew it." *Fortune*, July 6, pp. 42–46.

Labich, K. (1991). "An airline that soars on service." *Fortune*, December 31, pp. 94–96.

Labich, K. (1992). "Airbus takes off." *Fortune*, June 1, pp. 102–108.

Laffer, A. (1969). "Vertical integration by corporations: 1929–1965." *Review of Economics and Statistics*, 51, pp. 91–93.

Lambert, R. (1986). "Executive effort and selection of risky projects." *Rand Journal of Economics*, 13(2), pp. 369–378.

Lamphier, G. (1980). "Inco 'poison pill' plan is producing broad opposition." *Wall Street Journal*, October 20, p. A5.

Landro, L. (1995). "Giants talk synergy but few make it work." *Wall Street Journal*, September 25, p. B1+.

Landro, L., P. M. Reilly, and R. Turner (1993). "Cartoon clash: Disney relationship with Time Warner is a strained one." *Wall Street Journal*, April 14, p. A1.

Lang, H. P., and R. Stulz (1994). "Tobin's *q*, corporate diversification, and firm performance." *Journal of Political Economy*, 102, pp. 1248–1280.

Lau, L. J., and S. Tamura (1972). "Economies of scale, technical progress, and the nonhomothetic leontief production function." *Journal of Political Economy*, 80, pp. 1167–1187.

Lawrence, J., and P. Sloan (1992). "P&G plans big new Ivory push," *Advertising Age*, November 23, p. 12.

Learned, E. P., C. R. Christensen, K. R. Andrews, and W. Guth (1969). *Business Policy*. Homewood, IL: Irwin.

Lecraw, D. J. (1984). "Diversification strategy and performance." *Journal of Industrial Economics*, 33, pp. 179–198.

Leftwich, R. B. (1974). "U.S. multinational companies: Profitability, financial leverage and effective income tax rates." *Survey of Current Business*, May, pp. 27–36.

Leinster, C. (1993). "Vietnam: Business rushes to get in." *Fortune*, April 5, pp. 98–104.

Lessard, D. R. (1976). "World, country, and industry relationships in equity returns: Implications for risk reduction through international diversification." *Financial Analysts Journal*, 32, pp. 32–38.

Levine, J. (1995). "Entertainment systems for idiots." *Forbes*, May 22, p. 238.

Levitt, T. (1975). "Dinosaurs among the bears and bulls." *Harvard Business Review*, January/February, pp. 41–53.

Levy, D. T. (1985). "The transactions cost approach to vertical integration: An empirical investigation." *Review of Economics and Statistics*, 67, pp. 438–445.

Lieberman, M. B. (1982). *The learning curve, pricing and market structure in the chemical processing industries*. Unpublished doctoral dissertation, Harvard University.

Lieberman, M. B. (1987). "The learning curve, diffusion, and competitive strategy." *Strategic Management Journal*, 8, pp. 441–452.

Lieberman, M. B., and D. B. Montgomery (1988). "First-mover advantages." *Strategic Management Journal*, 9, pp. 41–58.

Lindenberg, E. B., and S. A. Ross (1981). "Tobin's q ratio and industrial organization." *Journal of Business*, 54(1), pp. 1–32.

Lipin, S. (1995a). "A list of laggards appears to back investor activism." *Wall Street Journal*, October 3, p. C1+.

Lipin, S. (1995b). "Mergers, acquisitions rose 20% in 1st half to record." *Wall Street Journal*, July 3, p. A3.

Lipman, J. (1992). "Advertising: Advertisers may be under Batman shadow." *Wall Street Journal*, June 23, p. B12.

Lipman, S., and R. Rumelt (1982). "Uncertain imitability: An analysis of inter-firm differences in efficiency under competition." *Bell Journal of Economics*, 13, pp. 418–438.

Livingstone, J. L., and G. L. Salamon (1971). "Relationship between the accounting and the internal rate of return measures: A synthesis and analysis." In J. L. Livingstone and T. J. Burns (eds.), *Income Theory and Rate of Return*. Columbus: Ohio State University Press.

Loeb, M. (1995a). "Empowerment that pays off." *Fortune*, March 20, pp. 145–146.

Loeb, M. (1995b). "Jack Welch lets fly on budgets, bonuses, and buddy boards." *Fortune*, May 29, pp. 145–147.

Logue, D. E. (1982). "An experiment in international diversification." *Journal of Portfolio Management*, 9, pp. 22–20.

London, H. (1995). "Bait and switch in academe." *Forbes*, May 22, p. 120.

Long, W. F., and D. J. Ravenscraft (1984). "The misuse of accounting rates of return: Comment." *American Economic Review*, 74, pp. 494–500.

Loomis, C. J. (1993). "Dinosaurs?" *Fortune*, May 3, pp. 36–42.

Lorsch, J. W. (1989). *Pawns or Potentates: The Reality of America's Corporate Boards*. Boston, MA: Harvard Business School Press.

Lubatkin, M. (1983). "Mergers and the performance of the acquiring firm." *Academy of Management Review*, 8, pp. 218–225.

Lubatkin, M. (1987). "Merger strategies and stockholder value." *Strategic Management Journal*, 8, pp. 39–53.

Lubatkin, M., and R. E. Shrieves (1986). "Toward reconciliation of market performance measures to strategic management research." *Academy of Management Review*, 11, pp. 497–512.

Lublin, J. S. (1995). "Give the board fewer perks, a panel urges." *Wall Street Journal*, June 19, p. B1.

Lublin, J. S., and C. Duff (1995). "How do you fire a CEO? Very, very slowly." *Wall Street Journal*, January 20, p. B1.

Lux, H. (1995a). "NASDAQ retains Nobel laureate for anti-trust case defense." *Investment Dealers Digest*, 61, March 13, pp. 3–4.

Lux, H. (1995b). "The big noise from Columbus." *Investment Dealers Digest*, May 22, pp. 110–111.

Lux, H. (1995c). "An economists' supergroup will review NASDAQ charges." *Investment Dealers Digest*, 61, July 3, pp. 5.

Maccoby, M. (1984). "A new way of managing." *IEEE Spectrum*, 21(6), pp. 69–72.

MacDonald, J. M. (1985). "Market exchange or vertical integration: An empirical analysis." *Review of Economics and Statistics*, 67, pp. 327–331.

Mack, T. (1990). "We're not perfect yet." *Forbes,* February 19, pp. 68–72.

MacLeod, W. B. (1985). "A theory of conscious parallelism." *European Economic Review*, 27(1), pp. 25–44.

MacMillan, I., D. C. Hambrick, and J. M. Pennings (1986). "Uncertainty reduction and the threat of supplier retaliation: Two views of the backward integration decision." *Organization Studies*, 7, pp. 263–278.

Maddigan, R. (1979). *The impact of vertical integration on business performance.* Unpublished doctoral dissertation, Indiana University, Bloomington.

Magnet, M. (1993). "What activist investors want." *Fortune*, March 8, pp. 59–63.

Mahoney, J. T., (1992). "The choice of organizational form: Vertical financial ownership versus other methods of vertical integration." *Strategic Management Journal*, 13, pp. 559–584.

Mahoney, J. T., and J. R. Pandian (1992). "The resource-based view within the conversation of strategic management." *Strategic Management Journal*, 13, pp. 363–380.

Mahoney, T., and W. Weitzel (1969). "Managerial models of organizational effectiveness." *Administrative Science Quarterly*, 14, pp. 357–365.

Main, O. W. (1955). *The Canadian Nickel Industry.* Toronto: University of Toronto Press.

Mansfield, E. (1985). "How rapidly does new industrial technology leak out?" *Journal of Industrial Economics*, 34(2), pp. 217–223.

Mansfield, E., M. Schwartz, and S. Wagner (1981). "Imitation costs and patents: An empirical study." *Economic Journal*, 91, pp. 907–918.

Marcus, A. (1982). "Risk sharing and the theory of the firm." *Bell Journal of Economics.*" 13(2), pp. 369–378.

Maremont, M. (1994). "Danger: Competition dead ahead." *Business Week*, January 10, p. 100.

Marin, D. (1990). "Tying in international trade: Evidence on countertrade." *World Economy*, 13(3), p. 445.

Marketing News (1992). "New marketing approach puts SuperAmerica in national spotlight." February 17, p. 3.

Markham, J. W. (1951). "The nature and significance of price leadership." *American Economic Review*, 41, pp. 891–905.

Markides, C., and P. J. Williamson (1994). "Related diversification, core competencies, and corporate performance." *Strategic Management Journal*, 15, pp. 149–165.

Markowitz, H. (1959). *Portfolio Selection*. New Haven, CT: Yale University Press.

Marshall, A. (1891). *Principles of Economics*. Philadelphia: Porcupine Press.

Maskin, E., and J. Tirole (1988). "A theory of dynamic oligopoly." *Econometrica*, 56, pp. 549–600.

Mason, E. S. (1939). "Price and production policies of large scale enterprises." *American Economic Review*, 29, pp. 61–74.

Mason, R. O., and I. I. Mitroff (1981). *Challenging Strategic Planning Assumptions: Theory, Cases, and Techniques*. New York: Wiley.

Masten, S., J. W. Meehan, and E. A. Snyder (1991). "The cost of organization." *Journal of Law, Economics and Organization*, 7, pp. 1–25.

Masulis, R. (1980). "Stock repurchases by tender offer: An analysis of the causes of common stock price changes." *Journal of Finance*, 35, pp. 305–319.

McCarthy, M. J. (1993). "The PEZ fancy is hard to explain, let alone justify." *Wall Street Journal*, March 10, p. A1.

McCormick, J., and N. Stone (1990). "From national champion to global competitor: An interview with Thomson's Alain Gomez." *Harvard Business Review*, May–June, pp. 126–135.

McGee, J., and H. Thomas (1986). "Strategic groups: Theory, research and taxonomy." *Strategic Management Journal*, 7, pp. 141–160.

McGinley L., and A. R. Karr (1991). "Airlines fight expansion of postal fleet." *Wall Street Journal*, July 2, p. B1.

McKelvey, W. (1982). *Organizational Systematics: Taxonomy, Evolution, Classification*. Los Angeles: University of California Press.

McWilliams, A., and J. B. Barney (1995). *Cooperative strategies in empty core markets*. Unpublished manuscript.

Mead, W. J. (1967). "Competitive significance of joint ventures." *Antitrust Bulletin*, 12, pp. 300–315.

Mendes, J. (1992). "A stereo brute from Russia." *Fortune*, May 18, p. 18.

Metz, T. (1988). "Promoter of the poison pill prescribes stronger remedy." *Wall Street Journal*, December 1, p. C1.

Meyer, M. W., and L. G. Zucker (1989). *Permanently Failing Organizations*, Newbury Park, CA: Sage.

Michel, A., and I. Shaked (1984). "Does business diversification affect performance?" *Financial Management*, 13(4), pp. 18–25.

Michel, A., and I. Shaked (1986). "Multinational corporations vs. domestic corporations: Financial performance and characteristics." *Journal of International Business*, 17, pp. 89–100.

Miles, R. H. (1980). *Macro Organizational Behavior*. Santa Monica, CA: Goodyear Publishing Co.

Miles, R. H., and K. S. Cameron (1982). *Coffin Nails and Corporate Strategies.* Englewood Cliffs, NJ: Prentice-Hall.

Miller, M. W., and L. Berton (1993). "Softer numbers: As IBM's woes grew, its accounting tactics got less conservative." *Wall Street Journal*, April 7, p. A1.

Mintzberg, H. (1973). "Strategy-making in three modes." *California Management Review*, 16(2), pp. 44–53.

Mintzberg, H. (1975). "The manager's job: Folklore and fact." *Harvard Business Review*, July–August, pp. 49–61.

Mintzberg, H. (1978). "Patterns in strategy formulation." *Management Science*, 24(9), pp. 934–948.

Mintzberg, H. (1985). "Of strategies, deliberate and emergent." *Strategic Management Journal*, 6(3), pp. 257–272.

Mintzberg, H. (1988). "Opening up the definition of strategy". In J. B. Quinn, H. Mintzberg, and R. M. James (eds.), *The Strategy Process* (pp. 13–20). Englewood Cliffs, NJ: Prentice-Hall.

Mintzberg, H. (1990). "The design school: Reconsidering the basic premises of strategic management." *Strategic Management Journal*, 11, pp. 171–195.

Mintzberg, H., and A. McHugh (1985). "Strategy formulation in an adhocracy." *Administrative Science Quarterly*, 30, pp. 160–197.

Mitchell, J. (1991). "Office-furniture firms struggle for sales." *Wall Street Journal*, August 9, p. B1.

Modigliani, F., and M. Miller (1958). "The cost of capital, corporation finance, and the theory of investment." *American Economic Review*, 48, pp. 201–297.

Modigliani, F., and M. Miller (1963). "Corporate income taxes and the cost of capital." *American Economic Review*, 53, pp. 433–443.

Moffett, M. (1993). "U.S. firms yell Olé to future in Mexico." *Wall Street Journal*, March 8, p. B1.

Mohr, J., and R. Spekman (1994). "Characteristics of partnership success: Partnership attributes, communication behavior, and conflict resolution techniques." *Strategic Management Journal*, 15, pp. 135–152.

Montgomery, C. A. (1989). "Sears, Roebuck and Co. in 1989." Harvard Business School, Case no. 9-391-147.

Montgomery, C. A. (1993). "Marks and Spencer Ltd. (A)." Harvard Business School, Case 9-391-089.

Montgomery, C. A., and H. Singh (1984). "Diversification strategy and systematic risk." *Strategic Management Journal*, 5, pp. 181–191.

Montgomery, C. A., and B. Wernerfelt (1988). "Diversification, Ricardian rents, and Tobin's q." *Rand Journal of Economics*, 19, pp. 623–632.

Montgomery, C. A., and B. Wernerfelt (1991). "Sources of superior performance: Market share versus industry effects in the U.S. brewing industry." *Management Science*, 37, pp. 954–959.

Montgomery, D. B. (1975). "New product distribution: An analysis of supermarket buyer decisions." *Journal of Marketing Research*, 12, pp. 255–264.

Moore, F. T. (1959). "Economies of scale: Some statistical evidence." *Quarterly Journal of Economics*, 73, pp. 232–245.

Moriarity, S., and C. Allen (1984). *Cost Accounting.* New York: Harper & Row.

Moritz, M., and B. Seaman (1984). *Going for Broke: Lee Iacocca's Battle to Save Chrysler.* Garden City, NJ: Anchor Press/Doubleday.

Murphey, K. (1990). "A new survey of executive compensation." *Harvard Business Review*, May–June, pp. 150–153.

Naj, A. K. (1993). "Shifting gears: Some manufacturers drop efforts to adopt Japanese techniques." *Wall Street Journal*, May 7, p. A1.

Narisetti, R. (1995). "Justice department is investigating tire makers for possible price fixing." *Wall Street Journal*, August 24, p. A3.

Nayyar, P. (1990). "Information asymmetries: A source of competitive advantage for diversified service firms." *Strategic Management Journal*, 11, pp. 513–519.

Nayyar, P. (1992). "On the measurement of corporate diversification strategy: Evidence from large U.S. service firms." *Strategic Management Journal*, 13, pp. 219–235.

Neff, T. J. (1990). "Outside directors and the CEO: Changing the rules," *The Corporate Board*, 11, pp. 7–10.

Nelson, R., and S. Winter (1982). *An Evolutionary Theory of Economic Change*. Cambridge, MA: Belknap Press,

Neumeier, S. (1992). "Companies to watch." *Fortune*, March 9, p. 63.

Nguyen, T., and T. Devinney (1990). "Diversification strategy and performance in Canadian manufacturing firms." *Strategic Management Journal*, 11, pp. 411–418.

Nielsen, R. P. (1988). "Cooperative strategy." *Strategic Management Journal*, 9, pp. 475–492.

Noldeke, G., and K. Schmidt (1995). "Option contracts and renegotiation: A solution to the holdup problem." *Rand Journal of Economics*, 26, 163–179.

Nulty, P. (1993). "Look what the unions want now." *Fortune*, February 8, pp. 128–135.

Nulty, P. (1995). "Digital imaging had better boom before Kodak film busts." *Fortune*, May 1, pp. 80–83.

Nystrom, P. C., and W. H. Starbuck (1984). "To avoid organizational crisis, unlearn." *Organizational Dynamics*, 12(4), pp. 53–65.

Oates, B. (1992). "What happened to the run-and-shoot revolution?" *Football Digest*, 22(2), pp. 28.

O'Brien, B. (1993). "Losing altitude: After long soaring, Delta Air Lines runs into financial clouds." *Wall Street Journal*, June 25, p. A1.

O'Reilly, B. (1990). "The inside story of AIDS drug." *Fortune*, November 5, pp. 112–129.

Olson, M. (1965). *The Logic of Collective Action: Public Goods and the Theory of Groups*. Cambridge, MA: Harvard University Press.

Ordover, J. A., and R. D. Willig (1985). "Antitrust for high-technology industries: Assessing research joint ventures and mergers." *Journal of Law & Economics*, 28, pp. 311–343.

Ortega-Reichert, A. (1967). *Models for Competitive Bidding Under Uncertainty*. Unpublished dissertation, Stanford University.

Ortega, B. (1995). "Life without Sam: What does Wal-Mart do if stock drop cuts into workers' morale?" *Wall Street Journal*, January 4, p. A1.

Osborn, R. N., and C. C. Baughn (1987). "New patterns in the formation of U.S./Japan cooperative ventures: The role of technology." *Columbia Journal of World Business*, 22, pp. 57–65.

Scott, W. R., A. B. Flood, W. Ewy, and W. H. Forrest, Jr. (1978). "Organizational effectiveness and the quality of surgical care in hospitals." In M. W. Meyer (ed.), *Environments and Organizations* (pp. 290–305). San Francisco: Jossey-Bass.

Sellers, P. (1995). "PepsiCo's shedding ugly pounds." *Fortune*, June 26, pp. 94–95.

Selznick, P. (1957). *Leadership in Administration.* New York: Harper & Row.

Senback, A. J., and W. L. Beedles (1980). "Is indirect international diversification desirable?" *Journal of Portfolio Management*, 6, pp. 49–57.

Serwer, A. E. (1994). "McDonald's conquers the world." *Fortune*, October 17, pp. 103–116.

Serwer, A. E. (1995). "Why bank mergers are good for your savings account." *Fortune*, October 2, p. 32.

Seth, A. (1990). "Sources of value creation in acquisitions: An empirical investigation." *Strategic Management Journal*, 11, pp. 431–446.

Severn, A. K. (1974). "Investor evaluation of foreign and domestic risk." *Journal of Finance*, 29, pp. 545–550.

Shaffer, R. A. (1995a). "Who wins home banking?" *Forbes*, August 14, p. 163.

Shaffer, R. A. (1995b). "Intel as conquistador." *Forbes*, February 27, p. 130.

Shan, W., G. Walker, and B. Kogut (1994). "Interfirm cooperation and startup innovation in the biotechnology industry." *Strategic Management Journal*, 15, pp. 387–394.

Shane, S. (1994). "The effect of national culture on the choice between licensing and direct foreign investment." *Strategic Management Journal*, 15, pp. 627–642.

Shanley, M., and M. Correa (1992). "Agreement between top management teams and expectations for post acquisition performance." *Strategic Management Journal*, 13, pp. 245–266.

Shapiro, E. (1993). "Cigarette burn: Price cut on Marlboro upsets rosy notions about tobacco profits." *Wall Street Journal*, April 5, p. A1.

Sharpe, W. F. (1966). "Mutual fund performance." *Journal of Business*, 39(1), Part II, pp. 119–138.

Shartell, S., and E. J. Zajac (1988). "Internal corporate joint ventures: Development processes and performance outcomes." *Strategic Management Journal*, 9, pp. 527–542.

Sherman, S. (1995). "Can you believe what you see at ITT?" *Fortune*, April 17, pp. 109–116.

Shleifer, A., and R. W. Vishny (1986). "Large shareholders and corporate control." *Journal of Political Economy*, 94, pp. 461–488.

Simmods, P. (1990). "The combined diversification breadth and mode dimensions and the performance of large diversified firms." *Strategic Management Journal*, 11, pp. 399–410.

Simon, H. A. (1976). *Administrative Behavior.* 3d ed. New York: Macmillan.

Simons, R. (1994). "How new top managers use control systems as levers of strategic renewal." *Strategic Management Journal*, 15, pp. 169–189.

Sims, J., and R. H. Lande (1986). "The end of antitrust: Or a new beginning." *Antitrust Bulletin*, 31(2), pp. 301–322.

Singh, H., and F. Harianto (1989). "Top management tenure, corporate ownership and the magnitude of golden parachutes." *Strategic Management Journal*, 10, pp. 143–156.

Singh, H., and C. A. Montgomery (1987). "Corporate acquisition strategies and economic performance." *Strategic Management Journal*, 8, pp. 377–386.

Slade, M. E. (1990). "Cheating on collusive agreements." *International Journal of Industrial Organization*, 8(4), pp. 519–543.

Smirlock, M., T. Gilligan, and W. Marshall (1984). "Tobin's *q* and the structure-performance relationship." *American Economic Review*, 74(5), pp. 1051–1060.

Smith, D. K., and R. C. Alexander (1988). *Fumbling the Future*. New York: William Morrow.

smith, f., and R. Wilson (1995). "The predictive validity of the Karnani and Wernerfelt model of multipoint competition." *Strategic Management Journal*, 16, pp. 143–160.

Smith, G. D., D. R. Arnold, and B. G. Bizzell (1988). *Business Strategy and Policy*. Boston: Houghton Mifflin.

Smith, L. (1993). "Can defense pain be turned to gain?" *Fortune*, February 8, pp. 84–96.

Smith, T. K., and E. Norton (1993). "Throwing curves: One baseball statistic remains a mystery." *Wall Street Journal*, April 2, p. A1.

Solomon, E. (1970). "Alternative rate of return concepts and their implications for utility regulation." *Bell Journal of Economics*, 1, pp. 65–81.

Solomon, J. (1994). "Mickey's trip to trouble." *Newsweek*, February 14, pp. 34–39.

Spence, A. M. (1973). *Market Signalling: Information Transfer in Hiring and Related Processes*. Cambridge, MA: Harvard University Press.

Spence, A. M. (1974). "Competitive and optimal responses to signals." *Journal of Economic Theory*, 7, pp. 298–315.

Spence, A. M. (1981). "The learning curve and competition." *Bell Journal of Economics*, 12, pp. 49–70.

Spender, J. C. (1989). *Industry Recipes: An Enquiry into the Nature and Sources of Managerial Judgement*. New York: Blackwell.

Spiller, E. A., Jr., and M. L. Gosman (1984). *Financial Accounting*. Homewood, IL: Irwin.

Stackelberg, H. von (1934). *Marktform und Gleichgewicht*. Vienna: Julius Springer.

Stalk, G., P. Evans, and L. Shulman (1992). "Competing on capabilities: The new rules of corporate strategy." *Harvard Business Review*, March–April, pp. 57–69.

Stapleton, R. C. (1982). "Mergers, debt capacity, and the valuation of corporate loans." In M. Keenan and L. J. White (eds.), *Mergers and Acquisitions* (Ch. 2). Lexington, MA: D. C. Heath.

Starr, C. (1993). "Orphan drug act: Celebrating a decade and 87 drugs later." *Drug Topics*, April 5, pp. 26–31.

Statman, M. (1981). "Betas compared: Merrill Lynch vs. Value Line." *Journal of Portfolio Management*, 7(2), pp. 41–44.

Stauffer, T. R. (1971). "The measurement of corporate rates of return: A generalized formulation." *Bell Journal of Economics*, 2, pp. 434–469.

Staw, B. M. (1981). "The escalation of commitment to a course of action." *Academy of Management Review*, 6, pp. 577–587.

Steiner, G. A. (1983). "Formal strategic planning in the United States today." *Long Range Planning*, 16(3), pp. 12–17.

Steiner, G. A., and J. B. Miner (1977). *Management Policy and Strategy: Text, Readings and Cases.* New York: Macmillan.

Stern, J., B. Stewart, and D. Chew (1995). "The EVA financial management system." *Journal of Applied Corporate Finance*, 8, pp. 32–46.

Stertz, B. A. (1991). "In a U-turn from past policy, Big Three at Detroit speed into era of cooperation." *Wall Street Journal*, June 28, p. B1+.

Steven, L. (1992). "Front line systems." *Computerworld*, March 2, pp. 61–63.

Stewart, T. A. (1991). "GE keeps those ideas coming." *Fortune*, August 12, pp. 40–49.

Stewart, T. A. (1993). "The king is dead," *Fortune*, January 11, pp. 34–41.

Stillman, R. (1983). "Examining antitrust policy toward horizontal mergers." *Journal of Financial Economics*, 11, pp. 225–240.

Stogdill, R. M. (1974). *Handbook of Leadership: A Survey of Theory and Research.* New York: Free Press.

Stopford, M., and L. Wells (1972). *Managing the Multinational Enterprise.* New York: Basic Books.

Stuckey, J. (1983). *Vertical Integration and Joint Ventures in the Aluminum Industry.* Cambridge, MA: Harvard University Press.

Suris, O. (1993a). "Big Three win joint patent, marking a first." *Wall Street Journal*, April 13, p. B1+.

Suris, O. (1993b). "IndyCar 'Honda rule' blocks fast track." *Wall Street Journal*, May 28, p. B1.

Sweezy, P. M. (1939). "Demand under conditions of oligopoly." *Journal of Political Economy*, 47, pp. 568–573.

Swieringa, R. J., and J. H. Waterhouse (1982). "Organizational views of transfer pricing." *Accounting, Organizations & Society*, 7(2), pp. 149–165.

Tannenbaum, J. A. (1993). "Once red-hot PIP faces legal assault by franchisees." *Wall Street Journal*, April 8, p. B2.

Tanouye, E. (1993). "Drug prices get dose of market pressure." *Wall Street Journal*, March 11, p. B1

Taylor, A., III (1991). "BMW and Mercedes make their move." *Fortune*, August 12, pp. 56–63.

Taylor, A., III (1994a). "New ideas from Europe's automakers." *Fortune*, December 12, pp. 159–172.

Taylor, A., III (1994b). "Iacocca's minivan." *Fortune*, May 30, pp. 56–66.

Taylor, A., III (1995). "GM: Some gain much pain." *Fortune*, May 29, pp. 78–84.

Teece, D. (1977). "Technology transfer by multinational firms." *Economic Journal*, 87, pp. 242–261.

Teece, D. (1980). "Economy of scope and the scope of the enterprise." *Journal of Economic Behavior and Organization*, 1, pp. 223–245.

Teitelbaum, R. S. (1992). "Eskimo pie." *Fortune*, June 15, p. 123.

Telser, L. G. (1978). *Economic Theory and the Core.* Chicago: University of Chicago Press.

Templeman, J. (1993). "Nestlé: A giant in a hurry." *Business Week*, March 22, pp. 50–54.

Terpstra, V., and K. David (1985). *The Cultural Environment of International Business*. Cincinnati, OH: South-Western.

Tetzeli, R. (1993). "Johnson Controls: Mining money in mature markets." *Fortune*, March 22, pp. 77–80.

Thompson, A. A., Jr., and A. J. Strickland, III (1987). *Strategic Management: Concepts and Cases*. 4th ed. Plano, TX: Business Publications.

Thompson, T., L. J. Tell, T. Vogel, J. E. Davis, J. R. Norman, and T. Mason (1987). "Bankruptcy court for Texaco: The lesser evil, barely." *Business Week*, April 27, pp. 102–108.

Tichy, N. M., and M. A. Devanna (1986). *The Transformational Leader*. New York: Wiley.

Tichy, N. M., and S. Sherman (1993). *Control Your Destiny or Someone Else Will: How Jack Welch Is Making General Electric the World's Most Competitive Corporation*. New York: Doubleday.

Tirole, J. (1988). *The Theory of Industrial Organization*. Cambridge, MA: MIT Press.

Titman, S. (1984). "The effect of capital structure on a firm's liquidation decision." *Journal of Financial Economics*, 13(1), pp. 137–151.

Tobin, J. (1958). "Liquidity preference as a behavior toward risk." *Review of Economic Studies*, 25, pp. 65–86.

Tobin, J. (1969). "A general equilibrium approach to monetary theory." *Journal of Money, Credit and Banking*, 1, pp. 15–29.

Tobin, J. (1978). "Monetary policies and the economy: The transmission mechanism." *Southern Economic Journal*, 37, pp. 421–431.

Tobin, J., and W. Brainard (1968). "Pitfalls in financial model building." *American Economic Review*, 58, pp. 99–122.

Tobin, J., and W. Brainard (1977). "Asset markets and the cost of capital." In B. Belassa and R. Nelson (eds.), *Economic Progress, Private Values and Public Policies: Essays in Honor of William Fellner*. Amsterdam: North-Holland.

Tomer, J. F. (1987). *Organizational Capital: The Path to Higher Productivity and Well-Being*. New York: Praeger.

Tomlinson, J. W. L. (1970). *The Joint Venture Process in International Business*. Cambridge, MA: MIT Press.

Tomsho, R. (1992). "Columbia Hospital is expanding, one market at a time." *Wall Street Journal*, December 4, p. B4.

Toy, S., and P. Dwyer (1994). "Is Disney headed to the Euro-trash heap?" *Business Week*, January 24, p. 52.

Trachtenberg, J. A. (1991). "Home economics: Ikea furniture chain pleases with its prices, not with its service." *Wall Street Journal*, September 17, p. A1.

Trachtenberg, J. A., and K. Pope (1995). "Poly Gram's Levy puts music firm further into movie-making." *Wall Street Journal*, June 15, p. A1+.

Trager, J. (1992). *The People's Chronology*. New York: Henry Holt.

Trautwein, I. (1990). "Merger motives and merger prescriptions." *Strategic Management Journal*, 11, pp. 283–295.

Treece, J. B. (1991). "Autos: Are the planets lining up at last for Saturn?" *Business Week*, April 8, pp. 32–34.

Treynor, J. L. (1965). "How to rate mutual fund performance." *Harvard Business Review*, January–February, pp. 63–75.

Tucker, I., and R. P. Wilder (1977). "Trends in vertical integration in the U.S. manufacturing sector." *Journal of Industrial Economics*, 26, pp. 81–94.

Tuller, L. W. (1991). *Going Global: New Opportunities for Growing Companies to Compete in World Markets*. Homewood, IL: Irwin.

Tully, S. (1990). "GE in Hungary: Let there be light." *Fortune*, October. 22, pp. 137–142.

Tully, S. (1992a). "How to cut those #$%* legal costs." *Fortune*, September 21, pp. 119–124.

Tully, S. (1992b). "What CEOs really make." *Fortune*, June 15, pp. 94–99.

Tully, S. (1993). "The real key to creating wealth." *Fortune*, September 20, pp. 38–50.

Tully, S. (1994). "You'll never guess who really makes . . ." *Fortune*, October 3, pp. 124–128.

Tully, S. (1995a). "So, Mr. Bossidy, we know you can cut. Now show us how to grow." *Fortune*, August 21, pp. 70–80.

Tully, S. (1995b). "Can EVA deliver profits to the post office?" *Fortune*, July 10, p. 22.

Turk, T. A. (1987). *The determinants of management responses to interfirm tender offers and their effect on shareholder wealth*. Unpublished doctoral dissertation, Graduate School of Management, University of California, Irvine.

Turk, T. (1992). "Takeover resistance information leakage, and target firm value." *Journal of Management*, 18, pp. 503–522.

Turner, R. (1991). "How MCA's relations with Motown Records went so sour so fast." *Wall Street Journal*, September 25, p. A1+.

Turner, R., and L. Hooper (1993). "IBM ventures to Hollywood in visual effects." *Wall Street Journal*, February 26, p. B1+.

Tyler, B., and H. K. Steensma (1995). "Evaluating technological collaborative opportunities: A cognitive modeling perspective." *Strategic Management Journal*, 16, pp. 43–70.

Utterback, J. M., and W. J. Abernathy (1975). "A dynamic model of process and product innovation." *Omega*, 3, pp. 639–656.

Vance, S. C. (1964). *Board of Directors: Structure and Performance*. Eugene, OR: University of Oregon Press.

Van de Ven, A., and R. Drazin (1985). "The concept of fit in contingency theory." In B. M. Staw and L. L. Cummings (eds.), *Research in Organizational Behavior*. Vol. 7 (pp. 333–365). Greenwich, CT: JAI Press.

Varadarajan, P. (1986). "Product diversity and firm performance: An empirical investigation." *Journal of Marketing*, 50(3), pp. 43–57.

Varadarajan, P., and V. Ramanujam (1987). "Diversification and performance: A reexamination using a new two-dimensional conceptualization of diversity in firms." *Academy of Management Journal*, 30, pp. 380–399.

Varaiya, N. (1985). *A test of Roll's hubris hypothesis of corporate takeovers*. Working paper, School of Business, Southern Methodist University.

Venkatesan, R. (1992). "Strategic sourcing: To make or not to make." *Harvard Business Review*, November–December, pp. 98–107.

Venkatraman, N., and V. Ramanujam (1987). "Measurement of business economic performance: An examination of method convergence." *Journal of Management*, 13, pp. 109–122.

Von Clausewitz, K. (1976). *On war, Volume I.* London: Kegan Paul.

Von Neumann, J., and O. Morgenstern (1944). *The Theory of Games and Economic Behavior.* New York: Wiley.

Wald, M. L. (1991). "ARCO reports new gasoline that sharply cuts pollutants." *New York Times*, July 11, p. A1.

Walker, G., and D. Weber (1984). "A transaction cost approach to make-or-buy decisions." *Administrative Science Quarterly*, 29, pp. 373–391.

Walkling, R., and M. Long (1984). "Agency theory, managerial welfare, and takeover bid resistance." *Rand Journal of Economics*, 15(1), pp. 54–68.

Wallace, J., and J. Erickson (1993). *Hard Drive: Bill Gates and the Making of the Microsoft Empire.* New York: Harper Business.

Wall Street Journal (1990). "GM's Opel unit to build plant in East Germany." December 11, p. A15.

Wall Street Journal. (1992). "Time Warner Inc.: HBO unit expands push into original programming." January 16, p. B6.

Walsh, J. (1988). "Top management turnover following mergers and acquisitions." *Strategic Management Journal*, 9, pp. 173–183.

Walsh, J. (1989). "Doing a deal: Merger and acquisition negotiations and their impact upon target company top management turnover." *Strategic Management Journal*, 10, pp. 307–322.

Walsh, J., and J. Ellwood (1991). "Mergers, acquisitions, and the pruning of managerial deadwood." *Strategic Management Journal*, 12, pp. 201–217.

Walter, G., and J. B. Barney (1990). "Management objectives in mergers and acquisitions." *Strategic Management Journal*, 11, pp. 79–86.

Walton, S. (1992). *Sam Walton, Made in America: My Story.* New York: Doubleday.

Warner, J. B. (1988). "Stock prices and top management changes." *Journal of Financial Economics*, 20, pp. 461–492.

Warner, J. B., R. Watts, and K. Wruck (1988). "Stock prices and top management changes," *Journal of Financial Economics*, 20, pp. 461–493.

Watts, R. L., and J. L. Zimmerman (1978). "Towards a positive theory of determination of accounting standards." *The Accounting Review*, 53, pp. 112–133.

Watts, R. L., and J. L. Zimmerman (1986). *Positive Accounting Theory*, Englewood Cliffs, NJ: Prentice Hall.

Watts, R. L., and J. L. Zimmerman (1990). "Positive accounting theory: A ten-year perspective." *Accounting Review*, 65, pp. 131–156.

Weick, K. E., and R. L. Daft (1982). "The effectiveness of interpretation systems." In K. S. Cameron and D. A. Whetton (eds.), *Organizational Effectiveness: A Comparison of Multiple Models.* New York: Academic Press.

Weidenbaum, M. L. (1986). "Updating the corporate board." *Journal of Business Strategy*, 7, pp. 77–83.

Weigelt, K., and C. Camerer (1988). "Reputation and corporate strategy: A review of recent theory and applications." *Strategic Management Journal*, 9, pp. 443–454.

Weiner, S. (1987). "The road most traveled." *Forbes*, October 19, pp. 60–64.

Weisbach, M. S. (1988). "Outside directors and CEO turnover." *Journal of Financial Economics*, 20, pp. 431–460.

Wernerfelt, B. (1984). "A resource-based view of the firm." *Strategic Management Journal*, 5, pp. 171–180.

Wernerfelt, B. (1986). "A special case of dynamic pricing policy." *Management Science*, 32, pp. 1562–1566.

Wernerfelt, B. (1988). "General equilibrium with real time search in labor and product markets." *Journal of Political Economy*, 96, pp. 821–831.

Wernerfelt, B., and A. Karnani (1987). "Competitive strategy under uncertainty." 8, *Strategic Management Journal*, pp. 187–194.

Westley, F. (1990). "Middle managers and strategy: Microdynamics of inclusion." *Strategic Management Journal*, 11, pp. 337–351.

Westley, F., and H. Mintzberg (1989). "Visionary leadership and strategic management." *Strategic Management Journal*, 10, pp. 17–32.

Weston, J. F., and S. K. Mansinghka (1971). "Tests of the efficiency performance of conglomerate firms." *Journal of Finance*, 26, pp. 919–936.

White, L. J. (1971). *The American Automobile Industry Since 1945*. Cambridge, MA: Harvard University Press.

William, J., B. L. Paez, and L. Sanders (1988). "Conglomerates revisited." *Strategic Management Journal*, 9, pp. 403–414.

Williams, M., and M. Kanabayashi (1993). "Mazda and Ford drop proposal to build cars together in Europe." *Wall Street Journal*, March 4, p. A14.

Williamson, O. E. (1975). *Markets and Hierarchies: Analysis and Antitrust Implications*. New York: Free Press.

Williamson, O. E. (1979). "Transaction cost economics: The governance of contractual relations." *Journal of Law & Economics*, 22, pp. 233–261.

Williamson, O. E. (1983). "Organizational form, residual claimants, and corporate control." *Journal of Law & Economics*, 26, pp. 351–366.

Williamson, O. E. (1985). *The Economic Institutions of Capitalism*. New York: Free Press.

Williamson, O. E. (1991). "Strategizing, economizing, and economic organization." *Strategic Management Journal*, 12, pp. 75–94.

Winslow, R. (1995). "Simple device to prop clogged arteries open changes coronary care." *Wall Street Journal*, October 23, p. A1+.

Womack, J. P., D. I. Jones, and D. Roos (1990). *The Machine That Changed the World*. New York: Rawson.

Woodman, R., R. E. Sawyer, and R. W. Griffin (1993). "Toward a theory of organizational creativity." *Academy of Management Review*, 18, pp. 293–321.

Woods, W. (1991). "Misery in the air." *Fortune*, December 16, pp. 88–89.

Wooldridge, B., and S. Floyd (1990). "The strategy process, middle management involvement, and organizational performance." *Strategic Management Journal*, 11, pp. 231–241.

Worthy, F. S. (1991). "Japan's smart secret weapon." *Fortune*, August 12, pp. 72–75.

Wrigley, L. (1970). *Divisional autonomy and diversification*. Unpublished doctoral dissertation, Harvard Business School, Harvard University.

Yan, A., and B. Gray (1994). "Bargaining power, management control, and performance in United States–China joint ventures: A comparative case study." *Academy of Management Journal*, 37, pp. 1478–1517.

Yoder, S. K. (1991). "A 1990 reorganization at Hewlett Packard is already paying off." *Wall Street Journal*, July 22, p. 1+.

Yoffie, D. B. (1992). "Apple Computer—1992." Harvard Business School, Case no. 9-792-081.

Yoshino, M., S. Hall, and T. Malnight (1991). "Whirlpool Corp." Harvard Business School, Case 9-391-037.

Yoshino, M. Y., and P. Stoneham (1992). "Proctor and Gamble Japan (A)." Harvard Business School, Case 9-793-035.

Yukl, G. (1989). "Managerial leadership: A review of theory and research." *Journal of Management*, 15(2), pp. 251–289.

Zachary, G. P. (1991). "IBM, Microsoft are deadlocked over royalties." *Wall Street Journal*, October 1, p. B1.

Zachary, P., and S. K. Yoder (1991). "Apple and IBM discuss a swap of technologies." *Wall Street Journal*, June 7, p. B1+.

Zaheer, A., and N. Venkatraman (1995). "Relational governance as an interorganizational strategy: An empirical test of the rate of trust in economic exchange." *Strategic Management Journal*, 16, 373–392.

Zahra, S. A., and J. A. Pearce, II (1989). "Boards of directors and corporate financial performance: A review and integrative model." *Journal of Management*, 15, pp. 291–334.

Zajac, E., and J. Westphal (1994). "The costs and benefits of managerial incentives and monitoring in large U.S. corporations: When is more not better?" *Strategic Management Journal*, 15, pp. 121–142.

Zenger, T. R. (1989). *Organizational diseconomies of scale: Pooling vs. separating labor contracts in Silicon Valley (California)*. Unpublished doctoral dissertation, University of California, Los Angeles.

Zimmerman, J. L. (1979). "The demand for and supply of accounting theories: The market for excuses." *Accounting Review*, 64, pp. 273–305.

Zimmerman, J. L. (1983). "Taxes and firm size." *Journal of Accounting & Economics*, 5(2), pp. 119–149.

Zimmerman, M. (1985). *How to Do Business with the Japanese*. New York: Random House.

Zmijewski, M. E., and R. L. Hagerman (1981). "An income strategy approach to the positive theory of accounting standard setting/choice." *Journal of Accounting & Economics*, 3(2), pp. 129–149.

INDEX

Starr, 95
Statman, 52
Stauffer, 42
Staw, 211, 376
Steensma, 339
Steiner, 8–10, 13, 16, 22
Stempel, Robert C., 405
Sterling Drug, 129T
Stern, 424
Stern Stewart, 425
Stertz, 289
Steven, 150
Stevens, 389T
Stevenson, 224
Stewart, 15, 408, 424
Stillman, 447
Stodgill, 137
Stone, 199
Stoneham, 482
Stopford, J. M., 514
Stopford, M., 291
Strategic alliances, 255–256
    acquisitions, 302, 304–305
    adverse selection, 296–297
    alliance management skills, 311
    antitrust liabilities, 305
    asymmetric, 294–295
    cheating, 296–300
    commitment, 311
    complementary resources, 292, 301
    contracts, 307
    cooperative cultures, 304
    cost sharing, 288–289
    distribution networks, 302–303
    economies of scale, 294–295, 299, 309
    entering a new industry, 292
    entry into new markets, 290–291
    flexibility, 305
    history, 311
    hold up, 298–299
    imitability, 301–306
    industry structure, 294–295
    internal development, 302
    interpersonal relations, 310
    intraorganizational cooperation and trust, 304, 306, 310–311
    legal constraints, 305
    linkages between firms, 247
    local partners, 291, 482
    mixed alliances, 294
    moral hazard, 297–298
    nonequity alliances, 285–286, 306, 309
    option-pricing theory, 293
    product differentiation strategy, 291
    proprietary technologies, 307
    rareness, 300–301
    reputation, 309
    research and development alliances, 289
    risk management, 288–289, 292
    symmetric alliances, 294–295
    synergies, 293
    tacit collusion, 289, 294–295

trade barriers, 291
transaction-specific investments, 309
uncertainty management, 293–294
    See also collusive strategies, corporate diversification, trust, vertical integration
Strategic bankruptcy, 35
Strategic groups, 99, 126
    cluster analyses, 130
    mobility barriers, 127, 128, 132
Strategic objectives and policies, 12–15, 17
Strategic tactics, 13–15, 17, 20
Strickland, 8–14, 22, 143
Structure-conduct-performance (S-C-P) Model, 66–69, 71, 99, 105, 120–123, 125, 127, 136, 145, 170, 172, 182, 237
    See also five forces framework
Stuckey, 287, 336
Stulz, 417
Substitutes, 95, 103, 151–152, 206, 214
    cost leadership, 214–215
    diversification, 391–392
    global strategies, 508
    product differentiation, 247–248
    strategic alliances, 302–306
    tacit collusion, 278–280
Sumitomo Corporation, 491
Suppliers, 206, 255, 285
Suris, 80, 81, 289
Survival, 35–36, 449
    See also accounting performance, economic profit, strategic bankruptcy
Sweezy, 269
Swieringa, 432–433
Switching costs, 239
    See also first movers
SWOT Analysis, 22, 99, 123, 141, 162, 164, 173, 175, 259
Synergy, 184, 286, 302–305, 359–360, 365, 372, 282, 440, 444–447, 451, 453–456, 458–459, 461–462, 464, 473, 513–514
    See also corporate diversification, economy of scope, mergers and acquisitions, strategic alliances
Syntex, 129T

Taco Bell, 102
Tamura, 188
Tannenbaum, 239, 297
Tanouye, 95
Target cost design system, 201
Tariff and non-tariff barriers
    See also barriers to entry, global strategies
Taylor, 85, 191, 200, 245, 249
Teams and teamwork, 214, 249, 252
Technology, 200
Technological software, 200, 209, 214
Technomed, 478
Teece, 13, 23, 36, 288, 303, 335, 392

Teitelbaum, 292
Tell, 35
Telser, 86–87
Templeman, 392
Tenneco, 157, 390, 405
Terpstra, 493
Tetzeli, 113
Texaco, 35
Texas Instruments, 119, 248–249, 361
Thomas, H., 378
Thomas, J., 126–127, 130, 132
Thompson, 8–14, 22, 35, 143
Threats,
    of buyers, 91–92, 95, 97
    of new entrants
    of rivals
    of substitutes, 96
    of suppliers, 95–96
    See also five forces framework
Tichy, 24, 157, 420
Time, 87
Time Warner, 381, 405, 473
Time compression diseconomies, 152
    See also imitation
Timex, 148, 186, 220
Timing, 245, 248
    See also history, path dependence
Tirole, 31, 66, 76, 79, 86, 122, 257, 263, 269, 272, 276, 309, 380, 382
Titman, 44
Tobin, 54
Tomer, 144, 200, 399
Tomlinson, 146, 291
Tomsho, 362
Toshiba, 84
Total quality management, 252
Toy, 481
Toyota, 68, 83, 85, 126, 201, 222, 287, 288, 498, 514
Trachtenberg, 202, 372
Trager, 489
Transactions-cost economics, 343–344, 338–339
Transaction-specific investments, 298–299
    See also hold-up
Transfer prices, 430–433
Transformational leaders, 157
Transnational strategies, 119
    See also global strategies
Transnational structure, 514–516
    See also global strategies
Transportation costs, 191
TransWorld Airlines (TWA), 21
Trautwein, 440
Treece, 199
Trout, 110
Trumpf Machine Tools, 232
Trust, 275, 335, 353
TRW, 491
Tucker, 318–319
Tuller, 80
Tully, 88, 337, 350, 424–425, 434, 501
Turk, 408, 455, 465–466, 469–470
Turner, 292, 297, 381
Turner Broadcasting, 305–306, 473